MOJAVE DESERT PEAKS

Hiking the Crown
of the California Desert

Michel Digonnet

Maps, illustrations, and book design by the author
Photographs by the author, unless otherwise specified

Publisher: Michel Digonnet
Volume Editor: Susan Cole
Copy Editor: Susan Cole
Cover Designer: Karen Frankel

Published in Palo Alto, California
Printed and bound in the United States of America

Front Cover: Black Mountains' badlands from Red Cathedral,
Death Valley National Park

Back Cover: Squaw Tank, Hexie Mountains,
Joshua Tree National Park
Sacred datura, Shadow Valley,
Kingston Range Wilderness

Library of Congress Control Number: 2018913243

ISBN: 978-0-9659178-8-9

To Marc
*In celebration of years
of friendship, desert trekking,
and fine Parisian cuisine*

By the same author:

Hiking Death Valley (two editions)
Hiking Western Death Valley National Park
Hiking the Mojave Desert
Hiking Joshua Tree National Park (in preparation)

WARNING

Many of the hikes suggested in this book are potentially dangerous. They involve hours of strenuous physical activity across often rugged terrain, with no water, little to no shade, in a hot desert. They should be attempted only by hikers in excellent physical condition, with prior experience in desert hiking and good route-finding skills. Although many of the dangers of specific routes are mentioned in the text, all of them cannot possibly be covered. The information contained in this book should not be considered a substitute for common sense. The author declines all responsibilities for any injuries, physical or otherwise, anyone might sustain while hiking any of the routes suggested herein.

ACKNOWLEDGMENTS

Once again I would like to thank my wife Susan for letting me pursue my passion for the desert and take the inordinate amount of time that it takes to write about it, and for proofreading this long book with her customary attention to detail.

Over the years, many friends and family members have contributed to the making of this book by joining me on some of the peak climbs described in these pages. I would like to thank in particular Francie Allen, Michael Closson, Nikki Cole, Sarah Cole-Burnett, Cliff Lawson, Ryan Lewis, Bruno Marchon, and Jeff Weintraub. A special credit goes to Janet Ader, the only one bold enough for attempting to climb Telescope Peak in one day; to John Arkwright, for braving slippery taluses more or less against his will; to Ralph Bergh, always willing to pack up at a moment's notice to go trekking just about anywhere; to Marc Fermigier, for sharing many adventures and mishaps, and always coming back for more; and to Susan again, for waiting for me patiently in the absolute middle of nowhere on many occasions while I pushed on to bag one more summit. I could not possibly end this list with anyone but my friend Alice Fermigier, who braved three-digit heat one memorable summer to hike into some of the most inaccessible corners of the Mojave Desert, always with a keen interest in all things natural, and a smile.

Several people from multiple government agencies have taken time off from their busy schedules to review the book manuscript. For the detailed comments they provided, I would like to thank Death Valley National Park Superintendent Mike Reynolds, Park Ranger Thomas Arnold, and Chief of Interpretation Patrick Taylor; Park Guide Matthew Caire in Mojave National Preserve; several staff members of Joshua Tree National Park, including Park Superintendent David Smith and Park Ranger Cynthia Anderson; Wilderness Coordinator Ramona Daniels at the BLM Field Office in Needles; and Archaeologist Donald Storm at the BLM Field Office in Ridgecrest.

I would like to thank again Jim Andre from the University of California at Irvine for identifying from photographs some of the more obscure desert plants that I ran across.

Finally, I extend a warm thank you to my friend Karen Frankel for lending me her artistic talents and designing the book cover.

PRAISES FOR THE AUTHOR'S DESERT BOOKS

Your books open the doors to show visitors (and employees) how to safely and respectfully journey into the amazing landscapes of Death Valley. Having worked in many other national parks, I have seldom seen other books that so single-handedly establish the culture of the backcountry. Your passion for this place is inspiring.

This is a superb book that provides a large amount of exceptionally useful information about Death Valley.

The author writes with true passion for his subject clearly borne of extensive, first-hand experience.

I have read it from cover to cover, and it is probably the best hiking book I have ever read.

You have inspired many hikers, walkers, readers and loafers with your poetry about the desert. Your words travel across each page and form trails to new and exciting adventures. So many people love and appreciate what you have written.

A must-have book for any desert rat.

This book covers an incredible amount of information and detail that will serve me for years to come and many more visits.

I can't tell you how much Hiking Death Valley has meant to my family...it was really the impetus to get up numerous washes and into canyons that we otherwise probably wouldn't have pursued.

Your books truly amaze me.

Your books sit on my shelf, but not for very long because I keep thumbing through them trying to figure out my next adventure.

If you are considering going to one of the areas on which he has written a guide book, do yourself a huge favor and get any of his books. All others will pale in comparison.

TABLE OF CONTENTS

FOREWORD

The Mojave Desert is an extraordinary region. There is, for one, the matter of size. In the state of California, it covers approximately 27,500 square miles, extending from northern Death Valley south to the edge of the Salton Sea, and from the foot of the Sierra Nevada east to the Colorado River. All of it is a quilt of luminous valleys stitched together by long colorful mountain ranges. If you have driven across it or flown over it, you have seen its vast, empty expanses of auburn and dusty-white land, capped on its high crests by forests or snow. Everything about it is huge—the distances, the mountains, the valleys, and the sky. It is, also, a country of staggering contrasts and diversity, in its geology, landforms, botany, wildlife, and human history. It is home to summits reaching above 11,000 feet and basins dipping close to or even below sea level, of oak and conifer forests intermixed with exotic cactus gardens, of valleys filled with eerie Joshua trees, of wind-sculpted dunes, mountains of boulders, and barren alkali flats fringed by unbelievably profuse wildflowers. It is fierce country, reputed for its rugged topography and extreme summer heat. Naturally guarded by its own inhospitable terrain and climate, it is one of the largest relatively intact ecosystems in the lower 48 states. It is preserved by six national park units, 31 wilderness areas, six state parks, and several other federal and state units. Together, these protected areas encompass 9.1 million acres, a little more than half of the whole desert. For outdoor recreation on a crowded planet, this is just about as wild as it gets.

Of all the terrains that can be explored on foot in the desert—canyons, dunes, playas, narrows, salt flats, or badlands—the most physically demanding and arguably most rewarding are mountain tops. All of these hiking goals are united by a common denominator. We seek them to fulfill our need for open spaces, our longing for solitude, and our appetite for discovery. Each terrain also has its own appeals. Canyons guide us to secret places hidden deep in the interior of mountains. We immerse ourselves in dunes for their sensuality, and in badlands for their alien topographies. Mountain climbing brings its own set of thrills. The targeted summit is often in plain view from miles away—there is little secrecy. Instead, we climb mountains for the awe of limitless space, for the physical accomplishment, and the aloneness that comes with it. We have a single destination in mind, that singular point in space where the land runs out and gives way to sky. There is no aimless ambling, no compromise—you have not conquered the mountain until you have reached that ultimate spot. Little compares to the exhilaration that rushes through your mind when you do, after a hard-won battle against gravity. The sense of personal victory is empowering. You are much of the time on top of the world, riding high on mazes of ridges overlooking glorious landscapes thousands of feet below. We seek desert summits for these rare bird's-eye views, as momentous as secrets, that embrace the vastness of the land.

In California's share of the Mojave Desert there are upward of 100 named ranges, mountains, hills, and buttes, and likely more than 800 named summits. This volume describes 130 peak climbs carefully selected among this copious menu. This selection was guided by a desire to reflect the Mojave Desert's remarkable diversity. Some summits were chosen because they are the highest, the greatest, or the most challenging; others because the route leading up to them passes by important historic mines, remote ghost towns, particularly scenic cactus gardens, stunning boulders, or exceptional Joshua tree forests. Another criterion was wildness. Given that the region has enough pristine summits to last a dedicated peakbagger more than a lifetime, summits degraded by paved roads, radio installations, or the proximity of freeways or power plants were excluded. Priority was given instead to summits located in designated wilderness, places wilder than most parks by the simple virtue of being roadless and sometimes less charismatic. Most wilderness summits are still just as scenic, yet they are climbed by only a handful of very small parties every year, and some years by no one at all. In most ranges, at least one relatively easy peak was included to appeal to a broader audience and encourage first timers to give desert mountains a try.

In these primitive desert landscapes, brutal and dramatic, there is tremendous beauty. We can only see it when we go out there, on foot in the scalding sun or maddening wind, or on a perfect spring day, and cover the rocky miles that it takes to visit properly—quietly, attentively, respectfully. Readers have expressed their gratitude that my desert books have given them the impetus to explore, the knowledge and confidence to strike out on their own into the most remote areas, and ultimately a deep appreciation of the desert. May this book serve too as a portal into ever more rugged landscapes, and inspire the same bewildered fondness for the desert's haunting beauty and timelessness. These hot, sweaty, blood-letting treks to the crown of the Mojave Desert could well become some of the greatest moments in your life.

Palo Alto, California
August 14, 2018

ABOUT THIS BOOK

General Organization

This volume is divided into eight parts. Parts 1, 2, and 3 provide background on the Mojave Desert's geography and climate, natural history, and human history, respectively. Part 4 covers safety tips, regulations, and ethics. The remaining four parts describe individual climbs in the four sub-regions, defined somewhat arbitrarily as:

• Northern Mojave Desert: north from the Avawatz Mountains and east from Eureka Valley, Saline Valley, and Panamint Valley;

• Eastern Mojave Desert: south from the Clark Mountain Range down to the southern boundary of Mojave Trails National Monument, and east from Barstow to Nevada and the Colorado River;

• Southern Mojave Desert: from Route 66 between Barstow and Amboy south to the eastern San Bernardino Mountains, Little San Bernardino Mountains, Pinto Mountains, and Sheep Hole Mountains;

• Western Mojave Desert: west of Barstow and the Panamint Range.

Each part begins with a general introduction of the sub-region and a map showing the location of the peaks covered in it. Each range in the sub-region is introduced with a two-page summary of highlights, topography, geology, mining, botany, and other salient features. Under each range, individual climbs are arranged from north to south. A table of climbs at the end of the book summarizes the distances and elevation gains of all the summits covered in the book.

Organization of individual climbs

Each individual climb description contains six sections: a summary of highlights as a quick guide, three sections titled "General Information," "Location and Access," and "Route Description," a distance and elevation chart, and a map. Occasionally, other sections are included to cover more detailed points of geology or history.

"General Information." This section provides a synopsis of the key facts about the climb, including the following entries.

The climb mentions the one-way distance, the total elevation gain, and the total elevation loss of the climb(s) described in the section. All elevation figures account for small local elevation changes.

The climb also rates the *overall difficulty* of the climb. This is often the only place where this rating is mentioned. Ratings are based on distance and elevation gain, but mostly on ruggedness and steepness of the terrain, and the number and seriousness of obstacles. They assume that the climb is done in one day (breaking up a long climb into a two-day backpacking trip may make it easier) and in cool to warm weather. In very hot weather, the difficulty worsens considerably, and these ratings underestimate the difficulty. The following scale is used:

• Very easy: a short climb on open, gentle slopes; a rare occurrence.

• Easy: a relatively short climb on obstacle-free terrain with modest grades; accessible to most people.

• Moderate: a longer climb (3–4 miles one way), with moderate grades and obstacles; accessible to anyone in reasonably good shape.

• Difficult: steep grades (1,000 feet per mile) over longer distances (4-5 miles one way), substantial elevation change (2,000 feet or more), rough terrain, uneasy footing; good physical condition is imperative.

• Very difficult: much the same but with steeper grades, larger elevation changes (3,000 feet or more) and distances (5-7 miles one way), and/or very rough terrain; good physical condition is imperative.

• Strenuous: one or more of the following: very steep grades (1,500 feet per mile or more), long distances (7 miles or more one way), large elevation changes (4,000 feet or more), and very challenging terrain; requires excellent physical condition, training, and practice.

This scale is obviously subjective. However, I did my best to be consistent throughout the book. So even if you disagree with it, you should still be able to use it effectively as a relative scale: just calibrate it against your own scale and adjust it accordingly. For example, you may decide that climbs I rate moderate are usually easy for you.

USGS topographic maps lists the USGS 7.5' maps that cover the entire route of the climb. When several maps are required, the most useful maps are identified with an asterisk.

Maps indicates, in this order, the page location for the climb of the hand-drawn contour map, marked by an asterisk; in some cases, other contour maps (no asterisk) showing the peak in relation to adjacent areas; and the general map identifying the regional location of the summit, shown in italics.

"Location and Access." This section provides driving directions to the starting point of the climb. The type of road (paved, graded, primitive) is mentioned, as well as the vehicle requirement for unpaved roads (assuming dry weather). Vehicle requirement is a *very subjective* topic, and in this book it reflects *only* my own experience. I tend to be tolerant of rocks and bushes occasionally scraping my car. I understand that not everyone feels this way. *So be aware that on most of the primitive roads that I claim can be driven with a standard-clearance vehicle, the NPS and BLM are more conservative and recommend stronger vehicles. If you have little experience driving desert roads, or you do not want to push your car too hard, follow their recommendations instead of mine.*

"Route Description." This is the main section. It describes the natural features, main attractions, physical challenges of the climb, and route finding. Unless otherwise specified, all cardinal directions are referenced to the true north (North Star). Only in a few stated instances does it refer to the magnetic north. The magnetic declination ranges approximately from 11.4° east to 13.5° east.

When warranted, the Yosemite Decimal System is used to rate the *technical* difficulty of a climb. These ratings are based on personal evaluations and are therefore again subjective. They should be viewed as estimates. Since climbers disagree rather strongly about the definitions of the five classes used in this system, here are the ones I used:

• Class 1: Walking with no need for hands.

• Class 2: Use of hands for scrambling or balance, or on short easy walls or dry falls with little exposure.

• Class 3: Use of hands to climb on steep and somewhat exposed rock surfaces; beginners may find the need for a rope. From this class on up, a fall could be fatal.

• Class 4: Simple climbing moves with high exposure; natural protection can be found, although a rope may be required.

• Class 5: Technical climbing on sheer or overhanging rock faces with small footholds and handholds; requires skill and training, and on high climbs a rope and other hardware for safety are needed. Class 5.0 to 5.15c labels climbs with progressively more difficult moves.

TOPOGRAPHIC MAPS LEGEND			
═(66)═	Highway/Paved road	———	Contour line
= = = = =	Unpaved road (2WD)	———	Contour line (every fifth line)
- - - - -	4WD-HC road	—8400—	Elevation, in feet
- - - - - - - -	Hiking trail	⌒⌒	Wash
· · · · · · · · · ·	Cross-country route	▨▨	Broad gravel or sand wash
— — — —	State boundaries	·-·-·-·-	Wash distributary
)(	Pass	⌒⊢⌒	Fall/Boulder jam/Chockstone
¦	Gate	▱	Sand dunes
·	Manmade structure	∩	Natural bridge/Arch
□	Ruin	△	Summit
+	Grave	⌂	Grotto
⚠	Campground	⬭	Pond/Lake
⬥	Ranger station	⌒	Spring
✕	Picnic area	○	Well
☉	Guzzler	·	Water tank
⠇⠄	Corral	⊱	Adit/tunnel
⚘	Windmill	⊁	Collapsed adit
·S	Starting point of climb	▫	Mine shaft
		⊗	Open pit/Surface mine
↑ -N- ¦	North Star	x	Prospect
		◀ *To Baker* *(25 mi)*	Mileage from edge of map

Distance and elevation charts. Each climb description contains a chart that tabulates key features along the route, each entry showing its elevation and the one-way distance to it from the starting point (mile 0). For features reached by a side trip to a point of interest, the one-way distance to it from the point of departure off the main route is indicated in parentheses. The distance to the next entry on the main route is again measured from mile 0, and it does not take the side trip into account. Most distances are accurate to ±10%.

Maps. Each climb description includes a topographic map of the route hand-drawn from USGS topographic maps. North (North Star) is parallel to one edge of the map to within 1°. These maps include natural and manmade features, as well as local names, that do not appear on USGS maps. Not all obstacles are shown, especially in areas away from the main route. The contour interval is 80 feet on most maps. On extensive climbs, especially with difficult orienteering, bring the USGS topographic maps as well.

■

— 1 —

GEOGRAPHY AND CLIMATE

Boundary

The smallest of the five main North American deserts, the Mojave Desert is an arid ecoregion of approximately 47,500 square miles that straddles eastern California, southern Nevada, the extreme southwestern corner of Utah, and northwestern Arizona. To the west lies the Sierra Nevada's alpine cordillera, to the north the Great Basin Desert, to the south the Sonoran Desert. This book focuses exclusively on the California portion, which is the largest and arguably the most scenic and popular for outdoor recreation. Its boundary is most accurately defined not by geology, topography, or climate, but by botany—its plant associations differ sufficiently from those of neighboring regions to delineate it with astonishing precision. As defined by eminent botanist Willis Jepson, the Mojave is bounded to the west by Eureka Valley, Saline Valley, the Sierra Nevada, and the Tehachapi Mountains; to the southeast by the San Gabriel and San Bernardino mountains, Coachella Valley, the Eagle, Coxcomb, Turtle, and Whipple mountains; and to the northeast by the border with Nevada and Arizona. This is a huge province. Driving along its western margin from Bishop near its north end to Indio near its south end via Mojave, Barstow, and Yucca Valley, all on paved roads, takes close to six hours. Returning along its east side, on backcountry roads, would take much longer.

Topography

Much of the Mojave Desert is Basin and Range country, a repetitive pattern of long parallel valleys oriented predominantly along a north-northwest axis and separated by high mountain ranges. This

7

quintessential American West landscape is most dramatic in the northern Mojave, where massive ranges tower 8,000 feet or more above low valleys near 1,000 feet of elevation or less. The most formidable is legendary Death Valley, a 140-mile trench that bottoms out at Badwater, 282 feet below sea level and the lowest point in the western hemisphere. It is framed to the west by the Panamint Range, capped by 11,049-foot Telescope Peak, the highest summit in California's Mojave Desert. In the Mojave Desert's southern third, the ranges gradually get smaller, lower, and less oriented, and the valleys grow in size. In the extreme southern area, compressive north-south forces along the San Andreas Fault have uplifted a 300-mile belt of mountains oriented east-west, across the prevailing direction. The San Bernardino and Little San Bernardino mountains are part of these renegade Transverse Ranges, which reach more than 2 miles above the sea.

Although California's Mojave Desert is not officially included in the Great Basin, by strict application of the definition of the Great Basin, most of it is part of the Great Basin: except for three eastern valleys that are part of the Colorado River drainage, all valleys have no outlet to the sea. Off and on during much wetter periods between about 186,000 and 11,000 years ago, every valley was flooded under a pluvial lake. Some lakes overflowed into each other and formed long convoluted chains. The largest one was the Owens Valley lake system, which linked Owens Valley to Death Valley via Owens Lake, China Lake, Searles Lake, Lake Panamint, and finally Lake Manly, 100 miles long and 600 feet deep. Many other valleys had prime beachfront properties, from Kelso Valley in the eastern Mojave Desert to Antelope Valley in the western Mojave and Sheep Hole Valley in the southern Mojave. The drying climate eventually desiccated all lakes, leaving behind playas of cracked mud or evaporites. Every depression now holds a dry lakebed, one of the flattest and eeriest landforms on the planet. Since then, in the vicinity of many playas wind-blown particles have accumulated into sensuous sand dunes.

Legacy

Seemingly limitless and still uncrowded, the Mojave Desert is a region of rough mountains and desolate valleys vibrant with light, a landscape so mysterious and little known that it makes an adventurer's heart long to return. Each sub-region has its own attractions, its own charm and personality. The northern Mojave is the home of Death Valley, the hottest spot on Earth, a place of massive mountain ranges gouged by long walled-in canyons, of valleys deeper than the Grand Canyon, of playas filled with giant salt crystals, and sumptuous

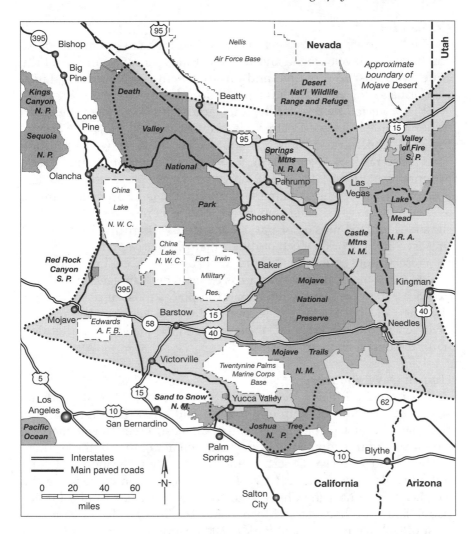

cliff-forming sedimentary formations. The eastern region is a glorious celebration of nature's immensity, where cinder cones, volcanic table-lands, and craggy mountains rise thousands of feet above huge valleys. It has singing dunes, limestone caves, outlandish cactus gardens and wildflower shows, and a blissful lack of modern commodities. The southern region is different still, a riveting outdoor museum of monumental rock sculptures polished to sensual shapes, of boulders falling over boulders, of high valleys green with oaks, conifers, and forests of Joshua trees that look like something from another galaxy. As a whole, it is a land of impossible contrasts, suffused with silence, astounding colors, and intoxicating solitude.

Conservancy

Thanks to its remarkable scenery, to its harsh environment poorly conducive to development, and to its fortuitous location in one of the country's most progressive and environmentally conscious states, California's Mojave Desert has a prestigious history of land conservancy. It is protected by three of the four largest desert parks in the coterminous United States—Death Valley National Park, Mojave National Preserve, and Mojave Trails National Monument—as well as Joshua Tree National Park, Sand to Snow National Monument, and Castle Mountains National Monument. Large tracks are preserved in 36 designated wilderness areas, some larger than a small European country, as well as scores of smaller state parks, botanical reserves, and wildlife sanctuaries. This mosaic of parks constitutes the fifth largest desert preserve in the world. Much of the rest is split between five large military reservations, public lands, and townships. Although military-controlled lands have been in some areas extensively damaged by training exercises, they are much wilder than the places most of us call home, and they receive far fewer visitors. Military bases are also actively involved in the conservation of plants, wildlife corridors, and critical natural habitats on their lands.

Human Developments

California's Mojave Desert has approximately 920,000 residents scattered in about 50 hamlets, towns, and cities. The largest city, Palmdale, has 160,000 inhabitants; the smallest, Essex, fewer than 10. About 86% of the population is concentrated along the southern fringe of the western Mojave Desert, from Mojave down through Antelope Valley to Barstow. The next two largest population centers are the Ridgecrest area near the China Lake Naval Air Warfare Center (33,000 people), also in the western Mojave, and the Yucca Valley area northwest of Joshua Tree National Park (60,000 people). The rest, more than 90% of the area, has fewer than 40,000 inhabitants and no large settlements. On the immediate periphery of the region, there are a few rural towns in Owens Valley and on the Nevada and Arizona sides, and a large population center around Palm Springs just south of Joshua Tree.

For over 150 years, the relative openness of the Mojave Desert's southern third has prompted its wholesale use as a transportation corridor. It is used today to move anything from humans on two interstates (I-15 and I-40) and three major highways (395, 58, and 95); freight on three railways (the Union Pacific, Santa Fe, and Parker branch); pressurized natural gas in many buried pipelines; water from the Arizona border and the eastern Sierras to southern California; and electrons on a grid of high-voltage steel-tower power lines. Since the 2000s, energy corporations have converted tens of thousands of pristine acres into power plants, concentrated mostly around Mojave, Fremont Valley, and Ivanpah Valley, and communication companies have erected microwave towers on dozens of mountains. The creation of Mojave Trails and Sand to Snow national monuments in 2016 was motivated in part by the need to offset this increasing loss of ecological integrity and degradation of viewshed, and to curtail further damage.

Climate

The Mojave Desert is a land of climatic extremes. Summers are stifling hot and parching, with a sky that will stay heartbreakingly clear for days on end. Winters are surprisingly cold, generally dry too, and often partly cloudy. In the middle of July in Death Valley the thermometer regularly reaches above 120°F and may not drop below 100°F, even at night, for several days. Even up at 8,000 feet, the midday temperature will still be in the three-digit range. In the middle of January on that same mountain it may be miserably cold, with snow and freezing winds. Although Death Valley is certainly the most extreme, these trends are similar elsewhere.

At any given time of year, the temperature can vary substantially across the desert. The reason is that the range of elevations is huge. Valley floors are typically between sea level and 3,000 feet and surrounded by mountains between half a mile and two miles higher. Except perhaps on the hottest days, the temperature drops relatively quickly with elevation, by roughly 4°F per thousand feet of elevation gain up to about 5,000 feet, and slightly faster higher up. In summer, when the generally lower summits of the eastern Mojave Desert are unbearably hot, the weather can be noticeably more pleasant on a 9,000-foot peak in the northern Mojave. The reverse is true in the dead of winter, at which time the lower desert is more comfortable.

The hot season starts earlier and lingers later in the year than in more temperate parts of the American West. Late October can be still sweltering, and April already unpleasantly hot. Springs and falls tend to be therefore comparatively short. In the fall the weather often switches from too hot to not warm enough in a matter of two or three weeks. In mid-October the valley temperatures can still be in the 90s, but by Thanksgiving the cold weather has settled in everywhere. Timing a fall visit correctly can be hit or miss. Year-round, the best guide is on-line weather forecasts. They are generally fairly accurate. The forecast being usually available only in valleys, use the 4°F-per-1,000-feet rule to estimate the temperature on nearby mountains.

Any time of year, weeks can go by without a drop of rain. The annual precipitation in the valleys averages around 5 inches. Olancha (3,650'), along Owens Lake, receives 7.4 inches; Ridgecrest (2,290'), in Indian Wells Valley, 4.7 inches; and Needles (1,600'), along the Colorado River, (5.1 inches). The Ranch at Death Valley (-180') is the driest—it gets less than 2 inches. The mountains are a little wetter—9 inches at 4,500 feet in the Granite Mountains or at 7,000 feet in the Panamints; 11 inches at Mountain Pass (4,650 feet); and at most 15 inches above 10,000 feet. The wettest period, December through March, receives 40% to 50% of the water. The moisture then comes from the Pacific Ocean; little of it reaches the desert because the desert lies in the rain shadow of the Sierra Nevada and San Bernardino Mountains. There is a spike of rainfall during the desert monsoon from July to September, originating in the Gulf of Mexico and the Gulf of California. It can generate thunderstorms with devastating power. The driest month is June. There is also a lull in rainfall in October.

High winds are common year-round, especially in winter and spring. They arise from strong temperature gradients between the lower valleys and the cooler surrounding ranges. They occur some- times several times a month, lasting generally a few hours only, although on occasion they will persist for a few days. In the northern Mojave, the long valleys trapped between parallel ranges also act as efficient wind tunnels, and storms often degenerate into sand storms. They will send thick clouds of dust hundreds of feet in the air and greatly reduce visibility. Wind storms tend to be milder elsewhere, though still powerful. Strong winds are most common on valley floors. They often prevail over thousands of square miles.

Snow graces the desert's highest summits off and on between December and March, and a late cold, wet front may apply one last coat as late as May. For a few weeks, sometimes longer, they become bright beacons visible from great distances—Telescope Peak, Clark Mountain, the Providence Mountains, Charleston Peak in Nevada, San Gorgonio Mountain and San Jacinto Peak just outside the Mojave Desert to the south, and of course the Sierra Nevada. Numerous sum- mits above about 6,000 feet can receive more amounts of snow. Snowfalls are more abundant on the higher northern ranges, and on the more western ranges, closest to the ocean. Occasionally a freak storm will blanket a large area down to 4,000 feet or even lower. The frequency and abundance of snowfalls have greatly diminished in the last decade. Summits that were white without fail in winter now often receive no snow at all. Like on Kilimanjaro, the snow may not return.

■

2

NATURAL HISTORY

Geology

   Proterozoic. The oldest rocks in the Mojave Desert belong to the underlying continental crust, which dates back to the Early Proterozoic. Between roughly 1.8 and 1.1 billion years ago, the region was intruded by huge quantities of magma, which led to turbulent mountain-building episodes. It involved intense faulting, folding, and metamorphism. Existing rocks as well as plutons implanted concurrently were subjected to extreme temperatures and pressures deep in the crust, and transformed into various forms of gneiss and schist. Their parentage can sometimes be traced to either sedimentary or igneous rocks. So we know that sedimentation took place even prior to that time, and that the region was submerged.

   Later, this Proterozoic complex and whatever rocks covered it were uplifted and exposed to a few hundred million years of erosion. Later still, especially in the Mesozoic, it was partly assimilated into rising magma. Today, these rocks are exposed in many ranges, although expectedly over generally very limited areas. The largest exposures are found at the base of some of the major ranges, where vertical tectonic movements have pushed up the crust high enough to exhume these deep-seated rocks. This is true on the south flank of the Little San Bernardino Mountains along the San Andreas Fault; in the western Black Mountains across from Death Valley's lowest point; and at the western base of the Panamints. Much larger areas are exposed on the east side of Clark Mountain and the Ivanpah Mountains, and on the north slopes of the New York Mountains. That area has the most complete sequence of Proterozoic rocks in California.

Late Proterozoic and Paleozoic. Around 1.1 billion years ago, near the close of the Middle Proterozoic, the Mojave Desert lay in a fault-bounded trough on the shore of supercontinent Rodinia. Over the next 465 million years, the area was alternatively eroded and flooded as the trough was uplifted, then subsided, three times. At each cycle the environment changed, and so did the sediments that accumulated in it. At first it was conglomerate and mudstone brought in by stream erosion of the surrounding Proterozoic uplands, then limestone formed in a warm sea, and finally siltstone and sandstone. These sediments became the Crystal Spring Formation. The next cycle deposited a thick sequence of carbonates known as Beck Spring Dolomite. During the last cycle, which produced the Kingston Peak Formation, the environment changed several times, leading to a complex sequence of limestone, sandstone, conglomerate, and three strata of unsorted rocks that record long periods of glaciation on a planetary scale.

At the end of that era, around 635 million years ago, a new trough opened that eventually broke through the crust and grew into an ocean. From then through the Paleozoic and until the Early Triassic, tens of thousands of cubic miles of sediments accumulated in this widening trench. As the shoreline shifted with fault movements, the sediments evolved. When the shore was near, as in much of the Late Proterozoic and earliest Paleozoic, sediments were predominantly gravel, sand, and mud washed down from the continent. Compressed by the enormous weight of subsequent sediments, they were metamorphosed into the quartzites and shales characteristic of that era. After that time, the continental shelf slowly subsided, and marine organisms became the main sediments. For the next 300 million years—most of the Paleozoic—they formed the thick interlayered strata of mostly dolomite and limestone that dominate units from that era. As an aggregate, these sedimentary formations reached some 5 *miles* in thickness, the lithified skeletons of myriad shelled animals.

Today, from the northern Mojave south to the Marble Mountains and into southwestern Nevada, many ranges are made at least in part, and sometimes almost exclusively, of the often spectacular sedimentary rocks deposited during this 960-million-year slice of history.

Mesozoic. By the end of the Paleozoic, Rodinia had broken up, and the land masses had reassembled themselves into a new supercontinent called Pangaea. In the Late Triassic, Pangaea started breaking up too. As the North American land mass drifted west, the ocean floor subducted under it. The continental shelf was uplifted, and for the first time in hundreds of millions of years, the ocean withdrew. As the

ERA	AGE Million years	MAIN EVENTS	LITHOLOGY
Cenozoic	~20 ~37 66	**Volcanism and tectonism**	Basalt, andesite, rhyolite, tuff, trachyte, dacite, cinder, scoria, pyroclastics, and breccia
		Sedimentation	Sandstone, mudstone, conglo.
		Erosion	
Mesozoic	252	**Volcanism, plutonism, and erosion**	Volcanics suites Monzonite, quartz monzonite Granite, monzogranite Diorite, monzodiorite Syenite, syenogranite Gabbro
Paleozoic	541 ~1100	**Marine sedimentation, rifting, and glaciations**	Limestone, dolomite, dolostone Shale Sandstone, siltstone Quartzite Diamictite
Proterozoic	~1800	**Erosion** **Plutonism, rifting, and metamorphism**	Granitoids Granitic gneiss, augen gneiss, amphibolite, migmatite Metasedimentary rocks, quartzite Hornblende or biotite schists

subducting plate ground against the continent's underbelly, it was shoved deep down into the mantle and melted into large reservoirs of magma. The phenomenal friction launched a series of compression waves through the continental margin, which folded and faulted older rocks. The magma found pathways up through these faults and erupted in a chain of volcanoes that rose along the edge of the continent. Over time, they emitted many thousands of feet of lava, building a shelf of volcanic rocks that extended more than 200 miles to the west.

Volcanism eased up in the Middle Jurassic to Early Cretaceous. Concurrently, and throughout the rest of the Mesozoic, magma also crystallized into enormous chambers of granitic rocks. The largest of these batholiths produced California's 400-mile-long Sierra Nevada. Dozens of smaller plutons, the largest covering more than 500 square miles, were implanted east and southeast of it, across the future Mojave Desert. The infiltrating magma either ingested existing formations or metamorphosed them into marble, quartzite, and metasedimentary gneisses. The magma crystallized into broad suites of rocks with a lexicon of tongue-twisting compositions. These batholiths, large and small, delivered many of the rich metal deposits mined in the 19th and 20th centuries. They intruded mostly the western and southern parts of the region, diminishing in intensity east from the Sierra Nevada, and had a much lighter impact in the northern Mojave and parts of the eastern Mojave, where the Paleozoic sedimentary formations still dominate. Plutonism stopped around 70 million years ago, near the end of the Mesozoic, when the ocean plate started subducting at a shallower angle and no longer reached deep enough to melt.

Cenozoic. The first part of the Cenozoic was a period of relative quiescence. For approximately 45 million years after plutonism had run its course, much of the region was an upland. Erosion removed some of the older rocks overlying the Mesozoic batholiths, which smoothed down some of the older, more mountainous relief. Up until at least the Early Miocene, 20 million years ago, the region had a subdued relief dotted with shallow lakes and streams.

The event responsible for the end of this interlude was renewed tectonism. At the south end of the Mojave Desert, about 25 million years ago compressive forces along the San Andreas Fault Zone started squeezing the Pacific Plate northward against the North American Plate. The resulting uplift produced southern California's long oriented east-west cordillera known as the Transverse Ranges. An even more major event started around 16 million years ago. From just east of the Sierra Nevada, through most of Nevada, and into western Utah and southern Idaho, the continental plate was pulled apart and started to stretch. This extension thinned and fractured the crust into fault-bounded blocks the size of mountains, generally oriented parallel to each other in an east-west to northeast-southwest direction. Pushed around by tectonic forces, these blocks rose, sank, and dipped, to become the landscape of long parallel mountains separated by deep basins typical of today's Basin and Range province.

This period of crustal thinning was also associated with intermittent outbursts of volcanism as magma rose through the faulted crust to the surface. Some eruptions were particularly violent, smothering thousands of square miles under thick ash flows or belching out tens of cubic miles of ejecta. The region witnessed many smaller eruptions, dozens in total, the most recent one less than 1,000 years ago. Throughout the Mojave, from the Providence Mountains to the Coso Range and from the Ord Mountains to the Greenwater Range, many ranges have sizable exposures of material spewed out by this wave of volcanism. Some, like the Piute Range and the Lava Mountains, are made almost exclusively of Miocene volcanic rocks.

Over the last few million years, as the valleys were sinking, they were periodically flooded under persistent lakes. During the last major flooding, in the last Ice Age, all major basins were submerged under interlinked pluvial lakes. The lakes' subsequent desiccation left behind huge playas of clay or salt, some covering hundreds of square miles. The lacustrine deposits beneath the larger ones reach down 3,000 feet to bedrock and record a nearly continuous history of sedimentation. Dunes were the last additions to the landscape. They formed after the lakes dried up and released the sand and silt they had accumulated.

Botany

At least 1,000 plant species grow in the Mojave Desert. Vast areas have not yet been inventoried; there are likely many more. This diversity stems in part from the desert's large range of elevations and broad variety of rock compositions. The environment in which a given species likes to grow is determined by its tolerance to many variables, particularly precipitation, moisture, temperature range, topography, soil texture and chemistry, drainage, and light exposure. Species with similar tolerances to these variables tend to gather in communities that often cover huge areas. Because elevation controls to a large extent several of these parameters, plant communities are often defined by elevation. Because elevation is not the only controlling factor, they often partly overlap. They are usually labelled after their dominant species, the plant that is most abundant and/or covers the most ground.

Wildflowers are a common denominator that permeates all plant communities. The blooming season starts on the lower alluvial fans and bajadas between early March and early April. If the winter rains have been evenly spaced and temperatures not too severe, annuals can carpet thousands of acres with vibrant flowers—pale yellow dandelion and tackstem, blue phacelia, bright-yellow desertgold, white evening primrose, and many others. For a few weeks, terrains normally dull brown turn tender green under a veneer of young shoots. Over time the flower displays migrate to higher ground, reaching the highest summits in summer. Common flowers include globemallow, Indian paintbrush, Mojave aster, penstemon, and Goodding's verbena. Fall brings another wave of flowers, smaller in magnitude and diversity. There are several classic beauties not to be missed, flowers that will stop you dead in your tracks: the masses of rose-purple blossoms of giant four o'clock, the deep-purple indigo bush, the arresting snow-white desert lily, the delicate pink globes of desert five spot, and the huge white trumpets of sacred datura. The most dazzling are unquestionably the cacti. Most species put forth a flood of large flowers in shades of pink, vermillion, red, magenta, and yellow so saturated that they seem out of place in the desert.

Alkali flat communities. At the bottom of the ladder are the chemical shores and playas of dry lakes, among the desert's most barren areas. The clay in the lakebed prevents rainwater from percolating. When the water evaporates, it deposits dissolved salts that accumulate in the soil. The high salinity limits plant life to the few species with taproots deep enough to reach water and offset the drying power of alkaline salts. This community is dominated by mesquite and desert holly. Mesquite is a low spiny tree with handsome green leaves. It is also well adapted to aridity, and common in washes. Desert holly is a remarkable plant that can grow in pure stands on the driest, poorest soils. It resembles a holiday holly sun-bleached to a ghostly ash color. When soaked by a good rainfall, playas can turn into green marshes of bulrush, pickleweed, and cattail spaced by scraggly lawns of saltgrass.

Saltbush scrub community. Away from dry lakes, the soil salinity drops and the plant diversity steadily increases. In this zone of typically well-spaced vegetation, the main species belong mostly to the hardy *Atriplex* genus—four-wing saltbush, shadscale, and allscale—as well as a few species of lycium. Saltbush is dominant, a large, pale-green shrub with a fluffy-looking crown. It has in fact the widest distribution of any true desert shrub in North American deserts. Its success is due in part to its tolerance to drought, its taxonomic variability, and its adaptation to a variety of soils and elevations, and to wind pollination. Its range extends far beyond this community. It survives equally well in sand dunes as in rocky canyons and on mountain slopes.

Creosote bush community. Alluvial fans and bajadas, which range from near sea level to about 3,500 feet or even higher in the eastern Mojave, are dominated by creosote bush scrub vegetation. The iconic creosote bush is the largest biomass, in part because of its larger size— it can reach 12 feet in height. After a rainstorm the air is filled with its pungent earthy smell. To increase water capture after a rainfall, it has developed a widespread root system. At lower elevations, it shares dominance with bursage, a small shrub also highly adapted to heat and aridity. To approach a mountain, we often wander for a few miles between these regularly spaced plants. The symmetry is inviting. It is the right proportion of ground and plants, enough space to walk yet not too barren. The repetitive pattern of dominant plants is occasional-ly broken by cheesebush, brittlebush, the spiky crown of a Mojave yucca, the blue-green pads of beavertail cactus, or a lone silver cholla.

Blackbrush community. This widespread vegetation type occupies at least 7.5 million acres throughout the Southwest, spanning a broad range of elevations between the creosote-bush community and pinyon-pine woodlands. Blackbrush either forms nearly pure stands, or it is more frequently mixed with these two communities and Joshua tree woodlands. It is an extensively branched shrub, usually 1 to 5 feet tall, named for its dark-gray to blackish bark. Where it grows in close ranks, it can be challenging to walk through without getting generous-ly scraped by its stiff, pointed branches. It grows in association with many minor species, most of which are common in other communi-ties—brittlebush, California buckwheat, ratany, desert almond, desert senna, turpentine broom, and several types of grass. This community, including the tough stems of blackbrush, provides ample food for rodents, birds, mule deer, and bighorn sheep.

Joshua tree woodlands. Joshua trees occur almost exclusively in the Mojave Desert, often in woodlands spread across entire valleys, passes, or other comparatively level areas. This iconic multi-branched yucca tipped with orbs of skewers does not grow everywhere, but if you see one you are probably in the Mojave. The subspecies found in the northern and eastern Mojave Desert, *jaegeriana*, is slightly shorter and has a denser crown, which gives it a more compact and symmetric appearance. The *brevifolia* subspecies, which has a taller trunk and larger leaves, lives in the southern and western Mojave.

In spite of this broad distribution, Joshua trees are particular about their habitat. They need well-drained loamy soil, at least 3 but no more than 12 inches of rain a year, and temperatures neither too high (they find it too hot in summer below about 3,500 feet) nor too low (winters are too cold for them above about 6,000 feet). They are widespread in the eastern and southern Mojave, although some areas have none.

Nolina, Kingston Range

Shadow Valley and Cima Dome in the eastern Mojave, and Lost Horse Valley in the southern Mojave, have some of the largest Joshua tree woodlands, and imposing specimens up to 40 feet tall. In the rest of the desert they are less common, and generally not as bulky.

Joshua tree woodlands include many mid-elevation species—lycium, squawbush, catclaw, brittlebush, paperbag bush, buckwheat, cactuses, chollas, and yuccas. Mojave yucca is the most common. Its unmistakable rosette gathers numerous yellowish-green stiff daggers 2–3 feet long edged by curly fibers, often at the top of a spine-covered trunk, sometimes in tall clusters. Nolinas have narrower, more flexible leaves than Mojave yuccas. They are locally abundant in the southern and eastern Mojave Desert. Chollas are easily distinguished by multiple branches composed of jointed cylindrical segments covered with needles. The silver cholla, a compact bush with a thick crown of shorter stem-joints, is the most widespread. The staghorn cholla is a close second, and the largest: its long untidy arms often dangle high above the ground. Six of the Mojave Desert's seven species of prickly-pear also live in Joshua tree woodlands. The beavertail cactus is most recognizable because of its spineless pads dotted with clumps of short bristles. Mature pancake prickly-pear look like a squat tree with Ping-Pong pads for branches. The other prickly-pears are prone plants, and less common.

Agaves grow at about 300 to 5,000 feet and overlap with Joshua tree woodlands. Unlike in yuccas, their rosettes have broader leaves edged with sharp teeth, and they have no trunk. Most agaves flower once and die. The rosette then sprouts a tall stalk crowned by profuse clusters of large creamy flowers. The desert agave grows in sandy washes and on rocky slopes in the western Wonderland of Rocks and Little San Bernardino Mountains. The simple desert agave occurs in the Ivanpah, Granite, and Old Woman mountains, and east from there. The smaller pigmy agave lives only in the Clark Mountain Range and the New York and Ivanpah mountains. Its rosette is a handsome sphere of leaves curved inward and tipped by a long, wispy thread.

Four species of oak, a genus not usually adapted to drought conditions, live in a few cooler and wetter ranges, congregating strictly in rocky terrains where water can percolate to their roots. They usually overlap with the upper Joshua tree and lower conifer woodlands. Scrub oak is a deciduous shrub or small tree that does not get much taller than 10 feet. It resembles the live oaks of California's coastal and inland regions, with curled leaves no more than an inch long protected by spiny margins. They are found in the New York Mountains, and two hybridized related species in the southern Mojave Desert. In contrast, canyon live oaks grow to be real trees, up to 30 feet tall. They are restricted to a few montane canyons in the eastern Mojave Desert.

Juniper-pinyon pine woodlands. Most desert ranges are sky islands, tracks of high country ringed by low desert valleys that cuts them off biologically from the rest of the world. Being higher, they are cooler and slightly wetter, which creates a microclimate hospitable to a greater variety of flora and fauna. Unable to make the journey across the much hotter and drier surrounding valleys, much of this richer life is stranded. Over time, sky islands have become refuge for species not found for tens of miles around—or anywhere else on Earth.

The most blatant manifestation of range insularity is pinyon-pine woodlands. Widespread throughout the North American deserts, they are the world's most extensive drought-resistant conifer forest. Juniper occur first, then a mixed zone of juniper and pinyon pine at higher elevation, and finally pinyon pine only. By far the most common is the Utah juniper. It is a sturdy tree, usually under 30 feet high, often with a twisted trunk and peeling bark. It often relinquishes some of its branches to dedicate its limited moisture to the remaining branches. Almost every major range has Utah juniper, either as extensive forests, dispersed stands, or scattered trees. The California juniper, on the other hand, is a shrubby tree with multiple trunks. It grows in particular in the Granite and San Bernardino mountains. Blue yucca is found in association with juniper. It looks like the Mojave yucca, with a slightly rounded rosette of blue-green spikes.

The dominant species is the single-leaved pinyon pine, an aromatic tree with a profuse crown of short needles arranged, unlike all other pine trees, in single needles. Slow-growing, they can reach a height of 40 feet and live to be about 200 years old. Mountain mahogany, a 15- to 25-foot-tall bush with lance-shaped leaves and the stature of a tree, is also conspicuous in this community. Thicker and greener, the ground cover is dominated by blackbrush, ephedra, cliffrose, and big sagebrush. Grizzly bear cactus is the most common prickly-pear. Its small pads are covered by a whitish mass of long flexible spines resembling tousled hair. Canyon floors generally have slightly different plant associations than the surrounding slopes, with a higher representation of rabbitbrush, mesquite, catclaw, as well as willows and baccharis near groundwater. In its lower reaches, especially in Joshua Tree, conifer forests grade into Joshua tree woodlands. These deep pockets of greenery provide shade, coolness, and higher humidity, and in hot weather a welcome break from the dryness and harsh light of the lower desert.

The highest crests are also home to relict groves of other conifers that were once much more widely distributed in the Mojave. White fir, a classic conifer shaped like a Christmas tree with handsome steely blue needles, has shriveled to small stands in the New York Mountains, on Clark Mountain, and in the Kingston Range. Limber pine is restricted to a few locations in the Grapevines and Panamints. Bristlecone pine, a skeletal tree with short stiff needles arranged like a bottlebrush, survives usually above about 10,000 feet. In the Mojave it grows only in the Panamint Mountains, and below its comfort zone in the Last Chance Range where a single tree still clings to life.

Wildlife

We do not come to the Mojave Desert for wildlife safaris. On a typical hike, sightings can be counted on the fingers of one hand—a few birds and lizards, perhaps a rabbit or a ground squirrel, and likely no larger animals. Desert wildlife is generally shy and elusive, and some of it is nocturnal, but in spite of appearances, it is comparatively abundant. Our extensive system of interlocked parks and wilderness helps wildlife by providing critical habitats to live and breed, and vital connecting corridors to move comparatively safely across the desert. Even this hottest of deserts hosts hundreds of species of mammals, reptiles, insects, amphibians, snails, fish, and even more birds. You may never see most of them, yet the simple knowledge of their presence and of their admirable adaptation adds richness to the experience. This said, encounters with wildlife can be surprisingly frequent in the spring, when the weather is more pleasant and almost every able creature is out there with one thing in mind—mating. At the end of a good day, you might actually feel that you have been on a minor safari.

Mammals. Of all the desert's large mammals, the bighorn sheep is one of the rarest and most charismatic. Sheep live in small groups, mostly in mountainous areas where they can get an advance warning of approaching predators and take full advantage of their remarkable agility in difficult terrain to flee. They will come down to lower elevations to access watering holes, often at dawn. Most main mountain ranges have bighorn. Herds range in size from a few in small mountains to 30 in the New York Mountains, 40 to 50 in the Wonderland of Rocks and Clipper Mountains, and perhaps a few hundred in the Panamints. Sheep generally respond poorly to human disturbance. In heavily visited areas, they bed and spend more time further away from humans. When disturbance exceeds their tolerance, they abandon the area. Most herds are declining. An encounter is usually a brief thrill, as sheep are shy and will dash off at great speed, even on the rockiest terrain, as soon as they spot a human. In a few areas, they have become habituated to humans and can be observed leisurely.

Mule deer, the largest native animal, are more common but still fairly scarce. Mojave National Preserve is a prime stronghold, as are major ranges like the Panamint and Little San Bernardino mountains. They live mostly in sagebrush and forested habitats in the high country. They are also present in a few ranges with little to no forest cover, from the El Paso to the Old Woman and Chemehuevi mountains. They roam over fairly small areas, often as individuals or in small herds. In hot weather, they try to drink daily, hide during the day in the shade, and browse in the evening or at night.

The top predators are mountain lions and coyotes. Mountain lions are extremely rare. They live almost exclusively in the most remote, spacious, and deserted mountain ranges—places like the Panamint, Providence, Granite, New York, and Little San Bernardino mountains. They probably number less than a few hundred in the entire Mojave.

Coyotes are far more numerous, in part because, to the contrary, they have adapted to almost every environment, from valleys to high mountains and asphalted suburbs. I have seen them bravely crossing huge dry lakes, slithering between bushes in high mountains, slugging over sand, and resolutely trotting along interstates. They can hunt by day or by night, in packs or alone, feast on a fresh kill or carrion, survive on wild berries or cholesterol-rich garbage, and thrive in deserts or in snow. In some heavily visited areas, they have sadly adapted in yet another way, and will pose along roadways for a food donation.

This versatility, combined with the coyote's wise inclination to make himself inconspicuous, has enabled the species to pull through centuries of persecution. Animals who have had limited exposure to people will only let you get a fleeting glimpse as they furtively vanish behind vegetation cover. Yet they are there, every night, hunting and playing, howling their chilling calls in the gray light of dawn. They were venerated by many Native American tribes, and deified by Mexico's ancient civilizations, and it is easy to see why.

Feral burros are the largest mammal in the Mojave Desert. Native to northeastern Africa, they were first introduced in the late 1800s by prospectors, who used them as beasts of burden. Burros proved to be well adapted to the arid climate, and they multiplied into large populations. The main problem is that they compete directly with the native bighorn sheep. They eat and drink more, congregate around springs, contaminate the water, scare away other wildlife, create extensive networks of trails, often uproot plants and increase soil erosion, and reproduce at the alarming rate of 20-25% a year. Since 1939, NPS has humanely removed some 10,000 burros from the Death Valley region. Burros are still doing quite well on BLM and U.S. Forest Service desert lands, where, ironically, they are protected. Over time, they are drifting out of these protected areas into NPS units. It is not uncommon to run into small groups in the southern Panamint and Owlshead mountains, in Shadow Valley, in the Argus Range, and on lands bordering military properties.

Black-tailed jackrabbit,
Wonderland of Rocks

Many smaller and often much more plentiful mammals live in the Mojave, often with no strong habitat specificity. Black-tailed jackrabbit and desert cottontail are common. In some areas, mountains or low lands, there might be more than 100 per square mile. In the lower desert you might be lucky and spot a kit fox, badger, ringtail cat, or bobcat. Higher elevations support some of the same species as well as gray and red fox (often in brushy and wooded terrain), skunks, ground squirrels, and occasional chipmunks. There is also a whole menagerie of mice, rats, and gophers, who often dwell in burrows in sandy soil. One of the most commonly sighted and charming is the kangaroo rat, a silky-furred critter with a head almost as big as the body and a tail nearly twice as long, who bounds away in elegant leaps like a kangaroo. Many species of bats also live in natural caves and mine workings. They are out only between the last and first hours of the day, and their numbers are declining, so they are not often seen.

Reptiles. Lizards are abundant and easy to spot: except on cold winter days, it is unusual not to catch a glimpse of a lizard scurrying to shelter. The creosote bush and scrub jungles of the lower fans are the hangouts of zebra-tailed lizards (especially sandy washes), western whiptails, side-blotched lizards, desert iguanas, and long-tailed brush lizards (especially shrubby washes). The upper fans are home to desert horned lizard, armored like a knight, and desert night lizards. Gilbert's skinks and western fence lizards live in woodlands of sky islands. Chuckwallas, among the largest and most colorful, have a predilection for rocky outcrops; when threatened, they wedge themselves in cracks, inflate their bodies, and wait it out. Collared lizards favor boulders at mid-elevations. The Mojave fringe-toed lizard is superbly adapted to life in sand. It has developed fringes of pointed scales on the edge of its toes to prevent it from sinking and to race across loose sand. It also uses them to "swim" into sand, to escape a prey or extreme weather. It lives in several areas with deep sand, from the Kelso and Cadiz dunes to the Hollow Hills. The Gila monster, largest and only venomous lizard in the country, may be the rarest in the state: it has been sighted only 26 times. Its beaded skin is marbled with black and coral. Its neurotoxic venom has effects comparable to the rattlesnake's, but fortunately, unless stepped on or pestered, it is normally docile.

The Mojave Desert provides habitats to about 24 species of snakes. There are five species of rattlesnakes, the Mojave, western diamondback, red diamond, and speckled rattlesnakes, and the sidewinder. Highly venomous, they are the most dangerous locals. To make matters worse, they are fairly common and well camouflaged, and live at most elevations (the sidewinder only up to about 5,000 feet). Some snakes have patterns that resemble a rattler's. The slim, cat-eyed lyre snake does, and it is mildly venomous. The common kingsnake does too, but it is harmless, although when on alert it might try to pass for a rattler by vibrating its upright tail. Learn to identify the dangerous snakes as a precaution and to enjoy viewing the harmless ones. If you see a suspicious snake with red, yellow, and black cross-bands, it is a long-nosed, a western shovel-nosed, or a ground snake—harmless.

The lithe and speedy coachwhip can exceed 8 feet in length. The worm-looking western blind snake is albino. The rosy boa kills the small animals it preys on by constriction. The gopher snake and red racer are also relatively common—all harmless.

Desert tortoises are another reptile perfectly adapted to the harsh desert environment. They inhabit gravelly washes and fans with creosote, thorny shrubs, and cacti. Like some plants, they are avoiders: they hibernate from October to March, and estivate in very hot weather. They are active mainly on sunny days between March and May, when plants are green and other *Gopherus agassizii* are around to mate. They like to sleep, bask in the sun, and eat, mostly grasses, cacti, and broad-leaved plants to build up their fat and water reserves. Much of their time is spent in burrows that they dig with their flattened front legs. It is a threatened species. Many areas are federally protected critical tortoise habitat, including wilderness areas, about half of Mojave National Preserve, and the Desert Tortoise Natural Area in Fremont Valley. They are seldom seen. If you see one, do not touch it, or you may pass on fatal diseases, and do not pick it up, or it may pee and lose precious water. Enjoy it from a distance. Patience helps: it may take a little wait before it decides to come out of its shell.

Birds. It is rare to spend a day without seeing a bird—several hundred species have been spotted in the Mojave Desert. A small fraction, perhaps less than 25%, are permanent residents. The rest is migratory birds. The species count is highest during the two main pulses of migration, March through May and August through October. In the summer, bird activity is very low except in the cooler hours of dusk and dawn. Springs are usually an exception; birds can be active there much of the day. Winter is the quietest time, although you might still be surprised by a solitary raven flying low on some secret mission.

There is generally a gradient of bird life with elevation. The drier fans and bajadas typically have limited breeding species, like sparrows, thrashers, and northern mockingbird. At higher altitudes, the vegetation diversifies and the list quickly gets longer. Among conspicuous species are ravens, turkey vulture, cactus wren, hummingbirds, and Gambel's quails, which liven many areas with their noisy clutches. Doves often rest on roads at dusk and night. Jays, mountain chickadee, and mountain quail live at even higher elevations. Raptors include golden eagle, American kestrel, northern harrier, prairie falcon, osprey, and hawks. If you tie something red to your tent or pack, hummingbirds will pay you a visit surprisingly often.

■

3

CULTURAL HISTORY

Native American History

Native Americans have lived in the Mojave Desert for at least 13,000 years. They were never numerous, but over the centuries many men and women lived and died and left marks of their passage. On the shores of Lake Manly in Death Valley and along the Colorado River, they abandoned crude stone tools now darkly patinated by prolonged weathering—scrapers, drills, blades, and gravers chipped out of local chert, jasper, and rhyolite. On Turquoise Mountain, northeast of Baker, there are ancient diggings where they mined turquoise off and on since at least 400 AD. Rock and cave shelters in the Providence and Woods mountains were littered with fragments of vessels, awls, hammerstones, basketry, and fire drills. The Coso Range holds tens of thousands of petroglyphs. An extensive network of prehistoric paths has been worn throughout the desert by repeated passages over desert pavement. The natives have left house circles, storage pits, bone tools, hunting blinds, bedrock mortars, dams, and irrigation ditches. From Panamint Valley to the Slate Range and the Colorado River, the desert is still decorated with the mysterious geoglyphs they built.

To eke out a living in the driest, hottest, and most forsaken North American desert, most native groups had adopted the harsh nomadic life of hunter-gatherers. They had adapted to a wide spectrum of ecological niches. They traveled from warmer valleys in the cold of winter to intermediate elevations in the spring, where they procured annuals and hunted the more abundant spring game. They escaped the summer heat by moving up into the mountains, where they also harvested pinyon nuts and high-elevation plants, and hunted large game. They had acquired a sophisticated knowledge of desert plants. Strands of willows and yucca roots were used for basketry. Arrowweed went into the construction of dwellings, windbreaks, and sweat houses. Hunting

Petroglyphs, Piute Range

bows were made of juniper and the arrows of willow. Through trial and error, and over probably considerable time, they had developed a fine medicine cabinet. They found out that creosote could heal many ailments or induce vomiting; that boiled cottonwood bark relieved headaches; that brittlebush was good for toothaches, big sagebrush for stomach aches, and sacred datura to get stoned. Their diet included dozens of species, from agave hearts to yucca buds. They knew how to increase the productivity of their lands with small prescribed burns of low severity.

Although a few bordering tribes like the Cahuilla made regular trips into the Mojave Desert, only five larger tribes inhabited the region—the Western Shoshone, Chemehuevi, Mohave, Kawaiisu, and Serrano. Their territories were generally not bound by hard frontiers but by porous, sometimes strongly overlapping boundaries that other tribes periodically crossed to access resources or sacred grounds, and to maintain trade relationships with far-away tribes. Except along the Colorado River, there was plenty of room to share.

The Western Shoshone. The Western Shoshone lived in the northern Mojave Desert. They were part of a much larger Shoshone Nation that inhabited a vast region stretching from western Wyoming to eastern Oregon, eastern California, and central Nevada. They were divided into small extended family groups, each concentrated in a particular area. Those who lived in Death Valley called themselves Timbisha. Their home was the mouth of Furnace Creek, where they enjoyed the abundant and reliable water of Travertine, Nevares, and Texas springs. Another group, the Panamint Shoshone, were based in northern Panamint Valley, and extended west to the Coso Range.

To meet their subsistence needs in the hottest place on Earth, they made use of just about every available resource, and they kept their numbers low. The Death Valley area was inhabited by few individuals, estimated around 100. The Western Shoshone moved frequently, following the rhythm of the seasons. In the wintertime they lived in the valleys in roofless brush shelters or in conical log dwellings. They hunted rabbits, rodents, birds, reptiles, and bighorn sheep. In spring they gathered wild plants, grasses, and mesquite beans. In summer they fed themselves on roasted pinyon-pine nuts up in the high mountains. Most of their time must have been dedicated to food gathering. Little time was left for other activities such as art, although they were deft pottery and basket makers.

Here as throughout the Mojave, the arrival of immigrants starting in the mid-1850s, and the influx of miners over the ensuing decades, destroyed this self-sufficient society. Newcomers established roads, camps, and mining districts, and manipulated water sources with disregard for prior Native American uses of the land. With their traditional hunting and foraging grounds gradually taken over, the natives became slowly acculturated. During the mining rush they often carried out manual labor for road building, construction, ranching, and mining. The beginning of tourism in the late 1920s further accelerated this disruption. A few families continued to visit the Death Valley area annually until the late 1930s, but eventually they also left or died.

Today, a few Timbisha Shoshone families live in a 314-acre village at the mouth of Furnace Creek. While other Shoshone and Paiute families share a few small reservations in Owens Valley, the Timbisha are faring much better. In 2000, 7,440 acres of tribal land were created outside Death Valley National Park. A huge area within the park, which includes the Panamint Range and portions of Mesquite Flat, Saline Valley, and Eureka Valley, was also earmarked for the tribe to carry out ecologically sustainable traditional practices.

The Chemehuevi. The Chemehuevi were originally Southern Piute who migrated from Nevada into California fairly recently, likely in the 17th century. They inhabited the region from around the Kingston Range south to near the Palo Verde Mountains, and from the Colorado River west to the Cady Mountains. At about 9,000 square miles, this was the largest geographic distribution of indigenous California people with a homogeneous dialect. They also occasionally ranged into the Tehachapi Mountains and as far as the Panamint Range, which they held sacred. Their lands ranked among the poorest in the state, and it was very thinly populated. The Chemehuevi likely numbered fewer than 1,000—on average, only one inhabitant per 10 square miles.

The Chemehuevi were famous for "visiting," which meant constantly being away. They could walk 20 miles a day for days without a break, arduous journeys they completed wearing moccasins and deerskin shirts. They lived and traveled in small groups, probably centered around a family nucleus. Their annual migration took them in a great circle around their territory. Chemehuevi men had the caricatural profile of weightlifters, with broad shoulders and slender waists. They walked very fast and carried a hook to pull small animals like gophers and rabbits out of their holes. They hunted pronghorn antelope and bighorn sheep with bows and arrows tipped with a stone point. They had mastered the fine art of weaving baskets, light and resistant vessels well adapted to migratory life. Their settlements ranged from temporary campsites to permanent villages. They occasionally farmed on small lots at well-watered springs, with limited success. Being very scattered and often on the move, it is doubtful that they had time to develop a new tribal identity. Culturally and linguistically, they remained indistinguishable from the Southern Piute.

That the Chemehuevi farmed under adverse conditions at desert springs rather than along the fertile Colorado River shores suggests that their difficult nomadic life was dictated in part by geopolitics. Yet, a more sedentary life along the river must have been a tempting alternative. Eventually, some Chemehuevi did move to the Colorado River. After the Halchidhoma left that area around 1829, the Mohave either invited or tolerated small bands of Chemehuevi to live there with them. The Chemehuevi adopted Mohave practices and began floodwater farming. During his historic visit in 1854, Lieutenant A. W. Whipple met some 50 Chemehuevi in today's Chemehuevi Valley. They were eager to trade their grain and vegetables with him, but cautious to stay away from the Mohave, who lived a short distance up the river.

The Mohave.   The Mohave have lived for a long time primarily along the Colorado River, in the vicinity of modern-day Needles. Four centuries ago, the Oñate expedition of 1604–1605 entered this region and met many Mohave, especially in Parker Valley where they lived in large numbers. They were the tallest of Native Americans, often taller than 6 feet, and excellent swimmers. Their religious beliefs made them go through life with heavy tattoos. Like the Yuma down the river, they had close cultural ties with the American Southwest. The river provided them reliable water, safety, minnows, shade, and greater comfort than the surrounding desert. On the arable river banks they grew maize, wheat, beans, squash, and tobacco. Mesquite beans, collected in the desert, were also a major staple. The Mohave also occasionally crossed the desert on foot to the coast to trade with local groups.

The river's banks where they lived were coveted land, and competition for it was fierce at times. Territorial war occasionally broke out between the river tribes. Between 1827 and 1829, after years of fighting against a Mohave-Yuma alliance, the Halchidhoma lost and evacuated the Colorado River corridor, leaving more space for the Mohave and for some Chemehuevi to settle. As emigrant settlements along the river displaced Chemehuevi families, the Chemehuevi responded with thefts and acts of violence, and the Mohave and Yuma often took the blame for it. In 1865, the year the Colorado River Indian Reservation was created, hostilities broke out between the Mohave, Yuma, and Yavapai in one camp, and the Chemehuevi and Piute in the other. The Chemehuevi were forced to retreat to the desert. When peace returned in 1867, the Mohave came back to Parker Valley, Chemehuevi Valley, and Cottonwood Island. In 1874 the reservation was expanded and the Chemehuevi were convinced by government officials to permanently settle on the river's west side. By then the eastern Mojave Desert had largely been abandoned by its indigenous population.

The Desert Kawaiisu. The Kawaiisu's homeland straddled two distinct geographic regions. The Mountain Kawaiisu had many settlements in the Tehachapi Mountains and the southern Sierra Nevada. The Desert Kawaiisu fanned out from there across the El Paso Mountains and the Slate Range to southern Death Valley. These two subgroups intermarried and shared the use of some desert areas. In spite of their westerly location, the Kawaiisu were culturally rooted in the Great Basin, like the Western Shoshone and the Southern Piute.

Because they inhabited a more temperate region of relatively high rainfall and richer vegetation, the Mountain Kawaiisu were likely more sedentary. The Desert Kawaiisu were more isolated and probably ranged far and wide. They collected salt on Koehn Lake, and hunted deer and bighorn sheep in the Argus Range. They had villages at such far apart locations as Little Lake, Hungry Bill's Ranch in the southern Panamints, and near Furnace Creek, these last two sites a mix of Kawaiisu and Western Shoshone. Coso Hot Springs was the site of an indigenous village and important ceremonial center. Southern Panamint Valley was largely inhabited by Kawaiisu, where their main settlement was Warm Springs—the Chemehuevi called the Kawaiisu *Panumunt*. It is likely that the Kawaiisu exploited the same resources as the Western Shoshone with whom they shared some of the land.

The El Paso Mountains, where the homelands of the two subgroups overlapped, held—and still hold—a special religious status. They were a major cultural and spiritual center, especially Black Mountain, which is sacred. It is likely that the Kawaiisu held annual mourning ceremonies there, as well as religious events similar to the Western Shoshone's, who believed in guardian spirits and shamanism.

The Serrano. The core region of the Serrano Indians was the high-lands of the San Bernardino Mountains and the Transverse Ranges, an area with more abundant resources (including water) that they shared with the Mountain Cahuilla. Some Serrano bands later extended east into the desert, along the Mojave River to around the western edge of the Cady Mountains. When Francisco Garcés visited the area in 1776, he found them more destitute than the highland Serrano. A quiet and inoffensive people, they wore coats made of rabbit pelt, and subsisted on acorn and small game that they trapped in snares made of wild hemp. Over the next century, these small bands suffered great losses from massacres by settlers and smallpox outbreaks after being forcibly relocated to missions—a common fate of Native Americans. The small remaining population of Serrano now lives in the general vicinity of the Santa Rosa Mountains on Cahuilla reservations. The two tribes have intermarried for so long that they are now difficult to distin-guish—the Serrano have been assimilated by both culture and nature.

Mining History

The desert has always fascinated fortune seekers. Its isolation, inhospitable geography, and harsh climate conveyed images of large tracts of unexplored land filled with hard-to-get riches waiting for hardy souls to discover. Between around 1860 and the end of the his-toric era about a century later, this overwhelming attraction inspired countless adventurers to brave the Mojave Desert in search of mineral treasures. From the Last Chance Range to the Hexie Mountains and from the Tehachapis to Needles, it is likely that more than 80,000 claims were filed over at least half a million acres. There is hardly a mountain range that was left unexplored. Gold and silver were the commodities of greatest interest, but many other metals and minerals were sought after—copper, lead, zinc, iron, tungsten, vanadium, tin, molybdenum, mercury, sulfur, talc, borax, barite, uranium, gems, and table salt. The vast majority of claims were never exploited. Most of the rest did not produce anything. But the small percentage of privi-leged mines that did make it took nothing short of epic proportions. They involved full-fledged companies, rowdy towns, elaborate mills, the blood and sweat of hundreds of hard-working people, and togeth-er they generated hundreds of millions of today's dollars.

The commodity that drew the first main wave of mining, starting production around 1870 and ending around 1893, was silver. During this era, the Darwin district, in the Argus Range, put out more than $20 million, most of it silver. Its neighbors, the Modoc and Minnietta Belle mines combined reached $2.9 million. The Ivanpah mines on

Clark Mountain grossed $3.8 million. For three years in the mid-1880s, the Bonanza King Mine, in the Providence Mountains, harvested $1.7 million. Several other mines had returns in the six figures. In the 1870s, high in the Panamints, Panamint City had many active mining properties. The bullion that came out of its monumental smelter was cast in 400-pound ingots too heavy for thieves to steal. Two decades later, the Alta Silver Mine in the Avawatz Mountains had ore so rich that it was shipped by express at a whopping cost of $135 a ton.

Throughout these early years, the price of gold was stable at about $20.70 per ounce. The value of silver, however, fluctuated in response to the market. When it dropped 40% between 1891 and 1894 and stayed down, miners turned to more valuable metals, especially gold and copper. Improved transportation by rail, advances in mining and ore-processing technologies, and a more stable economy, all combined to spark a new era for desert mining. During the ensuing two decades, through World War I, the Mojave Desert witnessed an explosion of mining activity. It prompted the construction of railroad spurs, which in turn reduced the cost of ore delivery to market and further stimulated mining. All over, new communities sprung up to support the miners. Every corner of the desert had its gold stars. The brightest one was the Yellow Aster Mine near Randsburg in the Rand Mountains. Until its clo-

Winch at the Contact Mine, Wonderland of Rocks

sure in 1942, it put out over $12 million from 15 *miles* of underground workings. A dozen other properties in the small Rand district brought in another $8 million. The Golden Queen Mine on Soledad Mountain south of the town of Mojave came in second, with more than $10 million; the nearby Cactus Queen Mine made $4 million. In Death Valley, the largest gold producer was the great Skidoo, the only mining area with a mill entirely powered by water pressure. The Keane Wonder Mine in the Funeral Mountains, for a time the state's largest gold producer, delivered upward of $1,000,000 of auriferous ore down one of the desert's most complex aerial tramways. Scores of smaller gold mines ended up with respectable six-figure productions—the Ashford and Inyo in the Black Mountains, the Ratcliff and the World Beater in the Panamints, the town of Vanderbilt, and the Reward, the Queen Esther, the Telegraph, the Elephant, the Lost Burro, and the Lost Horse.

Copper was not such a success. Many copper deposits failed to deliver because the ore did not extend at depth. The most resounding failure was the Greenwater rush. Starting in 1905, it quickly drew more than 2,000 people, stimulated the creation of four small towns and 73 mining companies, and attracted $30 million in investment. After the main shaft reached 1,400 feet and failed to turn up any copper, the site was abandoned overnight. The Ubehebe district in the Last Chance Range, the Willow Creek area in the Black Mountains, and several others, suffered similar fates. The only copper came out as secondary ore from mines seeking other metals. There were two notable exceptions. The Standard No. 1 Mine in the Ivanpah Mountains produced mostly copper—at least 320 tons between 1902 and 1919. So did the Copper World Mine on Clark Mountain. It was so rich that it had its own 50-ton smelter, to which the ore was delivered in the early years via twenty-mule team. From 1898 to the end of World War I, it extracted 3,300 tons of copper and became the largest historic copper producer in southern California.

During the Depression of the 1930s, there was a marked increase in mining as jobless people moved to the desert and resorted to small-time mining for survival. Small families reopened existing mines or reworked their tailings, using abandoned equipment and buildings, learning the trade on the spot. At the end of that era, in 1942, a government order closed down nearly all non-essential mines to encourage mining of base metals crucial to the war effort. Almost all gold mines shut down overnight and never reopened. The Carbonate King Mine in the Ivanpah Mountains and the mines on Zinc Hill in the Argus Range were among those that rose to the war challenge and generated record tonnages of zinc. So was the Vulcan Mine in the Providence Mountains: in five years it yielded 2.6 *million* tons of iron ore.

The Mojave Desert had good lead mines, although their returns were more modest. Operated from 1912 to 1928, then after 1938, the Shoshone Mines in the Nopah Range made $7 million. The Defense Mine in the Argus Range put out $1.3 million in the 1930s. On Clark Mountain, the Mohawk Mine yielded $600,000 from 1917 to 1952. The Queen of Sheba Mine, in the southern Panamints, was Death Valley's richest, although it produced only half as much. It became famous for the mysterious murder of its discoverer, Chester Pray, who was shot in 1913, likely by a competitor. There was also the lonesome Ubehebe and Lippincott mines out by the Racetrack; John Lemoigne's mine in the

Mengel's homestead in Butte Valley, southern Panamint Mountains

Cottonwoods, for which Old John turned down good offers even though it was not worth much; and Leadfield in the Grapevines, which was promoted with great fanfare but never delivered.

Many other commodities were mined not during a specific period but throughout the historic era. Over a period of five years in the 1880s, 20 million pounds of borax were harvested, refined, and hauled from Death Valley's Harmony Borax Works—a major portion of the country's supply. The Crater area on the crest of the Last Chance Range holds the second largest native sulfur deposit in the state. Between 1929 and 1969 it shipped 50,000 tons of sulfur, less than 2% of its reserve. Talc was extensively mined from a 70-mile talc-bearing arc that extends from the southern Panamints through the Ibex Hills, Avawatz Mountains, and Alexander Hills to the Kingston Range. This was one of the highest historic cash-making commodities, with a total yield of 1.2 million tons until 1959, extracted from about 30 mines.

The history of mining was shaped by the minds, skills, and deeds of many colorful characters—indefatigable prospectors, bold investors, visionary businessmen, chronic dreamers, and the inevitable crooks. Every era and area had its cast. In the eastern Mojave, the McFarlane brothers made the 1870 silver strikes that sparked the Ivanpah mines and masterminded their development. Their enterprise made millions and supported a whole town for nearly 20 years. In 1907, the Dawson brothers embezzled the money they had raised to develop a mine that did not exist. In 1934, a gentleman farmer named Earl Dorr published an affidavit in which he reported discovering a giant underground canyon filled with placer gold. Decades later, people are still looking for it. In the Ivanpah Mountains, World War I medic John "Riley" Bembry became a local legend by filing over 60 claims and acquiring many of the district's abandoned mines. Most of them had played out, and he reigned over a gutted empire. At the Lost Horse Mine, the most productive in the southern Mojave, co-owner Johnny Lang was caught stealing gold in the 1890s, forced to sell his shares, and went on to live off the stolen gold. The nearby Desert Queen Mine was for a time overtaken and controlled by a ruthless gang of cowboys headed by Jim McHaney, who later served seven years in a penitentiary for counterfeiting. In the 1940s and 1950s, Lee Foreman and William Skinner made a fortune reworking the Modoc Mine's old tailings.

Death Valley attracted the most heteroclite crowd. In 1882, prominent industrialist William Coleman built the Harmony Borax Works to process borax harvested on Cottonball Basin's salt flats, and became the tycoon of Death Valley's "white gold." His 20-mule teams heroically hauling refined borax across the desert are still an enduring symbol of the Death Valley days. Some prospectors, like Frank Shorty Harris, were so good that they made many lucrative strikes. Others did not do so well—like poet-prospector Clarence Eddy, who filed claims over thousands of acres in the sands of southern Death Valley, convinced that they held so much gold that "all the world will be rich." In 1909, gun-toting Johnnie Cyty murdered a claim jumper at his mine in the Funerals, was sentenced to jail, then acquitted, twice. Thomas Wright, a florist from LA, built an extravagant 30-mile monorail across a whole mountain to deliver... Epsom salts! And then there was Death Valley Scotty, who invented a rich gold mine to live off gullible investors, succeeded for a decade, and lived for years in the mansion that now bears his name, ironically built by one of the investors he had conned.

Mining fizzled rapidly after the 1950s. Only a handful of large corporate mines are in operation today. The Molycorp Mine, at Mountain Pass along Interstate 15, is exploiting a precious deposit of rare earths. Phosphates, sulfates, borates, and other salts are mined from Searles Lake, and borax from a huge pit at Boron along Highway 58. They have been active for over a century, and still have enough reserves for another century. In Panamint Valley, the C. R. Briggs Mine is still defacing the majestic Panamint Mountains. The Castle Mountain Mine, reopened in 2017, will be doing the same for ten years. Both mines extract gold so dilute that a thousand pounds of rocks must be blasted, crushed, and leached with cyanide to make a dollar...

■

4

SAFETY TIPS, REGULATIONS, AND ETHICS

The desert can be unforgiving. An emergency situation that would be taken care of with a simple phone call elsewhere can become life-threatening, as help may not arrive for days. This section provides a brief summary of what to do and not do to minimize both your chances of running into trouble and your impact on the desert. This is *not* a survival guide. Refer to one if you need more substantial advice.

Backcountry Driving
Road conditions and vehicle requirements. To climb summits in the Mojave, you will probably have to do some driving on primitive roads. Graded and maintained roads tend to be in decent shape and passable with standard two-wheel-drive vehicles. Unmaintained roads often require high clearance, sometimes four-wheel drive as well, especially up in mountains. These are only broad guidelines, as any unpaved road can deteriorate radically. After a heavy rain, an unpaved road can very quickly get muddy, flooded, or washed out, and be at least temporarily impracticable. If you are several miles out on a primitive road with a passenger car and it starts raining seriously, it is safest to drive back right away. Over longer periods of time, wear and tear can also turn a good road into a track rough enough to give pause to even a sturdy vehicle. The reverse happens when an agency, a company, or a rancher grades a damaged road. Bear in mind that the road conditions mentioned in this book assume dry weather, and that they may have become partially or completely incorrect.

Although a standard vehicle will do in many cases, driving the desert's longer primitive roads is safer in a more rugged vehicle. A high-clearance vehicle also greatly increases your chances of reaching your destination. Clearance is generally more critical than power. Four-wheel-drive sedans often do not fair much better than a normal vehicle because they lack clearance. Larger four-wheel-drive vehicles will generally make it easier to drive over rough spots because they have better clearance. Four-wheel drive and power are particularly critical to tackle roads with deep sand or steep and rocky grades.

The most common breakdown on unpaved desert roads is a flat tire. It is often caused by nothing bigger than a tiny sharp pebble that gets rammed into the treads. People driving SUVs or rental four-wheel-drive vehicles are particularly at risk. These vehicles are generally equipped with city tires too thin for dirt roads, and they get more flats. If possible, rent a four-wheel-drive vehicle with heavy-duty tires—they are available from several places throughout the Mojave Desert, in particular The Oasis at Death Valley and Yucca Valley. Drive slowly. Take a flat tire kit with you; it may fix the leak long enough to get you back to asphalt. Inspect your spare tire before each trip.

Even if you are adept at driving backcountry roads, it is advisable to inquire about road conditions beforehand. This information is often available from local land-management agencies (NPS or BLM). They will tell you whether a road is closed to motor vehicles, washed out, or closed due to snow, and possibly suggest alternate routes.

Getting unstuck. If you put in enough unpaved miles with a standard passenger car, sooner or later you will get stuck. A common scenario goes something like this: the car stops going forward, the wheels spin into soft ground, and bury themselves part way to the axles. As soon as the spinning starts, stop feeding gas. If you are on a slope, it is usually easy to get out of the soft spot by reversing the direction of travel or pushing your vehicle. On level ground, driving the car forward and backward repeatedly to acquire momentum can be effective. Otherwise, try to dig the wheels out. To this end, always keep in your trunk a shovel, a few sturdy boards or strips of carpet, and a jack. Dig a trench in front of the buried tires deep enough to jam a board underneath them for better traction, or jack up the car to slip a board, rocks, or a carpet underneath the tires and slowly drive out of the ruts.

Driving. Many desert paved roads are no longer in their prime and not suited for high speed. Respect posted speed limits (55 mph is a good safe speed). Graded roads are generally wide and straight, and they encourage a higher speed than is safe to travel. Sudden braking or swerving on their gravel surface can result in hydroplaning, loss of control, overturning, and dangerously long braking distances. Respect the posted speed limit, or the common-sense safe speed of 30–35 mph if none is posted. The incidence of a flat tire increases rapidly with speed. To minimize the risk, do not exceed 15 mph on primitive roads.

Whether your vehicle makes it over a poor road depends in part on your determination and willingness to push it. It may require plucking out rocks, filling in dips, trying different angles, and changing tires in three-digit heat. If you are new at this, take enough short drives to get exposed to, and learn how to handle, most hurdles—large stones, sharp rocks, washboards, sand, crowns, tight spots, washouts, lopsided bedrock, encroaching vegetation, mud, water, and more. It may take dozens of trips to be ready for longer distances.

If your vehicle gets stuck or breaks down, either call 911 or a towing company, or wait for help to come to you if you have no cell phone or no reception. Unless you are certain that you can walk to help safely, stay with your vehicle: it is much easier for rescuers to spot a vehicle than a person. Weather permitting, open all doors to make your vehicle more visible (and to provide shade if need be). Use the horn and headlights for signals. Always keep in your vehicle plenty of water and food, flashlights, matches, a rope, jumper cables, a toolbox, flares, and a good book. Always have proper sleeping gear in the winter: you must be able to survive overnight if it comes to that.

In many areas in the Mojave Desert, especially in parks, there are either no or infrequent gas stations. Always top off your tank at the last gas station—even a gallon can later save the day. Monitor your gas gauge frequently. Drive out to a gas station well before it is too late.

Hiking and Climbing Tips

Physical preparedness. Mountain climbing in the Mojave Desert is generally rough business. It involves hiking on ankle-twisting alluvial fans and gravel washes, over unstable sand and taluses, up steep and rocky canyons and ridges, and occasionally bushwhacking and technical rock climbing. On most mountains there is no trail; when there is one it is typically a steep mining road or an even steeper use trail. Cross-country climbing provides a greater sense of freedom, but it is often much more strenuous than most people care to put up with.

To tackle this uncompromising terrain, being in excellent physical shape is essential. Get in shape if you are not; make sure to stay in shape if you are. Hike near where you live once a week or more, covering occasionally the same distance and elevation change (if possible) as you plan to do in the desert. Cross train. Occasionally push yourself to assess your limits; it is safer to do this near home than in unfamiliar terrain. Make a habit of stretching before and after a hike. If you are pre-middle age it may well make no noticeable difference, but in the long run it reduces wear and tear on joints, tendons, and ligaments. It also increases the chance that you will be able to hike at a higher level of difficulty later in your life. Use lightweight hiking boots, especially if you have weak ankles. Try shoes padded with air or a gel. Though not as sturdy, they are lighter and on long hikes they reduce joint pain.

If you are new to desert hiking, test yourself on short, easy walks. If possible, hike with a friend who knows the desert. Keep track of your water and food needs, tolerance to sun and heat, hiking speed and fatigue. If possible, hike along old roads rather than cross-country; even if it means a slightly longer route, it will likely be easier and possibly faster. Do not take risks that far exceed your abilities. Build up your endurance and slowly work up to more substantial hikes. It may take a few dozen outings to graduate to a challenging full-day hike.

Orienteering. The widespread use of GPS to navigate vehicles and humans has created a new breed of drivers who cannot get around town, and hikers who cannot navigate in nature, without a GPS. If their GPS gives out in the wild, because of poor reception, dead battery, or failure, they may not find their way back. As Ellen Meloy put it in her customary spot-on wit, GPS "is a form of voluntary neutering."

My humble advice to hikers who have not yet succumbed to the GPS addiction is to develop and use their own orienteering skills; and to those who have succumbed, to kick the habit at least once in a while to keep their sense of direction honed. Fortunately, vast portions of the Mojave and other deserts are so open that orienteering is considerably easier than in regions with limited long-distance visibility. It is not uncommon to see your destination or its general vicinity from the start of your hike. All you have to do is locate your destination using a topographic map. If you do not know how to read topo maps and use a compass, take a crash course from a book or on the Internet, which is easy, and practice on sample hikes. On any climb, always take a topo map with you, or a copy of the map supplied in this book (which often shows features not shown on the original topo, as well as the route). All U.S. 7.5-minute topographic maps are available on-line from store.usgs.org and other sources. Unless you intend to cover a good fraction of a map, you may want to take with you only photocopies of the targeted areas. They are easier to carry and consult in the field.

When out on a desert hike, look back early on and identify at least one landmark that will help you locate your vehicle when you return. A peak or a notch on the skyline are preferable because they can be seen until well after sunset. Further into the hike, periodically memorize features you pass by—an unusual tree or outcrop perhaps—that can help find your way back. Canyons can be more troublesome than ridges because your line of sight is more limited. When traveling uphill in a canyon, chances of wandering off into the wrong fork are amazingly good. It can be a serious error if you are trying to get back to your car. Frequently keep good track of your location on your map.

Water needs. In the Mojave Desert, surface water is rare. You need to carry your own water. How much depends on several factors, starting with the season and elevation. During the cooler months (November through February at mid to low elevations, longer at high elevations), you need about as much water as in temperate regions. For any reasonable hiking distance, two quarts a day should be sufficient, depending on your metabolism. The rest of the year, with rocks too hot to touch, three-digit temperatures in the shade, and no shade, you will need a lot more. Your water needs will depend on humidity, the amount of shade and wind, level of physical activity, the terrain difficulty, your clothing, and your metabolism. As a rule of thumb, when hiking on level ground in 100°F heat, allow a minimum of one quart per hour. You will need less while resting, about one or two cups per hour. On steep uphill slopes, you may need as much as two quarts per hour. This may seem like a lot of liquid to ingest, but do not underestimate this most vital body need. A common mistake is to think that you can personally get by with drinking less and become dehydrated. If you have not done this before, start by monitoring your water consumption safely, on short, easy walks. Slowly work up to longer hikes, increasing the water you take with you accordingly.

In hot weather, you lose minerals and salts through perspiration. To offset this loss, take multi-vitamin/mineral tablets, or drink a mineralized drink instead of straight water. The salts and minerals prevent your muscles from cramping, in particular your stomach, and after a tiring hike they help keep the water down.

Water is dense. To complete a 10-hour hike in the summer you may need to start with 10 to 20 pounds of it on your back. The only redeeming feature is that your load will lighten up as you drink it and sweat it off, so that on the average you will be carrying only half what you start with. But this is still heavy, and it may adversely affect both your enjoyment and the distance you can cover. Being in excellent physical shape is again essential.

There are hundreds of seeps and springs in the Mojave Desert, so the chance of finding water is not nil. Most of those with surface water are used by wildlife, sometimes livestock, and they are likely biologically contaminated, in particular with giardia. Always purify the water by boiling or filtering, or chemically. Always carry with you a vial of iodine pills, and make sure to know how to use them properly. These treatments do not get rid of minerals. Heavily mineralized water may upset your stomach (which may be preferable to heat exhaustion).

A good way to handle the water weight problem on multiple-day desert treks is to cache water ahead of time along your anticipated route. It is also useful on an out-and-back day hike: stash one third of your water after traveling one third of the total distance, and pick it up on your way back. Keep your water in appropriately sized containers. When caching water containers for longer than a few hours, bury them so that animals do not chew through the plastic for a free drink. Make sure to retrieve all containers. Always keep at least a couple of gallons of water in your car, for both human and vehicle emergency needs.

Food. While out on a climb, eat small amounts of food often to keep your energy up. If you wait too long you might get too exhausted to feel like food. Bring a variety of foods—protein, carbs, nuts, cheese, bread, energy bars, dried fruit, banana, chocolate—and either listen to what your body is craving or experiment to determine what keeps you going the best. The closest town is often too far for a casual drive, and it may not be stocked in what you might consider to be food... Load up on food before heading out. Keep it in a good cooler with plenty of ice. In summer, a 20-pound bag of ice will last about two days.

Hiking time. On fairly level cross-country terrain, count on hiking at about 80% of your normal speed on established trails—from a typical 3 mph to 2.5 mph. With a light daypack you can expect to cover 12 to 14 miles in an eight-hour day, including breaks. Allow additional time when climbing, about 15 minutes per 1,000 feet depending on the grade and obstructions. If you are carrying a heavier pack like a backpack, count on 1.5 to 2 mph, including breaks, less in hot weather, when you might need to rest 10 minutes or so every hour.

Rock climbing. Some peak routes require technical climbing on dry falls or steep outcrops. Rock climbing in remote areas can be dangerous. The best advice for novices is not to climb alone. In case of an accident, having a partner can save your life. Also, where one person finds it impossible to climb, two people can sometimes make it by helping each other. To this end, bring a short length of rope or webbing and climbing shoes. Before climbing up, make sure that you can come back down, which is often more difficult than going up. If a climb looks too difficult, look for a safer way around it. If none is available, turn around. Train closer to home under more controlled conditions to learn basic moves and build up and maintain upper body strength.

Best Seasons to Climb. For most people the comfort zone in the Mojave Desert extends approximately from mid-October to mid-April, depending on elevation and personal tolerance for heat and cold. Consult the temperature charts in the introduction of each sub-region to assess the times that suit you best. February–April is ideal. The blooming season is then in full swing. The days are longer and more action-packed. Snow graces the higher summits, and wildlife is more abundant. Early fall is a good second best. It offers fairly balanced diurnal and nocturnal temperatures, and the days are still relatively long. The fall often has a small pulse of wildflowers, mostly at higher elevations. Fall days also tend to be clear and not as windy.

Between these two best periods, from mid-November to mid-February it may not be very warm during the day, and it may freeze at night above a few thousand feet. The days are disappointingly short, which reduces hiking and sightseeing time. To take best advantage of winter days, climb the generally lower summits in the eastern, southern, and western portions of the desert.

As expected, two of the three peak tourist seasons coincide with this comfort zone: Easter and Thanksgiving, the third being the Christmas season. During peak seasons, increased visitation is noticeable only in a few areas, in particular in the most popular canyons and valley-floor sites in Death Valley, in western Joshua Tree National Park, and on BLM lands near Barstow and Ridgecrest. Almost all other places are seldom visited year-round. Should this situation changes in the future, remember that most people dislike walking. Almost anywhere you can find solitude if you are willing to hike far.

Most Mojave Desert mountains are high enough to be noticeably cooler in summer than the low desert. Above about 5,000 feet, it is often "only" in the 90s during the day and low 80s at night. If you can take the heat, climbing mountains then is not as crazy as it may sound. The atmosphere is generally hazy, which somewhat defeats the purpose of seeking distant views. The best times to climb are after a rainstorm scrubs the air; and on partly cloudy days or in the evening, when clouds and shadows add depth to the landscape.

Summer hiking tips. My experience tells me that of the few serious perils that await a hiker in the desert, three are more likely to occur than others: physical exhaustion, dehydration, and heat exhaustion. When hiking in challenging terrain in a hot and physically stressful environment, these three conditions tend to occur in unison, and it helps to think of them as one combined issue. The first manifestation of dehydration is thirst, a signal that your body has lost too much water (between 0.5 to 1 quart, depending on your weight) and needs to be hydrated. A subsequent signal is dark urine. Prolonged exposure to heat without sufficient drinking produces further water loss and may lead to heat exhaustion. Blood is then directed away from the brain to irrigate and cool the skin, resulting in excessive sweating, dizziness, tiredness, and vomiting. If water loss and exertion persist, a heat stroke may occur. Blood becomes too thick to be pumped fast enough through the body and glands stop producing sweat. The body's main cooling mechanisms essentially shut down. The symptoms are red, dry skin, headache, fever, dizziness, delirium, and nausea.

These warnings foreshadow trouble. Learn to recognize them, and take timely measures. Always take plenty of water with you. Do not wander into the desert without water, even for an intended short walk. Thirst lags behind your body's need for water, so do not wait until you are thirsty to drink. Drink every 15 minutes, even if you think you do not need to. At the first signs of dehydration, start drinking more right away. If you feel you are getting into the second stage of dehydration, rest in a place sheltered from the sun and wind. Drink plenty of mineralized water, at least a couple of quarts. Often this will restore sufficient strength to return to your vehicle. The third stage is a serious condition that requires prompt medical attention. In the meantime, keep your body cool in the shade, covered with wet clothes, if possible.

Other simple preventative measures help deal with the heat. Wear a wide-brimmed hat to reduce evaporation through your head and exposure to harmful ultraviolet radiation. Dress lightly, but do wear a light-colored long-sleeve shirt and long pants. It will reduce water loss by insulating your body from the sun and wind. Use high-strength sunblock and lip balm, liberally and often. Avoid hiking around midday. When it is windy, your rate of dehydration can be significantly higher. Drink more, and stay out of the wind during the hottest hours.

If you run out of water, and you are too far from potable water to reach it without getting in more trouble, check your map for springs, creeks, wells, guzzlers, and windmills. Use questionable spring water to soak your clothes and a headband to cool you down.

Winter hiking tips. In the winter in the mountains the mercury often dips into the low 30s or even 20s, and the wind chill can make it feel a lot colder. In the morning, there can be frost on the ground and the water in your bottle may not be entirely liquid. There is often snow and ice in the highest mountains, especially in the northern Mojave Desert. Come as well prepared as for winter hiking in temperate regions. Take warm clothes, a warm sleeping bag and a good tent with you, for camping even if you are not planning to camp, in case you get stranded in a snow storm. Keep plenty of water and food in your vehicle, enough for a couple of days longer than your intended stay. While hiking, avoid protracted exposure to wet or cold without proper gear, which could lead to hypothermia. Be prepared for possible large daily temperature variations anywhere. Wear several layers, including a toasty jacket, gloves, a warm hat, and proper footwear. Symptoms of hypothermia include chills, shaking, upset stomach, and vomiting. If it happens not far from your vehicle, get back to it, turn the heater on to high, change to warm dry clothes, drink hot liquids, and go take a long hot shower if possible. If out in the wild, get into your sleeping bag and tent, preferably with another warm body in it with you. Stay dry.

Winter days are deceptively short. In December the sun rises around 7 a.m. and sets around 4:30–5:00 p.m. For long climbs, get an early start. Bring a flashlight in case you return at dark.

Altitude sickness. Only a few summits in the Mojave Desert are high enough to be concerned about altitude sickness. But to minimize the risk, when climbing above about 9,000 feet plan on acclimatizing yourself to the higher elevation for a day before the climb, especially if you live, like most of us do, near sea level.

Desert Hazards
Snakes. Of the several desert hazards that are largely out of our control, an encounter with a venomous snake is one of the most probable. Only a few species are venomous. The desert night snake and Sonoran lyre snake are mildly toxic and not considered dangerous to humans. Rattlesnakes are dangerous, and the ones to watch for. The Mojave rattlesnake is more aggressive than the speckled rattlesnake and the sidewinder, and its bite is more serious, because it injects both hemotoxins and neurotoxins. Hemotoxins attack muscles and the circulatory system, and may cause loss of motor skills. Neurotoxins affect the nervous system and may result in breathing difficulties or heart failure. A rattlesnake bite often, though not always, requires prompt medical attention. It can be painful, sometimes fatal, often temporarily disabling to the point of not being able to walk very far. Learn to identify rattlesnakes, by their triangular heads, the narrowing of their

necks, skin patterns, and rattles. Be familiar with the physiological effects of a bite, and learn how to take care of it. To reduce the chance of getting bitten, stay alert. Unless pestered or cornered, a rattler is more likely to warn you or escape than strike. If you hear rattling (the sound of a loud cricket) but do not see the snake, stop, locate it by sound or sight, then move away from it. If you cannot spot it, take one step on open ground and listen. If you are getting closer to it, the snake will crank up the volume. If you are moving away, it will soon reduce the rattling intensity. Above about 90°F rattlers do not survive long in full sun, and they hole up. So in hot weather it is relatively safe to walk in full sun. But do not jump into a shaded area or an area you cannot see. Apply particular caution when climbing up. That said, snakes are not numerous. They are largely nocturnal, and daytime encounters are rare. I see on average only about one rattler every 300 miles on foot.

Mines. Virtually every desert range has abandoned mines. Most mine adits are old, unsupported, and dangerous, and many shafts lie wide open. Sometimes a tunnel will lead into a hidden shaft. Tunnel roofs are often fractured and on the verge of collapse. Tunnels may be infected with hantavirus by rodents. The chance of getting in trouble is slight, but an accident could be deadly. For your personal safety, do not enter mine openings, and avoid camping near mines.

Wind. Persistent winds can cause irritability, anxiety, insomnia, and allergic reactions. They can also make hiking tedious and nights sleepless. If you are susceptible to these symptoms and high winds are forecast, you might want to postpone your trip. If the wind keeps you awake at night, try driving to a higher elevation, a sheltered spot, or sleeping in your vehicle. During the day, use a scarf to protect your eyes and nose from wind-blown dust.

Flashfloods. Flashfloods can occur in narrow canyons, especially in summer. If you are planning to hike in one, consult the weather forecast. If a major storm is predicted, postpone your trip, use another route, or be very careful. Periodically inspect the sky up canyon, and stay alert for advance warnings such as rumbling sounds. If a storm catches you in a canyon, climb to higher ground. Keep an eye open for escape routes to places at least 10 feet above the wash. Always camp at least 20 feet above a main wash, and never in narrows.

Insects and arachnids. Mosquitoes are not typically a problem in the Mojave Desert. There is just not enough standing water for them to breed in maddening numbers. However, in the spring or a few weeks after heavy rains, areas near valleys can be wet enough for gnats to be a nuisance. Where there are cattle or feral burros, black flies can be a ravening pest. Bring repellents if these insects bother you.

Arachnids are seldom a problem either. Tarantulas tend to be harmless. I have spotted only three scorpions in my life, and no black widow or brown recluse. Ticks are more common and troublesome. Encounters occur almost exclusively in the warm season. They crawl on you slowly in search of the best spot, sometimes for a long time. When a tick starts digging, it feels like a mosquito bite. A tick must stay in you at least 24 hours to infect you with Lyme disease. Only a small percentage of ticks carry the disease, typically the ticks the size of a pinhead. Learn to identify ticks; check your body and clothes carefully and often. Wearing long sleeves and pants helps. If you find a tick in you, do not pinch it to pull it out, which would flush its fluids into your body. Use a tick-removal tool, or cover it with oil to force it to come out for air. Save the tick's body to have it later tested for disease. Carry a first-aid kit for this and other minor treatments.

Mountain lions. Mountain lions are extremely rare in the Mojave Desert. They generally avoid contact with humans, but elsewhere they have occasionally attacked and sometimes killed humans, so be watchful. Should you encounter a lion displaying hostility, do not approach it. Do not run away either, which might trigger a chase. Do all you can to appear as large as possible, by spreading out your arms or opening your jacket. Do not crouch or bend over. Speak firmly in a low voice. If attacked, fight back. On occasion, throwing stones has been effective.

Hunters. Portions of the Mojave Desert are open to hunting, in particular Mojave National Preserve (year-round) and many wilderness areas. Most of the hunting is done in the fall and in the daytime. Game being relatively scarce, so are hunters. But while hiking, be aware of their possible presence. If you see a hunter, make your presence known. Shout if they cannot see you.

Regulations

The Mojave Desert's public lands are administered by the state of California, the NPS, BLM, or U.S. Forest Service. Regulations vary depending on the agency and the level of protection (national parks, monuments, and preserves, wilderness, and public lands). For lack of space, only some regulations are reproduced in this section. More complete regulations can be found in the brochures handed out at visitor centers and park entrances, on backcountry boards, on boards at the main entrances to BLM sub-regions, and on the agencies' websites.

Off-road driving. To spare the land and wildlife, driving off roads is strictly prohibited in all parks, in all designated wilderness, and on all public lands, except in off-highway vehicle areas. On almost all NPS units, roads closed to motorized traffic are clearly signed or barricaded. On BLM lands, driving is allowed only on designated roads. Any BLM road *without* a number at its start, usually posted on a flexible stake, is closed to motor vehicles. This inherently ambiguous policy may get you in trouble. People unaware of it who see a road without a closed sign or a barrier of sorts take it for granted that it is open, and drive it. Also, some open roads are *not* signed, usually because someone removed the sign. If you have good reasons to believe that an unsigned road is actually open, you can of course drive it to see whether it is signed further down. But then you may be driving a closed road... To stay on the right side of the law, keep track of your location by using this book's descriptions and maps, or by consulting the BLM's sub-region maps (some are available on-line and/or posted at some access points). If you see a road entering a wilderness improperly signed, let the BLM know; they welcome the information.

Entrance permits. To visit DVNP and JTNP, a permit is required. Permits can be purchased at an entrance station. If there are no entrance stations, you must stop and purchase one at a visitor center, a ranger station, or on-line. A single-entry pass is valid seven consecutive days in one park. An annual pass gives access to all NPS units for one year starting from the month of purchase. To be safe, display the permit in your vehicle at all times while visiting.

Backcountry camping. Regulations for backcountry camping also vary greatly from agency to agency and park to park. In Joshua Tree National Park, permits are required for backcountry camping, and car camping is not allowed anywhere. In Mojave National Preserve, designated wilderness, and on most BLM public lands, there is no permit or registration system. In DVNP, backpackers are encouraged to fill out a free voluntary permit, as are dispersed campers and other backcountry travelers. Some sensitive or heavily used areas in some parks are off limits to car camping and/or day-use only, and all camping is typically allowed some minimum distance from a paved road or developed area (1 mile in DVNP, 1/4 mile in MNP). Consult the regulatory agency's website to become familiar with their regulations. When in doubt, apply common sense. For example, to minimize impact select a camp-site that has been previously used; set up your tent off the road but leave your vehicle on the road if it does not block access; do not camp within 1/4 mile of water sources or known cultural sites. Store all food and garbage in a manner that will prevent access by wildlife.

Campfires. To prevent wildfires, in certain regions and during certain seasons campfires are prohibited, or allowed only in portable fire pans or existing fire rings. Consult the regulatory agency for details. To conserve the scant desert wood, the gathering of native wood, dead or alive, including kindling, is unlawful. So is burning lumber from historical structures. Bring all wood from outside the desert, or use a camp stove. Keep your fire small and use a fire pan, which makes it easy to pack out ashes. Do not leave fires smoldering or unattended.

Garbage. Carry plastic bags and pack out all garbage; do not bury any of it, biodegradable or not. Bury human waste in holes six to eight inches deep, at least 300 feet from water, camp, and trails. Pack out all toilet paper and hygiene products.

Weapons. The possession and discharge of weapons, in particular for target shooting, are prohibited in most parks. This applies to firearms, air guns, bows and arrows, slingshots, and similar weapons. All firearms transported within parks must be unloaded, broken down, and cased, except during lawful hunting activities.

Wildlife. Do not pester or harm wildlife. Feeding all wildlife is prohibited. Wild animals fed by humans tend to become dependent on this easy food source. They lose their ability to be self-sufficient and function properly in the wild, which puts their survival at risk. Some wild animals also carry communicable diseases, like rabies. Store all food and garbage in a manner that will prevent access by wildlife. If an animal comes begging for food, scare it away gently. For their own survival, they must learn that humans are their worst enemy.

Cultural resources. All cultural resources in the desert, under all jurisdictions, including historical structures (mines, mining camps, ghost towns, and railways) and archaeological sites, are protected by federal law. At historical sites, do not disturb, damage, burn, or remove anything, even the seemingly worthless bits of metal and wood lying around. The sea of broken artifacts littering many historic sites as a result of years of vandalism is a sad reminder of the high cost of ignorance. Leave everything where you find it so others have the pleasure of discovering it too. Sanctions for breaking this law include jail time and/or hefty fines.

It is equally illegal and punishable by law to disturb, damage, or remove anything from archaeological sites. This applies to rock art (which tarnishes and wears under repeated contact and should never be touched), rock alignments (which lose their significance when disturbed), artifacts, and camps. These sites are part of the heritage of contemporary Native American tribes. They are important to their traditions, and many of them are sacred. Treat them with respect.

Wilderness Ethics

Be considerate to others. When other hikers are nearby, speak quietly, or not at all. Do not play music out of a speaker; use earphones instead, leaving one ear free to listen to rattlesnakes and other possible imminent dangers. Avoid hiking in large groups. It violates the wilderness spirit, and it has a negative impact on the fragile desert environment. Large groups are also more noisy and visible, which is unfair to other visitors. Do not beep your car when locking or unlocking it in campgrounds or at trailheads. Close each car door only once while getting ready in the morning or late at night. Respect quiet hours.

Minimize the traces you leave behind: walk softly, on rocks rather than gravel, and on gravel rather than plants. Most perennial desert plants are slow growers and slow healers, and important fodder or habitat for wildlife. Avoid stepping on or near them. Practice low-impact camping. Pack out what you pack in. Do not discard organic matter, which often takes months to decompose.

Cairns are often resented by others as a blemish on nature. In DVNP and JTNP, building cairns and rock sculptures is considered as vandalism. On BLM lands build cairns only when necessary for *your* benefit, and destroy them on your way back. They may otherwise mislead other hikers. Do not build rock sculptures; they are also intrusive.

Disturbing natural areas, and the removal of rocks, plants, or animals, are strictly prohibited in NPS units. Do not write on rocks or plants; in many parks this is punishable by law. To limit damage to the desert crust, hike in washes, on rocky outcrops, or on existing trails.

Summit registers are an endearing tradition, but they are also an intrusion into the wilderness. Like litter and graffiti, they violate the old adage—leave only footprints. Do not put up new registers. In DVNP, they are prohibited except on the 46 peaks in Andy Zdon's *Desert Summits*.

∎

5

NORTHERN MOJAVE DESERT

The region. East from the long alignment of deep tectonic troughs known as Eureka, Saline, and Panamint valleys lies the northern Mojave Desert, the very grandest corner of the Mojave. This is archetypical Basin and Range country, majestic mountains and valleys marching in ranks eastward into the Silver State. What is different here is the sheer size of the topography. The western boundary is marked by the Panamint Range, a tremendous fault block 140 miles long capped by 11,049-foot Telescope Peak. On its east side the land drops more than two vertical miles into Death Valley, the most extreme in the land of extremes. Its lowest point, somewhere in Badwater Basin's vast hardpan of salt crystals, lies 282 feet below sea level. To the east looms the Amargosa Range, not as high but almost as long and just as formidable. In its southern reaches, the Black Mountains shoot up 6,000 feet in scarps so abrupt that they may never have been scaled. Over the next 60 miles east, the land rises and falls in four more tectonic waves, over ranges named Greenwater, Resting Spring, Nopah, and Kingston that divide empty, little-known valleys. In all of the Mojave Desert, these are the most magnificent mountains. They hide in their titanic ridges the longest and deepest canyons, the most luxuriant oases, the largest tracks of untrammeled wilderness, the boldest colors, the most outrageous landforms, and the most imposing summits.

Protection status. The exceptional beauty of this region was recognized early, and over the last century many have endeavored, quite successfully, to protect as much of it at the highest possible level. The northern Mojave Desert is now one of the most protected eco-regions

in the coterminous United States. About two thirds of its approximately 7,200 square miles has been set aside in Death Valley National Park,
America's largest desert park. Since its designation as a national monument in 1933, this enormous territory has been spared road building
and other developments. Many roads that existed then were closed
and have revegetated. Today, the park is a mosaic of large roadless
areas, and nearly 93% of it is designated wilderness. Outside the park,
13 wilderness areas covering 650,000 acres preserve large tracts of
mostly mountainous terrain. The extreme southern area, which
includes the Granite and Tiefort mountains, is part of the Fort Irwin
Military Reservation. Except for the Avawatz Mountains and three
small ranges around Silurian Valley, all 21 mountain ranges outside the
reservation are protected. The region's isolation, turbulent geography,
and extreme climate were also strong advocates for its preservation.
There are no interstates, no railways, no power lines, and, although
there is a proposal to turn Silurian Valley into the state's latest sacrifice
zone, no power plants. All around is land shaped almost entirely by
nature.

Geology.   The northern Mojave Desert is the legacy of nearly one
billion years of sedimentation. Much of the region's mountains are
made of huge chunks of the 10-mile-thick stack of sedimentary rocks
that were deposited between the Mid-Proterozoic and Early Triassic.
The older, deeper formations were metamorphosed by heat and pressure into marbles and schists. Over the last few million years, they
were exhumed by spasms of crustal deformations much more extreme
here than elsewhere. The fault blocks are longer, taller, bigger. Dragged
sideways by the regional motion of the San Andreas Fault at the western edge of the state, they rotated, collided, and slipped northward
over considerable distances—at least 50 miles in the case of the
Panamint Mountains. The blocks tended to tilt downward on their east
sides, exposing the oldest rocks on their lower western flanks. The 1.7-
billion-year basement and the Proterozoic formations that rest on it are
now exposed at several locations, in particular along the western base
of the Panamint Mountains, in the Black Mountains facing Death
Valley, and on the eastern flanks of the Kingston Range.

The dominance of sedimentary rocks has had a profound impact
on the region's topography. Because they have a broad range of physical and chemical properties, limestones, dolomites, shales, conglomer-
ates, and other sedimentary rocks erode into rougher and more diverse
landscapes. The summits are sharper, the slopes more often overwhelmed by cliffs, and the canyons more chaotic. Fossils of the sea life

Average temperatures (°F) in the northern Mojave Desert							
	Beatty, Nevada (3,300 feet)		The Ranch at Death Valley (-178 feet)		Shoshone (1,570 feet)		Baker (920 feet)	
	Low	High	Low	High	Low	High	Low	High
January	29	55	39	65	40	62	35	61
February	32	58	46	73	43	66	40	68
March	36	65	54	81	48	73	46	75
April	41	72	62	88	52	82	53	83
May	50	82	71	100	62	92	61	92
June	56	92	82	110	68	100	70	102
July	62	98	88	116	75	107	76	108
August	61	96	86	113	74	105	75	106
September	54	89	78	106	68	97	68	99
October	44	78	62	91	57	85	54	86
November	35	64	48	75	46	71	42	71
December	28	54	40	66	38	60	33	61

that built up these formations are common. Many areas display trilobites (Funeral Mountains and Nopah Range), corals and crinoids (Cottonwood and Panamint mountains), stromatolites (Kingston Range), conodonts (Nopah Range and Last Chance Range), and a whole evolution museum of bivalves scattered over most ranges.

Although the region was less affected than others by granitic intrusions in the Mesozoic and volcanism in the Miocene, igneous rocks occur in most ranges, albeit over limited areas. They become much more prevalent to the south and east (Greenwater Range, Owlshead Mountains, Avawatz Mountains, and Kingston Range). Some of the most colorful landscapes are volcanic—Red Pass in the Grapevine Mountains, the northern Black Mountains, and the southern Avawatz Mountains. The Ubehebe Crater area, at the north end of the Cottonwood Mountains, was last active as recently as 800 years ago. It is one of the youngest volcanic centers in California, and one of the seven areas most likely to erupt next in the state.

The northern Mojave Desert is unique in many ways, not least this superb lithology that brings together sedimentary, metamorphic, volcanic, and plutonic rocks. This remarkable diversity is at the root of the region's exceptional range of landforms. Visit after visit, this is land that will leave you breathless.

Climate. Between late spring and early fall a few low valleys in the northern Mojave Desert, in particular Panamint Valley, Silurian Valley, and of course Death Valley are noticeably hotter than the rest of the desert. This is offset by the fact that many of the surrounding summits are much higher, and therefore a little cooler. Nevertheless, traveling by car and camping in these valleys at such times, or hiking across alluvial fans to climb summits, can be taxing. The best times to climb lower summits are generally a little earlier (February to March) and later (late October to November) in the year than elsewhere. Most people will prefer the dead of winter over the height of summer. Summits above approximately 7,000 feet receive snow just about every winter, especially all along the Panamint Range, in the northern Grapevine Mountains, and in the Kingston Range. They should then be tackled only with proper hiking and survival gear, or in the warmer months. The Amargosa Range and ranges east from it lie in the rain shadow of the Panamint Range and generally do not get snow below 6,000 feet.

Botany and wildlife. The region's extreme aridity has significant repercussion on the fauna and flora. On the slopes facing Death Valley, many plant communities are shifted up in elevation to escape the intense summer heat. All high crests have a juniper-pinyon woodland, but the first trees do not appear until anywhere between 5,000 and 7,000 feet. Some ranges that reach above 6,000 feet, like the Black Mountains, are too dry for trees. At lower elevations, the vegetation is often more sparse and stunted. Cacti are usually not plentiful, in numbers or in diversity. Even Joshua trees are uncommon, except at a few places where they actually thrive, particularly in the Cottonwood Mountains and in Shadow Valley. In the ranges farther away from Death Valley, like between the Avawatz and Mesquite mountains, the distributions of plant zones are more similar to other parts of the desert. Several sky islands are home to trees rare or uncommon in the desert, such as mountain mahogany and bristlecone pine (Panamint Mountains), limber pine (Grapevine and Panamint mountains), and white fir (Kingston Range). Wildlife still manages to survive. The most common sightings are rodents, rabbits, and birds, especially at watered springs. Encounters with larger animals, in particular bighorn sheep, mule deer, coyote, bobcats, and burros, are much less frequent.

Climbing and services. In all of the Mojave Desert, the northern area is the wildest reach. Its monumental topography takes peak climbing to a whole new level. On average, it is noticeably more challenging. Most of the longest and roughest climbs in the California

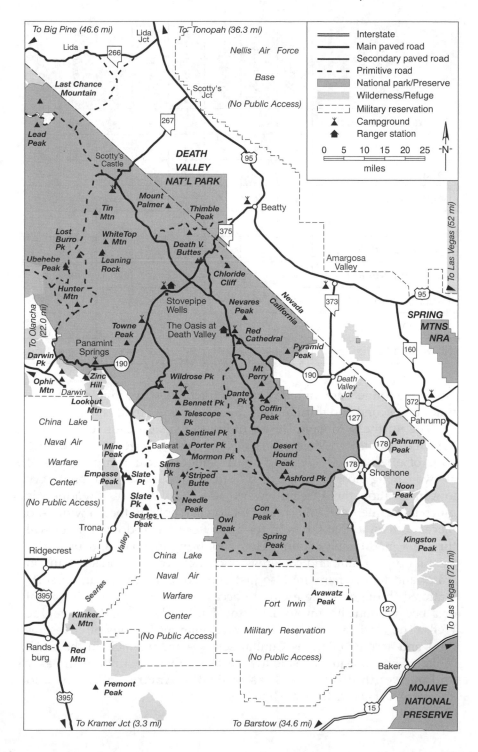

To Big Pine (46.6 mi)
Lida Jct
To Tonopah (36.3 mi)
Lida
266
Nellis Air Force
Base
(No Public Access)
Scotty's Jct
267
95
Last Chance Mountain
Lead Peak
Scotty's Castle
DEATH VALLEY NAT'L PARK
Beatty
Mount Palmer
Thimble Peak
Tin Mtn
375
Lost Burro Pk
WhiteTop Mtn
Death V. Buttes
Ubehebe Peak
Leaning Rock
Chloride Cliff
Hunter Mtn
Stovepipe Wells
Nevares Peak
Nevada
California
Amargosa Valley
95
373
SPRING MTNS NRA
Towne Peak
The Oasis at Death Valley
Red Cathedral
Pyramid Peak
160
To Olancha (22.0 mi)
Darwin Pk
Panamint Springs
190
Mt Perry
190
Death Valley Jct
372
Pahrump
Ophir Mtn
Zinc Hill
Darwin
Wildrose Pk
Dante Pk
127
Lookout Mtn
Bennett Pk
Coffin Peak
China Lake
Telescope Pk
178
Pahrump Peak
Naval Air
Mine Peak
Ballarat
Sentinel Pk
Desert Hound Peak
178
Warfare
Porter Pk
Shoshone
Center
Empasse Peak
Slate Pt
Slims Pk
Mormon Pk
Ashford Pk
Noon Peak
(No Public Access)
Slate Pk
Striped Butte
Searles Peak
Needle Peak
Con Peak
Kingston Peak
Trona
Owl Peak
Ridgecrest
China Lake
Spring Peak
395
Naval Air
Searles Valley
Warfare
Fort Irwin
Avawatz Peak
127
Klinker Mtn
Center
Military Reservation
To Las Vegas (72 mi)
Randsburg
Red Mtn
(No Public Access)
(No Public Access)
Baker
Fremont Peak
MOJAVE NATIONAL PRESERVE
395
15
To Kramer Jct (3.3 mi)
To Barstow (34.6 mi)

Legend:
- Interstate
- Main paved road
- Secondary paved road
- Primitive road
- National park/Preserve
- Wilderness/Refuge
- Military reservation
- Campground
- Ranger station

0 5 10 15 20 25
miles

–N–

To Las Vegas (52 mi)

	Restaurant	Groceries	Lodging	Campground	Gas station	Tire repair	Towing	Water
Amargosa Valley, Nev.	✓	✓	✓		✓	✓	✓	✓
Baker	✓	✓	✓	✓	✓	✓	✓	✓
Ballarat				✓				✓
Beatty, Nevada	✓	✓	✓		✓	✓		✓
Death Valley Junction	✓		✓					✓
Oasis at Death Valley	✓	✓	✓	✓	✓	✓		✓
Pahrump, Nevada	✓	✓	✓		✓			✓
Panamint Springs	✓	✓	✓	✓	✓			✓
Shoshone	✓	✓	✓	✓	✓			✓
Stovepipe Wells	✓	✓	✓	✓	✓			✓

desert are found here. In many ranges the highest summit, and sometimes the second and third highest, take a day-long trek.

The northern Mojave Desert offers the same major recreational
appeal as the eastern Mojave Desert. There are no large towns, no caravans of off-road vehicles and sharp shooters, car camping is still
allowed along most primitive roads, and backcountry visitation is very
low. In addition, there are far fewer roads, and the sense of wildness is
much more intense. If you choose to, you can hole up for a few days in
places so remote that the need for a shower or a sit-down dinner will
turn to a maddening craving. Here too, bring a cooler and plenty of
ice, fill up your tank and cooler every chance you get, and stock up on
water and food. There are also just enough small towns and resorts
scattered throughout the region to occasionally indulge in a hot meal
or a bed without having to drive too far. Inside the park, Stovepipe
Wells, The Oasis at Death Valley, and Panamint Springs offer restaurants and accommodations. Similar services are available in the small
town of Shoshone just outside the park's southeast boundary, in Baker
an hour south of it, as well as in Beatty, Amargosa Valley, and
Pahrump just across the state line.

∎

NOPAH RANGE

Known as the Chung Up Mountains in the 1880s, the Nopah Range (possibly meaning "no water") is a beautiful free-standing mountain range, the last chain east of Death Valley before the state of Nevada. Its rugged spine describes a pronounced arc across the desert, a 25-mile north-south comma punctuated with many distinct summits rising up to 4,300 feet above the valleys. Essentially roadless, it stands in the middle of a seldom-traveled region, bordered by pristine Chicago Valley and the Resting Spring Range to the west, and Pahrump Valley and California Valley to the east. This is a little-known region, rough, remote, and unrevered, well preserved by a mosaic of designated wilderness. The range itself is almost entirely preserved within the Nopah Range Wilderness (106,623 acres) and the South Nopah Range Wilderness (17,059 acres), divided by the only road that crosses the range, the historic Old Spanish Trail Highway. The Resting Spring Range Wilderness (76,312 acres) lies to the northwest, and the Pahrump Valley Wilderness (73,726 acres) to the east. The only developed area is central and northern Pahrump Valley to the northeast, home of the spread-out, thinly populated town of Pahrump, Nevada.

The Nopah Range is one of the great sedimentary mountains of the Mojave Desert. It is made of almost the entire sequence of sedimentary and metamorphosed sedimentary formations deposited between the Middle Proterozoic and the Pennsylvanian. This stack has been strongly tipped to the east-northeast, so that the formations tend to be exposed in narrow, staggered and faulted bands many miles long roughly parallel to the range's axis. At a given latitude, only a few formations span the range's narrow width, generally younger eastward and northward. The sequence starts with the Crystal Spring Formation at the toe of the range, and ends more than 800 million years later with the Bird Spring Formation at its head. In between, almost all intervening formations are present. Few other ranges in the Mojave Desert reach nearly continuously across this much geological time.

This exceptional record holds geological gems. Two formations, the Noonday Dolomite and the Nopah Formation, are globally better preserved here than anywhere else, and they have shed invaluable light on the paleoenvironment of their times. The chemistry and structure of two units of the Noonday Dolomite provide evidence that twice in the Late Proterozoic, the Earth was completely glaciated. Many formations are richly fossiliferous. The Pyramid Shale Member of the Carrara Formation, exposed for 11 miles along the western front of the southern range, is crawling with trilobites. Nearly 100 species have been exhumed from it, the most complete representation of Early to Middle Cambrian trilobites in North America.

Only the two extremities of the Nopah Range were mined, both for lead-silver-zinc ore. At the very north end, the Nancy Ann (Shaw) Mine produced from 1925 to 1928 and in 1943 a meager total of about $20,000. In contrast, the mines at the south end—the Gunsight, Noonday, Columbia, and War Eagle, among others—were for a time the second largest lead producer in the state. They generated an estimated $3 million between 1912 and 1928, and $4 million after 1938. This last effort focused on extracting argentiferous galena, cerussite, and anglesite from the Columbia and War Eagle mines. The area then had a bustling camp called Noonday City, with a large flotation plant and a crew of 45 that routinely handled 80 tons of ore a day.

While the older formations in the south end have eroded into a more subdued topography of sharp hills, the majority of the range holds the rugged signature of sedimentary rocks. If you have walked the desert long enough you can tell, even from far away, by the greater verticality, the colorful bands, the stair-like scarps, the massive shields of dolomite, and the deep canyons incised along 1,000-foot precipices. This is the Nopah Range legacy—heightened drama. The highest summits, Nopah Peak and Nopah Point, rank among the most challenging in the area. There are other perks. The west slopes of the central range has California's only known occurrence of ivory-spined agave—no other agave lives this far north or west. This is one of California's few ranges where you might spot a pineapple cactus, a handsome little barrel shielded by a tight armor of spines. There are wild horses and burros in Chicago Valley and California Valley, as well as in the central range, an area they share with bighorn sheep. The most precious commodities, however, are ruggedness and seclusion. The approaches from either valley are comparatively long, and the ridges often exceed 40% slope. For many hikers, one day is not quite long enough to reach the highest summits and return. If you try, you will likely be alone.

∎

PAHRUMP PEAK

Though not the hardest in this range, Pahrump Peak is one of the most strenuous summits to climb in this part of the Mojave Desert. The ascent is only about 4 miles, but most of the elevation change— nearly 3,500 feet—occurs in the second half, first in a bouldery canyon, then on loose, sheer ridges, and finally up the aerial fin that snakes up along the crest. The mountain is spectacular, with striking rocks, fossils, and ivory-spined agave all over. Few summits are this precipitous, this alluring, and this exhilarating.

General Information
Jurisdiction: Nopah Range Wilderness (BLM)
Road status: Trail in valley, rough trail in mountain; paved access road
The climb: 3.9 mi, 3,410 ft up, 60 ft down one way / strenuous
Main attractions: A rugged canyon, stunning knife-edge crest, geology
USGS 7.5' topo map: Twelvemile Spring
Maps: pp. 61*, 55

Location and Access
Pahrump Peak is the northernmost named summit in the Nopah Range, midway between Shoshone, California, and Pahrump, Nevada. From the junction of Highway 127 and Highway 178 in Shoshone (56 miles north of Baker), drive Highway 178 north by east 10.6 miles to a primitive road on the right. The road can be seen climbing northeast to a deep canyon in the Nopah Range a little less than 2 miles away. Two flat-top summits cap the crest above the canyon mouth. Pahrump Peak is the slightly higher one on the right. The road and the canyon are the way to the summit. The road is in the Nopah Range Wilderness; park on the shoulder. To get to this road from Highway 160 in Pahrump, drive Highway 372 (which becomes Highway 178 upon entering California) 12.6 miles southwest to the broad pass into Chicago Valley, marked by the dirt Shaw Mine Road on the left, then 3.8 miles south.

Route Description
The old road makes access to the canyon easy. In 1.9 miles it gains a modest 810 feet, crossing a well-behaved fan punctuated with occasional cactus. It ends at the mouth of the canyon, on a low shelf overlooking the wash. Right away you know what the next few hours of your life are going to be like. The wash is a river of tossed boulders,

59

chunks of dolomite, limestone, and sandstone shed by the thick Paleozoic strata that hang down from the mountain's crest. To move up through the canyon, much of the time you walk on the pointed tips of boulders, touching each one only briefly to hop onto the next one. There are, fortunately, short segments of use trail that bypass the wash and speed up progress. They are easy to locate: all of them are on the narrow gravel benches that occasionally line the wash.

The landscape is ample compensation for the rough terrain. The canyon is a monumental gash in the mountain's flank, its inner curls hemmed in by craggy slopes that grow taller, more jagged and vertical deeper in. At its head, less than a mile away, access to the crest is barred by a buttressed wall that rears up like a fortress. In plain view most of the way up, it is a striking sight, a broad drapery of undulating, sharply contrasted sedimentary beds. In the wash, rock surfaces are stamped with random veins of calcite, crisp white against the dark-grey stone, so aesthetically pleasing that they impelled me to stop and touch them. The stone is sharpened into a constellation of tiny thorns and razors. Panels are imprinted with the pale ghosts of Paleozoic tropical sea life—archipelagoes of corals, embossed pads of cyanobacteria colonies, wiggly channels of worm tracks, and the neat geometric coils of 3-inch snails. A boulder big enough to lounge on, ancient-Rome style, served a platter of shells that looked very much like oysters. The rocky slopes hold platoons of rare ivory-spined agave, a dwarf century plant armed with half-inch teeth and 6-inch nails.

About 0.8 mile in, the canyon forks. Stay with the wider and less steep left fork. In 0.3 mile there is a fall where a strata of bright sandstone straddles the canyon, an easy 8-foot climb (Class 2–3). Just above it the canyon forks again. Take the right fork. It bunches tighter and steepens a notch, the boulders get bigger, often heaped in tall clusters, and there is no more room for a trail. Over the next 0.3 mile, there is another 8-foot Class-3 fall, a series of slants, and finally a higher fall. As you approach it and the massive headwall behind it, with less than half a mile but still 1,000 feet to go, it becomes increasingly dubious that there is a way through. But there is one, albeit strenuous, and navigation is not so difficult, thanks to a nearly continuous use trail.

Just before the last fall, leave the wash and climb the very steep gully on the south slope. This section is tedious, on a slippery chute of loose rocks, although the trail helps. It exits at a shallow saddle on Pahrump Peak's southwest shoulder. Continue up the ridge, through notches between pillars of stone on its north side, and past a curious arch punched through a slab of brecciated dolomite. While riding this high rib of land, it is easy to feel small, surrounded by giant abutments

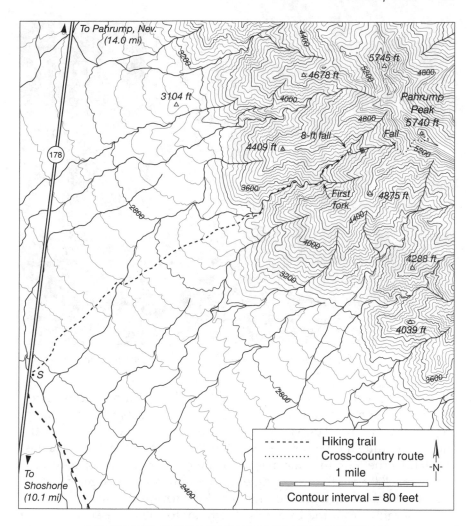

To Pahrump, Nev.
(14.0 mi)

5745 ft
△ 4678 ft
3104 ft
△
Pahrump
Peak
5740 ft
8-ft fall
Fall
4409 ft △
First
fork
△ 4875 ft

4288 ft
△

4039 ft
△

S

To
Shoshone
(10.1 mi)

- - - - - - - Hiking trail
. . . . Cross-country route
1 mile
-N-
Contour interval = 80 feet

Pahrump Peak

	Dist.(mi)	Elev.(ft)
Road (Highway 178)	0.0	2,392
End of road at canyon mouth	1.9	3,180
First fork (go left)	2.65	3,760
Second fork (go right)	2.9	4,100
Gully on south slope (go right)	3.3	4,725
Saddle	3.45	5,070
Crest	3.8	~5,650
Pahrump Peak	3.9	5,740

Pahrump Peak (upper right) from just below the sandstone fall

above and sheer cliffs below. This will lead shortly into a second gully climbing to the right, an even steeper and more unstable avalanche of cobbles that narrows down to 5 feet. Where the gully ends back on the ridge, continue a little north of east up the ridge to the crest. The last stretch to the summit, northwest on the crest, is the most awesome part. For 200 yards you scramble up a sinuous knife edge of naked, shattered limestone that dives into the sky, surrounded by thin air.

Emerging from the canyon's depths onto the exposed ridge and crest is liberating. To the east, the 180-degree view into the long alignment of Stewart Valley and Pahrump Valley borders on vertiginous. Even with sprawling Pahrump in the way, the huge Spring Range rearing up behind them is impressive. Spanning some 70 miles and capped by 2-mile-high Charleston Peak, it is too vast to fit between horizons. To the west, beyond desolate Chicago Valley, a backdrop of long ranges unfolds all the way to the Panamints. In spite of this stunning scenery, it is the crest of Pahrump Peak that wins the grand prize. Few summits in the Mojave are crowned by such a dramatic arête, perched high above abrupt drops, as keenly chiseled as young alpine mountains. This sight alone encapsulates Pahrump Peak's unique appeal.

∎

NOON PEAK

Although from a distance Noon Peak looks more like an overgrown hill than a full-size mountain, it offers a good opportunity to quickly gain a decent elevation and enjoy satisfying views of a little-known region of the California desert—the Nopah Range, Chicago Valley, Tecopa Basin, and the Kingston Range. The cactus are plentiful, the rock delightfully ancient and colorful, and the historic mines in the nearby foothills interesting goals to occupy the rest of the day.

General Information
Jurisdiction: South Nopah Range Wilderness (BLM)
Road status: Roadless; hiking from primitive road (2WD)
The climb: 1.4 mi, 1,400 ft up, 50 ft down one way / easy–moderate
Main attractions: Well-preserved mining ruins, cacti, views
USGS 7.5' topo map: Tecopa Pass
Maps: pp. 65*, 55

Location and Access
Noon Peak, the highest summit in the southern Nopah Range, is a few miles east of the small town of Tecopa. Drive Highway 127 8.3 miles south from the center of Shoshone (or 47.9 miles north of Baker) to the signed Old Spanish Trail on the east side. Follow this paved road 3.9 miles southeast to the junction to the even smaller town of Tecopa Hot Springs on the left. Continue straight, past Tecopa's cluster of houses, 1.5 miles to the Furnace Creek Road on the right. Take this road 1.8 miles to the turnoff to China Ranch, where it becomes graded, and continue on it 4.9 miles to an unsigned dirt road on the left, near the east end of a large opening in the Nopah Range to the north. Turn left on this road, passing by the ruins of Noonday City. This fairly recent ghost town has several house foundations, including the mine supervisor's house. The cinder-block building on the left side of the road is the vault where valuables were locked up. After 1.15 miles you will reach a complicated intersection at the foot of the Columbia Mine's wide tailing. Turn left, then immediately right on the road that skirts the tailing's west side. Go 0.5 mile on old potholed pavement to a fainter unpaved road on the left. Drive this spur 0.15 mile to a small loop at its north end and park. Noon Peak is the pale rocky summit about 1 air mile to the north-northeast. Standard-clearance vehicles should have no difficulty on these fairly smooth roads.

Route Description

Noon Peak's southern slope is dissected into several ridges that can all be used to access the summit, either directly, for example on the peak's southern shoulder, or via more westerly ridges up to the comparatively level western shoulder. The ridges trend mostly north-south, and they are separated by dominantly northeast-southwest ravines, so most routes require crossing one or more drainages. The route suggested here is a little circuitous, but it is a good compromise between distance and elevation gain.

From the end of the road, head north down the gentle slope to the nearby wash. Walk up the wash a short distance to where it splits, and take the left fork. After 50–100 yards the wash splits again. Head up the left fork 50 yards, then climb onto the low ridge to the right. Follow this ridge north, then north-northeast, 0.35 mile to a shallow saddle, just before it starts climbing more seriously. The rocky wash down below to the north makes a left bend northward. Drop into it, then take it uphill 0.25 mile, past a right bend, to a triple fork. Climb onto the ridge that separates the two rightmost washes. In 0.45 mile it ascends roughly north 700 feet to Noon Peak's western shoulder. It is then a short climb east along the shoulder to the summit. The walking is generally easy, along ridges that are mostly open. The only exception is the final pitch to the summit block, which is made of broken rocks and is locally steep and a little slippery.

Like most desert places, this area holds its own combination of attractions. The formations span a nearly continuous time period, from the upper member of the Johnnie Formation just past the road (~640 million years old) through the Stirling Quartzite and Wood Canyon Formation, to the Zabriskie Quartzite (~530 million years) at the summit. They have shed particularly colorful rocks all over the ridges, well-faceted quartzites tinted creamy, light apricot, or purple red, brown dolomite, dirty-white flat-pebble conglomerate, and pink or greenish-brown shales. Barrel and cottontop cacti grow in abundance right up to the top. Some barrel cactus reach respectable dimensions, standing 4 feet tall and 20 inches in girth. In the setting sun, the spherical heads of younger plants glow a surreal fluorescent pink. On the lower slopes, a sizable population of ground squirrels dwell in shallow burrows dug at the foot of large creosote. They are a frequent sight in the spring, running into hiding in long purposeful bounces. So are coyotes, perhaps drawn by the high density of meals on legs...

The California desert is a land of extreme contrasts, and Noon Peak is a grand observatory—albeit uncomfortably jagged—to take in this remarkable diversity. To the east, Charleston Peak looms more

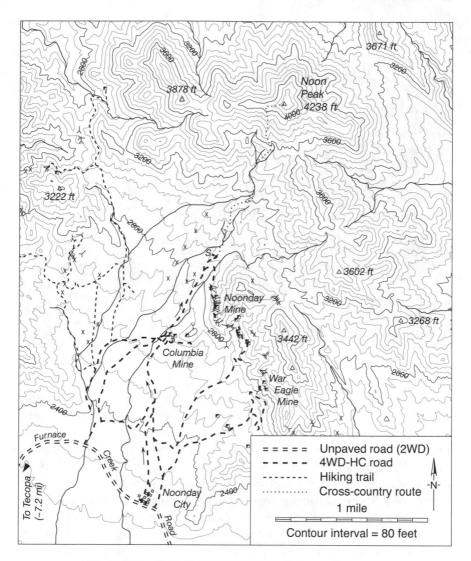

Noon Peak		
	Dist.(mi)	Elev.(ft)
End of road	0.0	2,895
Leave wash/climb onto ridge	0.15	2,935
Descend to wash	0.5	3,210
Leave wash/climb onto ridge	0.8	3,360
Western shoulder	1.25	4,040
Noon Peak	1.4	4,238

Chicago Valley and the Resting Spring Range from Noon Peak

than 8,000 feet higher, often blanketed with thick snow. Turn 180 degrees and you will be looking down 2,000 feet into Tecopa Basin and its bright salt lake. To the north, the smooth bajadas of Chicago Valley unfurl for miles, framed by the crinkled scarps of the Nopah Range. The hulking Kingston Range soars to the south, its crest dusted with evergreens. In the winter and spring, the most unusual element is the Amargosa River glittering in the sunlight, tracing the improbable course of a desert river on its way to sea level—and below.

The mines below Noon Peak have several well-preserved structures that are easily accessible either on foot or with a high-clearance vehicle. The largest and most enjoyable site is the Noonday Mine's tramway. Its slender railroad trestle spills 50 yards down the fan below the mine's bulky ore bin. The Columbia Mine has extensive mill foundations with some machinery, and a headframe in beautiful condition. An unusually tall twin-chute ore bin is still extent at the War Eagle Mine. Other remains are scattered throughout the rocky hills (all of it Noonday Dolomite), including can cemeteries, rusted cars, and ore chutes in various states of disrepair. You might well put in more miles looking for these treasures than climbing the peak itself!

KINGSTON RANGE AND AVAWATZ MOUNTAINS

Between Soda Lake and the great bend in the Amargosa River lies a small, seldom-visited valley by the name of Silurian. On its east side, huge alluvial fans ascend for miles to the imposing Kingston Range, its crenulated 7,000-foot crest dark with conifers, and the Shadow Mountains' rounded hills south of it. On its west side rise the Avawatz Mountains, a 37-mile-long crescent that climbs clockwise from 170 feet along the Amargosa River below the Owlshead Mountains to 6,154-foot Avawatz Peak, then descends south to meet the Soda Mountains. During the last Ice Age, when Death Valley was flooded under Lake Manly, some of its water intake came through Silurian Valley. The then-plentiful Mojave River replenished Soda Lake, which spilled over sequentially into Silver Lake, Lake Silurian, then the Amargosa River and Death Valley. Silurian Valley was then prime beach-front property, with a blue lake and green trees coming down close to its shores.

The Avawatz Mountains are a large fault block of plutonic rocks sandwiched between two local faults. The Mule Spring Fault wraps around the range's outer curve, facing Silurian Valley, and the Arrastre Spring Fault around its inner curve. Most of the plutonic rocks belong to the Avawatz Quartz Monzodiorite complex, an amalgam of multiple intrusions about 200 million years old with a wide range of compositions. A few remnants of Proterozoic and Paleozoic formations, mostly metamorphosed sedimentary rocks, survive near the crest. The southwestern flanks are composed mainly of Mesozoic volcanic rocks and the particularly colorful Avawatz Formation, a coarse conglomerate that accumulated on the fans of a tectonic trench controlled by the Arrastre Spring Fault in Eocene and Paleocene times.

The Kingston Range is more compact, about 17 miles long in a north-northeast direction and 12 miles wide. The majority of its main southern block, including Kingston Peak (7,336 feet), is a granite porphyry only 12.8 million years old, with large quartz and feldspar crystals dusted with biotite and hornblende. This hard rock is responsible for the signature hoodoos that crowd the high country. The northern half and southeastern edge of the Kingston Range are faulted jumbles of sedimentary marine formations deposited between about 1,100 and 630 million years ago. Three of them are so well represented here that they were named after local geographic features—the Crystal Spring Formation, Beck Spring Dolomite, and Kingston Peak Formation. The latter is famous for its conglomerate formed by glaciers dumping sediments into a tectonic sink when the Earth was covered in ice.

Mined since 1872 and until fairly recent times, the Avawatz Mountains produced mostly iron and talc, as well as silver, gold, copper, lead, and zinc, although none of them in great quantities. The Kingston Range was much richer. The Crystal Spring Formation contained huge talc and iron deposits that were exploited for decades starting in 1935. Between 1972 and 1987, the Beck Mine produced 1.2 million tons of iron. At least 140,000 tons of talc came out of five mines, the Excelsior Mine being the largest. Their snow-white tailings still dot the foothills along the road that crosses the northern Kingston Range.

The southern half of the Kingston Range is protected within the Kingston Range Wilderness, at nearly 200,000 acres the largest in the Mojave Desert. This wilderness also includes the Sperry Hills and Dumont Hills to the west, and most of the Shadow Mountains. The northeastern part of the Kingston Range lies within the 73,726-acre Pahrump Valley Wilderness. In contrast, the Avawatz Mountains are still unprotected. About 60% falls within Fort Irwin Military Reservation. Most of the rest, including the highest central crest, is now considered for protection in the 87,700-acre Avawatz Mountains Wilderness Study Area.

Both ranges are high enough to host a nearly full range of plant zones, from a creosote and blackbrush community to Joshua tree woodlands (more extensive in the Avawatz Mountains) and juniper–pinyon pine forests (much denser in the Kingston Range). The botany of the Kingston Range is one of the most diverse in the Mojave Desert, with over 500 native species and many species either uncommon or rare. Among the most noticeable are nolinas, far away from their strongholds in the southern Mojave Desert; pygmy agave, thriving on carbonate rocks; and a rare stand of about 150 white fir just north of Kingston Peak. Both ranges provide wildlife with water at a number of springs. Bighorn sheep live in both ranges, and feral burros in the northern Kingston Range. These mountains are also home to the usual gangs of desert critters—coyote, lizards, bobcats, rabbits, desert tortoise, a few dozen bird species, and the obligatory *Crotalus*.

■

KINGSTON PEAK

Highest summit in the Kingston Range, Kingston Peak is a tough nut to crack. You must first cross a brush-invaded valley, then scramble up a steep ravine, and finally traverse a long, hilly, forested crest smothered by armies of tall crags. Conquering this tortured terrain where nothing is straight and verticality reigns supreme may take four hours, and the return is not much faster. To anyone serious about desert climbing, this minor ordeal is a classic as spectacular as it is obligatory.

General Information

Jurisdiction: Kingston Range Wilderness
Road status: Mostly roadless; paved and graded access road
The climb: 4.4 mi, 2,980 ft up, 620 ft down one way/strenuous (Class 2)
Main attractions: A challenging brushy climb to a forested peak
USGS 7.5' topo maps: Horse Thief Springs, Kingston Peak
Maps: pp. 71*, 55

Location and Access

From the Cima Road exit on Interstate 15, take the Excelsior Mine Road north. This is a lonesome road, with a coarse pavement that occasionally fades to gravel, and more jackrabbits than cars. For more than 20 miles it descends into, then climbs through isolated Shadow Valley, abundantly dotted with Joshua trees, in full view of the Kingston Range and its high point to the north-northwest. At the end of Shadow Valley, the road crests a pass between the Kingston Range and the Mesquite Mountains, then slowly veers west to cross the range. After 28.3 miles, it passes by Horse Thief Springs, most of the year a flash of bright-green cottonwoods. Just past it is Tecopa Pass, marked by a cattle guard. Drive 0.9 mile further to a good dirt road on the left (a "detour" sign might direct you to it). Take this road 0.35 mile to a rougher road on the left, and park. Along the last mile, a broad valley on the south side cuts a deep bay into the range. Kingston Peak is way out of sight, beyond the high rim that walls the south end of the valley—you will not get to see it until two thirds of the way in.

Route Description

The first segment is easy at first. The road climbs to a low saddle next to the domed hill just south of the access road, passing below the

69

talc tailings of the Kingston Prospect. It then descends around the hill and climbs south across the valley. In this area the road points to a notch on the crest beyond the head of the valley—this is the route to the summit. After 0.65 mile, the road angles right, into the first side canyon. Leave it and continue generally south up the roadless valley. From there on, travel is rougher. The valley is a waist-high jungle of shinbone-swatting woody plants. Cattle have blazed miles of short paths, disjointed and unpredictable. They help, but not enough, and it is still a tortuous, blood-letting crossing. The main wash is narrow and often cluttered; walk parallel to it on the irregular benches west of it. Deeper in, imposing stone monuments stagger up and down the surrounding slopes, everything sharp and vertical. On both rims, the high tips of rocks stab the sky, a harbinger of challenges to come. Between the second and third side canyons, where the valley narrows and curves left, the east side is a little easier. You will trade tall thickets of manzanita and squawbush for steeper but less congested slopes.

The second segment starts at the third side canyon. The land tilts upward, creased along a ravine as steep as a mountain face. It is a short, brisk pull against gravity, 1,100 feet up over 0.7 mile, most of it rocky. The brush clears up a little at first, then comes a long strip of pinyon-pine woodland, a talus of tumbled boulders entrenched between narrow cliffs, and more prickly brush as the slope slowly levels off and you finally top the U-shaped saddle on the ridge.

The final segment, from the saddle southwest to the crest, then south along the crest, is the most challenging. The elevation gain is modest, but the crest is a crooked spine that weaves up and down over half a dozen local summits. Much of it is capped with stone reefs that have exfoliated into tight ranks of tall fins and pinnacles. Pine, juniper, and cliffrose have colonized the narrow gaps between outcrops, and stiff plants—nolina, buckwheat, big sagebrush, ephedra—occupy the

Kingston Peak		
	Dist.(mi)	Elev.(ft)
Excelsior Mine Road detour	0.0	4,990
Leave road	0.65	5,130
Start of steep ravine	1.85	5,560
Saddle on ridge	2.6	6,680
Crest	2.9	6,940
Main saddle	3.7	6,610
Kingston Peak	4.4	7,336

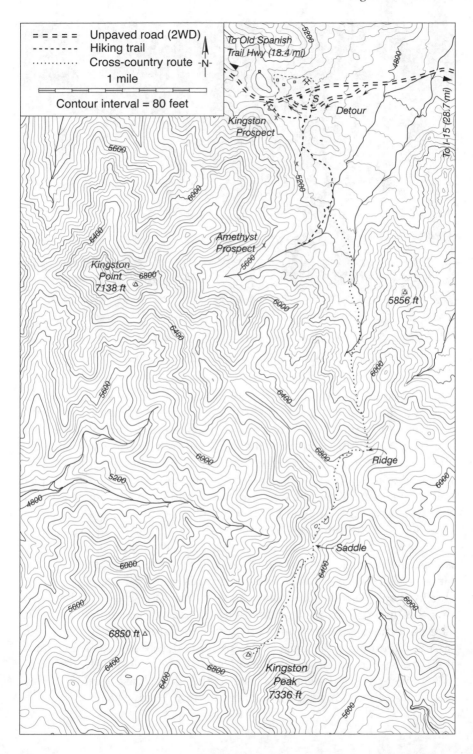

= = = = = Unpaved road (2WD)
- - - - - Hiking trail
············· Cross-country route -N-

1 mile

Contour interval = 80 feet

To Old Spanish
Trail Hwy (18.4 mi)

To I-15 (28.7 mi)

Detour

Kingston
Prospect

Kingston
Point
7138 ft

Amethyst
Prospect

5856 ft

Ridge

Saddle

6850 ft

Kingston
Peak
7336 ft

Standing rocks along the steep corridor to Kingston Peak

rest. Traversing this endless tangle of crags and trees is slow, painstaking, and demanding. You wiggle through sloping clefts choked with boulders, or bypass them on unstable hillsides. Occasionally the best option is to climb right over the rock columns. Often you end up stranded high above the trees or snagged on them, and you must look for another way. A few areas are open and have a faint use trail—just before the crest, before the deep midway saddle, and the burn around the last false summit. The hardest spot is the final Class-2 pitch, a crowded grove of tilted fins hanging high toward the abrupt summit.

Notwithstanding its roughness, this billowing maze of pale granite competing for majesty with stately gnarled pine trees is a spellbinding landscape. There is a sultry pleasure in this quest for secret passages, skirting cool, bone-naked walls as gray as fire ash, squeezing between fins that may go through or dead-end in shady alcoves with a view. The panorama changes constantly, over to Pahrump Valley and the Spring Mountains, the crop circles in bone-dry Mesquite Valley, and the massive mountains of southern Death Valley. Ultimately, the summit delivers a grand sweeping vista to the south, past Shadow Valley and Clark Mountain, over much of the eastern Mojave Desert.

∎

AVAWATZ PEAK

> *Climbing this remote summit is a superb celebration of the desert's astounding diversity. You first go up a tortuous canyon, then follow a windy mining road, scramble up a steep bluff studded with weathered cliffs, and end with a long airy walk up and down a crooked crest. The terrain is comparatively forgiving, but it is a long trek, over 14 miles round-trip with more than one vertical mile of elevation change, and it requires nothing short of dogged tenacity.*

General Information
Jurisdiction: Avawatz Mountains Wilderness Study Area (BLM)
Road status: Hiking from primitive road (HC)
The climb: 7.1 mi, 4,850 ft up, 730 ft down one way/strenuous
Main attractions: A remote peak, colorful mountains, unusual views
USGS 7.5' topo maps: Red Pass Lake NE, Sheep Creek Spring
Maps: pp. 75*, 55

Location and Access
From the Kelbaker Road exit on Interstate 15, take Highway 127 on the north side of the freeway and drive 19.1 miles to the primitive road to the Old Mormon Spring on the left, across from the southern half of Silurian Valley's dry lake. Coming from the north, this road is 10.6 miles south of the signed Harry Wade Road. Stay on it 4.5 miles west to a gentle ramp that descends into a wash at the base of the mountains. The road used to continue into the obvious canyon incised in the Avawatz Mountains up ahead, to a mine near the crest. Severe storms in the 2010s have erased most of it in the canyon. Park 100 feet further, where the road has been clipped by a flashflood. This is a slow road, with lots of rocks and a rough dip 3.8 miles in. It requires high clearance, and four-wheel drive for lighter vehicles.

Route Description
Even without the road, the canyon is an easy walk, an open wash of braided gravel with sparse vegetation. It slips into the mountains in short, random meanders, a secret passage that seems to be searching for a path through the mountain's maze of ridges. This is part of the Avawatz Quartz Monzodiorite complex, a mosaic of small intrusions with an unusual diversity of colors and compositions. Some exposures are highly cohesive bluish diorite, like the rough waves of bedrock that

73

fill the short constriction 1.1 miles in. In the canyon's interior, the walls rise 1,400 feet, draped in thin, tall taluses and fractured upsweeps of cream-colored quartz monzonite. Other creatures use this convenient avenue of the mountains. The gravel is stamped with countless imprints of bighorn hooves. In the dim light of dusk, I caught a fleeting glimpse of a coyote slithering like a ghost between the silent walls.

About 1 mile past the constriction, a feeder canyon comes in on the left (go straight), then another one 0.2 mile further (make a sharp left). The road resumes 0.6 mile up canyon on the right, where it climbs out of the wash. In 0.35 mile its battered grade crests at a small solar-powered radio antenna, then spills into the next canyon north. A few spurs drop to the mine shafts that probed the bowels of the canyon for lead, silver, zinc, and copper ores. The main road heads southwest, down a little then up, along the canyon's scalloped upper basin. It crosses the Avawatz Formation, an Eocene fanglomerate made of almost every rock type ranging in size from silt to jeep-size boulders. Its most plentiful constituent is a vivid granite filled with pink crystals. The hills to the north are a particularly colorful stack of Precambrian shales, quartzite, and dolomite stippled with Joshua trees and Mojave yucca.

About 0.6 mile past the antenna there is a tight hairpin left, to the south-southwest. Go 400 feet to the next bend (right), then 100 feet to a draw on the left. Leave the road and climb the draw to the canyon rim, then descend on the far side northwest to a saddle (0.2 mile). To the west, the long, neck-bending mountain block that carries Avawatz Peak shoots up 500 feet in a third of a mile. It is buttressed by a band of storied cliffs cleaved in pale-grey marbles of the famous Bonanza King Formation. Luckily, above the saddle the cliffs have been fragmented

	Avawatz Peak	
	Dist.(mi)	Elev.(ft)
End of road at edge of wash	0.0	2,100
First fork (go right)	2.15	3,540
Second fork (go left)	2.35	3,675
Start of old road	2.95	4,200
Radio antenna	3.3	4,530
Leave road	4.0	~4,620
Crest	4.55	5,120
1787T point	6.0	5,683
Deep saddle	6.6	5,725
Avawatz Peak	7.1	6,154

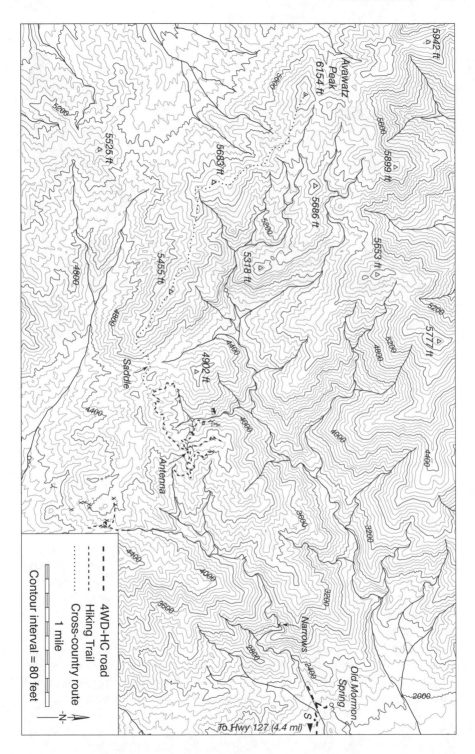

Avawatz
Peak
6154 ft △

5942 ft △

5899 ft △

5686 ft △

5683 ft △

5653 ft △

5525 ft △

5318 ft △

5777 ft △

5455 ft

4902 ft △

Saddle

Antenna

Narrows

Old Mormon
Spring

To Hwy 127 (4.4 mi)

4WD-HC road
Hiking Trail
Cross-country route

1 mile

Contour interval = 80 feet

-N-

Kelso Valley area from below the crest to Avawatz Peak

into individual outcrops. A few routes can be used to climb between them to the crest, a steep, Class-2 scramble over loose rocks.

The rest of the climb is northwest along the crest, a capricious 2.5-mile roller coaster that changes direction abruptly, rises and falls over no fewer than 15 prominences, and cumulates 2,200 feet of elevation gain. When Avawatz Peak finally comes into view after half a mile, it is still a distant ship on the horizon. The crest is locally steep but open ground of shattered stones—marble, then quartz granodiorite and granite—livened by Joshua trees and pinyon pine. It commands unorthodox views of the desert that we never get to see it from this angle. Silurian Valley is often in plain view, its slender dry lake surrounded by rugged ranges—the Kingston Range, the Shadow Mountains—and scores of colorful hills. There are unique perspectives over Silver Lake, Kelso Valley and its vast dunes, the Cronese Lakes and oddly symmetric Cave Mountain, and Fort Irwin's forbidden lands. Southern Death Valley spreads out to the north, from the crisp Saddle Peak Hills to the Owlshead Mountains. These unusual snapshots are alternatively revealed and eclipsed by towering hills, until you top the summit and they all coalesce into one sublime tableau.

■

GRAPEVINE MOUNTAINS

Long, massive, and rough, looming high above northern Death Valley's empty quarters, the Grapevine Mountains are one of the most imposing ranges in the northern Mojave Desert. Their most rugged southern section rises more than a mile above the sea-level valley floor. The highest summits are Grapevine Peak (8,738') and Wahguyhe Peak (8,628'), both in Nevada. Increasingly popular among diehard hikers for the deep and spectacular canyons that slice through their steep western scarp, the Grapevine Mountains are also home to several summits that are as difficult to reach as they are breathtaking.

This range is best known, however, not for its grand scenery but for its grandiose mansion—Scotty's Castle. Set amid lush springs in Grapevine Canyon in the northern reaches of the range, it was built in the mid-1920s by Albert Johnson, a wealthy insurance executive from Chicago with a life-long involvement in the area. Walter Scott, a con artist and would-be prospector better known as Death Valley Scotty, had been bankrolled by Johnson on his many infamous mining shenanigans. Over the years they became friends, and Scotty often entertained Johnson and his wife with his tall tales at their home. After Albert Johnson's death in 1948, Scott lived on the premises to entertain the tourists—and the mansion became known as Scotty's Castle.

Like all ranges east of Death Valley, the Grapevine Mountains lie in the rain shadow of the high Inyo Mountains and Panamint Range to the west. Springs and surface water are scarce. The most blatant exception is Grapevine Springs. Marked by green vegetation, they rise along a horizontal fault in the western foothills below Grapevine Canyon. Their water has been appropriated for human use at Scotty's Castle for decades. Despite their dryness, the Grapevine Mountains are high enough to support a relatively extensive pinyon pine-juniper woodland, as well as limber pine, on the two highest peaks.

The range's western foot is paralleled by the Furnace Creek Fault Zone, which is closely followed by the Scotty's Castle Road (recently renamed the North Highway by someone at CalTrans overflowing with romanticism) along Death Valley. Vertical displacements along this fault have created the mountains' very steep western escarpment, in contrast to the eastern side, which drops only a few thousand feet into high valleys—Nevada's Sarcobatus Flat and the Amargosa Desert. The most prevalent rocks belong to Paleozoic sedimentary formations. They make up most of the range's western front. From Grapevine Peak to Boundary Canyon, where the Grapevine Mountains nudge against the Funeral Mountains to the south, the southern crest is capped with Miocene volcanic rocks, mostly rhyolite. These rocks are fringed to the west by small, fault-bounded exposures of the Titus Canyon Formation, stream and lake deposits that formed around 40 million years ago when this area was probably a region of broad valleys and mountain ranges. It contains the fossilized remains of the mammals that lived here then—titanothere, tapir, horse, and rhinoceros. The hills between the fault and the western foot of the range, including the Kit Fox Hills, are mostly fanglomerates of the colorful Funeral Formation.

Although the portion of the Grapevine Mountains within the park was largely spared from mining, it witnessed two major booms. Between 1904 and 1908, the Bullfrog Hills, in the southeastern foothills in Nevada, was the site of one of the most feverish gold rushes in Death Valley's history. The area produced more gold than any other mine around. The second historically significant site is Leadfield, in a fork of Titus Canyon in the southern part of the range. In 1925 and 1926, prospectors and miners swarmed the area to investigate what was being hailed as the biggest lead-silver mine in the West. Although the venture quickly turned out to be unprofitable, the massive advertising campaign conducted by mining promoter Charles Julian raised a lot of interest in the property for a while, and left a lasting imprint on the local lore.

Only two roads cross this range, the scenic backcountry road through Titus Canyon, and the paved Bonnie Claire Road through Grapevine Canyon. The huge swath of land between these roads is rough mountainous terrain that is particularly difficult to reach. Many named and unnamed summits in that area, places like Mount Palmer and T89 High Peak, are far from the closest road and offer some of the most challenging mountaineering goals in the northern Mojave Desert. Fortunately, a few peaks in the southern part of the range can be reached relatively easily, especially Thimble Peak from the Titus Canyon Road, and Corkscrew Peak—though still no picnic—from the paved Daylight Pass Road in Boundary Canyon.

■

MOUNT PALMER

There is no easy way to Mount Palmer. Isolated in the remote central Grapevine Mountains, surrounded by a hundred square miles of roadless mountains, it is one of the most challenging summits in the region. The climb is long and difficult, impeded by mature trees, peaks, gnarly outcrops, thin air, and a spiked cliff just when you thought you were there. Notwithstanding its roughness, it is nothing short of outstanding. The views are sumptuous the whole way. The long curled causeway that leads up to the summit plunges on both sides thousands of feet into fall-ridden canyons, while up ahead Death Valley's great void coaxes us to get closer, and closer still. This is pure Death Valley excitement.

General Information
Jurisdiction: Death Valley National Park
Road status: Roadless; primitive access road (HC-4WD)
The climb: 5.7 mi, 2,940 ft up, 1,680 ft down, one way/strenuous
Main attractions: A long challenging climb to a remote peak
USGS 7.5' topo maps: Wahguyhe Peak (Nev.), Grapevine Peak (Nev.)
Maps: pp. 83*, 55

Location and Access
The best route to Mount Palmer from Death Valley is up Fall Canyon, a long and rough route that even well-trained hikers will have difficulty completing in a day. The easiest approach is from the Nevada side of the mountains. You will be trading some of the walking for a long bumpy ride.

First work your way to the small town of Beatty, Nevada, on Highway 95 about 115 miles northwest of Las Vegas. From the junction with Highway 374 in Beatty, drive 11.8 miles north on Highway 95 to a primitive road at 10 o'clock (the Phinney Canyon Road). There is a barbed-wire gate across it, with a "keep gate closed" sign in red stenciled letters. Drive this road west-southwest, first over a low rise, then across the vast open plain of Sarcobatus Flat—another cheerful local name. After 6.9 miles (go straight at all crossroads) there is a fork. Stay with the main road (left), which very soon crosses a cattle guard at the signed entrance into Death Valley National Park.

In 5.3 miles the road forks. The main road drops down to the left. Keep right instead. After 3 miles, the Phinney Canyon Road reaches the scenic foothills of the Grapevine Mountains, spotted with cholla and dwarf Joshua trees. About 17.1 miles from the highway, a ramp descends 0.1 mile into Phinney Canyon. Continue 3.5 miles up the increasingly forested canyon to a spacious pullout on the right (elev. 6,665') surrounded by pinyon pine. This route requires high clearance.

There are two possible starting points to Mount Palmer. The first one is the large pullout. The climb starts in the side canyon along the road 100 yards below the pullout. The second route starts at the pass at the end of the Phinney Canyon Road, 1 mile further on the mountains' crest. The drive is rough. After a quarter of a mile the road deteriorates quickly, with large holes and rocks requiring high-clearance, four-wheel-drive, and experience. If you cannot make it, park at the large pullout and either hike the road or take the first route.

There are two other classic summits in this area, Wahguyhe Peak and Grapevine Peak. Both are clearly visible from the access road on Sarcobatus Flat. Wahguyhe Peak's distinctive steep-sided cone rises almost straight ahead, while Grapevine Peak's pointed summit, the highest in this range, is about 3 miles to the right of it. From the large pullout, Wahguyhe Peak looms about 1 air mile to the south and looks deceptively easy, but the climb involves a frustrating slog up a very steep and unstable scree of loose slabs (1.5 miles and 2,000 feet up). The Grapevine Peak climb is the easiest. At the pass, just follow the crest to the north as it wanders up and over half a dozen small summits before the final 800-foot ridge to the summit (3.3 miles and 3,060 feet from the pullout). Since it takes a while to drive to this area, it makes sense to stay a second day to climb one or both of these peaks.

Route Description

Most people will prefer the road. It is easier and quicker, even if you end up walking it. When you reach the pass at road's end, follow the crooked ridge south to the first summit (~8,045') just past the 7,980-foot peak. The ridge is dark with thick-headed pinyon pine. The spaces between trees are mantled with pine cones and needles, ephedra and bitterbrush, cliffrose and big sagebrush. In the warm season lupine, Indian paintbrush, and other bloomers decorate the area. In the dead of winter there is enough snow to stop normal boots. On north-facing slopes, snow patches can linger well into the spring. On a nearby peak in early April I sank thigh deep in powdery drifts. Watch your timing: a little snow can be a useful source of water; too much of it can make life miserable. The summit area commands fine views of Mount Palmer to the south, and east down wooded Phinney Canyon, to pointed volcanic hills and wide-open Sarcobatus Flat.

The last leg of the long ridge leading across to Mount Palmer (far left) seen from Wahguyhe Peak; the crux is the steep rise to the right of Mount Palmer

I preferred the other route, up the side canyon, cross-country and wilder. From the pullout it starts 100 yards back down the Phinney Canyon Road, on the south side. Its entrance is marked by a tall angular outcrop of rhyolite on its west side. Over the first 0.2 mile the side canyon is overgrown, and some tree-whacking is unavoidable. Further on it becomes a shallow, narrow, steep-sided ravine crowded with pine and littered with logs and fallen branches. But the slope is modest and the walking fairly easy, at first beside the wash, then in the wash. After 0.8 mile, when it feels like the crest is near, climb out of the wash onto the low open bench on the south side, and continue up on the bench in the same direction toward the crest. The woodland quickly turns into a beautiful sub-alpine meadow of aromatic big sagebrush. It ends at the broad treeless crest overlooking Mount Palmer and the long wavering ridge leading to it, its deeply furrowed slopes rising straight from the bowels of Fall Canyon—an enticing preview of what is to come. To proceed, climb the ridge northwest of the crest, up a succession of three benches, to the same first summit (~8,045′).

From this summit the route follows a curved ridge in the shape of a half hexagon—it runs southwest 1.4 miles, then a little west of south

1.5 miles, and finally southeast 1.1 miles. Mount Palmer is 90 feet *lower* than the first summit, but the ridge has so many ups and downs that the total elevation change between the two summits is substantial—about 3,150 feet. First descend southwest, then west-southwest, along the ridge about 0.5 mile to a first saddle. Then climb over two more peaks to the third, shallowest saddle. Up to that point the exposures belong to a sequence of Tertiary sedimentary rocks, whitish tuff, and a lava flow, tentatively named Wahguyhe, that makes for relatively easy terrain. The next peak (7,710') rises straight ahead to the southwest. A ravine drops southeast into Fall Canyon. Between the peak and the ravine, about 450 feet down to the south, is the start of the long and skinny ridge to Mount Palmer. It is best not to climb the 7,710-foot peak, and not to drop into the ravine either. Instead, head due south across the peak's eastern slope, staying below the rocky outcrops higher on the slope and above the ravine. The hillside is steep and covered with trees and loose rocks, but bits of trail help a little.

The next objective is the prominent pointed peak (~7,725') visible up ahead, where the ridge swings to the left. From the last saddle on down you are in former titanothere territory. The rocks underfoot are part of the sedimentary Titus Canyon Formation, famous for its fossilized remains of numerous Oligocene mammals. Although still densely forested, the rolling terrain is more sedate, as it was when titanotheres ruled.

About half way to the 7,725-foot peak, in just a few steps time jumps back several hundred million years to the Devonian-Silurian era, and everything changes. The rest of the ridge is all Hidden Valley Dolomite, often sharpened to vertical serrations. As the ridge makes ingress into Death Valley's drying breath, the pines are gradually replaced by more heat-resistant juniper, then the forest thins down

	Mount Palmer	
	Dist.(mi)	Elev.(ft)
Large pullout	0.0	~6,700
Pass on road	1.05	~7,500
First summit	1.8	~8,045
Second summit (7780T point)	2.6	7,780
Third saddle	3.15	7,540
Fourth summit	4.7	~7,725
160-foot cliff	5.45	7,670
Mount Palmer	5.7	7,958

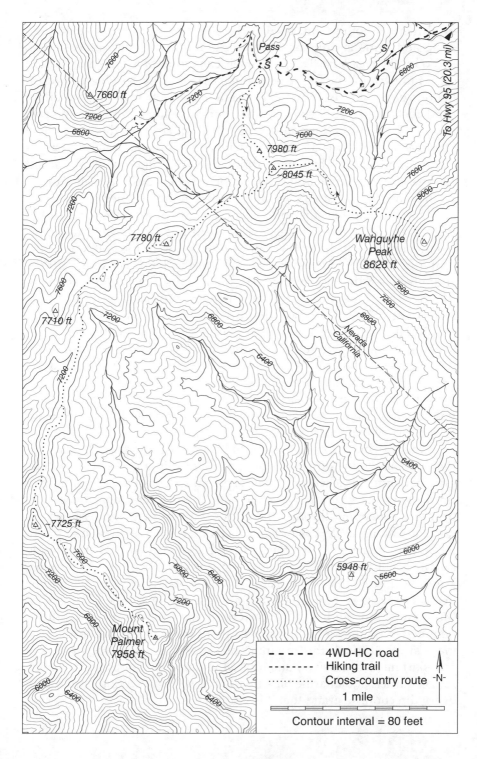

Pass
S
S
To Hwy 95 (20.3 mi)

△ 7660 ft

△ 7980 ft
△ ~8045 ft

7780 ft △

Wahguyhe
Peak
8628 ft △

△ 7710 ft

Nevada
California

△ ~7725 ft

5948 ft △

Mount
Palmer
7958 ft △

– – – – – 4WD-HC road
– – – – – Hiking trail
· · · · · · · Cross-country route   -N-
1 mile

Contour interval = 80 feet

until there is nothing but hard rock. The first outcrops are along the steep and sinuous ridge up to the 7,725-foot peak; they are easiest to avoid on the east side. The peak itself can either be climbed or skirted on a faint trail along its unstable east flank. The last leg to Mount Palmer, past the peak, is an intermittent obstacle course sculpted out of solid rock. Here too there is a trail, better defined, worn by the rare hikers who venture here and inevitably squeeze by the same most practicable spots. It is a broken, dusty, and capricious roller coaster— but it does the job. This long isthmus hanging high above the desert commands deep views into Fall Canyon on one side, Red Wall Canyon on the other, and Death Valley shimmering in the distance.

The crux is a short distance before Mount Palmer, a 160-foot cliff of weathered dolomite that steepens to verticality at its summit. Three parallel broken ribs hang vertically from the top of the cliff, one in the center of the cliff and two to the right of it. The direct route, up the chute between the two leftmost ribs, is a Class-3 climb, exposed near the top. The chute to the right of it is harder (Class 4 or 5). The least risky route (Class 2) bypasses the ribs. Start at the saddle at the foot of the cliff, lined up with a lone pine about 25 feet down to the right. Cut to the right across the hillside, climbing a little on a faint path while passing below the foot of the ribs. Just past the third rib, ascend the open slope to the left, paralleling the ribs. All routes involve steep loose talus and crumbly rock poorly fit to hold a human being, so be very careful. There is a little more Class-2 climbing and dodging small-er outcrops above the cliff, but nothing serious.

Mount Palmer is a slanted spit of broken Silurian seabed, held cap-tive high above the desert by cubic miles of thin air. The rock is pale-gray dolomite, bleached by metamorphism and blasted to a sandpaper finish. To the east, serrated fins and cliffs tumble hundreds of near-ver-tical feet, screaming through the Ordovician on their reckless descent into the Cambrian depths of Fall Canyon. This is the far-flung epicen-ter of the Grapevine Mountains, a jumble of cusped ridges plunging into abysmal canyons. To the east is the spacious head of Fall Canyon, a moth-colored punch bowl capped by the stately cone of Wahguyhe Peak. The western horizon is all high desert ranges—the Cottonwood Mountains and the Last Chance Range, the Inyos and the Whites— hemmed in by the Sierra Nevada's silvery fringe. Death Valley slices a giant swath through this mountainous province, its sinuous rivers of salt skirting the massive Panamint Mountains and fading into far-off ranges turned aquamarine blue by distance. It is a riveting spectacle in every direction, so grand that it is painful to leave.

■

THIMBLE PEAK

Up on the crest of the Grapevine Mountains a primitive trail swings high above the colorful walls of Titus Canyon, then peters out into wilderness. This is the route to Thimble Peak, a prominent landmark recognizable from all around Stovepipe Wells. Climbing the limestone cliffs that crown the peak is an exhilarating experience, rewarded by awesome bird's-eye views from the aerial summit. In one direction you will be gazing over the chiseled Grapevine Mountains, and in the other across the great gulf of Death Valley to Mesquite Flat and the great wall of the Panamint Range.

General Information
Jurisdiction: Death Valley National Park
Road status: Roadless; hiking from graded road
The climb: 1.8 mi, 1,390 ft up, 300 ft down, one way/moderate
Main attractions: Short steep climb, spectacular views of Mesquite Flat
USGS 7.5' topo maps: Daylight Pass, Thimble Peak*, Fall Canyon
Maps: pp. 87*, 55

Location and Access
Thimble Peak is the pointed summit that juts out on the southern crest of the Grapevine Mountains. The shortest route to it starts from the Titus Canyon Road at Red Pass. To get there, drive the Daylight Pass Road 6.9 miles east of Daylight Pass (or Highway 374 6.1 miles west of Beatty, Nevada) to the signed Titus Canyon Road, on the north side. Follow this graded road 12.6 miles to Red Pass and park at the small turn-out (take as little space as possible, as others might want to park there too while you are gone). This road is one-way westbound; after climbing the peak you will have to drive it down through Titus Canyon to get out. Since it is a long road with much to see (see *Hiking Death Valley*), get an early start to make the most of it. The NPS recommends a high-clearance vehicle to tackle this road. Although people occasionally drive it with more marginal vehicles, it is a good idea: this road is long, it has steep grades up to Red Pass, a few short stretches of soft gravel in the wash, and if in trouble you cannot turn around.

Route Description
Thimble Peak is visible off and on from the road before reaching Red Pass, but at the pass it is hidden by the tall ridge that rises to the

Titanothere Canyon and Corkscrew Peak from Thimble Peak

south. The general route to Thimble Peak goes up this ridge to a first, unnamed summit, drops down to a saddle, then proceeds up the far side to the peak. Up to near the first summit there is a primitive trail. It starts in the bend on the south side of the road, and climbs approximately along the spine of the ridge, wiggling its way between the low shrubs that cover the steep, rock-strewn slope. About half way up it passes below a rocky outcrop, eases up along a narrow, level stretch of ridge, then resumes climbing just as steeply. Shortly before the first summit Thimble Peak bursts into view, a tall pyramid capped by an abrupt rim of limestone cliffs. If rock climbing is not your thing, this sight might be a little discouraging, but do not give up just yet—scaling it is not as tough as it seems. In this area the trail fades at a short sweep of slickrock; it reappears shortly after, slightly to the right of the ridge line. Just before the first summit the trail veers right and ends soon after, about 1 mile from Red Pass.

Over time this use trail will be extended all the way to Thimble Peak, but until then the rest of the route is essentially cross-country. Work your way down the long band of low cliffs that slashes across the south side of the first summit (there are plenty of breaks in the cliffs), then descend along the ridge of your choice to the deep saddle

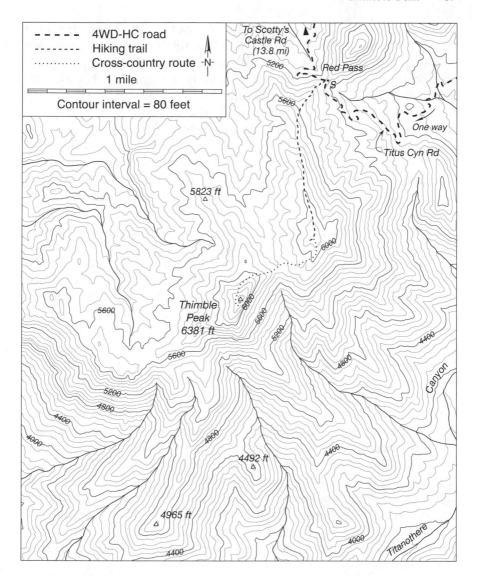

Thimble Peak

	Dist.(mi)	Elev.(ft)
Red Pass	0.0	5,290
End of trail near first summit	~1.0	~6,100
Saddle	1.3	5,820
Foot of summit block	1.65	~6,200
Thimble Peak	1.8	6,381

separating it from Thimble Peak (a 300-foot drop). Then climb up again, in the same general direction, to Thimble Peak's north shoulder. At this point you should be 100–200 yards from the summit block, a sheer cliff of rust-tinged limestone pierced by a large cave. Hike up the shoulder to the base of the cliff (a faint trail is developing). Then climb the loose talus that circles counter-clockwise up around the cliff's base to the southwest side of the peak, just before the peak's precipitous south face. This is the easiest route (about a Class 2) around the summit block. It is a short scramble up a slant of bare rock to an arête less than two feet wide. The last 10 feet to the summit are along this prickly spine suspended above hundreds of feet of nearly vertical land. If in doubt, it can always be crossed sitting. Some of the earlier routes are less exposed, but steeper.

This is a short hike—only 1.8 miles each way—but with about 1,700 feet of total elevation change it makes for a vigorous cardiovascular workout. As often, the desert knows how to reward adventurous souls. From the trail the views of Titus Canyon's colorful volcanic crags (Titus Canyon Formation) and the rugged Grapevine Mountains beyond it are stunning. A few uncommon, rare, or simply beautiful plants grow on the north slope of Thimble Peak—Mojave fishhook cactus, milkvetch, and a scattering of tousled cliffrose the size of small trees. Exceptionally large patches of velvety rock spiraea coat the foot of the cliffs. Beautiful cliffs of pink and dark-gray banded limestones wrap around the peak's east side, a gift from the Cambrian (likely the Bonanza King Formation). The views from the narrow summit are nothing short of awesome. To the southwest a jagged alignment of pointed cliffs drops precipitously into 3,000-foot-deep Titanothere Canyon. Beyond it rise the convoluted folds of Corkscrew Peak. Far to the west the Mesquite Dunes shimmer more than a mile below, bright against the dark escarpments of Tucki Mountain. In the summer the haze that fills the valley occludes much of this distant view, but it also turns the surrounding ranges into a monochromatic landscape, more alien than Vulcan.

■

DEATH VALLEY BUTTES

> *Thanks to their unique central position on the edge of Death Valley, the Death Valley Buttes command expansive views up and down the valley floor, from Mesquite Flat and the Mesquite Dunes to the salt flats. There is a trail most of the way, so novices can get a chance to visit the easier Eastern Butte, and enjoy the exercise and the panorama. The main butte's summit block, on the other hand, requires Class-3 climbing on sturdy base rock. It takes more stamina than it looks, and the climb is airy at places—this little mountain is more fun than many peaks several times its height.*

General Information

Jurisdiction: Death Valley National Park
Road status: Roadless; hiking from paved road
The climb (Eastern Butte): 0.8 mi, 660 ft up, 10 ft down one way / easy
The climb (Red Top Peak): 1.6 mi, 1,190 ft up, 270 ft down, one way /
      moderate, with Class-3 scrambling
Main attractions: Trail and rock climbing, views of Mesquite Dunes
USGS 7.5' topo maps: Chloride City*, Stovepipe Wells NE
Maps: pp. 91*, 55

Location and Access

The Death Valley Buttes are an alignment of three hills, the two easternmost buttes connected by a ridge and the third one separate, located at the southern tip of the Grapevine Mountains about 11 air miles northeast of Stovepipe Wells. They can be easily accessed from the paved Daylight Pass Road via a use trail that has developed over the last couple of decades. Coming from Stovepipe Wells, drive Highway 190 7.2 miles east and turn left on the North Highway. Go 0.6 mile and turn right on the Daylight Pass Road. The buttes will soon become visible to the north. Park 6.35 miles from the North Highway, within sight of Hells Gate, across from the eastern tip of the buttes. The trail is visible just on the north side of the tip. If you are coming from the south on Highway 190, it is a little shorter to take the Beatty Cutoff (10.5 miles north of the Visitor Center at The Ranch at Death Valley) to Hells Gate (10 miles), then make a left and park after 0.4 mile.

The price to pay for easy access is potential noise from car traffic on the Daylight Pass Road. It is manageable at normal times, but it can be intrusive on popular long weekends.

89

Route Description

Dwarfed by the Grapevine Mountains and Funeral Mountains that soar thousands of feet above them, the Death Valley Buttes may not look like much. Yet this modest mountain barely sticking out of the alluvial fan certainly holds its own. From the car park head across the bumpy fan 0.15 mile to the trailhead. The trail first climbs the eastern tip of the buttes to a first saddle, swings to the south side of the buttes' crest, then proceeds up to the top of the eastern butte, switching from one side of the crest to the other. The narrow trail heads practically straight up on the uphill sections, and it is steep and slippery with small loose rocks, but the going would be much harder without it.

The Death Valley Buttes are thought to be at their unorthodox position because of detachment faulting. They slipped off the southern face of the Grapevine Mountains along a low-angle fault plane. The mile-wide wash on the north side of the buttes traces the general location of the fault. This isolation from the runoffs and slightly higher humidity of the main mountain mass, combined with the low elevation, are likely responsible for the buttes' particularly drab vegetation. The only plants on this sun-beaten crag that show some chlorophyll are a scatter of emaciated creosote, desert holly, and cottontop cactus that look like they have not seen a drop of water in years.

The trail overlooks sumptuous panoramas essentially the whole way to the eastern butte. The Grapevine Mountains loom grandly to the north, capped by Thimble Peak and the colorful recumbent folds of Corkscrew Peak. To the south, Death Valley spreads out many miles to Cottonball Basin's salt flats and beyond, funneled between the massive Funeral Mountains on one side and Tucki Mountain on the other. If you are not going any further, the eastern butte's pointed summit is a fine second-best observatory to enjoy this magnificent scenery, and the stately main butte rearing up ahead.

From the eastern butte the trail descends very steeply in short switchbacks to the skinny saddle between the eastern butte and the main butte, known as Red Top Peak. The next stretch is nearly level, just on the north side of the ridge. There is little shade up to this point, so it makes sense to avoid coming here in the summer. The trail then ascends the sharp eastern shoulder of Red Top Peak, but not very far. About 0.15 mile short of the summit, the terrain changes abruptly to a compact jungle of outcrops and boulders, some of them enormous. For the remaining distance, other than very short segments there is just no room for a trail. On both sides of the sharp ridge the mountain drops precipitously, and the only way to proceed is by clambering, scrambling, and climbing over and between the rocks. All of it is a pretty

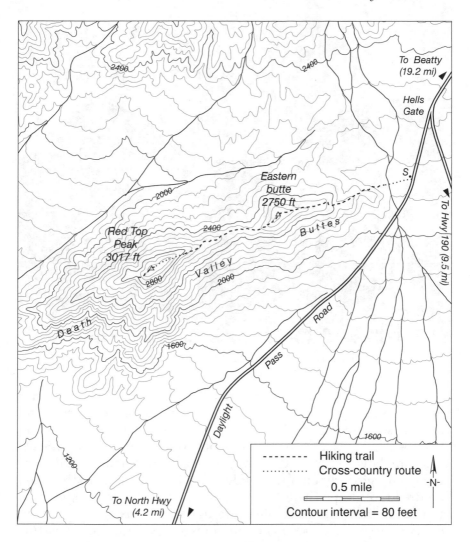

Death Valley Buttes

	Dist.(mi)	Elev.(ft)
Daylight Pass Road	0.0	~2,100
Trailhead	0.15	2,120
Eastern Butte	0.85	2,750
Saddle	1.0	~2,500
Lower end of rocky area	1.4	2,760
Red Top Peak	1.55	3,017

Red Top Peak and Mesquite Dunes from the eastern butte

quartzite with a golden sheen, cleaved in angular edges that offer plenty of sturdy handholds. There are many possible routes to get through, some requiring Class-5 technical moves, but with a little care it is possible to select a route that is not worse than a Class 3. Some areas are, however, very exposed—at one place I had to walk very slowly and gingerly on a foot-wide ledge between a cliff face and a hundred-foot drop. There is some shade along this stretch, even in summer. In the spring, blooming clumps of brittlebush grow right out of mere cracks in the rocks. The summit is just past the rocky area; the trail resumes briefly for an even better view further west.

Red Top Peak is a great place to let yourself get bewitched by Death Valley's spirit. The views of the Mesquite Dunes and Mesquite Flat that fill the valley floor to the west are amazing. The dunes draw a long arcuate veil across the desert, cocooned by imposing mountains, silent and timeless. The scenery is even more dramatic in the winter, when snow drapes the high Panamint Mountains to the south, and the air is so clear that the views extend well beyond the lowest point in the western hemisphere.

∎

FUNERAL MOUNTAINS

The Funeral Mountains form the eastern margin of central Death Valley, from Boundary Canyon (their boundary with the Grapevine Mountains) south to Furnace Creek Wash (their boundary with the Black Mountains and the Greenwater Range). Together with the Owlshead Mountains, they are the smallest (about 220 square miles) of the mountains bordering Death Valley, and among the lowest. Roughly in their center lies a broad low point called Indian Pass (about 3,050'), with high points at Boundary Peak (5,464') and Chloride Cliff (5,279') to the north and Pyramid Peak (6,703') to the south. In spite of these relatively modest statistics, and of their dreadful name, the Funeral Mountains exhibit some of the northern Mojave Desert's finest sculpted slopes and rugged peaks. On their west side, the alluvial fans rise for several miles from the floor of Death Valley to the western foot of the mountains, which shoot up 2,000 to 3,500 feet to their crest. On the east side, the Funeral Mountains slope down gently to the Amargosa Desert, dropping an average of only 2,000 feet over several miles. Most of the range is within Death Valley National Park. The southern tip of the mountains is protected as the 25,707-acre Funeral Mountains Wilderness.

North from Nevares Peak, the Funeral Mountains rise as a long and straight scarp along the Keane Wonder Fault, a minor, northwest-trending, 25-mile-long fault zone east of, and parallel to, the Furnace Creek Fault Zone. Movements along the Keane Wonder Fault have exposed different types of rocks on each side of it. East of the fault the mountains are one large block of Late to Middle Proterozoic metamorphic rocks, belonging mostly to the Crystal Spring Formation, Beck Spring Dolomite, Kingston Peak Formation, and Johnnie Formation. West of it the rocks are much younger, mostly Oligocene and Miocene nonmarine sedimentary formations.

The southern half of the Funeral Mountains, from Nevares Peak south to around Death Valley Junction, rises along the Furnace Creek

Fault, which defines the drainage of Furnace Creek Wash. The rocks there are largely of marine origin (Cambrian to Mississippian). The exception is a long exposure of Pliocene and Pleistocene nonmarine sedimentary deposits stretching from the Hole-in-the-Wall area north to the upper drainage of Echo Canyon. Oligocene nonmarine rocks are also exposed at the very southern tip of the Funeral Mountains. The marine formations define the well-stratified flanks of several of the mountains' most notable summits, especially Pyramid Peak and Bat Mountain. This unusual variety of formations is responsible for a particularly wide range of landforms, and unusually rugged and spectacular sedimentary summits.

Because of their low elevation and location in the rain shadow of the Panamint Range, the Funeral Mountains are among the driest in the region. Rain, which occurs mostly in the summer, and snow are even more rare than elsewhere. Summer downpours, however, can be especially violent, producing in particular devastating flashfloods in historic times along Furnace Creek Wash. Paradoxically, the largest springs in the park are found at the western foot of the Funerals. Travertine Springs, the largest of these, emit an average of 2,000 gallons per minute (gpm). Nearby Texas and Nevares springs discharge over 200 and 300 gpm, respectively. Half a dozen smaller springs carry enough flow to spawn pools and waterfalls. The main source of water is believed to be the large aquifer brooding under Pahrump Valley, about 50 miles to the southeast. Water travels along fractures through permeable carbonate rocks until it is intercepted by high-angle faults. At Travertine Springs, the water flows underground over an impermeable layer of mudstones; where the layer intersects the fan's surface, the water is forced to emerge. Year-round it feeds a lukewarm creek that runs openly along the bone-dry gravels of Furnace Creek Wash.

The Funeral Mountains witnessed the boom and bust of some of the most famous mines in Death Valley—Chloride Cliff, the Keane Wonder Mine, and the Inyo Mine. The Keane Wonder Mine was one of Death Valley's few rich properties: between 1906 and 1912 it produced nearly one million dollars in gold and became Death Valley's largest gold producer after legendary Skidoo itself. The Inyo Mine, deep in Echo Canyon, and the mines around Chloride City, on the mountain's sharp rim, were not as lucky, but they were also worked extensively. One of the assets of peak climbing in the Funeral Mountains is that several routes can be conceived to pass through some of these exceptional sites, which are still rich in obsolete machinery and well-preserved ghost mining camps.

■

CHLORIDE CLIFF

> Beneath the rumpled Proterozoic slopes that tumble down from the wind-swept heights of Chloride Cliff into Death Valley's blaze there was once more silver and gold than at any other place along the valley's entire 130-mile eastern rim. Spectacular Chloride Cliff can be accessed the easy way, on foot or by car, through the ruins of Chloride City, the oldest ghost town on the valley's east side. It can also be climbed the hard way, on a nearly 150-year-old wagon trail from the floor of Death Valley. On its epic ascent the trail passes by two of the region's best historic sites—the Keane Wonder Mine and its phenomenal aerial tramway, and the well-preserved ruins of the Big Bell Mine. Most of the way the views are stupendous.

General Information
Jurisdiction: Death Valley National Park
Road status: Roadless; hiking from graded or high-clearance road
The easy climb: 2.3 mi, 1,030 ft up, 110 ft down one way/easy-moderate
The hard climb: 4.6 mi, 4,280 ft up, 320 ft down, one way/strenuous
Main attractions: Historic mines, spectacular views, old mining trails
USGS 7.5' topo map: Chloride City
Maps: pp. 99*, 55

Location and Access
The shortest vehicular access to Chloride Cliff is the Monarch Canyon Road. It starts at the Daylight Pass Road 3.4 miles east of Hells Gate (see *Death Valley Buttes*), or 2.8 miles west of Daylight Pass, on the east side. After 5.2 miles, the road joins the Chloride Cliff Road. This itinerary requires high clearance after 2.3 miles, a little past Monarch Canyon. With the right stone-churning machine, one can drive the remaining 2.4 miles, over stretches of steep lopsided bedrock, through Chloride City and right up to Chloride Cliff, with full-fledged on-board life support and lattes rattling in the cup holders. I prefer to park at this junction and walk—a respectful way to visit a legendary site with a 90-year history.

To climb Chloride Cliff from the foot of the Funerals, start from the Keane Wonder Mill. From the main visitor center drive north on Highway 190 10.5 miles and turn right on the Beatty Cutoff. Head north 5.7 miles to the signed road to Keane Wonder. This well-graded road ends in 2.8 miles at a parking area within sight of the mill.

Route Description

The Chloride City route. In 1871, when Death Valley was still essentially unknown, a civil engineer named August Franklin assisting in the survey of the California-Nevada boundary discovered silver at the top of the Funerals. He founded the Chloride Cliff Company, likely a poetic amalgam of his silver chloride ore and the summit's sharp geography. With a small team of miners, starting in April 1872 he exposed and shipped some good ore. The 180-mile trek to present-day Barstow was negotiated by mule trains, which left loaded with ore and returned weeks later with long-awaited food and supplies. Inaccessibility made Franklin's mine unappealing to investors, and the silver rush of 1873 in the Panamints diverted what little funding was available. Franklin was forced to shut down after less than two years. He still hung on the rest of his life, dutifully carrying out his annual assessment work until his death in 1904. Ironically, the following year gold was discovered on his old turf. New outfits were soon feverishly working the hills, including George Franklin, who was running his father's mine. A small camp grandly named Chloride City sprung up behind the cliff. When new gold veins were exposed in 1910, the road to Rhyolite was improved for the delivery of a mill. But mine owners were all too aware of their district's limitations. The mill was a puny one-stamp affair that may never have been fired up for lack of water. Occasional shipments were made until 1912, likely not very rich. George Franklin was probably the only lucky one. In July 1906, after the San Francisco earthquake drained most funding, he sold his family mine for a reported $150,000. His father's dream had finally come true.

From the junction the Chloride Cliff Road climbs in two broad switchbacks 1.1 miles to a junction on a ridge top overlooking Chloride City. White-capped Chloride Cliff rises beyond to the south-southeast, across one air mile of barren rolling plateau. Chloride City was never a city, not even a town, but a dispersed community bound by the seductions of gold and solitude. It is crisscrossed by a spiderweb of roads that reach out to a host of mines, mills, cabins, dugouts, and junkyards, all bursting with stories. The side road on the right leads to the water tank, concrete pad, and lumber of J. Irving Crowell's extravagant five-ton mercury treatment plant. Erected in 1941, it burned down soon after it became operational. The main road (left) descends a little into a drainage to the cabin and grave of a James Mc Kay. The Lane mill, over the low ridge to the west, was put up in 1916 by the same unlucky Crowell—the well he dug for it ran dry after a few days. The road then crosses over a hump into a small ravine lined with the ruins of three stone dugouts, which probably housed miners during a brief revival in

Looking down the Funeral Mountains into Death Valley from Chloride Cliff

the 1940s. They once had elegant facades of carefully selected stones, glass windows, and smoky stoves to placate the bite of winter.

Chloride Cliff is just up the road, past Franklin's original tunnels. The exposed summit commands a spellbinding view of Death Valley. The valley floor stretches in both directions as far as the eye can see, its giant fans, crescent dunes, and sinuous alkali flats held captive by interminable alignments of towering mountains. The western horizon is fringed by the Sierra Nevada's lacy crest, more than a hundred miles away from the Silver State's bleak ranges to the east. The panorama is so grand that each and every time it holds me in insatiable rapture.

The mining trail route. Discovered in the spring of 1904 by two lucky prospectors, the Keane Wonder property was sold in June 1906 to Homer Wilson, a prosperous owner of Mother Lode mines. The mine being located 1,700 feet up a steep mountain, Wilson erected a mile-long aerial tramway to haul the ore down to an 80-ton milling complex at the foot of the range. The first gold bullion, worth around $20,000, was delivered to Rhyolite in November 1907. By December the mill was running around the clock, processing daily 70 to 75 tons averaging $19 per ton. Except for a few short interruptions, the mill and tramway performed almost flawlessly. This was one of the desert's

rare successes. Until the Keane Wonder shut down in the summer of
1912, it produced a steady stream of gold worth nearly $1,000,000.

The trail beyond the access road to the Keane Wonder Mill is the
road that was used to build and service the tramway. It passes by the
ghost of the mining camp and the site of the 20-stamp mill at the foot
of the tramway's massive lower terminal. The mill's concrete foundations, three-chute ore bin, and huge boiler give a good idea of its former size. It is an imposing site, overwhelmed by the terminal's timber
frame and the tramway towers strung up the slope above it. From
there the road shoots straight up the mountain, the aerial tramway a
constant presence a stone's throw away. The tramway is a masterpiece
of early-twentieth-century mining engineering. Supported by 13
wooden towers 18 to 30 feet high, it ascends 1,500 feet in 1.1 miles,
spanning at one place 1,280 feet across a chaotic canyon 500 feet deep.

When tectonism pushed up the northern Funerals, it exhumed the
region's deepest formations, billion-year-old sediments squeezed and
cooked to a host of metamorphic rocks. Quartzite sparkles all over.
Ancient marbles outcrop in creamy veins as crisp as ceramic. All the
way to Chloride Cliff the ground is sprinkled with mica schists afire
with sunlight. When brushed with a finger they leave a coat of powdery eyeshadow, silver and gold, the colors that first drew men here.

The road ends at the upper terminal, a huge structure of heavy
timber packed with wheels, hoists, rail tracks, tanks, wire cables, ore

Chloride Cliff		
	Dist.(mi)	Elev.(ft)
The Chloride Cliff route		
Monarch Canyon Road jct	0.0	4,360
Mercury mine junction	1.0	4,760
Stone dugouts	1.9	~5,020
Chloride Cliff	2.3	5,279
The mining trail route		
Keane Wonder Mine Road	0.0	1,320
Keane Wonder Mill	0.15	1,400
Tramway upper terminal	1.5	2,840
Keane Wonder Mine	1.6	~3,040
Fork in trail	2.9	3,800
Big Bell Mine / Cable road	3.15	~3,620
Road junction (go left)	4.05	4,970
Chloride Cliff	4.6	5,279

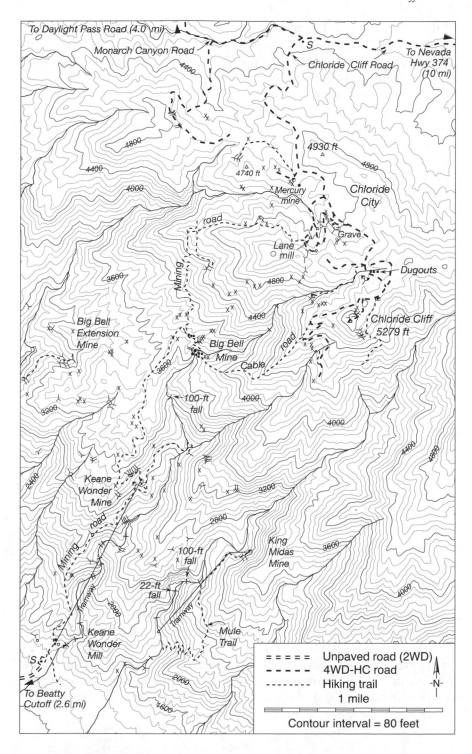

To Daylight Pass Road (4.0 mi)

Monarch Canyon Road

Chloride Cliff Road

S

To Nevada
Hwy 374
(10 mi)

4400

4800

4400

4000

4930 ft

4800

4740 ft

Mercury
mine

*Chloride
City*

3600

road

Mining

Grave

Lane
mill

4800

Dugouts

4400

Big Bell
Extension
Mine

road

Chloride Cliff
5279 ft

3600

Big Bell
Mine

Cable

3200

100-ft
fall

4000

4000

4400

4800

Keane
Wonder
Mine

3200

road

Mining

2800

King
Midas
Mine

3600

100-ft
fall

2400

22-ft
fall

Tramway

Tramway

4000

2000

Mule
Trail

Keane
Wonder
Mill

===== Unpaved road (2WD)
- - - - - 4WD-HC road
-------- Hiking trail
1 mile

-N-

S

To Beatty
Cutoff (2.6 mi)

2000

4400

Contour interval = 80 feet

chutes and buckets. The tramway was cleverly designed. The ore was crushed into 2-inch chunks in a jaw crusher, then loaded automatically into buckets that held about 600 pounds each. When the line was loaded, the descending full buckets pulled the empty buckets back up to the mine—and there was enough left-over power to run the crusher.

Past the upper terminal the road shrivels to a foot trail and climbs to the mine, visible on the cliff up behind the terminal. The trail soon goes right by a small open pit and the caved-in adits. This segment ranks high on the scenic scale, with widening views of Death Valley's north and south basins. After 2.9 miles, there is a fork just before a shallow rectangular pit on the south side. The mining trail continues straight to Chloride City. The right fork descends a short distance into a canyon and the Big Bell Mine.

The man behind the Big Bell Mine was Johnnie Cyty, a trigger-happy eccentric nicknamed "Johnnie-Behind-the-Gun." He and a part-ner located these gold claims in June 1904. Their holdings were first developed by Cyty and a few independent parties. When funds ran out in 1908, in an innovative attempt to raise money Cyty bet his entire company shares in a Rhyolite gambling hall—and lost. The Big Bell Mine remained idle until it was acquired in 1935. An ambitious infra-structure was put in place, including a ball mill, a pipeline from nearby Keane Spring, and an aerial tramway. It was a commendable effort, but the gold production did not even cover expenses. The mine shut down in 1941, leaving 30,000 tons of ore in the ground. The same isolation that spelled the Big Bell's demise also guaranteed its protection—it is today one of the park's most extensive historic mines. Its camp is a cluster of small cabins built on a terraced hill above the trail, shielded by a stone wall from the brutal winds. The mining complex still has its grizzly, ore bin, rail, and tramway, its mill and water tank, cyanide vats and tailings, shacks and tool sheds. Even the Mack truck in which the ore was winched up to Chloride City still rests along the cable road, up behind the mill. This road is the shortest route to Chloride Cliff, but it is one hell of a workout. It screams straight up a ridge so steep that gravity often wins over friction. The road is still lined with remains of the cable, of the short spikes that guided it, and of the pipeline.

The combination of visual, educational, and physical pleasures on this long hard climb is so acute that upon reaching the summit, Death Valley's formidable landscape may bring you to the giddy edge of euphoria. It is the kind of intensity that sets new standards. Years later, while climbing other mountains, I still find myself secretly hoping for a repeat performance of the glorious day I climbed Chloride Cliff.

■

NEVARES PEAK

Climbing this prominent range-front summit in the rugged central Funeral Mountains is a pure Death Valley adventure. The route crosses several miles of alluvial fans just to get to the base of the mountain, passing near Nevares Springs' lush oasis, then screams up an abrupt slope to the summit. The views of the valley, especially of the fan below Furnace Creek and Cottonball Basin, are sublime.

General Information

Jurisdiction: Death Valley National Park
Road status: Roadless; hiking from paved road
The climb: 6.1 mi, 3,080 ft up one way / difficult
Main attractions: Long fan, range-front peak overlooking Death Valley
USGS 7.5' topo maps: Beatty Junction, Nevares Peak
Maps: pp. 103*, 55

Location and Access

Nevares Peak is in the central Funeral Mountains, 5 miles northeast of The Ranch at Death Valley. The most direct route to the summit, via the Cow Creek Road and Nevares Springs Road, crosses the park's residential area and a firing range. *Both areas are off limits.* Do not drive or hike that way. Instead, start from Highway 190 1.7 miles north of the Cow Creek turnoff (or 6.0 miles south of Beatty Junction). Nevares Peak is the leftmost of the colorful striated summits on the front of the Funeral Mountains 4.5 air miles to the east-southeast.

Route Description

Fans can be deceiving. Although from the highway Nevares Peak seems to be looming over the alluvial fan that leads up to it, most of the walking and elevation gain on this climb occur on the fan. Any one of the washes that spill out of the opening in the hills due east of the starting point is a good way to start. They all lead into a short gulch that cuts through the hills, the most interesting area because of the greater relief and formations in its walls. Past the hills the wash is the main thoroughfare to the foot of Nevares Peak. It is wide and it goes through, and chances of erring off are comparatively small.

In this indolent sea of stones and creosote, distances are easily underestimated. It takes half an hour to silence the highway, an hour to notice progress, two hours to reach the mountain. Fortunately, fans of sedimentary origin like this one are quite varied and entertaining. The top of Nevares Peak is Cambrian dolomite of the Bonanza King Formation. The younger sedimentary formations that once covered it were removed by erosion and cast off to form this colossal fan. The rocks are a constant distraction—cream limestones, rose quartzites, blue-gray dolomites, khaki shales, orange sandstones, all weathering with distinct patterns. Some bear the round imprints of extinct coral reefs, others quiet layering, or the doodlings of wind-blown particles. As the elevation increases the rocks get bigger, as their prime mover— running water—loses its velocity downhill. The numerous steps on the lower fan's surface trace fault scarps where the fan snapped during earthquakes. Most of them are less than a thousand years old.

After around 3 miles, the tree tops of an unexpectedly green oasis appear over the fan's southern horizon—not a mirage, but Nevares Springs, Death Valley's second largest spring. Like the peak, they are named after Adolph Nevares, a soft-spoken prospector, farmer, and rancher who developed a homestead known as Cow Creek Ranch at the springs. In the late 1890s, then in his mid-twenties, he worked as a driver and handyman for the borax companies out of Daggett. His first contact with Death Valley was in August 1900, when he participated in the much-publicized search for Jim Dayton, caretaker of the Greenland Ranch (now The Ranch at Death Valley). Dayton had been missing, and Nevares volunteered to help find him. Although the rescue was a failure—Dayton was found dead—upon his return from this heroic trip Nevares was offered Dayton's job. In his own words, Death Valley was then dismissed as "a land to be shunned." But Nevares loved the desert, took the job, and stayed in Death Valley for 52 years. He bought a cabin from a nearby mining town and rebuilt it at the spring, where it still stands to this day. His time was split between his caretaker job, tending his ranch, and indulging in prospecting when the urge called. Right in the middle of Death Valley, he enjoyed the luxury of a hot

Nevares Peak		
	Dist.(mi)	Elev.(ft)
Highway 190	0.0	-215
Upper end of gulch	1.6	240
Tip of mountain	4.5	1,520
Leave wash at steep ravine	5.5	2,000
Saddle on crest	5.9	2,620
Nevares Peak	6.1	2,859

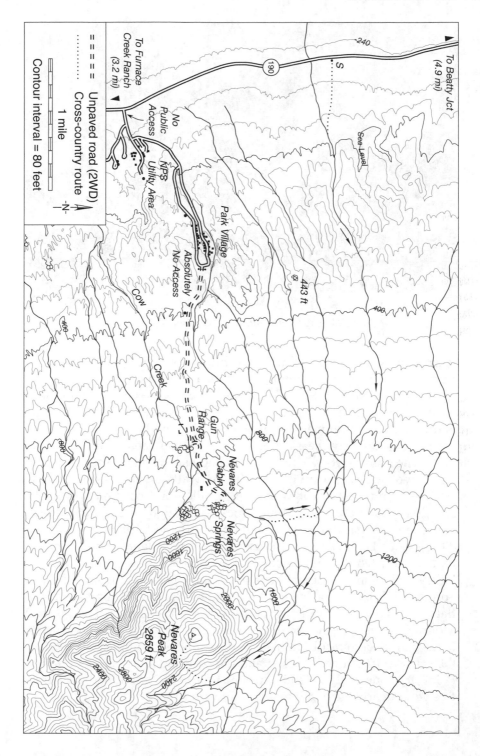

To Beatty Jct
(4.9 mi)

190

Sea Level

-240-

S

443 ft

400

To Furnace
Creek Ranch
(3.2 mi)

No
Public
Access

NPS
Utility Area

Park Village

Absolutely
No Access

Cow

Creek

Gun
Range

Nevares
Cabin

Nevares
Springs

800

800

1200

1200

1600

1600

2000

2400

2800

Nevares
Peak
2859 ft

Unpaved road (2WD)
Cross-country route

1 mile

Contour interval = 80 feet

-N-

Adolph Nevares old cabin at the foot of Nevares Peak

spring, tap water, and well-irrigated plots where he grew apricot and fig trees, beans, peppers, melons, squash, and even a small vineyard.

East from Nevares Springs the wash narrows, reaches the northern tip of the mountain, then slips along its eastern side. This abrupt slope is drained by a prominent, steep and shallow gully that climbs to the 2,620-foot saddle southeast of Nevares Peak, between it and a reddish peak. The gully starts where the wash begins to head due south, across from two side washes with low fluted walls on the east side. It is steep—it gains 600 feet in a third of a mile—and covered with rocks and gnarly old desert holly, but it does go through. The rest of the way along the crest has a steep pitch but it is short and fairly easy.

Nevares Peak is a great observatory of this "land to be shunned" that so attracted Adolph Nevares. It encompasses all of central Death Valley and the monumental Panamint Range behind it, from the green apron of Furnace Creek's fan to Cottonball Basin's shimmering alkali flats, the sensuous Salt Hills, and the Mesquite Dunes. The Funeral Mountains' crest to the south is an impressive grove of sharp peaks, both stark and colorful, desolate and exquisitely complex. Beyond lie the great walls of Echo Canyon and the pale badlands below Zabriskie Point. It is one of these landscapes instilled with a wildness so attractive yet unreachable that it makes you want to soar.

■

PYRAMID PEAK

If there was one last mountain I was given a chance to climb before the world comes to an end, Pyramid Peak would be on my short list. It is a spectacular place that encapsulates on its own the romance of the desert, the fascination of fathomless geological times, the wondrous beauty and colors of rocks and fossils, and the exhilaration when you reach a high summit after a long hard pull against gravity and succumb to a grandiose view.

General Information
Jurisdiction: Death Valley National Park
Road status: Climb cross-country and on use trail; paved access road
The climb: 4.9 mi, 3,730 ft up, 60 ft down one way/strenuous
Main attractions: Colorful geology, fossils, botany, awesome views
USGS 7.5' topo maps: East of Ryan, East of Echo Canyon*
Maps: pp. 107*, 55

Location and Access
When you take the long drive out of Death Valley east on Highway 190, you climb from below sea level up windy Furnace Creek Wash along the base of the craggy southern Funeral Mountains. Pyramid Peak, the range's high point, is the last summit before the road tops the long pass out of Death Valley and into the Amargosa Desert. To climb it, park off the highway 6.7 miles east of the signed junction to Dantes View (or 11.4 miles west of Highway 127), 0.5 mile west of a road that leads south to a huge parking area.

Route Description
This is quite a mountain. From its western base at Travertine Point it shoots up 4,000 feet over a handful of miles, a steeply canted stack of Paleozoic sedimentary beds crowned with serrations, vibrant with rich shades of cream, gray, and sienna. As it was uplifted over the past few million years, erosion gradually stripped off its top strata, etching through 200 million years down to the Ordovician. Pyramid Peak is the expression of this endless tug-of-war between tectonic and erosional forces. When you face the mountain from the road, you are looking at the leftover cross section of time, Cambrian at the base, Ordovician at the top. About 3 miles to the northeast, across the fan, a deep gash severs the range. The ridge that rises left from it to Pyramid Peak is the

Southern Funeral Mountains from below third saddle on Pyramid Peak

route to the summit. It is made of all three Ordovician formations. The most conspicuous one is the blazing-white Eureka Quartzite, visible left of the gap and at the summit. The charcoal crags that cap it are remnants of the younger, resilient Ely Springs Dolomite. The ruddy layers under the quartzite are the older Pogonip Group limestones. When climbing the ridge, you time-travel through this one geologic era, up a tilted seafloor that has not seen seawater in 445 million years.

Navigation is simple. First strike northeast up the fan toward the gap. The walking is easy, up a 5% grade free of large rocks; there is even a faint twin track on the main bench. After 2.6 miles, and about 0.6 mile inside the canyon that leads to the gap, a broad side canyon sunk in Eureka Quartzite opens up on the left. In 0.35 mile it forks at a left bend. The second fork quickly narrows to a ravine and squeezes into a tight spot with an 8-foot Class-2 fall. A few feet above it on the right, a use trail exits 20 feet out of the ravine. It then climbs 0.35 mile up this drainage to the first saddle on the main ridge. The trail is very steep, rubbly, slippery, and not very much fun, but it does the job.

From the first saddle it is a strenuous 1.5-mile slog 2,100 feet up the sinuous ridge to the summit, the relentless steepness tempered only briefly by two saddles. The use trail is there most of the way. The

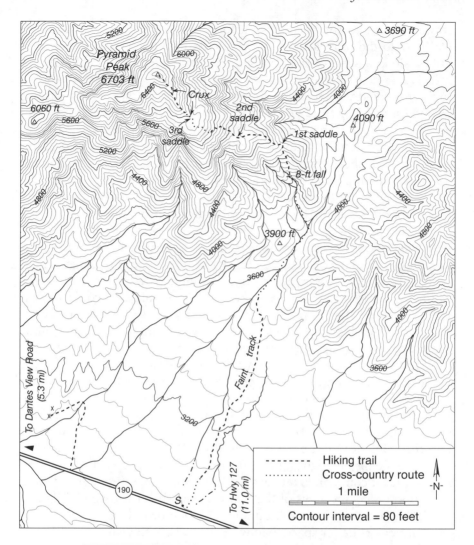

Pyramid Peak

	Dist.(mi)	Elev.(ft)
Highway 190	0.0	3,035
Side canyon	2.6	3,740
8-ft fall/Start of use trail	3.0	~3,870
First saddle	3.4	4,590
Second saddle	3.8	5,060
Third saddle	4.3	5,980
Pyramid Peak	4.9	6,703

first segment to the second saddle is the least steep and easiest. Halfway to the third saddle, the trail cuts to the left and shoots up a gutter along a slant of gray breccia with two small caves. Above it, a massive 45-degree scree of loose limestone plates screams 350 feet up to the third saddle. The last segment is the crux, over the ragged plug of Ely Springs Dolomite visible from the road. The trail zigzags up the middle of it to the sharp crest. It then crosses to the sheer west flank and proceeds across it to the quartzite stratum at the upper end of the dolomite. The short remaining stretch above it has a smaller and easier dolomitic outcrop that ends a few steps from the quartzite summit.

Nature has bestowed on this mountain scores of little gems. Just before the side canyon, the gravel hosts more pincushion cactus than I have seen at any one place. In the spring, the side canyon is flooded with the canary flowers of Mohavea. The lower ridge is sprinkled with handsome blocks of fractured Eureka Quartzite, oxidized to a pale orange. Bearpoppy, a rare and protected plant, grows above the second saddle, its bluish-green leaves fuzzy with silver hair. One could write a whole doctoral thesis on the intricate fossils of gastropods, trilobites, and deeply scalloped bivalves exposed on the ridge. Many are found in the Pogonip Group's top member, especially on the loose talus.

From the moment you reach the first saddle the views are awesome, split between the Amargosa Desert to the east and the sullen Greenwater Range to the west. The Funeral Mountains to the south are easily the most captivating, a complex tapestry of finely pleated ridges carved into colorfully banded strata. The line of sight eventually extends clear over them into Death Valley's spacious southern province. Being the highest point for tens of miles in any direction, the summit itself commands far-reaching views of the entire region. There are stunning perspectives of the Black Mountains' furrowed badlands, and of the warped Funeral Mountains to the north. On every horizon, more ranges jostle for space than we will ever get to visit.

On my way up the ridge I was treated to a rare drama. It rained. From the shelter of a shallow overhang, I watched engorged cumulus clouds scratch their bellies against mountain tops and burst open with rain. In minutes, champagne runoffs flushed the ground and tiny puddles pooled on the tops of rocks. The desert was deluged with mist, darkness, and the smell of wet shrubs. The temperature plummeted from too hot to cold. The lofty cliff that edges the ridge was glistening with sheets of flowing water. I waited a long time, struck by the age-old spectacle of erosion picking apart a mountain, carrying away the Ordovician piece by tiny piece, evening up the score against tectonism.

■

BLACK MOUNTAINS

The Black Mountains rank among the roughest and most spectacular ranges in the California desert. They are the home of world-famous Zabriskie Point and Dantes View, of brilliant badlands and superb geology, and of what is probably the most diverse collection of canyons and narrows in the Mojave Desert. For some 50 miles, from Furnace Creek Wash down the length of Badwater Basin's vast alkali flats to the broad inland delta of the Amargosa River, the Black Mountains' sheer western escarpment leaps out of Death Valley, rising in just a few miles from below sea level to above 6,000 feet. The combination of rapid uplifting and flashflood erosion has produced along this flank scores of deep, tight, and precipitous canyons blocked off by unscalable falls and hemmed in by abrupt slopes. Climbing on this fierce side can be extremely challenging, requiring serious rock-climbing skills and endurance, yet it offers some of the most rewarding high-level hiking in the desert. Most of the named summits—Mount Perry (5,739'), Coffin Peak (5,490'), Funeral Peak (6,384'), Smith Mountain (5,913'), and Epaulet Peak (4,766')—are generally climbed from the east side, facing Greenwater Valley, where the Black Mountains rise more gently out of the high desert.

The Black Mountains are wedged between two major northwest-trending fault zones, the Northern Death Valley Fault Zone, which runs along the foot of the western escarpment, and the Furnace Creek Fault Zone, which parallels the northeast side of the mountains along Furnace Creek Wash. The two combined faults, which merge into a single fault zone north of Furnace Creek, are among the longest active faults in California. The Northern Death Valley Fault is responsible for the Black Mountains' formidable western scarp. Land east of this fault has been uplifted, while land on the Death Valley side has been sinking. As a result, the fans along the western Black Mountains are generally steep, low, and short. Parts of the mountains are even fan-free. In contrast, the fans into Greenwater Valley have long and gentle grades.

Partly because of this tumultuous history of faulting and folding, the geology of the Black Mountains is among the most complex and varied in the region. The mountains can broadly be divided into four geological areas. The northern part, down to around Natural Bridge Canyon, is primarily made of Quaternary and Tertiary rocks from the Funeral, Furnace Creek, and Artist Drive formations. These soft sedimentary rocks have been deeply eroded into colorful badlands, dramatically typified near Zabriskie Point. The second area is the western scarp. From Natural Bridge Canyon south to near Saratoga Spring, the majority of it comprises either Late Proterozoic sedimentary rocks or Early Proterozoic metamorphic schist and gneiss. The metamorphism that altered these ancient rocks has been dated at around 1.7 billion years, which makes them the oldest exposures around Death Valley. The third area is the crest of the central Black Mountains, in particular just west of Dantes View and around Funeral Peak and Smith Mountain. It is made of granitic rocks of Mesozoic age. The fourth area, eastern flank of the mountains along Greenwater Valley, is mostly Miocene rhyolite and pockets of Pliocene volcanic rocks, in particular basalt and andesite. The general lack of limestone and dolomite formations makes the topography of the Black Mountains quite different from most other ranges around Death Valley.

Because the Black Mountains stand in the rain shadow of the Panamint Mountains, and because of their relatively low crest, they are among the driest in the region. The average annual precipitation has been estimated at 3 to 5 inches. Springs are few and far between, and not a single pine or juniper grows anywhere. The blatant anomaly is Willow Creek, east of Mormon Point in the south-central part of the range. This staggering narrow chasm filled with giant drop-offs is flushed by one of the longest perennial streams in Death Valley.

The Black Mountains were mined for borax in the northern foothills starting in the 1880s, for copper on their eastern slopes at Greenwater in 1905–1909, for copper, silver, and gold near Willow Creek in the southern range in 1906–1909, and for gold in the vicinity of Ashford Peak and Desert Hound Peak in the 1900s–1940s. Only borax was lucrative—the gold mines brought in more lawsuits than ore, and Greenwater was one of the most spectacular booms and magistral fiascos in the history of Death Valley. A century later, a few of these historic sites still have interesting physical remains, including the Ashford and Desert Hound mines, which adds another charm to climbing in these awesome mountains.

∎

RED CATHEDRAL

> *Red Cathedral, the high point of the colorful cliff band overlooking the world-famous Zabriskie Point badlands, is the lowest summit suggested in this book, one of the easiest to reach, and quite possibly the most scenic. The route follows a use trail worn by curious minds seeking new vantage points, up and down the sharp, sinuous arête that hovers high above the badlands' magnetic landscape. Unobstructed views start right away, and they only get better.*

General Information
Jurisdiction: Death Valley National Park
Road status: Roadless; trail hiking from paved road
The climb (Red Cathedral): 1.1 mi, 440 ft up, 110 ft down one way/easy
The climb (Palm Grove O.): 2 mi, 630 ft up, 380 ft down one way/easy
Main attractions: Easy trail climb with awesome views of badlands
USGS 7.5' topo map: Furnace Creek
Maps: pp. 113*, 55

Location and Access
This climb starts at Zabriskie Point, where every day from fall to spring thousands of visitors stream by like pilgrims to succumb to the knee-buckling view of Death Valley's surreal badlands. The viewpoint is right off Highway 190, 4.5 miles east from The Ranch at Death Valley (or 7.2 miles west from the Dantes View turnoff). Halfway up the scenic drive from the ranch, Travertine Springs' fingers of lush greenery slash the bare ivory hills east of the road. Underneath the tall hedges of tangled arrowweed that line the road, the spring water collects in an abandoned concrete flume. In the early hours of morning, coyotes often come down to it to quench their thirst. After the winter rains, when a small stream runs along Furnace Creek Wash across the road, they shun the springs' tepid water and chance crossing the road to drink out of the cooler stream instead. The deeply carved wall that rises to the south from the springs is the back side of Red Cathedral.

Route Description
The wide dirt path lined with rocks at the west end of the parking lot is the Golden Canyon Trail. It points roughly to Red Cathedral, the summit just visible behind the pointed bluff about a mile to the northwest. Take this trail 0.1 mile to a manmade gap looking west into the

Manly Beacon (left) and Red Cathedral (right) from the trail

badlands. The fainter, dusty path that climbs up onto the ridge just before the gap on the right is the trail to Red Cathedral.

This trail puts scenic to shame. After climbing 150 steep yards to the top of the ridge, it meanders languidly along the abrupt top of the cliff that towers above the Black Mountains' spectacular badlands. A few hundred feet below, the mountain has been worn down to a spacious amphitheater filled with wave upon wave of low ridges sculpted in soft stone, as naked as the sea. Narrow serpentine washes weave down countless gullies, bound for Death Valley's salt flats. Light dazzles every surface, ivory hillsides banded in pastel purple and coral, cinnamon hilltops, and mahogany upsweeps splashed with pale green. Every slope is wrinkled, furrowed, creased, and flanked by rhythmic ranks of rounded buttresses. Up ahead iconic Manly Beacon, a lone spire braced by fluted walls, looms over the badlands.

Red Cathedral's cliff is radically different. It is a layered cake of coarse gravel, cobbles, and small boulders oxidized to a maroon finish. The beddings are so strongly canted that they seem to be slipping. On the loose taluses below the rim, a rock buff could sit anywhere and find beauty in most rocks within arm's reach. The ground is a crumble

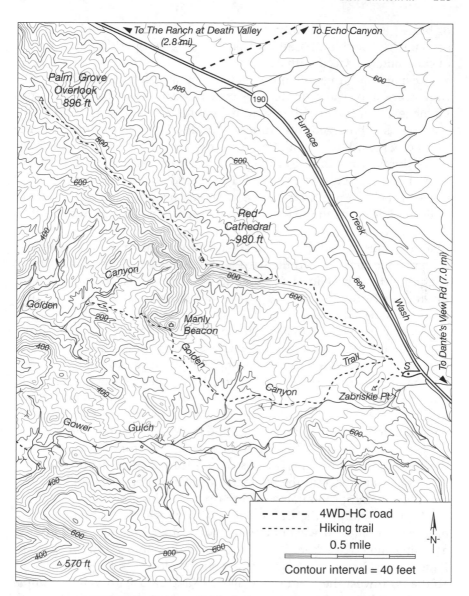

Red Cathedral

	Dist.(mi)	Elev.(ft)
Zabriskie Point parking	0.0	650
Trail junction (right)	0.1	650
Red Cathedral	1.05	~980
Palm Grove Overlook	2.0	896

of bluish limestone, creamy onyx, white quartzite, red bubble-filled scoria, sliced cobbles, basalt incrusted with green peridot, and lumps of conglomerate laced with calcite.

Disparate geology often points to disparate past worlds. Four million years ago, the climate was much wetter than today's. From Furnace Creek up to what would become Ubehebe Crater, Death Valley was submerged intermittently under the briny waters of Lake Furnace Creek. For 1.2 million years, the lake trapped cubic miles of fine sediments and erratic ash falls. Then the climate changed; the lake evaporated and erosion ran wild. Flashfloods broadcasted huge volumes of rocks torn from the Funeral Mountains over the dry lakebed, building thick fans that were later cemented into fanglomerates. After the uplift of the Black Mountains pushed up both formations, eons of rushing water carved the fragile lakebed sediments into these whimsical badlands, and cleaved the hard fanglomerates into Red Cathedral's rugged cliffs. The badlands come from a lost world of camels and mastodons browsing on grassy lakeshores. Red Cathedral was born from a desert that foreshadowed Death Valley's brutal future.

Hardly ever wider than a couple of feet, the trail constantly flirts with the cliff's precipitous edge. There is a lot of thin air, which gives unobstructed views and the occasional feeling of walking a tight rope. The badlands are a constant presence, barren yet sensual, so ethereal that they look artificial. Red Cathedral's pointed summit stands at the divide between Gower Gulch and Golden Canyon. The two canyons are separated by Manly Beacon and the impressively high and slender land bridge that links it to the summit. There are stunning views over the tops of red pinnacles, across to the frayed crest of the Funeral Mountains, and beyond the badlands into Badwater Basin's alkali flats and the Panamint Mountains rearing up two miles above them.

Past the summit the trail continues above Golden Canyon's even brighter badlands. It wavers up and down the cliff's high rim, briefly avoiding the edge where it gets too steep. In about a mile it reaches Palm Grove Overlook, a summit only slightly lower but equally scenic. To the northwest the palm grove at The Ranch at Death Valley stamps out a large lush square on the bare fan of Furnace Creek Wash. All along the fan's wide circular perimeter, the underground creek resurfaces and irrigates a green mesquite belt 200 feet below sea level. In the summer, the heat combined with the intensity of colors border on hallucinatory. The only sane time to climb these very low summits trapped in Death Valley's fiery breath is then dawn, when the badlands slowly emerge from darkness under an amethyst sky.

■

MOUNT PERRY

The primitive trail to Mount Perry is one of the most breathtaking. For several miles it courses the brightly colored volcanic crest of the Black Mountains, overlooking the mountains' vertiginous western slopes and Badwater Basin's immense salt flats swirling more than a mile below. Hiking even a portion of this awesome trail will not fail to impress anyone, even a seasoned desert hiker.

General Information
Jurisdiction: Death Valley National Park
Road status: Roadless; access from paved road
The climb: 4.5 mi, 1,470 ft up, 1,220 ft down one way / difficult
Main attraction: Spectacular views of Death Valley's salt pan
USGS 7.5' topo maps: Dantes View, Ryan
Maps: pp. 117*, 55

Location and Access
Named after John W. S. Perry, the foreman at the Harmony Borax Works who organized the famous twenty-mule teams in the early 1880s, Mount Perry is the highest peak in the northern half of the Black Mountains. The trail starts at Dantes View, a spectacular viewpoint reached by a paved road that splits off Highway 190 11.8 miles east of The Ranch at Death Valley. Drive this road 13.1 miles to its end at the viewpoint. The trailhead is 100 yards north of the parking lot.

Route Description
This trail is stunning. From start to finish it closely follows the crest of the Black Mountains and commands much of the way magnificent views of Badwater Basin and several desert ranges. From Dantes View, it first ascends 0.45 mile to Dante Peak, then drops 1.1 miles to a long saddle at the head of Bad Canyon's drainage. Over the next 1.4 miles, it climbs or skirts four minor summits to the fifth saddle, before the final 1.55-mile scramble up the rocky spine to Mount Perry. The elevation at Mount Perry is only 240 feet higher than at Dantes View, but all these ups and downs add up. By the time you crest the summit you will have gone over 2,700 feet of elevation change.

There is little shade, it is steep at places, and it takes stamina, but at least there is a trail. Much of it is well defined and not too rocky. The first exception is a short section near the middle, starting just past the saddle north of the 5,235-foot summit, where it is easy to wander off. At this point the trail does not contour the hill up ahead on its east side, but it cuts across the hill a little east of its high point. Someone with a limited understanding of wilderness ethics marked the route with spots of white paint on the rocks. The second exception is the last three quarters of a mile or so, where the terrain is very rocky and the trail is vague and intermittent. But by then the ridge is narrow and straight, and there is no ambiguity as to how to proceed.

From Dantes View to Mount Perry and points beyond, the crest is all volcanic terrain. It is made dominantly of rhyolite and rhyodacite, with minor amounts of other pyroclastic rocks and tuffaceous sedimentary rocks, from the pre-Miocene Tertiary. The exception is a small plug of younger Greenwater Volcanics (mainly vitrophyre rhyolite and rhyodacite) exposed for 0.8 mile in the group of three hills centered on the 5,235-foot summit. Combined with the pale monzonite and dark gneiss exposed down the rugged western scarp, and the eroded Quaternary alluvia of the soft foothills along Greenwater Valley, they compose a contrasted scenery rich in colors, landforms, and erosion patterns. Most striking is the summit block itself, a long and sharp wavering ridge of deep-red rhyodacite bristling with sharp rocks.

In spite of the fairly high elevation, few plants are in the way of our enjoyment of these colorful exposures. All that grows is a sparse cover of low, desiccated plants, including Heermann's buckwheat, often a skeletal shrub resembling a complex organic molecule. Scattered clumps of ephedra and spiny menodora are the only touches of green. At the same elevation 20 miles away across the valley, the Panamint Mountains are sprinkled with juniper. Trapped in the rain shadow of these major mountains, not high enough to catch a cloud, the Black Mountains are too parched to support much vegetation. Even the usually valiant cottontop cactus and cholla have trouble getting a foothold. It is remarkable that even in the midst of this hostile

Mount Perry		
	Dist.(mi)	Elev.(ft)
Dantes View	0.0	5,475
Dante Peak	0.45	5,704
First saddle	1.5	5,130
5,235T point	2.0	5,235
Fifth saddle	2.95	4,930
Mount Perry	4.5	5,716

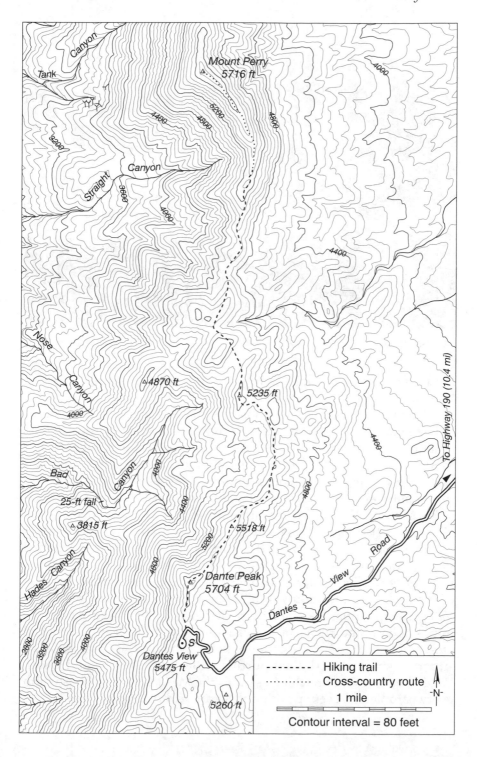

Tank

Canyon

Straight   Canyon

Mount Perry
5716 ft

To Highway 190 (10.4 mi)

Nose   Canyon

△4870 ft

△ 5235 ft

Bad   Canyon

25-ft fall

△ 3815 ft

△ 5518 ft

Hades   Canyon

Dante Peak
5704 ft

Road

View

Dantes

S

Dantes View
5475 ft

△ 5260 ft

- - - - - - -   Hiking trail
· · · · · · · ·   Cross-country route

1 mile

-N-

Contour interval = 80 feet

Crest line leading up to Mount Perry (left of central horizon) looking north

land a few diehards manage to eke out a living, including desert horned lizards and chuckwallas.

Ambling across this sere landscape suspended high above Death Valley's gaping void is a strangely primordial experience. You can look straight down at the salt flats (-282') just west of Badwater and at Mount Whitney (14,494') 90 air miles away, respectively the lowest and highest points in the contiguous United States. Badwater Basin is less than 4 miles away by line of sight and more than 1 mile down—this is as steep as the Grand Canyon at South Rim, and a little deeper. The view of the basin's immense salt flat changes gradually with position and the time of day. Toward the north end of the trail, Cottonball Basin's fractured expanses of snow-white salt make an appearance, sometimes flooded under a shallow lake. Depending on the vagaries of the trail, your attention will be drawn alternatively to Greenwater Valley's empty quarters, the Funeral Mountains' furrowed flanks, the imposing fans and ridges of the Panamints, and the beautiful rugged crest of the Black Mountains. Mount Perry combines all of these, plus a superb vista of the crinkled northern Black Mountains and Death Valley's barren sink stretching as far as the Mesquite Dunes. It is worth every hard breath, every prickle and scrape, every drop of sweat.

■

COFFIN PEAK

This short and almost easy hike in the vicinity of Dantes View crosses colorful volcanic exposures along a broad and well-behaved ridge. Strategically located at a narrowing in the Black Mountains, Coffin Peak commands beautiful vistas of Greenwater Valley and the southern Funeral Mountains on one side, and intensely colorful Coffin Canyon and Death Valley's awesome salt flats on the other. It would be tough to be disappointed.

General Information
Jurisdiction: Death Valley National Park
Road status: Roadless; access from paved road
The climb: 1.25 mi, 620 ft up, 290 ft down one way/easy–moderate
Main attractions: Spectacular views of Death Valley and Coffin Canyon
USGS 7.5' topo map: Dantes View
Maps: pp. 121*, 55

Location and Access
Coffin Peak is located approximately in the middle of the Black Mountains, 1.5 miles east-southeast of Dantes View. The climb starts from near the upper end of the Dantes View Road. Drive Highway 190 11.8 miles east from The Ranch at Death Valley (or 18.2 miles from Death Valley Junction) to the signed Dantes View Road, on the south side. Drive this paved road south, then southwest, 12.6 miles to a small parking loop with an outhouse on the left, in a pronounced right curve in sight of Dantes View up ahead. Coffin Peak is not visible from the parking loop, but it can be seen to the southwest where the road cross-es Greenwater Valley before entering the Black Mountains.

Route Description
At the parking loop's south end, take the shallow ravine that descends gently to the southeast. This is the top of one of the many tributaries that form the head of Coffin Canyon, a spectacular drainage that slices down through the Black Mountains and squeezes through an impassible fall-ridden chasm before emerging on the luminous edge of Badwater Basin. After 0.15 mile, the ravine reaches a scatter of boulders and widens to a wash of pure sand. From there to Coffin Peak the route essentially follows the ridge that starts just on the left. Over the next mile, the ridge changes direction several times. From the

Lower Coffin Canyon and Badwater Basin from Coffin Peak

wash it first climbs east up to a first summit (5,410T point), then angles northeast as it descends to a curved saddle. It then climbs east again to a second summit, where it veers to the south-southwest and slants gradually down to the Black Mountains' precipitous western rim. There, a use trail follows the undulating crest east to Coffin Peak.

This is all volcanic terrain. The broad slopes of the intermediate summits are partially covered with rhyolite boulders from the Pliocene, pale beige and heavily varnished. The boulders are generally low and flattish, which makes climbing the two summits a relatively easy affair. The open ground between boulders hosts plenty of wild-flowers in the spring, pink phlox, pale-blue phacelia, gardens of flam-ing red Indian paintbrush, and the bright magenta flowers of calico cactus—a healthy cluster thrives right at the summit. Along the rim the trail crosses a particularly vivid patchwork of Tertiary rhyolite that changes color abruptly, from purple grey to sand-color and reddish with white polka dots. Scenic beige and deep-red spikes of this same rhyolite line the rim on the final climb to the peak.

You do not have to wait long for the views. On the east side, the ridge overlooks Greenwater Valley and the more subdued Greenwater Range. The Death Valley narrow-gauge railroad that serviced Ryan, one of the most productive historic borax operations in the region, still

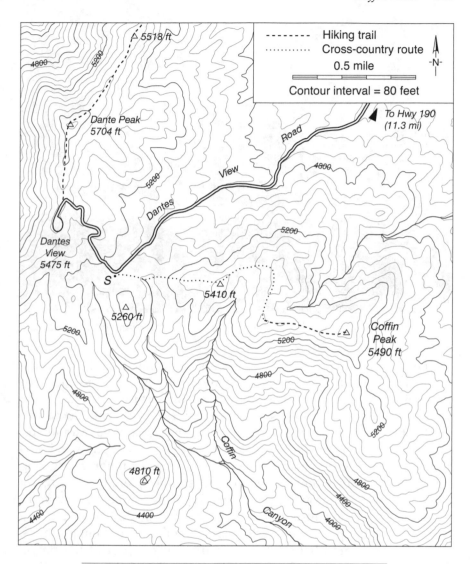

Coffin Peak

	Dist.(mi)	Elev.(ft)
Dantes View Road	0.0	5,160
First summit (5410T point)	0.45	~5,410
Saddle	0.55	~5,300
Second summit	0.75	5,460
Rim/trail	1.1	5,430
Coffin Peak	1.25	5,490

Greenwater Range and Funeral Mountains from the ridge to Coffin Peak

slashes a long horizontal white line across the range's flanks of choco-late-colored basalt. Behind the Greenwater Range rise the southern Funeral Mountains, a chain of summits as finely chiseled as any in the Mojave Desert—Winters Peak, steep-walled Schwaub Peak, the canted strata of Pyramid Peak, and the impressive sugarloaf of Bat Mountain.

The day I was on Coffin Peak was perfectly evil. The wind was howling. The sky was filled with white vapor pegged high above long banks of ominous clouds. The sun had trouble piercing through, a huge diffused ball glowing an unearthly orange over the Panamint Mountains. To the southwest, way below the peak, Coffin Canyon traced a crooked path through the Black Mountains tormented slopes, until it disappeared between sharp ridges at the foot of the range. Beyond the mountains' edge gaped Badwater Basin's immense sink of misshapen salt beds. Whisked off the alkaline pan by gale-force wind, salt dust rose up in thick white twisters tens of feet tall, advancing so fast that even from several miles away they were visibly moving. It was one of the most wicked sceneries I had the good fortune to wit-ness, a rare serendipitous conjunction of foul weather and awe-inspir-ing land. In the entire Mojave Desert there is, as I became aware long ago, no equal to Death Valley. Rain or shine, Coffin Peak is a perfect place to understand why.

■

ASHFORD PEAK

As dramatic as the views of southern Death Valley are from this seldom-visited summit, it is the route itself that may impress you the most. It first follows Ashford Canyon's tortuous corridor of beautiful ancient mica schist and gneiss, past narrows, falls, and long sculpted bedrock exposures of colorful conglomerate mosaics. It then swings by the cabins and ruins of the historic Ashford Mine, before finally ascending a hard ridge to Ashford Peak.

General Information

Jurisdiction: Death Valley National Park
Road status: Roadless; access via primitive road (HC)
The climb: 2.9 mi, 2,450 ft up, 60 ft down one way/strenuous
Main attractions: Mine and camp, canyon with falls, geology, views
USGS 7.5' topo map: Confidence Hills
Maps: pp. 125*, 55

Location and Access

Ashford Peak is the high point of the sharp ridge that forms the south wall of Ashford Canyon, in the southern Black Mountains. To get to this canyon, drive the Badwater Road 27.4 miles south of Badwater (or 2.1 miles north of the Harry Wade Road) to the signed turnoff to the Ashford Mill, on the west side. Take the Ashford Canyon Road instead, on the east side. Drive it 0.7 mile to a fork and make a left. Along the next mile, the low hills to the west represent some of the most colorful exposures of the Jubilee phase of the Amargosa Chaos (see *Desert Hound Peak*). The western slope of Ashford Peak, rising east of the road, is all Calico phase. Park 2.1 miles from the fork, at the top of a rise at the mouth of Ashford Canyon. This road is decent for about 0.5 mile, worse along the next mile (there can be a little sand past the fork), and the rest gets gradually steeper and rougher, with lots of rocks and wash crossings. It takes good clearance to make it through.

Route Description

Ashford Peak is named after the Ashford brothers, who developed in the canyon below the summit a little gold mine that mirrors the frustrated hopes of countless desert miners. It started on the wrong foot, in 1909, when Harold Ashford's claim to his property was contested in court by the owners of the nearby Desert Hound Mine.

123

Ashford won the case the following year—but losing it instead might have been a blessing in disguise. Harold and his two brothers worked their holdings sporadically; most of the mining was done by lessees. The first one, an oil industrialist from Los Angeles, built the road up to the mine and put up a 40-ton mill—today's Ashford Mill—below the canyon. For a short time in 1915, operations employed up to 28 men. But after a year, only about $100,000 had been taken out of the ground, $25,000 short of his investment, and he quit. After he failed to pay his year's lease, it was the Ashfords' turn to file a lawsuit. The property and equipment were eventually returned to them, but they never got their money back. In 1935 the mine was leased again. The new company gave up in 1938, after shipping only $18,000 worth of gold from high-grade pockets. By then the mine was essentially gutted, but somehow the Ashfords managed to lease it again. An aerial tramway was constructed to collect the ore from tunnels scattered up the mountain slope. The effort employed up to ten men, but the lessees found the deposit too poor and gave up in 1941. When the property was finally retired in the 1950s, some 4,000 feet of workings had been blasted, but the total yield covered only about half the investment.

From the mouth of Ashford Canyon the old road continues as a foot trail 0.3 mile east to the canyon wash. It then climbs out of the wash on the left to bypass a 0.3-mile stretch of canyon. The road is easier going than the canyon, but the canyon is much more fun. It has good narrows penned in by steep walls, short but action-packed if you like rock climbing. The narrows have four falls, each one requiring different moves, from low 5s to 5.8, with one overhang. The first two falls can be bypassed, so the lower narrows are accessible without climbing.

Ashford Canyon is sunk deep into the Black Mountains' metamorphic core, mostly gneiss, mica schist, migmatite, and quartzite from the

Ashford Peak		
	Dist.(mi)	Elev.(ft)
Mouth (knoll on road)	0.0	1,100
Wash/road bypass	0.3	1,220
End of road bypass	0.5	~1,430
Road resumes	1.8	2,240
Ashford Mine's camp	(0.3)	2,230
Side canyon	2.0	2,520
Saddle	2.5	3,100
Ashford Peak	2.9	3,547

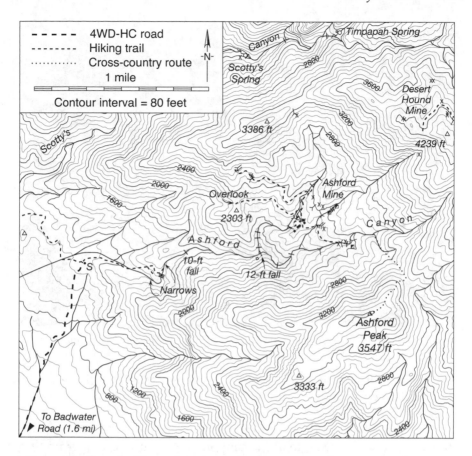

distant Archaean. The schists come in a variety of unusual colors and textures, gray to green, sparkling with mica, streaked with gneiss or folded veins of milky quartz and feldspar. Along the wash, billowing conglomerate bedrock has been polished into natural basins and exquisite mosaics. For a mile above the narrows, segments of road remain. Constructed above the wash to circumvent a few more falls, they were spared by floods. They can be used to avoid the falls, although the falls are a strong highlight, especially the first one, with its polished lip of vivid mosaics. The road resumes one last time up on the right side shortly past the second of two side canyons. It crosses the wash, swings around, and winds 0.3 mile to the Ashford Mine camp.

It is well worth visiting the little mine that caused so much grief. The camp has three wood cabins with partial furnishings. The largest one was the cook house and office. Low wooden doors give access to cool troglodytic rooms carved in solid rock. Just north of the camp lie remnants of a headframe and the collapsed lower terminal of the aerial

Ashford Peak (slightly left of center) from the Harry Wade Road

tramway built around 1938. If you like mining paraphernalia, you will have a field day: the surrounding hills are crawling with historic workings, some of them reached by old trails.

To climb Ashford Peak, continue up the main wash 0.2 mile, past a fall and a few workings, to a side canyon on the right. Clamber up this steep drainage, which soon turns into a ravine, about 0.4 mile up to the saddle between Ashford Peak to the southwest and much taller Desert Hound Peak to the northeast. About half way up to the saddle, the Archaean rocks are replaced by Calico phase lava and tuff. It makes up all of Ashford Peak and its colorful, deeply gouged south flank. From the saddle, proceed southwest up Ashford Peak's shoulder to the summit. From the wash to the summit the elevation gain is 1,030 feet in less than 1 mile. Expect some very steep stretches, and a few outcrops.

The summit has grand views of the Confidence Hills, the Narrows of the Amargosa River, and the Owlshead Mountains to the southwest. Across Death Valley to the west, the Panamint Mountains soar close to 1.5 miles higher and fill much of the landscape. To the north the ridge drops like a stone into the deep amphitheater of Ashford Canyon's upper drainage, framed by the dark heights of Desert Hound Peak and the corrugated crest of the Black Mountains.

■

DESERT HOUND PEAK

Desert Hound Peak, in the southern Black Mountains facing Death Valley, is easiest to reach from Ashford Canyon. The longer route suggested here, up Virgin Spring Canyon, gives an opportunity to check out a little spring and to enjoy vast exposures of the colorful Amargosa Chaos. It then follows a forgotten mining trail to the remote Desert Hound Mine just below the peak, a small gold mine with a connection to mysterious Death Valley Scotty. The trail and the summit overlook grand panoramas of southern Death Valley.

General Information
Jurisdiction: Death Valley National Park
Road status: Roadless; access by short primitive road (HC)
The climb: 6.9 mi, 3,440 ft up, 550 ft down one way/strenuous
Main attractions: The Desert Hound Mine, Virgin Spring, geology
USGS 7.5' topo maps: Epaulet Peak*, Funeral Peak, Shore Line Butte
Maps: pp. 131*, 55

Location and Access
The primitive road to Virgin Spring Canyon starts on the north side of Highway 178 0.4 mile west of Jubilee Pass (coming from Shoshone), or 33.4 miles south from Badwater. Drive it 1.35 miles to a small parking area, where a little sign will confirm that you are at the right place, and park. The mouth of Virgin Spring Canyon is the wide opening a little west of north, about 0.5 mile up the open wash. Starting 0.2 mile from the highway, the road has a few nasty sand traps. If you are driving a low-clearance vehicle, you might want to walk from the pavement.

History: Scotty's Secret Mine
The story of the Desert Hound Mine is intimately connected with Death Valley Scotty, a con man famous for his outrageous intrigues. In 1902, Scotty began claiming he had located a fabulously rich gold deposit in a remote area of Death Valley. His thinly veiled ploy was to convince investors to finance him—in principle to work his mine, in practice to take it easy. Since his mine was probably imaginary, it was instrumental that he kept its location secret. Scotty was resourceful, and he was successful for several years. In 1906, he managed to interest yet another group of investors in purchasing his by-then reputed

Epaulet Peak and the Amargosa Chaos from lower trail to Desert Hound Peak

mystery mine. The group requested that a mining expert be taken to the mine to assess its value. Put on the spot, Scotty led an expedition to Death Valley, resolved to pass off a mine owned by his friend Bill Keys, the Desert Hound Mine, as his own. The party included four investors and experts, Scotty's brothers Bill and Warner, Keys, and Scotty's friend Jack Brody. Concerned that Keys' modest property would not fool the experts, Scotty changed his mind along the way and decided to stage a little gun play to scare them off while crossing Wingate Pass. Keys and Brody, waiting in hiding, fired a few shots at the party, failed to miss, and wounded Warner. Mission accomplished: the expedition was aborted without anyone seeing the mine. Scotty and Keys were arrested, though charges were dismissed.

The Battle of Wingate Pass made headlines nationwide. Its publicity spiked the curiosity of investors, who decided to purchase Keys' Desert Hound and formed the Key Gold Mining Company in May 1906. Over the following months the company acquired as much of the surrounding ground as possible. The mine soon employed six men, and in the fall about $20,000 worth of gold ore was ready for shipment. In February 1908 a 600-pound furnace was hauled up the long, steep trail to the mine. Experts' reports were so enthusiastic that the company immediately planned for an on-site mill and a fancy aerial tramway to take the ore down to it. In February 1909 other workings were opened, and a plentiful supply of ore worth $80 to $100 a ton was reported. The company steadily increased its task force to about a dozen people by fall. In April 1911 the main adit was 1,300 feet long. Around that time 40 tons of ore worth about $12,000 were shipped to the smelter in Needles. But isolation was a tough enemy. Only the best ore could be profitably shipped out, and there was only so much of it. Mining continued through at least the beginning of 1912, at which point the Desert Hound Mine was shut down.

A one-man operation brought the mine back to life for a few years during the Great Depression. The enterprising man refurbished the trails to the mine and treated ore from the old tunnels at a small mill near Virgin Spring. Judging by the mill tailings, he may have spent more time building trails than mining. When the Desert Hound Mine was abandoned in the late 1930s, it is doubtful that it had produced much more than its purchase price. Scotty had indeed fooled them all. By then he was savoring his success in the comfort of Albert Johnson's mansion, the lavish castle that would eventually bear his name.

Route Description

The Virgin Spring Canyon area is a geological oddity. Among California-desert geologists, it is well-known as the prime locale of the Amargosa Chaos, an uncommon formation of highly disordered blocks ranging in size from tens of feet to a good fraction of a mile. Adjoining blocks are often made of rocks as disparate as dolomite, sandstone, basalt, marble, quartzite, and granitoids from almost all geologic times, all resting on the region's Archaean basement. A thrust fault roughly follows the contact between the chaos and the basement. The Amargosa Chaos was formed in the Tertiary by intense movements along the thrust fault. The overlying rocks were shoved over the basement like junk by a bulldozer, thoroughly faulting and shattering them into this phenomenal jumble.

Although lower Virgin Spring Canyon is wide and mostly straight, its colorful exposures of Amargosa Chaos very much make up for it. Except for a 1-mile stretch of crystalline basement starting 0.3 mile in, the Amargosa Chaos occurs all along the west side up to the main fork. The sweeping cliff about 0.2 mile in is a fine example. It has a few small faults, shattered rocks, and slickensides from being dragged over the basement. The two short side canyons around Virgin Spring also have typical outcrops. The best way to visualize the Amargosa Chaos is, however, from afar. It will become obvious when you gain elevation and look down at the random, multi-colored quilt that drapes the surrounding mountains.

After 2.2 miles a side canyon opens up on the west side, just before a lone, 8-foot high, cubic boulder in the wash. Take the next side canyon instead, 250 yards further, marked a short distance in by a similar boulder. About 0.1 mile inside the side canyon, on the left side, are the small, studded concrete foundations and small tailing of the mill from the 1930s revival of the Desert Hound Mine.

To check out Virgin Spring, a little off the main route, continue up the wash about 150 yards to the end of a right bend. A short trail climbs on the left to a low saddle. Walk across the saddle to the edge of the next side canyon south, which overlooks Virgin Spring. Dwarf mesquite grow in a steep, shallow ravine, among outcrops of blue-gray shale and a conglomerate of igneous fragments. The spring caved in and dried up decades ago; the NPS dug it up and installed a pipe to collect the water in a tub, for bighorn sheep and other wildlife. The water tank, drum, and rusted pipes lying around date from the 1906-1912 mining efforts.

The lower trail to the Desert Hound Mine starts a little past the mill foundations as a faint trace ascending the side canyon's right slope. For the next 1.4 miles, it climbs up to, then essentially follows, a sharp northwest-trending ridge. It then crosses the head of three drainages. Trail segments are missing, mostly around the wash crossings. The trail resumes about 0.6 mile before the junction with the upper trail. The remaining stretch to the old mining camp is in better shape and nearly level. This trail has been rarely used since the 1930s. Often a dim track, it has been taken out by multiple small slides and is

Desert Hound Peak		
	Dist.(mi)	Elev.(ft)
End of road	0.0	1,580
Mouth of Virgin Spring Cyn	0.5	1,660
Side canyon to lower trail	2.2	2,250
Start of lower trail	~2.4	~2,380
Virgin Spring overlook	(0.15)	2,420
Jct with Desert Hound Trail	5.3	3,970
Desert Hound Mine	6.1	~3,990
1906-1912 mining camp	6.4	~4,010
Desert Hound Peak	6.9	4,472

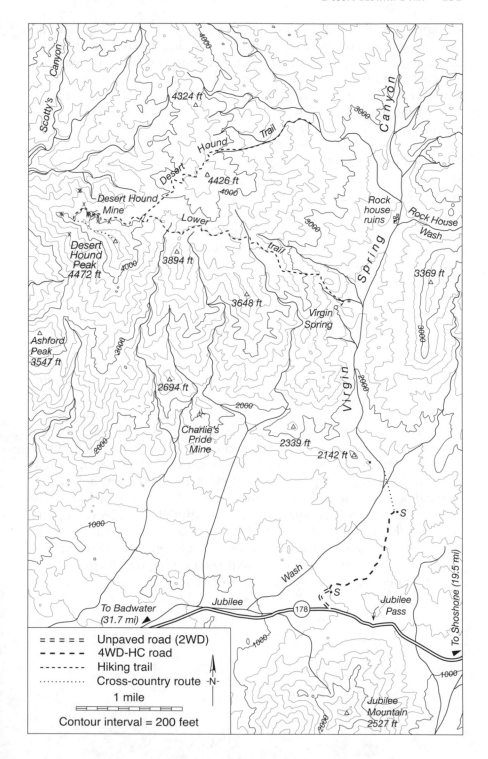

Scotty's Canyon

4324 ft

Desert Hound Trail

4426 ft
4000

Desert Hound Mine

Lower

Desert Hound Peak 4472 ft

3894 ft

trail

Rock house ruins

Rock House Wash

3369 ft

3648 ft

Virgin Spring

Ashford Peak 3547 ft

Canyon

Virgin Spring

2694 ft

2000

Charlie's Pride Mine

2339 ft

2142 ft

1000

Wash

S

To Badwater (31.7 mi)

Jubilee

178

S

Jubilee Pass

To Shoshone (19.5 mi)

= = = = = Unpaved road (2WD)
– – – – – 4WD-HC road
- - - - - - Hiking trail
· · · · · · · · · Cross-country route

-N-

1 mile

Contour interval = 200 feet

Jubilee Mountain 2527 ft

overgrown by thorny bushes. The lower portion is quite steep, hard on your lungs going up, hard on your knees coming down. However run-down it is, it does a decent job at minimizing elevation changes and distances, and it is far easier than the slick slopes it crosses. The main problem is that it is easy to lose. Frequently check your location against the map. If you lose it, chances are that by climbing to higher ground you will run into it again.

Desert Hound Peak and the crest around it are built of Archaean basement rocks 1.7 billion years old—the same rocks exposed all along the lower trail. Rocks this old are not usually uplifted this far up. The reason is that this crest is on the Desert Hound Anticline, a northwest-trending ripple, like the ridge on a bunched carpet. Located near the crest of the anticline, the Desert Hound Mine overlooks upper Scotty's Canyon and its wild scenery of chiseled slopes. A small camp was set up on a leveled terrace right by the trail. The main shaft, still shored with its original timber, gapes in the hillside beside the camp. The main tunnel is around the next bend in the trail. A long tailing, littered with rusted cans and trash, spills down the slope. The steel carcass stranded part way down is probably the 1908 furnace. The trail winds on for another half a mile to its end at a narrow divide, the site of the 1906-1912 mining camp. It is marked by a few tent sites, some of them well-preserved rock platforms, and the larger ruin of a rock shelter constructed partly in the hillside.

The summit is another 0.5 mile and 550 feet up along Desert Hound Peak's narrow northwest ridge. Between the old camp and the peaks, the views are awesome. Standing on the brink of Ashford Canyon, you look straight down the sweeping curvature of a great wall to the small camp of the Ashford Mine 2,000 feet below. Far beyond sprawls the pristine southern tip of Death Valley, framed by the Owlshead and Panamint mountains, with the Sierra Nevada peek-ing over them. It is strenuous, but it is a small price to pay for these glorious views, and for the thrill of visiting a legendary site no one has seen in a long time. Most people will need a long day for this climb; two days might be better, with water to match.

■

THE LAST CHANCE RANGE

The Last Chance Range is the long and narrow range that separates the extreme northern part of Death Valley from Eureka Valley
and Saline Valley to the west. It extends roughly north-south about 55
miles, from near the Nevada state line to south of Racetrack Valley.
With an elevation ranging from around 2,000 feet to above 8,500 feet, it
is the third highest range in Death Valley National Park. Except toward
its slightly lower southern end, the elevation of the crest exceeds 6,000
feet along most of the range. It is the least accessible range in the park,
most of it far from paved roads and reachable only from long primitive
roads. The closest services and water, at Scotty's Castle and Big Pine,
are nearly 80 miles apart. Since it takes so long to get to it, visitors are
infrequent. The isolation, combined with the austere beauty of the
range, make it a special place for climbing in perfect solitude.

The vast majority of the Last Chance Range north of Ubehebe Peak
is, like several other ranges in the northern Mojave Desert, emblematic
of the region's spectacular sedimentary formations. Along broad sections, especially overlooking Eureka Valley, striking banded slopes
hang high above the mountainsides. The Paleozoic is well represented
up through the Pennsylvanian, especially the Cambrian, Ordovician,
and Devonian. Although the stratigraphy is fairly complex, the formations tend to be younger toward the west side. Older formations
(mostly Cambrian and Ordovician) dominate north of Marble Peak,
and younger formations south of it. Many of them bear fossils.

Non-Paleozoic rocks are exposed in three main areas. The first one,
south from Ubehebe Peak, is composed largely of Jurassic granitic
rocks from the Hunter Mountain Pluton. The second area is the southwestern tip of the range, where it juts into Saline Valley east of the
springs. It is made of granite and Pliocene basalt. Finally, Tertiary
basalt and pyroclastic rocks are found on the east slope of the range
facing Ubehebe Crater. Several small exposures of similar Tertiary volcanic rocks also outcrop at a few locations near the foot of the range.

The Last Chance Range stands in the rain shadow of the high Inyo Mountains and the Sierra Nevada, and it is generally fairly dry. The main spring is the Last Chance Spring, near the north end of the range. The only other ones are around the southern boundary of the range, on the west slope of Hunter Mountain—Big Dodd and Little Dodd springs, which are dry most of the time, and Jackass Spring, which usually has a little flow. The highest areas can nevertheless receive quite a bit of snow in the winter. Last Chance Mountain and Dry Mountain are high enough to support some of the healthiest stands of conifers in the park. Joshua trees abound on the east side of the range, at the foot of Dry Mountain.

Only two areas in the Last Chance Range were mined in the past. The Racetrack Valley area witnessed nearly a century of mining. Copper, discovered in 1875, was mined starting in the mid-1890s, mostly on the slopes of Ubehebe Peak, on the sub-range east of the Racetrack, and around the Dodd springs. Production probably remained minimal, although after 1904 a few properties may have produced a little ore. The area was brought into the limelight by Jack Salsberry, a mining promoter who controlled some of the richest claims. To open the area, Salsberry completed a road to near Bonnie Claire, Nevada. By the fall of 1907, a weekly coach serviced the area. Mining continued until the middle of 1908, but soon after, perhaps as a result of the Panic of 1907, investments dried up and the project died.

Over the next 50 years or so, intermittent work at the best mines did produce copper—an estimated 120,000 pounds. Yet it was lead and gold that kept the district busy. The Ubehebe Mine, at the north end of the Racetrack, began to show promising lead veins in 1906, and remained active, albeit sporadically, longer than any other mine in the district. Up until the 1960s, it produced about 1,300 tons of lead and 2,600 pounds of silver. The Lippincott Mine, at the south end of the Racetrack, was active mostly between 1938 and 1952, and it became the third largest lead producer in Death Valley. The Lost Burro Mine, in nearby Hidden Valley, produced essentially all of the district's gold.

The area around Crater, in the northern Last Chance Range, boasts one of the largest sulfur deposits in the West. Discovered in 1917, it was mined from 1929 up until the 1940s and produced over 50,000 tons of nearly pure sulfur. Smaller-scale mining took place in the 1950s and continued sporadically until today. The area also produced 115 pounds of mercury in 1968-1971. There is still quite a bit of both elements in the ground, which was the reason for the exclusion of the Crater area's patented claims from the park.

■

LAST CHANCE MOUNTAIN

The little springs and forgotten mine at the foot of 8,456-foot Last Chance Mountain, and the mountain's forested slopes above them, make an excellent target for a strenuous climb in this remote corner of the Last Chance Range. In early spring the air is so clear that the views from the summit extend well over 100 miles.

General Information
Jurisdiction: Death Valley National Park
Road access: Roadless; access by long graded road and dirt road (HC)
The climb (short): 2.5 mi, 2,970 ft up, 150 ft down one way/strenuous
The climb (long): 3.4 mi, 3,230 ft up, 400 ft down one way/strenuous
Main attractions: A thickly forested peak, springs, mine
USGS 7.5' topo maps: Last Chance Mountain,* Hanging Rock Canyon
Maps: pp. 137*, 55

Location and Access
Last Chance Mountain is near the north end of the range, at the extreme northern tip of Death Valley. From the North Highway 2.9 miles southwest of Scotty's Castle (or 33.4 miles north of Highway 190), drive the Ubehebe Crater Road west 2.8 miles and turn right on the Big Pine Road. Go 21 miles to Crankshaft Junction, marked by a cemetery of rusted crankshafts. Turn right, and after 0.8 mile bear left. Park 2.7 miles up this road, where it ends at the site of the Last Chance Cabin. The Big Pine Road is graded, and although it is a bad washboard at places, a standard-clearance vehicle can usually make it. The road from Crankshaft Junction is a little rough, especially the last 2 miles, which are steeper and a little worse, and high clearance is preferable. But the crown is shallow and the rocks small, and by driving slowly and carefully one can make it with a compact car.

Route Description
The area at the end of the road was the heart of a small homestead and mine that were active from probably the 1930s until relatively recent times. Until it burned down in the early 2000s, its tin cabin was furnished with a fireplace, a table, and chairs, and it received rave reviews from the occasional visitors who spent the night in it.

This peaceful, remote setting on the edge of timberline has a few springs, all very different. One is in the ravine just below the road. A little water usually flows all of 200 feet along a narrow, algae-coated channel lined with rabbitbrush and cliffrose. The largest spring, surrounded by a wire fence, is up on the wide bench across the ravine. A faint trail climbs to it across the wash northwest of the end of the road. It is locally known as Fan Spring, presumably for its shape, visible from higher ground on the way up to Last Chance Mountain.

Given the odds of finding a mineral fortune right next to the only spring for miles, not much mining went on here. The workings, a short distance up the wash, consist of two deep shafts and a short tunnel. The shafts still have their access ladders, and a primitive hoist stands by the inclined shaft. The tailings are minimal, and so, probably, was the production.

The third spring, Last Chance Spring, is 0.15 mile up the wash from the end of the road. Water seeps out from under a low tangle of mesquite and grapevine, feeding a grassy slope and a cluster of cottonwoods. The runoff collects in a large steel tub, which is always full. In the old days, water was piped by gravity to the mine or the cabin—remnants of the pipeline are scattered below the spring. Bighorn sheep and other wildlife use this spring regularly.

For the shortest route to Last Chance Mountain, from Last Chance Spring hike up canyon, bearing left at the first two forks (within 300 yards of the spring). Just under 100 yards past the second fork there is an 18-foot fall, easy to scale or bypass. In another 250 yards, before the next fork, leave the wash and climb onto the ridge to the right. Follow it 0.6 mile up to the 7,141-foot summit, then 0.8 mile to the crest at a saddle near 8,110 feet (a use trail is starting to emerge). The last stretch is 0.5 mile west on the crest, over a false summit, to the true summit.

Last Chance Mountain		
	Dist.(mi)	Elev.(ft)
End of road	0.0	5,630
18-ft fall	~0.35	~5,945
Leave wash/climb onto ridge	0.5	6,100
Third fork (go left)	(0.05)	6,160
Bypass 7,978-foot summit	(1.5)	7,970
Saddle on crest	(2.35)	~8,110
7,141-foot summit	1.1	7,141
Saddle on crest	1.95	~8,110
False summit	2.1	~8,285
Last Chance Mountain	2.5	8,456

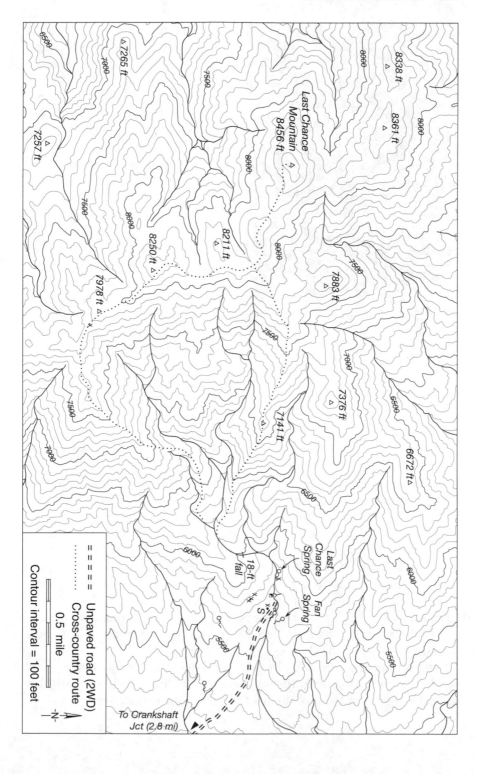

Old sign at Crankshaft Crossing

The route I prefer is about 1 mile and 500 feet of elevation gain longer, but it spends more time on the crest overlooking Eureka Valley. From the 18-foot fall, continue up canyon 400 yards to the next fork. Head up the left branch 100 yards and climb out of the wash onto the ridge on the right. Stay on it as it climbs steeply and curves southward to the crest (7,825 feet). Then follow the crest roughly northwest over four minor peaks to the summit.

Either way, this is a great climb. Last Chance Mountain is heavily forested with juniper and pinyon pine, and it makes for a refreshing climb, almost temperate. The density and size of the trees increase with elevation, until on the crest they reach magnificent proportions. In the thickest areas, you occasionally walk on the backs of fallen trees. Some trees are beautifully gnarled and varnished to a butterscotch finish, like they can be on much higher mountains near timberline.

From the summit the views are tremendous. You look straight down the shimmering sink of Death Valley all the way to the Black Mountains, with the high summit of Charleston Peak piercing the far edge of the horizon some 130 air miles away. Dry Mountain and Tin Mountain soar to the south, and far in the background Telescope Peak reaches even higher. But it is the views to the west that steal the show. Pristine Eureka Valley sprawls more than a mile below, its majestic sand dunes glowing a pale golden light. On its far side, the valley is framed by the stark hump of the Saline Range and the overwhelming barrier of the Inyo and the White Mountains. Still beyond, miles of the Sierra Nevada cap the skyline.

The best time for this climb is early to mid spring, when snow adds charm to this magnificent scenery. The downside is that there might be some on the ground. Mid-fall is a good second best.

■

LEAD PEAK

Lead Peak is a little beauty, a long hogback of angular quartzite towering over pristine Eureka Valley and its finely sculpted dunes. The climb is short and easy, across small historic mining properties that exploited mercury and the huge sulfur deposit that lies under the mountain. The surrounding hills are strikingly colorful, the old mine dumps hold vast quantities of unusual minerals, and the views of the valley and the banded Last Chance Range are wonderful.

General Information

Jurisdiction: Death Valley National Park
Road status: Access by rough road (HC/4WD); roadless beyond
The climb: 2.0 mi, 730 ft up, 50 ft down one way/easy
Main attractions: Easy peak climb, panoramas, sulfur mines and camps
USGS 7.5' topo map: Hanging Rock Canyon
Maps: pp. 141*, 55

Location and Access

Lead Peak borders the east side of Eureka Valley, a few miles north of the Eureka Dunes. It is a long and lonesome drive to get to it, on one of the least frequently traveled roads in California. From the sleepy town of Big Pine on Highway 395, take Highway 168 2.3 miles to the Big Pine Road on the right. This scenic byway, mostly paved and the rest graded, climbs the long western flank of the Inyo Mountains to a high pass above timberline. East of the pass it winds down through Little Cowhorn Valley, Joshua Flats, and several more mountainous miles to Eureka Valley. It then crosses the valley to the signed turn-off to the Eureka Dunes, 36.3 miles from Highway 168. Continue straight 4.7 miles, up the Last Chance Range, to a dirt road on the right, in sight of Crater's barren pit at 11 o'clock. If you reach the pass, you have gone 0.25 mile too far. Drive this road 150 yards to the smaller Lead Peak Road on the right, and park. The Lead Peak Road can be driven 1.8 miles to its end just north of Lead Peak (four-wheel drive is needed for the steep grade halfway through). I suggest walking it instead—it is easy, and it adds a little exercise to an otherwise very short climb.

Route Description

Lead Peak sits on top of a huge deposit of native sulfur. Sulfur rarely occurs as a native element: there are only ten native-sulfur deposits in California, and this is the second largest one. It was formed in the last 4,000,000 years by hydrothermal solutions related to magmatic activity, which makes it even more rare—only a few percent of the world's native sulfur has a volcanic origin. Together with the Saline Range, this is also one of only two places in the region with known mercury deposits. Sulfur was mined extensively between 1929 and 1943, then intermittently until 1969. Close to 200 claims were developed, but only three—the Crater, the Gulch, and the Fraction and Southwest Sulphur—became large producers. Crater, the richest, was operated by far the most consistently. A long list of owners and lessees gave it a try. The most productive outfit shipped 12,000 tons; all others did much more poorly. Sustained production was hindered by high shipping costs and the lack of water for on-site refining. Some companies erected steam retorts and trucked in thousands of gallons of water daily to run them. Operations were also hazardous. Over the years, at least two retorts were destroyed by sulfur-dust explosions. Although it barely made a dent in the estimated reserve of 3 million tons, the area's output was significant. Crater had produced nearly 30% of California's native sulfur by the mid-1950s, and over 50,000 tons by 1969.

You do not often run into sulfur or mercury mines in the wild. This climb is unique in that it gives access to both. The Lead Peak Road winds southwest along a shallow gulch, then climbs steeply out of it to the high crest of the Last Chance Range. Part way up the grade, a short spur cuts east to the Midas Mine and the Soliz and Vaseta Mine. Their long trenches explored a low-grade sulfur, mercury, hematite, and gold deposit in fractured Zabriskie Quartzite. On the crest the views from the road are spectacular, encompassing all of Eureka Valley to the west and tightly striated canyon walls to the east. In the late spring and summer the area is graced with Indian paintbrush, scented cryptantha, globemallow, phacelia, and uncommon purple owl's clover. The Aloha Prospect, by the right side of the road, has a shallow 100-foot trench with traces of cinnabar in shale and quartzite, and a little onyx. In the right bend just before the road ends, a trail on the left descends to the Rebecca No. 4 Mine's 100-foot open cut. The most interesting site is the Rebecca No. 2 Mine 0.25 mile below it, down very steep terrain slashed by bits of road. This small mercury mine was a latecomer that was run on a shoestring budget by one or two men for a time, and abandoned in the 1980s. Its photogenic camp has a plywood cabin, an elevated water tank, and a ramshackle tool shed. Cinnabar-stained quartzite was extracted from trenches up the slope, then crushed and screened. The homemade screens are still there, and so is the brick furnace where the ore was roasted, complete with its two slender smokestacks.

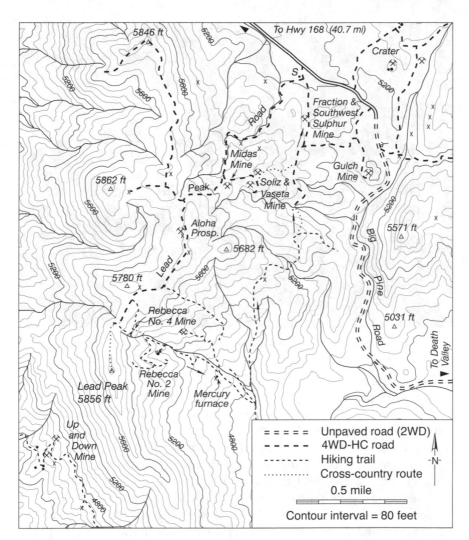

= = = = =	Unpaved road (2WD)		
- - - - -	4WD-HC road		
- - - - - - -	Hiking trail		
· · · · · · · · · · ·	Cross-country route		
	0.5 mile		
	Contour interval = 80 feet		

Lead Peak

	Dist.(mi)	Elev.(ft)
Lead Peak Road (right)	0.0	5,180
Junction to Midas Mine	0.75	5,540
Crest/road junction	1.0	5,740
Trail to Rebecca mines	1.7	5,740
Rebecca No. 2 Mine camp	(0.35)	5,320
End of road	1.75	5,740
Lead Peak	2.0	5,856

Eureka Dunes and the Last Chance Range from the Lead Peak area

From the end of the road Lead Peak is reached by scrambling 0.25 mile and all of 120 feet up the razor-sharp ridge to the south. The local rock is Carrara Formation quartzite and Zabriskie Quartzite, around 520 million years old. Along the ridge the quartzite layers have been upturned and broken into natural stairways. The summit deserves a special award for providing such breathtaking views at the cost of so little effort... To the west the land falls off sharply to eerie badlands drained by serpentine canyons, as black as scorched earth. Eureka Valley sprawls beyond, framed by the high Inyos and a fringe of the Sierra Nevada. To the south, the crisp Eureka Dunes glow brightly against the long and colorful arcuate flank of the Last Chance Range.

To add serious sulfur mines to this climb, from the Rebecca No. 2 Mine return east down the steep grade to the canyon wash below, then along the road that cuts north across the mountain's flank to join (via a short cross-country stretch) another road that passes by the Fraction and Southwest Sulphur Mine on its way back to your starting point (see map). Another option is to descend east from the Soliz and Vaseta Mine to this last road. The mine's long trench is covered with large outcrops of canary yellow brimstone, as fragrant as a volcano's throat. The nearby Gulch and Crater mines are even more colorful.

∎

UBEHEBE PEAK

From the edge of the Racetrack, an old mining trail climbs to the stark heights of Ubehebe Peak, across rocky slopes sparkling with heavily varnished plutonic rocks. The summit views of the Racetrack's eerie mud flats, Saline Valley's deep sink, and the surrounding ranges are so awesome that you might find it more difficult to leave than to get there.

General Information
Jurisdiction: Death Valley National Park
Road status: Roadless; 25-mile primitive access road (HC)
The climb: 2.6 mi, 2,190 ft up, 220 ft down one way / difficult
Main attractions: A spectacular climb, views of the Racetrack
USGS 7.5' topo map: Ubehebe Peak
Maps: pp. 145*, 55

Location and Access
Ubehebe Peak is the highest summit towering over the west side of Racetrack Valley, the scenic high-desert valley between the Cottonwood Mountains and the south end of the Last Chance Range. This valley is famous for its mysterious moving rocks, which are occasionally propelled by strong winds and leave long wandering tracks on the valley's ancient lakebed—better known as the Racetrack. From the paved loop at Ubehebe Crater in northern Death Valley, drive the Racetrack Valley Road 19.5 miles south to Teakettle Junction, a scenic ride over Joshua-tree-covered Tin Pass. Continue straight 5.4 miles to the turnout for the Grandstand, the island of dark rounded granite on the Racetrack. The trail to the Ubehebe Peak, which towers to the right, starts at the turnout. This road is long, and locally rough. The park often receives reports of disabled vehicles with flat tires, broken axles, or torn undercarriages. Although an experienced driver can make it with a standard-clearance car, I recommend a high-clearance vehicle. Camping along the road south of Teakettle Junction is prohibited except at the Homestake Dry Camp south of the Racetrack.

Route Description
This is one of the most spectacular climbs in this part of the desert. For a change there is a trail, most of the way, likely built by miners to access their mines and haul out their ore by mule. At the Grandstand

turnout, the trailhead is identified by rocks lined up on both sides of the trail. The trail first heads west part way up the short alluvial fan, then veers approximately northwest. It continues in this general direction up across the mountain's flank 1.4 miles before climbing steeply to a low saddle north of Ubehebe Peak, on the crest of the range. This is quite a good little trail, with a total of 36 switchbacks nicely pacing the climb, and increasingly fine views of Racetrack Valley. In the summer it is best to tackle it in the late afternoon, when it is in deep shade.

Most of the rocks along the way are porphyritic granite. Sometime in the Late Jurassic or Early Cretaceous, a batholith of quartz monzonite intruded this area. The contact between the magma and the native rocks produced a region tens to hundreds of feet thick where rocks on both sides were metamorphosed—the native rocks from being heated and crystallized, the intrusive rocks from being cooled, and both from exchanging chemical constituents. Shales were transformed into hornfels, dolomite into marble and tactite, quartz monzonite into granite, diorite, gabbro, or syenite. Later on, rising metal-bearing solutions preferentially soaked up the weakened metamorphosed rocks, slowly turning them into rich lodes. Subsequent uplifting and erosion exposed this pluton all over the southern Racetrack region. Ubehebe Peak, the mountain facing it across the playa, the north face of the Nelson Range, and Hunter Mountain, are all mostly quartz monzonite. Here and there, islands of the original sedimentary rocks are still exposed, and on their edges are the metal-rich contact zones that sparked the Ubehebe District mining rush in the early 1900s. When miners found metals, unbeknownst to them they were identifying contact metamorphic zones. On today's geology maps, their mines magically trace the complex outlines of the Mesozoic pluton. The granite on Ubehebe Peak contains little quartz or mica, and it is unusually dark. It is often stuffed with tabular orthoclase crystals, commonly over 2 inches long. Each crystal is twinned: it is made of two crystals that grew within each other. The difference in reflectivity between the two halves neatly divides the crystal down its length.

Little can prepare you for the views when you top the crest and first look down the far side into Saline Valley, half a mile lower than the Racetrack. There is perhaps no better place to appreciate what a deep trough it is. The salt lake at the bottom of the valley, 12 miles away and nearly 4,000 feet down, is dwarfed by the two-mile high wall of the Inyo Mountains behind it. In the late afternoon, when it is obscured by the mountains' shadow, the valley seems unfathomable.

At the crest the trail forks. The leftmost trail, lined with rocks and the most obvious of the two, goes to the peak. At first it climbs steeply

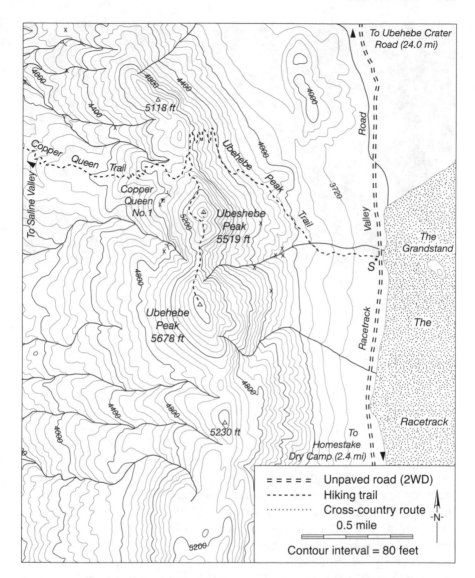

Ubehebe Peak

	Dist.(mi)	Elev.(ft)
Grandstand turnout	0.0	3,710
Saddle on crest	1.7	~4,900
Ubeshebe Peak	2.2	5,519
Saddle between peaks	2.3	~5,220
Ubehebe Peak	2.6	5,678

The Grandstand (foreground) and Ubehebe Peak (left) from the Racetrack

along the crest, then it circumvents the west flank of the subordinate peak north of Ubehebe Peak (a hiker with a good sense of humor called it "Ubeshebe"). In spite of a few switchbacks and rock stairs, this part is rougher than the lower trail. The trail then drops to the saddle between the two peaks. The rest of it is less well defined, but the route is straightforward, a little west of the ridge line. It is locally strenuous, up a slope approaching 45% covered with large rocks—not all of them rock steady. But as usual the rewards make it all well worth it. At several points, you will be looking down the ridge's razor-sharp eastern edge and enjoy breathtaking bird's-eye vistas of Racetrack Valley.

When you reach Ubehebe Peak's narrow summit you are confronted with two different worlds. On one side, you look, straight down it seems, at the bright Racetrack and its dark Grandstand, with the high Cottonwood Mountains sprawling in the background. A 180° turn and you are peering down into Saline Valley, its lake and dunes shining in the distance, completely isolated by high mountain ranges—the Nelson Range to the south, the Inyos to the west, the Saline Range to the north, and the Last Chance Range you are standing on. You may find, as I did, that two eyes are just not sufficient to take it all in.

■

COTTONWOOD MOUNTAINS

The second highest in Death Valley National Park, the Cottonwood Mountains rank among the most remote and spectacular ranges in the California desert. Their statistics are impressive. They frame the west side of northern Death Valley for some 45 miles and cover approximately 250 square miles. Together with adjacent alluvial fans and valley floors, they hold one of the largest roadless areas in the park. Their average crest elevation exceeds 5,000 feet. From north to south they are dominated by several peaks above 7,000 feet, including Tin Mountain (8,953'), their highest summit, White Top Mountain (7,607'), Hunter Mountain (7,454'), and Towne Peak (7,287'). Their physiography is as strikingly asymmetric as any range in the Death Valley region. On their west side they slope down only 1,000 or 2,000 feet into several high-desert intermountain basins—Hidden Valley, Racetrack Valley, Ulida Flat, and Sand Flat. In contrast, the eastern side drops precipitously into Death Valley, at places almost all the way to sea level, in only 4 or 5 miles.

The Cottonwood Mountains are generally poorly accessible. Just getting to the starting point of a climb and back can take a good part of a day. Most of their eastern base lies between 3 and 9 miles from paved roads (the North Highway and Highway 190). On their east side only Marble, Cottonwood, and Lemoigne canyons have access roads. None of them are through roads, and they all require a high-clearance and/or four-wheel-drive vehicle. On their west side, the Cottonwood Mountains can be accessed by three long backcountry roads, the Racetrack Valley Road from the north (starting at Ubehebe Crater), the Hunter Mountain Road from the south (starting from the Saline Valley Road), and the rough Lippincott Road from the west (starting at the south end of Saline Valley). The main backbone road, the Hunter Mountain Road, can be snowed-in and closed in the winter.

For the most part, the Cottonwood Mountains are made of Paleozoic sedimentary and metasedimentary rocks of marine origin.

With a few exceptions, these exposures stretch from around Mesquite Spring south to Goldbelt Spring, then resume south of Lemoigne Canyon. They are composed mostly of limestone and dolomite, with ages ranging from Ordovician to Pennsylvanian. The remaining central area, from Goldbelt Spring to Lemoigne Canyon, is a massive band of granitic rocks known as the Hunter Mountain Pluton (approximately 170 million years old). This signature pluton also outcrops around White Top Mountain and along the ridge separating Racetrack Valley from Hidden Valley. North from Mesquite Spring, mostly Tertiary nonmarine rocks and Cenozoic basalt flows are exposed, as well as quaternary volcanic rocks from the recent eruptions of Ubehebe Crater and smaller nearby craters. An extensive flow of Pleistocene basalt, several miles wide, also covers the south end of the Cottonwood Mountains. Finally, a few nonmarine deposits, Plio-Pleistocene in age, are exposed along the eastern front of the range on both sides of Cottonwood Canyon and west of Towne Pass.

The only significant mining in the Cottonwood Mountains took place east of Racetrack Valley, around Ulida Flat and Hidden Valley, and in Lemoigne Canyon. On the other hand, this range was highly prized by prehistoric cultures, as may be inferred from the large number of rock art sites—the highest concentration in the park.

Because of their more western location and high elevation, the Cottonwood Mountains receive the second highest amount of precipitation in the park, including snow just about every winter. This moisture feeds a relatively large number of widely scattered springs. In the southern reaches of the range, Cottonwood Creek is the longest perennial stream in the mountains surrounding Death Valley—it flows above ground for about half of a 5-mile run of canyon. The higher elevation and moisture create a favorable climate for pinyon pine–juniper communities, which thrive at several places. Hunter Mountain is covered with one of the park's thickest forests. Tin Mountain, White Top Mountain, Towne Peak, and other summits on the central crest have more scattered woodlands. Joshua trees are relatively common in the central Cottonwood Mountains, in particular around Hidden Valley and Ulida Flat.

Thanks to their size and rugged topography, the Cottonwood Mountains offer challenging first-class desert climbs that involve steep slopes, significant elevation gains, and sometimes long roadless approaches. Combined with their remoteness, low visitation, higher elevations, and cooler temperatures, these features make this range particularly appealing for overnight ascents.

∎

TIN MOUNTAIN

Tin Mountain is one of the harder non-technical climbs in the Mojave. From the access road, climbing the avalanches of broken rocks that drape the mountain looks formidable—and it is. The elevation change is 4,300 feet over 3.3 miles, with loose rocks, rocky spurs, sustained 35% grades, and little shade except for conifers along the last mile. The views from the highest summit in northern Death Valley are stunning, first of the long tectonic trench leading to Racetrack Valley, then of all of the northern Mojave Desert.

General Information
Jurisdiction: Death Valley National Park
Road status: Roadless; primitive access road (HC)
The climb: 3.3 mi, 4,250 ft up, 60 ft down one way / strenuous
Main attractions: Views of the Racetrack and Death Valley
USGS 7.5' topo maps: Dry Mountain, Tin Mountain*
Maps: pp. 151*, 55

Location and Access
Tin Mountain is near the north end of the Cottonwood Mountains, about 9 miles south of Ubehebe Crater. When viewed from the North Highway in northern Death Valley, it fills the western skyline, soaring 8,000 feet above the valley. The easiest route to it starts on the other side of the range, on the Racetrack Valley Road. From the paved loop at Ubehebe Crater, drive the Racetrack Valley Road 9.8 miles south to the entrance to a tighter passage between low banks, at a left bend to the south-southeast (elev. 4,665'). Go 0.35 mile further, just before a sharp right bend to the south, and park at a small pullout on the left. You should be just past a wash coming out of a break in the bank on the left (east). Refer to *Ubehebe Peak* for road conditions.

Route Description
From the pullout, first head east up the wash through the opening in the bank. Due east, a pointed front-range peak (~8,210') caps the horizon. Tin Mountain is barely visible behind and to the left of it. Continue up the broad wash. Up ahead the mountain is flanked by precipitous taluses 1,400-feet tall calved by the upper mountain. The fan is covered with dwarf Joshua trees and a sprinkling of cactus, silver cholla, and desiccated low shrubs. About two thirds of the way to

the base of the taluses, the wash narrows and deepens. Climb onto its north bank and follow it the rest of the way to the foothills, where the wash enters a shallow ravine. This is 0.8 mile from the road.

From this point most routes to Tin Mountain proceed via the 8,210-foot summit. The least painful way to this false summit is up the sharp ridge on the left at the mouth of the ravine. The ridge heads first northeast, following the edge of a deeper ravine on its north side, then south as it gets closest to this ravine, and finally east-southeast to the 8,210-foot peak. This is a long hard pull—the elevation gain is 2,360 feet over only 1.3 miles—on consolidated avalanche material, slippery patches of loose rocks, and rocky outcrops higher up. There is a use trail much of the way, but it goes mostly straight up and does not help much. The end of the last stretch, inclined at 35 degrees, is the roughest—you climb nearly a foot and a half per step. By then the Joshua trees have been replaced by a scatter of juniper, then large pinyon pine. The saving grace of this frustrating trudge is the stunning perspective of the long trench that connects Ubehebe Crater to Racetrack Valley, formed by tectonic activity along the Tin Mountain Fault. As the elevation rises, this perfect rift valley in the making opens up gradually, punctuated by miniature dry lakes. Eventually the Racetrack itself emerges from its ring of dark mountains at the distant southern end of the fault.

Past the false summit, which is avoided on the south side, continue up the ridge to ~8,560 feet, where Tin Mountain first becomes visible to the northeast across a sandy canyon. Up ahead the ridge is covered with hard spurs. It is easier to leave the ridge and cut a beeline northeast across the canyon to the summit. This area has beautiful vistas over the sharply sculpted cliffs that girdle the nearby summits. The rocks on Tin Mountain range from Silurian Hidden Valley Dolomite near the base to Tin Mountain Limestone on some of these cliffs. Widespread in the region, this smoky-gray limestone records a major

	Dist.(mi)	Elev.(ft)
Racetrack Valley Road	0.0	4,760
Foot of ridge	0.8	~5,600
Edge of ravine	0.95	5,800
Bypass 8,210-ft false summit	2.3	~8,160
Leave ridge	2.7	8,560
Tin Mountain	3.3	8,953

Tin Mountain

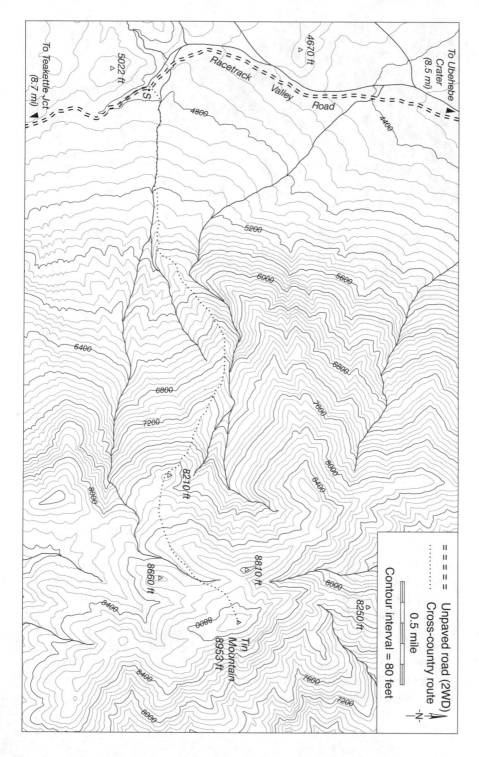

To Ubehebe Crater (8.5 mi)

To Teakettle Jct (8.7 mi)

Racetrack Valley Road

4670 ft

5022 ft

4800

4400

5200

6000

5600

6400

6800

7200

6800

7600

8000

8210 ft

8000

8660 ft

8400

8810 ft

8000

8000

8250 ft

Tin Mountain 8953 ft

8400

8000

7600

7200

= = = = = Unpaved road (2WD)
. . . . Cross-country route

0.5 mile

Contour interval = 80 feet

-N-

The route up to Tin Mountain follows the ridge that circles around on the left side of the photograph, taken from the Racetrack Valley Road

environmental shift during the Mississippian, from a lagoon or mud-flat to a deepening continental margin as the shore shifted eastward. Tin Mountain's outcrops, boulders, and taluses all serve up abundant remains of life on the reefs that thrived then—chips of gastropods, tubular corals, the severed thoraxes of trilobites, and, with luck, the ornate lilies of crinoids.

At the top of Tin Mountain you stand on a tilted ancient seabed jutting into a sky 60 miles wide. On a clear day it commands exceptionally gratifying views of northern Death Valley and the Grapevine Mountains. From the northern tip of the Last Chance Range to the Black Mountains the valley's popular icons are strewn across some 70 miles, from Lake Rogers and Ubehebe Crater to the Niter Beds, Mesquite Flat and the dunes, and distant Cottonball Basin. On one side you peer over the insanely dissected topography of the Grapevine Mountains into Nevada; on the other to the 14,000-foot dome of the White Mountains and a luminous 60-mile sweep of John Muir Wilderness. This spread of wildlands is so enormous that even Death Valley does not begin to fill it.

∎

WHITE TOP MOUNTAIN

The main appeal of White Top Mountain is its isolation. From the closest pavement at Ubehebe Crater to the foot of the mountain it is a 32-mile drive on primitive roads, not all in their prime, a two-hour, bone-rattling ride into little-traveled territory. The climb itself, a little over one mile and 1,000 feet of elevation gain, is a pleasant hike up a beautiful ridge of pale dolomite dotted with conifers. Towering nearly a mile and a half over northern Death Valley, the summit commands spectacular views of the region.

General Information
Jurisdiction: Death Valley National Park
Road status: Roadless; long access on primitive roads (HC-4WD)
The climb: 1.25 mi, 1,000 ft up, 50 ft down one way/easy
Main attractions: Isolation, geology, view of northern Death Valley
USGS 7.5' topo map: White Top Mountain
Maps: pp. 155*, 55

Location and Access
Half of the fun and excitement of climbing White Top is driving there. From the end of the pavement at Ubehebe Crater it is first a long dusty ride on the Racetrack Valley Road to Teakettle Junction (19.5 miles), along the deep corridor between the Cottonwood Mountains and the Last Chance Range. At the junction, after the obligatory inspection of the eclectic kettles hanging from the historic sign, it is another 3.2 miles east on the Hunter Mountain Road, between Lost Burro Gap's awesome Paleozoic walls, to the White Top Mountain Road on the left. It is then 8.9 miles up this road, along a deep canyon, to the starting point of the climb, a mining road on the mountain's north slope. By then you will have crossed Joshua tree woodlands, skirted two intramontane basins, spooked a dozen neurotic jackrabbits, and climbed 4,100 feet from a volcanic devastation to timberline. The mining road is faint and easy to miss. It is on the right in an area of pinyon pine, in a straight stretch of road 0.3 mile after exiting a tighter passage. It is still open to motor vehicles, but the climb is so short that it makes more sense to park at the junction and walk the road.

As mentioned under *Ubehebe Peak*, it is best to use a high-clearance vehicle on the Racetrack Valley Road—it would be a long and potentially dangerous walk out should your vehicle get stranded. A couple

Niter Beds and Mesquite Flat from the sheer rim of White Top Mountain

of miles up the White Top Mountain Road, a few small washouts will stop low-slung vehicles anyway. Further on, along the narrow wash of Rest Spring Gulch, erosion has exposed four bedrock slants two to four feet high across the road. Most urban SUVs will have trouble negotiating the hardest two without losing vital organs. High clearance and good traction are imperative to make it up these bumpy ramps of rock.

Route Description

You do not have to be an orienteering genius to find this summit: from the start of the mining road it is visible to the southeast through the trees. The road will take you halfway there, and the other half is a leisurely climb on the unobstructed crest. The mining road is an easy track, still in reasonable shape, that ascends only 400 feet to the crest of the Cottonwood Mountains. On its way up it zigzags across open slopes sprinkled with juniper, pinyon pine, cliffrose decked out in feathery blooms in the spring, and aromatic plants. We saw Indian paintbrush, penstemon, and an abundance of rock spiraea, a plant that normally shies away in shady nooks. The seductions of the desert were likely remote from the minds of the people who built this road in the late 1900s; they came here to mine asbestos... The Whitetop Mountain

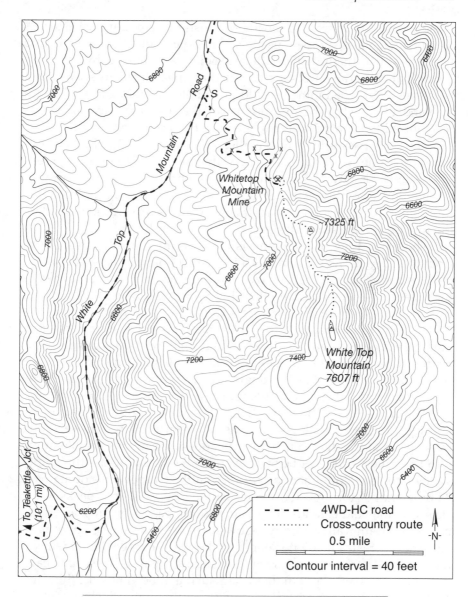

White Top Mountain

	Dist.(mi)	Elev.(ft)
White Top Mountain Road	0.0	6,708
Quarry/end of mining road	0.6	~7,100
False summit	0.85	~7,325
White Top Mountain	1.25	7,607

Mine worked four small deposits of mostly low-quality asbestos. A small tonnage was shipped, used as a mundane filler in plaster, before they gave up. In the 1950s the property was leased by Huntley Industrial Minerals, a Bishop outfit that specialized in scavenging whatever abandoned mine it could get a hold of, from garnet to tungsten and, obviously, asbestos. Judging by the size of the trees that have recolonized the quarry, it probably was not any more successful.

The road passes by three smaller asbestos deposits, then ends at the largest one, worked by a quarry that straddles the range's crest. The asbestos is now reduced to traces of chrysotile mixed with talc, calcite, and tremolite. All that is left is the host rock, a dolomite so thoroughly metamorphosed that it is as white as driven snow, its glare too intense to stare at in full sun.

The second leg of the climb is cross-country up the crest south from the quarry. The mountain is a bare shield of uplifted seafloor that reaches back through the Cenozoic and Mesozoic to the dark ages of the Paleozoic. It is made entirely of Ely Spring Dolomite, the solidified purée of the equatorial coral reefs that lived and died here in the Ordovician. The formation has eroded into expansive sweeps of hard, pale-gray shelves littered with occasional small rocks, as convenient as a stretched staircase. On single-digit winter days, when snow blankets the mountain, or during 100-degree heat waves in the summer, the scattered conifers dispense a little refuge and sanity.

The rare hikers who climb here do it for the giddy sensation of staring into Death Valley's immensity. From the summit, receding ranks of striated ridges coursed by meandering canyons tumble down into the valley 7,500 feet below. Several miles away, across the empty valley floor, the land rebounds abruptly at the Grapevine Mountains, a 35-mile wall of tortured formations capped by 8,000-foot peaks. On a clear day the void extends deep to the south, past flats, fans, and sand dunes to Death Valley's briny below-sea-level basins. The space is so vast that it creates its own silence. To the west, parallel alignments of mountains stretch out some 60 miles from the Inyos to Telescope Peak.

I am reasonably certain that I had such a good time on White Top Mountain because my friend Alice was there with me. She even let me beat her to the summit, an impossible feat at three times her age... We stood on the mountain's abrupt rim for a long time, mesmerized by the giant gulf below us, by the immutable sky and rock. We were bonded by the same closeness to nature, the calculated risks of exploration, and a common fascination for the animate and inanimate. Friendship is often most exalted in the isolation of wilderness.

∎

LEANING ROCK

> *Little-known Leaning Rock is one of these summits that takes you by surprise—the drive to its isolated location takes longer than the climb, yet the views from it are spectacular. Expect a short but steep ascent over scenic hills graced with Joshua trees, eerie vistas of Racetrack Valley and Hidden Valley, and an eye-filling perspective of Mesquite Flat. The nearby cliff-bounded bluff offers a little extra challenge and a deep view into Dry Bone Canyon's twisted narrows.*

General Information
Jurisdiction: Death Valley National Park
Road status: Roadless; access on long primitive road (HC)
The climb (Leaning Rock): 1.8 mi, 1,620 ft up one way / moderate
The climb (Hidden Valley Viewpoint): 2.3 mi, 1,730 ft up, 190 ft down
        one way / moderate
The climb (North Leaning Rock): 2.4 mi, 1,790 ft up, 260 ft down
        one way / difficult
Main attractions: Spectacular views of Hidden Valley and Mesquite Flat
USGS 7.5' topo map: Sand Flat
Maps: pp. 159*, 55

Location and Access
Leaning Rock (7,342') is on the crest of the central Cottonwood Mountains, between Hidden Valley and Dry Bone Canyon. Follow the directions to the four-way junction just east of Lost Burro Gap (see *Lost Burro Peak*). Turn left on the White Top Mountain Road and drive it west-northwest 3.25 miles to a parking area on the right, blocked off after about 100 feet by a wilderness-boundary sign. This is just before the road dips into a broad wash, and near the northern tip of a low hill about 200 yards to the east. High clearance is recommended (see *Ubehebe Peak* and *White Top Mountain* for details on road conditions), especially on the White Top Mountain Road, which has a couple of small washouts.

Route Description
If it weren't for the low hill just east of the White Top Mountain Road, it would be a straight shot from the spur road to Leaning Rock. To circumvent the hill, walk up the spur road 250 yards until it drops into a wash and the wash forks. The right fork circles around the

Ubehebe Peak, Inyo Mountains, and high Sierras from Leaning Rock

northern tip of the hill, reaching a 6-foot horseshoe-shaped wall in light-gray limestone in 100 yards, then another wall, breached in its center, shortly after. The summit area first comes into full view around there. To the east, a wide bajada slopes up about 1 mile to the foot of the steep mountain front. Leaning Rock is the small nipple on the relatively level crest above it. Neither a rock nor leaning, it is eclipsed by a stately cliff-bounded bluff that juts out just north of it. It may well be this bluff's pronounced tilt that inspired the name of Leaning Rock.

From the first fall, hike up the wash 150 yards as it veers south, to an area on the left buried under alluvia. This is the start of a wash that wanders southeast across the bajada to the foot of Leaning Rock. In 0.9 mile it reaches the southern base of the 6,631-foot hill below the crest. If you cannot find the wash, cut a beeline across the bajada to the same point. The walking is easy, across open ground covered with ephedra, bitterbrush, and small Joshua trees. In the late spring, this sad-looking flora comes alive with globemallow and prince's plume in bloom.

From the base of the hill, the rest of the route is straight up the steep southeast ridge south of the wash about 0.6 mile to the summit. The slope locally reaches a vigorous 45%, but the footing is generally sturdy. Near the top of this ridge there is a tall outcrop that can be bypassed on its north side. This shaded side is home to large fuzzy

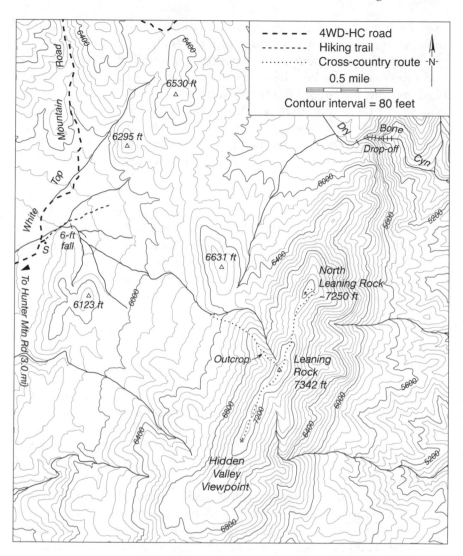

Leaning Rock

	Dist.(mi)	Elev.(ft)
White Top Mountain Road	0.0	5,720
Fork in wash (go right)	0.15	5,760
Base of 6,631-ft hill (leave wash)	1.25	6,320
Leaning Rock	1.8	7,342
Hidden Valley Viewpoint	(0.5)	~7,290
North Leaning Rock	2.4	~7,250

mats of uncommon rock spiraea. Above the outcrop, the rocks under-foot are loose, but a few opportune outcrops help.

This is Paleozoic country. The entire area is underlain by limestone and dolomite of the Lost Burro Formation, except for the cliff-bound bluff and the 6,631-foot hill (Tin Mountain Limestone). The corals and crinoids of these famously fossiliferous formations are common on outcrops and on the bajada. Native Americans cherished this area. They likely used the local reddish jasper littering the bajada to fashion stone tools. On smooth limestone breaks they pecked a lexicon of symbols with long-forgotten meanings.

The views from the summit are alien. To the west four increasingly taller alignments of ranges project their jagged skylines against each other's—the diminutive Dutton Mountains on the far side of Hidden Valley, the stark Ubehebe ridge, the Nelson Range and Inyo Mountains behind it, and the Range of Light looming on the horizon. Leaning Rock's eastern slope remains hidden until you take your final steps onto the narrow summit and the land ahead plummets down many miles to sea-level Mesquite Flat. In the distance rise the colorful Grapevine and Funeral mountains, overshadowed by Nevada's 2-mile-high Spring Mountains beyond. If you are familiar with the region, you will recognize dozens of geographical features across the 150-mile span of desert between Charleston Peak and Mount Whitney.

The best part of this climb is taking advantage of being up on high ground and exploring the crest. South from Leaning Rock it is open and gentle. Grizzled cliffrose cling to the rubble, their bleached trunks as thick as trees'. Mound cactus grow out of cracks in the limestone. It is an easy half-mile walk to a local summit with a good view of Hidden Valley and its shiny mud flat.

The tilted bluff north of Leaning Rock is more challenging. There are two outcrops on the way there, which can be bypassed on the west side, then a free-standing pillar with a striking resemblance to a gorilla's head. The bluff looms beyond, an impressive piece of geological engineering bounded by 70-foot cliffs of dark-gray limestone. It can be climbed by following the top of the loose talus along the bluff's scalloped eastern base, past neatly stratified walls stuffed with oblong black chert nodules. After about 200 yards, a Class-2 scramble up a very steep, fluid talus through a break in the cliffs leads to the craggy summit. North Leaning Rock commands great views north into Dry Bone Canyon's gorge winding half a mile below, and over the beautifully wrinkled slopes of the upper canyon rising 2,000 feet toward the lofty heights of Tin Mountain. Sunsets are dramatic, in every direction.

■

LOST BURRO PEAK

Rising sharply at the north end of Hidden Valley, Lost Burro Peak is a neatly striated stack of pale limestones, glaring intensely in the summer, as moody as a Scottish ben on a wintry day. The climb is short and delightful, past the historic camp, mill, and workings of the Lost Burro Mine, one of the richest in the Ubehebe Mining District. The views of Hidden Valley and the Racetrack Valley area from the broad limestone summit are outstanding.

General Information
Jurisdiction: Death Valley National Park
Road access: Roadless; access by long primitive road
The climb: 1.3 mi, 990 ft up, 210 ft down one way / moderate
Main attractions: Lost Burro Mine, geology, views of Hidden Valley
USGS 7.5' topo map: Ubehebe Peak
Maps: pp. 163*, 55

Location and Access
Lost Burro Peak is the high point near the north end of the small sub-range, once known as the Dutton Mountains, that frames the east side of Racetrack Valley. From the paved loop at Ubehebe Crater drive the Racetrack Valley Road 19.5 miles south to Teakettle Junction, and turn left on the Hunter Mountain Road. Continue 3.2 miles, through Lost Burro Gap and past the sheer east face of Lost Burro Peak on the right, to a four-way junction. Turn right and park after 1.1 miles at the Lost Burro Mine. A high-clearance vehicle is recommended on the Racetrack Valley Road (see *Ubehebe Peak*), as well as on the last mile.

Route Description
In April 1907, while rounding up his burros a prospector named Bert Shively spotted gold at the foot of a mountain east of Racetrack Valley. By wandering off, the burros with a flare for gold unwittingly set off a naming spree. Shively filed several claims in the area and named the two main claims Lost Burro. The mine that opened soon after inherited the name too, and so did the nearby mountain and the gap north of it. As it happens, Lost Burro Gap displays a good sequence of Devonian carbonates. In keeping with geologists' conventions, the gap was recorded as the official type locality for this formation, which became the now well-known Lost Burro Formation.

The small mining camp below the mill is a picturesque site, slumbering in timeless torpor, a little austere in its desolate hollow sprinkled with stunted Joshua trees. On my last visit it had a cabin, a dilapidated shelter, and an outhouse. The cabin was still furnished with odds and ends resting on dusty shelves, and parts of a stove. Yellowed newspaper and magazines from a long-gone era served as wallpaper.

Although early assays identified valuable ore, the Lost Burro Mine had slow beginnings. For several years its owners bonded it, leased it, and attempted to sell it. Each time the new operators developed the mine for a while, then called off the deal for one reason or another, and the property returned to the original owners, who eagerly worked it themselves while waiting for another offer. They made a little cash in the process, and the property was worked fairly diligently. The workings exploited a vein up to 10 feet thick and assaying $15 to $18 per ton, and a small pocket with samples worth up to $1,000 per ton. By 1909 $30,000 worth of gold-bearing ore had been stockpiled. The most glamorous era started in 1915, when the Montana-Tonopah Company bonded the property and proceeded with ambitious plans. Below the mine it began constructing a five-stamp, 50-ton mill that was to be powered by water piped from Burro Spring, some 8 miles away. The pipeline was eventually installed, but no records indicate whether the

Lost Burro Peak's striated east face from Hidden Valley

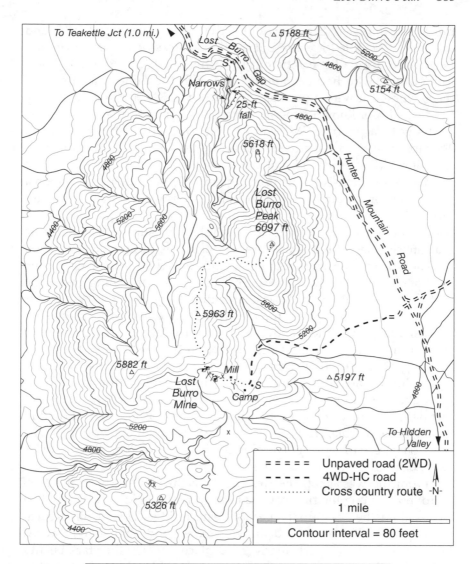

Lost Burro Peak

	Dist.(mi)	Elev.(ft)
Lost Burro Mine camp	0.0	5,320
Mill	0.1	~5,430
Lost Burro Mine (west shaft)	0.3	5,580
False summit (5,963T point)	0.6	5,963
Saddle	1.0	~5,780
Lost Burro Peak	1.3	6,097

mill was completed. This flurry of activity stopped around 1917, and the mine stood idle for years. But the deposit was rich, and it eventually yielded a nice little return. From the late 1920s to 1938, Andy McCormick, who had been associated with the mine since its early days, worked it with a partner and recovered $85,000 in gold. Shorty Borden, a lesser known miner in the region, relocated the claims in the 1940s with a partner, William Thompson. After Shorty's death, Thompson worked the mine sporadically until the 1970s. All told, the Lost Burro Mine produced probably close to $100,000 in gold.

The most extensive structure at the mine is the mill, pinned against the hill a short distance from the camp. Towering above several levels terraced into the hillside, it is an impressive sight. Its massive timber frame, darkened by a century of sunlight, still supports some of its machinery. The ore bin is more recent, and was probably constructed by Thompson. The workings are strung out along the steep ravine west of the mill, mostly on the south side. The lower mining area is the east shaft, at the top of the lowest large dump. It was connected underground to the middle area, the most productive, which was accessed by two adits, one 50 feet above the other. The upper area is the west shaft near the upper end of the ravine, on the north side. The gold-bearing vein occurred near the contact zone between a small syenodiorite pluton and Tin Mountain Limestone. The pluton is exposed throughout the mine. It contains sizeable crystals of biotite and hornblende. The contact zone, where the limestone was metamorphosed to nearly white marble, crops out across the wash from the workings. The west shaft area has fine samples of the marble. The limestone is exposed from the top of the mine to the summit.

From the west shaft the route to Lost Burro Peak is straightforward: north along the ridge over a false summit (5,963') and down to a twin saddle, then east up the peak's western ridge. The terrain is occasionally steep but open, and the views are good almost right away. Lost Burro Peak is a particularly good place to enjoy the stark beauty of Hidden Valley. To the east the mountain tumbles down 1,200 feet to the edge of the valley, exposing its prominent slice of Devonian history. Hidden Valley sprawls below, its small dry lake and pale shrub cover cocooned between moon-like hills—it is a quiet scene, infused with intense serenity. The view to the west is dominated by the sharp Ubehebe Peak crest and the massive Inyo Mountains behind it. The Racetrack is mostly hidden, but the false summit, or better yet the 5,882-foot promontory southwest of it, make up for it, commanding views even more dramatic than from Ubehebe Peak itself.

■

HUNTER MOUNTAIN

This is a short and uncommonly easy climb through a pleasant conifer forest peppered with aromatic plants and monzonite boulders. The summit's scenic repository of granitic outcrops, reached by an easy scramble, commands an exceptional view of Saline Valley's awesome sink and its majestic ring of mountains.

General Information

Jurisdiction: Death Valley National Park
Road status: Roadless; access by long primitive road (HC)
The climb: 1.0 mi, 360 ft up, 40 ft down one way / very easy
Main attractions: Forested summit, views of Saline Valley
USGS 7.5' topo map: Jackass Canyon
Maps: pp. 167*, 55

Location and Access

Hunter Mountain is a sprawling mountainous mass at the confluence of the Nelson Range to the west, the Last Chance Range to the north, and the Cottonwood Mountains to the east. Its high point, Jackass Peak, is but a short distance from the Hunter Mountain Road. To get to this road, work your way to the signed Saline Valley Road, on Highway 190 17.0 miles east of the junction with Highway 136 (or 13.7 miles west of Panamint Springs). Most of the time we want the driving done and over with so we start climbing sooner, but here the drive is very scenic and an integral part of the excitement. The Saline Valley Road wanders across the colorful rolling plateau of Santa Rosa Flat, then crosses the low Santa Rosa Hills. On the north side of the hills, 8.2 miles from the highway, is a Y junction at the south end of Lee Flat, a high desert valley hosting one of the most impressive Joshua tree forests in Death Valley National Park. Some of the trees reach over 30 feet and have exceptionally dense crowns. Take the right fork, into the rubbly volcanic foothills of Hunter Mountain. The scenery changes rapidly as the sparse desert vegetation morphs into a healthy conifer forest. The junction with the Hunter Mountain Road, known as South Pass, is 7.3 miles from the Y junction. Just before South Pass there is a magnificent vista point looking down the length of Panamint Valley.

At South Pass, turn right on the Hunter Mountain Road, and drive northeast 2.7 miles, up through an increasingly dense forest, then along Jackass Canyon and its spring-fed groves of willows, to a sharp

Saline Valley from the summit of Hunter Mountain

right U-shaped bend at the head of the canyon. The climb starts 0.1 mile further, at the low point in the road just after the next left bend. However, there is not much room to park without damaging roadside vegetation. Park 0.15 mile further, where there is a bare spot up on the left side. Jackass Peak is hidden behind the top of the forested slope less than a mile to the west.

Up to Lee Flat, the Saline Valley Road is partly paved, partly (and mostly) dirt. In dry weather, a standard-clearance vehicle can normally push on to South Pass. The Hunter Mountain Road is steep and locally rocky, and high clearance with good power is required.

Route Description

Hunter Mountain is named after William Lyle Hunter, an adventurer who moved to the Inyo Mountains–Saline Valley area in the late 1860s, when he was in his mid-twenties, and spent his life dabbling in all kinds of trades. He was for a time a mule skinner for the booming Cerro Gordo mines. He discovered valuable copper deposits on Ulida Flat in 1875, then rich silver outcrops near Cerro Gordo and gold in the Inyo Mountains in 1877. He worked his gold and copper ledges off and on for 16 years. He also had a ranch and a picturesque log cabin

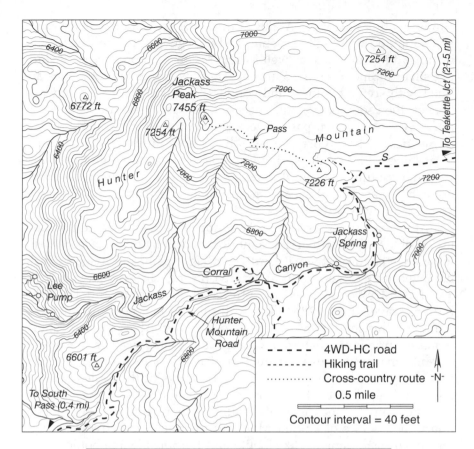

Hunter Mountain

	Dist.(mi)	Elev.(ft)
Hunter Mountain Road	0.0	~7,140
Leave road at wash/trail	0.15	7,100
Pass	0.7	7,310
Hunter Mountain	1.0	7,455

on the forested heights of what is now Hunter Mountain. In recognition of his pioneering contributions, his name was given to a record number of local features—a spring, two canyons, a formation, a peak, a road, a cabin, and a whole mountain.

From the car park, backtrack 250 yards to just before the next right bend in the road. A narrow trail, plowed by the cattle that roam this area, takes off on the right. It wanders off into a broad hollow that climbs gently to the west. At this altitude the vegetation is remarkably exuberant, a thigh-high carpeting of big sagebrush, bitterbrush, salt-bush, and Mormon tea, as well as several uncommon species, including silver lupine, rare in California. The low ridges on both sides are lined with scenic boulders and conifers. The trail meanders between bushes, then soon peters out. The slope of least resistance leads west-northwest to an open pass. Selected unnaturally by generations of domesticated herbivores, grasses have gone humorously berserk. Refreshingly lush in the springtime, they overcompensate in the dry season by putting out countless needle-shaped seeds with an obsessive appetite for socks and shoe linings, making walking an itchy misery. Weeks later I was still plucking the little pricks off my shoes.

At the pass the tree cover thickens abruptly. From there to the summit, visible to the northwest as a mound of chubby outcrops barely rising above the forest, there is hardly a straight path, and it takes a little bushwhacking to get around the pinyon pine, cliffrose, large shrubs, and fallen trunks. In prehistoric times, the Panamint and Timbisha indians traveled great distances to hunt and harvest pine nuts and plants on this mountain. It is easy to see why. Apart from its abundance of springs and natural resources, and cooler weather, it exudes a serenity that infiltrates your mind and makes you want to linger. If you do, you might run across the descendants of the mule deer and bighorn sheep that fed them—or escaped their arrows.

The summit block is a tall mound of hard plutonic boulders—quartz monzonite of Hunter Mountain of course. Relatively poor in ferromagnesian minerals like biotite and hornblende, the boulders are unusually pale and contrast sharply with the dark-green pine growing among them. The east side has only steep and exposed faces, but the south side has an easy route, over lower boulders huddled together, and only one 6-foot slant requiring hands.

This is the best approach for another reason: it gives no clue about how incredible the view is until the very last moment, when you reach the shallow V between the summit's twin knobs and peer over the edge into the shiny heart of Saline Valley. Hunter Mountain drops like a grand staircase into the valley's deep basin, its dune fields, salt lake, marshes, and hot springs dwarfed by the towering Inyo Mountains. Desert rats will recognize many of the classic summits that surround this stunning tectonic sink—Waucoba and Cerro Gordo, Saline and Dry and the twin chocolate cones of Ubehebe, and lonesome Galena. Together with the Salt Tramway Trail, this is one of the most spectacular views of one of the most spectacular desert valleys in California.

■

TOWNE PEAK

Climbing Towne Peak, perched on the high volcanic crest of the Cottonwood Mountains, is an aerial experience. Most of the time you are walking on an open ridge, peering down over the sharp rim of colorful Dolomite Canyon into the long trench of Panamint Valley sprawling a mile below. It is wild, rugged, and spectacular. The ultimate goal is the well-preserved wreckage of an amphibian plane that crashed decades ago on a sheer talus below the summit.

General Information
Jurisdiction: Death Valley National Park
Road status: Roadless; access from paved road
The climb (Towne Pk): 3.5 mi, 2,630 ft up, 300 ft down one way/difficult
The climb (Albatross crash site): 4.5 mi, 3,680 ft up, 1,420 ft down
      one way/strenuous
Main attractions: Views of Panamint Valley, geology, botany
USGS 7.5' topo map: Panamint Butte
Maps: pp. 171*, 55

Location and Access
Located at the head of Dolomite Canyon, Towne Peak is the highest summit in the southern Cottonwood Mountains. This climb starts at Towne Pass, on Highway 190 7.5 miles west of the Emigrant Canyon Road, or 11.3 miles east of the Panamint Valley Road. Towne Peak is not visible from the pass, but you can catch good views of its distinctive brownish mesa profile if you drive up from Panamint Valley. Park at the north end of the brake-check area, where a very short dirt track on the west side points to one of the easiest routes up the ridge.

Route Description
Towne Peak. West from Towne Pass the land rises steeply as a wide ridge to the crest of the Cottonwood Mountains. Small volcanic boulders litter the slope, usually with just enough space between them to walk. Where the grade eases up, erosion slows down, the density of boulders increases, and boulder hopping is the main mode of locomotion. The boulders are vesiculated olivine basalt, nearly black with desert varnish. They sparkle with tiny crystals and reflect light with a deep purple sheen. From start to finish the rocks are all volcanic. They were spewed out of vents disseminated over a wide area, especially

169

Dolomite Canyon and Panamint Valley from the crest below Towne Peak

just north of the Argus Range, between 5.5 and 3.9 million years ago. Collectively, these modest flows smothered at least 100 square miles under up to 400 feet of lava. Parts of them survive miles away on the Darwin Plateau, severed by the rifting of Panamint Valley.

At the crest, 800 feet above the receding pass, the scenery opens up as abruptly as if a door had been flung open. To the south and west the land drops into the rough, 2-mile-wide upper drainage of Dolomite Canyon, a singularly colorful caldron in which simmers a mosaic of faulted and warped Paleozoic formations. Below it the canyon wiggles through sharp ridges and hills before emerging into spacious Panamint Valley, bounded in the distance by the high Argus Range.

To the north the crest describes a crooked arc upward around the head of Dolomite Canyon, past two false summits and a few hills, to eventually reach lofty Towne Peak. It makes for an aerobic climb, with copious elevation change, no shade, and less oxygen than most of us are accustomed to. Basaltic boulders dominate for a while, then reddish scoriaceous rocks and volcanic breccia. Rainbows of lichen, white, orange, and fluorescent green, coat the north sides of boulders. The crest is mostly open, thinly covered with bitterbrush and Mormon tea, oddly green against the auburn ground. The one plant that stands out in this classic high-desert flora is a rare cactus called Mojave fishhook.

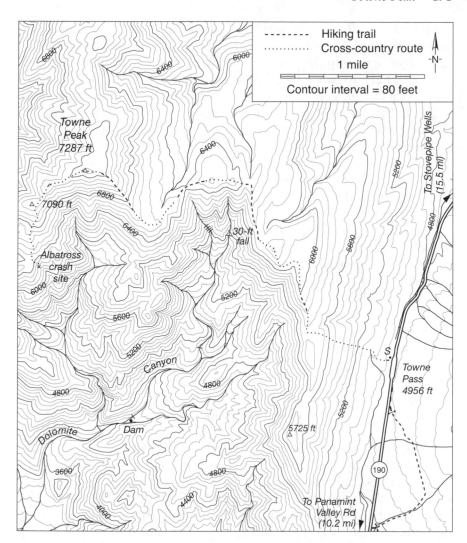

Towne Peak

	Dist.(mi)	Elev.(ft)
Towne Pass	0.0	~4,960
Crest	0.65	~5,770
First false summit	1.5	6,240
Second false summit	2.3	6,565
Towne Peak	3.5	7,287
Saddle	4.35	6,420
Albatross crash site	4.5	~6,220

I counted more than I had seen in a lifetime, and lost count after a full-grown speckled rattlesnake wandered across my path, its scales shining bright orange in the afternoon light. Faint use trails are emerging here and there, mostly along the steep inclines where the rare climbers tend to follow the same easiest route. Climbing the first false summit is a quick affair. The second one takes more effort. The final ascent, up Towne Peak's 30% southeast ridge, is a minor grind on loose slabs. These pretty silvery rocks (quartz-olivine basalt) were formed when lava flowed over wet ground and shattered. They pave the ground as neatly as tiled flooring and outcrop in peculiar mounds of close-packed vertical slabs. On a windless day, the silence is intense enough to hear the flaps of a raven passing high overhead. It is easy to be envious of a bird that effortlessly flies in a minute to places that will take us an hour to reach.

We painstakingly lift ourselves to these remote heights hoping for outrageous vistas that will remain forever imprinted in our memories. Towne Peak delivers. Along the crest the views of Panamint Valley open up gradually until they extend down its entire length to its salt lake and the far-off Slate Range. Towne Peak's broad summit overlooks an impressively vast region, from Grapevine Peak to Tucki Mountain, Telescope Peak, and the Sierras. The peak's north slope is just high and cool enough to host a dispersed woodland of ground-hugging, wind-brushed juniper. Their dark shade is a silent invitation to take a break and soak in this sumptuous panorama.

The Albatross crash site. During the night of January 24, 1952, a CIA Albatross flying from Idaho to San Diego crashed in these mountains after one of its twin engines failed. The six men on board parachuted in time and landed safely north of then Furnace Creek. The plane continued on course, scraped a couple of summits, then against all odds landed itself with surprisingly little damage on an insanely steep talus less than a mile south-southwest of Towne Peak.

The wreckage, severed in its midriff, its two halves resting at a mortal 90° angle, is clearly visible from the first false summit. Protected by isolation, much of the old plane is still there, and it is one of the most interesting plane crash sites in the U.S. From Towne Peak it is a steep mile-long descent to it along the crest. Looking for a way back among dark boulders at night in the bouncing beam of a headlamp is not everyone's idea of fun, but sometimes it is the right price to pay. Strangely, years from now, this may well be what you remember most vividly of the day you climbed Towne Peak.

∎

PANAMINT MOUNTAINS

The Panamint Mountains form the western margin of southern Death Valley, which they separate from Panamint Valley to the west. Covering about 820 square miles, they are the largest and highest in Death Valley National Park, and one of the most formidable ranges in the California desert. The crest has several summits above 10,000 feet, topped by Telescope Peak (11,049 feet). Between Wildrose and Porter peaks, a distance of 15.5 miles, the elevation hardly dips below 8,000 feet. The distance between Telescope Peak and Death Valley's salt pan is about 12 miles, for a vertical drop exceeding 2 miles. This is twice as deep as the Grand Canyon, and one of the steepest slopes this long in North America. This spectacular topography makes the Panamints a mecca for hard mountaineering. They offer an unusual variety of landforms, extensive historic sites, cooler and more shaded terrain, far-reaching views, and some of the highest desert climbs in California.

The Panamint Range is one of the largest fault blocks in the western Basin and Range. Over the last few million years its west side was uplifted along the Hunter Mountain Fault Zone, which runs along the east side of Panamint Valley, while its east side was sunk into Death Valley. The fault block was originally a stack of stratified marine deposits many miles thick, the result of nearly one billion years of sedimentation. As it was rising out of the ground, older and older formations were exhumed along the fault. At the same time, the younger layers at the top of the block were stripped off by erosion, exposing the underlying older rocks. The whole stack was eventually unearthed. Today, the western Panamint Mountains are made of the Proterozoic formations—Johnnie, Noonday, Kingston Peak, Beck Spring, and Crystal Spring—that were once the most deeply buried. The basement gneisses and schists also became exposed at a few places near the foot of the mountains, in particular at South Park Canyon. Between 1.35 and 1.82 billion years old, they are among the oldest rocks in the Mojave. On the east side, with a few exceptions, from Tucki Mountain to Warm Spring Canyon the youngest rocks are Devonian. Most of the central range dates from the Cambrian. Precambrian formations occur around Galena and Warm Spring canyons. Small Jurassic and Tertiary plutons outcrop on Manly Peak, around South Park Canyon, in upper Hanaupah Canyon, and in Hall Canyon.

The Panamints are high enough to capture some of the moisture from the Pacific Ocean that has managed to slip over the Sierra Nevada, and they receive a fair amount of precipitation. The average yearly rainfall is at least 9 inches at 7,000 feet, and up to 15 inches higher up. Snow usually blankets the highest summits until March, and sometimes as late as May. In the winter, ice can make them inaccessible without proper equipment. Rain and snowmelt that have percolated downward feed many springs and creeks throughout the mountains, some of them with fairly substantial flows. Reflecting this higher precipitation and the broad range of elevation, the vegetation is one of the most varied in the region, and it encompasses most of the local plant zones. The high Panamints support the most extensive woodland belt in the park, including pinyon, limber, and bristlecone pines. Larger mammals are more numerous. In forested areas it is not uncommon to flush out mule deer or bighorn sheep. Feral burros are often spotted at mid-elevations, especially in the southern range.

The Panamints have had a particularly long and rich mining history dating back to 1860, when antimony was discovered in Wildrose Canyon. The first major strike occurred in 1872, when a silver lode was exposed high in Surprise Canyon. In just two years, the town of Panamint City had burgeoned below the mines to a population of 2,000. It made national headlines and produced a fair amount of silver, although in the end investors lost money. Between 1896 and 1903, the Ratcliff Mine in Pleasant Canyon was the district's largest historic gold producer, with a return of $450,000. Its neighbor the World Beater Mine harvested another $180,000. There were dozens of less fortunate ventures, like the Lotus Mine in Goler Canyon, Jail Canyon's gold mine, and the Gold Bug Mine above Ballarat. The biggest bonanza, however, was talc. The huge deposits in Warm Spring Canyon, facing southern Death Valley, were for years the most largest talc producers in the western United States. From 1937 to the late 1980s, this and adjacent Galena Canyon yielded upward of 1,000,000 tons of talc worth tens of millions of dollars. The last active mine is the C. R. Briggs south of Ballarat. Opened in the mid-1990s, it has been steadily chewing the range's southwest front at the tune of 10,000 tons of rock a day to extract gold from a very poor but unfortunately very large deposit.

∎

WILDROSE PEAK

From Wildrose Canyon's historic charcoal kilns, the narrow trail to this lofty summit crosses sweeping slopes blanketed with a beautiful conifer forest. The second half of the trail overlooks central Death Valley, in a pleasant setting of fragrant high-desert vegetation. The barren summit commands spectacular views over many desert ranges between the Sierra Nevada and Nevada's Spring Mountains. Thanks to the trail, this is good testing ground, if you are in shape but lack desert experience, to conquer a superb major peak.

General Information
Jurisdiction: Death Valley National Park
Road status: Trail climb; access on graded road (2WD)
The climb: 4.2 mi, 2,390 ft up, 190 ft down one way / moderate–difficult
Main attractions: Forested trail to a spectacular peak, historic kilns
USGS 7.5' topo maps: Wildrose Peak*, Telescope Peak*
Maps: pp. 177*, 55

Location and Access
The Wildrose Peak Trail starts at the famous charcoal kilns in upper Wildrose Canyon, the largest canyon on the western slopes of the Panamint Mountains. From Highway 190 in Panamint Valley, drive the Panamint Valley Road south 13.8 miles to the Trona-Wildrose Road. This junction can alternatively be reached from Trona by driving approximately 14.5 miles north from the town center to the pass out of Searles Valley (Slate Range Crossing), then down scenic switchbacks into Panamint Valley. The junction is 16.8 miles from the pass. Turn left if you are coming from Highway 190, or continue straight otherwise. After 9.8 miles you will reach Wildrose Junction, where the main through-road angles sharply left. Continue straight instead, up Wildrose Canyon on the Mahogany Flat Road. In 0.3 mile it passes by Wildrose and its campground. Wildrose Canyon's charcoal kilns are 6.8 miles further. This stretch is partly paved, partly graded, and usually suitable for most passenger cars, unless snowed in.

Route Description
Wildrose Canyon's impressive kilns, high in the thickly forested upper canyon, are a wonder of early desert mining. They are connected to the rich silver boom that took place in 1875 at the Modoc Mine, in

Wildrose Peak area from trail

the Argus Range across Panamint Valley (see *Lookout Mountain*). Charcoal was needed to operate two smelters near the mines, and wood was needed to produce charcoal. The closest wood supply was the conifer forest up in Wildrose Canyon, nearly 25 miles away, but the distance did not stop the enterprising mine managers. By the spring of 1877, the ten huge furnaces had been erected and were ready to produce. They were loaded with 4-foot logs, which were left to burn for several days until the wood had turned to charcoal. The operation probably employed a small crew to cut the wood and stack, fire, and tend the kilns. The Modoc Mine remained active until the early 1890s. However, perhaps because it temporarily ran out of good ore, or perhaps because cheaper smelting was identified elsewhere, the kilns were last fired up in 1879.

The kilns are made of limestone blocks quarried locally and mortared with sand, lime, and gravel. Like other charcoal-burning ovens of that era, they were designed like an opera house, to reflect as much heat—which behaves in certain ways like sound—as possible. Inside a kiln, even the faintest sound is audibly reflected by the curved walls. The back portholes served to stack the logs. When the kilns were fired, the arched entranceways were closed with sheet-metal doors. The stone ruin behind the fourth kiln is a lime kiln. Loaded with wood, topped with limestone, and fired, it baked the limestone into

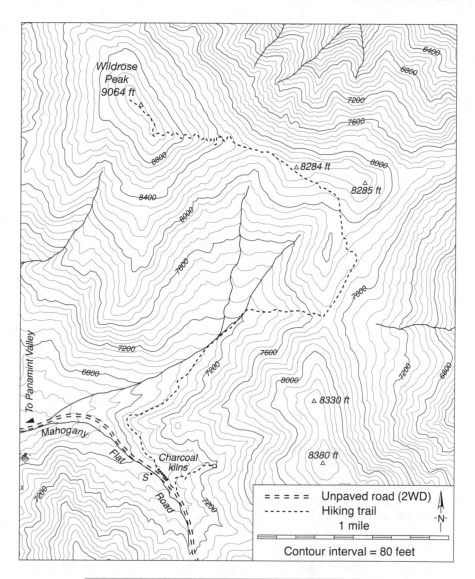

	Dist.(mi)	Elev.(ft)
Trailhead	0.0	6,870
Crest	1.75	7,740
False summit	2.95	8,280
Saddle	3.15	8,220
Wildrose Peak	4.2	9,064

Wildrose Peak

lime, which fell through a grate into a draw hole. The lime was probably used to make the kilns' mortar, and perhaps for ore milling and
cyaniding at the mine.

From the west end of the charcoal kilns the trail climbs steadily
along an open drainage, then more steeply through an increasingly
thick forest. The vegetation is largely mixed stands of pinyon pine (the
ground is covered with their fragrant cones) and Utah juniper (many
infested with mistletoe). The 100-year-old stumps along this part of the
trail are remains from logging operations when the kilns were active.
Many plants thrive here thanks to the higher elevations, including big
sagebrush, cliffrose, wild cabbage, tansybush, Panamint eriogonum,
and grizzly bear cactus. Several flowering species not so common in
the California desert bloom in the summer, including purple sage and
lupine. Surrounded on all sides by low desert, at that time of year this
sky island is a rare treat blessed with a comfortable mix of sun and
shade. After 1.7 miles the trail tops the crest, and the bright, sun-beat-
en expanse of Death Valley bursts into view. The scenery only gets better from here on up, but if your time or energy is limited, this is a great
place to enjoy the magnificent scenery before turning around.

The trail continues north near the crest, then reaches a false summit and a shallow saddle just beyond it. The last mile, most of it
switchbacks, is the steepest and most strenuous. Closer to the summit,
the greening process reverses itself. Discouraged by the nasty weather
that prevails several months of the year, the trees thin out and shrivel,
then disappear. The summit area is a long plateau of broken shale
where a scant cover of Mormon tea and patches of grizzly bear cactus
survive. In the winter it can be a bone-chilling place, covered with icy
snow and swept by fierce winds. The scenery then looks singularly
alpine, with muffled sounds and trees festooned with snow.

Wildrose Peak overlooks a huge territory. To the east the land tumbles more than 9,000 feet to Badwater Basin's and Cottonball Basin's
alkali flats, backed by the fierce scarp of the Black Mountains. To the
northeast rises the rugged wall of Trail Canyon, emblazoned with tilted parallel strata representing several hundred million years of
Paleozoic sedimentation. The white band in the middle of it is Eureka
Quartzite, a convenient geological marker that pinpoints the Middle
Ordovician, when sand rather than shells was deposited. The hulking
mass of Telescope Peak fills the southern horizon. To the west, beyond
the bleak volcanic expanse of the Darwin Plateau, the long sawtooth
crest of the Sierra Nevada shines brightly more than 60 miles away.

■

TELESCOPE PEAK

Named in 1861 by fortune seeker William Henderson, who was impressed by the vast panorama it commands, 11,049-foot Telescope Peak soars more than 2 miles above Death Valley and is one of the most prominent summits in the California desert. The 6.4-mile crest trail from Mahogany Flat to the summit is a scenic route across beautiful forested slopes. The other route—the grueling slog from the edge of Death Valley's salt flat, 253 feet below sea level, to the lofty summit—is Telescope Peak's greatest legacy, a unique opportunity to climb one of the largest continuous elevation gains under 15 miles in the conterminal U.S. Conquering this giant from this end is a tremendous experience charged with emotions. Both routes are memorable, and rewarded by sumptuous views covering tens of thousands of square miles.

General Information
Jurisdiction: Death Valley National Park
Road status: Hiking from graded or primitive road (HC)
The climb (Telescope Peak Trail): 6.4 mi, 3,200 ft up, 280 ft down
      one way / difficult–strenuous
The climb (Telescope Peak ridge): 14.6 mi, 11,800 ft up, 520 ft down
      one way / grueling
The climb (Bennett Pk): 3.0 mi, 1,950 ft up, 110 ft down one way / difficult
Main attractions: World-class trek, wet spring, forest, awesome views
USGS 7.5' topo maps: Hanaupah Canyon, Telescope Peak*
Maps: pp. 181*, 185*, 55

Location and Access
Telescope Peak is located near the middle of the Panamint Mountains. The Telescope Peak Trail starts in upper Wildrose Canyon, on the western slopes of the range. To get to it, drive to the charcoal kilns (see *Wildrose Peak*), then continue on the Mahogany Flat Road 1.6 miles to its end at Mahogany Flat. This last stretch is a little rough and steep at places, but in dry weather it is often manageable with a standard-clearance vehicle.

To climb Telescope Peak from Shorty's Well, from Highway 190 just south of The Ranch at Death Valley, drive the Badwater Road south 5.9 miles to the signed West Side Road on the right. Drive this good graded road 10.7 miles to a primitive road on the right, which is the Hanaupah Canyon Road, and park. Shorty's Well is located in the low mesquite grove to the east. If you are coming from the south on the Badwater Road, pick up the south end of the West Side Road instead, 28.9 miles from Highway 127 near Shoshone. Then drive the West Side Road 25.2 miles to the Hanaupah Canyon Road.

Route Description: Telescope Peak Trail

The maintained foot trail from Mahogany Flat to Telescope Peak is one of Death Valley's classics, and it is tackled every year by many visitors. The first part of the trail circles the east side of Rogers Peak, under a thick canopy of trees—mostly pinyon pine, with some juniper and scattered mountain mahogany. The small colorful slabs covering the ground are slate from the Johnnie Formation, a Proterozoic formation brought all the way up here by the same tectonic forces that pried Death Valley apart. In the summer, phlox, firecracker penstemon, purple sage, and many other flowering plants grow right between the slabs, in essentially humus-free ground. This somewhat steep stretch ends at Arcane Meadows, an open and barren pass, often wind-swept, offering the first glimpses of the Argus Range to the west.

If you cannot make it to Telescope Peak, try to push on to Bennett Peak, the summit south of Arcane Meadows. The route is straightforward, south up the narrow ridge about half a mile, with only 370 feet of elevation gain. Just shy of 10,000 feet, Bennett Peak commands great views of Death Valley and the precipitous upper drainage of Hanaupah Canyon, the carved flanks of Telescope Peak and the southern Panamint Mountains, and the Argus Range to the east—all this for less than half the effort of climbing Telescope Peak.

The next couple of miles essentially follow the high spine of the Panamints and are fairly level. The trail swings back and forth over the crest, and the views alternate between the east and the west sides. You will be continuously rewarded with awesome vistas of Death Valley,

Telescope Peak Trail		
	Dist.(mi)	Elev.(ft)
Trailhead	0.0	8,140
Arcane Meadows	2.5	~9,610
Bennett Peak	(0.5)	9,980
Fork to Eagle Spring	4.0	9,500
Eagle Spring	(1.1)	~9,300
Telescope Peak	6.4	11,049

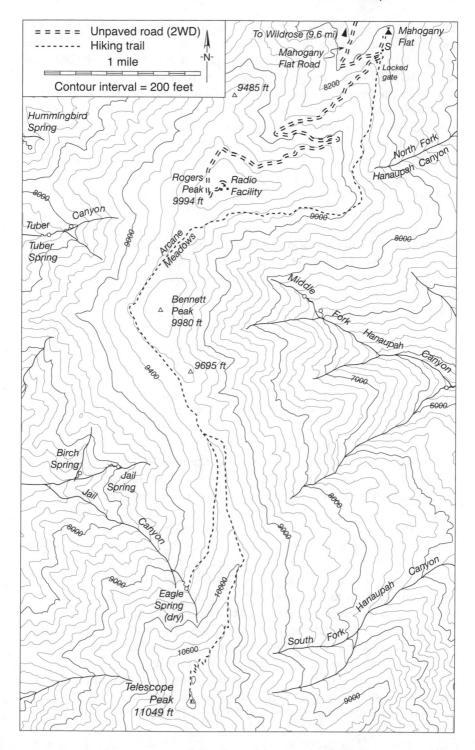

Unpaved road (2WD)
Hiking trail
1 mile
Contour interval = 200 feet

To Wildrose (9.6 mi)
Mahogany Flat Road
Mahogany Flat
Locked gate
9485 ft

Hummingbird Spring

North Fork
Hanaupah Canyon

Rogers Peak 9994 ft
Radio Facility

Tuber Canyon
Tuber Spring

Arcane Meadows

Middle Fork Hanaupah Canyon

Bennett Peak 9980 ft

9695 ft

Birch Spring
Jail Spring
Jail Canyon

Eagle Spring (dry)

South Fork

Hanaupah Canyon

Telescope Peak 11049 ft

Panamint Valley and the Argus Range, and several rugged canyons— Hanaupah Canyon on the east side, and Tuber and Jail canyons on the west side. The tree cover gradually thins to a woodland of limber pine and grizzled bristlecone pine. If you were transported to the same elevation in the Sierra Nevada, only 100 air miles away, you would be in the deep shade of a temperate forest, dwarfed by trees more than 100 feet tall. But as the Sierra Nevada robs most of the moisture from the Pacific Ocean, precipitation here is too scant, even this far up, to support such a luxuriant forest. Toward the end of this stretch, a side trail on the right climbs, then drops 1.1 miles into the drainage of Jail Canyon to Eagle Spring, the highest spring in the park.

The last segment is up tight switchbacks cut into the steep north face of Telescope Peak. Oxygen is a scarce commodity up here. If you are not used to this elevation you will grope for air and progress more slowly. Pause often to quiet your heart and smell the roses. Some of the largest trees in the park are found along here, impressive specimens several feet in diameter at the base and towering tens of feet overhead. Even late in the spring, high snow drifts may linger along the trail.

The ultimate rewards are the stunning views from Telescope Peak, which encompass much of the surrounding desert, from the hazy valley of Las Vegas to the southern Panamints' forest of mighty summits and the distant Sierra Nevada. From the rocky summit it is more than two vertical miles down to the eerie swirls of Death Valley's salt pan— to get higher above ground in the lower 48 states, you will have to fly.

Route Description: Climbing The Wall

The trek up "The Wall" is the one of the most challenging climbs in the California desert, second to the grueling San Jacinto Peak ascent from Coachella Valley. Crossing the Grand Canyon in one day is much easier—it is half as much elevation gain and there is a trail the whole way. Only a chosen few can do this climb in one day. Get a very early start. In the cooler season you will need all the hours of daylight you can get. In the warm season the hike up the fan is long, hot, and shadeless. Gaining as much elevation as possible before the sun is too high is essential. Since from the summit it is still 6.4 trail miles to return to the closest road, most people will want to take at least two days, and/or cache food, water, and camping gear along the trail. The most direct route has no water, unless there is snow on the ground, but then you do not want too much of it... Timing is everything.

From Shorty's Well, for the first 4.9 miles the Hanaupah Canyon Road traverses the canyon's gigantic alluvial fan. The slope averages a mere 8%, and the road makes for relatively smooth walking. About 1

Snow-covered Telescope Peak reflected in flooded Badwater Basin

mile up the fan it crosses the Hanaupah escarpment, a 50- to 75-foot step that parallels the mountains for miles, formed by block faulting during the sinking of Death Valley. The Panamint Mountains' eastern scarp soaring to the west is impressive. Few places in the desert offer such awesome perspectives of so much vertical land.

At the top of the fan, the road reaches the mouth of Hanaupah Canyon and drops along a steep ramp cut in the bank to the canyon's broad wash. It then proceeds up canyon 1.3 miles to the first major fork. Here you have to make a decision: either continue up the road, or climb onto the ridge separating the two forks. The first option will take you 2.1 miles into the south fork. You will get to stay longer on the road, enjoy the wet spring in the canyon, which will greatly alleviate the water limitation (do purify the spring water!), and it will shorten the cross-country portion of the climb, but the climb out of the canyon will be tougher. If you choose the ridge instead, the elevation change and distance will be sensibly the same and the climbing less brutal, but it will be cross-country and waterless the whole way.

Hanaupah Canyon's South Fork is one of Death Valley's grandest canyons. By the time you reach the end of the road, you are entrenched in a deep rocky gorge, and a little stream will likely have materialized in the wash—the first sign of Hanaupah Spring's remarkable oasis. About 1 mile further, the canyon opens up onto one of the lushest springs in Death Valley, acres upon acres of unbelievably green fields of grapevine, willow, and mesquite irrigated by a perennial creek. The contrast with the parched lower canyon and fan is stunning.

This area was once the base camp of Shorty Borden, a former U. S. Cavalry soldier who mined here in the 1930s. He built the original access road to Hanaupah Canyon, reportedly with hand tools, a burro, and a little dynamite, and dug the well that bears his name at the lower end of the road. His camp, on the south side of the wash, had a three-room house and a shower house. All that is left now is scattered junk, and the carcass of a bug-eyed car up canyon. Above the camp the vigorous stream plunges over boulders and bubbles into watercress-covered pools alive with water-skimmers, swarms of larvae, and toads. Fed by rain and snow from the high Panamints, it has one of the largest flows of any canyon in Death Valley—a respectable 50 to 200 gallons per minute. In the late summer and early fall, the wild grapevine bear small blue grapes that were part of the Panamint Indian diet. Many other plants abound—cattail, grasses, sacred datura, coyote melon, cliffrose, and carpets of prickly-pear. To avoid damaging this sensitive oasis, bypass it on the old road on its north side. Overgrown and badly damaged, it is a little tricky to find: look for small trails connecting to it northwest of Borden's camp.

After a few hundred yards, a narrow trail on the left drops back down to the wash. As spectacular as Hanaupah Canyon's south fork is (see *Hiking Death Valley*), I do not recommend it if your goal is to reach Telescope Peak in a day. It has serious obstacles, including an exposed Class-5 25-foot fall. Instead, climb out of the canyon starting at the trail, a Class-2 climb over a 40% grade covered with large slabs.

	Dist.(mi)	Elev.(ft)
The Wall: Shorty's Well to Telescope Peak		
Shorty's Well	0.0	-253
Grade to wash/Hanaupah Cyn	4.9	~1,700
North/South Fork confluence	6.2	2,200
East end of promontory	8.5	5,303
Start of steepest (last) segment	10.3	5,660
Telescope Peak Trail	~13.2	9,920
Telescope Peak	~14.6	11,049

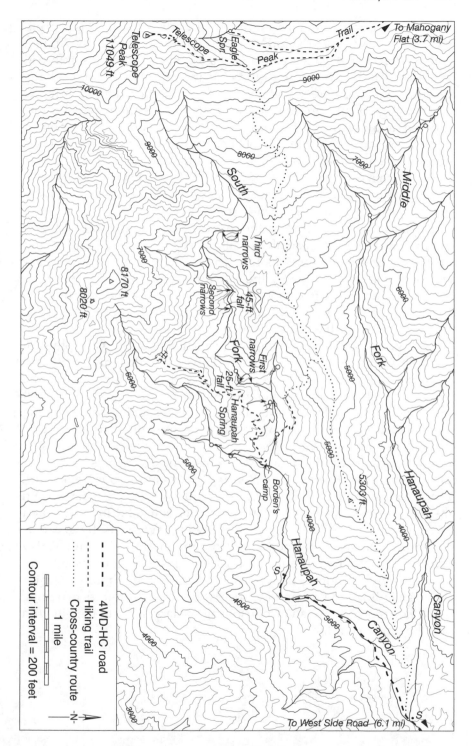

To Mahogany Flat (3.7 mi)

Telescope Peak 11049 ft

Telescope Peak Trail

Eagle Spr.

South

Third narrows

Second narrows

45-ft fall

First narrows

25-ft fall

Fork

Hanaupah Spring

8170 ft

8020 ft

Middle

Fork

Hanaupah

Borden's camp

5303 ft

Hanaupah Canyon

Canyon

To West Side Road (6.1 mi)

4WD-HC road
Hiking trail
Cross-country route

1 mile

Contour interval = 200 feet

-N-

The ridge route is much more straightforward—but it is a grind most of the way. From the fork to the trail it is approximately 7 miles, with 8,220 feet of elevation gain and 500 feet of elevation loss. In broad strokes, it can be divided into three segments about 2–3 miles long, each one with a different rhythm. The first one, from the wash to the eastern edge of the promontory at 5,303 feet, is the rockiest, most exposed, and much of it is quite steep. The first juniper, then pinyon pine, grow part way up this sun-baked segment. The second segment is unexpectedly level, a ridge that swells up and down half a dozen times but gains and loses only a few hundred feet of elevation. Its open forest provides welcome shade, although it too has some loose, ankle-twisting fields of slate. The third segment, from the saddle at 5,660 feet to the Telescope Peak Trail, is the longest, increasingly forested, and locally the steepest. Unusually rebellious vegetation, fallen trees, and unstable screes make portions of it frustratingly difficult. The upper end of this segment, roughly the last mile, is a steep open meadow essentially devoid of trees, mostly slices of slate partly embedded in softer ground. The ridge ends at the Telescope Peak Trail (elev. 9,920′), about 1.4 miles north of the summit.

It is grueling. It will challenge your mental strength, your physical endurance, and your ability to control swearing. But the payoffs are unequalled. From shortly after the start of the ridge you will be rewarded with constant eye-filling views of the Amargosa Range and the gulf of Death Valley to the east, gradually deepening and widening as you climb. Higher up you will be moving through a refreshing landscape dominated by trees, constantly looking up ahead at the forested ridge rising majestically to the distant crest. The diversity is as spectacular as the span in elevation. You will cross numerous vegetation zones, run across wildflowers almost any day of the year, travel from the driest environment to land where water is a solid in winter, and likely experience a 50°F temperature swing. Few sensations are as exhilarating as reaching the highest mountain around Death Valley after a journey of such epic proportions. From two miles up and almost anywhere along the last two hours of the climb, Badwater Basin's blinding salt flats and the succession of desert ranges marching to the horizon compose an awe-inspiring scenery likely to remain with you the rest of your life.

■

SENTINEL PEAK

Sentinel Peak puts up a great fight. Just to get to the mountain itself you will have to cross a lush oasis, climb through polished narrows flushed by a vivacious creek, and trudge up a deep canyon to the ruins of legendary Panamint City. It is then a hard climb through a forested canyon and up a sheer crest of liquid taluses to the barren summit where a relic grove of bristlecone pine survives. Few are the climbs that offer such thrilling diversity.

General Information
Jurisdiction: Surprise Canyon Wilderness, Death Valley National Park
Road status: Abandoned road in canyon; primitive access road (HC)
The climb: 8.5 mi, 7,040 ft up, 40 ft down one way/grueling in one day
Main attractions: Creek, narrows, ghost town, forest, a long hard climb
USGS 7.5' topo maps: Ballarat, Panamint
Maps: pp. 191*, 55

Location and Access
Sentinel Peak is on the high crest of the central Panamints, 5 air miles south of Telescope Peak. The rare people who tackle this challenging summit typically climb it from Panamint Valley via Surprise Canyon. To get there, drive Highway 190 to the Panamint Valley Road, which is 47.7 miles east from Olancha on Highway 395, or 28 miles west of Stovepipe Wells in Death Valley. Drive this road south 13.8 miles to its end at the Trona-Wildrose Road. Turn right and go 9.4 miles to the Ballarat Road on the left. Coming from the south, this junction is about 22 miles north of the market in Trona. The oiled Ballarat Road cuts northeast across the South Panamint Playa and ends in 3.6 miles at Ballarat, pop. 1. From Ballarat's general store, go 2 miles north on the graded Indian Ranch Road to a sign that points right to the Surprise Canyon Road. The road climbs 2.3 miles on the canyon fan, then 1.7 miles into Surprise Canyon to Chris Wicht Camp. It is an impressive ride, along a narrow wash dwarfed by colorful walls and sheer taluses. It is a little steep and usually requires good clearance.

Once a shady nook under thick cottonwoods, Chris Wicht Camp was occupied off and on for 130 years, starting in the 1870s. Chris Wicht, Ballarat's bartender, lived here for years. Rocky Novak and his father George moved in in the early 1980s, until the camp was destroyed by fire in 2006. Rocky became Ballarat's caretaker.

187

Route Description

This climb starts with a bang. From Chris Wicht Camp up to Limekiln Spring, a distance of 1.8 miles, Surprise Canyon is an idyllic oasis coursed by a spirited stream. You walk by a cottonwood-shaded creek, splashing through cold water at occasional crossings. By the time you reach the narrows, half a mile up canyon, you are walking *in* the creek. The walls are vertical, solid aplite nearly one billion years old, as white as driven snow. Every streamside rock surface has been polished into gleaming slickrock. Willows, grass, rush, and rare orchids border the banks. The narrows gradually tighten up, until there are no more banks, only hard rock and water. The creek gushes over bedrock lips, sluices down grooved chutes, and foams into dark potholes. There are even waterfalls, gently sloped and 4 to 15 feet high, negotiated on slippery boulders or up dry slickrock.

Past the narrows, the road resumes along the broad canyon. The water fun lasts another mile. The stream flows mostly in the road, switching abruptly from full sun to shady willows. Butterflies, dragon-flies (and horse flies in summer) are common. Little green frogs are often parked by the stream. Limekiln Spring is a billowing mass of grapevine spilling down the north canyon slope. Most of the stream gushes out from under it at hundreds of gallons per minute. The second outlet is in the wash around the next bend, hidden under willows and salt cedars. Above it, the tree cover ends and the canyon is dry. The next water is at Brewery Spring, a half-mile-long ribbon of willows that fills the wash. The road bypasses its lower half, then scoots under the spring's canopy and crosses it along cool tunnels of violet penumbra. A swift creek floods the road, irrigating sidewalks of water-cress and nettle. Together with Limekiln Spring, this is one of the few haunts of the rare Panamint alligator lizard. It is also the last chance to fill up: the remaining 2.4 miles to Panamint City are dry again.

Panamint City came to life in 1873, following the discovery of silver in a canyon so unexpectedly green that it became known as Surprise. It occurred in the wake of the rich strikes at Cerro Gordo and Nevada's Comstock, and it sparked a mad rush. By year's end every square foot of ground that showed the slightest promise had been claimed, and the town's mixed citizenry of miners and merchants had topped the 100 mark. The boom was fueled largely by the involvement of two Nevada senators. They purchased almost every claim in sight, organized a company to run the town, and erected a monumental mill and roasting furnace. During its brief life in 1875-1876, most days the mill put out $1,300 of nearly pure silver bullion. As a clever protection against Panamint City's thieves, the silver was cast into 400-pound

Surprise Canyon from below the slope northwest of Sentinel Peak

ingots, too heavy to lift. The company shipped $300,000 of silver by mule team without a single robbery. At its apogee Panamint City was as wild as any boom town in the West, with a population that peaked around 2,000 and a lawlessness that made national headlines. Main Street, the town's mile-long and only artery, offered saloons, gambling halls, and a red light district, fresh bread and cakes, oysters, meat, boots, garments, medication, and jewelry. It had a doctor, a barber, a stagecoach, its own newspaper, and even a French restaurant.

In spite of all the hype, silver was not so plentiful. By 1876 the best veins had played out. In May, two of the company principals were indicted for past fraudulent activities, and the mines went from boom to bust overnight. Until 1882, a few dozen workers remained and the mill was fired up off and on. By 1895 the town was a mere shadow of its former self. But its early fame incentivized sporadic mining until as late as the 1980s. By then the town's aging shacks were occupied by a handful of vets and hippies enjoying free rent on government land. In the end, Panamint City was a spectacular loss. A century of mining returned only about $600,000, most of it in the 1870s, a fraction of the total investment. But it was one of Death Valley's greatest adventures.

Panamint City is beautifully situated in a secluded valley enclosed by 3,000-foot forested slopes. The first signs of it are stone ruins along the road starting at Marvel Canyon: dozens of them, the ghosts of the 1870s homes and businesses that lined Main Street. There are rooms, walls, dugouts, stairs, and beds of ornamental irises decorating sidewalks long gone. The town center is announced by the improbably tall smokestack of Panamint City's smelter. Built of half a million bricks, it is a magnificent 45-foot tower tapering from a massive square base to an ornate crown. Erected in 1875 at a cost of $210,000, it was the Panamint mines' pride, and it survives today as their finest symbol.

The heart of town is just beyond, at a crossroad on the valley floor—a two-room plywood cabin, a large workshop, and a huge quarried-stone quadrangle. The cabin's glass windows and tap water have earned it the nickname of Panamint City Hilton. A row of four wooden cabins on the north side, and the colorful buildings of a mill on the south side, overlook the valley. Visitors sometimes use the cabins, huddling by their stove on chilly nights. The mill and valley-floor buildings were in use in the 1970s and 1980s when the Wyoming Mine and a few other mines were active. The town was then powered by the antique Pelton wheel housed in the easternmost cabin. The mill is the finest and most elaborate example of a modern mill in the park.

The traditional route to Sentinel Peak is southeast up Frenchman's Canyon to Panamint Pass, then south along the crest. From Panamint City, the main road goes 0.25 mile to the water tank at Slaughterhouse Spring. The wide forested opening 0.1 mile further on the right is Frenchman's Canyon. In historic times a road bounced along its tumbled wash and linked Panamint City to Swiss Ranch in Johnson

Sentinel Peak		
	Dist.(mi)	Elev.(ft)
Chris Wicht Camp	0.0	2,630
End of narrows	0.8	3,295
Limekiln Spring	1.8	3,945
Brewery Spring	3.1	4,810
Hemlock Mine Road	4.45	5,770
Panamint City (road junction)	5.45	~6,290
Frenchman's Canyon	~5.8	~6,480
Panamint Pass	7.4	8,070
Junction with ridge	7.75	8,680
Sentinel Peak	8.5	9,634

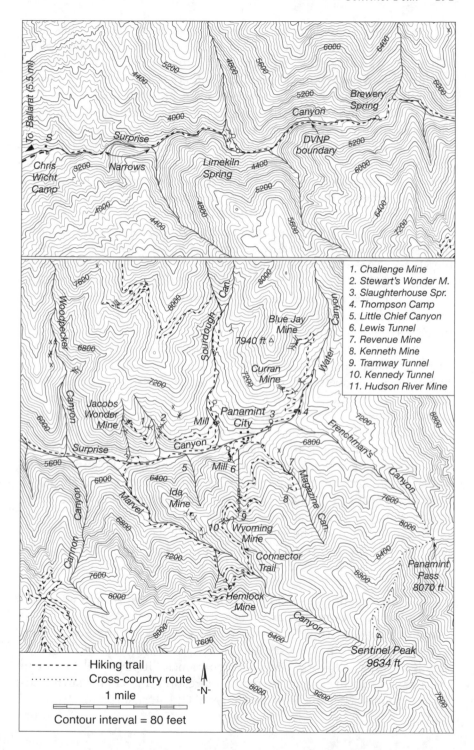

1. Challenge Mine
2. Stewart's Wonder M.
3. Slaughterhouse Spr.
4. Thompson Camp
5. Little Chief Canyon
6. Lewis Tunnel
7. Revenue Mine
8. Kenneth Mine
9. Tramway Tunnel
10. Kennedy Tunnel
11. Hudson River Mine

- - - - - - - Hiking trail
. . . . Cross-country route
1 mile
-N-

Contour interval = 80 feet

Canyon, which provided fresh vegetables. Much of the road has now been washed out, buried by slides, and reclaimed by pinyon pine. What little remains still helps climb the steep canyon. The wash is sprinkled with well-rounded granitic boulders, fragrant big sagebrush, and Indian paintbrush and other wildflowers after late spring.

Panamint Pass is a wooded saddle offering a tantalizing preview of panoramas to come. To the west it overlooks Surprise Canyon's lofty rim, and to the east Death Valley's blinding abyss. To the north the crest is straddled by a stunning band of reddish fins and cliffs, the Cretaceous formation known as Little Chief Porphyry that delivered the silver mined in the past. At this point you have covered nearly 90% of the distance but a fraction of the difficulty. To the south the crest shoots straight up through a forest sprinkled with outcrops. Obstacles must often be circumvented awkwardly, sideways across steep unstable slopes. The worst spot is a talus of loose rocks that careens hundreds of feet down at the angle of repose. At the junction with a ridge coming up from Surprise Canyon, the pinyon pine reach their limit and give up. Above, it is almost all bare rock, the product of a high desert too cold in winter, too hot in summer, and windy too often. The crest narrows to a precarious wedge, too precipitous to stand on the east side, steep and unstable on the west side. A series of rocky summits must be climbed or circumvented just to get to see Sentinel Peak, and a few more after to reach it. This is a wild landscape, stressed and emaciated, where frigid lichen, scrawny ephedra, and the twisted, erect trunks of dead pine accentuate more than hide the nakedness.

From the summit as from the ridge the views are superb, and constant excuses for a break. Below the summit the land falls into Death Valley like a stone, in tight battalions of sharp outcrops, too abrupt to hold but a scatter of valiant bristlecone pine. From nearly two miles up, the valley is daunting in its depth and immensity. Mountains ripple in every direction. The satisfaction of having conquered this persistently gnarly bit of ground is exhilarating. Years later, you may well remember this climb as your most extraordinary trip in the desert wilds.

For this strenuous ascent bordering on epic, most people will need to set up a base camp in Panamint City. Water is luckily available at Slaughterhouse Spring, in lower Water Canyon, at the Sourdough Canyon spring, at the largest cabin on the north side, and in Panamint City if the taps still work. Given the remoteness, it pays to throw in an extra day or two to explore the many interesting ruins in the surrounding mountains. They are Surprise Canyon's greatest surprise.

∎

SLIMS PEAK

From the great ghost town of Clair Camp in rugged Pleasant Canyon, this thrilling climb ascends the steep canyon wall, first on a twisted mining road, then cross country, to the high canyon rim and Slims Peak. There are plenty of opportunities to check out ruins of early-twentieth-century gold mining, the upper canyon is pleasantly forested, and the view into Panamint Valley a befitting climax.

General Information

Jurisdiction: Public lands (BLM)
Road status: Roadless; primitive access road (HC-4WD)
The climb: 2.8 mi, 2,280 ft up, 320 ft down one way / difficult
Main attractions: Ghost town, mines, burros, springs and creek, views
USGS 7.5' topo maps: Ballarat*, Panamint*
Maps: pp. 195*, 55

Location and Access

Slims Peak was named in honor of Charles Ferge, a prospector who came to Ballarat in the mid-1910s and lived there until his death in 1968. Tall and lean, prone to seclusion and grumpiness, he was known to all as Seldom Seen Slim. Ballarat had flourished between around 1890 and the early 1910s as a lively supply and entertainment center for miners working in the Panamints, and it was already declining when Slim arrived. Slim continued to make a living prospecting, mining, and selling rocks. He outlived all of the colorful characters who fueled the local mining history—Pete Aguereberry, Harry Porter, Carl Mengel, Chris Wicht, Shorty Harris—ultimately becoming Ballarat's sole resident and the last single-blanket jackass prospector.

You will first need to get to Ballarat, a lonesome drive from any direction (see *Sentinel Peak*). At the signed cross-road 50 yards south of the general store, head northeast up the Pleasant Canyon Road. At the two consecutive forks 0.5 mile out, bear right, and in 0.4 mile you will enter Pleasant Canyon. The rest requires high clearance, and four-wheel drive in spots. For the next 2 miles the road brushes by Pleasant Canyon's luxuriant spring of mesquite, baccharis, and willow festooned with grapevine, crossing its narrow creek half a dozen times.

After 6.1 miles is Clair Camp, at the base of a high-rising canyon wall. The small town sprang from the discovery of gold in 1896 at the nearby Ratcliff and World Beater mines. The gold rush put Ballarat on the map, and it opened the western Panamints to its second wave of mining, years after Panamint City had fizzled. Mostly active until 1903–1905, the mines produced $630,000 in gold. Around 1930 a man named W. D. Clair installed a large processing plant at the old camp to treat the Ratcliff's tailings, and he cleaned out another $80,000. Clair Camp is one of the region's greatest ghost towns. It has stone dugouts, several cabins from the 1930s, and Clair's elaborate mill. One of its crushers is a steel behemoth that ground the ore by tumbling it with sections of rail. The steam power plant's boilers and giant cogwheels are still there. From the partitioned ore bin above the mill the tramway cables point 1,800 feet up the mountain to the Ratcliff Mine. Slims Peak is almost directly past it, and as far up again. The Ratcliff Mine was re-opened by a small outfit in the early 2010s. Some camp cabins have been refurbished for the miners. Expect company, and respect all signs. The burros have recolonized the haunts of their forefathers, and they often hang around town and along the spring.

One mile past Clair Camp, a road on the right climbs to the World Beater and the Ratcliff mines. With a high-clearance, four-wheel-drive vehicle, it can get you much closer to Slims Peak. But it is a rough and hairy drive, and you may prefer to park and climb from this junction.

Route Description

The route to Slims Peak starts up Pleasant Canyon's south slope on the World Beater Mine Road to just above the Ratcliff Mine, then cross-country up to the canyon rim. The road first climbs moderately half a mile, past a nicely restored cabin, to a left U-bend next to the ruins of the World Beater Mine's 10-stamp mill. This historically significant site has many interesting remains. The mill's large steel boiler resting on its stone cradle is a fine example of a steam power plant. Concrete foundations, giant axles, and wheels bear witness to the size of the operations. The gold came out of half a dozen adits strewn above the mill. A cableway still connects the mill's ore bin to the main adit.

Past the World Beater Mine the road switchbacks up onto a broad ridge to timberline, then climbs straight up. About 800 feet above the mill it veers west and levels off as it cuts in and out of several sheer ravines, flirting with disaster along the plunging canyon wall. Across the deep gash of Pleasant Canyon, the opposite wall looks huge. After 1.3 miles the road crests as it crosses a northwest-southeast ridge, just before angling right and down toward the Ratcliff Mine. Slims Peak is the highest of the two adjacent bumps on the divide with Middle Park Canyon, 600 feet up to the southwest. The best route is up the ridge. The mountain is an open woodland of pinyon pine, some with forked

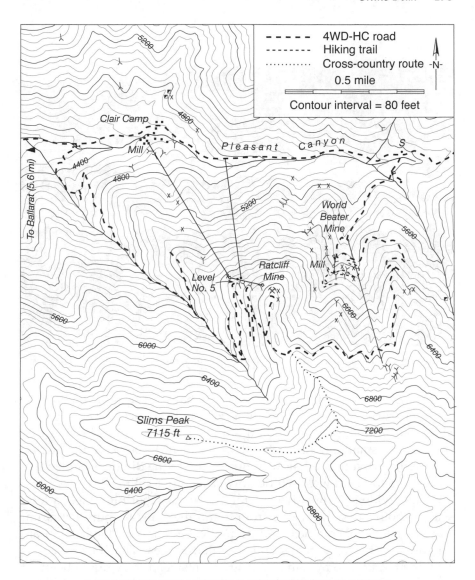

Slims Peak

	Dist.(mi)	Elev.(ft)
Foot of World Beater Mine Rd	0.0	5,160
World Beater Mine (mill)	0.5	5,520
Road crosses ridge (leave road)	1.8	6,520
Divide	2.2	7,280
Slims Peak	2.8	7,115

Panamint Valley's salt flats and Argus Range from ridge below Slims Peak

trunks over 30 feet tall. The valley plants have given way to ephedra, big sagebrush, and fuzzy spreads of grizzly bear cactus. The ascent is short but quite steep (40%!) and slippery, over unconsolidated dirt mixed with small angular slabs. It would help to be, as Slim claimed he was, half coyote and half wild burro... Once the divide is gained it is a breeze to follow it west, a little down then up, to Slims Peak.

The divide is impressive, a straight catwalk that plummets a long way on both sides. The views from it and the peak are pure Panamint Mountains, deep, complex, and dramatic. On almost all sides you are surrounded by lofty peaks and tumbled ridges. The centerpiece is Panamint Valley, compelling in its graceful sweep. Way down below it stretches for miles, from its slender salt playa to its dry lake and far-off star dunes pinned against Hunter Mountain. Across the valley rises the long wall of the Argus Range. Maturango Peak, its high point, is just across the way, its east face drained by a prominent canyon that issues onto the valley in a tremendous fan. If you go just a little further, you will get even better views west, and catch a glimpse of Ballarat's scattered buildings, Slim's home for more than 50 years and his final resting place, slowly dissolving into the landscape.

■

PORTER PEAK

This one takes determination. It is a long hard drive through remote, spring-fed Pleasant Canyon just to get to the start at historic Rogers Pass. The forested crest that winds up to Mormon Peak, then Porter Peak, is a steep roller coaster packed with trees and rock slides. The panorama is breathtaking, and the geology will break a rockhound's heart. The view changes constantly, from isolated Butte Valley to Middle Park and from Death Valley's vast alkali flats to the central Panamint Mountains' loftiest summits.

General Information
Jurisdiction: Death Valley National Park
Road status: Roadless; primitive access road (HC-4WD)
The climb (Mormon Pk): 1.2 mi, 1,180 ft up, 70 ft down one way / mod.
The climb (Porter Pk): 3.4 mi, 2,430 ft up, 490 ft down one way / difficult
Main attractions: A forested ridge with deep views, geology, wildlife
USGS 7.5' topo map: Panamint
Maps: pp. 199*, 55

Location and Access
Porter Peak (9,101') is on the crest of the southern Panamints north of Rogers Pass, at the head of Pleasant Canyon. Drive to Clair Camp in Pleasant Canyon (see *Slims Peak*), then continue up through the increasingly forested canyon. You will pass by the World Beater Mine Road on the right (1 mile), the Porter Mine Road (2.3 miles), Cooper Mine Road (2.35 miles), and Mormon Gulch Road (3.85 miles), all on the left, and the junction to the Pine Tree Cabin on the right (4.0 miles). Porter Peak is first visible around the Cooper Mine Road, soaring to the northeast. Mormon Peak is just south of it. Park at Rogers Pass on the crest, 5.4 miles from Clair Camp. In the early 2010s miners at the Ratcliff Mine graded the Pleasant Canyon Road up to Clair Camp, so this stretch is not too rough. The rest of the road is rocky and very slow going. Past the Pine Tree Cabin deep wavering trenches eroded in the center of the road make perfect traps for lighter vehicles. A four-wheel-drive vehicle with excess power and clearance is mandatory.

Route Description
Rogers Pass holds a special place in Death Valley's human history. It is here that on February 14, 1850, John Rogers and William Manly

197

famously led the Bennett-Arcane party out of Death Valley. The party waited and starved nearly a month at what is now Bennetts Well in the valley while the two men scouted a route to San Fernando and brought back supplies. Upon leaving the scene of their ordeal, one of the members uttered the famous words "Good bye, Death Valley!" that gave the valley its name. From the pass, the sight of rows of desert ranges was a befitting farewell to the country they had crossed—and perhaps a disheartening vision of the country that still lay ahead.

From Rogers Pass it is 1.2 miles north along the crest to Mormon Peak. There is a beat-up road at first, closed to vehicles, up and down a low hill, then up again until it fades in 0.6 mile. The rest is a steep cross-country ascent split into two types of terrain, open taluses of large angular rocks and smoother ground covered with trees. Much of the time you have to pick your battle. The ridge commands singular views into Butte Valley, not much different from what the 49ers must have seen. With as many as 200 trees per acre, the woodland is quite forest-like, mostly pinyon pine, some with trunks two feet across, and scattered mountain mahogany. Cliffrose, exalted by the altitude, grow with stout branches, shredding bark, and the dignity of a tree. Wildlife enjoys the four-season weather. We saw falcon, tens of quails, Steller's jays bickering in the trees, collared lizards, hyperactive ground squirrels and rabbits, and a bighorn so furtive it might have been a ghost.

The crest leads directly to Mormon Peak, a broad plateau too densely wooded for a panorama. Not that you would want to hang around, being as it is a stone's throw from a massive microwave repeater, installed in the 1980s to service Death Valley. But the outcrop west of the summit is a good wide-open spot to soak in the scenery, especially if this is your turning point. It overlooks Middle Park's curious suspended valley, Pleasant Canyon's crazy green slopes, and the long crest of the Panamint Mountains winding up to Porter Peak.

To continue to Porter Peak, first cross the summit plateau northeast about 0.2 mile, then stay on the crest as it veers northwest and hops down over rocky ledges. At the bottom, a long and slender land bridge braced by sheer slopes links Mormon Peak to the lower slopes of Porter Peak. On one side it plunges into forested Pleasant Canyon, on the other into Six Spring Canyon, dried bare by Death Valley's fiery breath. The fierce winds have sculpted the pine into stunted works of art. Badwater Basin's alkali sink sprawls a long way down, blinding against the Black Mountains' stark 50-mile escarpment. From the north end of the land bridge, the final pitch to Porter Peak is a similar mix of unstable taluses and mad woodland, except steeper—nearly 1,000 feet in only 0.6 mile—with even more rarefied oxygen.

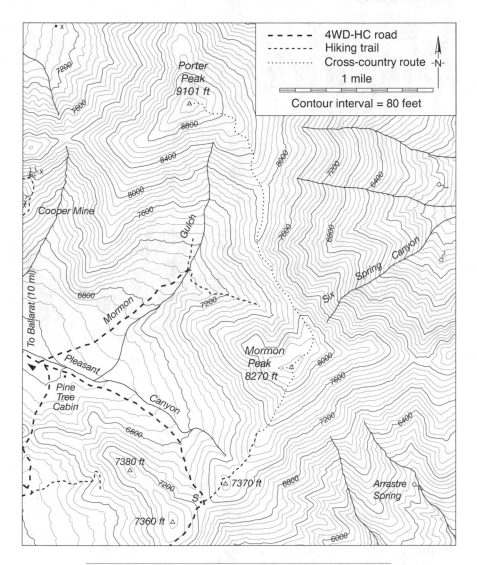

Porter Peak

	Dist.(mi)	Elev.(ft)
Rogers Pass	0.0	7,165
Hilltop (7,370T point)	0.2	7,370
Saddle	0.35	7,300
Mormon Peak	1.2	8,270
Middle of land bridge	1.8	7,860
Porter Peak	3.4	9,101

Six Spring Canyon and Badwater Basin from the land bridge to Porter Peak

What got me on this climb was the unusually diverse and atypical geology, almost all of it metamorphic. The lower taluses are all angular quartzite, whitish streaked with red stains. The middle section is dark-gray slate, its surface exfoliated in closed patterns as rhythmic as a written language. The ledges down to the land bridge are ancient sand beds hardened into pink sandstone and graywacke. The land bridge is the most impressive, a litter of small ink-black slate shingles peppered with tiny gold- and silver-colored flakes. The area is unexpectedly luminous, the isolated clumps of ephedra and grizzly bear cactus seemingly shining from within against the somber ground.

Porter Peak offers on a grander scale all of the views collected along the climb, plus a seldom-seen perspective of Sentinel Peak and Telescope Peak. To the south, Middle Park takes center stage, backed by creased ridges marching out to the Slate Range and Searles Lake's enormous salt lake beyond. Early morning in the wintertime, when the sun knifes in from Nevada, you might be lucky and witness a rare sight—the Amargosa River, resuscitated by rainstorms, shining in the sunlight on its age-old journey into Death Valley.

■

STRIPED BUTTE

> *Striped Butte is the beautifully sculpted small mountain stranded in the middle of Butte Valley, a scenic high-desert valley in the remote southern reaches of the Panamint Mountains. Composed of highly contrasted stratification of light-colored limestone, it is one of the most striking mountains in the Death Valley region. The climb is quite short and moderately, and from close up the striations are spectacular.*

General Information
Jurisdiction: Death Valley National Park
Road status: Roadless; long primitive HC-4WD access road
The climb: 0.6 mi, 840 ft one way / moderate
The loop climb: 2.4 mi, 1,860 ft loop / moderate
Main attractions: A remote scenic butte, wild burros, springs, camps
USGS 7.5' topo maps: Anvil Spring Canyon East, Anvil Spring Canyon West, Manly Peak*
Maps: pp. 203*, 55

Location and Access
To get to Butte Valley, from Highway 190 at The Ranch at Death Valley drive the Badwater Road 16.5 miles to Badwater, then 25.4 miles further to the south end of the West Side Road, on the right. Coming from the opposite direction, this junction is 8.5 miles from Jubilee Pass. Drive 2.9 miles north on the West Side Road to the Warm Spring Canyon Road, on the left. Take this road up through colorful Warm Spring Canyon, past Warm Spring Camp, shaded under well-watered cottonwoods, and the remains of several large historic talc mines. After 18.0 miles the canyon road crests the long open pass into Butte Valley. The road then descends southwest into Butte Valley and skirts the eastern foot of Striped Butte. About 2.5 miles from the pass, turn right onto the Redlands Canyon Road. Park after 0.7 mile, at a fork next to the butte's southern tip. The Warm Spring Canyon Road is in decent shape up to the camp, but the rest of this route is rocky and requires high clearance; four-wheel drive helps negotiate the few rougher areas.

Route Description
Rising sharply from Butte Valley's open floor like a forsaken pyramid, Striped Butte is a beautiful and enormously tempting destination.

Striped Butte looking north toward the pass into Warm Spring Canyon

All of it is made of the limestone beds of the Bird Spring Formation, which still display their tidy stratification in spite of severe tilting and folding. The west slope is a sinuous tapestry of upturned beds alternating between white, blue-gray, and dark gray. The east side is a sheer escarpment exposing a twisted core of tight recumbent folds. Striped Butte's singular location and its stratification's pronounced southeastward tilt are linked to the Butte Valley Fault, an enigmatic semi-circular fault that roughly follows northern Warm Spring Canyon and curves south into Butte Valley just west of the butte. Some evidence suggests that it is a thrust fault that has been active since at least the Late Jurassic. Striped Butte's tilt would then have been caused by dragging along the fault's lower plate. Other evidence hints that it might be instead a steep fault formed during the collapse of a caldera centered on upper Anvil Spring Canyon, just south of Butte Valley. The tilting would then have occurred when the butte slipped southeast toward the center of the sinking caldera.

The most spectacular route up Striped Butte is the south ridge, along the sharp edge of its eastern escarpment. From the butte's southern tip climb onto, then along the ridge. The slope increases gradually, eventually reaching 45% midway to the summit. There are lots of loose

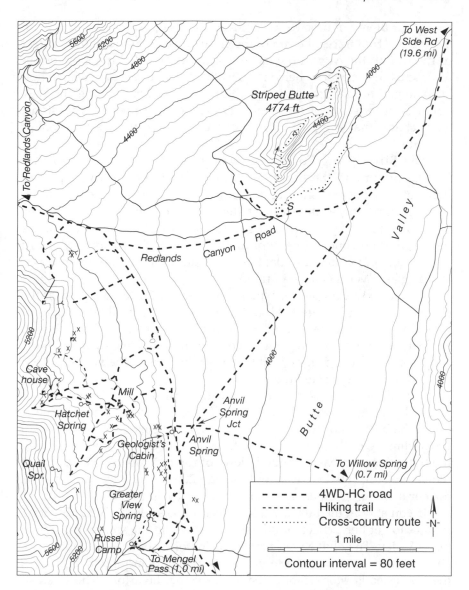

Striped Butte
4774 ft

To West
Side Rd
(19.6 mi)

To Redlands Canyon

Striped Butte
4774 ft

S

Valley

Redlands   Canyon   Road

Cave
house

Mill

Hatchet
Spring

Geologist's
Cabin

Anvil
Spring
Jct

Anvil
Spring

Butte

To Willow Spring
(0.7 mi)

Quail
Spr.

Greater
View
Spring

Russel
Camp

To Mengel
Pass (1.0 mi)

	4WD-HC road
	Hiking trail
	Cross-country route

-N-

1 mile

Contour interval = 80 feet

Striped Butte

	Dist.(mi)	Elev.(ft)
Western foot of Striped Butte	0.0	3,935
Striped Butte	0.6	4,774
Northern foot of Striped Butte	1.2	4,085
Back along east side	2.4	3,935

rocks, but plenty of base rocks for steady footing. Above the midpoint, a steep use trail traces the rim of the escarpment, staying within 50 feet of the rim all the way to the narrow summit. Small clumps of cotton-top cactus thrive everywhere, as do isolated beavertail cactus and cholla, pale-green ephedra, and rust-colored buckwheat. Along the way you will cross some of the steep channels etched into the limestone, giant chutes that wiggle hundreds of feet down to the western foot of the butte.

The Bird Spring Formation was deposited between the Late Mississippian and the Early Permian, when the region was part of Pangea's continental shelf and teeming with tropical life. The limestone is crawling with stromatolites (algae colonies), crinoids (sea lilies), fusulinids (amebas), and several species of corals. A few areas have septarian concretions, typical of carbonate formations. Mustard and orange jasper are abundant as loose pieces along the lower ridge, and as glassy veins near the summit.

The summit commands expansive views of Butte Valley, from the chiseled scarp of Needle Peak to Mengel Pass, the bouldery slopes of pine-dotted Manly Peak, and the improbably green springs pegged against the valley's dry vegetation cover. With binoculars you will likely spot some of the gangs of wild burros who live on the valley floor, if the NPS has not relocated them.

This climb is so short that it is worth returning a different way to enjoy this pretty butte a little longer. The most scenic return route is down the butte's northern spine, which is a little less steep and gives a good glimpse of the striated north face. Then follow the washes along the butte's eastern base for good views of the recumbent folds, some of which are bent 180 degrees over less than 200 yards. It is, indeed, as its former name proclaimed, a curious butte.

If you stay in the area a while, which makes sense given how long it takes to get here, check out the lush springs on the southwest side of Butte Valley. They have well-preserved historic homesteads, and some have surface water and shade trees. Some visitors indulge in a night in the homesteads' stone cabins (be aware of hantavarius). The interesting ruins of the Butte Valley Stamp Mill can be visited in the nearby hills, as well as an unusual cave house. Willow Spring, where Butte Valley funnels into Anvil Spring Canyon, has a shaded puddle and mill ruins (see *Needle Peak*). The seclusion is euphoric and the burros a constant treat, even though in the middle of the night their brays may make you jump out of your skin...

■

NEEDLE PEAK

Sculpted out of a thick accumulation of volcanic formations, Needle Peak is an imposing mountain bounded on all sides by abrupt slopes and ridges. The climb to this distant summit will take you past a lush spring, into a remote canyon lined with colorful outcrops, then up a sheer ridge studded with volcanic spires. The summit commands spectacular views of the Butte Valley area and the sprawling mountainous region south of Death Valley.

General Information
Jurisdiction: Death Valley National Park
Road status: Roadless; long primitive HC-4WD access road
The climb: 3.8 mi, 2,500 ft up, 280 ft down one way/difficult
Main attractions: Remote summit, volcanic formations, wildlife, spring
USGS 7.5' topo maps: Anvil Spring Canyon East, Anvil Spring Canyon
    West, Manly Peak*
Maps: pp. 207*, 203, 55

Location and Access
Needle Peak is the summit capping the prominent escarpment that looms over the southeastern corner of Butte Valley, in the southern Panamint Mountains. The climb starts at Willow Spring, at the bottleneck between Butte Valley and Anvil Spring Canyon. Follow the directions to Striped Butte. At the junction with the Redlands Canyon Road, continue straight (southwest) 1.8 miles to the next junction (Anvil Spring Junction), below Anvil Spring and the Geologist's Cabin. Make a left on the Anvil Spring Canyon Road and drive 1.5 miles southeast across Butte Valley to a fork. Take the right fork, and park after 0.2 mile at the end of the road, at the head of Willow Spring.

Route Description
Willow Spring is Butte Valley's largest spring. From its head it forms a river of greenery that fills the width of Anvil Spring Canyon's wash for a third of a mile. Much of it is impenetrable. A rocky burro trail heads down canyon along the spring's northern edge. The vegetation starts as a nearly pure stand of four-wing saltbush, then merges with an overgrown forest of willows, and ends in a cover of healthy rabbitbrush. This is a pretty spring, lush year round, pleasant for its higher humidity and patches of shade. In the late spring it is graced

Volcanic outcrops en route to Needle Peak

with the yellow blooms of prince's plume. The willows are festooned with flowering littleleaf mock orange, which attract colorful tarantula hawks. The trail passes by a misshapen stone cistern, water pipes, and the three-level stone foundations of a mill. These ruins are associated with the Willow Spring Claim, a placer that was active probably as early as the 1920s. Several building ruins, tunnels, and car bodies from that era are scattered throughout the adjoining hills.

After 0.25 mile the trail joins the Anvil Spring Canyon Road, which is soon blocked by a wilderness sign. Continue down the open wash along the eroding roadway. After 0.4 mile, on the south side of the wash, a well-defined track that the burros have fashioned for themselves climbs gently down-canyon across the canyon bank. In 0.2 mile this shortcut rounds the tip of a hill, then heads up along a wide side canyon and frays into a network of trails. If you miss this shortcut, continue about 350 yards down Anvil Spring Canyon, where it is easy to climb over the low bank into the side canyon.

It is 1.7 miles up the side canyon to a mountain-ringed amphitheater near its head. Most of it is a broad wash in uneventful rust-colored hills, although in May and June beavertail cactus and sandpaper plant cheer it up with their floral displays. Encounters with raptors, burros,

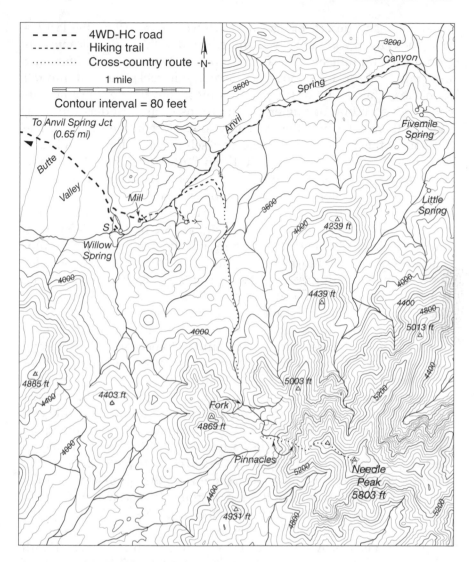

Needle Peak

	Dist.(mi)	Elev.(ft)
Willow Spring/end of road	0.0	3,585
Burro trail	0.65	~3,450
Fork/Amphitheater	2.65	4,240
Ridge/divide	3.05	4,650
False summit	3.5	~5,750
Needle Peak	3.8	5,803

jackrabbits, and desert tortoise are fairly common. Along the last 0.4 mile, the canyon walls are closer and covered with scenic volcanic outcrops. The amphitheater lies directly below Needle Peak's imposing west face, a sheer, 1,300-foot slope of volcanic rocks chiseled into tall pinnacles. This is one of the region's most impressive volcanic outcrops, the accretion of numerous emissions of ash, cinder, and lava, some of them explosive, that probably took place in the Miocene. The fun part of this climb is immersing yourself in this colorful jungle and searching for a way up through it. From Butte Valley it looks impassable; from close range and looking up, it looks even worse. But there is a way—albeit occasionally bordering on precipitous.

At the amphitheater, the canyon forks. For the most scenic approach, take the left fork. Then turn right at the first fork (125 yards), and right again 0.2 mile further. The ravine clambers over several broken slants of pretty whitish volcanic breccia with dark-gray lava inclusions, sprinkled with green shrubs. About 0.1 mile further, where the ravine makes a hard left, continue straight a few steps up to the ridge that marks the divide with Goler Canyon to the south.

The next 0.3-mile stretch is the crux. Climb east along the broad ridge, where the tireless burros have built yet another trail. The slope gradually steepens, up to an alignment of three outcrops perpendicular to the ridge; the trail passes between the two leftmost outcrops. The trail is more vague up to the next outcrop, a lone pinnacle that it skirts on the right. It then ascends in short switchbacks to the right side of a massive brown monument crowned by a pointed beige cap. To bypass it, follow the level ledge across its base to its left side, then scramble up the long, steep gully that flanks that side, choked with ephedra and loose rocks. Above this monument there are other pinnacles, but the path is more open, though still steep, to the ridge a few hundred feet higher. The false summit is 0.2 mile up the ridge. Needle Peak is on the far side of a steep 150-foot-deep saddle.

Needle Peak provides spectacular views of the southern Death Valley region. To the south and east the land falls off into a series of subordinate peaks to the wide swath of Wingate Wash and the fragmented Owlshead Mountains rising beyond it. In the distance the desert is bristling with mountains, a stark parade dominated by the Black Mountains, the Kingston Range, Clark Mountain, and the Avawatz Mountains. Even if you don't make the summit it is well worth climbing to the divide to enjoy the views in the other direction, west toward the blond sweep of Butte Valley and the barren hills of upper Goler Canyon.

■

OWLSHEAD MOUNTAINS

At the lonely south end of Death Valley, between the imposing Panamint Mountains and the Avawatz Mountains, the land gathers up into a circular aggregate of sub-ranges about 18 miles across surrounding two dry lakes, collectively known as the Owlshead Mountains. The name Owl's Head appears on early maps, in particular on Lieutenant G. M. Wheeler's 1871 map. It was reportedly inspired by the resemblance of the outline of Owlhead Peak, one of the range's summits, to an owl's head. It is an odd coincidence that decades later, after the area was fully mapped, the shape of the range turned out to also look like an owl's face, the two dry lakes—Lost and Owl—depicting the eyes.

The Owlshead Mountains consist mostly of granitic rocks and metamorphosed sedimentary rocks, especially marble, particularly in the eastern and northeastern areas and in the Owlshead Peak sub-range, as well as volcanic rocks and fanglomerates on the south and west sides. The metamorphosed rocks were likely deposited between the Late Precambrian and Paleozoic, and folded during subsequent mountain-building events. The plutons were emplaced during a series of intrusions around 100 million years ago. Erosion in the Tertiary, possibly assisted by uplifting, removed the overlying marble and exposed the plutonic rocks. The volcanic rocks are mostly lava flows and ash falls a few million years old. This abundance of granitic exposures, unique in Death Valley ranges, explains the profusion of sensuously weathered plutonic landforms, a significant perk when climbing here.

The Owlshead Mountains had a turbulent genesis. They happen to be trapped between two major faults, the east-west Garlock Fault to the south, which roughly overlaps with the Owlshead Mountains Road, and the northwest-southeast Southern Death Valley Fault Zone, traced by the Amargosa River in Death Valley to the northeast. In the last few million years, tectonic movements have transported the Owlshead Mountains 5 miles northwest along the Death Valley fault, and more than 25 miles west along the Garlock Fault. Before this crustal rearrangement, the Owlsheads lay *east* of the Avawatz Mountains. It is believed that they were formed as the wedge of land was squeezed up between the two faults, forcing it to bulge into a flattened dome. These extensional forces also resulted in the development of small local faults, the largest being the Owl Lake Fault on the south side of Owl Lake. These faults and increased erosion along them are responsible for the partial collapse of the dome, the abundance of fanglomerates around the base of the mountains, and the Owlshead Mountains' modern topography of a largely gutted ring of giant hills.

Base and precious metals were known to occur in the Owlshead Mountains as early as 1890. Around 1,000 claims were filed all over the range until the 1980s. Mineralization was generally poor; only a few mines were developed, and none produced very much. But the area did have two uncommon commodities that brought it some degree of fame—Epsom salts and manganese. The Epsom-salt deposit, located in the Crystal Hills west of the mountains, was exploited in the 1920s. To haul the salt to market, a spectacular monorail was erected across nearly 30 miles of rough desert terrain all the way to Searles Lake. The operation ended up being a dead loss, but the tramway became renown for its bold design and speed records. The manganese deposits were mostly on the southeast side near Owl Hole Springs. During the 1910s and 1940s sporadic activity at the Owl Hole, New Deal, and Black Magic mines yielded a total output likely between 15,000 and 20,000 tons, which was significant at the time. Decades later, in 1981–1982, in the same area the Ellie Iron Mine extracted 7,000 tons of hematite from a large iron deposit. The ore was trucked to Victorville for use in the manufacture of Portland cement. The mine shut down after six months because of waning demand for cement, leaving in the ground about one *billion* dollars' worth of iron. The Owlshead Mountains almost made a fortune, but in the end were spared from major strip-mining by the vagary of human affairs.

The Owlshead Mountains are home to the usual gang of characters—zebra-tailed, desert horned, and side-blotched lizards, chukars, kit fox, shrike, ground squirrels, tarantulas, and of course coyotes. But two desert dwellers are unusually common here. The first one is desert tortoise; their burrows locally reach impressive densities. The second is wild burros, who drifted in from adjacent BLM and military lands to the south. They like hanging around the southern Owlsheads and the dry lake areas. Accessed mostly by long primitive roads, and eclipsed by more formidable neighbors, this range sees infrequent visitors. You may well encounter more burros than humans.

∎

CON PEAK

Although the lowest of the three Owlsheads summits suggested here, Con Peak is the most difficult and the most diverse. You first descend below sea level, cross Death Valley at its narrowest, then climb through sculpted badlands to a remote canyon, and finally trudge up a very steep bouldery side canyon and a bumpy ridge to the summit plateau. It is a vigorous workout, the landscape is strewn with scenic granitic formations, and the summit area commands unconventional views of southern Death Valley.

General Information
Jurisdiction: Death Valley National Park
Road status: Roadless; hiking from primitive road (2WD)
The climb: 6.2 mi, 2,770 ft up, 200 ft down one way / strenuous
Main attractions: Badlands, granitic formations, views of Death Valley
USGS 7.5' topo maps: Shoreline Butte, Confidence Hills West*
Maps: pp. 213*, 55

Location and Access
Con Peak is a local summit on the ridge between Contact Canyon and Granite Canyon in the northeastern quadrant of the Owlshead Mountains. To get there via Contact Canyon, drive the Badwater Road to the signed Harry Wade Road near the south end of Death Valley. This is 29.1 miles south of Badwater coming from the north, or 4.7 miles west of Jubilee Pass coming from the east. Drive southeast on the Harry Wade Road about 2 miles and park. In spite of the "rough road" sign, this stretch is graded and suitable for most vehicles.

Route Description
From the road, Contact Canyon is marked by the pronounced notch on the crest to the southwest. Con Peak is at the south end of the broad plateau on the crest south of it. To start, strike out in the direction of Contact Canyon down the dissected, rocky fan. The Amargosa River is 0.7 mile down, famous for flowing below sea level, as it does in this vicinity—when it flows. Most of the time the river bed is all dusty stones and dry pools of salt-crusted cracked mud. Known as The Narrows, this area is particularly pretty, lined with green mesquite, encircled by summits more than a mile high. On the far side of the river bed, hike up the more gentle fan of sand and scattered cobbles,

aiming for the deeper bay in the Confidence Hills up ahead. This bay soon tapers into a short sandy gulch that winds up through scenic badlands, an upthrust of lake deposits (mudstone and conglomerate) crumpled by erosion. They contain beds of ash characteristic of known eruptions, in particular from Glass Mountain near Mono Lake, which enabled precise dating of their deposition—between 2.1 and 1.8 million years ago. Along the gulch, attractive stream-cut cliffs reveal the subsequent folding and dipping of the badlands' finely banded sediments. Forest-green pygmy cedar and pale desert holly cheer up the barren wash. Beyond the Confidence Hills, it is 1.1 miles to the two reddish ridges that frame the entrance to Contact Canyon. On the way up the wash, the sharp summits of the southern Black Mountains to the east compose a grandiose backdrop.

Contact Canyon first loops around a wide S-shaped bend, 0.7 mile long, beneath soaring slopes. Most of this canyon slices through the pale, coarse-grained Mesozoic adamellite typical of the Owlshead Mountains. Some exposures are radiant orange—at places due to oxidation, elsewhere from a high content in pinkish felspar. About 0.2 mile past the right bend, at an isolated low hill on the left side of the wash, a side canyon opens up in the left canyon wall. Con Peak can be reached by hiking much farther up Contact Canyon and backtracking along its south rim, but this side canyon is a good shortcut. A short distance in, the side canyon splits. Both forks eventually join the canyon rim, but the left fork is shorter and more eventful. Its sandy, boulder-ridden wash wiggles very steeply up the mountain, guided by V-shaped slopes of weathered outcrops. Just below its funnel-shaped head, where the side canyon first opens up (elev. 1,770′), access to the irregular ridge above is gained by scrambling up the steep rocky slope on the right. By then this coarse passageway has lifted you up nearly

	Dist.(mi)	Elev.(ft)
Con Peak		
Harry Wade Road	0.0	45
Amargosa River	0.7	-60
Confidence Hills (start)	1.4	130
Confidence Hills (end)	2.3	320
Contact Canyon mouth	~3.45	~770
Side canyon mouth	4.6	1,200
Rim (top of ridge)	5.7	2,400
Con Peak	6.2	2,621

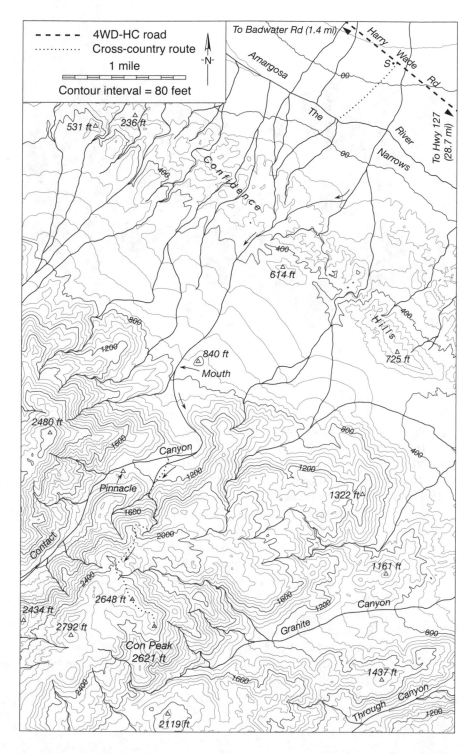

Legend:
- – – – – 4WD-HC road
- ········· Cross-country route
- 1 mile
- -N-
- Contour interval = 80 feet

To Badwater Rd (1.4 mi)
Harry Wade Rd
To Hwy 127 (28.7 mi)
Amargosa
The River Narrows
Confidence
Hills
531 ft
236 ft
614 ft
725 ft
840 ft
Mouth
2480 ft
Canyon
900
400
Pinnacle
1322 ft
Contact
1600
2000
1161 ft
2648 ft
Canyon
2434 ft
Granite
2792 ft
Con Peak
2621 ft
1437 ft
2119 ft
Through Canyon

Looking back at the Black Mountains from the gulch in the Confidence Hills

900 feet. The ridge above it climbs another 300 feet, roughly southwest in three steep giant steps, to the rim of Contact Canyon. The rest of the climb is much easier. The rim is a spacious plateau of soft knolls impregnated with light, gradually ascending to a small peak parading to the southeast. Con Peak, 25 feet lower, is hidden a third of a mile behind it, on the abrupt edge of Granite Canyon. The geology is pure Owlshead Mountains, warehouses of low adamellite boulders worn to artful rounded shapes, neatly displayed on open gravel slopes.

Well off the beaten track, Con Peak and the summit plateau over-look southern Death Valley at such unconventional angles that familiar landscapes appear oddly unfamiliar. Badwater Basin is no longer a static playa but a river of salt meandering between buttressed ranges. In the opposite direction, the Amargosa River seems to erupt from distant Silurian Valley, where in the Pleistocene a string of interconnected lakes overflowed into Lake Manly. To the northeast the Amargosa Chaos tiles the southern Black Mountains with amazingly colorful mosaics. Even the Owlshead Mountains are delightfully different, long narrow ridges dropping into Death Valley on one side, and the empty cauldron of Owl Lake on the other. These unsuspected perspectives are Con Peak's sweetest reward.

■

SPRING PEAK

> *The highest point in the eastern Owlshead Mountains, seldom-visited Spring Peak overlooks grand panoramas of Owl Lake Basin, the beautiful Avawatz Mountains, and much of the southern Death Valley region. A narrow canyon winds up to its dome of broken marble through colorful hills peppered with iron and manganese deposits. The mines that exploited them have interesting remains, relatively uncommon ores and minerals are plentiful, and a few climbable falls add a little challenge to this scenic climb.*

General Information
Jurisdiction: Death Valley National Park
Road status: Roadless; hiking from long primitive roads (2WD)
The climb (Spring Peak): 2.5 mi, 1,250 ft up one way/moderate
The loop climb (Spring Peak): 5.5 mi, 3,120 ft loop/moderate
The climb (Owl Lake V.): 3.5 mi, 1,450 ft up, 220 ft down one way/mod.
Main attractions: Views of southern Death Valley, falls, iron mines
USGS 7.5' topo map: Owl Lake
Maps: pp. 217*, 55

Location and Access
Spring Peak is located on the southeastern rim of the Owlshead Mountains, northwest of Owl Hole Springs. From Shoshone, drive Highway 127 26.5 miles south (or 29.7 miles north from Baker) to the Harry Wade Road on the west side (look for a large historical marker). Take this road 12.4 miles to a junction and turn left on the Owl Hole Springs Road. In 10.0 miles it reaches a fork at the springs. These roads are graded and usually suitable for most vehicles, in spite of road signs suggesting otherwise. Take the Ellie Iron Mine Road (right) and park after 0.75 mile. This last stretch is usually smooth, although there is a little sand at the fork. Spring Peak is the broad pale summit to the north visible off and on from the road. Alternatively, continue 3.85 miles to just before the road's high point southwest of Spring Peak (see map), and walk the remaining 0.2 mile to the summit. This road has rough washouts in the hills, and requires very good clearance.

Route Description
From the road, head up the broad embayment to the north until it tapers down to a canyon and forks after 1.1 miles. The surrounding

hills are a brilliant kaleidoscope of earth tones, a reflection of the area's fractured mosaic of marble, monzonite, and conglomerate. Take the right fork, an equally colorful ravine that narrows right away. The fun part of this climb is ambling up its twisted, rocky wash and negotiating the falls above its next fork (bear left). The first fall is about 12 feet high and sub-vertical, with good holds (Class 4). It can be bypassed on a steep gully on the east side. The second fall, also in monzonite, is two superposed slants totaling about 14 feet (Class 2). The last fall, in marble, is about 7 feet high and easy to bypass if needed. Shorter falls and a variety of rocks make for an entertaining climb. From the pass at the head of the ravine, 1.25 miles from the lower fork, it is a short walk northeast up an open ridge to Spring Peak's domed summit.

Spring Peak overlooks beautiful territory. The most striking scenery is the Avawatz Mountains to the south, their flanks as deeply wrinkled as badlands. This is one of the best spots to enjoy a global view of the Owlshead Mountains, including desolate Owl Lake to the north. At least a dozen ranges thrust their sharp crests on the horizon, from as far as the Slate Range to the New York Mountains, with little-visited places like the Shadow Mountains in between.

For even better views of Owl Lake, try the 3,300-foot summit (Owl Lake Viewpoint) west of the Black Magic Mine. Climb back down to the head of the ravine, then go 60 yards up in the same general direction to the Ellie Iron Mine Road. Follow this road's roller coaster west 0.7 mile to the well-preserved ore bin at the Black Magic Mine. A spur wanders generally north to a tall trench blasted in the side of a hill, rounds the tip of the hill, angles west as a track up the hillside, and

Spring Peak		
	Dist.(mi)	Elev.(ft)
Ellie Iron Mine Road	0.0	2,095
Start of ravine/fork	1.1	2,520
Pass at head of ravine	2.35	~3,165
Spring Peak	2.5	3,342
Black Magic Mine (ore bin)	(0.9)	3,135
Owl Lake Viewpoint (1,006 m)	(1.5)	3,300
Ellie Iron Mine (quarry)	3.1	3,180
Saddle at hilltop	3.3	3,060
Wash	3.4	~2,895
New Deal Mine	4.85	~2,320
Back to starting point	5.5	2,095

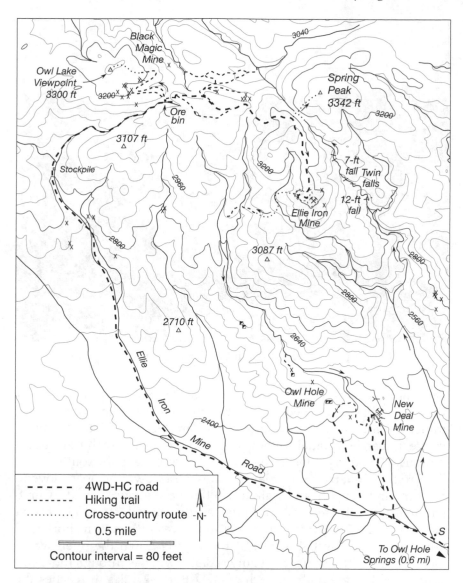

Black
Magic
Mine

Owl Lake
Viewpoint
3300 ft

3040

Spring
Peak
3342 ft

3200

Ore
bin

3200

3107 ft

Stockpile

2960

3200

7-ft
fall Twin
falls

12-ft
fall

Ellie Iron
Mine

3087 ft

2800

2800

2880

2560

2710 ft

2640

Ellie

Iron

Owl Hole
Mine

New
Deal
Mine

2400

Mine

Road

S

- - - -   4WD-HC road
· · · · · · · ·   Hiking trail
· · · · · · · · ·   Cross-country route -N-
0.5 mile

Contour interval = 80 feet

To Owl Hole
Springs (0.6 mi)

fizzles out (see map). The 3,300-foot summit is a short distance up the slope, topped by a small jagged outcrop of sparkling marble breccia. Owl Lake Basin spreads out below, its dry lake shining in a circle of hills, the Black Mountains parading grandly beyond.

For variety, return along the next canyon west. Walk the mining road south to its end at the Ellie Iron Mine. The ore body was exploited on three superposed terraces carved into the hillside. Vast quantities of ore are exposed, in piles of lustrous metallic boulders several tons

The Avawatz Mountains' wrinkled foothills from Spring Peak

each, on road cuts and tailings, and in the 20-foot pillar on the lower terrace. Jay black, streaked with rusty veins, the pillar hosts a surfeit of minerals embedded in hematite. There are tabular clusters of muscovite, jasper, botryoidal psilomelane, and vugs filled with translucent crystals. The quarry offers rare views of Leach Lake to the south.

From the quarry's lower level, climb west down the open slope to the bend in the wash, and walk down the wash about 75 yards. Climb southwest up the hillside to a low saddle, then descend northwest along a ravine 250 yards to the next main wash (there is a short road spur along the way). The rest of the way is down the open wash. Dotted with brittlebush and pygmy cedar, it wiggles through more colorful hills that gradually breach open. After 1.4 miles, it reaches the New Deal Mine, the area's largest manganese producer. Its ruddy waste heaps and bench cuts are loaded with minerals too. The workings include a collared two-compartment shaft (avoid walking around here at night!), and a cavernous tunnel framed with blood-red minerals. The Owl Hole Mine, a short walk to the west, has similar ores. From the New Deal Mine it is 0.5 mile down the mine's beat-up spur to the Ellie Iron Mine Road, a short distance northwest of your vehicle.

■

OWL PEAK

With an elevation of only 4,666 feet, Owl Peak is the lowest high point of the ranges surrounding Death Valley, as well as the most remote, which makes it both the longest to drive to and the easiest to climb. The ascent follows the gentle, elevated crest of the mountains, among colorful granitic and volcanic rocks. Most of it commands superb views of this little-known part of the California desert, including Long Valley and the beautiful Crystal Hills on one side, and Lost Lake and the fractured Owlshead Mountains on the other.

General Information
Jurisdiction: Death Valley National Park
Road status: Roadless; long primitive HC-4WD access road
The climb: 1.9 mi, 1,020 ft up, 250 ft down one way/moderate
Main attractions: Views of Wingate Wash and the Owlshead Mountains
USGS 7.5' topo maps: Old Ibex Pass, East of Owl Lake, Owl Lake, Quail
       Spring, Hidden Spring*
Maps: pp. 221*, 55

Location and Access
Owl Peak is in the Owlshead Mountains' westernmost sub-range, a couple of miles north of the radio facility at the end of the Owlshead Mountains Road. Follow the directions to Owl Hole Springs (see *Spring Peak*), and turn left on the Owlshead Mountains Road. Drive 1.2 miles to a junction (the left fork is gated shortly past this point). Turn right and go 16.2 miles, past Owl Lake Basin and into Lost Lake Valley, to a low pass on a ridge where the road angles right and starts climbing the mountain. Continue 2.15 miles up to a small pullout where the road reaches the crest, 0.2 mile before the radio installation, and park. A few rocky and rutted grades make high clearance mandatory.

Route Description
From the road, Owl Peak's broad and barren summit rises a couple of miles to the north-northeast, partly concealed behind intervening hills. Although anything but straight, the single-ridge crest of this portion of the Owlshead Mountains leads quietly up and over to it. West of the crest, long wrinkled ridges descend sharply to the wide-open plain of Long Valley at the head of Wingate Wash. To the east the crest skirts the steep, deeply fissured, funnel-shaped upper drainages of

Quail and Granite Mountains in the distance from the ridge to Owl Peak

four consecutive canyons. Much more sedate, the fairly narrow and gently undulating crest rides high above this fractured landscape, providing a generally easy path to the summit.

The crest marks the approximate boundary between two very different rocks, pale Mesozoic biotite adamellite on the east side and dark Miocene volcanic rocks to the west. The adamellite was locally intruded by aplite, rhyolite, and felsite. The terrain changes underfoot frequently, from adamellite to vesiculated basalt and back, sometimes over a few seconds of walking. Hydrothermal solutions locally altered the rocks and injected minor amounts of heavy metals, from around the end of the road to about 1 mile north of Owl Peak. The richest of these deposits is at the Kennedy Boys Mine (a spot hard to locate!).

Isolated from the rest of the world, the local burros are unused to humans and easily spooked. Where the going gets a little rough, they have blazed segments of trail, impeccably optimized to avoid the difficulty and elevation changes. One trail is at the first hill along the crest, which it bypasses on the east side. The second hill does not have a trail; even the burros find the terrain too deeply furrowed. Climbing over this hill is the best way to go. There are some very scenic areas along this stretch—sharp ridges dropping toward Long Valley, the

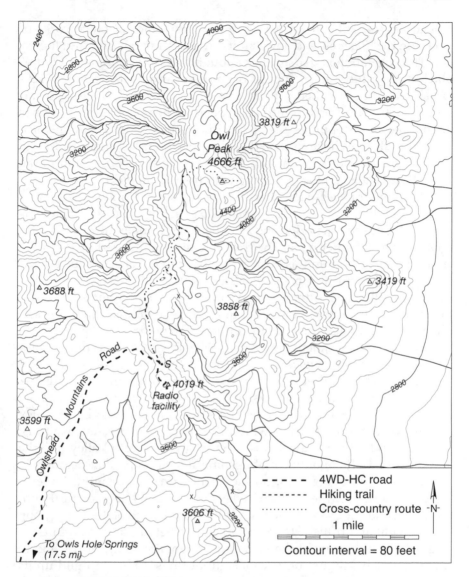

		4WD-HC road
		Hiking trail
		Cross-country route

1 mile

Contour interval = 80 feet

Owl Peak

	Dist.(mi)	Elev.(ft)
Owlshead Mountains Road	0.0	3,890
Second hill	0.7	~4,180
Enter wash	1.25	~4,075
Climb onto ridge	1.55	~4,265
Owl Peak	1.9	4,666

fractal Crystal Hills down below to the west, colorful patchworks of rocks on the hillsides, and angular outcrops jutting out here and there.

The vegetation is sparse, thick enough to be entertaining but not so thick to be a hindrance. Typical of mid-elevations, it includes blackbrush, bitterbrush, ephedra, and buckwheat. Clusters of cottontop and calico cactus are fairly common, especially near the summit. Other than trails and droppings, the burros' most obvious traces are the desiccated cacti they have uprooted to feed on the moist innards. In late winter, the ground is green with fiddleneck and coreopsis, and in the spring the cactus dot the landscape with their luminous blossoms.

The next trail segment, shortly after the second hill, is the longest (0.45 mile). It cuts a nearly level path just east of the ridge, then joins the wash between the ridge and Owl Peak, and finally heads north up this wash as a fainter track. The trail peters out a little before the wash ends at the crest. From this area, access back to the crest can be gained either by continuing up the wash or, better still, along any of the ravines on the east side. The final stretch is a steep but short jaunt southeast on the crest to the peak. In mild weather, this climb is easier than most. You might in fact wonder how you got there so quickly!

Owl Peak is a quietly powerful place, far from everything, commanding expansive views of government territory most of us never get to see. The southern horizon is lined with unfamiliar ranges— Robbers Mountain, Eagle Crags, and Fort Irwin reservation's Granite and Tiefort mountains. With binoculars one can follow in Long Valley to the west the road along which the twenty-mule-team wagons, creaking under their heavy loads of borax, exited Death Valley, and the darker track of the monumental Epsom salts monorail that parallels it. They lead to Wingate Pass, on the abrupt rim of Panamint Valley's very southern tip, where Death Valley Scotty staged his theatrical gunfight. Beyond the pass the horizon is bisected by the Slate Range, long and straight and ruffled. There is perhaps no better place to admire the rugged southern front of the Panamint Mountains to the north, and to appreciate the volumes of volcanic outpourings it took to build up its massive slopes. East from Owl Peak, a series of benches descend gently to a spectacular viewpoint of Lost Lake and its lonesome valley. Beyond, a procession of parallel ranges parades across eastern California, one behind the other, clear into Nevada. The only manmade object in sight is the elaborate radio tower, standing on its flattened hilltop like a spaceship about to return to the stars, a surreal vision in a surreal land.

∎

6

EASTERN MOJAVE DESERT

The region. The eastern Mojave Desert encompasses the land between just east of Barstow and the border with Nevada and Arizona, and from just south of the Avawatz Mountains and the Kingston Range to the Bullion, Old Woman, and Chemehuevi mountains included. This region of a little over 8,000 square miles is characterized by spacious high-elevation valleys interspersed with scores of mountains. The ranges exhibit conspicuous size and distribution patterns. To the north they tend to be tall and massive, and trend generally north-northwest in the parallel style of the Basin and Range Province, though not as prominently as elsewhere. The highest summit, Clark Mountain, tops out at just under 8,000 feet. Further south and east, the ranges generally get lower, more scattered, and less oriented, with a north-south orientation, while the valleys get bigger and lower. The lowest high point, in the Stepladder Mountains near the southeastern frontier, does not quite reach 3,000 feet. In that area, the valleys are only second in size to the giant bajadas of Imperial County to the south.

The region enjoys one of the strongest environmental protections in the country. Its core is preserved within Mojave National Preserve and most of Mojave Trails National Monument adjacent to it to the south, each 1.6 million acres in area. A good fraction of these units is designated wilderness. The land surrounding them is protected by Castle Mountains National Monument (20,920 acres), and seven designated wilderness areas covering about 560,000 acres. Some of these wilderness areas are larger than many national parks. The total protected acreage, not including military reservations, is about 3.36 million acres, or about two thirds of the land area.

Average temperatures (°F) in the eastern Mojave Desert							
Zzyzx (950 feet)		Mountain Pass (4,650 feet)		Granite Mountains (4,200 feet)		Needles (1,600 feet)	
Low	High	Low	High	Low	High	Low	High
January	34	61	30	50	36	50	37	62
February	40	69	32	54	38	54	44	68
March	46	74	36	59	41	59	48	75
April	53	83	41	66	48	68	57	85
May	61	93	50	76	54	75	66	94
June	70	103	59	87	63	85	74	103
July	77	109	66	93	67	90	82	108
August	75	107	64	90	66	89	80	105
September	68	100	57	84	61	83	73	101
October	55	87	46	72	52	73	61	87
November	43	73	36	59	41	59	48	72
December	34	62	30	51	34	50	42	64

This is a wild region, with ample room to roam, and some amazing mountains—the beautiful cordillera that slices through the heart of the preserve, the rough Old Woman Mountains, and the insanely crenulated Stepladder Mountains. Except for Lanfair, Piute, and Chemehuevi valleys at its easternmost edge, which are hydrologically linked to the Colorado River, valleys have no outlet to the sea. Most slopes drain toward expansive inland dry lakes; Danby Lake, the largest, is bigger than San Francisco. These ancient sinks are also home to spectacular dune fields, in particular the famous Kelso Dunes, part of a 25-mile sand desert known as the Devils Playground, and the marvelously isolated Cadiz Dunes. The Mojave Road, which traverses nearly the whole region from east to west, is one of the longest primitive roads in the contiguous United States that crosses no human habitations.

Geology. The eastern Mojave Desert's spectacular scenery was created by a tumultuous geologic past that spans more than 1.8 billion years. The area witnessed repeated igneous activity, turbulent mountain-building episodes, and intense metamorphism in the Proterozoic; sedimentation in the Paleozoic; the emplacement of multiple plutons in the Mesozoic; and volcanism, erosion, and major tectonic rearrangements in the Cenozoic. This remarkable diversity of geological events has produced an equally remarkable diversity of rocks exposed across a rugged geography of mountains, volcanoes, canyons, fans, bajadas, valleys, and dry lakebeds. Compared to the rest of the Mojave Desert, the region presents several major differences in its geological makeup, and therefore topography. First, it has considerably more volcanic terrain, much of it scattered throughout but with a higher concentration on the east side. Second, sedimentary formations are globally more poorly represented. They outcrop mostly in the northern half, especially in the preserve's mountainous heart. Their occurrence decreases abruptly to the south and east, with no sedimentary rocks in these areas. Finally, there is a predominance of granitic rocks throughout, getting stronger to the south and east. Many ranges are almost exclusively made of either intrusive or extrusive rocks, with often great diversity within a given range.

Botany. Except for variance in plant associations subtle to non-experts, the plant communities are similar to other parts of the Mojave Desert. The main and most enjoyable difference is the abundance of cactaceae. Many ranges hold extensive gardens of cactus, yucca, cholla, and agave, often astounding for their size, density, variety, and spring-time blossoms. Joshua trees, in particular, are abundant in the northern half of the region, and scarce in the southern half. A few ranges are home to uncommon or endemic species like the pygmy and simple desert agaves, fishhook cactus, and teddy bear cholla. The northern area also hosts a few groves of relict species of two-needle pinyon pine, white fir, scrub oak, and canyon live oak. The southernmost areas contain species that are typical of the Sonoran Desert immediately to the south, in particular striking larger plants such as nolinas and smoke trees. In all except minor ranges, the highest crests host stands of conifers, dense enough to qualify as forests in the northern half.

Climate. Here too the sun means business. In the summer, Baker's 13-story thermometer will reach above 120°F. It is often hottest around low-lying Needles. Up in the higher mountains, however, the daytime temperature usually does not exceed 100°F. Winter daytime temperatures are commonly in the 30s or 40s in the valleys, and much lower up on the mountains. The highest summits being lower than in the northern Mojave Desert, they tend to be a bit warmer year round. In the northern half of the region, snow blankets the highest crests almost every year, off and on between January and March, sometimes later in the spring. Snow is rarely thick enough to be an impediment to climbing. In the southern half, it hardly ever snows. Wind, perhaps more

	Restaurant	Groceries	Lodging	Campground	Gas station	Tire repair	Towing	Water
Afton Road exit				✓				
Amboy		✓			✓			✓
Baker	✓	✓	✓	✓	✓	✓	✓	✓
Barstow	✓	✓	✓	✓	✓	✓	✓	✓
Cima Road exit		✓			✓		✓	✓
Fenner	✓	✓			✓			✓
Hole-in-the-Wall				✓				✓
Kelso Depot	✓	✓						✓
Ludlow	✓	✓	✓		✓	✓	✓	✓
Mid Hills Campground				✓				
Needles	✓	✓	✓	✓	✓	✓	✓	✓
Newberry Springs	✓	✓		✓	✓	✓	✓	✓
Nipton	✓	✓	✓	✓				✓
Rasor Road exit		✓		✓	✓	✓	✓	✓
Searchlight	✓	✓	✓	✓	✓			✓

often than in other parts of the Mojave Desert, is often a nuisance. Encouraged by the more open geography, wind storms often occur on a regional scale, lasting sometimes several days, day and night.

Services, Regulations, and Climbing. The eastern Mojave Desert has several major recreational assets. For one, there are no large towns. The closest cities are Barstow to the west and Las Vegas to the east, both a respectable distance away. All settlements within the region are small. There is Needles near the Colorado River, garish Primm just inside Nevada, the service communities of Baker, Ludlow, and Fenner on the interstates, cannabis-friendly Nipton near the Nevada border, and not much else. Often you will not find comfortable amenities close

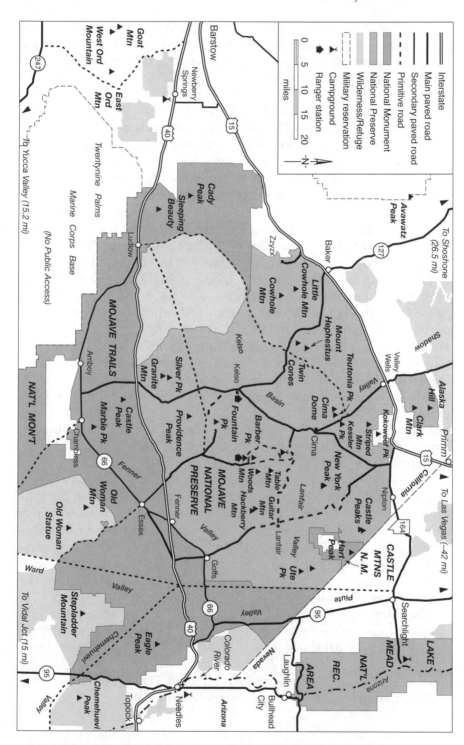

by to retire to, and the only food that might be available is conve-
nience-store cuisine. At the end of the day, unless you drive far, you
will have to set up camp near where you are, cook, and sleep under
the stars. Bring a well-stocked larder, replenish it with ice (and your
vehicle with gas) every chance you get, and bring much more water
than you think you will need. South of the preserve, except for the
interstates, Route 66, and Highway 95, most roads are dirt. To get to
most places, you will need a high-clearance vehicle. There is often,
blissfully, no reception. You must know what you are doing.

Another appeal is that camping regulations are comparatively lax.
Mojave National Preserve has literally hundreds of primitive camp
sites. At the end of a day of hiking, it is nice to be able to find a place to
spend the night without having to drive long distances. There is no
permit or registration system for backcountry camping. To minimize
impact, you are asked to select a site that has been previously used for
camping, as indicated by a fire ring (and yes, building new fire rings is
prohibited). Campfires are allowed only in fire rings or portable fire
pans. Camping is not allowed within 1/2 mile of a paved road or
developed area; in a small number of day-use areas; within 1/4 mile of
water sources and cultural sites; within 1/2 mile of Fort Piute and
Kelso Depot; and within 1 mile north or 1/4 mile south of the Kelso
Dunes Road. There are public campgrounds at Mid Hills and Hole-in-
the-Wall. The limit is eight people and two vehicles per site. The maxi-
mum stay is 14 consecutive days and 30 days per year. Regulations for
Mojave Trails National Monument have not yet been announced.
Apply the same rules until they are. On public lands, follow BLM regulations (see *Regulations* in Part 4).

One of the nicest attributes of hiking in the eastern Mojave Desert
is low visitation. Ironically, even though tens of millions of humans
drive through the region every year, the overwhelming majority never
stop to visit. Most desert enthusiasts also tend to spend their outdoors
time in other parts of the Mojave Desert—northern (which is more dramatic), southern (which is closer to home for many people), or western
(which is also closer, and more accessible). Oddly enough, in the
Union's most populous state, on most summits you will likely not see
another human. Yet the region is a treasure trove of summits. It encompasses upward of 40 ranges of all sizes open to the public, with elevations from under 3,000 feet to near 8,000 feet. Some ranges have a surprisingly large prominence, while many are quite easy, a drastic
change from Death Valley's grueling top dogs. There is room for every
ambition, from beginners to battle-scarred desert rats.

■

CASTLE MOUNTAINS AND PIUTE RANGE

At the far east end of Lanfair Valley, the skyline is broken by one last chain of mountains before the Silver State, the narrow 23-mile alignment of the Castle Mountains and the Piute Range. This is the southern edge of the Great Basin. Piute Valley to the east and most of Lanfair Valley to the west are not topographic sinks but genuine valleys that drain to the sea via the Colorado River. The two ranges share glorious views over these valleys' immense and largely empty bajadas, and a genesis rooted in protracted volcanism. One would be hard-pressed to find two adjacent volcanic ranges that are more different. The Castle Mountains are a scenic clutch of rhyolite domes, their golden flanks highlighted by white tuff and scattered juniper and Joshua trees. The Piute Range, fused against their south side, is a long straight ridge of somber, hard-baked lava.

The reason for this divergence is magma chemistry. Around 16.3 million years ago, Piute Range lavas started accumulating in a fault-bounded depression at the same time as intrusive domes were emplaced in the Castle Mountains depression to the north. In the Castle Mountains the magma was rich in silica—the main constituent of glass—and alkali, and it produced rhyolite and other light-colored rocks. In the Piute Range the magma tended to be silica-poor, and it formed flows and breccia of dark basalts and andesites. The main eruptions stopped in the Castle Mountains 12.8 millions ago. In the Piute Range they continued 4.8 million years longer, ultimately filling the southern depression with even more low-albedo rocks.

The dullness of the Piute Range is only skin deep. Throughout the range, dense cactus gardens flourish on the rich volcanic soil. Long after volcanism ended, rainwater flowing in Lanfair Valley's washes ponded against the range's western flank and formed a small lake. The thick lake sediments have since then been eroded into bright, sensual badlands. Below the badlands, Piute Gorge cuts a twisted corridor with 300-foot walls that expose the range's colorful core of oxidized volcanic breccia. In the lower gorge flows the region's only perennial creek. The vivacious stream nurses Piute Spring, a luxuriant oasis of cattail, arrowweed, willow, and whispering cottonwood. Native Americans lived and tended irrigated fields along the spring. On the Miocene boulders they incised a miniature zoo of petroglyphs. Starting in the late 1850s, the Mojave Trail passed through the spring on its way across the Mojave Desert. A small army outpost grandly called Fort Piute was garrisoned there for a brief time to protect travelers and freight wagons from natives. The steep pass over the Piute Range was said to be the most arduous spot along the entire trail.

While the Piute Range was never broken by a miner's pick, the Castle Mountains happen to host major gold deposits. Gold was discovered in 1907 at what became the Oro Belle and Big Chief mines. In spite of modest showings, a town named Hart sprung up and soon boasted hotels and stores, saloons, a dance hall, a newspaper, ladies of the night, and a jail. The mines were fully developed but little high-grade ore was found. The township was abolished in 1914, and mining stopped in 1918. There was a revival when kaolinite pits were exploited in the 1920s, then gold again from 1932 to 1944. After extensive low-concentration gold deposits were discovered near old Hart in 1986 by geologist Harold Linder, the Castle Mountain Mine ran a major heap-leach operation. From 1992 to 2001 it recovered over 28 tons of gold valued at $330 million. Today the site of Hart is betrayed by a lone chimney, a crooked headframe, and scattered junk. The modern mine left a pit and cyaniding ponds the size of 500 football fields.

When Mojave National Preserve was created in 1994, the Piute Range was included in it but not the Castle Mountains, being one of the largest reserves of minable gold in California. In 2016 then-president Barack Obama created Castle Mountains National Monument. The proclamation gave the mine permission to go after the remaining 28 tons of gold. When the project is completed, or after 10 years if no mining occurs, the property will be incorporated in the monument.

From California's coastal cities it is a long drive to these two ranges, the end of it on dusty, rocky, sandy tracks never touched by asphalt. All four named summits, including the Castle Mountains' highest point, unofficially and ironically named Linder Peak (5,581 feet), can be climbed from dirt roads along the western base of the two ranges. The three nearest towns—Nipton, Goffs, and Searchlight—have limited or no services. Everything bespeaks of emptiness, remoteness, and abandonment. You come here not for an encounter with the sublime, but to commune with the raw spirit of nowhere.

■

HART PEAK

Once the lava-filled chimney of a small volcano, Hart Peak is a dramatic vertical wedge of craggy rhyolite. The approach to its base crosses a striking high-desert grassland festooned with cactus, juniper, and Joshua trees. Although unusually short, the ascent of the summit block is hard enough to give a satisfying sense of accomplishment. It also provides a unique opportunity to enjoy multiple perspectives of the fantastically eroded ancient dikes, vents, and volcanoes that make up the colorful Castle Mountains.

General Information
Jurisdiction: Castle Mountains National Monument
Road status: Roadless; long standard-clearance access road
The climb: 2.0 mi, 1,130 ft up, 50 ft down one way / moderate–difficult
Main attractions: Tall volcanic plugs, geology, isolation
USGS 7.5' topo map: Hart Peak
Maps: pp. 233*, 227

Location and Access
The second highest point in the Castle Mountains, Hart Peak is near the north end of the range, less than a mile from the Nevada state line. From the Nipton Road exit on Interstate 15, drive the Nipton Road east 3.5 miles and turn right on the Ivanpah Road. Drive 16.7 miles south to the signed Hart Mine Road on the left. Follow this graded road 4.85 miles to a fork where it angles sharply right. Continue 2.3 miles east-southeast, past a white water tank on the right, to a fork, and angle left. After 0.9 mile, at a crossroad, turn left on the unmarked Walking Box Ranch Road. Drive northeast up to a low pass then down 4.2 miles to an old primitive road on the right at 5 o'clock, with Hart Peak rising to the east-northeast. With a high-clearance four-wheel-drive vehicle, this last road can be driven to the saddle at the southern base of Hart Peak (see map), but it is so short that it is not worth the effort. Park at this junction instead. These access roads are graded and in decent shape, and a standard-clearance vehicle can make it to this junction, although a little clearance helps at a couple of rougher spots.

Route Description
When you finally step out of your car you are in the middle of a postcard. On one side a blond savanna inundated with alien gardens

231

of cactus, blue yucca, Joshua trees, and Utah juniper sweeps down to a dramatic row of spiky summits. On the other side a magnificent fin rises abruptly in jagged glory, burning in shades of apricot and cinnamon against a cerulean sky. The spiky summits are the New York Mountains' iconic Castle Peaks. The giant fin is Hart Peak, a rim of razor-edged rhyolite crags too rough and abrupt to walk. Few Mojave Desert mountains this small command this much attention.

There are routes up this well-guarded summit that do not require technical skills. One of them is the northwest nose, which is all sharp upright rocks except for a convenient break that winds up through them. Most people will prefer the east face, which still occasionally requires hands but is not as steep. From the Walking Box Ranch Road you first follow the old primitive road 0.3 mile toward Hart Peak, in and out of two small washes, to where the road crests a knoll and makes a U bend to the south. You then leave the road, descend a very short distance north to a narrow wash, and follow its tortuous channel toward the saddle south of the summit. It is easy walking, between low banks positively green with Joshua trees, juniper, plump saltbush, and an enjoyable collection of cacti. The wash crosses a cove hemmed in by colorful hills capped with pointed rhyolite plugs. In 0.2 mile it splits; the way is to the right, a lazy arroyo occasionally occupied by a tree, to a beat-up road on the left bank 0.35 mile further. The road parallels the wash for a while, so it is easy to join it at any time. It climbs 0.75 mile up the talus that skirts the base of Hart Peak and crests on the saddle.

From closer up on the saddle, Hart Peak's south face looks even more daunting, a sheer ramp crowned with a forest of tall fins and pinnacles. There is less than half a mile left to go, but this last stretch is fairly rigorous. The first half is a steep open slope that climbs to a second saddle at the base of the summit block. Part way up, it is interrupted by a stocky spur. It can be avoided either on the left (west) side across a rocky talus, or on the right side up a Class-3 cleft in a 7-foot rise. The second saddle is not far above it, a grassy hillside beneath Hart Peak's serrated arête. By then other cacti have joined the show— the red heads of barrel cactus, erect clumps of pancake prickly-pear, and occasional brown-spined prickly-pear.

Most of the difficulty is concentrated in the second half. On its hidden east side, Hart Peak breaks up into a precipitous incline covered with low angular boulders. Fortunately, most of them are well anchored, and there is minimal loose material between them. The density of boulders increases steadily, and so does the grade, climaxing at 50% near the top. The saving grace is that there is no false summit to

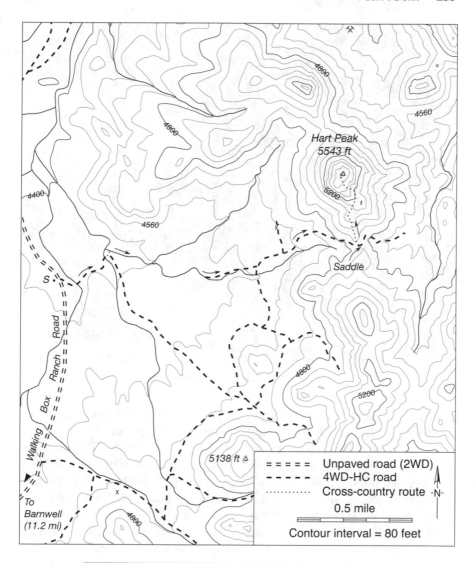

Hart Peak		
	Dist.(mi)	Elev.(ft)
Walking Box Ranch Road	0.0	4,460
Leave road at U bend	0.3	4,460
Join old road	0.85	4,510
First saddle (leave road)	1.6	~4,865
Second saddle	1.85	~5,170
Hart Peak	2.0	5,543

Second saddle (right) at base of Hart Peak's southern arête

fool you: when you crest the last visible outcrop and the sky suddenly opens up, you find yourself within 20 feet of the summit.

The view makes you very aware of the remoteness of this range. To the east you look across the state of Nevada's extreme southern wedge, occupied by the largely empty sweep of Piute Valley and the Newberry Mountains behind it. The valley's only buildings are those of the small communities of Searchlight and Cal-Nev-Ari. Beyond, out of sight, is the Colorado River, flooded under Lake Mohave, and on its far side the long rumpled crest line of the Black Mountains in Arizona. On Hart Peak you are practically immersed in the Castle Mountains, next to the fantastic skyline of the Castle Peaks' chiseled volcanoes. All around, the Castle Mountains show off their colorful hills of white ash flows and buff badlands pierced by sculpted dikes and vents of mahogany rhyolite. At sunset, when the shadows rise and the sunlight glows copper across its flanks, this little-known range looks richer than all the gold that it once held. Carefully picking your way through stubborn rocks and plants as you slowly return in waning light is a small price to pay.

■

UTE PEAK

Far off the beaten path, Ute Peak (4,908') is the highest point in the Piute Range, a stark mesa of sloped volcanic beds buttressed by weathered cliffs. It can be climbed two ways, one a short and comparatively easy cross-country route amid extravagant cactus gardens, the other up a long beat-up road that courses the yucca-dotted spine of the range. Both approaches encompass wide-open views of the California desert's desolate easternmost frontier.

General Information
Jurisdiction: Mojave National Preserve
Road status: Roadless; long primitive access road (HC)
The climb (cross-country): 1.4 mi, 1,240 ft up one way/moderate
The climb (trail): 7.0 mi, 1,380 ft up, 430 ft down one way/difficult
Main attractions: Scenic cactus gardens, view of Lanfair Valley
USGS 7.5' topo maps: East of Grotto Hills*, Hart Peak
Maps: pp. 237*, 227

Location and Access
Ute Peak is located in the middle of the Piute Range, at the far east end of Lanfair Valley. From all directions it is a long drive to get close to it. For the shortest approach, take the Fenner exit on Interstate 40. At the bottom of the westbound exit ramp, turn right on Goffs Road and drive northeast 10.4 miles to the signed Lanfair Road, on the left at the edge of the small community of Goffs. Go north on Lanfair Road 16.2 miles (the first 10.3 miles are paved, the rest well graded) to Lanfair, at the signed junction with the Cedar Canyon Road on the left. Continue north 100 yards to the unsigned Cedar Canyon Road eastern extension on the right. Drive this dirt road due east 9.5 miles to its end at the Badlands Road, at the foot of the Piute Range. Ignore all side roads; go straight at mile 2.1, at mile 3.65, and at the triple fork (mile 5.15). Turn left on the Badlands Road, and drive 4.6 miles north to a point due west of a low swell marked 1,222 m (4,009 ft). This is 0.1 mile past a sparsely vegetated flat, and 100 feet before a split in the road. Park here for the cross-country climb. To climb Ute Peak on the Piute Mesa Trail instead, continue 3.7 miles to a four-way junction. Turn right, drive 2.7 miles north to the next junction, and park. The poorer road to the right is the Piute Mesa Trail. High clearance is required up to the start of the cross-country route, and four-wheel drive as well beyond.

Route Description

From the start of the cross-country route, Ute Peak is the pimple about 1 mile and 1,200 feet up to the east-northeast, capped by a large cairn. To its right, the crest descends a little to a long saddle before dropping over short cliffs. Aim for the saddle across the open slopes north of the 4,009-foot swell, to a steep hillside covered with cavernous outcrops. Bypass it on the right, and climb the steep flank just south of it to the saddle. It is then an easy climb along the crest to the summit.

What makes this peak particularly enjoyable is the cactus gardens. As soon as the ground swells up to foothills, the vegetation morphs from the valley's creosote-bush forest into a thick belt of cacti. You are surrounded by bizarre plants growing right out of sunburnt rocks. Armies of red barrel cactus shoot out of the ground like an invasion of barbed fire hydrants. Staghorn cholla with shaggy crowns grow among gangs of 10-foot Mojave yucca shaped like electrocuted paint-brushes. They share the mountain with a thorny jungle of blackbrush, catclaw, and more subdued cactaceae—tufts of calico cactus, shiny sprigs of silver cholla, lone beavertail cactus, and diminutive fishhook cactus hiding between stones. Even during the chlorophyll lull of winter, this colorful cactus kingdom remains remarkably alive.

The eroded rubbles on Ute Peak's higher flanks record the vagaries of 8 million years of capricious Miocene volcanism. Pieces of basalt from runny lava are incrusted with long parallel grooves, each one a gas bubble that was stretched several times its original diameter as the lava freely flowed. The rhyolite is fine-grained or porphyritic, banded or chalky. Cleaved faces bear the serpentine eddies of turbulent flows. The upper slopes and the crest are littered with hunks of andesite, steel-grey cores encased in coffee-colored shells of heavy-metal oxides.

Ute Peak		
	Dist.(mi)	Elev.(ft)
Badlands Road	0.0	3,670
Foot of cavernous hillside	~0.9	~4,330
Crest	1.15	~4,720
Ute Peak	1.4	4,908
Piute Mesa Trail (trailhead)	0.0	3,960
High Table Mtn West End	4.5	4,793
Upper end of trail (viewpoint)	6.3	~4,895
Ute Peak	7.0	4,908

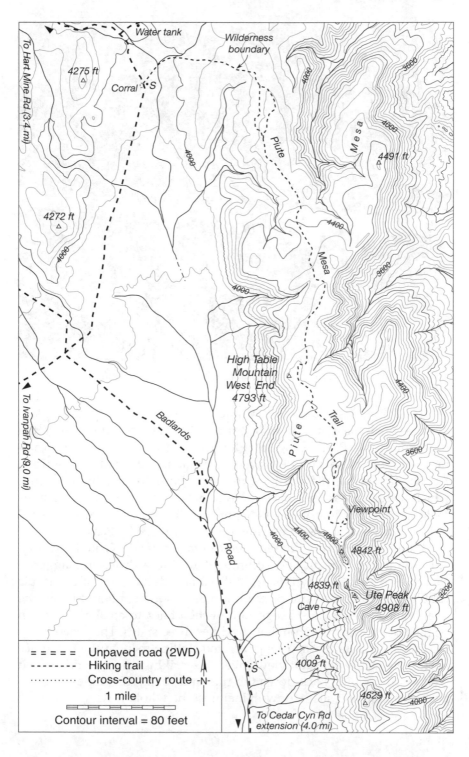

To Hart Mine Rd (3.4 mi)

Water tank

Wilderness boundary

4275 ft

Corral S

Piute

M e s a

4491 ft

4272 ft

4000

4400

Mesa

4000

3600

To Ivanpah Rd (9.0 mi)

High Table Mountain West End 4793 ft

Badlands

Piute Trail

3600

Viewpoint

4842 ft

4839 ft

4400

4000

Ute Peak 4908 ft

Cave

3200

Road

4009 ft

S

= = = = = Unpaved road (2WD)
- - - - - Hiking trail
· · · · · · Cross-country route

↑ -N-

4629 ft

4000

1 mile

⊨=====⊨⊨==⊨

Contour interval = 80 feet

To Cedar Cyn Rd extension (4.0 mi)

Cactus garden on the way to Ute Peak (left of center)

The Piute Mesa Trail offers a much more leisurely approach, gaining a comparable elevation in five times the distance. After 1 mile the road enters the Piute Range Wilderness and climbs a long gradual ramp to Piute Mesa, amid Mojave yucca, cacti, and small Joshua trees. At the start of the plateau it skirts High Table Mountain West End, which commands excellent views over precipitous slopes into Lanfair Valley. From the Piute Valley viewpoint at the end of the road, it is 0.7 mile along the crest, over three low rocky spurs, to Ute Peak.

Either way, it is a wild and scenic climb in rarely visited territory. All around the plateau and summit, Piute Mesa drops in staggered staircases of weathered cliffs and tall taluses draped in dark volcanic rubble. The panorama embraces hundreds of square miles of lonesome open valleys. The closest ranges are pushed back to a colorless crown pegged to a distant horizon that straddles three states. The exception is the Castle Mountains, their long serrated skyline rising just a few miles north. The nearly constant views over this striking range alone make it well worth looping back down the trail and road—13.4 miles of wildness, secluded and silent, downhill almost the whole way.

■

WOODS MOUNTAINS & HACKBERRY MOUNTAIN

The Woods Mountains and Hackberry Mountain just east of them are isolated volcanic ranges east of and adjacent to the northern end of the Providence Mountains. Together with the smaller Vontrigger Hills to the east, they form a 17-mile east-west mountainous alignment that loosely separates Lanfair Valley to the north from Clipper Valley and Fenner Valley to the south. With the exceptions of three short cherry-stemmed roads, the two ranges constitute the core of a large designated wilderness that extends well into Fenner Valley. Composed almost exclusively of ejecta from Miocene eruptions, each range holds one of the greatest diversities of volcanic rocks in the region. Suffused with the typical barrenness of volcanic ranges, home to prehistoric remains and tortuous canyons, they offer fine peaks to climb. Tortoise Shell Mountain alone, likely named after its symmetrical oblong dome, is begging to be climbed just for its wonderful name.

The Woods Mountains constitute a prime example of the devastation that volcanism can inflict essentially overnight. They are the product of many major eruptions that took place over a period of about 200,000 years starting around 17.8 million years ago. They came out of what is called a trap-door volcano. Its opening was defined by a circular fault hinged at one end, like a hinged lid on a mug. As magma approached the surface, superheated gases built up under the trap door until the phenomenal pressure blew it off. Clouds of volcanic ash were blasted across the countryside at near-supersonic speed. The sheer force of rising magma tore off chunks of basement rock the size of suburban houses, which were hurtled along with the ash. The bucolic landscape of lakes, marshes, and rivers that prevailed then was instantly wiped out. Below the ash, geologists have recovered the fossils of many animals and plants entombed alive by the cataclysm.

Within less than 100,000 years, a total of three ash eruptions took place. The total volume of ejecta was equivalent to a cube 3 miles on the side—at least 30 times what came out of Mount St. Helens in 1980.

The total released thermal energy was probably upward of 1,000 megatons. The blasts created a caldera 6 miles across and 2.5 miles deep, roughly centered on Tortoise Shell Mountain on the east side of the range. Its weakened gravity can still be detected nearly 18 million years later. The combined deposits formed a plateau of welded ash 230 square miles in area and 1,050 feet thick at its thickest—enough to bury the Eiffel Tower. This formation is known as the Wild Horse Mesa Tuff, after its prominent exposures on Wild Horse Mesa about 8 miles to the west, at the edge of the Providence Mountains. Over the next 100,000 years, a series of comparatively more tame rhyolite lava flows centered on the same caldera gave rise to the Tortoise Shell Mountain Rhyolite. This formation is exposed over most of the Woods Mountains. Subsequent erosion of parts of the extinct caldera has split the Woods Mountains into two blocks separated by mile-wide Woods Wash.

Hackberry Mountain was formed just a little earlier than the Woods Mountains. Almost all of it is made of Hackberry Spring Volcanics, a large field of interlayered lava and ash flows that accumulated from a series of vents starting 18.5 million years ago. The subsequent eruptions of the Woods Mountains caldera capped it with thick layers of Wild Horse Mesa Tuff. On Hackberry Mountain most of this tuff has eroded; it survives only on the northern slope and east of the southern tip. The narrow handle that extends south from there is made of Peach Springs Tuff, produced by an even larger Miocene eruption in northwestern Arizona, and Early Proterozoic gneiss and granitoids.

In spite of their modest elevation, the Woods Mountains have an open evergreen woodland around their northwestern corner. Although comparable in height, Hackberry Mountain has only a handful of juniper near its summit. The north side of Hackberry Mountain has also been scorched by the 2005 Hackberry Fire Complex (see *Mid Hills*). In winter both ranges can be blanketed with snow down to their bases, a striking contrast from the fiery furnace they are in summer.

Despite their general bleakness, wildlife is comparatively plentiful in both ranges. It is not uncommon to see jackrabbits, ground squirrels, finches, hummingbirds, turkey vultures, chukars, and other birds, especially down in the slightly wetter and cooler canyons. A small band of desert bighorn lives in these two ranges, as do rattlesnakes.

The Woods Mountains hold relatively abundant signs of prehistoric occupation. Remains range from shelters to stone tools and a surprising number of sizable petroglyph sites. The natives may have been attracted by the abundance of cliffs suitable as dwellings, and of prime medium to do their art—fairly soft, darkly varnished volcanic rocks.

■

WOODS MOUNTAIN

> *This delightful climb is a tale of two worlds, one a canyon at the core of a volcano that congealed 18 million years ago, the other the sculpted shell of a mountain that has been eroding for just as long. The canyon is a vibrant symphony of underworld colors, the mountain a celebration of wide open spaces, and they stand united by a luminous patchwork of desert vegetation. Given time, nature can convert the most devastated land into a sweet slice of paradise.*

General Information
Jurisdiction: Mojave National Preserve
Road status: Roadless; standard-clearance primitive access road
The climb: 3.0 mi, 1,740 ft up, 190 ft down one way / difficult
Main attractions: A scenic box canyon, volcanic rocks, botany
USGS 7.5' topo maps: Columbia Mountain, Woods Mountain*
Maps: pp. 243*, 227

Location and Access
The unnamed high point of the Woods Mountains, sometimes referred to as Woods Mountain, is at the extreme northwestern corner of the range. It can be climbed from many directions, most shorter than the Rustler Canyon route, but none as scenic. From the Hole-in-the-Wall area, the Woods Mountains are the long sculpted mesa rising abruptly 1 mile east, emblazoned with long horizontal ribs. The summit is clearly visible; Rustler Canyon runs right behind the crest. To get to the canyon, from the turnoff to the Hole-in-the-Wall Information Center (see *Table Mountain* for directions), drive the Black Canyon Road 0.75 mile south to a primitive road on the left. Drive it 1.1 miles to its end at the wilderness boundary, staying left at the two forks, and park. This road has a small crown but it is passable with most vehicles.

Route Description
From the end of the road walk 0.2 mile, across sandy Black Canyon Wash, to the prominent low cliffs to the north. Go west along the base of the cliffs, then north around their tip, into Rustler Canyon. This is quite a pretty canyon, with impressive geology, plenty of large cacti of all sorts, and enough evergreen deeper in to make it a little festive. The idea is to proceed up canyon until the mood strikes to climb to its western rim, then to follow the crest north to the summit.

Rustler Canyon starts as a shallow wash meandering lazily between steep-walled mesas. The cattle that live here have designed optimum paths across the benches to shortcut bends and avoid rougher areas. A pygmy forest of desert willow and catclaw thrives in the wash. When they bear leaves and flashy trumpet-like flowers decorate the desert willows, the area feels like a small oasis. The slopes are green in their own way, thick with Mojave yucca, spindly cholla, and the bulbous heads of barrel cactus. Little by little the benches get narrower and the rims grow taller. Low cliffs of welded tuff coated with rich desert varnish rise along the wash. Erosion and freezing–heating cycles have carved them into overhangs, scores of gaping grottoes, and on one large wall an alien face with giant hollowed eyes.

By the time you reach the first side canyon, a pinkish chute of scooped slickrock 1.6 miles in, the canyon has closed up. The upper canyon up ahead is rougher, but it is also the prettiest. It has boulders, falls fortunately easy to handle, and an impregnable thicket that must be bypassed on a cactus-choked hillside. Stands of cliffrose, hollyleaf redberry, ephedra, and blackbrush grow in the wash, then pinyon pine and juniper, and cactus everywhere. Sunk deep into the caldera's rim, the canyon exposes mind-boggling cross-sections of extrusive rocks. It is littered with veined rhyolite, pale tuffs, clumpy breccia, and grades of volcanic rocks that defy cataloging. In the last quarter of a mile, exposures get larger at an accelerating pace, until the canyon dead-ends at a magnificent amphitheater rimmed by ominous banded cliffs.

The dilemma is whether to go into the upper canyon, at the price of a harder climb to the crest, or to bail out earlier but miss it. Exit routes out of the upper canyon are fewer and tend to have more outcrops. The last manageable one starts at about 4,800 feet, where the main wash is bedrock, along the south side of the second side canyon. Exiting at the amphitheater likely requires Class-5 moves. It is easiest to climb out on any number of possible routes up to the first side canyon. A good take-off point is 1.1 miles in the canyon (elev. ~4,310'),

Woods Mountain		
	Dist.(mi)	Elev.(ft)
End of road	0.0	4,040
Mouth of Rustler Canyon	~0.3	4,090
Leave wash	1.45	4,310
Saddle on canyon's west rim	1.7	4,715
Woods Mountain	3.0	5,590

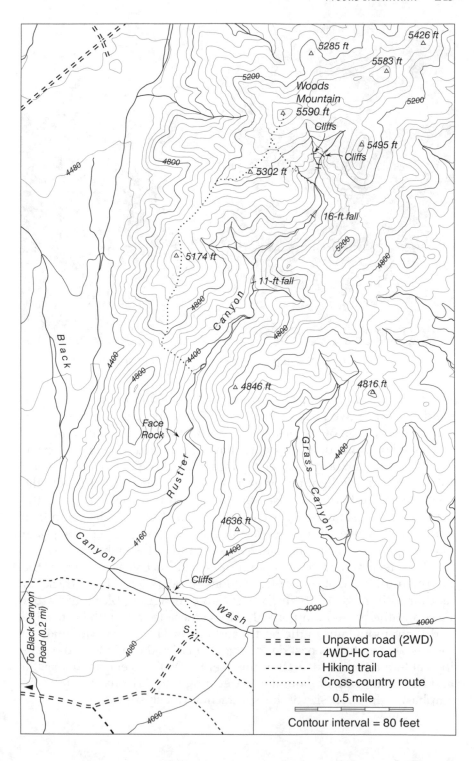

5426 ft
5285 ft
5583 ft
5200
Woods
Mountain
5590 ft
5200
Cliffs
4480
4800
5495 ft
Cliffs
5302 ft
16-ft fall
5200
4800
5174 ft
4800
11-ft fall
Canyon
4800
Black
4400
4800
4400
4846 ft
4816 ft
Face
Rock
4400
Grass
Canyon
Rustler
4636 ft
4400
Canyon
4160
Cliffs
4400
To Black Canyon Road (0.2 mi)
Wash
4000
4000
4080
S.
4000

===== Unpaved road (2WD)
- - - - 4WD-HC road
------ Hiking trail
············ Cross-country route

0.5 mile

Contour interval = 80 feet

Volcanic buttes along Rustler Canyon's mid section

where the wash veers north-northeast. It is a 400-foot scramble to the saddle between two mesas on the crest. The slopes are steep but open, with the exception of a series of long horizontal cliffs, broken and easily crossed or avoided. It is a scenic climb, through luminous gardens of barrel cactus, cholla, yucca, and pancake prickly-pear. The rocks are interesting, mostly light-tan or gray tuffs and white ash flows. On the crest, there are two low mesas to cross, then the final incline to the thinly wooded summit. Each mesa is encircled by low discontinuous cliffs and crowned with green bosques of pine and juniper. The going gets steep at places, but there are ways around or through the cliffs.

The steep-walled conical summit is a perfect vista to survey the aftermath of a mighty volcano. Millions of years later, large tracks of land are still made of its thick ejecta—the intriguing bluffs of Barber Peak and the broad hump of Wild Horse Mesa to the southwest, Table and Pinto mountains to the north, and bits of Hackberry Mountain to the east. Down below, past dark crags and twisted canyons, is the gaping caldera that spawned all of this. Lanfair Valley's enormous bajada and its distant ring of mountains stretching into Arizona dramatically emphasize the sheer size of this spectacular cataclysm.

■

HACKBERRY MOUNTAIN AND GUITAR MOUNTAIN

Rising 1,600 feet from Lanfair Valley's vast floodplain, Hackberry Mountain is the remnant of an extensive volcanic field that smothered this area around 18 million years ago. The short, steep climbs to its barren summit and neighboring Guitar Mountain provide an opportunity to discover isolated springs and a wealth of colorful extrusive rocks, and ultimately to embrace far-reaching panoramas of this remote corner of the California desert.

General Information
Jurisdiction: Mojave National Preserve
Road status: Roadless; primitive access road (HC)
The climb (Hackberry Mountain): 1.0 mi, 1,030 ft one way / moderate
The climb (Guitar Mountain): 2.0 mi, 1,020 ft one way / moderate
Main attractions: Volcanic peaks, geology, views of Lanfair Valley
USGS 7.5' topo map: Hackberry Mountain
Maps: pp. 249*, 227

Location and Access
The most conspicuous feature on Hackberry Mountain is a strongly tilted mesa shaped like a guitar resting on a high pedestal, on the range's north front. Long ago, when the Lanfair area was an active ranching and farming community, homesteaders referred to it as Guitar Mountain. It is easy to spot, a few miles south of the Cedar Canyon Road west of Lanfair, now a lonesome intersection. Hackberry Mountain, the high point of the range, is about a mile southeast of Guitar Mountain, a little north of the center of the range. The starting points to climb these summits are close to each other, so they can be climbed both in one day, or one can be reached from the other.

On Interstate 40 take the Fenner exit (57.2 miles east of Ludlow, or 35.2 miles west of the J Street exit in Needles). At the bottom of the westbound exit ramp, turn right on Goffs Road and go northeast 10.4 miles to the Lanfair Road on the left. This junction is in the small town of Goffs, 250 yards west of the railroad crossing. Drive the Lanfair Road 14.0 miles north to a dirt road on the left that heads southwest. Coming from inside the preserve, this junction is 2.2 miles south of the Cedar Canyon Road. Follow this road toward Hackberry Mountain 1.7 miles to a junction by some corrals. The road has a few ruts and a little sand at the corrals, but with care an entry-level sedan can make it.

To climb Hackberry Mountain, turn left on the Hackberry Spring Road. The road enters Hackberry Mountain along an open valley peppered with lava pillars and knolls. Before the Hackberry Fire Complex, this valley had an exceptional forest of giant Mojave yucca up to 10 feet tall. Now their gray trunks look like androids on a bad-hair day. The valley slowly pinches down to a scenic canyon dwarfed by tall taluses of rust-colored basalt streaked with white and mustard tuffs. For the shortest climb, proceed 2.5 miles to the end of the road just below Hackberry Spring. This road is rough, with large rocks, deep gashes, and catclaw jutting in on both sides. A high-clearance vehicle is mandatory. To hike the summit loop, park 0.5 mile earlier, at the fork in the canyon, which cuts down on the gnarly driving.

For Guitar Mountain, turn right at the corrals. This high-clearance road skirts the northern foot of Hackberry Mountain along the wilderness boundary. After 1.4 miles, make a left at a faint junction. Continue 0.6 mile to an old road on the left, closed to motor vehicles, and park.

Route Description

Hackberry Mountain. If you start from the fork in the canyon, walk the road to its end just below Hackberry Spring. Although this spring has also been singed, its thickets of catclaw are still standing. It usually has no surface water, but at times it discharges a few gallons per minute. In the springtime, it is blanketed with green grass and the myriad blooms of storksbill and fiddleneck. The catclaw's nickname—wait-a-minute bush—will take all its meaning if you cross the spring a little hastily and get hooked on the plants' curved spines.

From afar, Hackberry Mountain's elongated crest is reminiscent of a medieval castle ringed by impregnable ramparts. The least steep route to the summit is up the draw on the right just past the spring. The wash soon runs into tight narrows occluded by high falls. When the first fall is in sight, bypass the narrows up the draw's open southern slope. After 200 feet of elevation gain, you will reach the more level shoulder that wraps around most of Hackberry Mountain. If the wind has not blown it over, there should be a lone juniper about 100 yards to the west. Walk past it into the draw's upper drainage, then climb in the drainage southwest up to the crest. The rest of the route is along the narrow, mostly level crest. The cliffs that rim the final mountain block have plenty of breaks that are easy to climb. This climb requires little scrambling. But the climbing takes place on rock-strewn slopes along 30% of the distance, so this is not exactly a walk in the park.

Hackberry Mountain is a bleak desolation, dark-toned and sparsely vegetated, swept by icy winds in winter, scorched to three-digit

Approaching Guitar Mountain

temperatures in summer. Yet there is something captivating about this unrevered slice of desert. The massive outpourings that created it spawned a wilderness of minerals. Sheer bluffs dissected into fins of dark-brown tephra leap out of the slopes. White tuff outcrops in long scalloped cliffs. With the exception of Hackberry Spring Volcanics around the spring, this is all Wild Horse Mesa Tuff. Some of it is stuffed with large boulders propelled by the eruptions. There are trachyte dikes and rhyolite plugs, attractive olivine and pyroxene, and a rare horizon of beautiful spherical silicate crystals. The summit overlooks two dozen ranges, from the Providence Mountains to the

Hualapai Mountains in Arizona, and from Nevada's McCullough Range to Joshua Tree country. Wildlife blissfully ignores the threats of this unforgiving environment. Chukars quacked at the spring. A herd of bighorn sheep effortlessly climbed the crest near the open grove of juniper below the summit. Wispy bunch grass and flaming rock pea brightened even the most lifeless ground. That there is so much more than meets the eye is the best lesson this little mountain teaches us.

To return a different way, walk the crest back 0.2 mile to the false summit, then drop into the steep ravine northeast of it. After reaching the shoulder, cross it to the prominent flat bench to the southeast, then find the route of your choice down into the drainage to the west, which is the south fork of the access canyon. This descent is steeper than the climb, but it gives an opportunity to explore the pretty south fork. Its head is festooned with tall monuments of Hackberry Spring Volcanics. The unobstructed lower canyon leads back down to the road, past relict groves of catclaw and yucca and three small springs. The upper one was once tapped by a pipeline whose dislocated segments can still be traced all along the canyon. The middle spring has a grassy knoll and a manmade trench. The larger lower spring has a few willow and mesquite, and a small grove of cattail. You might hear, faintly rising from under it, the joyful sound of gurgling water.

Hackberry Mountain		
	Dist.(mi)	Elev.(ft)
Hackberry Mountain		
End of Hackberry Spring Rd	0.0	4,365
Hackberry Spring	~0.05	~4,420
Crest	~0.6	5,215
Hackberry Mountain	1.0	5,390
Wash in south fork	1.85	4,460
Lower spring in south fork	2.0	~4,420
Road at canyon junction	2.6	4,230
Back to starting point	3.1	4,365
Guitar Mountain		
Trailhead	0.0	4,010
Leave road toward saddle	0.65	~4,060
Ridgeline at saddle	0.85	4,190
Guitar Mountain	2.0	5,003
Saddle	2.4	4,710
Hackberry Mountain	3.4	5,390

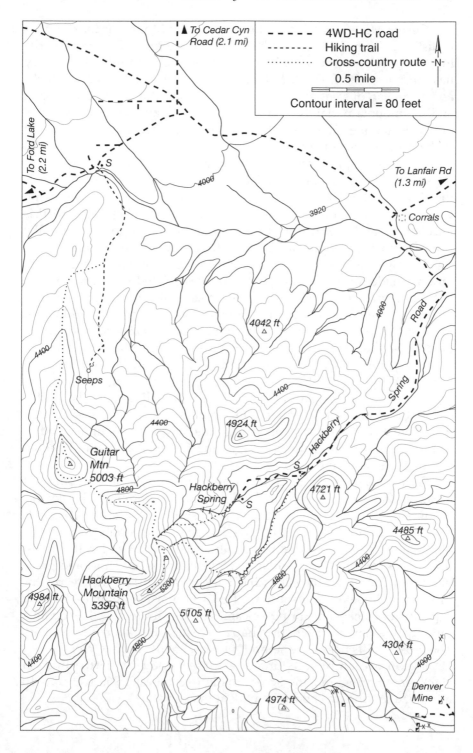

To Cedar Cyn
Road (2.1 mi)

4WD-HC road
Hiking trail
Cross-country route
-N-

0.5 mile

Contour interval = 80 feet

To Ford Lake
(2.2 mi)

S

4000

3920

To Lanfair Rd
(1.3 mi)

Corrals

Spring Road

4000

4042 ft

Seeps

4400

4400

4400

4400

4924 ft

Hackberry

S

Guitar
Mtn
5003 ft

4800

Hackberry
Spring

S

4721 ft

4485 ft

4400

Hackberry
Mountain
5390 ft

5200

4800

4984 ft

5105 ft

4304 ft

4900

4800

4400

4974 ft

Denver
Mine

Guitar Mountain. From close up Guitar Mountain looks oddly realistic, a cliff-bound slab of dark Wild Horse Mesa Tuff proudly rising skyward like a misplaced monument to rock and roll. The scenery has affinities with a Dali masterpiece; you half expect melted clocks and a caravan of slender-legged elephants. Because the terrain is open and the mountain plainly visible most of the way, this climb requires little orienteering. The hill a short distance southwest of the trailhead is the northern tip of the ridge that descends from Guitar Mountain. For the most foolproof route, climb this hill and follow the ridgeline to the summit. For greater diversity, hike the old road; it roughly parallels the ridge on the flat east of it. After 0.65 mile, leave the road, climb west to the saddle on the ridge, and follow the ridgeline. The road is locally faint and overgrown. If you lose it, just climb to the top of the ridge from wherever you are. Both routes are about 2 miles long.

The first part of this climb, along the road or ridge, is over soft ground made mostly of pale pebbles of vesiculated lava. The wildfire left scant survivors, although as usual several opportunistic plants, including a few species of eriogonum and a host of tiny wildflowers, have reclaimed the emptiness with unbridled exuberance. The second part, up on the guitar itself, is a canted tiling of rhyolitic slabs. The guitar was spared by the flames; the spaces between rocks are filled with grasses and green shrubs—ephedra, Wright buckwheat, and aromatic Mojave sage. The best part is the summit itself. All around, the land is sheared off into a girdle of dark cliffs plunging as much as 80 vertical feet. Here as all along the upper ridge the views are about as good as from Hackberry Mountain, encompassing Lanfair Valley and its timeless ring of sawtooth ranges.

Guitar Mountain's cliffs are largely unscalable, but a couple of breaks in the west-side cliffs make it possible to continue to Hackberry Mountain with little backtracking. The closest break is about 150 yards down (north) from the summit. The descent requires only easy scrambling on tall rock steps. The next break down is even easier. If all fails, hike to the bottom of the guitar, where the drops are short and gradual. From the foot of the cliff, circle back up (south) on the steep talus to the saddle below the southern tip of Guitar Mountain—the only exposure of Hackberry Spring Volcanics on this route. It is then about 1 mile up the narrow, seahorse-shaped crest to Hackberry Mountain. The broken cliffs below the summit plateau are not hard to cross.

If you are ambitious, make a longer loop by returning via Hackberry Spring and the access roads (8.8 miles, 1,960 feet up). To minimize driving on bad roads, park at the corrals.

∎

NEW YORK MOUNTAINS

The New York Mountains form the northeastern tip of the long cordillera that slashes across the eastern Mojave Desert. About 25 miles long and reaching 7,532 feet above sea level, they are the second highest range in Mojave National Preserve. They receive more moisture than most places in the region, and a good portion is covered with conifers. Combined with slightly cooler weather, spectacular geology, a long mining history, and an abundance of scenic canyons with seasonal streams or springs, this attribute makes this range unusually attractive for mountaineering in beautiful forested settings.

The New York Mountains feature an unusually diverse geology. The sensuous landscapes in the southwestern part of the range are composed of Mid Hills Adamellite. Directly against this pluton, near the east end of the main mountain block, lies a discontinuous band of sedimentary rocks, oriented roughly north-south and stretching from Carruthers Canyon to the mouth of Willow Wash. It is the remnant of a sequence of Paleozoic and Triassic carbonate formations, mostly Bird Spring Formation, Monte Cristo Limestone, and Sultan Limestone. The northeastern section is different still. Its south slope is made mostly of Miocene andesite and basalt, while its north slope is a faulted patchwork of gneisses, granites, and migmatite around 1.7 billion years old. Not too many desert ranges hold such a cross-section of rocks, and the variety of landforms that comes with it.

This range also hosts a remarkable botanical diversity. Aside from the usual associations of cactaceae grading into Joshua trees and conifers as the elevation increases, several unexpected species occur here. Two species of oak, scrub oak and canyon live oak, are found in the four main canyons on the south side. Scrub oak shrublands are rare in California, while canyon live oaks occur only in the eastern part of the Mojave Desert. In Carruthers Canyon, the larger canyon live oaks are found in nearly pure stands covering a good fraction of an acre. In Live Oak Canyon they form a thick green corridor, with specimens standing 30 feet tall. Much larger areas are occupied by chaparral plants such as manzanita and desert mountain lilac, more commonly indigenous to the California coast. Higher elevations, in particular in Carruthers Canyon and the highest ridges, are home to two-needle pinyon pine, also rare in the Mojave Desert. The rarest resident is the white fir. A tiny stand of about 30 trees grows on 2.5 acres sheltered on a steep ridge north of the highest summit, the last remnant of a once extensive boreal forest.

The New York Mountains were among the first in the region to yield valuable minerals. Copper was discovered in Carruthers Canyon possibly as early as the 1860s, and silver in Sagamore Canyon in 1870. Silver might also have been mined and even milled in the early 1860s. The Sagamore Canyon mines produced a little lead and silver off and on until the 1920s, then copper and zinc in the early 1940s. The Vanderbilt gold mines, active from 1891 to around 1942, were among the most diligently worked. For about a decade Vanderbilt was a boisterous town supported by several mills and numerous properties. All other mines, including in Carruthers, Keystone, and Cliff canyons, were far less productive. In 1969, the Goldome Mine installed a large mill and chemical complex to recover Vanderbilt's leftover gold and silver. The historic mines combined probably produced at most a few hundred thousand dollars, yet by establishing early on the presence of mineral assets in the region, they were a major mining catalyst in the east Mojave Desert. They sparked further prospecting and strikes. To service this and other districts further north, a reduction plant was installed in Needles as early as 1881. A railway was constructed across Lanfair Valley to the south to connect the mines to the mill. The Barnwell and Searchlight Railway, later grafted onto it, brought in business from Nevada. In turn, these rails helped open Lanfair Valley to homesteaders and supported mines as far north as Death Valley.

The closest place to dine and sleep indoors while in the area is Nipton, in Ivanpah Valley north of the mountains. Once a lively crossroad that faithfully served the railroad and local mines, Nipton is now a funky small community whose architecture and people reflect both its historic roots and more recent efforts to support tourism and a few artists. Hotel Nipton, a picturesque adobe building with an Old-West decor, is the only bed and breakfast for miles. You can also rent one of the Eco-Lodge Tented Cabins, heated with a wood-burning stove in the cold season. The Whistle Stop Oasis doubles up as the town's bar and restaurant. The Union Pacific runs right by the hotel, so a night in Nipton can be an adventure in itself...

■

CASTLE PEAKS

The imposing volcanic monuments known as Castle Peaks that cap the northern New York Mountains' crest are distinctive landmarks of the eastern Mojave Desert. For each peak the difficulty increases exponentially closer to the top, culminating with a vertical pitch that requires technical climbing. But climbing even part way up will deliver stunning bird's-eye views of these magnificent spires riding high above a green sea of cactus, juniper, and Joshua trees.

General Information
Jurisdiction: Mojave National Preserve
Road status: Roadless; primitive access roads (HC)
The climb (Dove Pk): 2.8 mi, 1,060 ft up, 180 ft down one way / difficult
The climb (North Castle Butte): 3.1 mi, 1,160 ft up, 210 ft down
        one way / difficult
Main attractions: Volcanic monuments, fantastic views, technical climbs
USGS 7.5' topo maps: Castle Peaks*, Crescent Peak
Maps: pp. 255*, 229

Location and Access
Castle Peaks are in the northern New York Mountains, about 9 miles southeast of the small railroad town of Nipton. From the Nipton Road exit on Interstate 15, drive the Nipton Road east 3.5 miles and turn right on the Ivanpah Road. Drive 16.7 miles south to the signed Hart Mine Road on the left. Follow this graded road 4.85 miles to a sharp right bend. At the start of the bend, a primitive road continues straight. This road, and the portion of the Hart Mine Road you drove on, are the abandoned berm of the Barnwell and Searchlight Railway, a 23-mile track that operated between 1907 and 1924. Continue straight on the berm 0.9 mile to a four-way junction and turn left. Go 2.3 miles to the rocky grade that climbs the side of an earth dam, then 0.6 mile to the wilderness boundary, marked by green metal posts. If you are driving a standard-clearance vehicle, the couple of rougher spots along this last road may stop you. Even if they don't, park at the foot of the grade, which requires good clearance, and walk from there.

Route Description
The approach to the peaks is along a shallow canyon that curls leisurely up to the crest of the mountains. Its slopes are forested with a

green spread of shrubs, Joshua trees, and Utah juniper. The walking is easy, either along the narrow sandy wash or the few surviving segments of road that parallel it. In the warm season the ground is brightened by Indian paintbrush, Goodding's verbena, globemallow, desertgold, phacelia, phlox, desert mariposa, and the usual gang of high-elevation cacti in bloom. After 1.3 miles the road goes over a first summit, descends a little to a fork (keep left), then climbs to a pass over the New York Mountains' crest. This area of subdued relief is a beautiful desert garden, and a vivid example of segregation in the plant kingdom. The ground cover is a patchwork of prickly-pear here, blue yucca over there, and staghorn cholla a little further. Barrel cactus, as often, almost exclusively congregate on steep south-facing slopes.

The pass offers the first good views of Castle Peaks' majestic spires. Sheer-walled and scarred by tall vertical gouges, they stand defiantly astride the mountain crest, like invincible sails riding colossal waves. The first one from the right, which I refer to as Blade, is an impressively thin fin. The second one is unnamed. The smaller third peak is concealed behind it. The fourth one is Dove Peak. The fifth has been largely eroded. The sixth, capped by a rectangular block, is the highest. It is sometimes referred to as North Castle Butte. All peaks require Class-4 or Class-5 ascents. Like the many pinnacles that line the nearby ridges, they are composed largely of andesite breccia. Named after the Andes, this rock has the same composition as diorite: it contains mainly feldspars and dark minerals like biotite, but no quartz. It is usually the product of explosive volcanoes, often above subduction zones, and this andesite may not be an exception. It erupted around 25 million years ago, when the Farallon Plate was subducting beneath the North American continent.

To climb Dove Peak, 100 yards beyond the pass leave the road and cross the rolling talus on a northeasterly course parallel to the spires. After 0.6 mile, climb to the fourth pass, south of Dove Peak. Then scramble up along the peak's narrow south spine to the stocky summit block. This is an airy Class-3 ascent on steep bare rock, not always stable, with vertical drops on both sides. The technical portion is on the east side of the gnarled summit block, up a 20-foot wedge. It requires a combination of low-5 stemming and face climbing (an anchor can be set up at the top). The breccia tends to break off when loaded, so be very careful. From the top, it is a short Class-3 scramble to the summit.

The view south from Dove Peak is awesome. You will be standing on the narrow platform looking *down* at the southern peaks towering above the open desert. Fortunately, it is not essential to reach the summit—the views from the upper part of the ridge are almost as good.

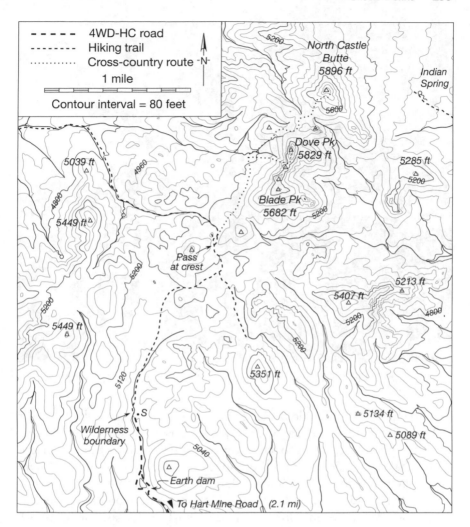

	4WD-HC road
	Hiking trail
	Cross-country route

1 mile

Contour interval = 80 feet

Castle Peaks

	Dist.(mi)	Elev.(ft)
Road's end (wilderness bdry)	0.0	4,965
Fork in road	1.3	5,165
Pass at crest	1.5	5,250
Climb to fourth pass	2.2	5,160
Fourth pass	(0.3)	5,620
Dove Peak	(0.6)	5,829
Sixth pass	2.8	5,470
North Castle Butte	3.1	5,896

Castle Peaks and Joshua trees: Dove (far left) and Blade (right)

To climb North Castle Butte, go 0.6 mile further across the talus (or 1.3 miles from the pass) to the grassy sixth pass, just south of the summit. The most direct approach is up the talus ridge to the left of the gully that drains down from the middle of North Castle Butte. Where the ridge meets the cliffs, there is a large cave. Circumvent this outcrop up on its left side, then angle to the right above it. Soon after, you will have to climb a 15-foot cliff, the hardest part of this ascent (Class 4). The summit block is made of beautiful brecciated andesite covered with knobby dark-brown fragments—pieces of mosaic straight from the center of the Earth. It can be climbed up a series of Class-3 outcrops, easier than the crux but locally exposed. It is an adrenaline-rich ascent, only for experienced rock climbers, but the payoff is matched— eerie views of the peaks to the south, and of the small army of odd-shaped pinnacles along the gulch southeast of the pass. Here too, however, all that is needed to get good views is walking up to the base of the cliffs. Both summits also offer fine panoramas of the region, particularly the Castle Mountains' notched skyline to the southeast, Ivanpah Valley to the north, and the Providence Mountains to the south.

■

NEW YORK PEAK

New York Peak, the highest point in this range, is reached by a scenic hike up Carruthers Canyon. This enchanting place is an artfully sculpted landscape of granite boulders, cliffs, outcrops, and pinnacles parading before an audience of oak and conifers. A beat-up road climbs through the lower canyon to a little mine sprinkled with blue-green minerals. The roadless upper canyon wanders into a handsome conifer forest. The rocky summit block itself, reached by a Class-3 scramble, overlooks some of the finest views in the desert.

General Information

Jurisdiction: Mojave National Preserve
Road status: Roadless upper canyon; 4WD road in lower canyon
The climb: 2.5 mi, 2,120 ft up, 210 ft down one way / strenuous
Main attractions: Forested canyon, spectacular monzonite formations
USGS 7.5' topo maps: Pinto Valley, Ivanpah
Maps: pp. 259*, 227

Location and Access

The most scenic of the four canyons that lead up to New York Peak, in the range's southern quarter, is Carruthers Canyon. From the Nipton Road exit on Interstate 15, drive the Nipton Road east 3.5 miles and turn right on the Ivanpah Road. Drive 24.1 miles (11.9 miles paved, then graded) south to the signed New York Mountains Road on the right. Follow it 5.6 miles west and turn right on the Carruthers Canyon Road. It enters the canyon about 0.4 mile further, a peaceful wide meadow funneled between steep monzonite slopes peppered with conifers. Ignore the side roads, which are all on the left and dead-end at campsites. In 1.6 miles, the road crosses the overgrown canyon wash. On the opposite side, 200 yards further, it curves left and passes by the first of a few forested campsites on the right side. From there on the road seriously deteriorates. Park and continue on foot.

Route Description

Carruthers Canyon is a rare treat. Most of it is a beautiful field of Cretaceous quartz monzonite fashioned by erosion into countless hoodoos. The lower road passes by Easter Island Rock, a slender monolith that rests on a contact point so narrow that it seems to violate the laws of gravity. About 150 yards past it, a spectacular wonderland of rounded monoliths spills out below the road. Foot Rock is 100 yards further—a giant bare foot seen from the bottom, toes wiggling in the air. The pale sculptures are enhanced by the greens of the chaparral—manzanita, hollyleaf redberry, desert mountain lilac, silktassel, and scrub oak. In late spring, mound and grizzly bear cactus, globemallow, penstemon, and many annuals bloom brightly all over.

After 0.4 mile, the road splits inconspicuously. The main road (left) continues steeply up the narrowing canyon. Great inclines of reddish monzonite rise hundreds of feet, diced into jointed fins, bulging boulders, and obese pinnacles. Up on the high rims loom even more formidable monuments. The road ends past a pointed mountain shaped like a Chinese hat, at the main tailing of the Giant Ledge Mine. This copper and gold deposit, likely discovered in the 1860s, was exploited mostly in the 1900s, when a few workings were dug in a copper-rich quartz ledge. If it was prosperous, it was not for long—it has been mostly idle ever since. Bornite, chalcopyrite, galena, scheelite, and huebnerite still sparkle on the slender tailings. Between two shallow pits, a rock face is coated with a saturated palette of azurite and malachite.

Past the mine, the upper canyon is filled with trees. Progress gets gradually slower—dodging pines, circling around boulders, and bushwhacking when all else fails. Not far up, the wash describes a long arc along the base of an awesome slickrock wall, a swollen nose of polished monzonite that soars over the canyon's west side. In the summertime, hawks often circle overhead; hummingbirds buzz by, drawn by the Indian paintbrush. In early spring or after a rainstorm, a little water flows over the wash's bumpy bedrock.

From the slickrock wall the peak is only half a mile away as the crow flies, but nearly 1,400 feet up, and hard work across the thickly forested upper drainage. When bushwhacking near the wash gets too tedious, follow the north slope instead a little above the wash. This very steep, lopsided stretch ends at North New York Peak. The rest is

New York Peak		
	Dist.(mi)	Elev.(ft)
First forested campsite	0.0	5,620
Fork in road (go left)	0.4	5,700
Giant Ledge Mine (tunnel)	1.15	6,100
Slickrock wall (start)	1.35	~6,160
North New York Peak	2.3	7,463
New York Peak	~2.5	7,532

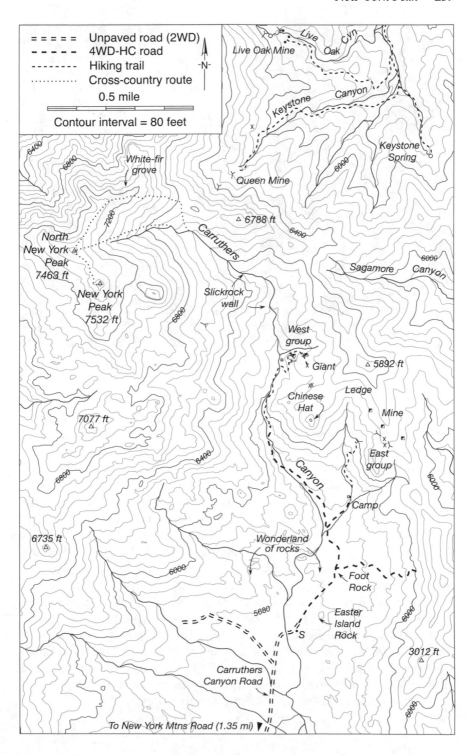

= = = = = Unpaved road (2WD)
- - - - -   4WD-HC road
- - - - - -   Hiking trail
....   Cross-country route

-N-

0.5 mile

Contour interval = 80 feet

Live Oak Mine
Live Oak Cyn
Oak
Keystone Canyon
Keystone Spring
6000

White-fir grove

6400
6800
Queen Mine
△ 6788 ft
6400
Carruthers
Sagamore Canyon
6000

North New York Peak 7463 ft
7200
New York Peak 7532 ft
6800
Slickrock wall
West group
Giant
△ 5892 ft
Chinese Hat
Ledge
Mine
7077 ft
6400
East group
6800
6600
6400
Canyon
6000
6735 ft
Camp
6000
Wonderland of rocks
Foot Rock
5680
Easter Island Rock
S
3012 ft
6000
6800
Carruthers Canyon Road

To New York Mtns Road (1.35 mi) ▼

Wonderland of quartz monzonite on the way to New York Peak

across a gentle saddle to the base of New York Peak. The summit block is an impressive pyramid of tightly packed fins and spires rising about the heads of pine. Several routes zigzag up to its small summit, all at least a Class-3 scramble, with some exposure. The easiest access is from the west, but the north side is a go too—it is a matter of taste.

For a more aerial route, 0.25 mile past the end of the slickrock wall scramble up the canyon's steep north slope to the divide with Keystone Canyon to the northeast. Continue up the even steeper ridge west-northwest to the main crest, around the head of Carruthers Canyon to the two peaks. This is about 0.25 mile longer, with more outcrops but less brush. It also passes right above the rare grove of white fir that graces the mountain's abrupt north slope.

The summit commands one of the most breathtaking panoramas in the eastern Mojave Desert. The south slope is a fantastic landscape worthy of a science-fiction masterpiece, bristling with hundreds of sharp pinnacles. Below it, a rolling sea of pine and juniper washes down to the bright edge of Lanfair Valley. On a clear day you will gaze across thousands of square miles of largely empty desert, from the San Bernardino Mountains to Arizona and Death Valley country.

■

PINTO MOUNTAIN

Of the few remaining exposures of the colossal lake of molten lava and ash that flooded the Lanfair Valley area in the Miocene, Pinto Mountain is the most colorful. Its south face is a striking mesa capped by a mile-long cliff balanced high on sheer taluses. The valley below it is a luminous grassland dotted with conifers that sweep up the graceful arc of the mountain's flank. In contrast, the north side has a subdued topography softened by erosion and stripped bare by the 2005 wildfire. When you climb Pinto Mountain, you swing from one side of it to the other and sample both worlds — the arboreal pre-fire desert, and the slowly healing post-fire holocaust.

General Information
Jurisdiction: Mojave National Preserve
Road status: Roadless; good graded access road
The climb: 2.3 mi, 1,100 ft up, 70 ft down one way / moderate
Main attractions: Forested canyon, easy climb, views of the preserve
USGS 7.5' topo maps: Mid Hills, Pinto Valley
Maps: pp. 263*, 227

Location and Access
Pinto Mountain is part of the narrow southern brow of the New York Mountains, overlooking the Mid Hills to the south and the spacious plains of Lanfair Valley to the east. If you drive long and scenic Cedar Canyon Road across Mojave National Preserve east toward the remote ghost town of Lanfair, it is the first unmistakable landmark you will come upon as you reach the top of Cedar Canyon and enter Lanfair Valley. To get there, from the service station at the Cima Road exit on Interstate 15, drive the Cima Road 17.5 miles south to its end at Cima's railroad yard. At the stop sign just before the railroad, turn right on the Kelso-Cima Road, toward Kelso. Go south 4.6 miles to the signed Cedar Canyon Road on the left (coming from the south, this junction is 14.2 miles north of Kelso). Drive the Cedar Canyon Road east 6.0 miles to the Wild Horse Canyon Road on the right, then 0.9 mile past it to where Cedar Canyon opens up. Pinto Mountain will be the cliff-bounded mesa rearing up half a mile to the northeast. Look for a small dirt road on the left (the way to the summit), facing a dirt road on the right, and park near this intersection. The Cedar Canyon Road is paved for the first 2.3 miles, then it is a good, broad, graded road.

Route Description

The beginning is leisurely, up along the easy grade of the dirt road on the north side of the Cedar Canyon Road. In 100 yards it reaches a wilderness boundary and angles right, along the boundary. Go straight instead, into the wilderness, up an abandoned track that aims toward the obvious canyon at the west end of Pinto Mountain. This area is particularly scenic. It is a grassy flood plain sprinkled with evergreens, Joshua trees, and occasional cactuses, right under the mountain's colorful cliffs. The mountain's west face records two major regional volcanic eruptions. The top cliffs are made of locally famous Wild Horse Mesa Tuff, the same formation that makes up the wildly pitted escarpments at Hole-in-the-Wall. The lower layer is a bulging drop of fluted tuff as gray as ash, the top layer a crew cut of columnar basalt in warm earth tones. Smaller cliffs protrude from the abrupt taluses well below them, which are the remaining ledges of the older Peach Springs Tuff.

After 0.5 mile, where the track comes down to the sandy wash just inside the canyon, leave it and continue up the wash. In 0.4 mile, and 50 yards before the first sharp right bend, a side canyon opens up on the right, pointing northeast. It is walled in on its left by a low ridge with vertical outcrops and stately pine. A 35-foot rock fall is visible blocking the way 0.1 mile up the side canyon's narrow wash. Walk up to the fall, which is easy to climb, a few Class-2 moves over large boulders and bedrock. Here as in the canyon, the country rock is Rock Spring Monzodiorite, nearly white monzonite grading into black hornblende diorite. This small pluton from 97 million years ago was named after a nearby spring with perennial pools deep enough to drown.

From the sandy patch at the top of the fall, count 130 steps and you will come to a fork. Both forks will get you to the summit, but take the right fork, where route finding is a bit easier. Above the fall the original forest is intact, and you find yourself instantly immersed in totally different terrain. You walk in a narrow, dimly lit wash that meanders in a tight ravine thickly forested with juniper, barberry, pinyon pine, and squawbush. Many trees seem too large for a desert, easily centennial, with deeply carved trunks and roots clutching at boulders. You have to duck under low branches, climb over fallen trees, and brush against juniper garlanded with strips of peeling barks.

A tenth of a mile past the fork the forest ends at the edge of the burn, and the scenery changes again. The rest of the way, the land has been torched by the blaze. Everywhere the grey ghosts of juniper claw at the air. Another 0.1 mile up the ravine, a naked gully opens up on the left. Climb it to the top of a ridge, where Pinto Mountain's squat summit first becomes visible, less than a mile due east. Descend 70 feet

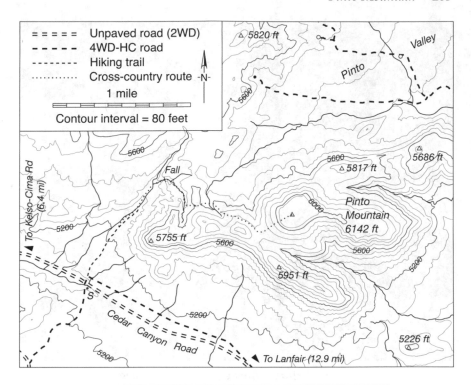

Pinto Mountain

	Dist.(mi)	Elev.(ft)
Cedar Canyon Road	0.0	5,115
Side canyon (right)	0.9	5,305
Fork (go right)	1.1	5,420
Gully (go left)	1.3	5,505
Top of ridge	1.45	5,615
Saddle on crest	2.0	5,785
Pinto Mountain	2.3	6,142

into the ravine directly below, cross it, and continue up the ravine's west flank to an eroded bench on the side of the hill west of the summit. Then contour the hillside to the saddle between that hill and the summit. The rest is up Pinto Mountain's broad southwest shoulder, a steep but short and unobstructed slope, and likely the only place where you might puff a little.

The summit is a desolate plateau fortified by needle grass scattered with grizzly bear cactus and blue yucca, a meager garnish that barely

Pinto Mountain from Cedar Canyon Road

keeps the soil from being blown off to bedrock. It is so broad and flat that it clips the view in most directions; the half-mile walk around the plateau is a better way to enjoy this central observatory. The views extend remarkably far and touch on all the preserve's major ranges. On the horizon, from Nevada and Arizona to the edge of southern California, more remote ranges collapsed by distance rise in single, hazy-blue ridges, too far to identify, except for the formidable hump of the San Bernardino Mountains.

This is certainly not the desert's most charismatic summit. But during certain times and seasons, it is transfigured by light. In the spring, the whole mountain comes alive with the myriad orange-red blossoms of thousands of globemallow. In late fall and winter, brittlebush flood the washes with pale-green fluorescence. In the slanting rays of late afternoons, every bush on every hillside glows gold and trails a long blue shadow across the land. In the final hours of a sunny day, the cliffs burn from within in deepening shades of apricot, as spellbinding as alpenglow.

■

MID HILLS

From Butcher Knife Canyon at their north end to just north of Columbia Mountain at their south end, the Mid Hills are all of about 10 miles long and 6,430 feet high. More the whim of a forgotten cartographer than a well-defined range, they are a squat collection of hills that links two giants—the New York Mountains to the north, and the Providence Mountains to the south. As diminutive as it may be, this range has merits of its own. Rich in granitic rocks, it is a scenery-charged collage of iconic boulders. Obliterated by a major fire in 2005, much of its woodlands have been transformed into a surreal world of bleached trunks and naked rocks. The comparatively subdued topography makes it a good place to indulge in easy climbs and seek these post-apocalypse landscapes and hidden vestiges of the original forest.

The Mid Hills are made largely of weathered 93-million-year-old Mid Hills Adamellite. It is by far the largest of the seven plutons that make up the Teutonia batholith: it extends nearly continuously from near Slaughterhouse Spring in the New York Mountains to Macedonia Canyon in the Providence Mountains. Much of it is monzogranite and fairly uniform—light-colored, with even-sized medium grains. Some outcrops contain very large feldspar crystals, dark gray hornblende, and olivine. Although this pluton exhibits intense mineralization elsewhere, in the Mid Hills much of it is bare, and mining was very limited. Some of the region's most ancient rocks—gneisses and granitoids between 1.66 and 1.7 billion years of age—extend in a narrow north-south band generally slightly east of the crest, from Live Oak Spring to south of the Mid Hills Campground. The only non-intrusive rocks are the Peach Springs Tuff and Wild Horse Mesa Tuff in the tablelands at the eastern and southern edges of the Mid Hills, in particular colorful Table Mountain and Wild Horse Mesa.

In June 2005 almost all of the Mid Hills were destroyed by a devastating fire. It was a complex of fires, ignited by hundreds of dry lightning strikes throughout the core of Mojave National Preserve over a relatively short time, starting on Hackberry Mountain. A coalition of unfortunate factors made it particularly damaging. The previous winter and spring had brought an average rainfall of 20 inches over the area, more than twice the normal amount, which had given rise to exceptionally thick vegetation. By June, all this biomass was dry and poised as a formidable reservoir of fuel. On the day the fire started, winds up to 40 miles per hour raged over the high desert. It was a perfect storm. Firefighters could not contain the blaze, which died out on its own when the wind subsided three days later. By then almost 71,000 acres had been consumed, much of it to the ground, including extensive evergreen and Joshua tree woodlands, from the northern Providence Mountains to the southern New York Mountains, and from the Mid Hills east to Hackberry Mountain. It was the greatest natural makeover to hit the preserve in human history.

Almost everywhere you go in the Mid Hills, you will be confronted with charcoaled ground and decimated vegetation. It is easy to think of this aftermath as a heart-breaking finality. It is harder to see it as a new beginning that spawned a different kind of beauty. For eons entire landscapes have been destroyed and reborn; Earth is a recovering mosaic of past catastrophes. The Mid Hills happen to be going through the rebirth phase of one of these endless cycles. Habitats are changing. Plants that had taken decades to grow, like juniper, are largely gone. Plants that did not have enough space, light, or water to flourish before the burn are now thriving. Springtime floods the newly created open spaces with more annuals than might have grown here in centuries. By 2010 much ground had been partially reclaimed, albeit by different combinations of species. It will take years for shrubs to mature and for diversity to build up, 20 to 30 years for trees to become established, and 100 to 150 years for old growth to rule again. As transient visitors, we are witnessing in slow motion a snapshot of a long dynamic process. It gives us a unique opportunity to observe how plants and animals cope with this extreme change in environment, and what brand new worlds rise from the ashes.

A well-developed network of graded and primitive roads makes the Mid Hills easily accessible. The Mid Hills Campground, in the southeastern part of the range, still has much of its original forest, and it is a refreshingly shaded place to camp in hot weather. The Mid Hills are small but packed with interesting features. Besides more than a dozen springs, there are countless areas for scrambling and bouldering, beautiful exposures of weather-worn outcrops, and good views from the range's low and generally easily climbable crest.

■

EAGLE ROCKS

Eagle Rocks are the two majestic peaks of bare granitic rock that crown the Mid Hills, a prominent landmark visible from much of the preserve. It is a walk in the park to the foot of these monuments, through a cool conifer forest and an eerie stretch of burnt land, but the last 100 feet to the summits are nearly vertical and require good technical climbing skills. The surrounding field of gargantuan boulders and outcrops offer plenty of less challenging alternatives, and equally breathtaking vistas of Cima Dome and Kelso Basin.

General Information

Jurisdiction: Mojave National Preserve
Road status: Roadless; access on short primitive road (2WD)
The climb: 0.9 mi, 380 ft up, 170 ft down one way/technical climbing
The loop climb: 2.1 mi, 1,070 ft loop/moderate, with scrambling
Main attractions: Granitic spires, boulders, rock climbing, pine forest
USGS 7.5' topo maps: Columbia Mountain, Mid Hills*
Maps: pp. 269*, 227

Location and Access

Eagle Rocks are in the southern Mid Hills, within easy walking distance of the Mid Hills Campground. To get to the trailhead, from the Essex Road's westbound exit on Interstate 40, drive the Essex Road north 9.7 miles to the Black Canyon Road on the right. Follow this road 9.75 miles north to the turn-off to the Hole-in-the-Wall Information Center. Stay on the Black Canyon Road, which becomes graded soon after, 6.7 miles north to the signed Wild Horse Canyon Road on the left. Drive this good graded road 2.7 miles to a primitive road on the right, just before a left bend. Take this road 0.15 mile to a fork. Along the way, you will see Eagle Rocks occasionally poking over the horizon up ahead. Turn right, and park after 0.15 mile in a tiny pullout on the right, 20 yards before the junction with the left fork (see map). Most vehicles can make this road. The trail to Eagle Rocks starts just beyond the wilderness boundary signs on the north side of the road.

Route Description

The trail to Eagle Rocks is an aging road that climbs up a little, then descends gently along a broad canyon. It traverses an exceptionally dense forest of pinyon pine and juniper, their crowns brushing

Southern peak (left) at Eagle Rocks

against each other. The air smells of sap, big sagebrush, herbaceous plants, and warm desert soil. Even on the hottest days large patches of cool shade flood the sticky carpets of pine needles. The forest soon disappears at the sharp edge of the 2005 burn. Encouraged by increased sunlight, opportunistic plants are proliferating on the open ground studded with upright charred trees. From mid-spring through summer wildflowers often flood this area, especially globemallow, giant four o'clock, Goodding's verbena, and evening primrose. Shortly into the burn Eagle Rocks come gradually into view, two magnificent sugarloaves of naked stone protruding 200 feet above the crest to the west. After about 0.5 mile the trail angles left towards them. A fainter trail marked by a wilderness sign branches off to the right. Stay on the road. It climbs a short slope to a low crest, passes in front of the southern peak, then crosses the head of the west-draining ravine that separates the two peaks. The road finally continues as a vague track a very short distance to end at the base of the northern peak.

This is a beautiful site. The northern peak is a towering monument bounded on all sides by nearly vertical walls. The southern peak is slashed by deep parallel fractures. They are both surrounded by chaotic skirts of huge boulders, smoothly rounded by erosion. All of this is

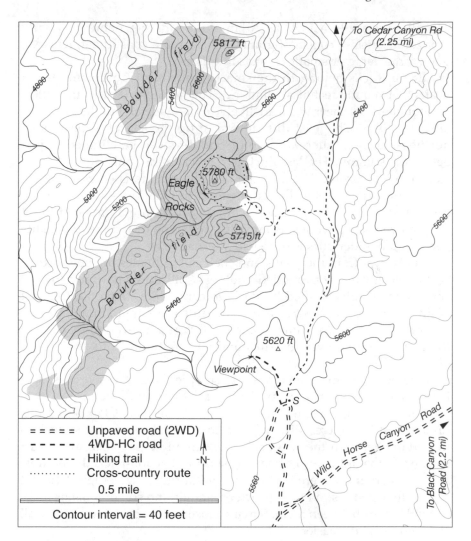

Eagle Rocks

	Dist.(mi)	Elev.(ft)
Trailhead	0.0	5,570
Jct (trail to Cedar Cyn Rd)	0.55	5,465
Cedar Canyon Road	(2.75)	4,575
Crest at Eagle Rocks/end of rd	0.7	5,555
North end of trail	~0.8	5,600
Back to trail via peak loop	1.35	5,595
Back to trailhead	2.1	5,570

93-million-year-old Mid Hills Adamellite—another name for quartz monzonite, a close cousin of granite whose main constituent, feldspar, often forms large prismatic crystals in this area.

Eagle Rocks belong to the small minority of California-desert peaks that require technical climbing. The northern peak is the tallest and toughest. Its sheer walls are likely to dissuade all but the most resolute climbers. The least difficult route up the southern peak is its northeast corner, where a ramp of boulders can be climbed to just below the summit. The last pitch is a crack climb, only around 12-15 feet high but a solid 5.9 and exposed. The granite is coarse-grained, and friction is good, but the grains tend to flake off—apply extreme caution. If you are serious about climbing here, come prepared to set up removable protections. Scrambling up some of the lower satellite peaks and boulder piles is not a bad alternative...

The views from the peaks and their subordinates are spectacular. To the west, waves of rounded boulders spill down abruptly toward eerie pointed hills slashed by dark volcanic dikes. Beyond, the vast plains of Kelso Basin stretch out for miles to Cima Dome and the Granite Mountains. In summer, the landscape gets even more alien as the heat haze dissolves the surrounding mountains into an ethereal blur.

The best way for non-climbers to sample the impressive west side is to circumvent the highest peak. From the end of the faint trail, proceed north into the ravine at the north end of the trail. Clamber up this ravine west to the crest. Then find a route south beneath the peak to the ravine between the two peaks, and finally climb this ravine east back up to the old road. This loop is short but action-packed. The west side is steep and covered with massive boulders. Averaging 10 feet across, they just rest on top of each other, with no soil or smaller rocks to fill the gaps between them. Staying closer to the peak's western wall is generally a little easier.

This 300-acre playground is loaded with surprises. Here and there, small enclaves of vegetation have been spared by the flames. Sacred datura, manzanita, locoweed, bitterbrush, and grasses thrive in the lifesaving shade of a few thick hollyleaf redberry and pinyon pine. Against the western base of the peak, a row of chiseled dolmens point skyward like prehistoric temples to the stars. A 3,000-ton behemoth rests in impossible equilibrium against a nearly vertical surface. The south-side ravine is obstructed by a long monolith the size of a small house. If you enjoy scrambling or bouldering, the sky is the limit.

■

TABLE MOUNTAIN

The climb to Table Mountain's high plateau is one of the eastern Mojave Desert's unavoidable classics. It calls for navigating through the mountain's surreal core of granitic boulders to reach the seemingly impregnable cliff-bound volcanic mesa that caps the mountain. The exercise is aerobic, the volcanic rocks are wild, and the desolate mesa commands far-reaching views of the Lanfair Valley area.

General Information
Jurisdiction: Mojave National Preserve
Road status: Roadless; primitive access road (HC)
The climb: 2.0 mi, 970 ft up, 80 ft down one way/moderate
The loop climb: 5.3 mi, 2,600 ft loop/moderate–difficult
Main attractions: A volcanic plateau, views, granitic boulders
USGS 7.5' topo maps: Columbia Mountain, Woods Mountain
Maps: pp. 273*, 227

Location and Access
The shortest route up to Table Mountain starts from the end of the ridge that extends west from the mountain. To get there, from the Essex Road's westbound exit on Interstate 40, drive the Essex Road north 9.7 miles to the signed Black Canyon Road on the right. Follow this road 9.75 miles north to the turn-off to the Hole-in-the-Wall Information Center. Stay on the Black Canyon Road, which turns from paved to graded soon after, 5.15 miles north to a primitive road on the right side, just past a cattle guard. Table Mountain's mesa profile rising to the northeast is clearly visible along the last few miles. Drive this spur road 0.65 mile until it runs into another road, and make a hard left. Continue 0.6 mile to a windmill and water tanks at the southern foot of the Table Mountain ridge, and park. High clearance is required to handle a couple of rutted spots near the start of the spur.

Route Description
Table Mountain is one of several insular remnants of the huge plateau of lava and volcanic ash spewed out by the Woods Mountains' caldera around 17.8 million years ago (see *Woods Mountain*). Its free-standing geometric outline protruding from the high-desert plain is an eye-catching landmark visible from many locations throughout the

Woods Mountains from Table Mountain's bouldery western ridge

eastern part of Mojave National Preserve. It can be ascended either from the open plain on the south side of the mountain, or along the ridge. I recommend climbing the first route, which gets you to the summit faster, and returning along the rougher ridge, which will keep your interest peaked even after the high of the climb.

From the windmill, head southeast along the long fence that parallels the ridge. After about 0.6 mile, cross the fence and cut a beeline east toward the cove at the base of the ridge below the western tip of the mountain. Two broad gullies converge at the east end of the cove; one drops from the northeast, the other from the east. Climb the latter, then continue in the same general direction, staying in the boulder-free areas when possible. After 0.3 mile of moderate climbing, angle left (northeast) and climb the remaining 0.1 mile to the ridge's crest. A broad, grass-covered gully framed by boulders traces the crest. Follow it east up to a local rise (~5,870 feet), then down a lopsided incline to a saddle at the foot of the long talus that shoots up to Table Mountain. The most demanding part of this hike is ascending this 40° slope of soil sprinkled with juniper, pinyon pine, and rocks. The talus ends at the western foot of Table Mountain's circle of cliffs, layers of cream and chantilly volcanic ash capped by milk-chocolate columnar basalt. Work your way south along the base of the cliffs about 80 yards to a rock-

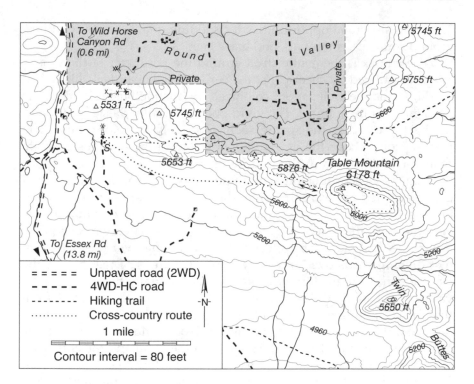

Table Mountain

	Dist.(mi)	Elev.(ft)
Windmill	0.0	5,290
Cross fence	~0.6	~5,395
End of cove	1.1	5,410
Ridge crest	1.5	5,810
Table Mountain	2.0	6,178
Table Mountain (east end)	2.5	6,135
Return via ridge	5.3	5,290

strewn breach in the cliffs, then climb up through the breach to the rim. The summit, all of 10 feet higher, is just 50 yards north.

This is a fun climb, short and easier than it looks—scrambling is not even necessary. The volcanic rocks are remarkably diverse, the cliffs imposing, and the vegetation has healed enough since the 2005 fire to liven up the desert again. The area is home to quite a variety of wildflowers. Sacred datura, white tidy-tips, Goodding's verbena, mound cactus, and giant four o'clock are among the most striking.

There are also good opportunities for spotting quails, turkey vultures, ground squirrels, cottontails, and black beetles.

The climax is the gentle stroll around the perimeter of the mountain top. Isolated by sheer cliffs, the eerily flat plateau feels like a lost world, far above civilization, colonized by anemic bushes and dwarf trees, most of them burnt. The vivid pools of woolly daisies that flood the bare ground in the spring seem too lively to belong here. The plateau floats above the desert like an island in the sea, closer to sky than earth. Sit down in the middle of it and its edges become your horizon, as closed-in as on a tiny planet. On the south side, a small grove survived the blaze. Inside it, the warm fragrance of juniper and big sagebrush brings back a modicum of earthiness. As you circumvent the mesa the desert revolves slowly, superb in every direction. At the mesa's east end, slabs of congealed lava hang over the sharp rim like diving boards over an empty pool. Hundreds of feet below, the land rebounds in great granitic waves that gradually dissolve into the vastness of Lanfair Valley. Range after range rise on the horizon, from the Castle Mountains to the Old Woman Mountains. To the southeast lies ground zero, the gaping void in the Woods Mountains where the caldera blew its top. There is no sound but the wind and the cliff swallows darting in and out of the cliffs below to perform reckless aerobics. Everyone should be so lucky to see this spectacle once in a lifetime.

After you tear yourself away from this spacious scenery, try returning along the more challenging ridge. Getting lost is not easy; the only difficulty is occasionally applying trial and error to search for a path through the jumble of boulders that cover much of the hilly ridge. The least obstructed route is always south of the crest; the north side is often steeper and clogged with boulders. The terrain is relatively open the first third of the way. The middle third is the roughest. There is no way to cross this wall-to-wall accumulation of close-packed boulders without getting intimate with the rocks. Some routes require minimal scrambling; others can be a welcome excuse to indulge in bouldering. Past this stretch progress is easier again, across more open, wavy terrain to the head of a steep ravine. The last leg is down this rock-filled drainage, where you might need hands again.

Wandering across this spectacular warehouse of boulders is one of the greatest rewards of this hike. Plump and well rounded, ranging in size from basketball to blimp, the boulders compose an ever-changing landscape suspended high against thin air. The blackened crowns of the dead trees add a tangible touch of hellishness. On many occasions the scenery literally stopped me dead in my tracks.

■

PROVIDENCE MOUNTAINS

With nearly 30 miles of rugged crest line rearing up from the high desert like an impassable barrier, the Providence Mountains rank among the most impressive ranges in the eastern Mojave Desert. Thanks to a particularly varied terrain and elevations spanning from around 2,500 feet to over 7,000 feet, they offer one of the region's greatest varieties of terrains and natural features—limestone caves, volcanic tablelands, heaps of boulders, rough canyons, forested slopes, and many springs. Add to this cornucopia spectacular cactus and yucca gardens, locally rare plants like simple desert agave, an unusually high density of derelict mines, mills, and mining camps, and you are looking at more action-packed mountaineering days than most people get to experience in a lifetime.

Most of this range lies within Mojave National Preserve. A 5,900-acre enclave on the eastern slopes, the state-owned Providence Mountains State Recreation Area (SRA), protects the famous Mitchell Caverns and the range's spectacular sawtoothed crest, including Fountain Peak (6,988') and Edgar Peak (7,162'), the range's highest point and one of the highest summits in the eastern Mojave Desert. Only one road was ever built across the Providence Mountains, a gas and power-line service road that scoots over Foshay Pass, a low notch in the crest just south of the central mountain block. The Macedonia Canyon Road clips the very northern tip of the mountains. All other roads are cul-de-sacs that go only as far as the foothills.

The Providence Mountains have the greatest geological diversity in the preserve. Volcanic, intrusive, metamorphic, and sedimentary rocks vie for space on the mountains' convoluted geologic map. The northern third, from around Columbia Mountain down to the large canyon east of Kelso, is composed mostly of ancient gneiss around 1.7 billion years old. The middle third, down to Foshay Pass, exposes the region's incomplete sequence of sedimentary formations, generally getting younger eastward, from Stirling Quartzite (Late Proterozoic) to the Bird Spring Formation (into the Permian). The exception is a few square miles of Fountain Peak Rhyolite (Middle Jurassic) on and around Fountain and Edgar peaks, responsible for the scenic spires on the highest crest. The southern third, south from Foshay Pass, is almost all Middle Jurassic intrusive rocks. Much of it is Quartz Monzonite of Goldstone, with small Jurassic–Cretaceous stocks of syenogranite at the Horse Hills and quartz syenite on Providence Peak. Finally, the Wild Horse Mesa area, which abuts the northeast flank of the mountains, exposes a thick stack of richly colored Miocene volcanics, mostly ash-flow tuff and lava flows. Two sizeable faults cut through the mountains, the East Providence Fault Zone along much of the length near the crest, and the Hidden Hill Fault Zone in the southern reaches.

Between the first discovery of mineral assets in 1880 and the 1950s, close to 170 mines were opened in the Providence Mountains, by far the largest number in the preserve. The greatest concentrations were along the west side between Macedonia Canyon and Tough Nut Spring, in the Colton Hills, around Goldstone Spring, and on the southeastern slope between Providence Peak and Hidden Hill. Most impressive are the two mines that made this range famous. The Bonanza King Mine, on the east side, was the area's second largest silver producer: between 1880 and 1924 it made close to $1.9 million. The Vulcan Mine, west of Foshay Pass, was the region's richest historic mine, bar none. In just a few years around World War II it harvested nearly $7.5 million in iron. A few other properties fared honorably. Between 1898 and 1943 the Big Horn Mine put out at least $130,000 worth of gold. In the 1895–1914 period the Hidden Hill Mine produced about half as much. The Francis Copper Mine probably reached the $50,000 mark in copper. Most other mines shipped either only a few tons of high-grade ore or nothing at all.

There are more good hard climbs to glean out of these mountains than any other range in the preserve. Fountain Peak and Edgar Peak in the SRA rank among the most strenuous. Neighboring Mitchell Peak can be climbed from the Bonanza King Mine up a demanding rocky ridge. For a taste of rough canyoneering and mountaineering, the west side of the main mountain block holds some of the very best in this part of the Mojave Desert. There are also many more accessible ascents. The abandoned dirt road to the summit of Columbia Mountain, at the north end of the range, is a good option for an easy climb. Hidden Hill, the lone sentinel on the southeastern edge of the Providence Mountains, commands spacious views of the preserve's boundless southeastern valleys and their ring of eroded volcanoes.

■

BARBER PEAK

Barber Peak is a tall, steep-walled mesa composed of a particularly colorful stack of volcanic cliffs and taluses, the legacy of phenomenal Miocene eruptions. The climb to its flat top is very short but particularly steep, on 45% inclines studded with rocks, cactus, grasses, and photogenic charred trees, and crowned near the rim with pinyon pine and juniper. The tilted summit plateau commands awesome views of the deeply sculpted surrounding volcanic country.

General Information
Jurisdiction: Mojave National Preserve
Road status: Roadless; access from graded or primitive road (HC)
The climb: 0.9 mi, 910 ft up, 40 feet down one way/moderate
Main attractions: Colorful volcanic rocks, views of Wild Horse Mesa
USGS 7.5' topo map: Columbia Mountain
Maps: pp. 279*, 227

Location and Access
Barber Peak parades at the heart of Hole-in-the-Wall, the popular area of vivid, eroded volcanic formations at the northeastern tip of the Providence Mountains. To get there, take the Essex Road exit on Interstate 40. From the north side of the freeway, drive the Essex Road northwest 9.7 miles to the signed Black Canyon Road on the right. Drive this road 9.75 miles north to the signed turn-off to the Hole-in-the-Wall Information Center. Barber Peak is the mesa across the road to the northwest. To access the shortest of several possible routes, continue on the Black Canyon Road 0.9 mile to a graded road on the left. Drive it northwest 0.3 mile to an old corral on the left, just past a 90° right bend. Turn left on a smaller primitive road that goes through the corral. Drive it 0.8 mile, along the northeastern base of Barber Peak, to a faint spur on the left, near the western tip of a low hill to the right, and park. This last road has a few bumps that require decent clearance. The route to the summit goes up the long ramp of alluvia that extends out from the base of the mountain to the south-southwest.

Alternatively, you can turn left off the Black Canyon Road and drive to the information center (0.3 mile), then park 0.15 mile further at the Hole-in-the-Wall picnic area (see map). You can then hike the Barber Peak Loop Trail, which starts at the west end of the picnic area, 1.6 miles counter-clockwise to the foot of the ramp.

Wild Horse Mesa from the western edge of Barber Peak's mesa

Route Description

Barber Peak is an island of Wild Horse Mesa Tuff, the compounded outpourings that erupted, sometimes violently, from the Woods Mountains caldera beginning 17.8 million years ago (see *Woods Mountain*). It is one of several mesas that remain after erosion removed most of this massive volcanic field. The mesa's flanks display colorful exposures of this formation, which stacks a great variety of volcanic materials. Short banks of white volcanic ash slash the mountain's lower reaches, chiseled into intriguing hoodoos. Higher up, the mountain is divided into four discontinuous bands of cliffs, gray cavernous tuff and columnar rhyolite the color of cocoa, spaced by steep taluses.

The alluvial ramp is the lower end of a narrow landslide that drops from rim to base and spills over all four cliff bands, providing a convenient passage over them. From the road, descend toward it across the open fan, until you reach the narrow Barber Peak Loop Trail (0.2 mile). Cross it, then the wash just beyond it. The ramp starts right across the wash. Its short nose climbs steeply to a longer, more level bench, crisscrossed by cattle tracks, that soon meets the foot of the mountain (0.15 mile). From there it is a stiff climb up the mesa's steepening flank to the mesa's rim—an elevation gain of 600 feet in 0.3 mile.

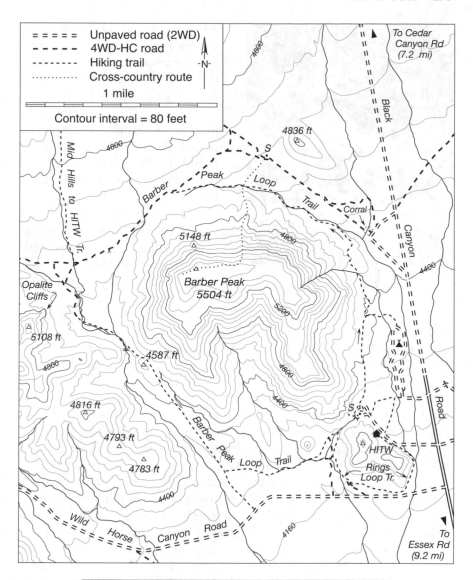

Barber Peak

	Dist.(mi)	Elev.(ft)
Road	0.0	4,629
Crossing Barber Peak Loop Tr.	0.2	4,590
Mesa's rim	0.65	~5,415
Barber Peak	0.9	5,504
Wild Horse Mesa viewpoint	1.0	~5,480

*Sculpted ash beds
on the flank of Barber Peak*

At the first two cliff crossings, the ramp pinches down to a narrow neck littered with boulders. The third crossing is almost imperceptible. The last one, just below the rim, is a jumble of large angular boulders choked with woody shrubs (hands help). The rest is an easy walk up the gently tilted mesa top to the subdued summit.

Since the area was ravaged by the 2005 wildfire, the vegetation has selectively recovered. Grasses dominate, and most types of cactaceae have grown back—barrel and calico cactus, chollas, pancake prickly-pear, and blue yucca. The whole mountain is studded with the silver and charcoal skeletons of the many pinyon pines that succumbed to the blaze. The highest slopes are still green with pygmy cedar, Mormon tea, and the full crowns of the lucky pines that survived. The broad, sloping mesa top is a scrawny tundra of small rocks and dwarf shrubs combed by the strong local winds—tuffs of blond grass, vermillion buckwheat, silvery grizzly bear cactus—and a scatter of juniper. It is a disquieting place, populated by a silent army of tree ghosts, permeated with the quiet sadness of desolation.

Barber Peak's lopsided plateau offers many good vista points, best discovered by walking along the abrupt edge of its irregular perimeter. On all sides the mesa drops precipitously to grassy valleys—Gold Valley, Wild Horse Canyon, Black Canyon Wash, and their braided distributaries—each one as radiant as an African savanna. From the eastern rim and on the way up, there are great views of Table Mountain's iconic silhouette and of the Woods Mountains' long, prominently banded mesa. The highlight is the alien viewpoint at the mesa's west end. Sharp volcanic peaks bristling with pinnacles rise way down below, buttressed at their tip by the white fluted bluffs of the Opalite Cliffs. The terraced cliffs of Wild Horse Mesa rear up behind them, capped on the horizon by the spiky outline of the Providence Mountains' high summits. It is a spellbinding landscape, tormented and primeval, carved right into the bowels of an apocalypse.

■

FOUNTAIN PEAK

Loaded with loose rocks, fierce plants, and Class-2 or 3 climbs, the short but strenuous ascent of Fountain Peak is one of the most spectacular in the eastern Mojave Desert. On the mountain's precipitous slopes, nature has arranged a blind date between some of the region's most dramatic formations and thickest cactus and yucca gardens. The views from the pine-dotted summit are unforgettable, embracing millions of acres of mountainous desert.

General Information
Jurisdiction: Providence Mountains State Recreation Area
Road status: Roadless, climb partly on trail; paved access road
The climb: 2.4 mi, 2,840 ft up one way / strenuous
Main attractions: A hard Class-2 peak climb, far-reaching views, botany
USGS 7.5' topo map: Fountain Peak
Maps: pp. 283*, 227

Location and Access
Fountain Peak is the southernmost of the Providence Mountains' three highest summits. On Interstate 40, drive to the Essex Road exit, which is about 100 miles east of Barstow, or 42.6 miles west of the J Street exit in Needles. Take the paved Essex Road northwest, into Mojave National Preserve, 15.6 miles to its end at the Providence Mountains SRA's visitor center. If you are coming from inside the preserve, take the Black Canyon Road south to the stop sign at the Essex Road and turn right. It is 6.0 miles to the visitor center.

The SRA is currently open only Friday through Sunday and holiday Mondays, and hours are limited. A good alternative that can be climbed anytime is the ~6,920-ft peak 0.3 mile south-southwest of Fountain Peak. At the junction between the Essex and Black Canyon roads, a wide high-clearance dirt road that services a gas pipeline runs straight west. Proceed on it 7 miles to Foshay Pass, marked by a yellow gas valve, and park. From the pass, hike the crest more or less the whole way to the ~6,920-ft summit (2.3 miles, 2,630 ft).

Route Description
From the visitor center, Fountain Peak is the sugarloaf summit that caps the mountains' crest; Edgar Peak is the next peak north, the highest in this range. The infrequent climbers who tackle Fountain Peak

tend to take the ridge on either side of the deep open canyon behind the visitor center. The Crystal Spring Trail climbs from the visitor center part way into the canyon, and cuts through some of the region's most awesome scenery. The slopes are bearded with a jungle of cacti more lush than almost anywhere in the preserve. Just about every local resident is represented, from ephedra to yucca, and spring flowers throw sparks of gold, blue, and vermilion against the greenery. Small boulders outcrop randomly, stained with vivid ochres and cloaked with colorful lichens. Switchbacks and stairways constructed with local rocks make for easy navigation through the uneven terrain. Less than half a mile away, the mountains rise in a sweeping amphitheater 2,000 feet tall, bristling with old pinyon pine and massive spires of reddish rhyodacite. The pipeline that parallels the trail on the north side of the canyon was built by Jesse and Ida Mitchell in 1934–1935 to bring water from the spring to their homestead at the caverns. After 0.7 mile the trail crosses Crystal Spring, a long grove entrenched in the narrow canyon, too thick to cross. The dominant species are willows and silktassel, a coastal evergreen shrub that resembles oak. Sometimes crystal-clear water fills small pools along the wash. The area is often active with quails, jackrabbits, and white-tailed antelope squirrels.

On the north side of the spring the trail climbs the canyon slope and ends shortly at a pointed outcrop with great views 3,000 feet down across Fenner Valley. For the northern route, climb up to the prominent saddle on the ridge 150 yards north. Then follow the ridge southwest to the false summit at the crest. You will need to gain 1,400 feet in 0.8 mile, across a terrain anything but cooperative. The main problem is the rhyolite towers that outcrop along the ridge. Some can be climbed, while others are best to bypass. The scrambling is fun, and it does not have to get technical. But all the trial and error consumes time and energy—it can take over an hour to cover this gnarly bit of ground.

For the southern route, get to the south ridge up the larger wash that the trail crosses 0.5 mile in. This ridge has fewer outcrops, and it is a little easier, but it still calls for some Class-3 scrambling and a few bypasses. Near the top of the ridge, route finding can be a little tricky. Make sure not to confuse the false summit with the slightly lower 6,617-ft summit southeast of it. You will need to get off the ridge on its north side and aim between these two summits, then climb up the steep ravine below to the south side of the false summit.

Either way, it is not an easy ascent. Negotiating the rhyolite plugs and the loose rocks is demanding. On more level terrain, there is often not enough space between cacti for a whole human foot. Chances of stumbling onto something eminently prickly are high. Gloves and

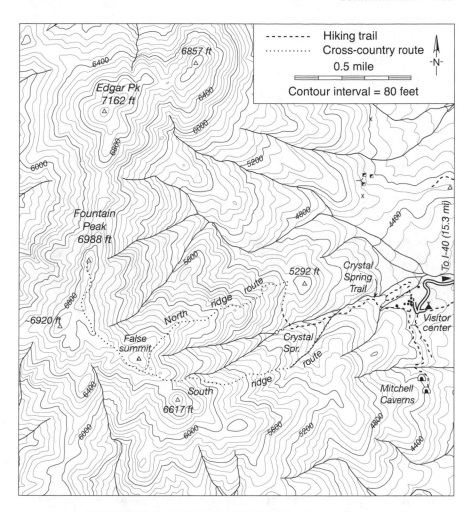

Fountain Peak

	Dist.(mi)	Elev.(ft)
Crystal Spring trailhead	0.0	4,310
Wash crossing/start south route	0.5	4,630
Join north route on crest	(1.05)	6,600
Fountain Peak	(2.2)	6,988
Crystal Spring crossing	0.7	4,890
End of trail at pointed outcrop	0.8	~5,120
Saddle on north ridge	0.9	5,220
Route jct below false summit	1.75	6,600
Fountain Peak	2.4	6,988

Wild Horse Mesa and Woods Mountains from north ridge to Fountain Peak

trekking poles come in handy. The upside is that both routes are aerial, with views stretching into Arizona. Mature pines grace the slopes and provide deep shade. A sizeable herd of bighorn sheep inhabits this region, so chances of an encounter are comparatively high.

When you reach the crest below the false summit, cairns will guide you around its south side, first down a short talus slope, then back up again. The next stretch is along a narrow, gently sloped ridgeline covered with an open pinyon-pine forest. The first peak to the west is not Fountain Peak. Continue along the sharp craggy ridge to the north instead. About halfway along this final stretch, another bypass is required, on the east side, just before getting to Fountain Peak.

The narrow summit commands dizzying views down the sheer slopes of the mountains, and magnificent vistas of most of the preserve. The tree-studded pointed summit of Edgar Peak rises majestically to the north. Spin slowly clockwise and you will see one after the other the iconic mesas of Hole-in-the-Wall, the New York Mountains and Piute Range, the Clipper and the Granite mountains, the Kelso Dunes, and the sprawling mass of the San Bernardino Mountains halfway to the Pacific Ocean. Another small turn and, if the sky is clear, you might make out the distant mountains of Death Valley.

∎

PROVIDENCE PEAK

> *Providence Peak encapsulates the most characteristic features of the Providence Mountains' high summits: the climb is comparatively short, rocky, steep, demanding, and it crosses hordes of cactus. To negotiate the tall ribs of granite near the crest, you may have to experiment and try different routes to keep it a Class-2 ascent. The summit area offers far-reaching vistas of most of the eastern Mojave Desert, millions of acres of endless valleys receding to crowns of distant ranges, including the magnificent Kelso Dunes.*

General Information
Jurisdiction: Mojave National Preserve
Road status: Roadless, climb partly on trail; primitive access road (HC)
The climb: 2.4 mi, 2,770 ft up, 40 ft down one way / strenuous
Main attractions: Fabulous views of the Mojave Desert, cactus gardens
USGS 7.5' topo maps: Fountain Peak, Van Winkle Spring*
Maps: pp. 287*, 227

Location and Access
Providence Peak is the highest summit in the southern portion of the Providence Mountains. It can be climbed from the Providence Mine, which is accessed by a dirt road in Clipper Valley, on the east side of the range. On Interstate 40, drive to the Essex Road exit, which is 49.7 miles east of Ludlow, the last place for gas and a fast-food fix, or 42.6 miles west of the J Street exit in Needles. Take the paved Essex Road northwest, into Mojave National Preserve, 9.7 miles to its junction with the signed Black Canyon Road on the right. A wide graded road cuts east-west through this junction, along a power line. Follow this road west (left) 0.45 mile and turn left on the unsigned Clipper Valley Road. Stay on it 4.85 miles in Clipper Valley to a primitive road on the right (Providence Mine Road). There are actually two roads within 70 yards of each other: this is the second, southernmost one. After driving 2.25 miles up the Providence Mine Road, a road comes in from the right at 7 o'clock. Continue straight 0.15 mile to a fork; look closely at your mileage, as there is a wash that is easy to mistake for a road just before it. Go 1.1 miles and park on the left side, just before a rocky, canted grade up. The Clipper Valley Road is graded and can be driven with a standard-clearance vehicle. The Providence Mine Road has a crown, serious ruts, and rocks, and high clearance is imperative.

Route Description

After argentiferous lead seams were discovered below Providence Peak about a century ago, for twenty-some years miners took turns developing a dozen properties. For a time the mountain echoed with the harsh sounds of hard-rock mining—drills, blasts, pumps, trucks, compressors, concentrators, generators, nearby mills, and the odd miner's snore at night. What little ore was pulled out barely paid for the dynamite, the whiskey, and the bullets that put jackrabbit on the menu. By the 1930s everyone had moved on, and Providence Peak had returned to its blissful age-old obscurity. Today's only visitors are a handful of hard-core hikers each year, and a few skittish cows in search of food and relief from the summer heat.

The easiest route to the summit starts on the mining trail to the area's most remote diggings. If you continue on the access road 120 yards, up the grade and around a left bend, it will be there on the left. Heavily damaged, hemmed in by thorns, this narrow twin track climbs slowly across a dissected hillside and enters into a deep cove in the mountain front. Providence Peak and the range's cliff-bounded crest loom steeply up ahead, a silent intimation of the hard labor to come. Here as elsewhere in this range, the desert has sprouted a remarkably verdant cactus garden. Several species have succumbed to gigantism, with staghorn cholla 5 feet high, Mojave yucca sporting multiple branches, and barrel cactus as puffy as fire hydrants. If it weren't for the trail, it would be tricky to get through without getting punctured.

After 0.6 mile, the trail angles 90° to the left as it narrows to a single track, descends a little to a small wash, and makes a right U bend across it. On the far side, it climbs gently 0.1 mile over the lower tip of Providence Peak's eastern shoulder—the way to the peak. Although it is tempting to continue on the trail to the mine, gaining access to this shoulder from the mine is an unpleasant trudge up a very steep and brushy ravine. It is easier to climb up the shoulder from this point.

	Providence Peak	
	Dist.(mi)	Elev.(ft)
Road at Providence Mine	0.0	3,890
Trailhead	0.05	3,910
Eastern shoulder	0.75	4,290
Saddle on ridge	1.5	5,215
Crest	~2.1	6,330
Providence Peak	2.4	6,612

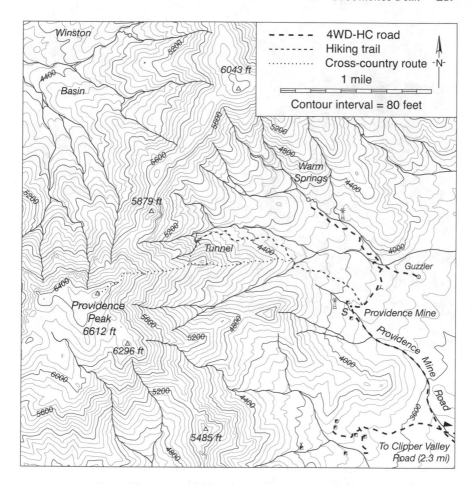

Providence Peak's eastern shoulder is fairly open and moderately steep at first. The lower elevation cactus garden extends up along it, thinner and mixed with pinyon pine. After 0.65 mile the ridge is interrupted by the first obstacle, a plug of granite artfully festooned with cactus, easily contoured on the left. Just behind it there is a shallow saddle. From there to the crest the terrain gets progressively rougher. The first part, up to about 5,600 feet, is still fairly open but much steeper, with more trees and boulders. Some of the climbing is done on the faint tracks gouged by the few temerarious cows that made it this far up. This is one of the few haunts in the Mojave for the simple desert agave, a handsome mescal with a thick blue-green rosette.

The second part is much more challenging. There the ridge is steeper still, and buried under a dorsal of tall granitic outcrops. Unless you tackle the Class 4–5 climbs on the shattered outcrops, the only

Mining trail and eastern shoulder ramping up to Providence Peak (left)

option is the steep flanks on either side of them. This stretch is ridiculously short—0.2 mile—yet so resilient that crossing it borders on com-
ical. You slip and slide on steep loose dirt and clamber sideways over
tumbles of wobbly angular rocks. You fight prickly plants on the south
flank, thick pine on the north flank, and fallen logs on both. To find
your way you have to accept being occasionally redirected.

Once on the crest, the summit is a short hike south, up a much easier open woodland of juniper and pinyon accented with low rounded
boulders. Up there you are suspended high between desert and sky;
the vistas are astounding, encompassing most of the eastern Mojave
Desert, from Nevada west to the Cady Mountains, and from the
Kingston Range southwest to the edge of la-la land. On a clear day the
panorama is as crisp as a diorama, each range neatly separated from
its neighbors. The middle ground is bristling with individual summits—the spiky crests of the Providence and Granite mountains, the
Bristol Mountains' sprawling archipelago, the somber lava terraces of
the Hackberry Mountains. Here too the Kelso Dunes hold center stage,
a long graceful island of luminous sand stretched out nearly one vertical mile below. This is an exhilarating sight to be remembered.

■

GRANITE MOUNTAINS

Rising majestically at the south end of the long chain of mountains that slashes across the eastern Mojave Desert, the Granite Mountains are the second highest in Mojave National Preserve, and quite possibly the most scenic. Their namesake dominates much of the range and composes striking landscapes of abrupt walls, slickrock, knobby ridges, and mountainsides of boulders. The southern and eastern foothills are dissected into beautiful coves nestled within silvery cliffs, many graced with verdant springs. The remote interior hosts rugged basins, serpentine canyons, and conifer woodlands inhabited by deer, bighorn sheep, and a few mountain lions. Unlike other nearby ranges, the Granite Mountains were virtually left untouched by miners; other than a couple of mining roads, they are as pristine as they ever were. About 9,000 acres, centered on the east side, are preserved as the Sweeney Granite Mountains Desert Research Center, managed by the University of California and off-limits to the public, including access to Silver Peak and Granite Mountain via Cottonwood Basin. Most of the rest is protected as a designated wilderness, and open to everyone willing to walk.

Rarely has a mountain range been so aptly named. At one time the area covered by the Granite Mountains was all Paleozoic sedimentary rocks. In the Mesozoic these formations were pushed up by the intrusion of multiple plutons. The overlying Paleozoic rocks were subsequently eroded, so that today the Granite Mountains are made almost exclusively of Mesozoic plutonic rocks. About 75% are a gift from the turbulent Cretaceous. The rest, mostly on the northern and northwestern fringes of the range and along much of Bull Canyon, date back to the Jurassic. One of the Granite Mountains' greatest assets is this fortuitous suite covering a wide spectrum of compositions, from monzogranite (the most common) to diorite, granite, quartz monzonite, quartz monzodiorite, and syenogranite. They also display many textures (fine-grained to porphyritic), structures (unaltered to gneiss), and colors (brown to dark grey and nearly white). Very few other areas in the eastern Mojave Desert showcase such extensive natural features carved out of granitic rocks, the plutonic equivalent, on a far more modest scale, of southern Utah's sensuous sandstone legacy.

The Granite Mountains are known for their exceptional biodiversity, which stems from a combination of a wide range of elevations and habitats, large variations in hydrology, and the fact that they face all cardinal points. They are home to nearly 500 species of vascular plants, 138 birds, 42 mammals, 34 reptiles, and 2 amphibians. There are chuckwallas and fringe-toed lizards, speckled rattlesnakes and rosy boas, ringtail cats, falcons and finches, foxes and feral burros, California juniper and rare agaves. Several drainages have seasonal or permanent streams with abundant flows, especially Bull Canyon and Budweiser Canyon. Some 50 springs are scattered throughout the range, a few with large groves of cottonwoods and willows. High elevations, typically above 5,000 feet, support open forests of pinyon pine and Utah juniper, some as tall as 25 feet and 500 years old. Individual trees and small stands also grow at unusually low elevation—as low as 3,600 feet—thanks to the propitious shelter and higher humidity offered by large aggregates of boulders. Smoke trees, rare in the preserve, grow on the open fan south of Granite Cove. In a single day in the Granite Mountains you might see toads, a deer trotting among blue yucca, oaks and Joshua trees, a golden eagle, and gorgeous bladderpods in bloom. This cohabitation of seemingly inconsonant species is one of the many charms of the Granite Mountains.

The Granite Mountains are a mecca for mountaineering and rock climbing. There is a nearly limitless selection of places for scrambling as well as technical bouldering and rock climbing on all kinds of near vertical surfaces, from boulders to cliffs. The granite varies greatly in cohesion and rugosity, but at many places it is quite strong. Boulders render many ridges impracticable, leaving canyons as the main means of reaching remote summits in the mountains' interior. Even so, progress in most canyons is generally difficult and slow because of the high density of outcrops and uncooperative vegetation. Climbing in this range may appeal mostly to seasoned desert hikers.

The Granite Mountains are also known for their extensive displays of rock art. Dozens of panels of polychromatic pictographs are scattered throughout the range. Most of them are abstract; some representing human or animal figures. The quest for these ancient messages in this 35,000-acre playground of igneous labyrinths can itself fuel a few years' worth of exploration on foot.

■

SILVER PEAK

The least painful legal route to Silver Peak, isolated near the center of the range, is up Devils Playground Canyon, one of the preserve's prettiest and roughest canyons. Its long chasm of sun-drenched stone threads through the mountains up a long brushy stairway of boulders and giant falls. After nothing short of an epic it leads to Bighorn Basin, an amphitheater of 6,000-foot peaks, and the steep finale up Silver Peak's forested north face. It takes perseverance, stamina, and patience to make it through this rebellious tract of nature where normal walking is often not an option.

General Information
Jurisdiction: Mojave National Preserve
Road status: Roadless; mostly standard-clearance access road
The climb: 5.7 mi, 3,630 ft up, 420 ft down one way / strenuous
Main attractions: A canyon with falls, springs, creeks, and boulders
USGS 7.5' topo map: Bighorn Basin
Maps: pp. 293*, 299, 227

Location and Access
To get to Devils Playground Canyon, from the westbound Kelbaker Road exit on Interstate 40 drive north into Mojave National Preserve 7.7 miles to Granite Pass, then 3.4 miles to a primitive road on the left side (it is easy to miss). Follow it 2.6 miles to a junction, passing by two roads on the left, and make a left. Park 0.15 mile further at the wilderness boundary. This last stretch is a little rocky and requires decent clearance, but the rest can be done with a normal vehicle.

Route Description
Things look rosy at first: the old road (El Compache Trail) to the Comanche Mine gives easy foot access into lower Devils Playground Canyon. It skirts foothills packed with granite boulders and outcrops, then switchbacks up a ridge with sweeping views of the southern Providence Mountains to the east, and Bighorn Basin and Silver Peak to the south. At the ridge's crest the Kelso Dunes burst into view, aberrantly bright in the dark V of the canyon walls. The trail ends after 1.65 miles in Devils Playground Canyon, and everything changes. Much of the rest of the way is up a wash and slopes overrun by monoliths carved out of the mountains' igneous core. The boulders jams are low

at first. The first high fall is climbable, or easily bypassed on the east side. The first main obstruction is more serious, a cove of bare granite blocked by a 20-foot fall that I named Fern, after its thick fur of maidenhair—a rare plant in the Mojave. Stands of cattail and willow shoots grow below it by a pool of stagnant water saturated with gecko-green algae. The least difficult bypass is up the tall east-side talus, although the broken chute down its far side is a crumbly Class-2 descent.

Thanks to its higher elevation, Bighorn Basin can receive a fair amount of rain and snow. After a wet winter, all this water pours over normally dry falls, splashes between boulders, and irrigates patches of green grass. Signs of this spirited creek are ubiquitous even months after it has retired underground—dried mud in the wash, black streaks on rock faces, and countless works of art polished in bedrock. Including Fern Fall, at eight places a hard plug of granite forms a high fall that dams up the water under the upstream gravel and holds at its wet lip a bosque of greenery. The next obstruction is at the lower spring, halfway to the second fork, a grand sweep of sensual slickrock capped by boils of cottonwoods and stately pinyon pine. Between this and the upper spring at the third fork lies the heart of Bighorn Basin, and the roughest stretch of canyon. There is a horseshoe-shaped fall of naked stone at the second fork, dense shrubs and trees held captive in its cusp. Between it and the next high fall, plants flood the wash at several places. For several hundred feet before the third fork the upper spring rules the canyon, almost too thick to cross. Some falls can be climbed, others must be circumvented across slopes seized by trees and boulders. A choice must constantly be made between bushwhacking, scrambling, climbing, or taking the long way around.

The third fork is ringed by a crescent of high summits crowned by the sugarloaf profile of Silver Peak. The easiest route to the crest is

	Silver Peak	
	Dist.(mi)	Elev.(ft)
El Compache trailhead	0.0	3,160
Devils Playground Canyon	1.65	3,280
Fern Fall	2.25	3,500
First fork	2.75	3,735
Lower spring	3.0	3,970
Second fork	3.25	4,115
Third fork/upper spring	4.0	4,545
Silver Peak	5.7	6,368

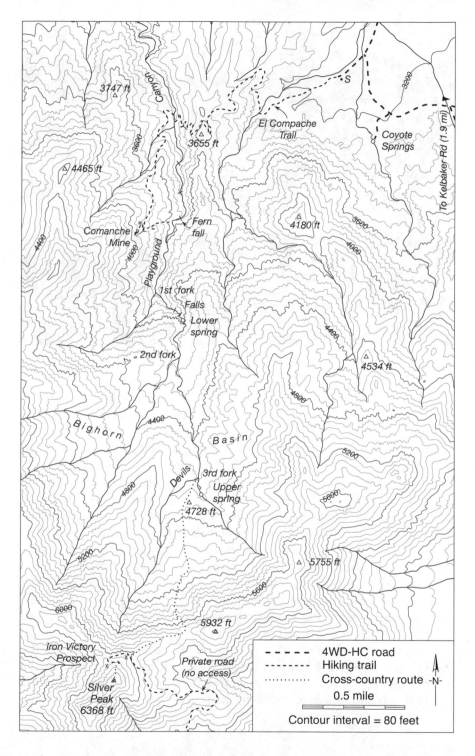

Silver Peak 6368 ft

Iron Victory Prospect

Private road (no access)

5932 ft

6000

5200

4800

Devils

4728 ft

Upper spring

3rd fork

Basin

Bighorn

4400

2nd fork

Lower spring

Falls

1st fork

Playground

Fern fall

Comanche Mine

4600

4400

4800

4400

4800

5600

5600

5600

5200

5755 ft

4534 ft

4800

4400

4000

4180 ft

3600

El Compache Trail

Coyote Springs

S

To Kelbaker Rd (1.9 mi)

3600

3655 ft

3600

Canyon

3747 ft

4465 ft

	4WD-HC road
....	Hiking trail
....	Cross-country route

-N-

0.5 mile

Contour interval = 80 feet

Southern Providence Mountains from the El Compache Trail

south up the low ridge between the two forks, toward the road and small marble pits of the Iron Victory Prospect visible just below the summit. At timberline half a mile up, cut southwest toward a ravine at a large outcrop across from it, cross it, and proceed up the ridge above the outcrop. Animal tracks zigzag up among sweet-scented pine the remaining third of a mile to Silver Peak's east shoulder. The road to the prospect is the same distance again up the open shoulder. The prospect, staked around 1912, explored a cluster of small skarns containing magnetite and hematite. Too small to be exploited, its 110,000-ton reserve of iron ore is still in the ground. The final struggle is a steep quarter-mile jaunt from the end of the prospect road to the summit.

In all directions, the views from Silver Peak are astounding. The summit is literally engulfed in the Granite Mountains—the deep gash of Bull Canyon on one side, Cottonwood Basin on the other, and Granite Mountain a forested horizon to the south, tens of square miles of igneous chaos right out of the Mesozoic. The grand prize goes to the Kelso Dunes nearly 4,000 feet below to the north, rising against the barren desert in majestic defiance, and the Devils Playground sands sprawling behind them for miles to the ivory shores of Soda Lake.

∎

GRANITE MOUNTAIN

There is no easy way up Granite Mountain. The route described here follows Bull Canyon, a long and tortuous swath blessed with narrows, slickrock, wildly decorated granitic walls, and perennial water that supports pockets of cattail, stately willows, and small waterfalls. With 4,400 feet of elevation gain over nearly 9 miles, this is one of the most demanding ascents in the Mojave Desert. Count on a very long day for this rough canyoneering trek copiously sprinkled with falls, tangles of vegetation, and giant boulders. Some people will prefer to take two or three days.

General Information
Jurisdiction: Mojave National Preserve
Road status: Roadless; mostly standard-clearance access road
The climb: 8.8 mi, 4,400 ft up one way / strenuous
Main attractions: Remote canyon, narrows, falls, springs
USGS 7.5' topo maps: Kelso Dunes, Bighorn Basin
Maps: pp. 299*, 227

Location and Access
Granite Mountain, the apex of the Granite Mountains, is on the rough southern crest of the range, overlooking Cadiz Valley to the south. The easiest route to it, from the northeast through Cottonwood Basin, is part of the Sweeney Granite Mountains Desert Research Center and closed to the public. The next shortest routes, from Willow Spring Basin to the south, are brutal slogs up washes and ridges overrun by boulders and ruthless brush. The route described here approaches it from the northwest along Bull Canyon.

To get to the mouth of Bull Canyon, from the westbound Kelbaker Road exit on Interstate 40 drive north 14.4 miles to the signed Kelso Dunes Road on the left. Coming from the other direction, this is 7.7 miles south of the stop sign at Kelso. Drive the Kelso Dunes Road 4.0 miles west-southwest to its end near the main dunes. Turn left on the smaller road that connects to a power-line road (0.15 mile). Turn right on this graded road and follow it 1.6 miles to a junction at the foot of a hill. With a standard-clearance vehicle, you will likely not be able to drive further; park and hike from here. Otherwise take the road on the left, which swings over the hill and meets the other road (0.35 mile). Then drive 0.3 mile to the next power-line tower. The very wide area between this tower and the next one west is Bull Canyon's floodplain. The main wash crosses the road 0.1 mile further. Park in this vicinity.

Route Description

Hidden in the Granite Mountains' convoluted foothills, Bull Canyon is hard to spot from the road. Its mouth is barely visible as a low notch in the hills a little over a mile to the south-southeast (145° magnetic bearing). A main wash leads up to it, surrounded by a braided network of narrower washes. The walking is much easier on the slightly higher ground between washes. The burros appear to agree: this is where they have blazed their trails. In the summer and fall, the floodplain is brightened by the many light-green desert willows and catclaw that thrive in the washes.

More than any other canyon around, Bull Canyon has "water" written all over it. All along the lower canyon, sweeps of water-worn bedrock alternate with a wash of rounded cobbles caked with dried mud and algae. Almost every mineral obstacle in the wash has a water-gouged plunge pool at its base, some several feet deep. One would be hard pressed to find in this desert a place with so many water-loving plants—so many groves of cattail, so many oases of tall willows, and thickets of narrowleaf willows. Even at the end of the long dry season, water survives in rivulets and countless pools held in slickrock hollows. So much water makes for tougher hiking. Stands of baccharis occupy large portions of the wash. Bushwhacking is often necessary, more frequently as the elevation increases. Progress is generally not too difficult where baccharis grows alone. The harder spots are where larger woody plants—catclaw, mesquite, willow, and tamarisk—congregate.

In spite of these hurdles, Bull Canyon is a pleasure to explore. The geology is off the chart, the flora uncommonly lush, and the scenery wild. The lower canyon cuts through dark-gray diorite and other Jurassic granitoids, commonly cleaved into flat surfaces coated with chocolate varnish. Thick white dikes draw wiggly courses across walls and slickrock. At four places the wash squeezes through short narrows trapped between these igneous rocks. The prettiest is the first one, a twisted wedge of naked stone lined with smooth chutes and shallow basins. Colonies of red-tinged barrel cactus and isolated calico cactus cling to the walls. Longstem evening primrose, a rare plant found in the preserve only at a handful of places, decorate large areas in the fall with their papery yellow flowers on 3-foot stalks. This is the home of quails, white-tailed antelope squirrels, scorpions, jackrabbits, bighorn sheep ossuaries, the rare simple desert agave, and burros gone wild.

The lower canyon ends at the first high fall, a wavy 18-foot slant of light-gray quartz-diorite gneiss bisected by a moss-covered chute. Bull Canyon's inner gorge starts just above it. Climbing this fall is at most a 5.7. There is a second fall shortly above it, a slick chimney about 14 feet high recessed at the head of a narrow passage of polished gneiss. Like the first fall, it can be climbed on the right side, and the difficulty and exposure are comparable. Both falls can alternatively be bypassed by scrambling up the steep rock-strewn ravine on the east side 100 yards below the first fall. After gaining about 200 feet of elevation and clearing the sheer spur to the south, work your way up canyon at roughly constant elevation about 60 yards to a ravine with a pine near its bottom. Then drop along this ravine back to the canyon wash, which will put you 80 yards above the second fall.

Waterfall at the first fall in Bull Canyon

The half-mile stretch above the falls is the tightest part of Bull Canyon. It starts with a stark passage beneath towering walls. The walls exhibit again the enigmatic artistry of igneous rocks, black, gray, and white exhibits of convoluted gneiss slashed by wandering veins. Further on, the canyon pinches through a shallow trench crowded by bulging walls of polished rock. Thick stands of cattail, desert willow, and tamarisk have invaded the narrow water-filled basins along the trench, leaving little space to squeeze by. Further still, slickrock and boulders take over, and bushwhacking gets a notch harder.

The inner gorge ends at the junction with the first major side canyon, where Bull Canyon makes a hard right. Beyond this point, the canyon retains some of its earlier character. It winds between high rock walls, past slickrock benches, inundated clumps of cattail, meadows of dark-green rush, desert willow, and an 8-foot waterfall concealed by exuberant vegetation. The bushwhacking intensifies gradually. Past a broad bend to the southeast, then the next two major side canyons a tenth of a mile apart on the right, the canyon enters the Granite Mountains' extensive conifer woodland.

The rest of the way, Bull Canyon is a beautiful V-shaped valley filled with hefty monzogranite boulders. Long monuments of this attractive Cretaceous porphyritic rock outcrop on the tall slopes. This last stretch is wild, remote, and the roughest. It takes nothing short of a blood-letting thrash to get through this chaos of brush, trees, fallen logs, and boulders and reach the broad saddle at the head of the canyon. From this saddle overlooking Cottonwood Basin to the east, the ultimate stretch is up Granite Mountain's northeast shoulder. This is a rough finale, a 1,070-foot ascent in 0.7 mile up a very steep forested ridge crowned by a large rocky outcrop.

Granite Mountain		
	Dist.(mi)	Elev.(ft)
Power-line road	0.0	2,360
Mouth of Bull Canyon	~1.4	~2,640
First narrows	2.6	2,950
18-foot fall	3.9	3,410
First major side canyon	4.4	3,600
Third major side canyon	5.1	3,835
Upper spring	7.3	4,890
Saddle at head of Bull Canyon	8.1	~5,690
Granite Mountain	8.8	6,762

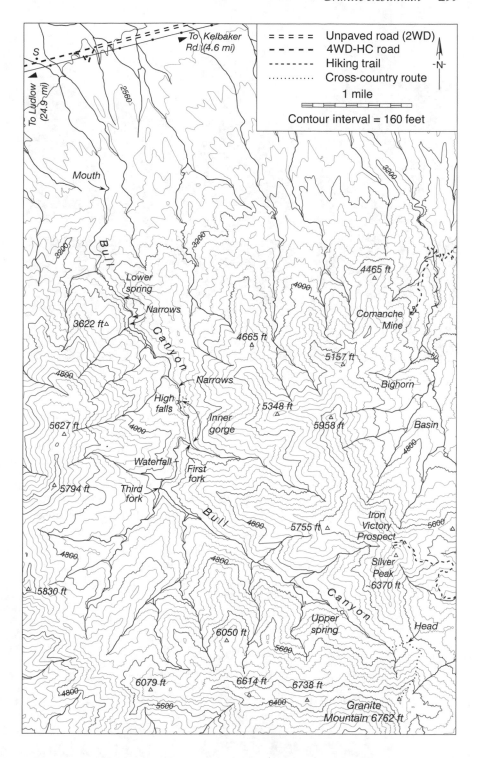

To Kelbaker Rd (4.6 mi)

===== Unpaved road (2WD)
----- 4WD-HC road
- - - - Hiking trail
·········· Cross-country route
-N-
1 mile
Contour interval = 160 feet

To Ludlow (24.9 mi)

S

Mouth

2560

3200

3200

Bull

Lower spring

Narrows

3622 ft

4665 ft

4465 ft

Comanche Mine

5157 ft

4900

Bighorn

4800

Canyon

Narrows

High falls

Inner gorge

5348 ft

5958 ft

Basin

5627 ft

4800

4800

Waterfall

First fork

5794 ft

Third fork

Bull

4800

5755 ft

5600

Iron Victory Prospect

5830 ft

4800

4800

Silver Peak 6370 ft

Canyon

Upper spring

Head

6050 ft

5600

6079 ft

6614 ft

6738 ft

5600

6400

Granite Mountain 6762 ft

4800

Bull Canyon above the third fork; Granite Mountain in the distance

On the quest for Granite Mountain, getting there is much more than the customary half the fun. Most of the time you are entrapped within the recesses of a deep canyon. The constant proximity to the physical world engages your senses on many more levels than most ridges ever do. The canyon holds you in rapture, and the spectacle from the summit is only the icing on the cake. The views are still wonderful. When you finally pull yourself up the ultimate ridge, the desert opens up all around with unexpected suddenness. Granite Mountain overlooks the Kelso Dunes, the Devils Playground, the Marble and Clipper mountains, and beyond them the heart of Mojave Trails National Monument, bounded by far ranges pegged at the blue edge of Earth's curvature.

■

CLARK MOUNTAIN RANGE

About 15 miles long, the Clark Mountain Range is a northeast-trending mountain that stretches from Mountain Pass along Interstate 15 to the Nevada border at Stateline Pass. To the south lies the Mescal Range, and to the north Nevada's vast Spring Mountains. Bounded on three-sides by extensive sinks—Shadow Valley to the west, Mesquite Valley to the north, and Ivanpah Valley to the east—it stands prominently above its surroundings. Its south end, including the rugged main mountain block, is protected as a separate unit of Mojave National Preserve. At its core lies a spellbinding 13,560-acre designated wilderness crowned by the carved rimrock of 7,930-foot Clark Mountain, the highest point in the eastern Mojave Desert and home to some of the best technical climbing on limestone cliffs in the country.

The Clark Mountain Range is one of the best representatives of sedimentary and meta-sedimentary rocks in the eastern Mojave Desert. It is a shattered mosaic of sandstone, siltstone, dolomite, limestone, shale, and quartzite. Around the main mountain block, the original stratigraphy has been majorly disturbed by movements along two roughly parallel, northwest-trending faults. The Mesquite Thrust Fault passes just east of the summit. The Clark Mountain Fault runs about 1.5 miles east of it. The sedimentary and meta-sedimentary rocks west of the Mesquite Thrust Fault have been shoved over the block sandwiched between the faults. They have thus eroded faster and been stripped of their younger top formations. What remains on that side is the older part of the sequence, from the Nopah to the Kingston Peak formations, generally getting older toward the western base of the mountain. The middle block, between the two faults, still preserves younger formations; from east to west it is made of Sultan Limestone, Monte Cristo Limestone, and Bird Spring Formation. These three units, exposed in an arcuate band that wraps around the summit's east-side scarp, are responsible for the majestic cliffs framing that most vertical flank of the mountain. The Monte Cristo Limestone and the Bird

Spring Formation host numerous species of mollusk shells, bryozoans, horn and tabulate corals, fusulinids, and crinoids. On the east side of the Clark Mountain Fault, all the sedimentary strata were removed by erosion. What is left is the continent's ancient crystalline basement, Early Proterozoic gneisses and pegmatites that extend from Mesquite Pass down to the eastern Ivanpah Mountains. Just north of Mountain Pass they contain a 1.4-billion-year-old intrusion of carbonatite. This rock is geochemically unique: it is based on carbonates instead of silicates, and stuffed with rare-earth minerals.

Clark Mountain has been a major mining center for more than 150 years. In 1868 it was the site of the region's earliest major strike. It led to the development of several particularly rich silver mines on Alaska Hill, northwest of the summit, which supported the thriving town of Ivanpah and brought in more than 3.7 million dollars. In 1898, after the best silver had run out, the Copper World Mine took over on the southwest side of the mountain. Twenty years later it had become the largest copper producer in southern California, with more than 1.3 million dollars in revenues. In the 1910s and from 1944 to 1952 the Mohawk Mine, south of Clark Mountain, put out more than $600,000, two thirds of it in lead, the rest in zinc, silver, and copper. The grand finale was yet to come: between 1987 and 1993, the Colosseum Mine ripped up from the range's ancient crystalline core more than 10 *tons* of gold. The area is still actively mined today: rare-earth minerals are being extracted at the Molycorp Mine in the foothills just north of Mountain Pass along Interstate 15—indeed a rare commodity found in important quantities at only a few locations on Earth. Our technological world uses rare earths in tiny quantities but in billions of devices, so what little it needs is vital. Without the rare earth called erbium for example, there would be no high-speed Internet.

This range is one of the strongholds of a few rare plants. One of them is the pygmy agave—also known as Clark Mountain agave. In California, it is known to occur only in this range, in the Kingston Range, and in the Ivanpah and New York mountains. It is easily recognizable by its neatly spherical rosette of narrow, yucca-like leaves fringed with sharp teeth and tipped with a long and slender spine, like a Cylon's nail. Another exceptional occurrence is white fir, one of the rarest trees in the California desert. A sizable forest of white fir and its attendant understory of single-leaf ash and mountain maple, both uncommon in the desert, thrives high on the northeastern slope of Clark Mountain.

■

ALASKA HILL

During the famous silver boom of the 1870s, Clark Mountain's richest mines were concentrated on a little mountain then known as Alaska Hill. If you have a penchant for history and grand vistas, you will enjoy climbing through the ruins of this historic mining district, up tall slopes peppered with Joshua trees, agave, juniper, and pinyon pine, to the top of this sharp hill overlooking Shadow Valley and Clark Mountain's sheer forested ridges.

General Information
Jurisdiction: Mojave National Preserve
Road status: Hiking cross-country and on roads; HC access road
The climb: 1.5 mi, 1,450 ft up, 160 ft down one way/moderate
The loop climb: 4.9 mi, 2,060 ft up loop/moderate
Main attractions: Historic silver mines, ruins, geology, botany, views
USGS 7.5' topo map: Clark Mountain
Maps: pp. 305*, 227

Location and Access
Alaska Hill is a compact, cone-shaped hill 3 miles north of Clark Mountain. From the southbound Cima Road exit on Interstate 15 drive the paved Excelsior Mine Road 8.5 miles north to a graded power-line road crossing the road. Turn right and drive it 6 miles to the Yates Well Road on the right. Go 1.2 miles on this road to a crossing and turn left on a primitive road. In 0.1 mile there will be a five-way junction. Take the second road from the left (northeast). Continue 0.8 mile (ignore the left fork halfway through) as the road curves right to an open area with large stone ruins on the right, and park. The power-line road is fairly good, but the last 3 miles have a dozen long steep grades that will stop low-power cars. The other roads require high clearance.

Route Description
Alaska Hill holds the distinction of being both the oldest and richest historic mining district in California's eastern Mojave Desert. Base metals were first discovered on its steep slopes in 1868, in the wake of Nevada's legendary silver rush, and in just a few months Alaska Hill was buzzing. Teamsters brought in supplies from San Bernardino, and returned loaded with raw ore worth as much as $800 a ton. Late in 1869, to accommodate the growing citizenry of miners, prospectors,

303

False summit to Alaska Hill from divide at top of Monitor Mine

merchants, and adventurers, a 160-acre town named Ivanpah was laid out around small springs on the other side of Clark Mountain. For a time the town was owned by the Ivanpah Con, which operated the Monitor and Beatrice mines, run by the McFarlane brothers. The next richest property was the Lizzie Bullock Mine, owned and operated by a seasoned miner named Julius Bidwell. After the McFarlanes put up a five-stamp mill in 1875, Bidwell raised the ante and installed his own ten-stamp mill. At its peak around 1879, Ivanpah boasted hotels, saloons, stores, blacksmiths, shoemakers, a post office, and a butcher shop, and a population of a few hundred. For a change the hard work paid off. Alaska Hill remained active until most of the good ore played out around 1891. By then it had churned out 100 tons of pure silver.

One of the pleasures of climbing Alaska Hill is exploring along the way its repository of antiques going back to the 1870s. From the trailhead the first goal is the Beatrice Mine, marked by the cabin pinned on the high ridge about half a mile to the south-southeast. The southern extension of the access road provides easy egress towards it at first. The road soon follows a narrow wash lined with the rubbled quarters of forgotten miners. It then enters a canyon so steep that erosion has ripped it apart. Joshua trees, yuccas, staghorn cholla, barrel cactus, and platoons of pygmy agave share the hillsides. After 0.3 mile the canyon

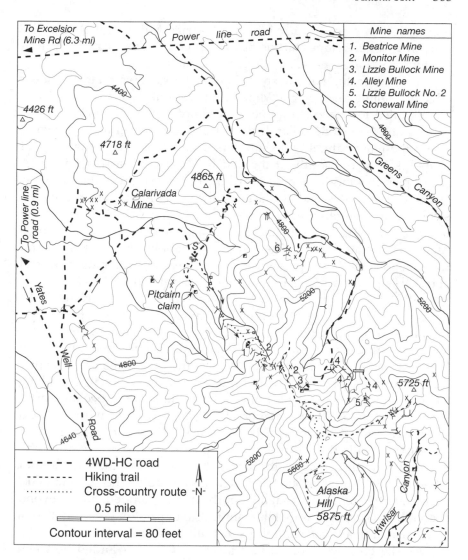

Mine names

1. Beatrice Mine
2. Monitor Mine
3. Lizzie Bullock Mine
4. Alley Mine
5. Lizzie Bullock No. 2
6. Stonewall Mine

- - - - 4WD-HC road
- - - - - Hiking trail
.... Cross-country route

0.5 mile

Contour interval = 80 feet

Alaska Hill

	Dist.(mi)	Elev.(ft)
Stone ruins at end of road	0.0	4,590
Beatrice Mine (cabin)	0.5	~5,080
Divide/trail	0.85	5,400
False summit	1.15	~5,760
Alaska Hill	1.5	5,875
Back via Lizzie Bullock Mine	4.9	4,590

angles left at a fork. To reach the Beatrice Mine, climb onto the canyon's western ridge starting at the left end of the long benchcut at the fork, and follow the rocky ridge to the cabin.

Trapped on the narrow space between a rock wall and the sheer edge of a tailing, the Beatrice Mine cabin is a funky patchwork of sheet metal nailed to a wooden frame, with empty shelves, a rickety table, and an attached stone cellar. It would be hard to find a shorter commute: the main tunnel and shafts are mere steps away; the furthest tunnel is 50 yards south, at the end of a tall and narrow tailing. A scenic picture window gapes toward the open desert way down below.

To continue, descend northeast to the wash. From there on up, the steep wash is largely buried under the Monitor Mine's overlapping tailings, testifying that this faulted Paleozoic block carried in its fractures considerable value. The fun part is looking for a path around these massive slants of pulverized rock. There is something powerful about this place, a persistent haunting stimulated by a sea of relics from the past, anything from bits of trails to mittens, stone ruins, and a spectacular collection of tunnels. Many of them have interesting remains—strap rails, inclined railways, rough-hewn ties, and stopes shored with trellises of pine logs. All around, the crumbled outcrops of blue-gray limestone are pinpricked with the quiet green of ephedra, juniper, and pinyon pine. The last major working is the largest, a long trench ending at three dank tunnels. From there, cut a beeline northeast up to the last three smaller tailings. The divide with the next canyon east is just above them, below Alaska Hill's looming summit.

At the divide there is a shaft. Just past it, a mostly level foot trail cuts south-southeast across the slope. It passes above the last Monitor Mine tunnel, then after 800 feet it reaches a saddle. The summit is 0.5 mile and 500 feet away, roughly south up the rounded ridge beyond the saddle. There is a stony false summit to bypass on the right, then a low hill, and finally the summit's short pine-covered north slope.

Alaska Hill overlooks a vast stretch of land stranded between parks, an ignored yet beautiful province of roomy valleys and prominent mountains. Here as along most of the climb the panorama is overwhelmed by pristine Shadow Valley and the rugged wilderness of the Kingston Range. To the north it looks out into Mesquite Valley, its small town of Sandy and oval dry lake dwarfed by the lofty Spring Mountains. On the hilly crest the view opens up abruptly to the south onto Clark Mountain's forested north face, rising impressively in deeply chiseled limestone buttresses. On a clear winter day there might be half a dozen summits in sight competing for snow.

■

CLARK MOUNTAIN

At nearly 8,000 feet, Clark Mountain is the highest summit in the eastern Mojave Desert. Its thrilling ascent calls for mandatory rock climbing to negotiate a long wall tipped with jagged outcrops called the Knife Edge. You will be rewarded with shaded pinyon-pine forests, extensive stands of a rare agave, spectacular cliffs, and the eastern Mojave Desert's largest grove of white fir. If all goes well, you will still remember the views when you knock on heaven's door.

General Information
Jurisdiction: Mojave National Preserve
Road access: Roadless; primitive access road (HC)
The climb: 1.8 mi, 1,880 ft up, 90 ft down one way/difficult, with rock
    climbing
Main attractions: Forested slopes, spectacular views, agave, white-fir
    grove, fossils, rock climbing
USGS 7.5′ topo maps: Mescal Range, Clark Mountain*
Maps: pp. 309*, 227

Location and Access
For the shortest route up Clark Mountain, the starting point is a picnic area in the mountain's forested foothills, about 1 air mile southeast of the summit. From the southbound Cima Road exit on Interstate 15, drive the paved Excelsior Mine Road north 0.7 mile and turn right on the power-line road (NN 388). Drive this road 4.1 miles until it merges with a better road coming in from the right. Keep left, go 0.2 mile to a fork, and turn left, leaving the better road. Proceed 2.7 miles to another fork, and make a left, now leaving the power-line road. After 1.3 miles, the road ends at a larger road. Bear left. This last road soon drops into a wash and follows it uphill. There is yet another split after 0.65 mile (make a hard left), then a last fork 0.45 mile further. Continue straight; the picnic area is 0.1 mile up ahead. It is easy to get lost: a topographic map definitely helps. High clearance is required.

Route Description
As you drive the last stretch of road, you will notice up ahead the long cliff band that slashes sideways from base to crest across the face of Clark Mountain. It is the result of movements along the Mesquite Thrust Fault. The summit is the first prominence left of where the cliff

The Knife Edge and the final ridge to Clark Mountain

joins the crest. As much as 180 feet thick, this cliff is the sheer edge of an immense dolomite slab, and the single major impediment to reaching the summit from this side or from the north side.

Start along the wash in the ravine a few yards east of the picnic area. After 200 yards or so, climb onto the ridge to the right, then follow the ridge about 1 mile to the crest east of Clark Mountain. Besides the constant tug of gravity, this part of the climb presents no particular obstacle. It is a fairly even grind up a slope averaging 30%, sprinkled in the middle with more level stretches to catch your breath, and near the top with pitches exceeding 40% to raise the ante. Hiking is a little easier 50 to 100 feet west of the ridge line, where the ground is more open and faint segments of trail are starting to emerge. The limestone exposed along the ridge, first Monte Cristo Limestone, then the Bird Spring Formation, has sheared off into a fluid litter of rubble unstable underfoot and locally crawling with fossils. The most common are tangles of short, light-gray segments on darker limestone plates, probably the imprints of invertebrate burrows.

As the elevation increases, the land opens up to the south and the Mescal Range comes into view, then Cima Dome, and ultimately the entire chain of mountains that cuts across the eastern Mojave Desert.

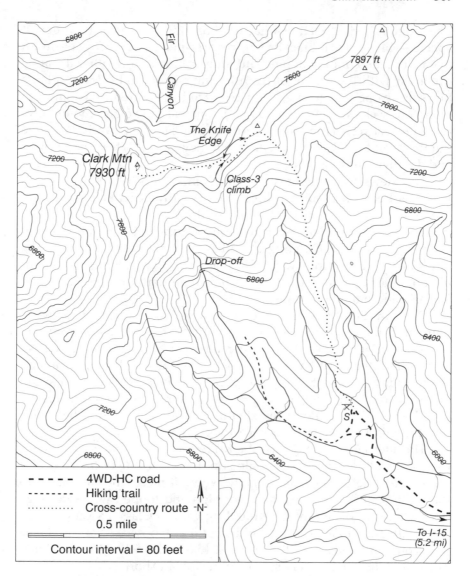

Clark Mountain

	Dist.(mi)	Elev.(ft)
Picnic area	0.0	6,140
East end of Knife Edge	1.3	7,680
White-fir forest	(0.1)	~7,640
Class-3 climb (via talus)	~1.45	~7,740
Clark Mountain	1.8	7,930

The ridge is a rich botanical garden boasting dozens of high-desert species—blue yucca, blackbrush, prickly-pear, and cliffrose—in an open woodland of pinyon pine and juniper. In warm weather the air is pregnant with the aroma of resin basking in sunlight. Many plants blossom in the late spring, from the striking scented penstemon to giant four o'clock, flax, wooly daisies, longleaf phlox, and mound cactus. The best treat is the rare pygmy agave. Here they thrive in huge numbers, and armies of the tall stalks they sprout when they flower and die cover the hillsides.

The views from the crest are awesome. Clark Mountain's north face has been cleaved into high silvery cliffs streaked with long draperies of orange lichen. The base of the cliffs is plated with grand prismatic pinnacles. Nestled below this abrupt rim is a rare forest of white fir. About 1,000 strong, it spills down into Fir Canyon to the north in a long verdant sweep of alpine aberration. It is easy to scramble down for a closer look at this relict community of currant, single-leaf ash, and mountain maple.

The summit is only 0.4 mile away and 300 feet up, but between you and it the crest pinches down to a high arcuate wall of upturned dolomite, about 150 yards long and barely 4 feet wide at its widest. The Knife Edge, as it has been aptly named, resembles a gargantuan jawbone. If you cross it along its top, you will be precariously balanced on its narrow teeth, high above the tree tops on both sides. The rock is pitted by erosion, friction is excellent, and the holds tend to be generous. But this is an aerial experience, exposed and dangerous.

The alternative is to bypass the Knife Edge. From the Knife Edge's east end, walk down the steep talus on the south side of the crest and follow the base of the Knife Edge to where it meets the cliff band. To the right, a steep wall, about 20 feet high and topped with two large trees, climbs to the top of the Knife Edge. It is a Class-3 ascent up this wall, with good foot and hand holds, but it is exposed. A rope and harness come in handy. It will stop most hikers disinclined to climbing. The rest of the climb is very steep and rocky but short.

The greatest reward is the stupendous panorama from the summit. To the south it encompasses all of western Mojave National Preserve and several ranges beyond. To the northeast Clark Mountain drops off abruptly toward isolated Mesquite Valley, flanked in the distance by the massive Kingston Range. In this monochromatic landscape of neutral browns, Mesquite Lake's white evaporites stand out like a bleak anomaly. On a clear day one can scan across 130 miles of desert bliss between Wildrose Peak and the Granite Mountains.

∎

IVANPAH MOUNTAINS

Covering only about 30 square miles, the Ivanpah Mountains are among the smallest of Mojave National Preserve's main ranges. Long and skinny, they are more like an aggregate of massive hills than a main mountain block. Their largest elevation differential, at the foot of 6,163-feet Kessler Peak, is only about 1,800 feet. But they make up for this unfortunate oversight of nature with a passion. Their rugged look, scenic granitic outcrops, and colorful limestone formations put them in a class of their own. They are also home to some of the best preserved camps and mining-related ruins in the region. Many primitive roads give access to much of the range. The Kessler Peak Road follows most of the mountains' west side, from near Kessler Peak to the southern base of Kokoweef Peak. It passes by several historic mines and summits, including eye-catching Striped Mountain. The area's most scenic byway is the Zinc Mine Road. From the Cima Road it climbs leisurely to and through Piute Valley, the serene high-desert valley that separates the Ivanpah Mountains from the Mescal Range, and ends after many miles at Mountain Pass. This little-traveled valley is covered with one of the densest, most extensive, and most beautiful Joshua tree forests in the preserve.

A major regional fault called the Clark Mountain Fault slices diagonally across the Ivanpah Mountains, from just east of Kokoweef Peak to the mouth of Oro Wash. North of this fault are the oldest rocks in the eastern Mojave Desert—gneiss, migmatite, and granitoids. This swath of ancient rocks extends continuously from the northern part of the range up to the east side of the Clark Mountain Range. The presence of migmatite is the signature of the Ivanpah Orogeny, a major mountain-building event that deformed and metamorphosed pre-existing granitoids 1.71 billion years ago. The younger granitoids were emplaced over a vast region during the subsequent 50 million years. Only a few enlightened geologists are likely to recognize these peculiar rocks—metagabbro, pelitic gneiss, meta-quartz diorite, and many more—yet their variety will impress anyone with a keen sense of observation. Directly south of the fault the geology is radically different. Paleozoic formations are exposed in a mile-wide band from New Trail Canyon to Kokoweef Peak. Similar carbonate formations crop out at the western tip of Copper Cove and on Striped Mountain. The rest of the range—all of the southern half—is made of 145-million-year-old Ivanpah Granite. This unit of coarse-grained syenogranite and monzogranite makes up the Ivanpah Mountains' handsome signature of dark-pink, weather-worn formations.

This little range generated more mining excitement than many ranges ten times its size. Precious and base metals were mined starting at least in 1879, when the Bullion Mine in New Trail Canyon was rumored to have shipped rich silver ore all the way to Wales for refining. In the course of its long subsequent history, the Ivanpah Mountains made headlines on a remarkable number of occasions. Altogether, fewer than 20 mines were in operation, but several of them broke records. In 1906 the district gained notoriety when the Standard No. 1 Mine shipped a large tonnage of very rich copper ore. By 1919 it had yielded $140,000. Over the next 30 years, the New Trail Mine matched this record. In the 1930s there was another strike with the discovery of tin ore at the Evening Star Mine. The output was modest—about $30,000—but it became famous for being the sole tin producer in the eastern Mojave Desert. The area was in the limelight again soon after, with Earl Dorr's alleged discovery of a prodigiously rich river of gold in the presumed vicinity of Kokoweef Peak. After he died without revealing its location, his secret became legend. Since then numerous adventurers have probed cave-bearing Kokoweef Peak in search of his lost lode. Between 1940 and 1951, the Carbonate King Mine on Kokoweef Peak's western flank brought in about $640,000 in zinc, the second largest zinc production in this part of the Mojave Desert. The last hurrah was the Morning Star Mine. From the early 1980s to 1993 it strip-mined a chunk of the eastern Ivanpah Mountains and leached out of it more than $10 million in gold.

Each range has something different to offer. Because of their smaller dimensions and the abundance of access roads, in the Ivanpah Mountains you are never more than a couple of miles from a road. Most summits can be reached via short climbs. In the southern part of the range, much of the scenery is composed of striking displays of carved granite, often enhanced by Joshua trees and juniper. The Ivanpah Mountains are also home to locally sizable populations of uncommon pygmy agave and simple desert agave.

■

KOKOWEEF PEAK

Kokoweef Peak is an isolated limestone mountain 1,000 feet high in the northern Ivanpah Mountains with a strange claim to fame. It is said to be resting on top of a vast canyon flushed by an underground river of gold. Spawned in the 1930s by a prospector with a vivid imagination, this legend has drawn legions of fortune seekers. Climbing Kokoweef Peak, which is still actively explored, is a rare opportunity to share the excitement of a modern tale.

General Information

Jurisdiction: Private property
Road status: Roadless; standard-clearance primitive access road
The climb: 1.2 mi, 880 ft one way / moderate
Main attractions: Legend of Dorr's lost river of gold, botany
USGS 7.5' topo maps: Cima Dome, Mescal Range, Mineral Hill*
Maps: pp. 315*, 227

Location and Access

On Interstate 15, take the Bailey Road exit. At the bottom of the northbound exit ramp, turn right, go 70 yards, and turn left on the frontage road (Zinc Mine Road). After 0.75 mile, it veers right and turns to dirt. At the fork 0.45 mile further, make a left. Continue 1.8 miles to a fork just beyond the pass into Piute Valley. The Zinc Mine Road continues straight; turn left (southeast) instead. After 1.1 miles, turn right at the fork just below Kokoweef Peak, then go 0.1 mile to a road coming in from the left. Turn right. Park at the camp of Kokoweef 0.3 mile down the road. This route can usually be driven with a standard vehicle. The area is actively mined. Do not climb this summit without obtaining permission from someone in charge at Kokoweef.

Route Description

Kokoweef Peak was immortalized by Earl L. Dorr, a blue-eyed, gun-toting gentleman farmer who came to this area in the 1920s, hoping to strike it rich. In 1934, he reported in an affidavit how he and a partner had explored, at an undisclosed location in the county, eight miles of underground passages that led 5,000 feet down to a river of gold. The cave was "divided into many caverns or chambers [...] embellished with stalactites and stalagmites..." and "encrusted with crystals." They ultimately reached a canyon that rivaled in depth with

313

The Ivanpah Mountains' crest south from Kokoweef Peak

the Grand Canyon. At the bottom of it, a wide river flowed past 100-foot banks of black sand thick with placer gold. The sand Dorr brought back was reportedly immensely rich, assaying $2,000 per cubic yard. After his return, Dorr blasted the cavern shut to protect it from looters—and lost track of its entrance. In 1940, he published another sworn affidavit in the *California Mining Journal*, but it failed to interest investors in financing the recovery of his gold. When the Carbonate King Mine opened up that year on the mountain's west flank, it scoffed the river of gold and made a mint producing zinc instead. The rest of his life, Dorr was consumed by the search for his lost lode. He died in 1957, still holding on to his secret.

Dorr's story is a fabulous tale, instilled with the same sense of wonder as Jules Verne's fantastic *Voyage au Centre de la Terre*, an unbelievable epic rooted in excess, yet so magical that it makes us want to believe in it. Kokoweef Peak does have sizable caves called Quién Sabe, Crystal, and Kokoweef, and it became the prime contender. Numerous cavers and mining outfits have probed it diligently for Dorr's alleged river of gold, all moved by the staunch obstinacy that can only be fueled by passions, riches, or insanity. Kokoweef (pop. 3) is

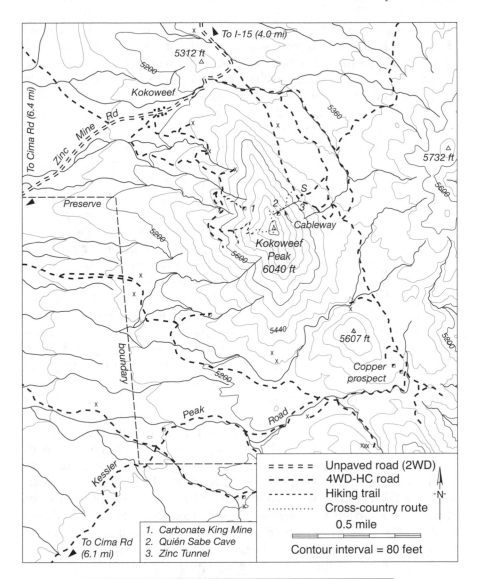

To I-15 (4.0 mi)

5312 ft

5200

Kokoweef

5360

Zinc Mine Rd

To Cima Rd (6.4 mi)

5732 ft

5600

Preserve

S

1   2   3

Cableway

Kokoweef
Peak
6040 ft

5200

5600

boundary

5440

5607 ft

5200

Copper
prospect

Peak   Road

Kessler

	Unpaved road (2WD)
=====	Unpaved road (2WD)
-----	4WD-HC road
--------	Hiking trail
....	Cross-country route

-N-

0.5 mile

To Cima Rd
(6.1 mi)

1. Carbonate King Mine
2. Quién Sabe Cave
3. Zinc Tunnel

Contour interval = 80 feet

Kokoweef Peak

	Dist.(mi)	Elev.(ft)
Kokoweef	0.0	5,160
Zinc Tunnel	0.85	5,545
Kokoweef Peak	1.2	6,040
Upper end of mining road	1.35	5,795
Kokoweef	2.4	5,160

the mining camp of the latest venture. The residential end, stretched thin on both sides of the road, is a time-warp of cabins and trailers in a forest of Joshua trees. The business end is an avalanche of high-testosterone cranes, graders, flatbeds, trucks, and drilling rigs. On weekends a motley crew of believers—store keepers, waitresses, and construction workers from Las Vegas and Los Angeles—come over and tirelessly search for a giant void that reason tells us must be imaginary.

Kokoweef Peak is a relatively subdued prominence that can be climbed from almost any direction—the roads that encircle it offer a few loops to go up one way and return another. The only route that is a bit of a workout—and the most fun—is the bank of cliffs on the east side. From Kokoweef, walk east up the main road to the steep grade on the east flank, and the Zinc Tunnel at its end. The grade closely follows the Clark Mountain Fault. Movements along it have made strange bedfellows: the carbonates on the mountain side abut on the downhill side a city-size block of Proterozoic gneiss and pegmatite—a time gap of 1.5 billion years. Starting 20 yards north of the tunnel, hike up the talus to a downed cableway directly uphill from the tunnel. Follow it to the blocked entrance of the Quién Sabe Cave. This ascent is short but tedious, over outcrops, loose slides, and thorny plants. From the cave, climb at 45° to the right (when facing uphill) to the only break in the cliffs, a rocky couloir lined with juniper and shrubs, just north of where the cableway is tethered to the crest. A little scrambling leads to the crest. The summit is 250 yards south up the open crest.

From a distance, Kokoweef Peak is not the most remarkable mountain, but closeness reveals hidden riches. The slopes are covered with Joshua trees, juniper, cliffrose, and pygmy agave. Clumps of uncommon mat rock spiraea cling to the naked rock. The bulk of the mountain is a thick sequence of sedimentary formations spanning most of the Paleozoic, from the Permian around Kokoweef to the Cambrian south of the peak. The Ordovician–Cambrian middle of the stack crops out all along the crest's scenic hogbacks in beautiful upturned smoky limestone. Between the summit's rocky spine and the horizon, a hardscrabble piece of real estate spreads in all directions and laps in the distance with a ring of intriguing mountain backbones. Presiding over this unruly landscape is the crenulated crest of the Ivanpahs, the hump of Cima Dome, and the eastern Mojave Desert's 70-mile chain unfolding from Nevada's McCullough Range to the Granite Mountains. Yet perhaps the most powerful inspiration is not the mountain itself but the pull of the legend, the constant awareness that you might be walking on top of a river of gold... We would be fools not to dream.

■

STRIPED MOUNTAIN

This is a fun little mountain to climb, easy and obstacle free, across the contrasted sequence of Paleozoic limestone strata that gave it its striking appearance and name. The area was the home of a famous miner who collected local mines and left his mark all over, including at the silver-tungsten mine on the way to the summit. This is a luminous place, peppered with Joshua trees, blue yucca, and rare agave, with an openness and a quality of light that invite lingering.

General Information
Jurisdiction: Mojave National Preserve
Road status: Mostly roadless; standard-clearance access road
The climb: 1.1 mi, 860 ft up, 120 ft down one way/easy–moderate
Main attractions: Geology, mines, history, botany, long views
USGS 7.5' topo map: Mescal Range
Maps: pp. 319*, 227

Location and Access
Striped Mountain is a crescent-shaped ridge joined to the western flank of the Ivanpah Mountains by a low isthmus. The starting point is the decrepit road to the Silverado Mine, on the mountain's east side. From the gas station at the Cima Road exit on Interstate 15, drive the Cima Road 7.1 miles south to two large water tanks on the left. From the other direction, this is 10.5 miles north of Cima. A hard-packed dirt road starts on the left side of the tanks. Follow it east 2.9 miles, through a densely vegetated woodland of imposing Joshua trees that come right up to the road, and past Striped Mountain's striated slope to the left, to a four-way junction. The small mountain-ringed valley up ahead is Copper Cove, where several mines were active from 1890 to the 1940s. Turn left (northeast) on the Kessler Peak Road. At the fork after 1.1 miles, keep left. In 0.6 mile, just past a right bend in a ravine, the rough road to the Silverado Mine splits off at 10 o'clock. Park 100 yards up this road, at a cutoff on the right. This route is rock-free and suitable for most vehicles, with care at the few ruts if clearance is low.

Route Description
The Silverado Mine dates back to the late 1880s. The ruins of a stone house stand by the roadside a short distance in; two more are along a faint track that loops up on the hillside to the west. One was an

assay office, the other a little cabin with a chimney and three walls enclosing bedrock. The road climbs a little, hooks a sharp left, then ends in 0.25 mile on a low ridge in full view of Striped Mountain's twin peaks. The mine's main 60-foot shaft and several shallower shafts are aligned down the ridge to the south, neatly tracing the skarn that they explored. The skarn was formed in the Jurassic, when the horn-blende-diorite pluton exposed just east of the mine intruded the Cambrian carbonates west of it. Notwithstanding its glamorous name, the Silverado Mine was not the richest. Its only known production was a few tons of silver ore in the 1880s and 1890s. Its main claim to fame is its connection with John "Riley" Bembry, a World War I medic who came here in 1928 and became a local legend by amassing an impressive portfolio of mines. Until 1981 he filed over 60 claims and acquired most of the district's abandoned mines. Many had played out, so he reigned over a gutted empire. He acquired the Silverado Mine in 1938, perhaps hoping for tungsten, which had just been discovered at the nearby Evening Star Mine. By 1950, the mine had indeed been expanded to include tungsten claims and renamed Silverado Tungstite. But the tungsten ore—scheelite—was too sparse to have commercial value. Bembry supplemented his meager miner's income with a stable job at the Molycorp Mine at Mountain Pass.

From the end of the mining road, follow the rougher, overgrown road that heads north along the ridge, past the small pits of the Silverado Tungstite Mine. After 0.25 mile, the road ends. Cut a beeline across the hillside, aiming for the white tailings on the low ridge to the northwest. Up there you will join a quarry at the upper end of another road. This was one of many claims held by the Georgia Marble Company since 1980–1981, most of which were never developed.

From the quarry the route is in plain view, generally west down to a shallow saddle and up the mountain's shoulder to the first summit, then northwest across a short saddle to the summit. From saddle to summit it is a steepish ascent, 550 feet up and down in less than 0.5 mile. You travel from the Middle Devonian to the Late Mississippian, 48 million years of rocks built on the lives and deaths of a quadrillion hard-shelled sea creatures. They stacked up on the sea floor in strata shaped by the vagaries of climate and tectonic plates. The strata now carve across the ridge parallel bands of limestones and dolomites, an alternation of cream, blue gray, and smoky white. The thickest striations bulge out in short strips of bumpy slickrock spaced by splintered rubble. Each strip holds a few hundred thousand years of ocean memory. The thinnest are fine parallel striations within the striations, as thin as a nail, less than a century's worth of sedimentation. The open

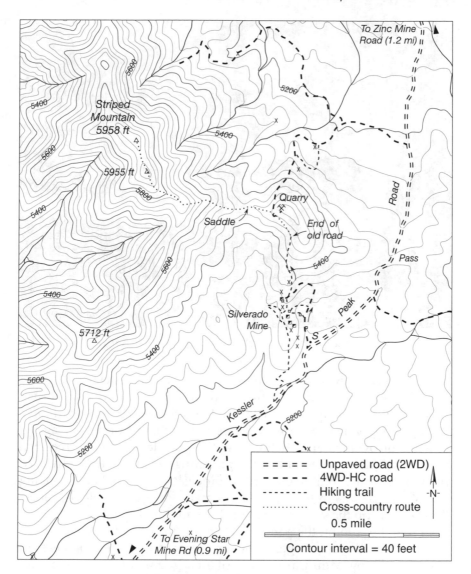

Striped Mountain

	Dist.(mi)	Elev.(ft)
Kessler Peak Road	0.0	5,220
Silverado Mine (ridge)	0.25	5,330
North end of road	0.45	5,480
Quarry road	0.5	5,520
Striped Mountain	1.1	5,958

Striped Mountain lit up against the Mescal Range

ridge is freckled with Joshua trees and blue yucca, blackbrush, green ephedra, and bitterbrush, and occasional juniper and big sagebrush higher up. Just about every cactaceae live up here, content with mere cracks in the bone-dry bedrock. There are battalions of pygmy agave, clusters of overgrown artichokes with spiky leaves and three-inch nails; startlingly big mound cactus gathering well over 100 individual plants; and small bulbous heads of pincushion cactus barely poking out of rock debris. In this open land barely shielded by plants, reflection ratchets up the sun's glare to the brilliance of driven snow.

From the summit the panorama extends for tens of miles to a horizon lined with giant ranges—the San Bernardino Mountains east of LA, the Spring Mountains west of Las Vegas, and the Avawatz Mountains north of nowhere. The Mescal Range looms close by, a colorful tapestry of upturned beddings. At least two dozen mountains dot the landscape, from Cima Dome's bulge to the Castle Mountains' spires and the Bristol Mountains' sprawling crest. Down to the southeast is Copper Cove, the lifelong haunt of Riley Bembry, whose story is so intimately linked to this mountain. They are all there, spread across his sleepy hollow—the mines where he toiled, the scenic granite knolls where he lived, and the tiny cemetery where he now rests.

■

KESSLER PEAK

The highest point in the Ivanpah Mountains, Kessler Peak is a delightful summit to climb. The route is only moderately difficult, and the slopes are covered with a vivid mixture of dark-pink granite outcrops, green juniper and Joshua trees, and all manner of cacti. The views from the top extend over much of western Mojave National Preserve and well into the northern Mojave Desert.

General Information
Jurisdiction: Mojave National Preserve
Road status: Roadless; standard- and high-clearance access roads
The climb: 1.9 mi, 1,150 ft up, 25 ft down one way/moderate
The loop climb: 4.2 mi, 2,570 ft loop (or more)/moderate
Main attractions: Joshua trees and juniper forest, scenic views
USGS 7.5' topo map: Cima Dome
Maps: pp. 323*, 227

Location and Access
Kessler Peak is near the very south end of the Ivanpah Mountains. As you drive to it on the Cima Road, its sharp profile stands out up ahead for miles. From the service station at the Cima Road exit on Interstate 15, drive the Cima Road south 11.3 miles to the signed Teutonia Peak Trail, then another 0.6 mile, to a primitive road at a sharp angle on the left, just before a right bend. This is the Kessler Peak Road. Coming from the other direction, this road is 5.8 miles north of Cima. Drive the Kessler Peak Road 1 mile north to a first junction. Turn right and go 0.3 mile to where this rougher road angles left and another road continues straight along a sandy wash. Park near this junction. Kessler Peak is the dome-shaped mountain to the southeast. A standard-clearance vehicle can usually make it to the first junction. High clearance is helpful beyond.

Route Description
There are many ways to climb Kessler Peak. Several steep routes up the peak's west slope are possible starting from near the south end of the Kessler Peak Road. They are the most direct, but trees are scarce and Kessler Springs Ranch spoils the views. The route suggested here, up a more gradual wash on the north face, is much wilder. From the suggested starting point, follow the road east as it winds along a

Shadow Valley and Mescal Range on the way to Kessler Peak

nearly level sandy wash. After 0.45 mile, past the tip of a low promontory pointing north, leave the road and head up the broad floodplain that opens up to the south. It is crisscrossed by narrow braided gullies at first, but a well-defined wash soon emerges. Follow it for about 0.6 mile, where it reaches tall granite outcrops at the foot of Kessler Peak. The wash angles right along the outcrops, then left (0.2 mile), and starts climbing more steeply. After half a mile of climbing (keep right at the two forks) you will reach the prominent east-west ridge of Kessler Peak. The summit is 0.2 mile east up the ridge.

This route is nowhere very steep, and the wash is a little rocky but never too brushy. Considering how minimal of a workout this is, the payoff is quite good. Along the base of the mountain, Joshua trees thrive in a vast belt intermixed with mature Utah juniper. Both trees grow right up to the summit, albeit stunted by high winds. Staghorn cholla, pancake prickly-pear, grizzly bear cactus, calico cactus, and mound cactus are plentiful at lower elevations, and they are gradually supplanted higher up by Mormon tea, squawbush, and cliffrose. Much of Kessler Peak's north face is covered with granite outcrops chiseled into pinnacles and vertical fins.

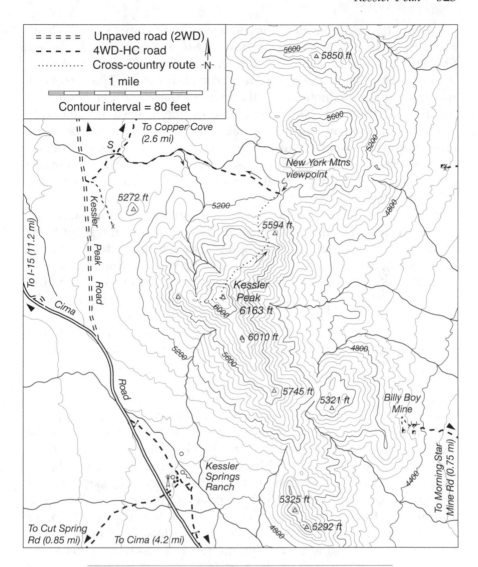

Legend:
- = = = = = Unpaved road (2WD)
- – – – – – 4WD-HC road
- ·········· Cross-country route
- -N-
- 1 mile
- Contour interval = 80 feet

Map labels:
- 5600
- 5850 ft
- 5600
- 5200
- New York Mtns viewpoint
- To Copper Cove (2.6 mi)
- S.
- 5272 ft
- 5200
- 5594 ft
- 4800
- Kessler Peak Road
- Kessler Peak 6163 ft
- 6000
- 6010 ft
- 5200
- 5600
- 4800
- To I-15 (11.2 mi)
- Cima
- Road
- 5745 ft
- 5321 ft
- Billy Boy Mine
- Kessler Springs Ranch
- 4800
- 4400
- To Morning Star Mine Rd (0.75 mi)
- 5325 ft
- 5292 ft
- To Cut Spring Rd (0.85 mi)
- To Cima (4.2 mi)
- 4800

Kessler Peak

	Dist.(mi)	Elev.(ft)
Access road (junction)	0.0	5,033
Leave road up broad wash	0.45	5,085
Ridge	1.7	5,770
Kessler Peak	1.9	6,163
New York Mtns viewpoint	3.0	5,200
Back to starting point	4.2	5,033

From its central position this modest summit commands a sweeping perspective of the western half of Mojave National Preserve. Striped Mountain, the Mescal Range, and Clark Mountain profiled against each other to the north are particularly scenic. The preserve's magnificent mountainous core fills up all of the eastern and southern horizons. To the southwest, Cima Dome's smooth curvature is sharply delineated against the Kelso Mountains and the pointed humps of the cinder cones. I was here in Indian summer, and several localized storms were adding drama to this grand scenery. Entire mountain ranges were obscured by ominous clouds and black curtains of slanted rain. Yet here and there vast tracks of land remained inundated with sunlight, from the Kelso Dunes to Death Valley's Black Mountains.

If you feel, as I did, that it would be a waste to interrupt these views too soon, consider prolonging them by returning along the crest. One option is to follow it south, then to drop along the drainage of your choice and loop back along the foot of the Ivanpah Mountains. Kessler Springs Ranch is NPS residential property; to avoid it, do not return any farther south than the 5,745-foot peak (see map).

I much preferred the other direction, northeast along the crest to the deep gap in the mountains, then back along the access road. All along the billowing ridge, Joshua trees, juniper, grasses, and granite outcrops compose a lively foreground floating high above the surrounding valleys. Here as all over Kessler Peak, the rock is Jurassic Ivanpah Granite, a variety of granite that contains very little biotite or other dark minerals, hence its light appearance. Some fresh cuts on the ridge are nearly pure white feldspar. The views alternate between the New York Mountains and the Mescal Range, depending on which side of the ridge the rocks and the path of least resistance take you. The descent is very steep, strewn with boulders and cactuses at lower elevations; it is the hardest part of this hike, but it is fairly short. Aim for the east end of the access road visible down below. Like many ranges, the Ivanpah Mountains are not symmetric, and nowhere is this asymmetry as impressive as from this final descent. On the west side, the mountains are buried right up to their crest under a long alluvial fan that sweeps down gently into Shadow Valley. On the east side they drop abruptly 700 feet to the edge of Ivanpah Valley. The access road ends on the edge of this prominent discontinuity, overlooking the New York Mountains on one side and nothing much on the other.

Try to time your return to walk the road back to your vehicle at the end of the day. It crosses dense stands of large Joshua trees, and the sunsets can be stupendous.

■

CIMA DOME

Cima Dome is in the north-central part of Mojave National Preserve, at the head of Shadow Valley and just south of the Ivanpah Mountains. Although more like a sprawling swell than a true mountain, it is a special place: it is host to the world's largest Joshua tree forest, it is flanked by a rare and extensive field of cinder cones, and it is capped by the most symmetrical dome in the United States. Its distinctive shape is one of the most curious landmarks in the eastern Mojave Desert, visible from great distances in many directions. Almost all of Cima Dome is protected by adjacent designated wilderness areas.

Geologically speaking, Cima Dome is the expression of a mountain in its final throes, its penultimate stage before its complete disappearance. When erosion wears down a mountain, upland material tends to erode faster, and waste rock is washed down and deposited away from the mountain. The area between the degrading upland and the aggrading lowland is a pediment, a transition zone below the base of the mountain over which waste rock is transported. Pediments are typically featureless and gently sloped surfaces that undergo little erosion and are fairly stable. As the mountain front retreats, the pediment grows toward higher elevation. Given enough time, pediments will eventually consume the whole mountain, as happened on Cima Dome. There are countless pediments on the planet, under many climatic and geomorphic settings. They take many forms, a common one being an apron extending down from a mountain front. What makes Cima Dome's pediment special is that it is dome-shaped and remarkably symmetric: over a radius of nearly 1 mile centered on its summit, its contour lines are almost perfectly concentric ovals. This unusual symmetry may be simply because the stock of the original mountain block, Teutonia Adamellite, was fairly symmetrical and homogeneous. Cima Dome is actually not a dome but mostly a cone: only its very top has the convex shape of a dome. Much of the slope, at least 6 miles out from the summit, and in all directions but east, is relatively constant.

One blatant exception is the striking region of cinder cones and lava beds that protrudes from 60 square miles of Cima Dome's southwestern slope. Known to geologists as the Cima volcanic field, it is composed of about 40 cinder cones, ranging in height from less than 100 feet to 560 feet, and a complex mosaic of more than 60 lava flows. They were produced by three periods of volcanism. The earliest one started 7.6 million years ago and lasted, off and on, 1.1 million years. The only exposures from this period are a few highly degraded cones and flows at the eastern edge of the field, especially around Whitney Peak. The second period, from 4.5 to 3.6 million years ago, occurred in the northern half of the field. It was by far the most intense. Thick molten rock flowed mostly eastward toward Shadow Valley, building overlapping sheets of basalt up to 400 feet thick. The third period began about one million years ago and ended as recently as 15,000 years ago. This time the lava drained westward, toward Soda Lake. These younger vents and flows dominate the field's southern half. The outstanding geologic significance of this volcanic field was acknowledged in 1973 with its designation as a National Natural Landmark.

In their proverbial wisdom, geologists found a way to measure the rate of removal of a mountain that no longer exists. Under the cinder cones lies a portion of Cima Dome's pediment that has been protected from erosion by hard coats of basalt ever since the basalt erupted. By comparing the intact buried pediment and the surrounding weathered pediment, geologists were able to determine the thickness of pediment that has eroded since the eruption. By measuring the age of the basalt, they were able to infer the rate of erosion. They found that Cima Dome is at least 4.5 million years old, that every million years it has been on average down-wearing about 95 feet and retreating about 1,100 feet. That the older cinders are still standing after more than 7 million years shows that erosion takes much longer to turn a cinder cone to rubble than it took tectonism to create Death Valley.

Cima Dome's other claim to fame, its sprawling Joshua tree forest, is indeed imposing. All over the dome and points beyond, dense covers of shaggy giants dwarf surrounding shrubs and cacti to mere understory. Their dense crowns cast shadows as cool as those of deciduous trees. In some areas large specimens are so numerous that it is impossible to pick the tallest, thickest, or widest. The Joshua tree's predilection for Cima Dome stems in part from the dome's fine-gravel slopes, and in part from the nearly ideal mean elevation and annual precipitation. The trees' unusual density is also the result of selective grazing, which favors them and other plants cattle do not care for.

■

TEUTONIA PEAK

Teutonia Peak is a small isolated inselberg ("rock island") that protrudes prominently from the northeastern slope of Cima Dome. The Teutonia Peak Trail goes most of the way there, amid scenic gardens of desert shrubs, cacti, and Joshua trees, and it ends shy of its namesake, at the vertical edge of the monolithic mountain. The trail is popular, but few are the visitors who search the summit block's miniature maze of textured granite formations for the technical route to the top—and far fewer find it.

General Information

Jurisdiction: Mojave National Preserve
Road status: Roadless; paved access road
The climb (Teutonia Peak): 2.0 mi, 820 ft up, 90 ft down one way / moderate
The climb (South Teutonia Peak): 2.3 mi, 830 ft up, 140 ft down one way / moderate
Main attractions: Short peak climbs, rock formations, botany, views
USGS 7.5' topo map: Cima Dome
Maps: pp. 329*, 333, 227

Location and Access

To get to the Teutonia Peak Trail, drive the Cima Road 11.3 miles south of the gas station at the Cima Road exit on Interstate 15 (or 6.4 miles north of Cima in the preserve) to the signed trailhead on the west side. Teutonia Peak is the ill-defined high point of the serrated ridge less than 1.5 miles away to the southwest, rising from the smooth swell of Cima Dome like a megafaunal jawbone.

Route Description

The trail first ambles gently to the foot of the inselberg, across a scenic plain studded with Joshua trees. The area is famous for its flora. Rain water penetrates fairly deeply in the sandy soil, which fosters a surprising plant diversity. Along this short trail alone dozens of species thrive, from ephedra to bitterbrush, desert almond, spiny menodora, hopsage, most of the local cacti, and a smattering of juniper.

After 0.5 mile, the trail crosses the Cut Spring Road, then continues 0.45 mile to an old mining road. This area was the site of a small mine called Teutonia. First worked in 1896, it was soon idle, until it was picked up again 10 years later by a man named Charles Toegel. In spite of the property's modest showings, Toegel managed to raise a little capital to develop it. He built a small camp consisting of a few cabins, a blacksmith, and a general store, which he grandly named Toegel City. His hopes were short-lived. Over the next few years, he shipped all of 100 tons of ore bearing at most 150 ounces of silver per ton, and a little lead. A decade later the mine and the camp were gathering dust. The main shafts are to the right along the road, the camp to the left. Dug in friable soil, many of the shafts have caved in, their former collars now splintered lumber. The only visible ore is yellowish coatings of limonite and smearings of copper ore. The camp is now reduced to the large wooden floor and collapsed walls of what may have been the store, nicely patinaed after decades of suntanning.

Make a right on the old mining road; the trail resumes 75 yards further on the left. In 150 yards, it crosses a third road, and switchbacks 0.25 mile up to a low saddle on the inselberg's ridge. To the northwest, across a forested ravine, the ridge continues as a dramatic alignment of fins and turrets. The trail veers south and closely follows the ridge line, along displays of sculpted granite. Unlike the bulk of Cima Dome, the exposures here and on Teutonia Peak are not Teutonia Adamellite but Jurassic Ivanpah Granite. Harder than the adamellite, the granite has resisted erosion and now stands prominently above the dome's worn surface. The trail ends in 0.4 mile at a tall gap between sheer cliffs, at the edge of the mountain block.

Such high-caliber vistas for so little effort is a steal. To the east rise Kessler Peak, the Ivanpah Mountains, and the rugged New York Mountains. To the northwest, Shadow Valley's immense creosote plain stretches out for miles, bounded in the far distance by Clark Mountain and the lofty Kingston Range. The highest summit visible to the northwest is no other than Telescope Peak itself, more than 100 miles away...

As scenic and educational as the trail is, the best part is yet to come—climbing the summit. The first challenge is finding the route to it; the second one is climbing the crux. From the end of the trail go back about 100 steps to an opening on the right (east). Turn right and work your way down the slope just far enough to get a good view down the length of the mountain block. About 400 yards to the southeast, at the same elevation, a saddle connects the south end of the mountain block to a 60-foot outcrop east of it. The summit is on the central part of the block, which is separated from the rest of the mountain by two narrow, sheer-walled trenches 40 to 80 feet deep. To get to the summit, continue toward the saddle, paralleling the crest, 100 yards down a first declivity, then up its far side 100 yards to a local

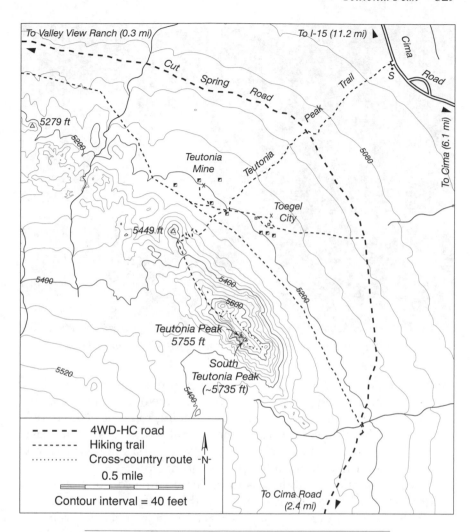

To Valley View Ranch (0.3 mi)
To I-15 (11.2 mi)
Cima Road
Cut Spring Road
Peak Trail
S
To Cima (6.1 mi)
5279 ft
5200
Teutonia Mine
Teutonia
5080
5449 ft
Toegel City
5400
5400
5600
5200
Teutonia Peak 5755 ft
South Teutonia Peak (~5735 ft)
5520
5400

- - - - 4WD-HC road
- - - - Hiking trail
· · · · · · Cross-country route
-N-
0.5 mile
Contour interval = 40 feet

To Cima Road (2.4 mi)

Teutonia Peak

	Dist.(mi)	Elev.(ft)
Trailhead	0.0	5,025
Junction at Teutonia Mine	0.95	5,200
Toegel City	(0.2)	5,180
Road crossing	1.05	5,225
Saddle on ridge	1.3	5,400
End of Teutonia Peak Trail	~1.7	5,700
Teutonia Peak	(0.2)	5,755
South Teutonia Peak	(0.35)	~5,735

Granite fins and spires near the trench north of Teutonia Peak

high point. About 20 yards past it, look up to the right for a break in the cliff. Scrambling up to it will take you into the northern trench. The summit can be reached via a circuitous climbing route near the trench entrance, at the northern corner of the central block. It is not an easy climb, it is exposed, and if you peel you may fall a long way. Apply extreme caution, and do not attempt this ascent alone.

If you cannot make it, there is fortunately a fine consolation prize. South Teutonia Peak, a stone's throw to the south, is only a few feet lower than the summit yet easy to reach, without even a scramble. From the local high point continue in the same direction 200 yards or so, down and out of another declivity, to the saddle. Climb the short slope west of the saddle to the crest, then follow the slickrock northwest to the summit near the rim of the southern trench.

Exploring this area is exhilarating for multiple reasons. The views from the summits are even better than from the trail, especially of the sweeping curve of Cima Dome spreading right under your feet. But the views are eclipsed by the sheer delight of wandering through the cool underworld of slots, cliffs, and hoodoos that make up Teutonia Peak's chaotic ridge. The quest for the summit becomes its own reward, more enticing than the summit itself.

■

CIMA DOME

Cima Dome is a geological oddity, home to an amazingly lush and diverse vegetation, and easy to climb, so it is hard to pass it up. On its southern slope an old loop road climbs leisurely through its extensive wilderness of Joshua trees and juniper to the dome's seldom-visited apex. The views from the broad summit are surprisingly far-reaching views for such a little mountain.

General Information
Jurisdiction: Mojave National Preserve
Road status: Hiking on abandoned roads; primitive access roads (HC)
The climb: 1.8 mi, 420 ft up one way/easy
Loop climb: 6.6 mi, 1,540 ft loop/moderate
Main attractions: World's densest Joshua tree forest, botany, geology
USGS 7.5' topo map: Cima Dome
Maps: pp. 333*, 227

Location and Access
Cima Dome can be climbed on one of three old roads, now foot trails, that start at Deer Spring on the east side of the summit, Valley View Ranch on the north side, and Cut Spring on the west side. Cut Spring and Valley View Ranch are privately owned, so it is easier and quicker to start from Deer Spring. To get there, take the Cima Road exit on Interstate 15. From the gas station, drive on Cima Road 9.9 miles south to the signed Valley View Ranch Road. Coming from the other direction, this junction is 10.5 miles north of Cima, a siding on the Union Pacific. Follow this well-graded road 1.7 miles to Valley View Ranch (respect the privacy of the residents and just drive through). Turn left on the Deer Spring Road. Keep right at the fork after 200 yards, and drive 2.8 miles to the end of the road at a corral and Deer Spring, marked by a tall thicket of cattail and a strip of green grass irrigated by a trickle of water. The road requires a high-clearance vehicle, although with standard clearance you will be able to drive it part way.

Route Description
Just east of the corral at Deer Spring, stakes block vehicular access to a beat-up abandoned road I refer to as Springs Trail. It swings around the south side of Cima Dome and ends in about 3 miles just before Cut Spring on the southeast side. After 0.6 mile up this trail, an

old fence road (Cima Dome Trail) takes off on the mountain side and climbs to the dome's summit.

The main attraction of this trivial ascent—all of 260 feet over 1.2 miles—is Cima Dome's mixed forest of Joshua trees and juniper. The Joshua trees are plentiful and locally reach respectable proportions. The exuberant ground cover is composed of dozens of species arranged in ever-changing spectra, from the bluish nuances of yucca and beavertail cactus to the yellower tones of chollas and the deeper shades of juniper. Numerous chollas poke as much as 5 feet above the ground. In May and June they decorate the landscape with their brilliant flowers, yellowish green for the silver cholla and dark orange for the staghorn cholla. Wildlife loves this slightly cooler area. You will likely spot ground squirrels bouncing hurriedly across the road, turkey vultures and hawks circling the sky, beetles and ravens, lizards and butterflies, and maybe a coyote or a deer. On a bright September day, I saw here more roadrunners than in a lifetime of desert wanderings.

Because of the modest grade and the trees, the views are limited at first, but they do improve near the top. The summit area is an undulating upland of shallow swales and rises; it is hard to decide which rise is the highest. From any of them, the low desert is concealed by the bulk of the dome, but the preserve's central chain protrudes majestically across the eastern horizon, unbroken from the Granite Mountains to Clark Mountain. An even better observation point is the curious 100-foot-long outcrop visible north of the trail and west of the summit. It is a curvaceous hump of naked Teutonia Adamellite, freckled with mustard and russet lichens and resembling a sea cucumber. All of 16 feet high, its spine commands views that stretch out to the Kingston Range and, on a clear day, the mighty mountains of Death Valley.

This short hike can be extended by continuing on the Cima Dome Trail down Cima Dome's southeast slope toward Cut Spring, then

	Dist.(mi)	Elev.(ft)
Cima Dome		
West end of Springs Trail	0.0	5,340
Cima Dome Trail	0.6	5,500
Cima Dome	1.8	5,745
Outcrop on south side	3.3	5,210
Backtrack and leave trail	3.4	5,260
Join Springs Trail	~3.6	~5,255
West end of Springs Trail	6.6	5,340

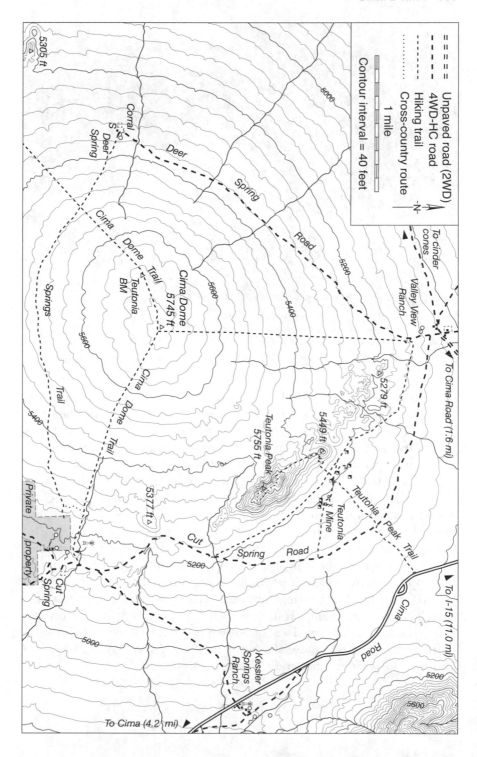

Unpaved road (2WD)
4WD-HC road
Hiking trail
Cross-country route

1 mile
Contour interval = 40 feet

-N-

To cinder
cones

To Cima Road (1.6 mi)

Valley View
Ranch

5279 ft

5000

5200

5400

Deer

Spring

Road

Corral

S Deer
Spring

5305 ft

Cima

Dome

Trail

Cima Dome
5745 ft

Teutonia
BM

5600

5600

5600

Springs

Trail

5400

Cima

Dome

Trail

5377 ft

Teutonia Peak
5755 ft

5449 ft

Teutonia
Mine

Teutonia

Peak

Trail

Cut

Spring   Road

5200

Private

property

Cut

Spring

5000

Kessler
Springs
Ranch

5200

5600

Cima

Road

To I-15 (11.0 mi)

To Cima (4.2 mi)

Clark Mountain Range and Joshua trees from Sea Cucumber Rock

returning along Springs Trail. Little known and almost all in a designated wilderness, this is a perfect loop to explore the quiet heart of
Cima Dome. The eastern segment of the Cima Dome Trail commands
fine views of the crumpled mass of Teutonia Peak and Kessler Peak.
The small springs near the bottom of the trail, mostly concealed by
trees, have thick groves of squawbush, baccharis, blackbrush, and
sometimes a little water. Handsome outcrops of polished adamellite
are abundant in this area. The largest spring is Cut Spring. The Cima
Dome Trail enters the inholding just before getting to it (see map). The
western boundary of this property is not marked. To avoid trespassing,
hike 1.5 miles from the trail junction at the summit to the first trail-side
outcrop in nearly a mile (Cut Spring's windmill should be visible up
ahead). Backtrack 0.1 mile, then head cross-country southwest less
than 300 yards to Springs Trail. It is then 3 miles, roughly west, on this
trail back to Deer Spring. This loop is 6.6 miles for 770 feet of elevation
gain. There are quite a few shaded places along the way, and even in
summer the temperature tends to be fairly decent.

■

MOUNT HEPHESTUS

Cima Dome's scenic wilderness of extinct volcanoes is one of only a few fairly recent volcanic fields in the American deserts. Of the area's several dozen cinder cones, the two suggested here stand out for one being the youngest, and the other the tallest. Both offer a unique opportunity to sample and admire from above this stark region of conical hills, dark lava flows, and intriguing formations.

General Information

Jurisdiction: Mojave National Preserve
Road status: Roadless; primitive access roads (2WD or HC)
The climb (Twin Cone): 2.5 mi, 1,000 ft loop/easy
The climb (Mt Hephestus): 3.6 mi, 980 ft up, 50 ft down one way/mod.
Main attractions: Classic volcanoes, geology, wildflowers
USGS 7.5' topo maps: Indian Spring
Maps: pp. 337*, 227

Location and Access

To reach the south end of the Cima volcanic field, which has the youngest and best preserved cinder cones, drive to Baker on Interstate 15 and get off at the Kelbaker Road exit. From the northbound exit, go 17.5 miles east-southeast on the Kelbaker Road to a dirt road on the left. Drive this road 0.3 mile to the sharp drop into Willow Wash. The youngest cone, which I refer to as Twin Cone, is the closest one, due north. The tallest cone (Mt Hephestus) is mostly hidden about 2 miles behind it. Willow Wash has steep banks that require a strong vehicle and skill. If unsure, park at the pullout at the edge of the wash and walk from there. Otherwise drive the road northeast 0.65 mile to the foot of the youngest cone, or another 1.25 miles north to the wilderness boundary to climb the tallest cone (see description below for details).

Route Description

Twin Cone. From Willow Wash it is a nearly level walk to the foot of the youngest cinder cone. Formed only 15,000 years ago, it is made of two cones, the main one and a smaller satellitic cone attached to its south side. After 0.5 mile the road crests a low swell at the eastern foot of the satellite, then crosses a small wash. A fainter road branches off at 10 o'clock 20 yards further. It climbs the satellite's lower flank to an open pit, crosses a few shallow trenches, then reaches a junction. The

Young lava flow spilling out of the west flank of Twin Cone

road on the left winds up to the crease between the two cones, then ascends the main cone to its sharp rim.

From base to rim this small mountain is nothing but cinder, a strange and beautiful rock. It forms when low-viscosity magma is ejected into the atmosphere. The pressure of the hot gases splatters the magma into small lumps that cool rapidly and trap gas bubbles inside the cinder. It typically takes a single eruption lasting a few weeks or months to form a cinder cone. Steam often wafts through the cinder for months, even years, after the eruption, oxidizing the iron in the cinder and giving it its red color. A cone can later emit lava. The lava often flows not from the structurally weak crater, but from the cone's base or side, and it usually carries away with it a portion of the cone. This little volcano is a fine example. Its rim overlooks the slanted edge of its gutted core. Down below, spreading for a mile, is the great tongue of lava that spilled out from under it and created this giant wound. The lava is so young that it is still black and deeply scalloped. Large chunks of cinnamon-red scoria outcrop in the roadcuts, clinkery and oddly light, its surface a fractal labyrinth of depressions and razor-sharp asperities.

Only a few tenacious plants cling to this chemical desert—except for spring wildflowers, which can thrive in unbelievable numbers. I saw here uncommon plants like spotted langloisia, and a mushroom

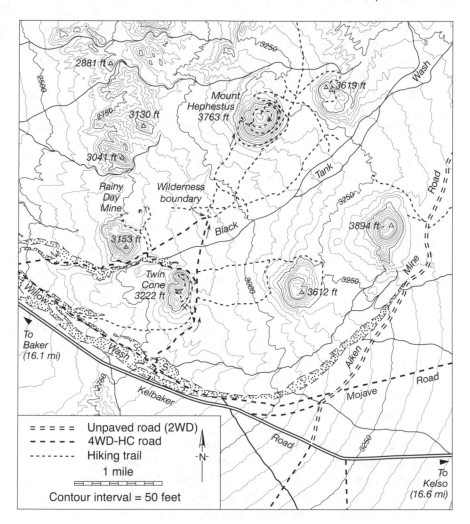

Mount Hephestus

	Dist.(mi)	Elev.(ft)
Willow Wash crossing	0.0	~2,780
Y junction (left to Twin Cone)	0.65	~2,880
Spiral road to Twin Cone	(0.3)	2,975
Twin Cone	(0.6)	3,222
Back to Y junction via rim	(1.25)	~2,880
End of road / wilderness bdry	1.9	2,930
T jct at base of Mt Hephestus	2.9	3,200
Mount Hephestus	3.6	3,763

called desert puffball, but what made my day was the profusion of desert five spots. One can go years without seeing a single one of these arresting beauties. Here there were hundreds, their globe-like shocking-pink corollas floating above the dark cinder.

On the rim, the road circles half way around the crater, then descends steeply on the north slope. At its lower end, it stops abruptly. Just slide down to a road 20 feet below it, which joins the main road.

Mount Hephestus. From the junction at the southeastern foot of Twin Cone, continue north on the main road across the wide braided floodplain of Black Tank Wash. In 1.25 miles the road reaches a wilderness boundary, at a junction with a road coming in from the left, in full view of Mount Hephestus to the north-northeast. Several roads crisscross the area up ahead, offering several ways to ascend it. For the shortest route, take the road that heads roughly north at first, then slightly left of the cone's summit. After just over 1 mile (ignore side roads), at the base of the cone, it runs into a road that climbs clockwise around the flank of the cone. Turn left on it. After 0.2 mile, shortly before this road ends, a fainter road on the right climbs straight up the spine of the cone. In 0.1 mile it reaches a junction. Take the road up and to the left (northeast), which climbs the last 125-yard stretch to the crater's rim. Finally, turn right on the rim road. The summit is 0.3 mile up and down this road, on the eastern rim.

All along this approach the terrain is a newborn volcanic wilderness. You will cross a vast plain of cinder pebbles, bypass lava flows, and enjoy increasingly fine views of this imposing, highly symmetric and well-preserved cone. The desolation is barely tempered by a scatter of Mojave yucca. In the spring, large spreads of sand verbena and showy mimulus often decorate the ground, and the entire cone is covered with tiny white flowers. The ascent itself, with its plunging views down the cone's unobstructed 45% slope, is an aerial thrill.

Circumnavigating this neat oval crater along the faint road that traces its closed rim is an unusual experience. In its shallow cup the crater holds a miniature dry playa, the fine sediments washed down and collected by this tiny suspended basin since it cooled down 22,000 years ago. Cinder cones rise all around, welded together by tumbled fields of lava. Even after so long the lava flows seem to be animated, pouring down Cima Dome's subtle curve and draping its pale granitic shield with dark currents and whirlpools of the once-fluid rock. This is a desolate land, miles upon miles of slowly recovering destruction, animated only by the wind singing over the volcanic jags.

■

COWHOLE MOUNTAINS

The Cowhole Mountains are a beautiful accretion of low desert peaks rising dramatically from the open shore of Soda Lake, at the boundless confluence of the Devils Playground's sand plains and the Mojave River Sink's alkali wasteland. Although small by desert standards—they are only about 12 miles long by 2.5 miles wide at their widest—their complex topography of craggy summits delineated by pronounced saddles and bays gives them the visual appeal of a full-fledged range. They are composed of three main blocks, from north to south Little Cowhole Mountain and Cowhole Mountain, itself subdivided in two distinct blocks. An alignment of dispersed sand-chocked hills completes the range to the south. Because of their geological similarities, geologists informally refer to Little Cowhole Mountain and Cowhole Mountain collectively as the Cowhole Mountains.

The Cowhole Mountains are special, not only because of their alien beauty but because in spite of their relatively small size, they pack in an amazing geological diversity. Their makeup reflects many of the major geologic events that shaped the eastern Mojave Desert—regional metamorphism and deformation around 1.7 billion years ago, 300 million years of marine sedimentation during the Paleozoic, plutonism and volcanism in the Mesozoic, and extensive faulting in the Mesozoic and Cenozoic. This miniature range even has its own pluton—a quartz monzonite exposed on the west side of all three blocks called Granitoid Rocks of Cowhole Mountain. It also has its own fault—the Cowhole Thrust—exposed below the highest summit.

The formation responsible for the stunningly colorful cliffs of the Red Rock Canyon National Conservation Area west of Las Vegas—Aztec Sandstone—is exposed in long screes on the south side of the main block. It was formed in the Jurassic, in a poorly drained region of sand dunes and silt pans. Dinosaurs barely made it to what little of California existed then, but they did roam the Aztec sandscape. In the Mescal Range 30 miles to the northeast, this same formation holds trackways of a flying dinosaur called pterosaur, and of coelurosaurs, a feathered bipedal dinosaur about the size of an ostrich.

Because all these formations are confined to a small space, to climb the Cowhole Mountains is to travel through time at an even more accelerated pace than elsewhere. One can cross, in less time than it takes to develop a sweat, from Proterozoic crystalline basement to Mesozoic monzonite, Cambrian quartzite, and limestone stuffed with Mississippian corals. The ground surfaces are as diverse in color and texture as they are in erosional patterns.

Sand is prevalent around the Cowhole Mountains, especially the southern hills, which are inundated with sand drifts, and the southern slopes of Little Cowhole Mountain, festooned with a few small dunes. This sand is part of and has the same origin as the Devils Playground, the enormous eolian deposit that extends 25 miles from Soda Lake southeast to the Granite Mountains. The composition and shape of the sand grains suggest that most of it came from the distant San Bernardino Mountains. Eroded from the mountains' abundant granites, the sand was transported 120 miles north and east along the Mojave River, then herded southeastward by the prevailing winds. Local winds are responsible for this sand getting blown onto Little Cowhole Mountain.

Mining never made it big in these mountains, although people certainly tried. All three mountain blocks were prospected for precious metals, especially the Cowhole Pluton exposures. Shafts were even sunk on Little Cowhole Mountain, and hopes were high enough that a small mill called Green Rock was erected at its southwest corner. It likely did not produce even a pocketful of gold.

The Cowhole Mountains are part of Mojave National Preserve, and all in a designated wilderness except for Little Cowhole Mountain. For decades the area was used for cattle ranching. The mountain's unglamorous name is said to have been inspired by watering holes sunk by ranchers at the foot of the mountains. The grazing allotment was retired in 2001, and wildlife has again the whole place to itself. Coyote are occasionally seen crossing the surrounding low lands, as are kit fox and more rarely bighorn sheep.

This area has the lowest elevations in the preserve. In the late fall and winter, this is the warmest spot to climb a desert peak without having to contend with the biting cold on higher peaks. In the spring, the bajadas around the Cowhole Mountains can be vibrant with dandelion and primrose in bloom. This is also a good area to spot the striking white flowers of desert lilies growing right out of the desert sands.

■

LITTLE COWHOLE MOUNTAIN

Little Cowhole Mountain is an unusual mountain to climb—most of its short ascent takes place on a sand dune. This fun mountain will appeal to hikers new to desert mountaineering, who may find it less inhibiting and easier testing ground than full-size mountains, and to anyone looking for one last quick climb before the long drive back home. Made of Paleozoic dolomite deeply corrugated by sandblasting, the windy summit offers good views of the Mojave River Sink and its ring of distant mountains.

General Information
Jurisdiction: Mojave National Preserve
Road status: Climbing on old road and cross-country; HC access road
The climb (north side): 1.1 mi, 590 ft up one way / easy
The climb (south side): 1.25 mi, 690 ft up one way / easy
Main attractions: A scenic climb on a dune, views of Mojave River Sink
USGS 7.5' topo maps: Soda Lake North*, Seventeenmile Point
Maps: pp. 343*, 227

Location and Access
Little Cowhole Mountain is about 7 miles as the crow flies south-southeast of Baker. From Interstate 15's northbound exit at Kelbaker Road in Baker, drive the paved Kelbaker Road 0.9 mile east-southeast to a left bend. Two primitive roads branch off on the right. Take the first one (south-southwest). After 1.5 miles, turn left at a Y junction between two small hills. In 0.1 mile the road reaches the northwest corner of the former Baker dump (fenced). Turn left, follow the enclosure 0.2 mile to its northeast corner, and make a right. After 0.25 mile, at the southeast corner, turn left (east-southeast). In 1.15 miles the road veers right (south) and merges with a smaller road coming in from the left. Continue south 1.9 miles to a road on the left. To climb the mountain from the north, take this road and park after approximately 1.9 miles. Little Cowhole Mountain's summit is the narrow dome 1 mile south.

To climb the mountain from the south, at the last junction continue straight (south) instead of turning left. This portion of the drive is shown on the accompanying map. The road passes between Soda Lake and Little Cowhole Mountain, then crosses a short, normally dry stretch of Soda Lake (do not attempt crossing it when wet). Stay on the tracks closest to the mountain; a metal post indicates where the road

341

resumes on normal ground. After 2.6 miles the road angles left at the southwest corner of the mountain and reaches a wide road crossing. The road on the left (northeast) goes to the large concrete foundations of the Green Rock Mill visible up ahead. Take the second road from the left (east-northeast) instead. After 1 mile it merges with the Mojave Road. Continue east 125 yards to a three-way split, and park. The high point of Little Cowhole Mountain is visible to the north. The smaller, leftmost road can get you a little closer, but it is a bit rough, and walking it is just as easy. The roads to either starting point are level and generally smooth, but a few short lopsided sections will stop some standard-clearance vehicles. A high-clearance vehicle makes it easier.

If you are coming from the direction of Kelso, follow the directions to Cowhole Mountain. After driving the Mojave Road 6.9 miles to the fainter road on the left where you would turn left to climb Cowhole Mountain, continue straight 1.1 miles to the three-way split and park. This itinerary has some deep sand and requires high clearance.

Route Description

On the north side the climb starts on the smooth fan that smothers the mountain. The fan is usually dominated by a monoculture of scattered creosote, as preened as a manmade garden. After the first heavy rains in the fall and winter, the sandy ground becomes for a short time a green lawn of young shoots. At the top of the fan it is easy to navigate among the low open hills to the saddle north of the summit. From there it is a short scramble over a rocky slope to the summit. The local rocks are all light-grey dolomite from the Cambrian–Ordovician era. Sand and salt particles blown in by the often strong local winds have blasted and chemically etched into them intricate markings of rills and points, as sharp as steel needles. Every single exposed surface has a unique texture and pattern, as beautiful as it is dangerously abrasive.

The climb from the south side is more interesting, and it offers better views on the way up. From the three-way split, walk up the leftmost road (north-northeast) toward the deep bay that cuts into the mountain. Most of the tall dune that covers the steep slope up ahead has been colonized by a tight cover of blond grasses. To avoid damaging this fragile vegetation working hard at stabilizing the dune, do not climb on that part of the dune. Instead, go 0.65 mile up the road, then leave it and head northwest across a shallow wash to the closest (southernmost) end of the dune, which has no grass. Climb east to the top of the dune—the only steep part of the climb. From there head north across the grass-free top of the dune to just below the shallow saddle south of the summit. The dune is covered with an interesting

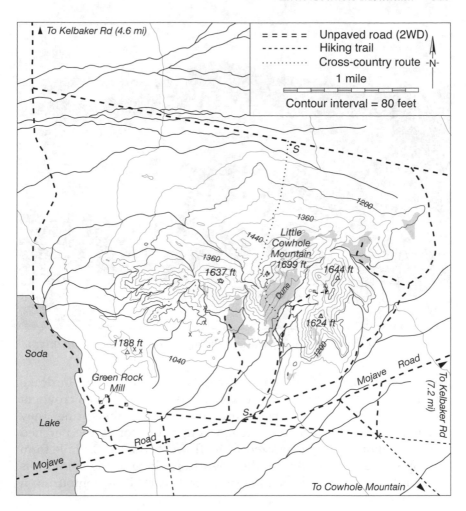

Little Cowhole Mountain

	Dist.(mi)	Elev.(ft)
North-side climb		
Road	0.0	1,105
Little Cowhole Mountain	1.1	1,699
South-side climb		
Mojave Road	0.0	1,015
Leave mining road	0.65	1,100
Upper end of sand dune	1.15	1,575
Little Cowhole Mountain	1.25	1,699

View south down the sandy slope below the top of Little Cowhole Mountain

assortment of plants, from scattered cholla to beavertail and birdcage evening primrose. In the colder season, the primrose's barren crown of white stems curl inward like an arthritic hand. In the spring, they transform themselves beyond recognition and decorate the parched sand with thousands of oversized white flowers. The last 0.1 mile from the top of the dune to the saddle, then from there to the summit, is over broken bedrock. The summit is easiest reached by contouring it on the east side.

Thanks to its central location, the small rocky summit of Little Cowhole Mountain commands sweeping vistas of the vast Mojave River Sink, encompassing the briny salt flats of Soda Lake, the austere Soda Mountains, Turquoise Mountain, the rough scarp of Old Dad Mountain, and the sprawling sawtooth crest of the Bristol Mountains. If you cannot make Cowhole Mountain, this is a worthy second prize.

Being circumvented by primitive roads, Little Cowhole Mountain can be readily climbed from many other directions, and a variety of loop hikes can be conceived to climb it one way and return another. The summit west of the high point, for example, has even better, unobstructed views of Soda Lake. The summit east of the high point is more rugged and challenging.

∎

COWHOLE MOUNTAIN

> *Climbing Cowhole Mountain's abrupt high point is hard work,
> along an insanely steep gully towards the end, but I cannot praise
> this breathtaking ascent enough. The physical effort is exhilarating,
> the variety of rocks and fossils impressive, and the views from the
> summit rank among the most otherworldly in the Mojave Desert.
> On a clear day, this is a perfect place for a wild winter workout.*

General Information

Jurisdiction: Mojave National Preserve
Road status: Roadless; primitive access road (HC)
The climb: 1.9 mi, 1,230 ft up, 50 ft down one way/difficult
Main attractions: A scenic peak climb, awesome views, geology
USGS 7.5' topo maps: Seventeenmile Point*, Cowhole Mountain
Maps: pp. 347*, 227

Location and Access

Cowhole Mountain can be climbed from a side road off the historic
Mojave Road. From the northbound exit on Interstate 15 at Baker, take
the Kelbaker Road south into the preserve 12.1 miles to a primitive
road on the west (right) side. Drive this road 0.8 mile until it merges
with the Mojave Road. Follow the latter 4.2 miles to a four-way junction (this stretch is sandy and requires good clearance), then continue
straight 2.7 miles to a fainter road on the south side (left). The flat-
topped summit to the south is Cowhole Mountain. Turn left and park
after 0.4 mile at a five-road junction (the two roads ahead are blocked
off by a wilderness boundary sign).

Coming from Baker, there is an alternative route that is shorter and
less troublesome for standard-clearance vehicles, although it should
still be undertaken with care, and a high-clearance vehicle is best.
Refer to directions to the starting point for the south-side climb of
Little Cowhole Mountain. Instead of parking at the three-way split to
climb that mountain, continue east-northeast on the Mojave Road 1.1
miles to the fainter road on the south side mentioned earlier. Turn
right, drive 0.4 mile, and park.

Route Description

Of the many possible routes to Cowhole Mountain, the one suggested here is the shortest and most straightforward. From the

The lunar landscape looking southeast from Cowhole Mountain

wilderness boundary head due south down the gently sloped creosote plain, aiming for the deep cove that cuts into the base of the mountain directly below the summit. After 0.9 mile you will cross a large wash coming down from the east, then start climbing into the cove. Two parallel washes drain the cove; take the one on the left, the one that squeezes up ahead through a gap in a dark dike transverse to the wash. (Better yet, follow the low bench that parallels this wash on the east side; it offers easier footing and ends at the dike). Just after crossing the dike, the wash splits. Take the left fork and stay in this steep and fairly straight rock-strewn gully until it emerges on the crest at a V notch just east of the summit block. The rest of the way (~0.1 mile) is north up along the crest, mostly across bumpy limestone slickrock.

Considering its modest size, Cowhole Mountain certainly holds its own. The total elevation gain is only about 1,200 feet, but most of it occurs in 0.4 mile up the gully, over terrain progressively steeper and rougher. Starting as a narrow field of sturdy boulders, the gully soon runs into a few falls, then it becomes so steep that gravity has stripped off all large boulders, leaving behind a slippery river of loose cobbles tipped at a reckless 50° angle. It is a grind (trekking poles help on the way back down), but at least it is short and plants are scarce. Even climbing part way has its rewards: the abrupt slope commands great

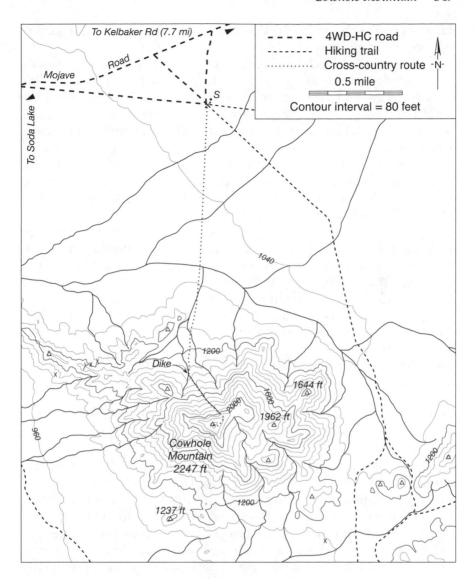

Cowhole Mountain

	Dist.(mi)	Elev.(ft)
End of road / wilderness bdry	0.0	1,066
Major wash crossing	0.9	1,020
Dike crossing	1.5	1,300
Ridge	1.8	2,150
Cowhole Mountain	1.9	2,247

views of Soda Lake and Little Cowhole Mountain, encrusted in generous coulees of virgin sand.

One of the perks of this climb is the variety of rocks. The wind-swept sandy plain leading down to the mountain is sprinkled with beautifully gnarled ventifacts, mostly black and red chunks of vesiculated lava flushed all the way down here from the cinder cones area. Up on the mountain, at least seven formations outcrop on the north face alone. The dikes at lower elevations are beige-gray felsite thickly coated with auburn desert varnish. The profusion of crags on the lower half are pink quartz monzonite (Granitoid Rocks of Cowhole Mountain). They are topped by thin-bedded shale, siltstone, and limestone (Carrara Formation), and above it by mostly dark dolomites (Bonanza King and Nopah formations to possibly Ely Springs Dolomite). The thick tilted limestone beds forming the summit block belong to yet another one, the Bird Spring Formation. Most of the boulders in the gully are made of this distinctive light-gray limestone. Wind-blasted to a skin-shredding finish, they provide good anchors to hang on for dear life as you scramble up. They are crawling with fossils, especially corals and primitive amebas called fusulinids. The several species of fusulinids that have been found here are particularly important: they have helped geologists reconstruct the evolution of the vast inland sea that sliced across the Americas in the Permian, at a time the equator passed close to Cowhole Mountain. There is an excellent exposure of fusulinids at the crest about 10 yards west of the gully's upper end—dark-gray grains of rice swimming across a tilted face of limestone.

The geology, the workout, and the setting all add up to a great climb, but it is the views that make it so exceptional. When I crested the ridge and first stared down at the southern portion of the Cowhole Mountains, my jaw dropped. Down below, clinging to the foreground like a nightmarish vision, a stark range of jagged peaks and ridges jutted sharply above a desert floor swirling with bleak shades of browns, grays, and reds. Beyond it, the range's dark southern hills were poking out of a sea of sand like the weathered ruins of a forgotten city. Still beyond, the Devils Playground stretched for many empty miles, past deeply furrowed Old Dad Mountain, to the ghostly Kelso Dunes outlined against the Granite Mountains. I gazed a long time at this forsaken moonscape, mesmerized by its primordial attraction. Even after I left and headed back down, the summit's edges were so precipitous that I was still floating above it.

■

SACRAMENTO AND CHEMEHUEVI MOUNTAINS

The Sacramento and Chemehuevi mountains are contiguous ranges along the Colorado River, west and south of the old railroad town of Needles, at the extreme southeastern corner of California's portion of the Mojave Desert. The northwest-trending Sacramento Mountains are about 22 miles long and 8 miles wide at their widest. The Chemehuevi Mountains to the south are shaped like a tight, crescent with a 20-mile spine facing the sunrise. To the west they drop quickly 1,000 to 1,500 feet into Ward Valley and Chemehuevi Valley. To the east, they descend as much as 3,000 feet over longer distances to the low-desert open shore of the Colorado River. Less than 4,000 feet tall, they rank among the lowest ranges in the Mojave Desert. In spite of this modest prominence, they are surprisingly rugged. Drained on all sides by dendritic networks of twisted washes and canyons, they rise as long wrinkled ridges capped by a surfeit of crags and peaks. The region's only paved roads are Interstate 40, which clips the north end of the Sacramento Mountains, and Highway 95, which crosses the broad saddle linking the two ranges at Lobecks Pass. Both ranges are well protected. The Sacramento Mountains lie entirely within Mojave Trails National Monument, and the Chemehuevi Mountains within the 85,864-acre Chemehuevi Mountains Wilderness. The two ranges adjoin, along their eastern borders, the Fort Mojave Indian Reservation and the Havasu National Wildlife Refuge in Arizona, and the Chemehuevi Indian Reservation in California.

Between about 23 and 13 million years ago, most rocks in both ranges were deformed, often severely, by major crustal extension. In the Chemehuevi Mountains, three roughly parallel detachment faults split the crust into a stack of plates dipping to the northeast. The first one to break was the Mohave Wash Fault; pulled down by gravity, the thick plate above it slipped over time a little over one mile. The second one, the Devils Elbow Fault, opened up a few thousand feet higher; it sheared the top of the plate and shoved it several miles into Arizona.

The third and youngest, the Chemehuevi Fault, sliced the plate between the two older faults in half and transported its top portion another 5 miles. In the Sacramento Mountains, even more severe structural deformations took place along two detachment faults, cumulating 30 miles of displacement in the southern reaches. In the process, in both ranges the original bedrock of Mesozoic granitoids and ancient gneiss, schist, and migmatite was locally buckled, grated, crushed into micro-breccia, and fragmented by swarms of small faults. Erosion subsequently carved into these weakened rocks the two range's finely chiseled landscapes. The geologic map looks like a quilt designed by insanity. All over, these profound tectonic rearrangements have brought together, over short distances, rocks as different as Miocene lava and ash-flow tuffs, Cretaceous diorite and porphyritic granites, and garnet-bearing gneiss up to 1.7 billion years old.

Both ranges have other unusual treasures. Chemehuevi Valley, which wraps around the west and south sides of the Chemehuevi Mountains, is one of the largest drainage systems in this part of the desert. It has some of the best desert-tortoise habitats in the Mojave Desert. Teddy bear cholla, uncommon in California, are common in both ranges. The largest population in the state is found in the northwestern Sacramento Mountains, in the 14,645-acre Bigelow Cholla Garden Wilderness. Crucifixion thorn, a rare and endangered, shaggy shrub up to 12 feet tall with thorns several inches long, grows around the small Sawtooth Range west of Chemehuevi Peak.

Native Americans made extensive use of these two ranges and surrounding valleys, as living spaces, hunting and foraging grounds, and for travel. Numerous archaeological sites have been found; some of them were active 120 centuries ago. Many areas have sleeping circles, grinding surfaces, shards of toolstones, and other pre-contact cultural remains. In and around the Sacramento Mountains, prehistoric paths are lined with galleries of small boulders engraved with rock-art images. They might have been portals to sacred grounds, or a sign of welcome to outsiders entering the harsh desert from the east.

The Sacramento Mountains have five officially named peaks, ranging from 3,314 feet (Bannock Peak) to 2,838 feet (Sacram Peak). The Chemehuevi Mountains have three—Whale Mountain (2,774'), Chemehuevi Peak (3,694'), and Rocky 2 Peak (3,551'). When climbing any of them, the Colorado River is a constant presence that commands attention, by its spirit if not by its size. In this utterly waterless land, it is a blatant anomaly with the calming effect that water has where water is scarce, and the quiet might of eternity.

∎

EAGLE PEAK

Eagle Peak is an extinct volcano that last erupted millions of years ago, during the Miocene's protracted volcanic mayhem. Its conical summit commands expansive views of the Mojave Desert's desolate southeastern province, with grand vistas of the Sacramento Mountains and a rare bird-eye perspective of the Colorado River. But the cover charge is steep... Climbing the sheer summit block, up a 40% couloir of precarious rocks flanked by hard spurs, is a short Class-2 grind that will get your heart pumping.

General Information
Jurisdiction: Mojave Trails National Monument (BLM)
Road status: Roadless; primitive access road (HC-4WD)
The climb: 1.5 mi, 1,540 ft up, 120 ft down one way / difficult
Main attractions: Exhilarating Class-2 climb, views of Colorado River
USGS 7.5' topo map: Flattop Mountain
Maps: pp. 353*, 227

Location and Access
The second highest summit in the Sacramento Mountains, Eagle Peak is roughly in the middle of the range, about 10 air miles south-west of Needles. If starting from Needles, get off at the J street exit on Interstate 40. At the eastbound exit stop sign, make a left on J Street, and go under the freeway 0.2 mile to West Broadway. Turn left and go 0.15 mile to S L Street. Turn left, and drive back under the freeway 0.1 mile to the Eagle Pass Road, on the right just past the overpass. Set your odometer to zero at this corner. Follow this road 0.4 mile as it parallels the freeway, veers west near the railroad, then crosses an open area by a towing yard. Continue west, 50 yards over and across a raised roadway, then down 50 yards to a fork; take the left fork. In 50 yards the road crosses a dirt road. Right after it, take the left fork (straight), signed NS 099. The Eagle Pass Road soon veers southwest, and maintains this general bearing up to the Sacramento Mountains visible ahead. It is very coarse gravel until it enters the mountains in 7.5 miles, then a washboard in a broad wash of soft gravel. Four-wheel drive and high clearance are imperative. Eagle Peak is the main summit visible up ahead most of the way. After about 10.2 miles, the road reaches Eagle Pass, not a true pass but a 1-mile stretch of narrower wash along the southeastern foot of Eagle Peak. After 11.7 miles, 0.8

mile past the peak, the Eagle Pass Road forks in the wash. Park in this area, below Eagle Peak's southwest shoulder (look for a grove of teddy bear cholla on its sloped shelf about 50 feet above the wash).

If coming from the west, this second itinerary is a little faster and the roads of better quality. Get off Interstate 40 at the Water Road exit, 69.9 miles east of Ludlow. At the eastbound exit stop sign, turn right and go 0.2 mile to the end of the pavement at a multiple-road junction. Continue straight. The road soon curves to the southeast and aligns itself with a steel-tower power line. From the stop sign it is 9.6 miles on this good graded road to the Eagle Pass Road on the left, signed NS 085 (this is 0.25 mile past another road on the left). Stay on this road 3.7 miles to an open pass with a lot of short ups and downs (one of them requires four-wheel drive westbound), then 3.0 miles, mostly down a gravel wash, to the wash below Eagle Peak. Park 0.1 mile farther, across the wash and a little to the left, below the cholla garden.

Route Description

In the vicinity of Eagle Pass, the road gives sobering glimpses of Eagle Peak's rugged topography. It skirts impassable cliffs along the peak's east base, then the army of tall spurs that crowds the south shoulder, and finally the precipitous west-facing summit block. The southwest shoulder offers the least difficult route to this uncooperative summit: it is a little steep but unobstructed up to the 2,800-foot knoll west of the summit, leaving the crux—the summit block—for the very end. It is also a good place to enjoy teddy bear cholla. One could climb most summits in this book and not see a single one of these deceptively cuddly-looking cactus. Cliquish to a fault, they live in this area in close-packed colonies of 50 to 250 plants, their fuzzy crowns haloed with warm lime-green light.

The southwest shoulder is an alignment of three inclines, the first one the slope right behind the cholla patch, the second one a much shorter rise, and finally the 2,800-foot knoll. The slopes are tightly

	Dist.(mi)	Elev.(ft)
Road	0.0	1,890
False summit (knoll)	1.05	~2,800
Saddle below crux	1.15	2,675
Crest (top of crux)	1.45	3,230
Eagle Peak	1.5	3,308

Eagle Peak

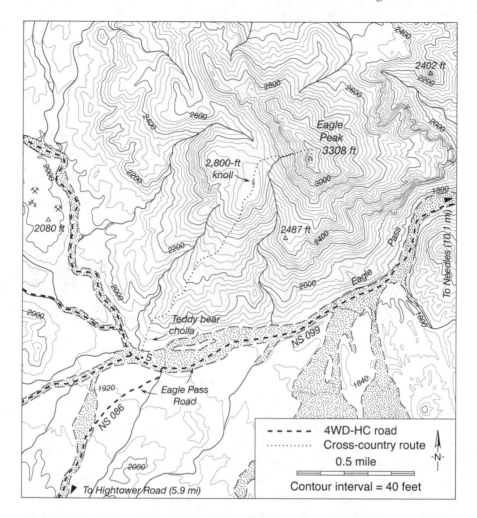

packed with angular cobbles of rhyolite, chocolate-brown from heavy patination. On the more level areas between hillsides the rhyolite has been crushed to a litter of pale beige pebbles. The vegetation is a sparse cover of low bushes with desert names like burro, brittle, salt, creosote, and wishbone. In the late winter, it is hard to find a stepping place without phacelia and evening primrose underfoot, so thickly do they cover the ground. The steepest hill is the last one, leading to the knoll's flat top, a wind-swept malpais of stones and barrel cactus.

The knoll looks out straight across a 120-foot-deep saddle at Eagle Peak's impressive summit block. From the saddle to the crest the mountain is draped in tall crags and taluses that tumble down 550 feet in a third of a mile. For the least painful route, from the knoll descend

Sacramento Mountains' sloped volcanic mesas looking north from Eagle Peak

north-northeast to the saddle. Then scramble up the broader couloir that starts east of the saddle and climbs to the first saddle on the crest north of the summit. It is not technically difficult, but it is a strenuous Class-2 ascent. You are almost constantly off balance on an avalanche of large rocks, spying at every step a suitably stable-looking spot for your next step. Once the saddle on the crest is reached, it is a short and easier climb south along the crest's sturdier spine of cleaved bedrock.

For miles in every direction Eagle Peak stands high above everything else. Lone actor on a vacant stage, the Sacramento Mountains easily steal the show. They drop north to a long ruptured stairway of maroon volcanic mesas clipped by erosion, south to a wrinkled sprawl of pale granitic hills rimmed by dark volcanic chimneys. Other than a hint of the Dead and Chemehuevi mountains farther afield, the rest of the scenery is a carousel of vast valleys—Fenner, Piute, Mohave, Chemehuevi, and Ward—bounded 30, 40, 50 miles away by a haze of aquamarine ranges. It is a harsh and uncompromising land, daunting by its sheer size, and piercingly beautiful. The aloneness is tempered only by the lazy stretch of Colorado River flowing along Mohave Valley, edged by a faint tide of life—the small town of Needles, and a checkerboard of green fields straddling the California–Arizona border.

■

CHEMEHUEVI PEAK

> *Midway in difficulty between its neighbors Eagle Peak and Old Woman Mountain, this is an imposing and spirited mountain to climb. Standing at the transition between two deserts, the fan that leads up to its base is covered with some of the most extensive colonies of teddy bear cholla and cactus gardens in the state. In the mountain, the climb is a trudge up steep drainages choked with boulders, beneath imposing granitic ledges. The views from the final ridge and the summit encompass an awe-inspiring territory, including the dramatic Turtle Mountains, the vast Chemehuevi Mountains, and a rare peek at the mighty Colorado River.*

General Information
Jurisdiction: Chemehuevi Mountains Wilderness
Road status: Roadless; standard-clearance access road
The climb: 3.8 mi, 2,000 ft up, 40 ft down one way / very difficult
Main attractions: Cacti, granitic formations, views of Colorado River
USGS 7.5' topo map: Chemehuevi Peak
Maps: pp. 357*, 227

Location and Access
The apex of the Chemehuevi Mountains, this summit is near the south end of the range, overlooking Chemehuevi Valley. From Needles, take Interstate 40 to the Highway 95 exit (East Broadway) near the south end of town. At the stop sign at the eastbound exit, turn right and drive Highway 95 south 19.6 miles to a power-line road that crosses the highway, just past a steel-tower power line. Coming from the south, this is 0.15 mile north of the Havasu Lake Road. Turn left (southeast) on the power-line road, which is well graded and suitable for all vehicles. Go 3.2 miles to where it first crosses under and to the north side of the power line. Park 0.8 mile further, at the third tower past the crossing, the last tower before the next crossing. Chemehuevi Peak is the prominent summit 3 air miles to the northeast.

Route Description
Chemehuevi Peak is an impressive summit. Viewed from the road it has the shape of a steep-sided pyramid rising up from a long transverse ridge crowned with rocky spurs. Its southwestern face is a tapestry of glistening granitic cliffs slashed by black volcanic dikes. The

355

primary route is up a canyon, not visible from the road, to the deep saddle west of the summit, then up the western shoulder, a 45-degree arête that hints of heart-pumping moments to come.

The beginning is easy enough, a stroll up a gradual alluvial fan to the base of the mountain. To avoid getting into the wrong canyon, aim slightly east of the summit (33° magnetic north). A number of braided washes will get you there, first across a series of low hills, then in more open terrain. What is most enjoyable on this part of the hike is the cactuses. The fan is crowded with one of the highest densities of teddy bear cholla in the Mojave Desert. Their fluffy heads pop up everywhere, thousands on the way to the mountain, mixed with spidery ocotillo, brick-red barrel cactus, tousled staghorn cholla, and simple desert agave. It is hard to go through here without getting snagged at least once on a stray spine or one of countless fallen stem-joints.

After 2 miles you will reach the mouth of the canyon that climbs to the saddle. Make sure you are not in the shorter parallel canyon just west of it—you should be in an embayment a third of a mile wide, bounded to the east by a long spiky ridge. The gravel wash makes a broad left bend, then after 0.75 mile it enters bedrock and turns into a chaos of boulders. For the next 0.7 mile to the saddle area, you walk mostly on rocks, up a canyon that quickly roughens to a steep staircase walled up in a trench. Passage is obstructed by two falls (15–18 feet, Class 2), and several cabin-size angular blocks. There are propitious bits of trail, mostly on the west side, etched into loose taluses by generations of deer, bighorn sheep, and, lately, humans. One trail starts just past the side canyon on the left blocked by a monster fall. The next one starts just below facing twin blocks. The third and longest (650 feet) begins below the conspicuous turret that caps the west rim; it bypasses the narrowest and roughest stretch. It ends at the more gently sloped head of the canyon, a few short bends from the saddle at the crest.

This is stunning country. Along the canyon, the mountain is a solid mass of sculpted plutonic rocks that leap skyward in giant steps streaked with desert varnish. The vegetation is an open mix of desert lavender, creosote, catclaw, and nolina, spiced up with teddy bear cholla and other cacti. In the spring, the rocky slopes come alive with wildflowers, white desert chicory, yellow brittlebush and blazing star, blue lupine and phacelias, and flaming-red penstemon. It is not necessary to climb to the saddle, except that it has one last good cactus garden, scenic slickrock, and a nice vista of the central Chemehuevis.

From the saddle area, an imposing monzonite dome looms to the southeast, a quarter of a mile across, bulging with jointed outcrops and slanted slickrock. Chemehuevi Peak is hidden above it, trivially close

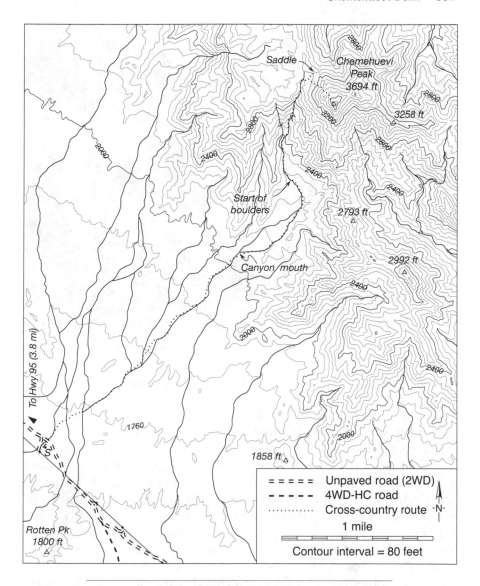

Chemehuevi Peak

	Dist.(mi)	Elev.(ft)
Power-line road	0.0	1,720
Canyon mouth	2.0	~2,025
Top of canyon	3.5	3,060
Saddle at crest	(0.1)	3,135
Chemehuevi Peak	3.8	3,694

Monzonite hoodoos at the saddle below Chemehuevi Peak

but 600 feet higher. The easiest way to tackle this final pitch is up the gully that slices down the middle of the dome. Although there is no technical difficulty, it is the hardest stretch. It is steeper, and the boulders may force you to scramble briefly onto one slope or the other. Even this far up you will be in the company of agave and ocotillo.

The summit is an airy spine of exfoliating monzonite so packed with outstanding views that it demands contemplation. All around, the Chemehuevis fall off in massive waves as furrowed as badlands, capped by hundreds of sharp crests. Desert classics rise further out— the Stepladders, the Old Womans, and the sere Mohave Mountains in Arizona. Here as most of the way up, the center of attention is the fantastic Turtle Mountains to the southwest, a long rampart of spires unlike any other range in the California desert. Yet the most remarkable element in this grand landscape is the Colorado, a true river lapping at the bone-dry flanks of the Mojave Desert. It appears and disappears all along the eastern base of the mountains, from the clutch of spires called the Needles that gave the town its name down to Havasu Lake, snaking past the sprawling Whipple Mountains on its way to the Sea of Cortez. It is a landmark so emblematic that you stare, like standing on an alpine meadow with a grizzly, struck by awe and respect.

∎

STEPLADDER AND OLD WOMAN MOUNTAINS

The Mojave Desert's extreme southeastern frontier is a remote region of rugged mountains buried up to their shoulders in cubic miles of bajadas that coalesce into immense north-south valleys. At its heart lies Ward Valley, a 65-mile-long trench flanked by multiple ranges. On its east side are the Stepladder Mountains, a fractured arc only 13 miles long and 1,100 feet high, yet possibly the most jagged range in the Mojave. On the west side are the Old Woman Mountains, which span 29 serrated miles from Fenner Valley south to Danby Lake, and loom 3,500 feet above their surroundings. Cadiz Valley unfurls on their west flank, hundreds of square miles of bajadas, salt flats, and sand dunes. Most of all this—the valleys, the mountains, the silence, the beauty—is preserved within the 165,172-acre Old Woman Mountains Wilderness, Mojave Trails National Monument, the 83,195-acre Stepladder Mountains Wilderness, and the 2,560-acre Old Woman Mountains Preserve, owned by the Native American Land Conservancy.

The magic of the Old Woman Mountains starts with these three syllables, a name that evokes a wise and wrinkled matriarch guarding immemorial secrets. This range was indeed named after a monolith perched on its crest that bears a striking resemblance to what the Chemehuevi called "Nomopeoits," their term for old woman. In a range artfully sculpted by erosion, this is the most recognizable of many formations. The Old Woman Mountains have seven named summits to enjoy this chaos of bare stone and their rich cultural history.

The Old Woman Mountains have been severely eroded by long broadening canyons. Viewed from the air, they look like a giant fish bone of high ridges stemming from a common spine. A little more than half is granites, mostly 71-million-year-old granodiorite of the Old Woman pluton. It makes up most of the central area. The northwestern area is mostly Fenner Gneiss, a very coarse rock metamorphosed from porphyritic granites around 1.68 billion years ago. The southern third is dominantly Kilbeck Gneiss, a striped rock of similar age and origin.

The Stepladder Mountains are even more skeletal, broken up into four discontinuous blocks that shrivel from south to north. Almost all of this is volcanic, a colorful medley of tuffs, basalt, rhyolite, and stony breccia. For several miles the main crest is a chain of burned-out volcanoes, a comb of sheer chimneys so ruined by erosion that reason alone tells us surely they must be ancient. This skyline is so impressive that it gives this range a presence wholly disproportionate to its small size.

Both ranges are located near the boundary between two deserts. On the Stepladder bajadas live plants normally associated with the Sonoran Desert—palo verde, smoke tree, teddy bear cholla, ocotillo, and a small stand of crucifixion thorn. The southern third of the Old Woman Mountains is actually in the Sonoran. This transitional location, combined with the range's large size and span of elevations, and multiple springs, attract a broad diversity of plants and wildlife. The high crests are dotted with open stands of pinyon pine and a mix of Utah and California junipers. A small band of bighorn sheep lives here, as well as mule deer, badgers, jackrabbits, and ground squirrels. They are kept in check by a cohort of alert and underfed coyote, bobcat, gray fox, kit fox, and even a few mountain lions. Rattlesnakes are common: I saw or heard one every day I spent here. Several rare or endangered bird species also nest in this range, including saw-whet and elf owls. Near both ranges the bajadas are home to some of California's largest populations of desert tortoise.

The Stepladder Mountains were likely explored for minerals but never mined. The Old Woman Mountains, on the other hand, witnesses a fair amount of mining from 1889 until the 1930s. About two dozen mines were running off and on, mostly in the northern half. The main commodity was silver at first, then mostly gold, as well as some lead-zinc, tungsten, and copper. The combined returns probably did not reach half a million dollars. The range is still haunted by the ruins of the camps, bunkhouses, blacksmith shops, cabins, corrals, water tanks, tramways, ore bins, and mills that supported the mining activities.

This mining district was not the world's richest. But it did have one of the world's rarest minerals—a magnificent 3-ton boulder of coarse octahedrite iron from outer space. The Old Woman meteorite was discovered in 1976 near the Black Metal Mine by two prospectors searching for a fabled lost Spanish gold mine. The discovery was extraordinary. It is the second largest meteorite found on U.S. soil, and it contains rare crystals that have shed invaluable new light on the formation of asteroids. It is on display at the BLM's Desert Information Center in Barstow, minus two chunks sawed off in the name of science.

■

STEPLADDER MOUNTAIN

The high point of a long sculpted volcanic ridge rising sharply above remote Chemehuevi Valley, Stepladder Mountain is an impressive piece of geological architecture crowned by a cliff seemingly too abrupt to scale. This is a gem of a climb. Most of it is a long hike on easy valley and canyon floors; the obstacles and most of the elevation gain come only in the last third of a mile. The greatest satisfaction is finding and scrambling up the narrow ledges that zigzag across the summit cliff. The greatest visual rewards are wandering through the range's spiky monuments, and admiring this surreal landscape from above. The greatest challenge, for the hard-core hikers who brave the desert without assistance, is locating their car when they return...

General Information
Jurisdiction: Stepladder Mountains Wilderness (BLM)
Road status: Roadless; primitive access road (HC)
The climb: 4.8 mi, 1,280 ft up, 120 ft down one way / difficult
Main attractions: Great Class-2 cliff climb, jagged volcanic landscape
USGS 7.5' topo maps: Stepladder Mountains*, Stepladder Mtns SW
Maps: pp. 363*, 227

Location and Access
To get to the Stepladder Mountains from the north, take Interstate 40 to the Water Road exit, 69.9 miles east of Ludlow. At the eastbound-exit stop sign, turn right and go 0.2 mile to a multiple-road junction. Continue straight on the Hightower Road (NS 056). It soon curves to the southeast along a power line. From the stop sign, it is 15.8 miles on this good graded road to the intersection with a graded pipeline road signed NS 203. To reach this junction from the south, from Vidal Junction drive 27.6 miles north on Highway 95 to the Havasu Lake Road. Go 0.15 mile past it to the Hightower Road on the left. Follow this road northwest 11.3 miles to the NS 203 road. Drive 0.55 mile west on NS 203 to an inconspicuous primitive road on the left signed NS 254. This road makes an immediate left, parallels NS 203 eastward for 50 yards, then veers right (south). It then keeps this course along the west side of Chemehuevi Valley, paralleling the Stepladder Mountains a couple of miles to the west. Park after 5.5 miles at the wilderness boundary sign. This last road cuts across hundreds of shallow erosional channels. It would be painfully slow without decent clearance.

Route Description

Viewed from the road, Stepladder Mountain's broad summit cliff is clearly visible 4 miles to the west-southwest, at the north end of the range's long, deeply notched crest. The route is a little circuitous, but not difficult. First cut a beeline across the valley in a 230° magnetic bearing, to the prominent ridge in the foothills 16° south of the summit. It is an easy 2.3-mile walk, on level, compacted sandy gravel and intermittent desert pavement. On the south side of the hill, a broad canyon cuts east-northeast into the Stepladder Mountains. Go about 1.4 miles into it, along its easier southernmost wash, to a pronounced gap in the south wall. Then cross over the gap's 60-foot saddle to the next canyon south, and continue northwest up this canyon's wash.

This first part is a pleasant walk across scenic open desert, against the grain of dry washes. The valley is flooded with creosote mixed with barrel cactus, giant staghorn cholla, and patches of spidery ocotillo, all prime real estate for desert tortoise. The mountain washes are lined with meadows of brittlebush, fragrant desert lavender, and the occasional nasty catclaw. All around loom the ruins of sharp volcanic chimneys. The rocks are a particularly colorful mix of gneiss, granitoids, scoria, tuffs, and basalt. Stepladder Mountain is a nearly constant presence, growing more impressive with proximity.

About 0.5 mile up the wash, soon after it gets rocky and brushy, a wash splits off on the left, right below the summit. Between there and the summit, there is a barrier of 100-foot crags that must be crossed. This side wash will take you up to a draw that crosses it, but it is a bit rough. Instead, go 400 feet further up the main wash and head west up the slope to the next draw. Scramble up this very steep, rocky chute to a talus at the top of the crags. The summit cliff, now in plain view, is slashed by two tall vertical clefts. Segments of use trails will take you up the steep (~40%) and slippery talus to the base of the left cleft.

Stepladder Mountain		
	Dist.(mi)	Elev.(ft)
NS 254 road at boundary	0.0	1,770
Foot of hill at canyon mouth	2.3	~1,840
Leave wash to cross saddle	3.75	2,000
Next wash south	4.0	2,040
Side wash on left	4.45	~2,165
Foot of mountain block	4.7	~2,640
Stepladder Mountain	4.8	2,926

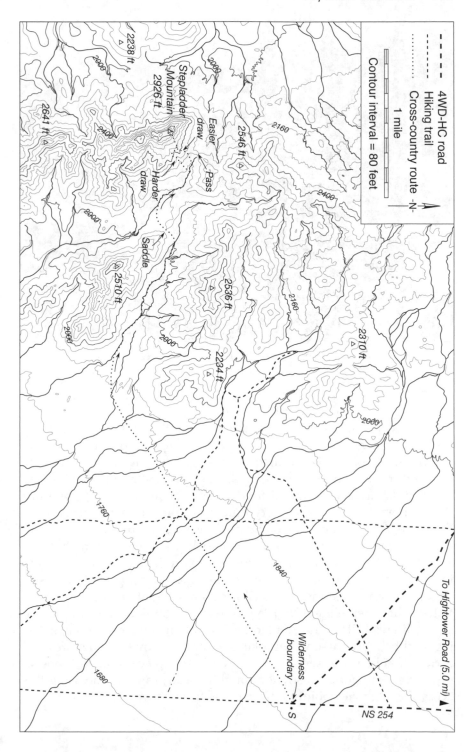

Looking southwest at the Stepladder Mountains from the summit

It is astonishing that although even up to this point the cliff seems hopelessly impassible, there is actually a way, and an easy way at that. The first step is on the 40–45° slant just left of the cleft. It climbs 25–30 feet to an overhang in a left curve, and to a 5-foot step just past it. The rest is a fortuitous series of three short ledges that zigzag up across the cliff, left, right, and left. The second ledge ends at a high fall back in the cleft. Climb instead the 12-foot wall on the left before it. The third ledge above this wall ends very quickly at the summit. Cairns mark the route. All the climbs are on Stepladder's signature breccia of basalt cobbles cemented in gray ash, a sturdy rock with large bulging holds.

The view from this remote summit is exceptional. You are engulfed in giant valleys. The closest ranges are miles away, pasted against a distant skyline—the Piute and Old Woman mountains beyond Ward Valley, the Chemehuevi and Whipple mountains on the far side of Chemehuevi Valley. The Stepladder Mountains take center stage, rising starkly out of these vacant plains in fantastically shaped spires and turrets. Geology has served us again a masterpiece of alien topography, a vertical world mostly too rough to scale, carefully devising this accessible high viewpoint for us to enjoy from above.

∎

OLD WOMAN MOUNTAIN

The highest point in the extreme southeastern province of the Mojave Desert, this prominent summit far away from everything embodies the wild spirit of the Old Woman Mountains. The ascent is only 2 miles, but with an elevation gain of 2,200 feet it is a slow and hard pull, up a canyon with an exponential grade consumed by a chaotic tide of boulders. You come here for the rough ride, the remoteness, the satisfaction of fighting a worthy opponent, a chance to spot a rare agave, and ultimately a sensational view of this extensive range rising starkly from alien desert valleys.

General Information

Jurisdiction: Old Woman Mountains Wilderness (BLM)
Road status: Roadless; primitive access road (HC-4WD)
The climb: 2.0 mi, 2,210 ft up, 30 ft down one way / strenuous
Main attractions: A rough boulder-filled canyon, botany, seclusion
USGS 7.5' topo map: Old Woman Statue
Maps: pp. 367*, 227

Location and Access

Old Woman Mountain (5,325') looms over the north end of the range, overlooking to the north Fenner Valley and the tiny community of Essex (pop. 7). It can be climbed on its north side via the Florence Mine, but because the road to the mine is closed it is a longer route. The southern route, starting in Carbonate Gulch, is shorter, less brushy, and more secluded, albeit at the price of a longer and more challenging drive.

To get there, take Interstate 40 to the Kelbaker Road exit, 28.2 miles east of Ludlow, and head south 11.4 miles on Kelbaker Road to its end at Route 66. Turn left on Route 66 and go 17.6 miles, past Chambless and Cadiz Summit near the south end of the Marble Mountains, to the signed Danby Road on the right. Drive this wide graded road 1.7 miles to the Santa Fe Railroad crossing. Across the tracks, a road signed NS 200 continues in the same direction (southeast) straight toward the Old Woman Mountains. Take the first road on the right instead, known as Skeleton Pass Road and signed NS 195 (not the second one, which parallels the tracks as NS 180). Drive it 5.3 miles to a road crossing (Sheep Mountain Road) with a pumping station on the left. Continue straight on Skeleton Pass Road 1.1 miles to Skeleton Pass, a broad passage

Nolinas and boulders in the mid-canyon to Old Woman Mountain

between low hills at the north end of the Ship Mountains, then 0.5 mile to the Carbonate Gulch Road on the left (NS 403). Drive this mostly slow road east 5.0 miles toward Old Woman Mountain, to a ramp that drops into the wash at the mouth of Carbonate Gulch. Park 2.25 miles up the canyon, at the narrow opening of a side canyon beside the road on the left, which is the way to the summit. Skeleton Pass Road is sandy north of the pass, and the canyon road is mostly deep sand, with a few rocky stretches. You will need four-wheel drive, high clearance, and experience; even then you might have to park earlier to avoid getting mired down in the middle of nowhere.

Route Description

It starts easily enough. The lower reaches of the side canyon is a sedate corridor of gravel sandwiched for 200 yards between perpendicular walls. At the fork a little less than half a mile in, you are still mostly on gravel. At this point you have a choice. The right fork, longer, has a lower average grade. The left fork, more direct, is likely more difficult but for a shorter time, and it is the one I chose. Less than 100 yards up, it has short narrows too, with two Class-3, 6-foot falls.

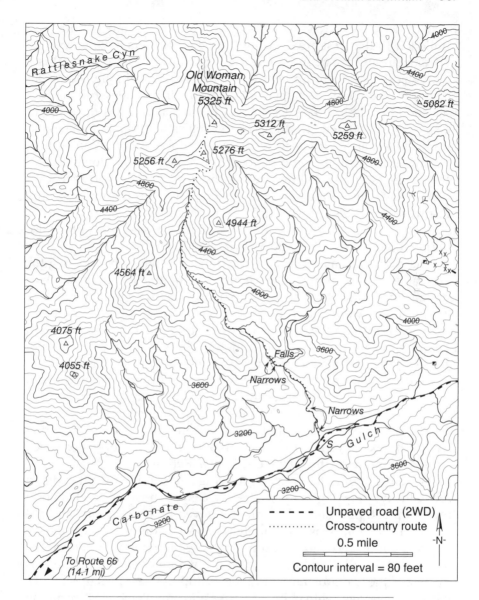

Old Woman Mountain

	Dist.(mi)	Elev.(ft)
Carbonate Gulch Road	0.0	3,145
Fork in canyon	0.45	3,355
South shoulder	1.8	5,100
Old Woman Mountain	2.0	5,325

Beyond them, the canyon remains open. There is not much more than a mile left to the crest area, but by then the boulders have moved in, and they are in to stay. As ridiculously short as this may seem, it is a strenuous slog, straight up nearly a third of a vertical mile, almost all shadeless, and all of it a hopeless avalanche of boulders. It would be bad enough without the rocks. Most of the canyon has no wash to speak of, just boulders, anything from cobbles to pregnant whales. To add insult to injury, bushes thrive in every nook that rocks can bestow, usually right where it would be most convenient to put down a boot. Near its head, about 300 feet below the crest, the canyon reaches a feverish 45% pitch. One option is to plug away up the ravine to the crest west of the false summit (5,276'). The other one is to traverse east to the rockier rim, then follow it north around the west side of the false summit. Both are short but superb grinds.

The mountain compensates for its harshness with a bounty of gifts. The land is a complex mix of metamorphic and igneous rocks, laminated walls of gunmetal schists in the narrows, sand-colored granite and salt-and-pepper granodiorite in the wash, and a jungle of shattered cliffs up and down the slopes. Whole gneiss boulders layered with sheets of mica glitter like liquid metal. The vegetation gathers the usual culprits but also less common species like nolinas, coyote tobacco, Mojave thistle, and rock pea. Live-forever in full pink-and-green regalia sprout out of the tiniest cracks. In the narrows the air is perfumed with desert lavender. The most delightful resident is the simple desert agave, a perennial that blooms once and dies, a selflessness that may partly explain its rarity. The canyon is home to dozens of specimens, ten times more than I have seen in a lifetime.

You emerge from the canyon on a ridge mercifully uncluttered and free of the tyranny of gravity, where it is easy to move, through an odd forest of plush pine and spiky yucca, buoyed by fresh air and the elation of victory. Old Woman Mountain is not the desert's tallest mountain, or the most recognizable. But as the highest summit for at least 80 miles in almost all directions, it delivers a whopper of a view. The perspective of the Old Woman Mountains is impressive, ranks upon ranks of transverse ridges with chiseled flanks and crenulated crests rippling down for 20 miles into the Sonoran Desert. The ridges taper to the west into a desolate Martian landscape of immense sand valleys studded with isolated ranges, where Matt Damon would have needed just as much luck to pinpoint a buried space probe. On a clear winter day the air is so crisp that even Mount San Jacinto pokes through, pegged on the far side of Palm Springs 100 miles away.

■

OLD WOMAN STATUE

> *Old Woman Statue is one of those places so enormously gratifying that one wonders how it can possibly still be lying in near-complete obscurity. Only a few people pay the venerable lady a visit each year. Yet it has all the attributes of a great destination—remoteness, an exceptional diversity of landscapes, exuberant wildflowers, cactus gardens, shady conifers, superb views, and a creative collection of stone sculptures, including the Old Woman herself.*

General Information
Jurisdiction: Old Woman Mountains Wilderness (BLM)
Road status: Roadless; primitive access road (HC)
The climb: 3.6 mi, 2,350 ft up, 350 ft down one way / difficult
Main attractions: Old Woman Statue and other striking formations
USGS 7.5' topo maps: Painted Rock Wash, Old Woman Statue*
Maps: pp. 371*, 227

Location and Access
Located approximately in the middle of the range, at least 25 miles from the closest asphalt, Old Woman Statue is just about as remote as it gets in the eastern Mojave Desert. You will first have to get to the Water Road exit on Interstate 40, 22.4 miles west of Needles. At the eastbound exit stop sign, turn right and go 0.2 mile to the end of the pavement. Turn right on the Metropolitan Water District Road; a power line parallels it to the right. Stay on this good graded road 23.3 miles down Ward Valley to a dirt road on the right (NS 420), at the south base of a tower. Take this road 4.3 miles west-northwest to NS 407. Old Woman Statue is distinctly visible on the crest to the west-southwest. Make a hard left on NS 407 and go south 1.6 miles to a parking area with interpretive signs at Painted Rock. The last two roads are a little sandy and require good clearance. This area is part of the Old Woman Mountains Preserve. This is a day use only area.

Route Description
The gated road on the right (west) as you drive in is the way to the Old Woman Statue. This rutted ranching road wanders leisurely into a scenic cove, along the curvy base of the mountain. You are following the edge of a secluded valley flushed with green creosote, saltbush, catclaw, yucca, ratany, and ultimately juniper, interspaced with patches

of sun-bleached grasses. In the spring, the cove is resplendent with the profuse canary flowers of desert senna. On the road's south side, the high-rising mountain is swarming with islands of granitic bedrock polished into forms so intriguing that one could easily forfeit the climb and explore them instead. In 1.4 miles the road reaches a creaking windmill. A third of a mile northwest of it the mountain comes down to a misshapen ridge of reddish granite. Strike a course across the open cove to the steep draw just beyond it, then climb up the draw to the saddle on the crest south of the 4,688-foot peak (1,429 m). The draw's narrow wash is filled with huge boulders and vegetation. It is less work to ascend its southern slope, although it, too, is a minor obstacle course, with catclaw, trees, tons of rocks, and the odd rattlesnake.

The Old Woman Statue first comes into view at the saddle. From this point the narrow, crescent-shaped crest wraps around the mile-wide head of a huge bay that drops over many miles into Ward Valley. The statue stands across the gap, the last and tallest of a rake of pinnacles that crowns the crest. The next stretch is along the crest, up and down a series of small peaks. The first one (4,688') is best bypassed. Instead of bypassing it *down*, it saves time to climb up its spine a little, gaining about 80 feet of elevation. There, a less cluttered bench offers a relatively easy path northwest to the saddle west of the peak. From there to the second 4,688-foot peak the terrain is a little easier. It is in this area that the Old Woman's shape becomes fully apparent, sitting slightly forward with her right arm resting on her knee, her skirt flaring below her, her head tilted a little, as if listening to eternity.

The ultimate stretch, from the second 4,688-foot peak to the base of the statue, is the most difficult. You first climb part way up a very steep ridge interrupted by a few outcrops, all avoided on the north side. You then cut a beeline southwest to bypass the massive cluster of pillars that caps the 5,164-foot summit north of the statue. From there the crest is bristling with pinnacles as sharp as teeth. They can be laboriously negotiated either up close and personal (Class 3) or avoided on

Old Woman Statue		
	Dist.(mi)	Elev.(ft)
End of road at Painted Rock	0.0	3,080
Old windmill	1.4	3,560
Saddle south of 1st 4,688-ft pk	2.4	4,380
Saddle west of 2nd 4,688-ft pk	3.0	4,640
Old Woman Statue	3.6	5,105

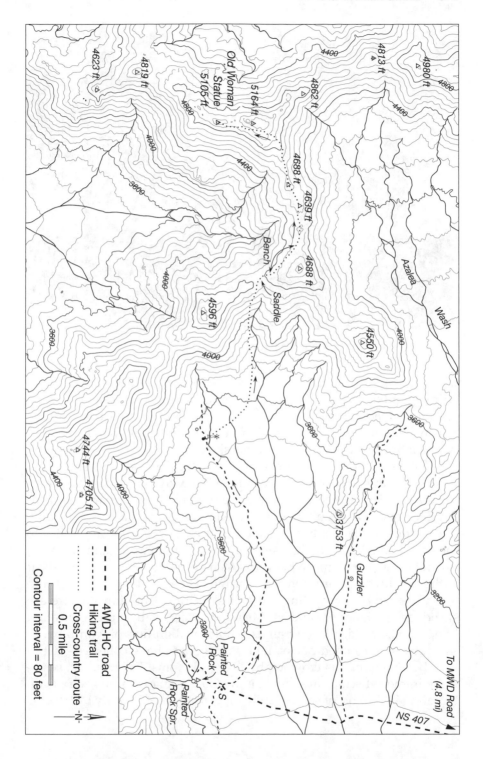

Old Woman Statue 5105 ft
4623 ft
4819 ft
5164 ft
4862 ft
4813 ft
4980 ft
4688 ft
4639 ft
4688 ft
Bench
Saddle
4596 ft
4550 ft
Azalea Wash
4744 ft
4705 ft
3753 ft
Guzzler
Painted Rock
Painted Rock Spr.
NS 407
To MWD Road (4.8 mi)

4WD-HC road
Hiking trail
Cross-country route
0.5 mile
Contour interval = 80 feet
-N-

Final ridge to the pinnacles (right) and the Old Woman Statue (left)

the east slope below them, across a precipitous field of boulders and spiny plants. The top of the Old Woman Statue's domed head is reached via a bolted, 25-foot, technical climb (5.7) up a crack on the northwest side. Most climbers will find it reward enough to respectfully touch the hem of the elderly lady's skirt.

The crest is in its final geological breath. Four advancing embayments, one in each cardinal direction, are slowly but inexorably eroding it away. The perspectives into these massive corridors are spectacular. Each one is a green, mile-wide lowland entrenched between spiky linear ridges that taper down to their distant terminus—Ward Valley to the east, Cadiz Valley to the west. Beyond, alien ranges stand etched in fine relief against cerulean heavens. As inspiring as the panorama is, it is the handiwork of erosion that got me. The crest is wearing off into an ever-changing recycling yard of striking formations. There are sliced fins, balanced boulders, blistered walls, standing gnomes and lying giants, on display for an assembly of dignified pinyon pine. In secluded rock-rimmed nooks, fallen pine cones have collected next to lone beavertail cactus crowned by brazen blooms. Everywhere, seemingly immortal sculptures are, like the Old Woman Statue itself, disintegrating into pools of sand, slowly dispossessed of identity by time.

■

MARBLE MOUNTAINS

Between the tiny service town of Ludlow and the Colorado River 100 air miles east, Route 66 crosses the heart of the Mojave Desert, one of the loneliest stretches of America's loneliest desert byways. It passes by deserted whistle-stops named Siberia and Bagdad, and largely abandoned towns like Amboy, Chambless, and Essex where boarded-up stores and antiquated gas-station signs speak of a long-gone era and prosperity. The Marble Mountains stand at the edge of this vast empty territory, a slender, 17-mile-long crest of finely sculpted granite and limestone peaks. To the north they overlook Fenner Valley and the eastern Mojave Desert's high cordillera. To the south their abrupt escarpment drops 1,500 feet to an immense bajada that descends for miles toward Cadiz Valley's huge salt flats and rippling sand dunes.

For such a small range, the Marble Mountains pack in a surprising geological diversity. About half, roughly the east side, is volcanic, most of it Miocene basaltic lava flows with some interbedded tuffs, and Quaternary flows and cinder cones on and north of Castle Peak. South of Castle Peak the western slope is Precambrian basement granite and gneiss, Teutonia Adamellite, a sequence of Cambrian formations (north of Chambless), and more basement at the south end. This variety makes for a spectacular mix of terrains, from domes to badlands, cliffs, plateaus, ridges, and ranks of impressively sharp peaks.

The Marble Mountains are famous for their trilobites, hard-shelled creatures that lived in the Earth's seas starting around 540 million years ago. They resembled today's horseshoe crab, typically oval and flattened bodies with a large head (the cephalon) and a ribbed thorax that tapered continuously to a blunt tail (the pygidium). They thrived all over, from the equator to the poles and from inter-tidal waters to the deep ocean. Until their extinction at the end of the Permian 252 million years ago, they evolved into the most diverse organisms to become fossilized. Most trilobites were about an inch long, but some were as small as a gnat and others more than a foot long. Some had horns, others spikes on their backs or flanks. What makes them special is that they were the first recorded animals to develop complex eyes. They had two eyes, each a two-dimensional array of tiny calcite lenses—up to a thousand—shaped like hexagonal cylinders that focused light onto a photosensitive area. The Marble Mountains' trilobites are found mostly in the Latham Shale, a bed of greenish shale about 50 feet thick in the midst of the sequence of Cambrian formations. At least twelve species have been recovered, as well as mollusks, ancient sea urchins, and brachiopods. The trilobites were of exceptional quality, and the site easily accessible. For decades, rockhounds and paleontologists drove to the site and, armed with chisels or sledge hammers or rocks, pried open the slate and harvested thousands of specimens. Here as elsewhere, this unbridled enthusiasm was threatening to give rise to what is referred to with bittersweet humor as the trilobites' second extinction. In 1994 the heart of the mountains was protected as the Trilobite Wilderness in part as a preservation measure. Ironically, the Marble Mountains were saved by an extinct species. Other than their northern tip located in Mojave National Preserve, they are now part of the Mojave Trails National Monument, and collecting is prohibited.

Before trilobites, from the 1880s to the 1900s it was gold, silver, and copper that attracted people to this range, mostly around the Castle Mine on the northwest side. The area still has the foundations of houses and of a gold cyaniding mill, a well, old diggings, and small shafts from subsequent one-man operations. The mines north of Chambless were all looking for iron, mostly magnetite, hematite, and a little pyrrhotite. The Iron Hat Mine was the largest of them. There were also attempts to mine limestone for cement, and ornamental slabs out of the Chambless Formation by an outfit called the Vaughan Marble Company, all short-lived ventures plagued by remoteness.

Bighorn sheep are fond of this place. The high country is peppered with the shallow depressions they have pawed into the gravel to make it more comfortable to lay down or sleep. Their beds are all strategically positioned on craggy high ridges, where they can get an advanced warning of approaching predators and a better chance to outrun them. Some beds have long been abandoned. Others, ruffled like morning sheets and rimmed with shiny pellets, were occupied only days before my visits. Perhaps the local band of *Ovis* migrates seasonally from the larger Old Woman Mountains to the southeast. Perhaps they returned after human visitation decreased following the trilobite hunting ban. I certainly gave them no reason to flee in a hurry, as I inched my way up their steep homeland, my lungs rasping like ceremonial bagpipes.

∎

CASTLE PEAK

This is a short, moderate climb to the high point of the Marble Mountains, across mostly open slopes covered with a variety of colorful volcanic rocks, desert pavement, wildflowers in the spring, and interesting plants. Other than the sheer ecstasy of isolation, the main reward is the view of the Cadiz Valley area from the crest, and of the spectacular army of sharp volcanic peaks that form the heart of this range.

General Information
Jurisdiction: Mojave Trails National Monument (BLM)
Road status: Roadless; primitive access road (4WD)
The climb: 1.9 mi, 1,110 ft up, 50 ft down one way/moderate
Main attractions: Spectacular views of the central Marble Mountains
USGS 7.5' topo map: Van Winkle Wash
Maps: pp. 377*, 227

Location and Access
Castle Peak is the highest point in the Marble Mountains. Located in the northern reaches of the range, it overlooks Clipper Valley to the northeast and Bristol Lake to the south. The starting point of this climb is conveniently reached by a wide graded gas-pipeline road, although unfortunately it has a few long steep grades that may stop two-wheel-drive vehicles. To get to this road, take the Kelbaker Road exit on Interstate 40, which is 28.2 miles east of Ludlow, or 64.1 miles west of the J Street exit in Needles. The pipeline road (NS 203) crosses the Kelbaker Road 1.35 miles south of the eastbound exit stop sign. Turn left on it and drive 2.4 miles up through a wide open gap in the Marble Mountains to a pass. Continue 1.9 miles down a broadening bajada to a narrow twin-track on the right, at 2 o'clock. This side road is inside the Trilobite Wilderness, so park at this junction. It is overgrown and easy to miss; if you miss it, park in this vicinity and cut a beeline toward Castle Peak, the dark volcanic ridge to the south-southwest.

Route Description
There are multiple ways to climb Castle Peak—via the trail with various points of departure toward the summit, via the other trail a mile to the west, cross-country up the wash that slices up the peak's north flank, or the more direct route suggested here, up the north-

Central Marble Mountains' sawtoothed crest from Castle Peak

northeast shoulder. All these routes are easier than most, free of large boulders and brush, and moderately steep. What I liked about the shoulder route is that you are on the crest and enjoy the views longer.

From the road, strike roughly south-southwest towards the broad shoulder that climbs to the prominent conical false summit (3,589') on this side of Castle Peak. In a third of a mile you will cross Cut Wash, the wide sand river that traces the entire north base of the Marble Mountains. Continue in the same general direction, up easy inclines of desert pavement and rounded basaltic cobblestones, to the first local high point. At the shallow saddle just past it, angle south to bypass the steep and rocky false summit on its west side. This is the only hard stretch, a ten-minute canted climb up a rock-strewn hillside to gain the saddle just south of the false summit. The rest of it is easy again, along the gentle curve of the open crest to the peak at the west end of it.

This is a pleasant ascent, short and unobstructed, loaded with little attractions. This is volcanic country, most of it basaltic flows that likely erupted from Miocene volcanoes to the north and/or east. Many intermittent eruptions covered the land north of the Marble Mountains under up to at least 2,000 feet of lava. The rocks are mostly varnished basalt, purplish andesite, and a desert pavement of scoria on the crest,

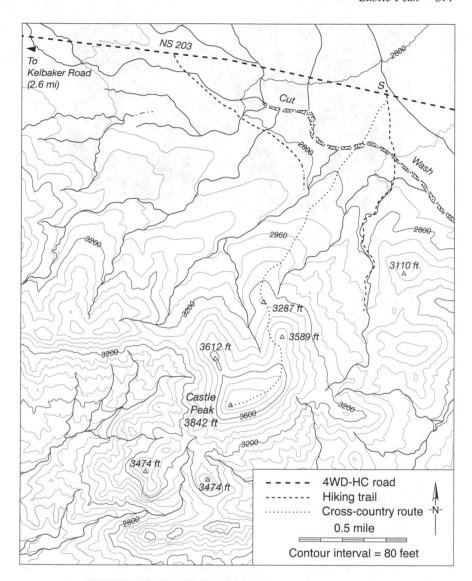

NS 203

To
Kelbaker Road
(2.6 mi)

Cut

S

Wash

2800

2960

3110 ft

3287 ft

3589 ft

3612 ft

3200

3200

3200

Castle
Peak
3842 ft

3600

3200

3474 ft

3474 ft

2800

	4WD-HC road
	Hiking trail
	Cross-country route

-N-

0.5 mile

Contour interval = 80 feet

Castle Peak

	Dist.(mi)	Elev.(ft)
Pipeline road	0.0	2,776
Wash	0.3	2,735
3,287-ft point	1.2	3,287
Saddle south of false summit	1.5	~3,560
Castle Peak	1.9	3,842

Smoke trees along Cut Wash, Castle Peak in background (center)

gray, purple, and brick red. Cream and lavender tuff beds streak the hills north of the crest. Cut Wash carries enough underground water to support a green belt of baccharis, willow, puffy smoke trees, and cat-claw laden with clumps of red mistletoe. In the spring the sand is peppered with white primrose and gravel ghost, yellow dandelion, and blue phacelia. When in bloom, the indigo bush blossoms hold a purple so deep that it borders on ultraviolet. The foothills are then surprisingly green, a forest of creosote sprinkled with small clusters of yucca and diamond cholla. On the mountain the annuals live in self-imposed segregation, monocultural pockets of Mojave aster, daisies, globemallow, and brittlebush.

From the rim of Castle Peak I could see the entire desert. The imposing pine-dusted scarps of the Granite and Providence mountains rise a few miles to the north, and the Clipper Mountains next to them. But in most other directions the view is unbroken, no less than 50 miles to the seam between land and sky, islands of blue mountain ranges from as far as Joshua Tree country to the hazy edge of la-la land. But what makes the view so breathtaking is the Marble Mountains themselves. Castle Peak looks out over the mountains' volcanic core, ranks upon ranks of deeply sawtoothed ridges marching along the range's narrow spine. Beyond lies 1,000 square miles of bajadas, sand dunes, and the ghosts of immense Pleistocene lakes. There is nothing remotely castle-like about this summit, but perhaps it was named not after itself but in commemoration of this fantastic topography of castellated peaks.

■

MARBLE PEAK

Marble Peak is a scaled-down version of a big mountain—flanked on one side by a staircase of cliffs, on the other by a very steep dip slope of Cambrian seabed, and a knife-edge crest in between. So in spite of its low prominence, it puts up a good fight. The approach is along a canyon infested with boulders, the route to the crest follows long upturned beds of corrugated dolomite, and the crest is a battlefield of jagged crags. The rewards are expansive views of Cadiz Valley and of the particularly angular geography of this part of the range.

General Information
Jurisdiction: Mojave Trails National Monument (BLM)
Road status: Roadless; primitive access road (HC)
The climb: 1.5 mi, 1,360 ft up, 90 ft down one way/difficult
Main attractions: Geology, views of Marble Mountains & Cadiz Valley
USGS 7.5' topo map: Cadiz
Maps: pp. 381*, 227

Location and Access
Marble Peak is in the southern Marble Mountains, above the famous Latham Shale trilobite site. If you are coming from the west, the scenic route to get there is from Ludlow on Interstate 40. Pick up historic Route 66 on the south side of the interstate and go 39.7 miles, east by southeast, to the signed road to Cadiz in the sleepy settlement of Chambless. The quicker alternative is to take the Kelbaker Road exit on Interstate 40, 28.2 miles east of Ludlow, and to drive Kelbaker Road south 11.4 miles to Route 66, passing by the Marble Mountains on the left. Turn left on Route 66 and go 5.6 miles to the Cadiz Road. Marble Peak is the high point on the crest 3 miles to the northeast. Continue east on Route 66 1.1 miles and turn left on a primitive road. This road forks after 0.1 mile. Angle left and go 0.8 mile to a junction. Turn right, and in 0.3 mile the road will fork at a cairn of cobbles painted white. The left fork goes to the trilobite site, but Marble Peak is a rough climb from there. Take the right fork instead and drive 1.3 miles up into a canyon to the Trilobite Wilderness boundary, which may not be signed. It is just before a side canyon on the left, which is the way to the summit. This last road is a bit rocky but OK with standard clearance up to where it angles left and joins the canyon wash. The last 0.7 mile is in the sandy wash, and it requires better clearance and a little traction.

The crest below Marble Peak, looking southeast at the Ship Mountains (left)

Route Description

From the edge of the wilderness the general route to Marble Peak is first up the side canyon on the left, which circles counterclockwise to end on a ridge, then up this ridge southwest to the crest, and finally northwest along the crest to the summit. The side canyon is well-behaved at first, with more gravel than rocks and an open landscaping of creosote, catclaw, smoke tree, and desert lavender. Soon rocks take over, and boulder hopping is the only way through the chaotic wash. The canyon is colorful, flanked to the west by tall slants of smoky-gray dolomite, and to the east by a volcanic mesa, then a band of reddish and beige volcanic cliff. There is an interesting short fall carved in conglomerate, bedrock of white ash, and many grades of basalt. Where the wash gets too congested, following the west-side bench instead helps. Where the cliff band begins, the most practical route is back in the wash, still overrun by boulder jams. At the end of the cliff band the wash ends. The saddle at the head of the canyon, marked by a spill of white limestone visible from some distance back, is reached by scrambling up a steep, bouldery talus.

The saddle is on a transverse ridge that ascends southwest to the crest, in full view of Marble Peak. The terrain up ahead is all Bonanza King Formation, the dolomite strata that cap the mountains' stack of

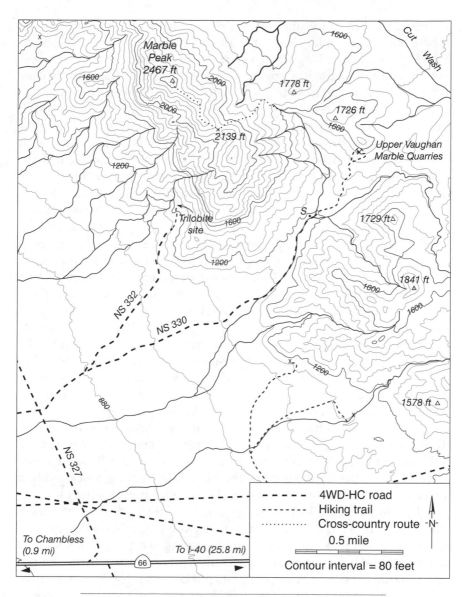

Marble Peak

	Dist.(mi)	Elev.(ft)
Access road / Wilderness bdry	0.0	1,200
Ridge at head of side canyon	0.85	1,760
Crest at saddle	1.15	2,139
Marble Peak	1.5	2,467

Cambrian sedimentary units. When the mountains were uplifted, the whole stack was folded and tilted toward you, south and east. From the ridge you are looking up at a giant wave of Cambrian seafloor that curves up to the crest at a gravity-defying 45° angle. The ridge is easy for a short distance, up to the next saddle. Then it swells to a massive craggy bluff that is best to bypass across its north slope. Not easy still, but easier. There the parallel strata protrude markedly, marching up to the crest in one direction and cascading down the mountainside in giant steps in the other. Any of these steps is a fairly convenient channel—steep uphill and slippery with loose rocks, but comparatively level toward the slope—to gain the crest near the 2,139-foot saddle.

The crest is a sharp knife of land squeezed between the mountains' abrupt escarpment on the west side and the long precipitous seabed on the east side. Oriented perpendicular to the Bonanza King's bedding, it crosses the hard broken tips of a series of strata, each one jutting up like a saurian tooth. There are a dozen teeth to climb, a few feet to tens of feet tall, up then down to get to the next one, most of them too narrow and uneven to stand on. This is a fun and scenic crux, with perilously thin air on all sides, although people with a fear of heights might beg to differ. The dolomite is beautiful, solid and angular, its surface a spidery web of erosional fissures, coated with tiny pricks that break skin on careless contact. It still preserves the topography of the ancient seabed, imprinted with countless crisscrossing fossil tracks of the primitive life that crawled on it half a billion years ago.

The views from the crest and summit are worth every battle scar. To the south the crest's curvy comb of jagged teeth you just crossed fills all of the foreground, overlooking tilted, finely banded cliffs. Beyond them, the southern tip of the Marble Mountains tapers off in a graceful arc toward the crisp sail of the Ship Mountains, the long serrated skyline of the Old Woman Mountains, and Cadiz Valley's luminous heart. To the north the crest plunges into a mind-bending geological chaos, complex sculpted walls exposing warped, crushed, and overturned beds folded by extreme compressive stresses during mountain building. Jumbled Paleozoic units poke out randomly in a brilliant kaleidoscope reminiscent of Death Valley's famous Amargosa Chaos.

When I left, a sand storm was brewing over the Cadiz Dunes. A sudden wall of wind rushed over the scarp, sending quivers through the ghostly desert holly. In moments the cobalt sky turned the color of granite. The turkey vulture that was soaring below me wisely sailed off ahead of the blizzard. The descent, usually harder, was harder still.

■

CADY MOUNTAINS

The first wagon road across the Mojave Desert, now known as the Mojave Road, was opened in early 1858. It connected the Colorado River to present-day Barstow across what is now Mojave National Preserve. When later that year the first trains of emigrants arrived from Arizona to the Colorado River to cross the desert on the newly opened road, they were attacked by Native Americans, who were upset at the growing incursion on their ancestral land. In the spring of 1859, more than 500 soldiers were sent to the Colorado River in retaliation. As trouble with local Indians continued, in April 1860 a camp was established near the other end of the Mojave Road, where the Mojave River flows above ground, 25 miles east of Barstow. The camp served as a base for troops searching the area for dissident natives. It was named Camp Cady, after Major Albemarle Cady of the 6th U.S. Infantry, then in command of Fort Yuma. Camp Cady was active off and on for only about 6 of the following 11 years. But the name stuck, and the range south of the camp became the Cady Mountains.

The sprawling Cady Mountains cover about 500 square miles confined to the wedge between I-15 and I-40 east of Barstow. Their geography is defined not by the linear symmetry of tectonic blocks but by incidental proximity. They can be loosely divided into seven irregular mountainous masses separated by miles-wide fans, bajadas, and washes. The west end, facing Troy Lake and Barstow, is two clusters of low hills dominated by Soldier Mountain (2,534') and Troy Peak (2,643'). The taller central portion has four groups, centered around Afton Peak (2,690'); Flat Top Peak (3,100') and Mellon Peak (3,634'); Top Peak (3,878') and Cady Peak (at 4,627' the highest point); and Sleeping Beauty (3,979'). The east end is a sharp ridge capped by Junction Peak (2,565'), overlooking Broadwell Lake and the Bristol Mountains to the east. To the north the Cady Mountains are bounded by the mostly dry Mojave River, where it cuts through scenic Afton Canyon, nicknamed the Grand Canyon of the Mojave for its striking sculpted cliffs.

383

More than 90% of the Cady Mountains are made of volcanic rocks produced by dozens of eruptions between the Oligocene and the Early Miocene, roughly from 36 to 10 million years ago. Legendary USGS geologist Tom Dibblee, who mapped in his prestigious professional life nearly one fourth of the state of California, synthesized this geologically complex country in exquisitely detailed maps. He rendered the randomness of the volcanic, tectonic, and erosional processes that created this range's tormented topography in bright canvases streaked with punk reds and yellows, like the work of an artist seized by lunacy and advanced cataracts. The mountains are an equally vivid kaleidoscope, dark-grey basalts and andesites, pale-beige rhyolites, pastel green and red tuffs, and polka-dotted breccias. Parts of these volcanic formations were later broken down and cast over huge alluvial fans, consolidated into knobby fanglomerates, rolled into fields of cobbles, or squeezed into foliated metavolcanic rocks. The rest of the Cady Mountains, about 6% in area, is the pre-existing granite and quartz monzonite onto which these volcanic rocks were laid down. Much of the underlying basement rock is likely made of these older Mesozoic igneous rocks.

The Cady Mountains were explored for a surprising number of mineral commodities. Miners looked for bentonitic clay on Soldier Mountain, manganese near Sleeping Beauty (Lavic Mountain, Black Butte, and Paymaster mines) and on Cady Peak (Logan Mine), talc and zeolite south of Troy Peak, copper near Junction Peak (Old Dominion Mine), and fluorite, travertine, and semi-precious agate and jasper on the eastern slope of Piston Peak. Only a few properties produced more than a small tonnage; by the 1960s they had all been abandoned.

The last major range in the California desert to receive federal protection, the Cady Mountains were preserved in 2016 with the creation of the Mojave Trails National Monument. Except for their extreme western margin, they are contained entirely within the monument. They are still relatively undisturbed, with only one transmission line cutting through their southeastern corner, and a long primitive road reaching into a central depression known as Hidden Valley. All other roads make only short incursions into the edges of the mountains. In the heart of the range, you are surrounded by miles of undeveloped desert in all directions. This is a sere wilderness, with no springs, not enough elevation for a juniper, and sparse vegetation. But it is particularly colorful, blessed with pretty rocks and expansive views onto itself, and it holds in its fractured topography an abundance of named summits to climb in complete isolation.

■

CADY PEAK

This is an exciting climb, longer and a little more demanding than most, and blessed with great ecological diversity. It starts in a scenic canyon haunted by ethereal smoke trees, proceeds up a steep ravine clogged with rocks and short falls, and ends up on a sheer high ridge of fluid rubble. The prominent summit commands exhilarating 360° views of the range's sea of pointed peaks and luminous bajadas.

General Information
Jurisdiction: Mojave Trails National Monument (BLM)
Road status: Roadless; standard-clearance access road
The climb: 3.2 mi, 2,010 ft up one way / difficult
Main attractions: Climb along canyon, spectacular views of Cady Mtns
USGS 7.5' topo map: Sleeping Beauty
Maps: pp. 387*, 227

Location and Access
Cady Peak (4,627') is the apex of the Cady Mountains' most prominent sub-range, a little south of the mountains' geometric center. The transmission line that cuts diagonally across the mountains' southeastern corner provides the closest access to it. To reach this road, take the Hector Road exit on Interstate 40 (31.7 miles east of the East Main Street exit in Barstow, or 17.5 miles west of Ludlow). At the bottom of the eastbound off-ramp, turn right and go 100 yards to Route 66. Turn left and drive 4.6 miles east on Route 66, alongside I-40, to a road crossing. Turn left onto a paved road (PC 8620) that crosses under I-40, angles left, parallels I-40 westbound, and ends after 1.3 miles at the triple transmission line. Turn right on the transmission line's right-of-way (later signed PC 8685) and follow it 4.65 miles northeast to a pass, where a road on the left (PC 8680) climbs to a radio facility. Drive 1.35 miles beyond the pass to a very short side road on the left that climbs a little then veers sharply left to a steel tower (numbered 733) on the leftmost transmission line. This is a good area to park. Cady Peak, hidden from view, is about 3 air miles to the north-northwest. This access road is generally good enough for a standard-clearance vehicle.

Route Description
Most of this climb traces the large canyon gouged into the peak's south slope. From tower 733 this canyon can be reached by walking

The broad canyon that leads up to Cady Peak, seen from the summit

either north-northwest on the low bank and merging soon after with the broad wash on the right; or walking northeast down the access road 75 yards, where the road crosses the wash, and heading left up the wash. The canyon starts half a mile up the wash. Its floor is a broad and gently sloped wall-to-wall floodplain of fine gravel, hard-packed and devoid of large rocks. After 1 mile a side canyon branches out on the left, while the canyon angles widely to the right and narrows to a 300-foot corridor. Cady Peak first comes into view then, rising high behind a ridge crested with vertical daggers. In another mile, at a three-way fork, stay with the main left fork as it veers left, passes by a small overhang in the western wall, then veers right (north) again. Soon after, the wash reaches the sawtoothed ridge; here too, continue north along the wider main wash. In 0.2 mile it squeezes between the sawtoothed ridge on the right and a steep 150-foot headland on the left, then skirts the left side of a long gravel bank. At the bank's upper end, 2.6 miles in, the canyon finally tapers down as it reaches its first obstruction, a 14-foot fall framed by low bluffs of jointed granite.

In cooler weather this longish walk is a breeze; in summertime it can be hellishly hot, with hardly a shady spot to take refuge from the sun. The native flora grows in oddly harmonious anarchy. In the lower

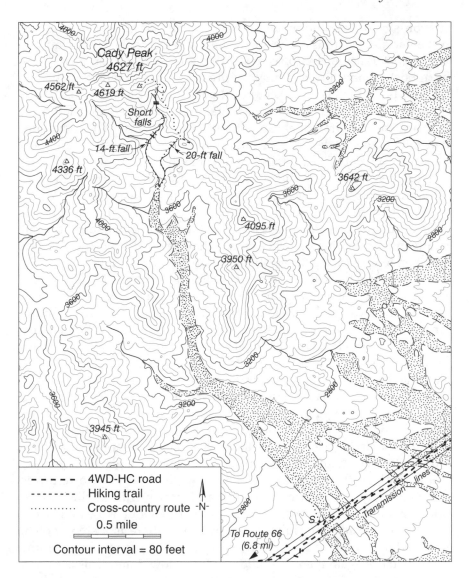

	4WD-HC road
	Hiking trail
	Cross-country route
	0.5 mile
	Contour interval = 80 feet

Cady Peak

	Dist.(mi)	Elev.(ft)
Transmission-line road	0.0	2,635
Foot of sawtoothed ridge	2.3	3,580
14-foot fall	2.6	3,820
Leave wash	2.95	4,260
Cady Peak	3.2	4,627

canyon smoke trees dominate, most of them scraggly skeletons, the rest emaciated, victims of fire and a sinking water table. Higher up, the vegetation transitions into scattered diamond cholla, then a creosote-burrobush community, and finally a predominance of rabbitbrush.

The 14-foot fall is a cracked, polished slant easy to scale. Just above it the canyon splits. The main wash makes a sharp 90-degree left turn. The side canyon straight ahead is the way to the peak. The remaining half mile is the hardest—it is right away steep and messy, with boulders and half a dozen easy falls 6 to 8 feet high. After a few wiggles the canyon splays into very steep ravines separated by narrow fins that fan up a scenic amphitheater of standing rocks. When the ravine gets too deeply entrenched, it is easier to climb onto the rightmost fin and follow it up to Cady Peak's eastern shoulder. It is steep and rubbly but relatively stable going up. Once on the shoulder it is a short, very steep climb on loose rocks to the crest, then a stroll to the summit.

When I first reached the ridge, then the summit, I broke into a round of spontaneous applause as the desert finally burst into view. The weather was partially cloudy that day, and in every direction the land was dotted with countless vapor shadows. To the north the Cady Mountains sprawled as an archipelago of sharp hills floating on fluid bajadas, every ridge and valley outlined against light or darkness in a dynamic ballet that changed every minute as the clouds drifted. Way down below, the broad access canyon wiggled out between furrowed ridges towards Sleeping Beauty's arresting volcanic crags. Broadwell Lake, the canyon's ultimate outlet, was camouflaged by patchy shadows. Far behind it, clear across the vast Bristol Mountains, the Kelso Dunes gleamed against the eastern Mojave Desert's high cordillera.

To prolong the enjoyment of the view, the best way to return is down the canyon's east rim. It is steep and strewn with smallish rocks, but there are no major obstructions. On the rim about 300 yards below where you crested the ridge on the way up, there is a steep notch, followed by a knife edge that can be bypassed on the west side. In the same distance again there is a saddle before a low dome. This is a good spot to drop back into the canyon, down the steep, broad, shallow ravine on the right. At its bottom this side wash levels off, angles left, and merges soon after with the main wash at the southern tip of the gravel ramp. Both routes are about 0.7 mile. To climb up Cady Peak this way, look for this side wash where it branches off inconspicuously on the right side of the gravel bank's lower end. Go up this side wash 300 yards, past the dome up on the canyon rim, to the second side ravine on the right, and climb it to the obvious saddle on the rim.

■

SLEEPING BEAUTY

Sleeping Beauty is a striking sculpted volcano at the southern edge of the Cady Mountains, the dramatic backdrop for the isolated town of Ludlow along Interstate 40. For anyone even remotely interested in climbing desert peaks, this spectacular mountain is a must. The chaotic canyon leading up to it passes through a rainbow of volcanic rocks. The summit is a superb observation deck to contemplate the transition zone between the eastern and western provinces of the Mojave Desert.

General Information
Jurisdiction: Mojave Trails National Monument (BLM)
Road status: Essentially roadless; primitive access road (4WD)
The climb: 2.6 mi, 1,650 ft up, 40 ft down one way / difficult
Main attractions: Colorful volcano, geology, views of eastern Mojave
USGS 7.5' topo map: Sleeping Beauty
Maps: pp. 391*, 227

Location and Access
If you are coming from the west along Interstate 40, take the Hector Road exit, approximately 50 miles east of Barstow. At the bottom of the off-ramp, turn right and go 0.1 mile to Route 66. Turn left on the pitted paved road and follow it east along the interstate. After 9.4 miles Route 66 angles sharply left, crosses over the interstate (0.25 mile), then angles sharply right. From this corner it is 0.55 mile to a primitive road on the left (BL 8655) that heads north toward Sleeping Beauty. To get to this road from the east, get off at Ludlow, pick up Route 66 on the north side of the interstate, and follow it west 7.55 miles.

From Route 66, drive 1.7 miles north on BL 8655 up to the second east-west graded road (BL 8660), just past a transmission line. BL 8655 is in fair shape except for a 100-yard stretch of deep sand at its very start, which requires four-wheel drive. Turn right on the transmission-line road, and drive it 1.2 miles to a road on the left. Of the two roads that fork right away, the rightmost road can be driven about 1 mile inside the canyon that drains southeast from Sleeping Beauty's summit. This road quickly gets a little rocky and sandy, so it is just as easy to park at the junction on the transmission-line road and walk the road instead.

Route Description

Sleeping Beauty has slumbered for a very long time. It erupted around 18.5 million years ago, many times and from multiple vents, spewing out a fury of burning rocks and laying down one of the desert's most colorful mountains. When driving up from Route 66, it rears up as dramatic auburn cones streaked with green ash flows, its maze of ridges bristling with chocolate lava plugs. The mountain can be climbed on its south side, but all routes involve convoluted and arduous ups and downs on steep rubbly slopes to circumvent the abrupt former vents. The approach suggested here, up the canyon that drains the mountain's southeast side, is more straightforward, though still tough, and it gives a chance to peer into the volcano's very core.

The canyon is pretty, at first an easy sandy wash surrounded by low rounded hills. It is lined with smoke tree, catclaw, and creosote, mixed with pygmy cedar farther in. Sleeping Beauty's fantastic silhouette is soon in full view, its summit capped by three sheer sugarloaves. In the mid-canyon the wash squeezes through short narrows in beige volcanic breccia, their low walls carved into grotesque bulges and pinnacles. There are three falls 7 to 9 feet tall, all Class 2 except the last one (Class 3). They can be easily bypassed together on the west side.

Above the narrows, the canyon tapers down and gets increasingly clogged with small boulders and low falls. The west-side bench, more gradual and less rocky, offers an easier path, until the canyon walls converge and the wash is the only way to proceed. This is approximately below the top of the cliff-bound dome on the canyon's east rim. At the fork, go up the right branch. It soon passes right below a first pinnacle, then a second one with a fall at its base, both on the right. At this point it is best to climb onto the canyon's east rim by scrambling up the ravine just behind the second pinnacle. It is steep and bouldery, although some bedrock comes in handy. I climbed part way to the slender pinnacle up the ravine, then angled slightly to the right to gain the ridge a little higher than the saddle north of the cliff-bound dome.

From this point to the summit the ridge has three rocky spurs. The first and lowest one is the crux. It is a 50° climb to its base, then a solid Class 2 to get over the spur's stack of boulders. The second spur is bypassed on the right side, and the last spur on the left side. From there I cut a beeline across the hillside to Sleeping Beauty's summit.

Sleeping Beauty holds one of the greatest diversities of volcanic rocks in the Mojave Desert. There are warehouses of basalt, solid, banded, or vesiculated, pale brown to a rich mahogany, overlaid with slickensides or mats of calcite crystals. There are andesites, a'a lava, volcanic bombs, breccia stuffed with half-ton boulders, 60-foot cliffs of

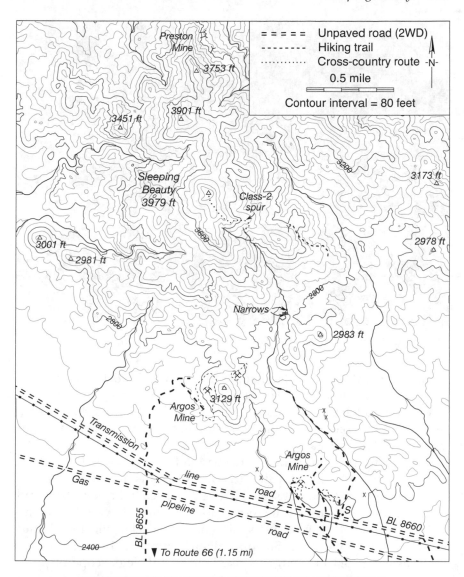

Sleeping Beauty

	Dist.(mi)	Elev.(ft)
Transmission line road	0.0	2,370
Narrows	1.55	2,790
Junction with ravine	2.1	3,390
Ridge below Class-2 spur	2.2	3,490
Sleeping Beauty	2.6	3,979

Volcanic pinnacles in the upper canyon; ravine angles right from the center

columnar basalt, and badlands of jade and blood-red tuffs. The area around the ravine is the heart of the volcano, a fantasyland of chimneys and hoodoos. In late afternoon the light comes from the bedrock itself, pouring golden from the brilliant breccia, a spectacle that makes you want to sit and stare.

The views from the summit are outstanding. On one side you look across Broadwell Lake and the Bristol Mountains at Kelso Basin, its vast valley of sand and salt sealed in the distance by the New York and Providence mountains. On the other side you gaze down into the valley at Pisgah Crater's vast lava spills, charcoal black against the blinding shores of Lavic Lake. Sleeping Beauty sprawls down below, its foothills encrusted in sand, its spiked ridges a kaleidoscope of pyroclastic colors. Dwarfed by distance, the endless procession of freight trains lumbering across the valley below looks like toy models. The mountain's name may have been inspired by romanticism, an astute reference to the volcano's natural beauty and the chance that it may be dormant rather than extinct. With apologies to physics, I like to think that the trains' low-frequency vibrations will one day act as the fabled Prince Charming's magical kiss and awaken the sleeping beauty, and she will once again unleash her pyrotechnics...

■

7

SOUTHERN MOJAVE DESERT

The region. The southern Mojave Desert is bounded to the west and east by the meridians going through Barstow and Chambless, to the north by Route 66 (which parallels Interstate 40 west of Ludlow), and to the south by the Mojave Desert's extreme southern limit. This region is also one of the world's champions in conservancy, a tight mosaic of national parks, national monuments, and designated wilderness. The western area is protected in a portion of Sand to Snow National Monument and four wilderness areas; the southern area in Joshua Tree National Park and the Pinto Mountains Wilderness; the eastern area in a portion of Mojave Trails National Monument and the Cleghorn Lakes Wilderness; and the northern area in the Marine Corps Air Ground Combat Center and two large off-highway-vehicle recreation areas, all three considerably more natural than a subdivision. The only areas that are unprotected are sections of the chain of valleys in the central and northwestern sectors, along Highways 62 and 247—Morongo Basin, Homestead Valley, Johnson Valley, Lucerne Valley, and Stoddard Valley—a small percentage of the total land area.

Geology. The region's mountains are composed mostly of granitic, volcanic, and metamorphic rocks formed as a result of subduction of the Pacific Plate under the North American Plate during the Jurassic and Cretaceous. For the best part of 140 million years, large-scale blending of the rising magma with mantle and crust material created a suite of igneous rocks with a broad spectrum of compositions and textures, including rocks intermediate between basalt and granite. Pre-existing gneiss from the distant Proterozoic were also metamorphosed, in their case a second time, which created a beautiful, twice-cooked gneiss. These delightfully complex rocks, spotted or foliated, layered with garnet or pegmatite, or imprinted with the tight curls of eddies, are a common hallmark of the southern Mojave Desert.

In the southern half of the region, the volcanic rocks from that era have long been worn away. Only a few small volcanic exposures from more recent activity remain. In the northern half, volcanic rocks are generally much better represented. It ranges from the Newberry Mountains, which are almost entirely volcanic, to the Ord and Rodman mountains, which have a good mix of volcanic and granitic rocks, and the Fry Mountains, which are almost entirely granitic. On the other hand, gneisses are generally less common than in the southern half, being widely exposed only in the Ord and Sheep Hole mountains.

The southern half of the region is part of an anomalous system of mountains that goes against the geologic grain, marching nearly eastward in a province where most ranges trend northwest. Known as the Transverse Ranges, this mountainous belt soaring up to 11,500 feet extends eastward 300 miles from the 90° bend in the California Coast west of Santa Barbara through Joshua Tree National Park. It owes its odd orientation to a couple of jogs in the San Andreas Fault. Along most of its length, the San Andreas follows a fairly straight southeasterly course. Where it enters southern California at the coastal bend, it angles nearly east, cuts straight across to the Salton Sea's north shore, then veers southeast again toward Mexico. Along this east-west segment, the Pacific and North American plates are transverse to their direction of motion. When the crust gives way, the Pacific Plate pushes north against the North American Plate. The Transverse Ranges were formed over the last 25 million years as these compressive forces fractured the edges of the plates and shoved up the pieces into mountains. In the western half of the park, this extended uplift has created an elevated plateau between 3,500 and 5,000 feet covered with interconnected ranges oriented roughly east-west. In contrast, away from the San Andreas Fault in the northern half of the region, the topography follows the classical arrangement of the Basin and Range province.

The massive jumbles of sculpted rocks emblematic of Joshua Tree National Park are a much more recent addition also created by plate tectonics, combined with the handiwork of erosion. Compressive stresses on the crust broke it along conjugate joints, two sets of parallel cracks at a 60-degree angle, like the lozenge pattern on a jester's suit. Horizontal fractures also develop as erosion removes surface rock and the underlying granite stock floats back up, like a ship after unloading its cargo. Since the Pliocene, ground water percolating to the water

Average temperatures (°F) in the southern Mojave Desert							
	Yucca Valley (3,200 feet)		Old Dale (1,270 feet)		Palm Springs (520 feet)		Coachella (-70 feet)	
	Low	High	Low	High	Low	High	Low	High
January	38	61	37	65	46	69	37	69
February	39	61	42	68	48	73	42	73
March	40	69	46	75	53	79	46	78
April	44	74	54	83	57	85	53	86
May	54	86	64	92	65	93	60	93
June	60	92	72	103	71	102	68	100
July	72	102	78	107	77	107	75	105
August	68	99	75	107	78	106	73	104
September	64	96	67	99	73	100	68	100
October	53	80	55	86	62	89	55	89
November	44	70	43	73	52	77	44	78
December	36	58	38	63	44	67	37	69

table has been decomposing bedrock preferentially along these joints, breaking it into piles of giant boulders. These buried structures were eventually uplifted, exposed by top-soil erosion, and further sculpted by rain and wind. They are not common because they exist only where the granitic stock is strong and homogeneous enough to break into large chunks over large areas. Their visual appeal lies in the pleasing symmetry they inherited from conjugate joints—rows of look-alike pinnacles, cliffs slashed by repetitive patterns of cracks, or heaps of boulders with similar shapes. These dramatic displays occur elsewhere in the Mojave Desert, but they are nowhere as striking and abundant as in the southern region. They are what attracts hikers and sightseers to Joshua Tree, and what makes it a unique space for rock climbing.

Botany. The southern section inside the park being largely a highland, the valleys receive slightly higher precipitation and are generally surprisingly green. They all host healthy mixed woodlands of Joshua trees, oaks, juniper, and pinyon pine, places for many desert dwellers to find food and shade. The ground is often densely covered with large shrubs that bear the colors and scents of the high desert—blackbrush, saltbush, cliffrose, ephedra, manzanita, mesquite, and squawbush. The juxtaposition of smooth sand-colored stone and deep-green plants creates the inviting landscapes filled with natural grace and vibrant harmony symbolic of the southern Mojave Desert. The soil and subsoil of mixed sand and rocks encourage colorful displays of cactaceae. Almost all the Mojave Desert species are represented, sometimes gathered over small areas, and in sizes and quantities that surpass almost all other regions. This is especially true of Joshua trees. They find here perfect living conditions—sandy soil and the ideal ranges of temperature, elevation, and annual precipitation—and thrive in forests larger and thicker than almost anywhere else.

Climate. Being on average higher than most areas of comparable size in the Mojave Desert, western Joshua Tree National Park is generally cooler year round. Not by much, only between about 5 and 10°F depending on location and time of year. In the summer, when every degree counts, this small difference can go a long way to improve comfort when mountain climbing. Conversely, in winter it may feel noticeably colder, especially at night. For several months, San Gorgonio Mountain, the highest summit in the San Bernardino Mountains, and San Jacinto Peak to the southwest, are bright snow-capped beacons visible from much of the region. It can snow also on the park's highest summits, and very occasionally on the valley floors, less frequently in recent decades. To be a little warmer in winter, it is best to climb in the northern half of the region or other low-lying parts of the Mojave.

Climbing and Regulations. Unlike the rest of the Mojave Desert, the southern region is relatively populated. Joshua Tree National Park is hemmed in on three sides by human developments. Morongo Basin, along the park's northern boundary, is lined with towns that essentially run into each other—Yucca Valley, Joshua Tree, Twentynine Palms, and rural Wonder Valley, larger in area than Paris and London combined. Coachella Valley along the Mojave Desert's southern boundary is even more developed, overtaken by a seamless string of cities sprawling 35 miles from Palm Springs to Thermal and home to 370,000 residents. Sand to Snow National Monument is also surrounded by towns on two sides. Other reasons add to the crowdedness: the relative proximity to southern California's coastal megapolis, the park being a world-class rock-climbing destination, and the park's main attractions being confined to a relatively small area.

These combined factors translate into heavy visitation. The park received 2.85 million visitors in 2017. On a typical spring weekend, the line of cars at the most popular north entrance can be 45 minutes long. There can even be a wait in the evening to exit the park. On the most

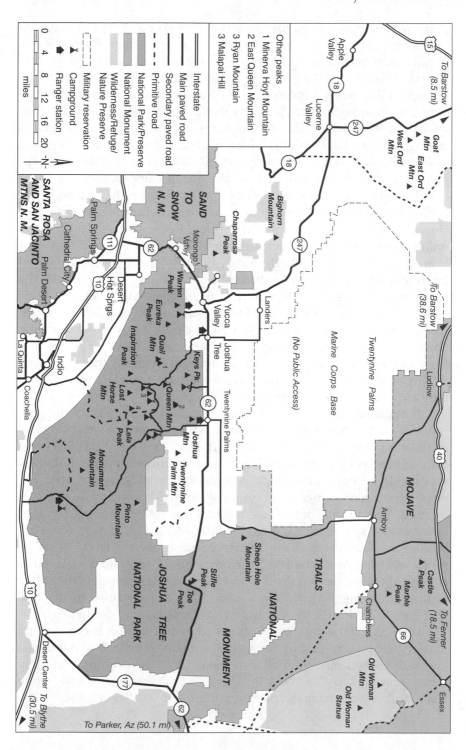

popular peaks and trails, just about any weekend except perhaps on Super Bowl Sunday it is rare not to see another hiker. Even the less popular trailless peaks are climbed with some frequency.

With heavier visitation come tighter regulations to minimize the impact on the park's fragile resources. Some popular areas are day-use only. Car camping and backcountry campfires are prohibited. To sleep overnight in the park, the only options are staying in a designated campground or backpacking. The park has 8 campgrounds, 3 group campgrounds, and 8 family campgrounds. Reserving in advance helps guarantee a spot (it is required for the group campgrounds), as does on-site registration early in the day. Depending on the season, some campgrounds require reservations, others are first come first served, or closed. Check on-line for the latest rules. Reservations can be made online at recreation.gov. Backpacking is restricted to trails that start from one of the park's 13 backcountry boards. You must self-register at the trailhead. Car camping outside the park is also more limited. The best areas are the Pinto Mountains' foothills south of Highway 62 between Twentynine Palms and Dale Lake, the New Dixie Mine Road corridor west of Landers, and a few BLM campsites south of the park. Some areas are prized among locals, who often drive in bright and early or linger until late in the night for target shooting, four wheeling, or dirt biking. These are not always the desert's quietest hounds, but they are usually quieter than public campgrounds.

The consequence of the proximity of cities is that much of the park is not as wild as the eastern or northern Mojave. You are never far from civilization, which has its merits. Because the park has no services and car camping is prohibited, hiking takes on a different rhythm. Unless you stay in a campground, each evening you must leave the park. The neighboring towns offer a full range of services, from fast-food places to ethnic restaurants, hotels, gas stations, car rentals, towing services, body shops, sports shops, coffee shops, and ATMs to pay for it all. Because most of the park's primitive backcountry roads are closed to motor vehicles, most climbs start from a paved or graded road. For a change, there is often no need for a high-clearance vehicle. About half of the climbs suggested in this section have a maintained or use trail that goes to or close to the summit, which makes for easier hiking.

That said, if the park's crowds get to you, seclusion is not very far away. The northern half of the region is much more lightly populated and visited. You can climb all day, then spend the evening and night where you parked your vehicle. There the mountains are still free of trails, and you can have the pleasure of finding your own route.

■

ORD MOUNTAINS

Halfway between its headwaters on the snowy crest of the San Bernardino Mountains and its terminus in parched Soda Lake, the Mojave River makes a wide curve from north to east as it passes through the dusty railroad town of Barstow. In the cradle of this 40-mile bend of wind-blown sand rises a cluster of four small desert mountains named Stoddard, Ord, Rodman, and Newberry. This is a no man's land anchored to two desert provinces—the BLM's western Mojave Desert empire, perilously close to southern California's sprawl, and the far wilder eastern Mojave Desert. With a high point at 6,309 feet, the Ord Mountains are the tallest of the group. Their irregular crest is shaped like a toppled "C" 12 miles across that curls around a series of small valleys and basins. To the south the valleys drain into the spacious expanses of Lucerne Valley and its dusting of far-apart ranch houses from the 1950s. To the northwest lies the Stoddard Valley Off-Highway Vehicle Area, an even emptier 35-square-mile creosote monoculture where all smaller plants have been crushed to fan-shaped road kills. Unlike the Newberry and Rodman mountains to the northeast and east, the Ord Mountains have not yet been deemed worthy of preservation. They remain unrevered, closer to civilization and more noticeably impacted by roads, antennas, illegal dumps, and shooting alleys. You are more likely to run into a local ATV rider than a hiker, and most likely to run into no one at all. This is not for lack of spectacle. With a vertical relief exceeding 3,000 feet, a nicely sculpted topography, and a name recognized by few, the Ord Mountains offer plenty of silence, solitude, inspiring scenery, and far-reaching vistas.

The Ord Mountains are topographically divided into three adjacent blocks—West Ord, Ord, and East Ord mountain—connected by low land bridges. The largest block, West Ord Mountain, is separated from the others by the northwest-trending Lenwood Fault, named after a strip-mall suburb of Barstow. It is composed of Precambrian gneiss and schist derived from plutonic rocks, and by plutonic rocks of different compositions (quartz monzonite, granite, quartz diorite, and hornblende diorite gabbro) that crystallized at different times in the Mesozoic. In contrast, Ord Mountain and East Ord Mountain are made in approximately equal proportions of volcanic rocks (basalt and latite porphyry) on the mountain blocks, and some of the same plutonic and gneissic rocks on their peripheries. On all three mountains many areas were more recently intruded by swarms of parallel felsite dikes. These resilient fine-grained volcanic rocks, as well as the gneissic rocks, are responsible for the scenic outcrops that abundantly poke out of the mountains' flanks and ridges.

The Ord Mountains' lower slopes are stained with the dumps of more than 30 mining operations, most of them active in the first half of the twentieth century. They searched for an extensive menu of commodities, from gold (Ord Mountain Group, Grand View, Ford, New Deal, and Gold Belt mines) to iron (Maumee Mine), silver, copper, tungsten, molybdenum, fluoride, barite, and uranium. Most of them did not graduate beyond the level of prospect. Only a handful had a documented production. The Gold Belt Mine, below the summit of Goat Mountain, was rich enough to keep an on-site 40-stamp mill busy from 1930 to 1932. The spread-out Ord Mountain Group, on the northwest slope of Ord Mountain, was active off and on for more than 50 years ending in 1942. Interestingly, this range was named after a claim or group of claims that were themselves named after General Ord by a prospector who may have served under him. Edward Otho Cresap Ord was an engineer and U.S. Army General involved in the Indian Wars and in the Civil War, where he played a key role in forcing the surrender of Confederate Army General Robert E. Lee. The original Ord claim (or claims) may have been part of the Ord Mountain Group, which is likely the oldest mine in this range.

Climbing in the Ord Mountains is generally a little easier than in most ranges. The slopes tend to be more modest, and neither rocks nor plants are usually a hindrance. The vegetation is about as scant as it gets, intergrading with increasing elevation from a creosote to a blackbrush community, with scattered colonies of chollas and Mojave yucca, and a sparse but nearly complete representation of Mojave Desert cactaceae. Of the named summits, Goat Mountain is the easiest. The road to the radio tower on Ord Mountain, the range's highest peak, makes it the second easiest (and the radiation-induced DNA mutations at the top are free). West Ord Mountain comes next. The hardest is East Ord Mountain—steeper and rockier.

■

WEST ORD MOUNTAIN

The lowest and easiest of the three main summits in this range, West Ord Mountain is a fun peak to climb. The access road is relatively short and smooth, directions are straightforward, and most of the climb is on surprisingly unobstructed terrain, albeit steep at places. The route follows the meandering spine of a ridge lined with eroded dikes of pale plutonic rocks. The summit area has good vistas of Lucerne Valley, little-known Tyler Valley and its hidden dry lake, and the range's main summits.

General Information
Jurisdiction: Public lands (BLM)
Road status: Roadless; primitive access road (2WD)
The climb: 1.65 mi, 1,510 ft up, 70 ft down one way/moderate
Main attractions: Botany, rock formations, views of Lucerne Valley
USGS 7.5' topo map: West Ord Mountain
Maps: pp. 403*, 397

Location and Access
West Ord Mountain is the westernmost of the Ord Mountains' three separate units, north of Lucerne Lake in Lucerne Valley. The climb starts at the mountain's western base, reached by a relatively smooth primitive road that branches off Highway 247 south of Barstow. From the Barstow Road exit on Interstate 40, turn south on Highway 247. Drive over a pass into Stoddard Valley, a local mecca for off-road vehicles. Part way through the valley the road passes by the colorful Slash X Ranch Café, then it climbs gradually in a straight line to a pass (elev. 4,148') between Stoddard Ridge on the right and West Ord Mountain on the left. This pass is 17.2 miles from the signal light at the Barstow Road eastbound exit. Slightly over 1 mile beyond the pass and just before the road angles right, a primitive road drops down on the left. This is between the last two power-line poles on the left side of the road. Coming from the south on Highway 247, this road is 14.7 miles north of Highway 18 in the town of Lucerne Valley.

Drive this road 0.8 mile up a broad canyon to a Y junction, and take the right fork. Park 0.5 mile further at a cattle guard. The road is smooth and hard-packed, with no crown and no large rocks that cannot easily be avoided, and only one spot near the start is a little rocky. A two-wheel drive vehicle with standard clearance is all that it takes.

Broken gneiss outcrop along the ridge to West Ord Mountain

Route Description

West Ord Mountain's summit is not visible from the starting point, but the easiest route to it is the obvious one on the USGS map: up the ridge that rises steeply to the east. This ridge can be gained directly from the road. A narrow rocky dike traces the ridge's crest, but it is generally straightforward to avoid it on the open slope along its south side. Other than a narrow dike of porphyritic felsite that crosses it just before the first false summit, this part of the ridge is made of Mesozoic diorite gabbro, a mottled, dark-gray plutonic rock rich in darker minerals like hornblende. Resistant to erosion, it weathers into faceted outcrops and small flat boulders convenient to step on.

Of the many plants that bloom on this mountain in the flowering seasons, the two most striking are the calico cactus and Canterbury bell. One holds a flamboyant crown of large purple-pink flowers, the other bouquets of deep-blue bell-shaped flowers with open throats. In a land overwhelmed by browns and grays, both are shockingly monochromatic. Along the access road the wash is flooded with flashy desert senna, a usually unremarkable leafless shrub several feet tall transformed for a few weeks into a solid mass of bright yellow flowers. Several less common plants grow on the slopes—mariposa blooms

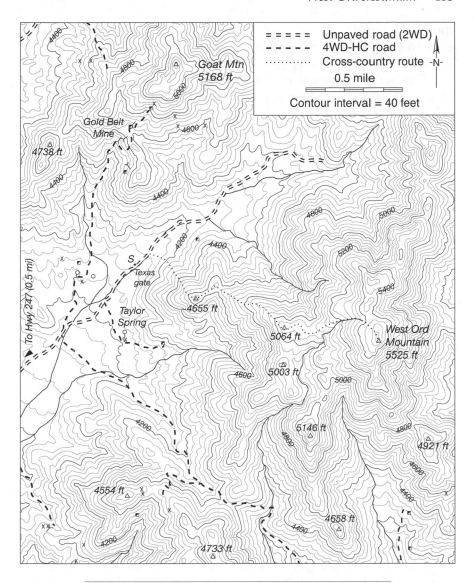

West Ord Mountain

	Dist.(mi)	Elev.(ft)
Access road (cattle guard)	0.0	4,090
First false summit	0.45	~4,655
Second false summit	1.0	5,064
Ravine	1.35	~5,200
West Ord Mountain	1.65	5,525

the color of apricot, live-forever in rocky cracks, diamond cholla a bit everywhere, and coyote tobacco, generously sprinkled with white tubular flowers in late spring—a plant the natives dried and smoked.

This is the steepest part of this ascent—the slope reaches close to 40%, though the exercise does not last very long. After 0.45 mile the ridge reaches a first high point (elev. ~4,655′), and the first vista of the summit. It then descends a little to a shallow saddle occupied by a small grove of Mojave yucca, then the climb resumes. The rest of the way, and much of West Ord Mountain, is Precambrian granite gneiss, a pale metamorphic rock faintly layered with darker mica-rich laminae. Spiky outcrops and stocky boulders of this highly cohesive formation protrude from the ridge's spine in an irregular dorsal. In another 0.6 mile there is a second false summit (elev. 5,064′). Above it the ridge levels off again and meanders a little before steepening on its final ascent to the peak north of West Ord Mountain's summit. It is shorter and easier to leave the ridge before getting there. Near an elevation of 5,200 feet, join the shallow ravine that drains the wide slope between the two peaks. Once in the ravine, continue up its unobstructed wash east about a tenth of a mile, then cut southeast up the more gradual slope to the summit. This climb is unusual in that almost everywhere there are plenty of smooth slopes free of rocks and thorns. The summit block, surrounded by large squarish boulders, is the only place that might require hands. For people new to desert-peak climbing, this is a good place for practice.

The summit has an inviting spread of slickrock with scattered right-angled blocks to use as backrests while gazing at the scenery. To the south, West Ord Mountain peters out in a series of diminishing isolated peaks to the mud-colored playa of Lucerne Lake, greened by cultivations near Lucerne Valley's sparse community. Goat Mountain and Stoddard Ridge rise to the west. When I was there the view east was the most dramatic, looking out beyond hidden Tyler Valley to the long outlines of Ord and East Ord mountains, both consumed by an electrifying thunderstorm. Obscured by a mile-high bank of cumulus clouds, their crests were pelted by lightning and translucent curtains of rain. I had luckily picked the right Ord Mountain to climb that day.

To extend this short climb, consider nearby Goat Mountain. The rough road to the Gold Belt Mine ascends almost to its south rim, leaving only a short scramble up a very steep talus of black granite (diorite gabbro) to the summit (1.8 miles, 1,230 feet of elevation gain). Goat Mountain has excellent views of Stoddard Valley and the unusually dissected flanks and crest of Stoddard Ridge.

■

EAST ORD MOUNTAIN

A rough-hewn volcano that became dormant in the distant Mesozoic, East Ord Mountain is much more imposing than the rest of the range. Its flanks are studded with the weathered spikes left by ephemeral vents, and its high ridges crowded with stocky crags where lava pooled and solidified over and over again. The climb is on the southeast side, where erosion has removed a great chunk of crest and gauged below it a straight ravine that plummets down the mountain. This rough channel, filled with rocks, trapped between vertical bluffs, and precipitous, is the passage to the summit—a 1,650-foot ascent in a little less than a mile.

General Information

Jurisdiction: Public lands (BLM)
Road status: Roadless; rough primitive access road (HC-4WD)
The climb: 1.4 mi, 1,950 ft one way / difficult
Main attractions: Geology, very steep short climb
USGS 7.5' topo maps: Grand View Mine, Fry Mtns, Ord Mountain*
Maps: pp. 407*, 397

Location and Access

The summit of East Ord Mountain is 24 air miles southeast of Barstow, in the Ord Mountains' eastern sub-range. About 8 miles east of town, take the Daggett exit off Interstate 40. At the eastbound exit stop sign, turn right and go 80 yards to a T junction signed Pendleton Road. Turn left on the unsigned Camp Rock Road and follow it east 1 mile along the freeway to a right bend, where the pavement ends. From there, stay 22.3 miles on this very good graded road. It first climbs to, then curves through, the Newberry Mountains' western foothills to a wide pass. Just before the pass, at mile 9, keep left where the Ord Mountain Road splits off. The Camp Rock Road then traverses a secluded high-desert valley used for ranching, between the Rodman (north) and Ord (south) mountains. At mile 17.1, turn right at the signed junction with Troy Road. Continue south-southeast to mile 22.3, all downhill, where the road goes under a triple power line.

Between the second and third power line, a graded service road merges in from the left, and a dirt road signed OM 6600 takes off on the right, aligned with it. Take this road, and immediately turn right at the fork on OM 6659. Drive north up a broad alluvial fan toward East

Ord Mountain 0.95 mile to a fork. Take the left fork, signed OM 6659, 0.7 mile up to a guzzler on the right, just inside a canyon at the base of the mountain. Park 100 yards further, where the road drops into the canyon wash. These two BLM roads are steep and covered with loose sharp rocks. Without high clearance and power, you will have to walk. As you drive up these roads, East Ord Mountain's angular summit block will be fully visible up ahead slightly west of north; the ravine leading up to it is below the narrow saddle just west of the summit.

Route Description

From the edge of the main wash, walk up the road a quarter of a mile to where it climbs out of the wash on the left. The opening on the right by the road is the start of the ravine to the summit. After 250 yards and a couple of twists, there is a low, open twin fall in rounded dark-gray rock. From the top of it, count 30 steps to a pile of small gray boulders against the ravine's right flank. The side ravine that leads to the summit forks off to the right just above the boulders. It starts with another twin fall, purplish and lumpy, trapped in a short constriction between low angular walls. From there it is a little less than a mile up this ravine to the narrow saddle on the mountain's crest. The summit is then very close, a Class-2 scramble up a steep-walled volcanic plug.

This climb is short but by no means easy. From start to saddle, the ravine screams up 1,550 feet at an average 33% slope. It would not be so bad if it weren't for the tumble of boulders in the wash, which make for slow, tedious navigation. In the ravine's lower reaches it is easier to stay out of the wash and follow instead the more open west-side bench. The bench ends at steep rocky bluffs at an elevation of about 4,960 feet. Beyond this point, the ravine traverses an impressive channel framed by towering dissected bluffs. The only sane direction of travel is the wash. The boulders grow in size and number, and the slope increases exponentially. At its upper end, the ravine turns into a gravity-defying couloir that gains 800 feet in a third of a mile.

East Ord Mountain		
	Dist.(mi)	Elev.(ft)
Road at edge of wash	0.0	4,220
Fork in ravine (right)	0.45	4,515
Start of couloir	1.0	5,280
Saddle at crest	1.35	~6,060
East Ord Mountain	1.4	6,168

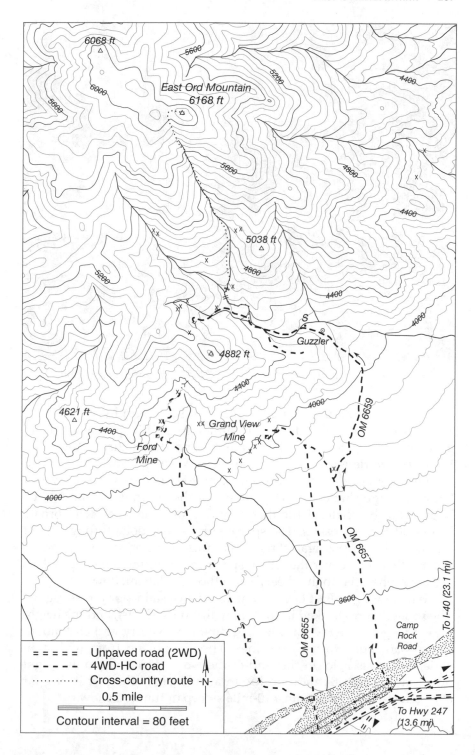

6068 ft

East Ord Mountain
6168 ft

5038 ft

4882 ft

4621 ft

Grand View
Mine

Ford
Mine

S
Guzzler

OM 6659

OM 6657

OM 6655

Camp
Rock
Road

To I-40 (23.1 mi)

To Hwy 247
(13.6 mi)

= = = = =   Unpaved road (2WD)
- - - - -   4WD-HC road
· · · · · · ·   Cross-country route   -N-
0.5 mile

Contour interval = 80 feet

The rocky upper ravine leading up to East Ord Mountain (right of center)

East Ord Mountain is a giant block of latite porphyry, a slightly more alkaline form of andesite uncommon in the Mojave Desert. Fine-grained and resilient, it is laid bare up and down the ravine in an impressive variety of shapes and surfaces. Most exposures are gray to brown, others pale orange, crimson, or mottled like fossilized waves of batter. A huge shattered section north of the summit has shed large boulders of brecciated latite that now decorate the wash with ornate black-and-white mosaics. The sparse shrubs that poke through stand out in starling greens against the dusky rock. The spring flowers are so diverse that they cover the whole spectrum, from the blues of Mojave aster and phacelias to the cheery vermillion of globemallow.

When I was on East Ord Mountain a fierce sand storm was raging. The valleys were chocked in shifting whirlpools of dust, and the neigh-boring ranges—the Fry, Lava Bed, Rodman, Newberry, and Ord mountains—had faded to hazy outlines. The air glowed from within an eerie, sulfurous halo. In this end-of-the-world vision the only bright note was the San Bernardino Mountains, their high crest lifting far above the frantic maelstrom a 10-mile sweep of tranquil snow.

■

SAN BERNARDINO MOUNTAINS

The San Bernardino Mountains are the most imposing of the Transverse Ranges. From their west end near historic Cajon Pass facing the San Gabriel Mountains, to their east end overlooking the Little San Bernardino Mountains in Joshua Tree, they run nearly 60 miles. Their main crest rises above 10,000 feet for close to 10 miles. Their high point, San Gorgonio Mountain (11,499'), is the highest summit in southern California. This alpine beacon is visible from tens of miles in any direction, and on rare clear days from as far away as the Dodger Stadium. North of it is Big Bear Lake, where Angelenos come to pull clean mountain air into their lungs and indulge in snow sports high above the desert.

Only the eastern and northern foothills of the range belong to the Mojave Desert. This region of rolling hills is a comparatively green transition zone between the highest summits to the west and the high-desert valleys and plateaus to the east. Until recently, only parts of it were protected by the Bighorn Mountain and Whitewater River National Recreation Lands, the Bighorn Mountain Wilderness, and the Pioneertown Mountains Preserve. In 2016 the protected acreage and level of protection were greatly increased with the creation of Sand to Snow National Monument, which covers the southeastern corner of the San Bernardino Mountains and much of their desert tip.

The majority of the San Bernardino Mountains' east end is a large monolithic shield of massive, gray-white Mesozoic quartz monzonite. The north flank, where the mountains descend steeply into Johnson Valley, is a collage of large pendants, mostly a suite of Paleozoic quartzite and schists known as Saragossa Quartzite. On its precipitous southern edge, uplift along the San Andreas Fault has exhumed a wide band of much older gneiss from the Proterozoic. Probably the same unit as in the Pinto Mountains, it is often striated in striking black and white laminae of biotite mica, hornblende, quartz, and feldspar. This area is lacerated by faults. Where Highway 247 climbs steeply from low to high desert along canted Morongo Valley, the Morongo Valley Fault split open the Transverse Ranges, severing the San Bernardino Mountains from the Little San Bernardino Mountains to the east. From near San Gorgonio Pass, the Pinto Mountain Fault slices 45 miles east along the park's northern boundary clear across to Twentynine Palms Mountain. The mighty San Andreas Fault runs along the entire abrupt southern base of the San Bernardino Mountains to San Bernardino, then well past them to Los Angeles and beyond. The prominent volcanic buttes at the eastern foot of the mountains are the most recent additions, basalt that cooled down just a few million years old.

The San Bernardino Mountains have been ranked one of the most biologically diverse ranges in the country. The primary factors are their large range of elevation, and their location at the crossroad of three major provinces—the Mojave Desert to the north and east, the Sonoran Desert to the south, and coastal chaparral and woodlands to the west. Although this diversity takes its fullest expression deeper in the mountains, it extends down into and benefits the range's desert fringes. The lower desert elevations hold a mosaic of ecosystems ranging from creosote bush scrub to chaparral, open Joshua tree forests, oak woodlands, riparian forests near creeks, and conifer forests. These habitats are home to jackrabbits and cottontails, mule deer, bighorn sheep, desert tortoise, and dozens of species of birds. This is also the only place in the Mojave Desert where there is a chance, albeit slight, to run into a black bear. A relatively large population of *Ursus americanus* live in the San Bernardino Mountains' forested highlands. A bear will occasionally mosey on down into the eastern foothills, in particular near the wetlands in the Pioneertown Mountains Preserve, perhaps for a change of scenery or for a lower elevation menu.

The traditions of the Cahuilla, Serrano, and Luiseño hold San Gorgonio Mountain sacred. The Serrano and Cahuilla maintained their homeland near the mountain, a productive area that provided them with relatively abundant resources. They harvested plants for food, medicinal, and ceremonial purposes, and hunted rabbits, deer, and perhaps an occasional bear or mountain lion. Scattered on the mountain are the ruins of the house pits, irrigation ditches, cooking stations, grinding stones, and ceremonial sites that were central to their lives. On Black Lava Butte and Flat Top Mesa, a sacred place the Serrano called *Ate 'Ivyat* at the eastern terminus of the mountains, boulders carved out of both the old quartz monzonite and the recent basalt are crawling with one of the densest collections of petroglyphs in the West. We were not first to cherish this exceptional range.

∎

BIGHORN MOUNTAIN

The hard part about this climb is the long bumpy ride on primitive roads to the trailhead, across terrain crisscrossed with a mess of roads. Once you get there the climb is made easy by a road that winds up and down all the way to the summit, across peaceful rounded hills dotted with Joshua trees and pockets of open pine woodlands. On the broad summit plateau several striking vista points look out over very different landscapes, from largely empty Johnson Valley to the hilly region you just crossed and the high crest of the San Bernardino Mountains.

General Information
Jurisdiction: Bighorn Mountain Wilderness (BLM)
Road status: Trail to summit; primitive access road (HC)
The climb: 2.9 mi, 890 ft up, 330 ft down one way / easy–moderate
Main attractions: Easy, lightly forested summit, view of Johnson Valley
USGS 7.5' topo maps: Bighorn Canyon, Rattlesnake Canyon
Maps: pp. 413*, 397

Location and Access
Bighorn Mountain lies within the Bighorn Mountain Wilderness, at the extreme northeastern tip of the San Bernardino Mountains. A rough primitive road goes all the way to the summit. The last mile or so is inside the wilderness and closed to motor vehicles, although people regularly trespass with impunity. The BLM has plans to fix the problem, by, for one thing, posting a wilderness boundary sign.

To get there, from Highway 62 in Yucca Valley drive north on Highway 247 11.3 miles to the signed New Dixie Mine Road on the left. Coming from the other direction, this intersection is 33.3 miles east then southeast on Highway 247 from the stop sign near Highway 18 in Lucerne Valley. Drive the New Dixie Mine Road, signed RC 2330, 1.05 miles west to a BLM board. The area up ahead has so many roads that the map posted on the board is of limited use, but it is a good idea to take a picture of it for general orientation. Keep left on the New Dixie Mine Road and go 8.0 miles west to a junction. There are many side roads and forks along the way, all signed except this junction, so keep track of your mileage. Take the right fork, then right again 100 feet further on the signed RC 2342 road. This road descends slowly 0.8 mile to a wash, where it angles left and starts climbing. Continue 0.7 mile to a

411

Joshua trees on the way to Bighorn Mountain

fork, and turn left onto RC 2358. In 0.5 mile this road reaches a local high point and begins a steeper wiggly descent (this is where the road changes to "4WD" on the USGS map). The remaining 1.9 miles to the wilderness boundary have a few very steep rutted grades that only some motorcycles, monster trucks, and ATVs dare negotiate. It is safer to park at this high point and hike the rest of the way.

This is a scenic ride along a pleasantly forested open canyon. The road is generally free of rocks, but it is long and twisted, with several uncomfortable series of deep waves 10 to 30 feet long, and a few rough spots that require clearance. Plan on an hour to get there.

Route Description

To gain the summit the road wanders northwest across the foothills of Bighorn Mountain along a course crooked in every direction—vertically and horizontally. At the foot of the first short descent it crosses a wash, then climbs over a ridge to drop on the far side into a second wash. It curves up along the wash, then soon climbs over another ridge and drops into a third drainage, which it also follows for a while. After 1.4 miles of roller-coasting, it winds up one last hill to the crest. The road crosses briefly in and out of the wilderness, then

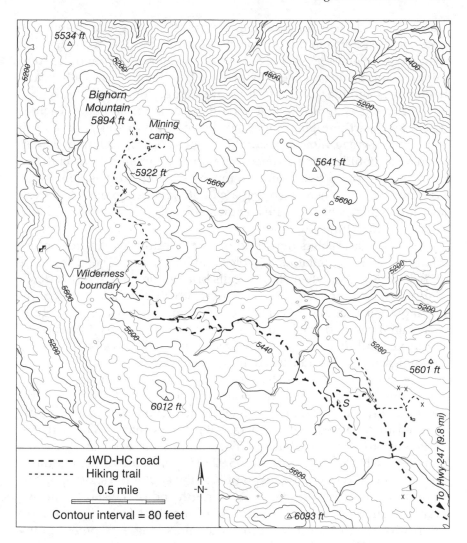

Bighorn Mountain		
	Dist.(mi)	Elev.(ft)
Bighorn Mountain Road	0.0	5,340
Third wash	1.2	5,410
Wilderness boundary	1.9	~5,800
Crest	2.2	~5,895
Upper fork	2.8	~5,875
Mining camp	(0.1)	~5,890
Bighorn Mountain	2.9	5,894

enters the wilderness for good half way up this last grade. It then follows the crest north to the summit. It would be hard to get lost. Other than the dead-end fork on the left shortly into the climb, and the summit loop, this is the only well-defined road, although it is locally heavily damaged and the steepest inclines are slippery downhill.

The topography is different from most desert mountains. There is no endless heart-pumping slopes, no cleaved cliffs or spiky summits. It is instead a serene, almost pastoral landscape of low rolling hills scattered with boulders and livened by a sparse community of cliffrose, blackbrush, Joshua trees, and pinyon pine, some surprisingly large. Wildlife likes it up here, enjoying a climate less extreme than the valleys and high mountains, with an adjustable mixture of sun and shade. We saw a fox slithering among the brush, and plenty of fresh deer tracks. A few jackrabbits ran ahead of us in random zigzags to confuse what they saw as predators. Coyotes had left plenty of solid evidence of their passage, and their chilling calls briefly filled the desert at dusk.

Like the countryside, the rocks are relatively subdued but interesting, a potpourri of granites and gneiss in exposures just big enough to reflect an unusual diversity over short spaces. They vary from orange to purple, dull to sparkling, laminated to twirled, and good old crisp salt-and-pepper with translucent bluish crystals.

The stroll along the gentle crest is particularly delightful. The road splits into a loop just past the mountain's high point. The two forks head roughly west 0.2 mile to join again at a small mining camp, now reduced to collapsed walls and wooden floors that still hold rusted beds and enameled appliances. The summit plateau has three fine viewpoints. The high point (elev. ~5,922') is just south of the middle of the right fork. The second viewpoint is at the end of the short spur east from the camp. The third one is at the north end of the short spur that branches off on the left at the middle of the right fork. It is the most impressive. To the north Bighorn Mountain's long escarpment plummets half a vertical mile to the flat desert expanses of Johnson Valley, framed in the distance by the Ord Mountains, the rust-colored Lava Bed Mountains, and other stark ranges few people know by name. To the southeast the low rolling hills unfold for miles to the cinnamon volcanic plateaus on the edge of Homestead Valley where the natives recorded a whole dictionary of inscrutable symbols. To the west the land rises in ever taller ridges to summits nearly 10,000-feet high that receive fresh coats of snow several times a year. The appeal lies in the diversity of vistas on this scenic headland stranded between parched desert and a sub-alpine cordillera.

∎

CHAPARROSA PEAK

From a secluded valley north of little-known Pioneertown a little trail twists its way up and down, over open slopes and through a delightfully bouldered canyon, to the volcanic heights of Chaparrosa Peak. The area is slowly being recolonized by an interesting post-fire plant succession in which dark oaks are the new king. The summit overlooks a striking transition region between the southern and eastern Mojave Desert and the forested San Bernardino Mountains.

General Information
Jurisdiction: Pipes Canyon Wilderness (The Wildlands Conservancy)
Road status: Abandoned road and trail to summit; graded access road
The climb: 2.8 mi, 1,320 ft up, 230 ft down one way/moderate
Main attractions: Views of San Bernardino Mountains, granite canyon
USGS 7.5' topo map: Rimrock
Maps: pp. 417*, 397

Location and Access
Chaparrosa Peak is a small mountain in the southeastern foothills of the San Bernardino Mountains, near Little Morongo Canyon. It is in the 20,000-acre Pipes Canyon Wilderness, which is itself part of the Pioneertown Mountains Preserve, administered by The Wildlands Conservancy. In Yucca Valley, drive Highway 62 1.9 miles west of Highway 247 to the signed Pioneertown Road on the right. Drive it northeast 4.2 miles to Pioneertown. The small town center looks like a Hollywood set for a Western production—and it is. Financed in the mid 1940s by Roy Rogers and other investors, it was built for a 1980s movie set that doubled as residences for the actors. It has been used since then for several Westerns and TV shows. Some buildings are still in use, including the former cantina, converted to a lively hamburger joint called Pappy & Harriet's. Continue 3.3 miles, across the south end of Bowden Flat, to the signed Pipes Canyon Road. Turn left on this graded road, and go 0.9 mile to the parking lot at the preserve's visitor center. The signed Chaparrosa Peak Trail starts at the upper (overflow) parking lot. The trail is open from 8 a.m. to 5 p.m. only.

Route Description
This climb starts leisurely, along an old road, then a constructed foot trail that winds down into a narrow wash lined with green willow

415

School of dolphins and the boulder-filled canyon seen from the upper trail

thickets. It then climbs a little to merge with an old road that follows Chaparrosa Peak's northeast shoulder part way to the summit. Like many desert roads, this one was originally bladed to access a prospect that turned out to be a dud. The road overlooks Bowden Flat, pin-pricked with a few sleepy ranches. To the east the valley is bounded by a scenic archipelago of broad mesas, places with suggestive names like Black Lava Butte and Flat Top, all steep-sided and coated with dark-brown basalt. There are fine views of the Sawtooths to the southeast, an aptly named ridge bristling with scenic spires of jointed granite.

Chaparrosa Peak's ridges were once pleasantly shaded by pinyon pine and juniper. In July 2006, lightning strikes a few miles to the south ignited the Sawtooth Complex Fire, an exceptionally fierce blaze that consumed nearly 100 square miles of desert hills, including much of the preserve. A decade later, the damage is still obvious, although the bare ground is speckled with green plants again, interspersed with the still-standing black-and-white skeletons of charred trees. Oaks have made a particularly prompt recovery and now dominate. Yucca, noli-na, blackbrush, and California buckwheat are also coming along, more slowly. Chia, penstemon, nama, wooly daisy, white tidy-tips, and beavertail cactus can put on quite a show in the late spring. Although

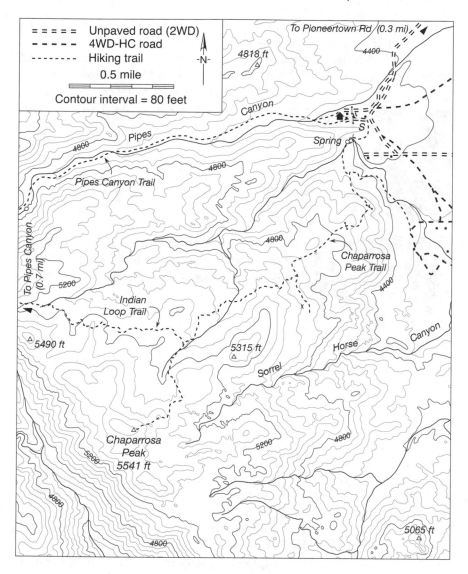

Contour interval = 80 feet		

Legend:
- = = = = = Unpaved road (2WD)
- – – – – 4WD-HC road
- - - - - - Hiking trail
- 0.5 mile

Chaparrosa Peak

	Dist.(mi)	Elev.(ft)
Trailhead (upper parking lot)	0.0	4,460
Wash crossing at spring	0.15	4,400
Trail junction	1.15	4,910
Indian Loop Trail junction	2.05	5,135
Chaparrosa Peak	2.8	5,541

quails are decreasing in numbers because of wildfires, it is not uncommon to flush out a noisy covey somewhere along the way.

After 1.15 miles and about 500 feet of elevation gain, near the end of the road, a signed trail branches off on the right. It continues a little up the broad northeast shoulder, then slips off its west side into an unnamed canyon. Chaparrosa Peak comes into view for the first time, the furthest of three subdued summits on the canyon's south rim up ahead. This is the most scenic part of the climb. Eroded into pale granite, the canyon is a chaotic jumble of odd-shaped outcrops, broken cliffs and oblong boulders scattered over its open slopes. Beautiful porphyritic veins hold inch-size crystals of quartz, felspar, and muscovite. The forest is gone, but along the wash, where it was the thickest, its presence can still be felt in the crooked shadows cast by its scorched trees.

California buckwheat

The primitive trail hugs the canyon's sandy wash, wandering up through a surreal landscape that artfully combines polished stone and bedraggled trees.

In the canyon's upper reaches the trail climbs back to the northeast shoulder and follows it to the summit. This is the only portion that is a little steep and gouged by erosion. The ground is gradually overrun by a thickening veneer of vesiculated basalt cobbles, dark brown against the underlying granite.

On Chaparrosa Peak you are standing at a geographical crossroad. To the west rise the San Bernardino Mountains, the Swiss Alps of southern California. Their highest crest is hidden behind the Three Sisters Peaks and other forested summits, all towering half a mile higher. The irregular skyline of Joshua Tree National Park, the heart of the southern Mojave Desert, frames the southern horizon. To the northeast, past the volcanic mesas, the vast Bullion Mountains stretch 40 miles in the distance, seemingly floating above a sea of sand. Behind them is the eastern Mojave Desert. In the winter, the contrast between the snow-capped mountains on one side and the desert on the other is stunning.

■

LITTLE SAN BERNARDINO MOUNTAINS

About 43 miles long by 13 miles wide at their widest, the Little San Bernardino Mountains are Joshua Tree National Park's huge southwestern backbone, its tallest range, and its largest mountain mass. To the south, they drop nearly one vertical mile in waves of eroded ridges into Coachella Valley's below-sea-level trench. When you drive the long steep grade on Highway 62 from Palm Springs to the park's north side, you squeeze right between their west end to the right and the San Bernardino Mountains to the left. After the road circles around to the north side of the Little San Bernardino Mountains and crests the high desert in Yucca Valley, the mountains look completely different, a long creased crest dotted with the green orbs of oak, pine, and juniper. Rising gently above small flats populated by Joshua trees, they beam a spare and sensuous beauty. The majority of this range is in the park. Its western tip is part of Sand to Snow National Monument. Only its very southern foothills along Coachella Valley are mostly unprotected.

Part of the Transverse Ranges, the Little San Bernardino Mountains have the crumpled asymmetrical topography of violent tectonism. Compressive forces along the San Andreas Fault, which bisects the entire length of Coachella Valley below the mountains, lifted them out of the ground while the valley was sinking. In the past 1,200 years, this fault segment has seen five titanic earthquakes powerful enough to rupture the earth's surface. The average time between them was about 215 years. The last one was around 1680. This part of California is overdue for a major re-arrangement of tectonic plates. Because the zone of deformation extends miles on both sides of the fault, the next big one could well happen in the mountains themselves. It would be good news for Coachella Valley's crowded desert cities, perhaps not so good for the tunnel that bores through almost the full length of the mountains and carries Colorado River water to Los Angeles.

This range is made of a similar assemblage of crystallized rocks as its neighbors. The eastern half of the crest to Covington Flat is a broad swath of Mesozoic rocks grading from granite to granodiorite to quartz monzonite. The crest's western half, Lost Horse Mountain, and Ryan Mountain expose a complex suite of Proterozoic gneiss. These pretty metasedimentary and metavolcanic rocks are among the most unusual in the park. They are often strongly migmatized, their metamorphic components mixed on a short length scale—often inches—with granitic intrusions to form complex structures as captivating as art. Although all these rocks have eroded into muted landforms, they often vary greatly in composition and texture over short distances, sometimes just a few steps. The White Tank Monzogranite exposed along the mountains' northern edge makes up for this generally subdued character with abundant abrupt outcrops and elegant boulders.

The Little San Bernardino Mountains also rank high in botanical diversity. They support a low-desert creosote community in their southern foothills, lush wetlands alive with dozens of bird species, and high-desert flats with extensive groves of yuccas and Joshua trees. Where it has not been scorched by wildfires in recent decades, the western crest is covered with beautiful emerald pelts of oaks and conifers more mature than most at this modest altitude.

Considering its size, this range saw comparatively little mining, but it did have two important sites, both in its eastern section facing Pleasant Valley. One was the Lost Horse Mine, the largest gold producer in the park. Operated between 1894 and 1936, it returned an estimated $260,000, most of it in the first two and a half years. Its mill is among the best preserved in the California desert. The other site was the Pinyon Mill, in a canyon at the only significant source of water for miles. Its well and two-stamp mill, erected around 1890, treated the ore of many local mines for years, including the Lost Horse and Desert Queen. From 1918 until the late 1930s, the water was piped 8.5 miles across the Hexie Mountains to run the mill at the rich Eldorado Mine.

The Little San Bernardino Mountains are a mecca for peak climbing: protected almost entirely in a designated wilderness, they have more peaks named on the USGS maps (42!) than any other range in the Mojave Desert. This unusual abundance gives a broad range of options for novices as well as seasoned desert rats, from short strolls on mere pimples in the Coachella Valley foothills to day-long trudges to respectable summits. The central and eastern mountains are largely undeveloped and seldom visited. The west end has a tight network of popular trails that see dozens of hikers on weekend days. The best time for peace and quiet is in the summer and on weekdays in the colder months—temperature extremes are still an effective deterrent.

■

WARREN PEAK

This is an easy climb, along a popular trail that wanders up almost imperceptibly along a rock-free sandy wash to the crest of the Little San Bernardino Mountains. The scenery is a peaceful landscape of sharp hills generously forested with an incongruous medley of oak, pinyon pine, juniper, and Joshua trees. The views from the summit encompass the Morongo Basin and Bullion Mountains to the north, the towering San Jacinto Mountains to the south, and the finely sculpted flanks of the San Bernardino Mountains to the west.

General Information

Jurisdiction: Joshua Tree National Park
Road status: Trails to summit; paved access road
The climb: 3.0 mi, 1,140 ft up, 20 ft down one way / easy
Main attractions: Trail climb, botany, views of San Bernardino Mtns
USGS 7.5' topo map: Yucca Valley South
Maps: pp. 423*, 427, 397

Location and Access

Warren Peak is the highest of the named summits near the west end of the Little San Bernardino Mountains, about two miles southwest of the Black Rock Canyon Ranger Station. It was named in honor of Mark Warren, a settler who came to Morongo Basin around 1880 and dug a well there in 1881. His ranch grew to be a stop on the stage coach from Dale to Banning starting in 1898, then a social center for local ranchers, and it seeded the settlement that became Yucca Valley.

To get to the ranger station, in Yucca Valley take Highway 62 to Avalon Avenue, 1.7 miles east of Highway 247. Drive 0.95 mile south to Yucca Trail, where Avalon Avenue becomes Palomar Avenue. Continue south on Palomar Avenue 2.0 miles and turn left on Joshua Lane. At the T junction 0.9 mile further, turn right on San Marino Drive. Follow this road, which soon veers 90° left and turns into Black Rock Canyon Road, 0.35 mile to the backcountry board on the left side, 100 yards after the road divides. There is a one-lane parking area along the east side of the road. If it is full, park at the ranger station 0.2 mile further. The trail to the summit starts at the backcountry board. Alternatively, park at the ranger station and walk uphill through the campground. A foot trail at campsite #30 connects via a water tank through scenic hills to the Black Rock Canyon Trail (0.6 mile, see map).

Sunset over stormy Morongo Valley from Warren Peak

Route Description

At their slender west end the Little San Bernardino Mountains are about as little as they get, their crest a thin rim of hills pegged to a low horizon. South from the campground the desert is an irregular undulating valley that rises gently to the flank of the mountains. Warren Peak is the local highest summit, hidden from view by nearby hills. Like other parts of the high desert that have been spared the indignity of fire since prehistory, this area is surprisingly lush. The understory is an unruly sagebrush rebellion of plump blackbrush, thorny ephedras, bushy rabbitbrush, frazzled yucca and cactus, and a smattering of squawbush. From it rises an eclectic mix of trees that seem to have been plucked from the state's four corners, canyon live oak, juniper, Joshua trees, and pinyon pine. Against the burnt hills to the south, shiny in their nakedness, the desert looks all dressed up.

The climb is about as easy as it gets. From the backcountry board, first take the unsigned California Riding and Hiking Trail 300 yards down, then up, to a fork. The trail on the right follows the wash of a minor drainage grandly named Black Rock Canyon, a swath of sand that lazily traces shallow creases in the terrain. Most of the walking is in this soft gradual wash churned daily by dozens of boots. Cold metal signs religiously signal the few trail junctions. In the summer the hills

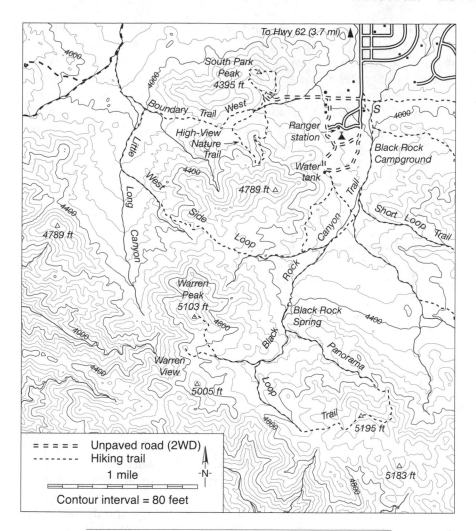

To Hwy 62 (3.7 mi)

South Park Peak 4395 ft

Boundary Trail West

High-View Nature Trail

Ranger station

S

4000

Black Rock Campground

Little Long Canyon

West

4400

Side Loop

4789 ft △

Water tank

Rock Canyon Trail

Short Loop Trail

△ 4789 ft

4400

Warren Peak 5103 ft

4800

Black Rock Spring

4400

Black Loop

Panorama

Warren View

△ 5005 ft

4000

4400

4800

Trail

5195 ft

△ 5183 ft

4800

===== Unpaved road (2WD)
-------- Hiking trail
1 mile
-N-
Contour interval = 80 feet

Warren Peak

	Dist.(mi)	Elev.(ft)
Black Rock Canyon Trail	0.0	3,980
Burnt Hill Trail	0.8	4,130
Black Rock Spring	1.6	4,365
Panorama Loop Trail (nth end)	1.8	4,435
Panorama Loop Trail (sth end)	2.15	4,560
Viewpoint Trail	2.45	~4,715
Warren View	(0.25)	4,890
Warren Peak	3.0	5,103

dissolved in shadeless torpor, and canteen water was hot enough to brew Darjeeling. Now, in late November, the pallid sun barely rose on its low arc and filled every wrinkle with crisp violet shadows. Water was a few degrees warmer than ice. Halfway to the crest the wash enters the only part of Black Rock Canyon that passes for a canyon, a shallow defile between broken perpendicular outcrops. Black Rock Spring is tucked just inside the defile. On wet years it spawns a frail creek. After a few rainless seasons it shrivels to a hole of murky water at the base of a blocky wall, barely big enough for a coyote's thirst. Hairy hedges of dark-green baccharis frame the spring, betraying underground water even during protracted droughts. The curvy forested passage beyond it has beautiful exposures of intensely metamorphosed gneiss. Heat and pressure folded the ancient rock upon itself in black twirls embroidered with rose felspar and silvery mica.

Above the canyon the trail cuts up through more open hilly country. Up there the trail markers are still old-fashioned organic wooden posts, signed with the hand-painted initials of the trail—PL for Panorama Loop, WP for Warren Peak, WV for Warren View. They will likely not survive long, to be replaced by sturdier metal signs as romantic as steel. Only then, at the very end, just past the last junction to a fine viewpoint on the crest, does the grade steepen as the trail wiggles up the last half a mile along the peak's rock-strewn western spine.

At the crest the thin rim reveals with unexpected suddenness what it had been hiding all along. To the west the land rolls off nearly one vertical mile into the bowels of Coachella Valley, only to scream up the corrugated wall of the San Jacinto Mountains on the opposite side. As we approached the crest the dispersed clouds coalesced and shut off the sun, compromising the views. Brilliance turned instantly into gloom. A hardening chill seeped into every surface, magnified by the slightest air current. Way down below, Palm Springs' untidy suburban sprawl was lost in perpetual haze. But just as we reached the summit everything changed. Somewhere over San Jacinto Peak the sun broke through holes in the stormy clouds and beamed across the valley long spokes of light solidified by veils of smog. It was, ironically, a most dramatic sunset, the sunbeams spotlighting a fairyland of furrowed hills out of the penumbra below us. The popular summit was deserted, drained of humans early that day by the call of turkey dinner. My wife and I sat on the cramped summit on our own for a long time, huddled against a rock spur and each other for warmth, mesmerized by a scene so surreal and color-saturated that it could have been computer generated. The desert had once again managed to surprise us.

■

EUREKA PEAK

Eureka Peak tests our laziness. It can be climbed with little effort by driving a long primitive road to very near the summit, or by taking a moderate but long hike using any number of combinations of a dozen hiking trails. The road and the trails cross particularly scenic valleys in the vicinity of Covington Flat, an area resplendent in its profuse high-desert vegetation. The summit encompasses expansive views of upper Coachella Valley and several 10,000-foot summits.

General Information
Jurisdiction: Joshua Tree National Park
Road status: Trails to summit; paved or primitive access road (2WD)
The climb (road): 0.15 mi, 60 ft up one way / very easy
The climb (trail): 4.7 mi, 1,670 ft up, 130 ft down one way / moderate
Main attractions: Green desert hills, views of Coachella Valley area
USGS 7.5' topo maps: Yucca Valley South, Joshua Tree South
Maps: pp. 427*, 397

Location and Access
To climb Eureka Peak the easy way, work your way to La Contenta Road, a signed city street that crosses Highway 62 2.7 miles east of Highway 247, at the east end of Yucca Valley. Drive La Contenta Road 1 mile south to its crossing with Alta Loma Drive. Continue south (from this crossing La Contenta Road is graded) 1.8 miles to a fork. Turn left onto the Vermiculate Mine Road, which leads in 1.7 miles to the entrance sign into Joshua Tree National Park. For the next 4.2 miles the road follows Lower Covington Flat to a junction. Turn right, and climb over some low hills 1.8 miles to a T junction in Upper Covington Flat. Turn right again. The road ends in 1.3 miles, in sight of Eureka Peak to the north. This road is hard-packed dirt, and in dry weather it is drivable with a standard-clearance vehicle. A very short trail (0.15 mile, 60 feet of elevation gain) connects the end of the road to the peak.

To climb Eureka Peak on one of the trails from the Black Rock Canyon Ranger Station, follow the directions to the backcountry board near the ranger station (see *Warren Peak*).

Route Description
The mountain leading up to Eureka Peak does not have the hard edge of desert mountains or the flourish of Joshua Tree's signature

landscapes. No outrageous castles of boulders, no defying ridges inclined at gravity-busting tilts. The countryside is a more gentle topography of narrow valleys and canyons confined between low billowy ridges. Mostly untouched by fire in recent decades, it is flush with oak, juniper, bitterbrush, desert almond, and pinyon pine linked in a puzzle of jade, moss, bottle green, and emerald. Joshua trees are ubiquitous, their lime-colored rosettes saturated with sunlight. It is a striking place, crisp and intimate, so bursting with potentials that it instantly ignites our craving for beauty.

This exceptional landscape did not go unnoticed—between Black Rock Canyon and the summit, the mountain is crisscrossed with some 25 miles of foot and hoof trails. Four main trails converge toward Eureka Peak, generally following canyon bottoms, and five shorter trails hop over ridges to interconnect them. One could climb this summit a dozen times and never take the exact same route. Most junctions are duly signed; even a GPS addict on withdrawal should not go missing.

The most direct route, and the backbone to which the other main trails eventually hook up, is the Eureka Peak Trail. From the trailhead at the backcountry board it is reached by following the California Riding and Hiking (CRH) Trail 300 yards south to the Black Rock Canyon Trail on the right. Stay on the CRH Trail (left) 1.15 miles, over scenic hilly terrain, to the Fault Trail branching off on the right. The Fault Trail cuts south 0.45 mile across the side of a low hill to the Eureka Peak Trail. The latter follows the sandy wash of a canyon and the remaining 2.9 miles to the summit. The canyon changes character several times. It starts as a twisted passage, goes through a straight corridor between steep facing hillsides, twists some more, then opens up before finally worming up a steepening ravine to the crest just below Eureka Peak. This is the shortest route, and it is the most scenic. The landscape is enchanting, in a spiny sort of way, generously dotted with large shrubs and trees. The proximity of the hills traps the canyon wash in a seclusion that breeds a deep sense of closeness. The Bigfoot Trail is a close second best when it comes to windiness. So is the Canyon View Trail. More open and occasionally up on higher ground, it offers low-angle perspectives of the surrounding desert country.

When all is said and done, the choice of trail is secondary. The trails are all delightful primitive tracks, sandy and unruly, often wandering off around intervening trees, adapting to rather than altering nature. Each trail gives us contentment in an economy of motion that reveals the value of details. I found myself stopping often to check out the tiny lobes of a bitterbrush, the silky veins on a slab of gneiss, the

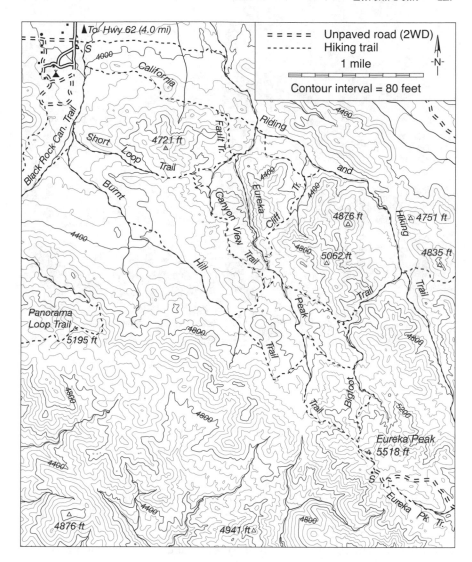

Eureka Peak

	Dist.(mi)	Elev.(ft)
Backcountry board	0.0	3,980
Fault Trail (right)	1.35	4,150
Eureka Peak Trail (left)	1.8	4,200
Canyon View Trail junction	2.9	4,500
Burnt Hill Trail junction	3.5	4,720
Eureka Peak	4.7	5,518

Coachella Valley and San Jacinto Mountains from Eureka Peak

mistletoe on a juniper, or the ossified remains of a hapless cholla. Like people-watching, the Joshua trees are an endless source of amusement—they are all there, the infants shaped like fuzzy bottlebrushes, the gawky teenagers, the ascetic marathon runners, the alpha males on steroids, and the saggy elders struggling to stay upright. Many trees with impressively thick crowns loom tall above the trails.

All approaches, be it the road or any of the trails, are entrenched below hilltops and offer limited distant views until the very last moment, when you crest the final ridge and Coachella Valley bursts open way down below. It is a sight to remember—the chiseled foothills freckled with oak and juniper rolling down into the valley, the spacious valley sloping gently to the distant shores of the Salton Sea, and the two-mile-high San Jacinto Mountains leaping out of the valley floor. The western horizon is closed off by the stately San Bernardino Mountains, their long ridge of ten-thousand-foot peaks crowned by the silvery dome of San Gorgonio Mountain. Another quarter of a turn and you are staring out at the sprawling Bullion Mountains and the bright Mojave Desert. The sudden encounter with this sumptuous panorama is Eureka Peak's greatest gift.

∎

QUAIL MOUNTAIN

At 5,813 feet, Quail Mountain is the highest point in Joshua Tree National Park. By Mojave Desert standards it is not very high, and it stands only 2,000 feet above its surroundings. But the classic route to it is fairly long and circuitous, across a small valley, through a winding open canyon, and finally up the mountain's tortuous eastern shoulder. The payoffs are interesting geology, scattered woodlands, a small historic mine associated with a local figure, and far-reaching views from the summit. Quail Mountain's neighbor Mount Minerva Hoyt is a good alternative, being a little closer yet offering similar views.

General Information

Jurisdiction: Joshua Tree National Park
Road status: Climbing on trail and cross-country; paved access road
The climb (Mt Minerva Hoyt): 4.4 mi, 1,790 ft up, 260 ft down one way /
    difficult
The climb (Quail Mountain): 5.8 mi, 2,450 ft up, 510 ft down one way /
    difficult
Main attractions: Views of Wonderland of Rocks, geology, mining
    history, botany
USGS 7.5' topo map: Indian Cove
Maps: pp. 433*, 397

Location and Access

Quail Mountain is the high point of an 11-mile northwest-trending ridge on the west flank of the Little San Bernardino Mountains, separated from the main range by Covington Flat's narrow valley. From any direction it is a relatively long way to it. The route described here goes up Johnny Lang Canyon, on a trail that comes within a couple of miles of the summit. Mount Minerva Hoyt, a recently officially named subsidiary summit, is also along this route, northeast of Quail Mountain and half way between it and the canyon.

To reach the trailhead, from Highway 62 in the town of Joshua Tree drive to Park Boulevard, which is well signed as the west park entrance. Drive it south, then east, 5.1 miles to the west entrance station. Continue 5.8 miles to the signed Quail Springs picnic area on the right. The Quail Springs Historic Trail starts at the west end of the parking loop. For a shorter access, go only 3.9 miles from the entrance station, and park at a small paved pullout on the left side at 3,875 feet. Quail Mountain is the bulky dome visible to the south-southwest, and Mount Minerva Hoyt the pointed summit to the left of it.

Route Description

Much of this route, and portions of Quail Mountain itself, were destroyed by the Memorial Fire of May 1999. The largest historic wildfire in the park, it burned for four days and consumed 14,000 acres. From the picnic area to Johnny Lang Canyon, much of the Quail Springs Historic Trail crosses the eastern edge of the burn. The scenery is much prettier from the small parking on Park Boulevard. The valley floor slopes gently through a scenic Joshua tree forest, with good views of Quail Mountain through the trees. Aim for the boulder-packed ridge at the valley floor level below Quail Mountain; it marks the south side of the entrance into Johnny Lang Canyon. The major east-west wash that drains the bottom of the valley two thirds of the way to the canyon was an effective fire break. The burn starts abruptly just south of it, an empty plain littered with the splayed skeletons of fallen Joshua trees.

Johnny Lang Canyon begins as a wide opening between low hills. A trail weaves through the lower and mid canyon, starting as the abandoned twin-track that once ran up to the Lang Copper Mine in the upper canyon. Combined with the modest incline, it makes for quick progress. Most of the larger shrubs and trees that once flushed the lower canyon with pleasing greens—the catclaw, Mojave yucca, Joshua trees, and many others—have been torched. But unlike in the valley below, smaller plants have been steadily returning. In the spring, grasses and annuals coat the canyon floor with a green five o'clock shadow. Beavertail and calico cactus scream for attention with arrestingly large bouquets of bright-red blossoms. Daisy-like white tidy-tips grow like weeds. The few burnt Joshua trees that are still standing now provide shade and nutrients to new shoots.

A little less than a mile in the canyon, the scenery changes radically. The transition occurs at a small spring in the wash, dry but announced loudly by two bright-green cottonwoods. On a hot day the cottonwood leaves vibrating in the breeze will fool your mind with the illusion of rain. The remains of a small camp and an even smaller assaying office stand nearby, likely associated with the Lang Copper Mine. By then the hills have grown taller and moved in, and the more protected wash is lined with greenery. There are thickets of saltbush and desert almond, thorny ephedra, pale rabbitbrush, and spikes of nolinas and Mojave yucca. The rounded heads of oak and California

Mount Minerva Hoyt (left) and Quail Mountain (left of center) from trailhead

juniper make an appearance higher up, then pinyon pine. Fairly uncommon species find refuge in this canyon—rock pea, a succulent enticingly called live-forever, and sacred sage, a stately shrub with broad star-shaped leaves. The hills up canyon are capped by scenic monzonite boulders and cleaved bedrock. The gneiss exposures along the trail are wild, coursed by fine wavering veins, sparkling with golden mica, or intruded by distorted dikes of pale monzonite.

Past the spring the trail becomes a single track worn into compacted coarse sand. It avoids the rocky wash by staying mostly on its west side, occasionally following the wash or splitting into two trails, on opposite sides of the wash. The mining road used to start its climb out of the wash to the mine half a mile past the spring, at 4,070 feet. A shallow ravine comes in from the south, with the first open views up ahead of the granitic domes in the upper canyon. The road used to take off on the right at the ravine; it is now hard to tell there ever was a road. Strike south up on the low swell between this ravine and the next one 100 yards east, and after 250 yards drop left into this second ravine. From this area the road is visible across the wash, climbing southeast up a hillside. In 200 feet it reaches a ridge, angles right, climbs the ridge to the 4,549-foot point, then loses a little elevation to a saddle. The Lang Copper Mine's tailing becomes visible around here, spilling down from about half way up the hill to the south-southeast. At the saddle the road veers left and parallels a wash for 300 yards, crosses the wash, and climbs as a single track to the mine. The distance from main wash to mine is just under a mile.

This canyon was named after John Lang, a shady character who co-owned and worked at the Lost Horse Mine in the 1890s (see *Lost Horse Mountain*). His partners, the Ryan family, noticed that Lang produced much less gold during his night shifts than they did during the day. In spite of his treachery—Lang had been diverting about half of his production for himself—the Ryans bought him out for a generous $12,000. Lang moved to an abandoned cabin in this canyon, and reportedly filed claims to the Lang Copper Mine around 1900. He developed this small copper-bismuth deposit in subsequent years, and 20 tons of bismuth (likely bismuthinite) were produced around 1904. Not much of his operation is left today, mostly the shaft and a short adit along the trail below the shaft. Lang did not make a mint on bismuth, but he had it made anyway. Over time he sold the gold stolen from the Lost Horse Mine for nearly $18,000. It would have been more than enough, back in the 1920s, to purchase a luxury Victorian house in San Francisco...

For the highest summit in hundreds of square miles, Quail Mountain is a little hard to find, hidden most of the time behind the sharp peaks on the western rim of Johnny Lang Canyon. The tallest of them, 600 feet higher across the drainage east of the shaft, is Mount Minerva Hoyt. Climb first toward the false summit (5,041') south of

Quail Mountain		
	Dist.(mi)	Elev.(ft)
Park Avenue	0.0	~3,875
Johnny Lang Canyon Trail (jct)	0.9	3,812
Quail Springs picnic area	(1.9)	3,980
Dry spring	2.2	3,960
Leave wash toward mine	2.8	4,070
Join mining road	2.9	~4,155
Lang Copper Mine	3.65	4,780
Bypassing 5,041-ft summit	3.8	~5,000
Mount Minerva Hoyt	4.4	5,405
Low point on ridge	5.0	5,190
Quail Mountain	5.8	5,813

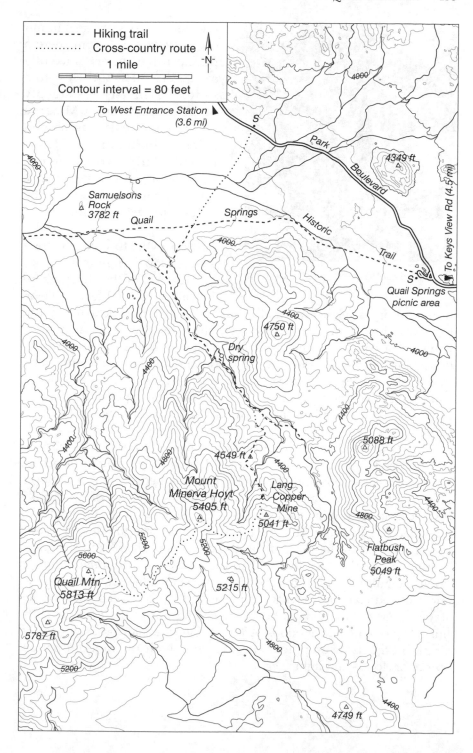

Hiking trail
Cross-country route
1 mile
-N-
Contour interval = 80 feet

To West Entrance Station ▶
(3.6 mi)

S

Park

Boulevard

4000

4349 ft
△

To Keys View Rd (4.5 mi)

Samuelsons
Rock
3782 ft
△

Quail   Springs

Historic

Trail

Quail Springs
picnic area

S

4000

4400

Dry
spring

4750 ft
△

4400

4000

4400

5088 ft
△

4400

4549 ft △

4800

Mount
Minerva Hoyt
5405 ft
△

Lang
Copper
Mine
△

5041 ft

4800

Flatbush
Peak
5049 ft
△

4800

4800

5600

5200

Quail Mtn
5813 ft
△

5215 ft
△

5600

5787 ft
△

5200

4800

4400

4749 ft
△

Beavertail cactus, Johnny Lang Canyon

the mine, and skirt its summit on its west side. From there a plump ridge curves gracefully as it descends southwest to a saddle, then ascends steeply northwest to Mount Minerva Hoyt. This peak was named recently in honor of a determined lady from South Pasadena who developed a passion for the desert in the 1910s and was instrumental in convincing President Franklin D. Roosevelt to create Joshua Tree National Monument.

The rest of the climb, about 1.4 miles and 700 feet of elevation gain, is easier, with Quail Mountain a constant beacon. Mount Minerva Hoyt's broad southwestern shoulder drops down in slow waves to a pass at the head of two facing drainages. Spared by the blaze, this area has kept its original woodland and offers the only good tree shade since the mine area. The final stretch is up Quail Mountain's southeastern shoulder, steep only briefly near its upper end. This is a long route, but the ridges are open and outcrops are few and easy to avoid.

The two summits are very different. Quail Mountain is a spacious and exposed plateau, too hostile to hold but a smattering of bleached, wind-combed shrubs and aberrantly green ephedra. Mount Minerva Hoyt is a high nipple encrusted with angular fragments of beautifully lustrous, dark gray igneous schists. They share similar views, luminous and breathtaking. To the west the land is a rough sea of rounded ridges, crossed in the distance by the daunting sails of San Gorgonio Mountain and San Jacinto Peak. To the east Quail Mountain bounces down languidly to a fragmented landscape of interconnected valleys and isolated stands of peaks. The Wonderland of Rocks takes center stage, its erratic mounds of boulders boiling out of the Earth in a 10-mile strip of fantastic hoodoos. After a winter rainstorm has wiped the air clean, this is a sumptuous theater, filled with the random performance of clouds and light.

■

INSPIRATION PEAK

This is a delightful short climb, up and down a steep primitive trail that closely follows the abrupt rim of the Little San Bernardino Mountains. It offers remarkable views of the mountains' rumpled southern scarp, of all of Coachella Valley from the Salton Sea to Palm Springs, and of the San Jacinto Mountains soaring like a wall out of the valley floor. With its intact pocket of vegetation spared by the wildfire that ravaged the area, the summit is a refreshing island of clean air and greenery.

General Information
Jurisdiction: Joshua Tree National Park
Road status: Climbing mostly on use trail; paved access road
The climb: 1.0 mi, 620 ft up, 210 ft down one way/easy–moderate
Main attractions: Gorgeous views of the southern Joshua Tree region
USGS 7.5' topo map: Keys View
Maps: pp. 437*, 397

Location and Access
Inspiration Peak is approximately in the middle of the Little San Bernardino Mountains, near the popular observation point at Keys View. To get to Keys View, from Highway 62 in the business district of the town of Joshua Tree take Park Boulevard 5.1 miles south, then east, to the Joshua Tree National Park's west entrance station. In the park, drive generally southeast 10.5 miles to Keys View Road and turn right (south). This scenic byway crosses Lost Horse Valley and one of the park's thickest and most impressive forests of Joshua trees, many of them taller than 15 feet. It ends at the viewpoint after 5.5 miles. Inspiration Peak is less than 1 air mile up the ridge to the northwest, hidden by a false summit. The faint trail to it starts on the north side of the parking area, near two adjacent curbside boulders.

Route Description
The views are awesome the whole way. From start to finish the sharp-edged ridge leading up to Inspiration Peak overlooks the expansive southern slopes of the Little San Bernardino Mountains, a dissected scarp that drops 5,000 feet into the sprawling lowlands of Coachella Valley. The unbroken chain of the Santa Rosa and San Jacinto mountains loom in the distance, draped with snow in winter. There is a little

Southern Little San Bernardino Mountains from ridge to Inspiration Peak

trail most of the way to the top, fortunately not much of one, and not yet soiled by signs or cairns. It winds its way, often straight up the rock-strewn slope, occasionally looping around a couple of loose switchbacks, gaining 325 feet to a first false summit. It then drops to a saddle overlooking Lost Horse Valley and its army of pointed inselbergs to the north.

A wildfire raged through this area in recent years. The barren ground is still littered with blackened wood debris and Joshua tree bark. Many plants have started to grow back, especially yucca and ephedra. One of the annuals that has recovered most quickly is chia, a handsome herb with erect leafless stems that bear pale-blue flowers arranged on spiky spheres. Long after the flowers have withered the spheres continue to decorate the dried plant. The Cahuilla were fond of chia seeds, which they harvested with a seed beater and prepared into a drink or a cake. They periodically applied prescribed burns to stimulate the growth of the plant. The proliferation of chia on these burnt slopes shows that they knew what they were doing.

Past the saddle the ridge climbs again to a second false summit (5,558') crowned by an interesting outcrop of gnarled and layered gneiss. A little further the ridge is capped by a mound of close-packed

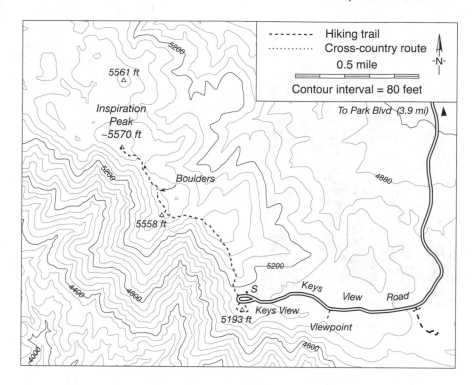

Inspiration Peak		
	Dist.(mi)	Elev.(ft)
Keys View	0.0	5,160
False summit	0.35	~5,485
5,558T point	0.65	5,558
Boulders area	0.7	~5,550
Inspiration Peak	1.0	~5,570

monzogranite boulders deformed by erosion. For the shortest route, clamber over and between the boulders. Large scrub oak live among them, spared from the blaze by their shield of boulders. The trail resumes just beyond, drops into a second saddle, then ascends one last pitch to Inspiration Peak.

The summit area is a scenic billowing plateau sprinkled with boulders and high-desert vegetation. Spiny plants like Mojave yucca, nolina, Joshua trees, silver cholla, and scattered cactuses grow intermixed with softer species like oak and juniper. Isolated pinyon pine stand on the rim of the mountain like lone sentinels guarding the high desert

Nolina near Inspiration Peak

from the encroaching cities below. All around lies dry hot desert, but up here everything is suddenly greener, cooler, and more fragrant, a secret world stolen from the desert.

The panorama from the summit is spectacular. It is not vastly different from Keys View, but it will be all yours, and the serenity won't be disturbed by cars beeping. To the south the mountain falls in long wrinkled waves to the distant floor of Coachella Valley. On a clear day, usually after a rainstorm has scrubbed the atmosphere, one can clearly see the main agent responsible for this great upthrust of land—the San Andreas Fault, marked by a long line of low hills at the base of the mountains. The views then extend from the Salton Sea and the Santa Rosa Mountains to the southeast, to Palm Springs and 11,499-foot San Gorgonio Mountain to the west. Much like Death Valley and Owens Valley, Coachella Valley is a place of staggering proportions, a huge tectonic sink much deeper than most, surrounded by mountains much taller than most. Its low point, the Salton Sea, lies some 288 ft below sea level, while San Jacinto Peak soars 10,804 ft above sea level. From base to summit San Jacinto's elevation differential is about 10,000 feet in 9 air miles, one of the steepest mountain fronts this tall in the conterminal United States.

Inspiration Peak was named decades ago, when Coachella Valley was still relatively unspoiled. Things have changed. When climbing down in the evening, the lights of the cities piercing through the smog reveal the disturbing extent of the suburban sprawl down in the valley, now home to several hundred thousand people. The inspiration that once came from marveling at so much wilderness is now tempered by sorrow over what we have lost. The bittersweet mixture of emotions reinforces our appreciation for the dedicated organizations that have been toiling to preserve what has not yet been paved over.

■

RYAN MOUNTAIN

This popular summit is a great perch to admire Lost Horse Valley and its outlandish piles of boulders—Joshua Tree's most distinctive signature. It is reached on a gradual trail with artful stairways built of beautiful local gneiss. The route offers close-up views of several imposing outcrops of polished monzogranite, especially Saddle Rocks, a superb cluster of towering sugarloaves. The desert flora is equally striking, green desert gardens that combine Joshua trees and juniper, yucca and nolina, and cactus of all sizes and shapes.

General Information

Jurisdiction: Joshua Tree National Park
Road status: Trail to summit; paved access road
The climb: 1.4 mi, 1,070 ft one way / easy–moderate
Main attractions: Striking formations, views of Wonderland of Rocks
USGS 7.5' topo maps: Indian Cove, Keys View*
Maps: pp. 441*, 397

Location and Access

Ryan Mountain is at the center of the popular western section of Joshua Tree National Park, between Lost Horse Valley to the west and Queen Valley to the east. In the business section of the town of Joshua Tree on Highway 62, look for Park Boulevard, which is well signed from either direction. Drive it south, then east, 5.1 miles to the park's west entrance station. In the park, drive generally southeast 10.5 miles to the junction with Keys View Road. Continue straight on Park Boulevard 2 miles to the signed parking area for the Ryan Mountain Trail on the right, and park. The trailhead is near the east end of the parking area. Ryan Mountain rises directly to the south.

Route Description

This is a Joshua Tree classic climb, true to the National Park Service's dedication to developing well-built trails to particularly scenic areas. The path to Ryan Mountain is indeed a perfectly groomed trail, hard dirt where the terrain is nearly level, and elegant staircases of granitic slabs where the slope exceeds a few percent, which is often. It makes for unusually easy walking, and greater ease to observe the surroundings. It also draws a cohort of hikers and joggers year round, so expect company.

Saddle Rocks from the Ryan Mountain Trail

The trail starts with a bang. It squeezes by a group of stunning formations, monumental humps of jointed White Tank Monzogranite polished into fantastic shapes. The westernmost outcrop is the site of Indian Cave, a series of natural chambers among boulders that local bands of Native Americans—Cahuilla, Serrano, and Chemehuevi—used as seasonal shelters. Past these outcrops the trail ascends the open western flank of Ryan Mountain at a leisurely angle. The steep slope above and below it are covered with gardens of low juniper, blackbrush, ephedra, young Joshua trees, and Mojave yucca, some of them boasting plump trunks the size of small trees. Dehydrated calico cactus, flaming-red cottontop cactus, and blue-green beavertail cactus grow between the rock litters, as do full-grown pancake cactus. This luxuriant community is all the more valuable since several nearby areas have been decimated by wildfires.

Because of the views it commands, this portion of the route is the most scenic. Lost Horse Valley sprawls below, pinpricked with an impressive density of Joshua trees right up to the Wonderland of Rocks to the north. The scenery's most exceptional element is Saddle Rocks, the stately outcrop of sculpted monzogranite that bulges out of the side of the mountain. Its four piggybacked sugarloaf summits rise

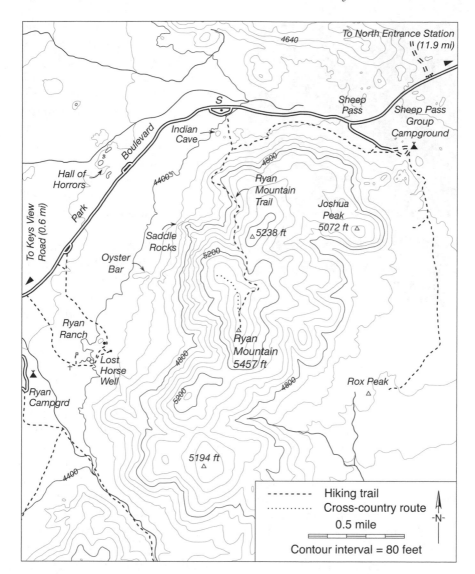

Ryan Mountain		
	Dist.(mi)	Elev.(ft)
Park Boulevard	0.0	4,390
Trail junction	0.2	4,520
Sheep Pass Group Campg.	(1.0)	4,530
Saddle on ridge	0.9	5,150
Ryan Mountain	1.4	5,457

Stairs along the Ryan Mountain Trail

proudly from a scree of boulders peppered with pinyon pine. This is one of the tallest formations in the park—and the only one that requires four pitches to be climbed. It is highly prized among rock climbers, who scale it along routes with funky names like Right On and Walk on The Wild Side.

After 0.9 mile the trail reaches a shallow ravine and climbs along it a short distance to the ridge. A tall pinyon pine lives right below the ridge. In the middle of the day in the summertime, it provides the only deep shade around. The trail then enters a scenic hollow at the crest, sprinkled with similar but greener and denser vegetation. From there it is a short meandering climb across the west side of this small hanging valley to the top of Ryan Mountain.

The summit itself is unfortunately disappointing. Stripped bare by some climbers' meaningless practice of harvesting local rocks and piling them up at the summit, it has all the charm of a vacant lot under construction. To add insult to injury, a bureaucrat who missed Wilderness 101 further defaced the site by erecting a sign that announces the summit, should anyone think they inadvertently climbed Everest. But the views of the park are good, north into the Wonderland of Rocks' surreal boulder piles, west to the rocky Little San Bernardino Mountains, and south to the Santa Rosa and San Jacinto mountains. This hike is short enough that it is not too hard to be here around the two best times of the day, shortly after daybreak when the sun slowly chases shadows from the mountains, and in the evening when light and shadows switch roles. The pristine, slightly lower summit 0.3 mile to the north-northwest offers even better, unobstructed panoramic views of Lost Horse Valley and the Wonderland of Rocks.

■

LOST HORSE MOUNTAIN

> *Most hikers come here not to climb the peak but to visit the Lost Horse Mine just below it, a rich gold property that has spawned more than its fair share of lore. It is an easy ascent on the popular historic mining road to the well-preserved ruins of its 1890s mill, then on a faint trail to the summit. The mountaintop commands great views of Pleasant Valley, the Hexie Mountains, and the Wonderland of Rocks. An enjoyable trail winds back to the starting point though the hilly southern end of this little mountain.*

General Information
Jurisdiction: Joshua Tree National Park
Road status: Climbing on trail and cross-country; graded access road
The climb: 2.2 mi, 810 ft up, 90 ft down one way/easy
Main attractions: Well-preserved mill, history, views of Joshua Tree
USGS 7.5' topo map: Keys View
Maps: pp. 445*, 397

Location and Access
Lost Horse Mountain is a small sub-range on the northern flank of the eastern Little San Bernardino Mountains. In Joshua Tree National Park, follow Park Boulevard to its junction with Keys View Road (see *Ryan Mountain*). Turn south on Keys View Road and drive 2.4 miles to the signed Lost Horse Mine Road. Turn left and park at the end of this good graded road (1 mile), just inside a gulch in the foothills.

Route Description
The character most central to the history of the Lost Horse Mine is Johnny Lang, a lanky rancher turned miner who came to this area in 1893. He and his father George were then traveling from Arizona with a large herd of cattle they wanted to sell in southern California. According to one version of the discovery, while grazing their animals near Witch Springs (now Lost Horse Well), they met a prospector named Frank Diebold, who told them about a rich gold strike he had made on a nearby mountain. For some years the area had been under the control of a gang of cattle rustlers headed by Jim McHaney, who had bullied and driven Diebold off the land. Johnny Lang himself had had a run-in with the McHaney gang. One of his horses had wandered off into their camp, and he had been unable to get it back from them.

Pleasant Valley and the Hexie Mountains from Lost Horse Mountain

Perhaps in revenge, Lang inspected Diebold's find, liked it, and bought it from him for $1,000. In December he took three partners as protection against the gang, and they filed multiple claims, befittingly naming the best one Lost Horse.

The Lost Horse Mine rapidly became the region's most productive gold property. Johnny Lang and his partners worked it first. The highest grade ore was hand-sorted, and the rest processed at a nearby two-stamp mill. The richest specimen was a museum-quality piece of quartz as big as an apple and laced with gold. In 1895 the mine was sold to the Ryan family, long-time friends of the Langs, while Johnny Lang retained an interest and continued to work at the mine. The Ryans improved it and developed a small ranch at Witch Springs to host the miners. In April 1897 a 10-stamp mill recycled from a mine in the Chuckwalla Mountains was brought in, and a 3.3-mile pipeline was deployed from the springs to run it. The mine played out at the end of 1899. Subsequent efforts by the Ryans and other parties, including cyaniding the tailings and mining underground pillars in 1936, were much less fruitful. But the Lost Horse was indeed rich. Until it closed in 1936 it shipped ore for 17 years and recovered 16,400 ounces of silver and 10,750 ounces of gold—a cube 10 inches on the side.

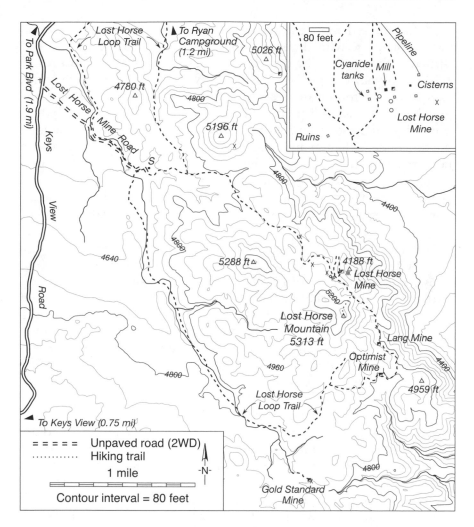

Lost Horse Mountain

	Dist.(mi)	Elev.(ft)
Lost Horse Mine Road (end)	0.0	4,590
Junction to Lost Horse Mine	1.8	5,000
Lost Horse Mine (mill)	(0.25)	5,090
Trail junction below saddle	2.0	5,110
Lost Horse Mountain	(0.2)	5,313
Lang Mine	2.4	4,805
Optimist Mine	2.8	4,785
Back to starting point	6.3	4,590

After more than a century of erosion, the aging road to the mine has become one with the landscape—rocky, ravined, lopsided, and dusted with gravel. Long stretches are lined with wavy exposures of 1.7-billion-year-old gneiss smoothed by a million boots. Dazzling exposures outcrop on the slopes, coursed by sinuous veins of dark-gray biotite that sparkle in the sunlight. The road winds slowly up and down into the mountain, past a scraggly cover of juniper, Mojave yucca, nolina, ephedra, and small Joshua trees. One better appreciates how green the high desert is when reaching the burn part way up, a stripped open space of sienna soil pinpricked with bare rocks and charred trees. Freed of competition, wildflowers grow with total abandon. In the spring the road is lined with the pale-blue ray flowers of Mojave aster, the cream clusters of California buckwheat, and the myriad pink blossoms of wishbone bush.

The mine pops into view suddenly, at a bend in the road, hanging high on a satellite peak of Lost Horse Mountain. At a junction, a side road on the left switchbacks up to it, past flat-topped tailings and the eroding cyanide heaps from the 1930s. Refurbished by the NPS, the mill is a mammoth construction of tanned lumber and steel. One would have to travel far to find another one with its stamp battery, camshafts, antediluvian generator, and concrete cisterns. The winch that hoisted the ore out of the shaft is a mechanical gem—and at 110 years of age its handbrake still works...

Shortly past the mine the main trail reaches its high point. Just before it a vague path on the right climbs 300 yards, straight up, to the top of Lost Horse Mountain. To the east the rock-strewn summit overlooks secluded Pleasant Valley, Malapai Hill's chocolate domes, and the Hexie Mountains beyond. Quail Mountain and the Wonderland of Rocks' saw-toothed skyline dominate the northern horizon. This is the perfect spot to survey what was the stage for Johnny Lang's protracted tribulations. During the mine's heyday, Lang was caught stealing ore. His partners gave him the option to sell his share or to turn him to the authorities. Lang sold and moved to an abandoned cabin in the canyon that now bears his name, just east of Quail Mountain. He made a scant living working a small mine, selling over time the gold he had skimmed at the Lost Horse, and occasionally bagging a vagrant cow to put meat on his plate. On January 25, 1926, at the age of 76, he set off to town for supplies, but never made it back. Two months later Bill Keys and a couple of friends found his desiccated body, still wrapped in his bedroll. A carved tombstone marks the spot where he was found and buried, ironically right by the road to the Lost Horse Mine.

■

WONDERLAND OF ROCKS

By conventional standards, the Wonderland of Rocks does not look like a mountain. Once a taller granitic range, it has been majorly degraded by erosion to what is today much closer to a fragmented sloping plateau. But the same erosional forces that wore it down have also sculpted what remains into a vast playground of fantastically shaped hoodoos, tens of square miles tightly packed with pale domes, slickrock, spires, jointed walls, and boulder piles immersed in green desert gardens. It is one of the most fascinating landscapes in the American West. No other area in the Mojave Desert holds bare-rock moonscapes so diverse, so extensive, and so spectacular. This uniqueness defines Joshua Tree National Park more vividly than its emblematic Joshua trees.

The Wonderland of Rocks generally designates the most scenic portion of this region, roughly confined between Indian Cove to the north and Hidden Valley to the south. Because of the similarity in terrain and geology, by extension it refers here to the larger mountainous mass encircled by Park Boulevard inside the park and Highway 62 north of it. Geographically it is bounded to the north by Morongo Basin, to the east by the Pinto Mountains, to the south by Queen Valley and Lost Horse Valley, and to the west by the Little San Bernardino Mountains. The majority of it is made of White Tank Monzogranite, the priceless formation without which the Wonderland of Rocks—and the park—would just not be the same. The rest of it, occupying a square block at the northeastern corner of the range north from Queen Mountain, is mostly Queen Mountain Monzogranite, with an island of Oasis Monzogranite west of Joshua Mountain, and a fringe of Twentynine Palms porphyritic quartz monzonite overlooking Twentynine Palms. This last formation crystallized in the Triassic, and all others in the Cretaceous. Small outcrops of Proterozoic gneiss are scattered throughout the range. The park's most photogenic spots—Indian Cove, Hidden Valley, Jumbo Rocks, White Tank, among many others—are underlain by the smooth, light-colored, fine-grained White Tank pluton. The Queen Mountain Monzogranite is a close second: this hard, fractured, slightly darker stock is responsible for the extensive region of bold domes and cliffs on and north of Queen Mountain.

The Wonderland of Rocks' deeply carved landscape results from differential chemical and mechanical weathering. Most of it was caused by the many direct and indirect actions of water—frost and heat cycles, chemical action of slightly acidic or basic water, and running water—which led to gradual exfoliation. Erosion progresses considerably faster along fractures and exposed corners and edges, the reason for the myriad walls of jointed blocks and spheroidal boulders that abound throughout this range. It took place mostly between the Miocene and Quaternary, when the climate was a little wetter and cooler than today. As erosion proceeded, the range's southern front, along Queen Mountain, receded northward, gradually shedding off the pediment surfaces that became Lost Horse Valley and Queen Valley immediately south of it. Both valleys are prime examples of the vestigial planed bedrock ground down during the removal of a mountain. The otherworldly inselbergs strewn across them are the harder core stones that have resisted erosion.

With such a profusion of smooth, cohesive, high-quality vertical surfaces laced with crevasses, pits, knobs, holes, pimples, and indentations for powerful fingers and nimble toes to cling to, the Wonderland of Rocks has been for decades a world-class site that attracts climbers from all over the planet. Any serious climber has skinned knuckles on White Tank Monzogranite. At many places in the Wonderland of Rocks you are likely to run into climbers, sampling a scramble or pushing back the impossible one more notch. Due to its extreme popularity, this entire range is day use only.

This contorted geography gave us another gift, remarkable for the desert. Big vertical rocks create shade, relative protection from the wind, and microsites that retain moisture. As a result of this serendipitous combination and of the relatively high elevation, the vegetation in the Wonderland of Rocks is among the densest, greenest, and most diverse at this altitude in the Mojave Desert. Very different plant zones co-exist in the same area in some free-for-all botanical nirvana. Low-desert creosote, catclaw, and silver cholla grow next to mid-elevation species like yucca, nolina, and Joshua trees, and plants found normally at higher elevations like juniper, oaks, and pine. Nearby mountains hundreds of feet taller do not even support a single evergreen.

■

KEYS PEAK

This scenery-charged climb comes in two stages, first a nearly level walk across a vast plain with a limitless supply of cacti and Joshua trees, then a rigorous scramble up a steep, 360-foot hillside smothered in boulders to the summit of Keys Peak. This is vintage Joshua Tree landscape, the chaotic topography that greets and instantly enthralls countless park visitors every year. Even a partial climb will deliver inspiring views of the Wonderland of Rocks' otherworldly jumble of standing stones.

General Information
Jurisdiction: Joshua Tree National Park
Road status: Climbing on trail and cross-country; paved access road
The climb: 3.6 mi, 540 ft up, 100 ft down one way / moderate–difficult
Main attractions: A leisurely trail to a steep bouldery peak, close-up
      views of the Wonderland of Rocks
USGS 7.5' topo map: Indian Cove
Maps: pp. 451*, 397

Location and Access
Keys Peak is a free-standing conical inselberg at the western margin of the Wonderland of Rocks. The most direct way to get to it is to hike the Boy Scout Trail from its south end at Park Boulevard. The well-signed trailhead is 6.5 miles southeast from the park's west entrance station, on the left side. Coming from the other direction, it is 4 miles northwest from the Keys View Road turnoff. From the large dirt parking area at the trailhead, Keys Peak is visible between the Joshua trees about 3 miles a little west of north.

Route Description
From the trailhead to the foot of Keys Peak the terrain is a spacious plain generously covered with desert vegetation. Platoons of Joshua trees stand guard all around, their spiked bodies competing for oddness, in ranks tight enough to paint the horizon solid green. Desolate stands of rounded boulders rise nearby. Up ahead in the distance, the horizon is closed off abruptly by the Wonderland of Rocks, a long wall of jointed stones dissected in turrets and battlements in the style of a medieval town. It is the kind of scenery between reality and fiction that makes you wonder whether you just got spontaneously stoned.

449

Stoned or not, it would be hard to wander astray. Most of the Boy Scout Trail is to trails what freeways are to roads—broad, straight, and impeccably manicured, mostly level and hard surfaced, signed with metal posts and plates designed to survive a nuclear conflict. There is only one junction along the way, 1.2 miles from the trailhead. This is quite a popular trail, enjoyed by hikers any day of the year, but at this junction most of the traffic heads right to Willow Hole. The rest of the way to Keys Peak, a further distance of 2.2 miles on the Boy Scout Trail (left fork), is generally less traveled.

The most spectacular areas along the trail are where it comes close to the Wonderland of Rocks, especially at the majestic cliffs near the junction, and at the smaller outcrop a little over half a mile further. Rock climbers often scale the popular routes in these two areas. In the hot months small bosques of juniper and pinyon pine below the cliffs offer welcome shade. The valley is host to many typical Mojave Desert plants—blackbrush, saltbush, and clusters of tall diamond cholla, occasional thornbush, calico and mound cactus, and less common plants like rock pea and live-forever in the rockier swales below the peak. On a good year the wildflowers are unbelievably prolific. Vast tracks are blanketed in chia, Canterbury bells, pincushion, globemallow, and wooly daisies.

As it approaches Keys Peak the trail narrows and starts to wiggle, climbs a little, and wanders up and down over a rolling pass on the peak's southwest shoulder. It then bends to the north-northeast and starts its long gradual descent to Indian Cove as it skirts the western base of the peak. The easiest route to the summit is up the steep gully in the peak's northwestern face. This is about 0.3 mile past the bend, just past the peak's slight but conspicuously rockier western shoulder.

Keys Peak is a hearty Class-2 scramble, up a slowly steepening slide overrun by boulders. What little room is not occupied by rocks has been annexed by Mojave yucca, juniper, young Joshua trees, and a few pinyon pine near the top. Most of the way you never touch

Keys Peak		
	Dist.(mi)	Elev.(ft)
Boy Scout Trail at Park Blvd	0.0	4,040
Willow Hole junction	1.2	4,142
Pass (Keys Peak's SW shoulder)	3.0	~4,160
Northwestern foot of Keys Pk	3.4	4,125
Keys Peak	3.6	4,483

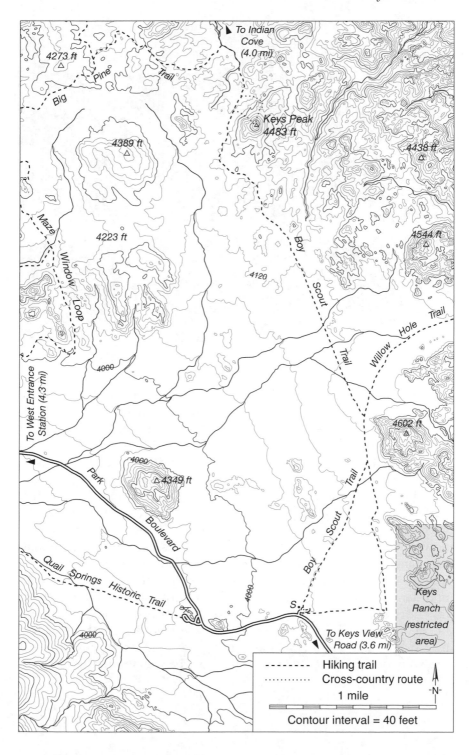

Keys Peak
4483 ft

To Indian
Cove
(4.0 mi)

4273 ft

Big

Pine

Trail

4389 ft

4438 ft

Maze

Window Loop

4223 ft

4120

4544 ft

Boy

Scout

Trail

Willow Hole Trail

4000

4602 ft

To West Entrance
Station (4.3 mi)

Park

4000

△ 4349 ft

Boulevard

Boy

Scout

Trail

Quail Springs Historic Trail

4000

4000

S

Keys
Ranch
(restricted
area)

To Keys View
Road (3.6 mi)

- - - - - Hiking trail

· · · · · · Cross-country route

-N-

1 mile

Contour interval = 40 feet

The route up Keys Peak from the Boy Scout Trail

ground but hop from stone to stone. It is a demanding little mountain; you have to make concessions, and accept having to give up on a route to try another one. It is generally best to favor the left (north) side of the gully, which has smaller rocks than the middle and fewer trees than the right side. Near the top it is easiest to drift back to the gully to avoid the larger boulders that frame it on both sides.

The summit is a remnant of the original mountain range, a flattish surface broken into 90-degree jointed boulders colonized by a few yucca and dwarf pine. The rocks make perfect front-row benches to sit down and take in the Wonderland of Rocks, its fantastic crest a miniature range of knolls, domes, nipples, and hoodoos unfurling from the foot of Keys Peak for several miles. In the late afternoon, every cliff, boulder, and spindle takes on a pale apricot glow as long bolts of lavender shadows fill in the notches and hollows between them. Beyond lie the wind-swept vastness of Morongo Basin, a haze of further ranges, and mountains high enough to hold deep snow. Even if this scenery were the only reward, it would be well worth the climb.

■

QUEEN MOUNTAIN

Queen Mountain is a lofty mesa of carved monzogranite that drops 1,000 feet from the edge of the Wonderland of Rocks into Queen Valley's scenic arboretums. The climb from valley floor to rimrock is hard work, up a sheer rock-strewn ravine traced by a rough use trail. Even if you cannot make the final rock-climbing to the two neighboring summits, from much of this ascent the views of the colossal sculptures surrounding the mountain are breathtaking.

General Information

Jurisdiction: Joshua Tree National Park
Road status: Roadless; graded access road (2WD)
The climb: ~2.0 mi, 1,230 ft up, 30 ft down one way / difficult
Main attractions: Scenic cactus gardens, views of Wonderland of Rocks
USGS 7.5' topo map: Queen Mountain
Maps: pp. 455*, 397

Location and Access

In the western section of Joshua Tree National Park, work your way to the signed Big Horn Pass Road, a graded road that starts off Park Boulevard 5.0 miles east from the junction with Keys View Road (see *Ryan Mountain* for directions to this junction). The Big Horn Pass Road heads northwest across Queen Valley towards the Wonderland of Rocks. After 0.4 mile, turn right at a fork onto the unsigned O'Dell Road. At the four-road crossing 0.6 mile further, continue straight toward Queen Mountain's twin summits, slightly east of north. Drive 0.9 mile to the small loop at the end of the road and park. These roads are passable with a standard-clearance vehicle.

Route Description

Queen Mountain is shaped like a mesa more than a desert mountain, a 1.5-mile long, 600-foot thick plateau of exceptionally hard monzogranite that drops from sky to valley like a pleated curtain. The rock is so resilient that the combined erosional powers of water, wind, heat, frost, and gravity have not cut a single canyon into it. But they have carved in the mountain's flank a spectacular mile-long parapet of hulking towers and sheared cliffs revered like a shrine by hard-core climbers for their remote, high-quality routes. The most striking outcrop is the Cirque of the Climbables, a rack of vertical ribs hanging above a sheer ravine. A couple of climbers will occasionally hike up the aging trail beyond the road and painstakingly trudge up the ravine to scale the Cirque. Queen Mountain stands above it, a bulb of naked stone surrounded by a capricious geography.

To those who lack the agility of a spider monkey the mountain has given an alternative, a ravine a little less rough that does not require levitating on footholds the size of bread crumbs. It is about a mile northeast of the end of the road, hidden by a fold in the mountain. If you walk due east from the end of the road about 400 yards, the second wash you will cross is the wash that drains out from the ravine. Walking up the wash's ribbon of fine sand across Queen Valley's serene countryside is a delight. It passes by a collage of desert gardens delineated by tiny washes, low swells, and erratic boulders. Monocultures of grizzly bear cactus alternate with stands of juvenile Joshua trees, hillsides of yucca and pancake cactus, and scenic coves of juniper and silver cholla, all growing out of a meager granitic soil. The wash soon crosses a line of low hills at a slanted fall of layered monzo-granite, then wanders on to the ravine at the foot of the range.

The ravine is impressive. A shallow, 30-foot wide trench, it screams up the mountain on a high parabola, funneled between raised rims of pale boulders at its base, some the size of a Cadillac. Its wash is cluttered with large flat-topped boulders and angular falls, and it is *steep*. Where the boulders became too crowded I exited up a propitious side drainage onto the east rim, where the climbing was easier, though not for long. The rim soon ran into a cliff that forced me back down into the ravine. The wash uphill from that point is clogged with vertical boulders. I crossed it and found salvation—a dusty use trail that took me the rest of the way and most of the ascent—to the crest. It is crooked, rocky, slippery, and it occasionally flirts with eminently prickly plants, but it is better than nothing.

At the crest the trail enters a serene cove sheltered by sheer bluffs. Large pine and oak, tall yucca, and pancake cactus grow in this unexpected garden high above the valley. The taller bluff on the west side is Queen Mountain. The one on the east side is too—so says the 1937 USGS benchmark irreverently glued to it. Yes, Queen Mountain has not one but two summits—*noblesse oblige*. The true high point (west) is girdled on its north, west, and south sides with hard cliffs, climbing routes like G Spot and Cactus Slump that will burn through muscles faster than it takes to fall. Its more sedate east side, facing the cove, is the only spot left for ordinary humans to reach the top, up tilted slabs.

From the cove the 10-foot shorter eastern twin looks even more daunting, but here too Queen Mountain offers an easier option. The

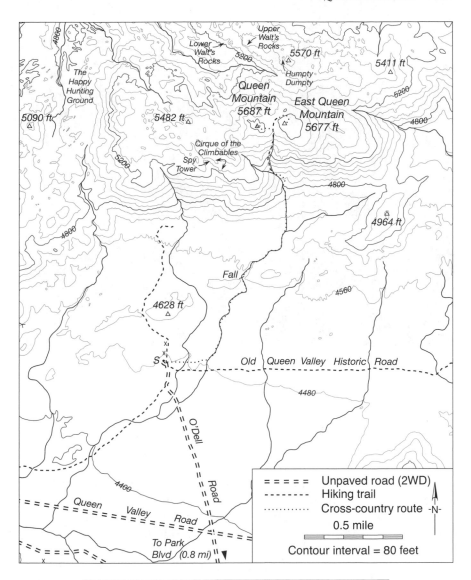

Queen Mountain

	Dist.(mi)	Elev.(ft)
O'Dell Road	0.0	4,475
Foot of ravine	1.1	4,600
Cove at crest	1.8	~5,530
East Queen Mountain	(0.15)	5,677
Queen Mountain	1.95	5,687

The Wonderland of Rocks from below East Queen Mountain

trail cuts north across the cove, then descends a little as it circles clock-wise to the northeast side of this second summit. From there it is an easy cross-country climb, first up a short talus spotted with pine, then through a small jungle of oak and giant nolinas to the eastern foot of the summit block, and finally up stepped slickrock to the top.

In every direction the view is beautiful. The true summit looks west over the G Spot at a maze of fins so dislocated that a ewe would have trouble finding her lamb. To the north a canyon with bulging cliffs flows gracefully down toward the Wonderland of Rocks' petri-fied waves of stone, past Walt's Rocks and other premier climbing sites, its wash a pigmy forest of oak and evergreen. To the south, the mountain plunges over its own rim and disappears. Queen Valley spreads out half a mile beyond, dotted with sharp hills and boulder islands, edged far away by a high cordillera of mountains. In the late afternoon every rock in the valley glows against its own shadow, a tableau so crisp one could reach out and touch it. An evening return down the precipitous ravine has the dreamy quality of a descent on a hot-air balloon, an intemporal suspension in space, Queen Valley a brilliant fantasy slowly turning to amber, then ash.

■

JOSHUA MOUNTAIN

Joshua Mountain is an imposing cliff-bound tower perched high on the chaotic eastern front of the Wonderland of Rocks. The climb is short, exhilarating, and a little demanding, first on a rough primitive trail up an abrupt ravine filled with boulders of beautiful megaporphyritic monzonite, then up the summit block on an exposed ramp of inclined slickrock. The peak offers a fine perspective of the small town of Twentynine Palms, the eastern Morongo Basin, and the sand-encrusted Bullion Mountains in the background.

General Information
Jurisdiction: Joshua Tree National Park
Road status: Climbing mostly on rough use trail; paved access road
The climb: 1.35 mi, 1,150 ft up, 40 ft down one way/moderate–difficult
Main attractions: A short, vigorous climb to a tall sculpted monolith
USGS 7.5' topo map: Queen Mountain
Maps: pp. 459*, 397

Location and Access
Joshua Mountain is at the very eastern edge of the Wonderland of Rocks, where the range drops precipitously into the small valley that separates it from Twentynine Palms Mountain to the east. Its stocky summit block protruding high above the range is a conspicuous landmark visible from the road to the park's north entrance. On Highway 62 in Twentynine Palms, about a mile east of the town center, turn south on Utah Trail (look for signs to the park's north entrance). Drive this road 3.0 miles to the signed Wellock Road on the left. Coming from inside the park, this is 1.1 miles north of the north entrance station. Joshua Mountain soars about 1 air mile and 1,100 feet higher to the west, at the top of the ridge. The curb makes it hard to park on the paved road, so park on dirt at the start of Wellock Road.

Route Description
Joshua Mountain is a stately rock. Its monolithic summit block stands sentinel high above the desert like a fortress anchored on an invincible rock. Below it, the sheer mountain front is overflowing with enormous outcrops. The boulder-choked ravine that tumbles straight down from the summit's southern brow to the foot of the range is obviously the shortest route. It is also the least difficult, though by no

457

means easy: it plunges about 950 feet in 0.6 air mile—a sustained 30% slope, most of it encumbered by large rocks.

From the road, first cross the short stretch of valley floor almost due west to the mouth of the ravine. This area is an interesting piece of desert real estate, dissected by many small sandy washes and a large one near the base of the mountain. Storm waters seem to have churned not only the terrain but the plant community as well. A surprising number of plants not too common in this type of habitat live inter-mixed with more typical flora, an eclectic blend of desert lavender, manzanita, coyote melon, desert larkspur, Mojave linanthus, and even smoke trees—which do not normally grow at this high elevation.

The easiest way up the ravine is not in the wash itself, where boul-ders are a major hindrance, but on the slightly more open slope on the south side. There is now a developing trail, never farther than about 100 feet from the wash. It starts at the foot of the low ridge of finer alluvia that frames the south of the ravine at its mouth. Misguided people had marked the trail with cairns and reflectors. If you are think-ing of putting up markers again, remember that others are resentful of signage in the wild, because it takes away their elemental pleasure of finding the way on their own. If you do not find the trail right away, you will likely run into it higher up, and once you have found it, it takes little effort to keep track of its whereabouts. Most of it is steep, gravelly, and slippery, meandering tightly between rocks. Even if you do not find it at all it is no big deal; the trail makes the ascent only marginally easier. The ravine climbs in two steep pitches separated by a short and more level stretch about a third of the way up. Joshua Mountain first emerges above the mountain's heads of boulders at the top of the first pitch, its sculpted cliffs slowly rotating and getting more ominous as you climb. Not far below it the ravine splits. The trail continues on the same side of the wash a little longer, then crosses the

Joshua Mountain		
	Dist.(mi)	Elev.(ft)
Utah Trail at Wellock Road	0.0	2,570
Foot of mountain	0.4	2,540
Across from fork in ravine	1.0	~3,260
Top of ravine	1.15	3,520
Foot of summit block	1.25	3,530
Joshua Mountain	1.35	3,682

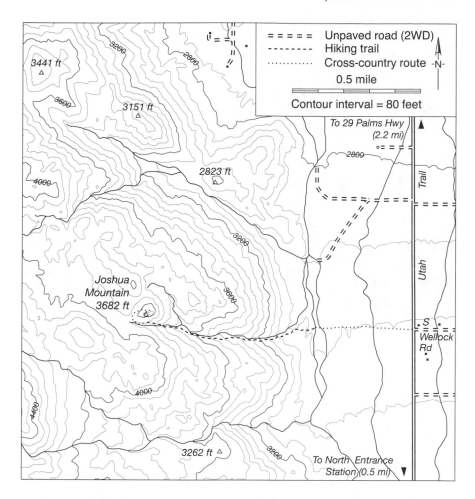

boulder-filled wash to the north side. It then stays on that side the short remaining distance to the top of the ravine.

One of the great pleasures of this climb is the rocks. All of Joshua Mountain is megaporphyritic monzonite, an unusual Mesozoic intrusive rock that contains huge feldspar crystals. Most of the boulders and exposures along the ravine are loaded with these eye-catching pink and white megacrysts, often perfect rectangles up to 4 inches in length. On flat surfaces they stand out sharply against the monzonite's darker groundmass, discordant tokens of order in the midst of chaos.

The head of the ravine is flush with the foot of the mountain block. Up ahead a long cirque of sand and creosote opens up, enclosed on the valley side by bouldery hills. From the head of the ravine it is a short stroll clockwise to the west side of the mountain block, where a long

Joshua Mountain's summit block from the fork in the ravine

ramp climbs steadily the 160 remaining feet to the summit. This last stretch is aerial, up bumpy, sloped slickrock overlooking the range's abrupt eastern flank. Just below and east of the summit there are two abrupt 5-foot steps in the slickrock. They can be avoided by going far enough south and winding around them, although it is very exposed.

The summit is a bald plug of exfoliating stone rising high above thin air. When the wind is blowing hard, it seems too small to safely stand. Bighorn sheep know of it. After a good rain, when the small tinaja etched into the summit is full of water, a ram will occasionally trot up here to take a sip, lay down, and fertilize the slickrock while contemplating the view. The summit does command an inspiring 180° panorama of Morongo Basin. The focus is Twentynine Palms, its compact grid of rectangular streets posed like a toy town on the edge of the basin's large reserve of undeveloped land. The proliferation of roads crossing the valley to single dwellings may inspire ruminations on whether there is still room to grow or still time to preserve. A consortium of government agencies and private organizations concluded the latter years ago, and have been saving this little jewel of a desert valley piece by piece ever since, before it turns into another desert city.

∎

HEXIE MOUNTAINS

The Hexie Mountains are the central piece in the jigsaw of mountain ranges that tile Joshua Tree National Park's high-desert plateau. Relatively compact, they are entirely contained in the park, sandwiched between the Pinto Mountains to the north and the Little San Bernardino Mountains and the Cottonwood Mountains to the south. It is a little bit of an odd range, slashed by faults that slip the wrong way, the home of Bingo Peak and Fried Liver Wash, of a mine once run by a clergyman who converted to gold, and of just one spring so tiny that it couldn't quench a desert rat's thirst. Most of it is a stark desolation of burnt-sienna ridges too low to hold a single juniper, occasionally heightened by eruptions of granitic shards the color of dried blood. Preserved in a designated wilderness, roadless for decades, it is a good place for solace and silence, away from the crowds that invade with clockwork regularity more charismatic areas.

The Hexie Mountains straddle two deserts—their body lies in the Mojave Desert while their eastern toes dip into the Sonoran Desert. When you climb down out of the mountains eastward, you slip from one desert into the other along an invisible boundary drawn by vegetation. The differences are subtle until you run into a plant so different that it surely has no business in the Mojave. It could be a palo verde, so fond of chlorophyll that its trunk and branches are green. Or perhaps a grove of smoke trees, a deceivingly attractive puff of turquoise cloud woven out of thorns that can skewer a small bird. There are others—the rare ironwood; the chuparosa in bloom, its thick mane of vermillion flowers screaming for hummingbirds' attention; or the ocotillo, a plumed seaweed plucked out of *Twenty Thousand Leagues Under the Sea*.

The geology of the Hexie Mountains is complex in its details but simple in its overview. Gneiss makes up 90% of the range, rocks occasionally similar to Pinto Gneiss, often beautifully migmatized—mixed with schists or much younger intrusive rocks. The rest is granitoids

461

from the Mesozoic, confined to the range's extreme eastern end, on both sides of Porcupine Wash's long estuary. Together with a fringe of White Tank Monzogranite along the northwestern front of the mountains, these eroded hills of pale granodiorite and quartz diorite, sometimes lightly metamorphosed, are easily the most scenic in this range.

Like all other ranges in the region, the Hexie Mountains were extensively eroded in the Tertiary and Quaternary. Two fault zones slice east-west across them, the Blue Cut Fault and the Porcupine Wash Fault south of it. A third one, the Smoke Tree Wash Fault, is slowly severing this range from the Cottonwood Mountains. Most faults in California, like the San Andreas, are right-lateral—if you stand on one side of the fault, the opposite side is displaced to the right. All three faults in the Hexie Mountains shift in the opposite direction. The mountains' three pieces have been sheared with respect to each other by one to two miles, each chunk to the *west* of its southern neighbor.

The Hexie Mountains had a dozen mines, most of them searching for gold above Pinto Basin, all marginal except for one hero. The Eldorado Mine, just inside a straight canyon along the Blue Cut Fault, had a choppy life, with at least six different lessees and owners, including the aforementioned clergyman, and work proceeded in fits and starts. But from its opening in 1901 until its final days in 1939 it was well developed. It did best in the years preceding the world wars—1911 to 1916 and 1936 to 1938. It recovered mostly gold, about 2,000 ounces—the size of a handball—but also lead, vanadium, molybdenum, and tungsten, strategic elements in high demand during wartime. Over time the Eldorado Mine had two mills, a cyaniding and amalgamation plant, and a camp that rose and fell with the fortunes of the business. When the 500-foot shaft played out in the early 1930s, the mill, a ten-stamp monster with an ambitious 1,000-ton capacity but no fresh ore to crunch, was put to work in other ways. For several years, it reprocessed the mine's old tailings, then it was used as a custom mill, treating the ore of neighboring mines like the Blue Bell and the Hexahedron. It was a match made in mining heaven, the mill and the mines providing each other business and extending each other's life span. In its lifetime the Eldorado Mine produced more than $100,000, a small fortune at the time.

■

MALAPAI HILL

Rising steeply 500 feet at the muted divide between Queen Valley and Pleasant Valley, Malapai Hill is an old stock of magma that intruded a mountain of granite but fell short of erupting as flowing lava. Climbing it is short and sweet—a peaceful stroll through an open desert garden, a brief vigorous climb, and you are there. The cooling magma formed intriguing columnar joints exposed among cliffs near the summit. The broad volcano overlooks the two spacious valleys and their alien plantations of Joshua trees and inselbergs.

General Information
Jurisdiction: Joshua Tree National Park
Road status: Roadless; graded access road (2WD)
The climb: 0.8 mi, 480 ft up, 40 ft down one way / easy–moderate
Main attractions: Volcanic hill, balanced boulder, columnar joints
USGS 7.5' topo map: Malapai Hill
Maps: pp. 465*, 397

Location and Access
From Park Boulevard in Joshua Tree National Park drive to the signed Geology Tour Road, which is 9.6 miles from the north entrance station, or 21.3 miles from the west entrance station. Drive south on the graded Geology Tour Road 4.65 miles to a steep sandy pullout on the west (right) side, across from a boulder pile to the west. Malapai Hill is the isolated mountain about half a mile west of the road—it is clearly visible along the last 3 miles. Park at the pullout. Standard-clearance vehicles routinely make it down this well-graded road.

Route Description
Malapai Hill is a peculiar mountain. Its dark twin domes seem to have been plopped down onto Queen Valley's bajada like two discarded scoops of partly melted chocolate ice cream. The hill is made of congealed magma that rose in at least two pulses of volcanism starting 16 million years ago when the crust was thinned by extensional tectonic forces, possibly related to the San Andreas Fault. The magma may have brought along with it the hydrothermal solutions that mineralized the rich deposits at the nearby Lost Horse Mine.

Being unusually symmetrical, Malapai Hill can be climbed via many routes of comparable difficulty. The most direct route is up the

Balanced boulder below Malapai Hill

saddle on the crest following a course north of the crease between the two humps, then along the gentle crest to either of the two summits. From the pullout on the Geology Tour Road it is a pleasant stroll southwest toward the base of the hill, skirting south of the boulder pile that stands half way there. The approach is inviting, across a peaceful desert garden on an open bajada of compacted coarse sand peppered with boulders. Every plant seems to have its place, as carefully positioned as in a manicured garden. Small Joshua trees, Mojave yucca, silver cholla, ephedra, manzanita, honey mesquite, and even tufts of grass, all grow a respectful distance from each other, unwilling to share too little rain with too many. The area is home to healthy diamond cholla, armed to the teeth with golden rosettes of two-inch spines. A local landmark not to miss is the impressive balanced boulder 150 yards south of the boulder pile's west end. About 16 feet tall and up to 20 feet across, shaped like a hot-air balloon, it stands on a base much narrower than its girth.

From the balanced boulder, the elevation drops a little to the wash that runs along the eastern base of Malapai Hill. Originally buried under White Tank Monzogranite, the hill's lower slopes were subsequently exhumed by erosion. A small field of white boulders was left behind up ahead. Just south of it, a long talus of darker basalt spills

Malapai Hill		
	Dist.(mi)	Elev.(ft)
Geology Tour Road	0.0	3,840
Balanced boulder	0.25	3,835
Wash at foot of eastern slope	0.4	3,810
Saddle at crest	0.7	4,000
Malapai Hill	0.8	~4,280

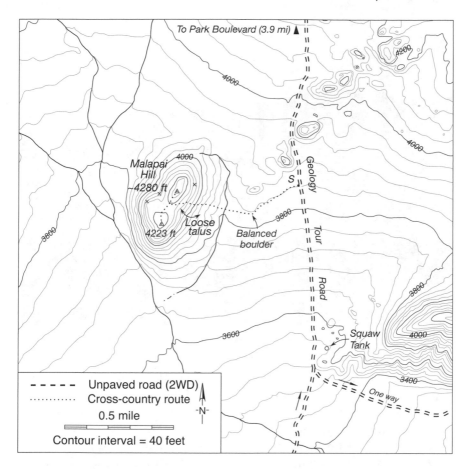

down the flank of Malapai Hill. The talus is free of vegetation and slightly more gradual, but it is made of loose rocks of precisely the wrong size, too small to step on and too large to ignore. The best route to the saddle starts below the boulder field. Cut a beeline up across it toward the saddle, then continue in the same direction, avoiding the talus by staying north of it. The hillside is an iconic wasteland of steel-grey basalt cobbles sun-baked to burnt sienna. The vegetation quickly thins down to a meager cover of tousled grasses, desiccated shrubs, and scrawny yucca. Even the calico cactus seem to have a hard time, although occasionally a red-spined cottontop cactus radiating with life illuminates the slope. For a diminutive mountain, Malapai Hill manages to put up a good fight shortly above the boulders, where the pitch steepens to a healthy 40%, but the crest is not far away.

When magma cools, especially in contact with groundwater, it contracts and fractures in hexagonal cracks that propagate through the

Malapai Hill (center) from the loop along the Geology Tour Road

solidifying rock and form tall stacks of parallel prismatic columns. There are many world-famous examples of imposing columnar joints, Wyoming's Devils Tower being one of the most striking in the U.S. Malapai Hills has columnar joints of its own, albeit on a small scale. The largest exposure is in the irregular cliffs west of the saddle. In a steep cleft below the rim, the wall is coated with inclined columns, a magical place like the inside of a giant geode. There is another outcrop, more accessible but more eroded, on the open slope northeast of the summit.

The views from the summit embrace two valleys of very different origin, cupped in a ring of desolate mountains. Pleasant Valley to the south is a structural basin formed by the sinking of two mountain blocks. Long ago, when the rains were generous, it held a small pluvial lake at the tip of the Hexie Mountains. Queen Valley to the north is the tilted pediment left behind by the erosion of a mountain. Whimsical boulder piles knife out of its bulging bajada. When the sun slips over the Little San Bernardino Mountains, every single boulder glows like amber, and for a few minutes the valley radiates a thousand points of light. Malapai Hill is close and easy enough that it gives us the luxury to attend a glorious sunset and return before full darkness.

■

LELA PEAK

Lela Peak is a nice little mountain that can be climbed via two very different routes, one a fairly quick ramble up a short rock-strewn canyon, the other a tougher scramble up through an exciting ravine clogged with boulders. It is a delightful stroll through a scenic cove to the foot of the range, the mountain has plenty of interesting cacti and rocks, and the summit commands tremendous views over Queen Valley and the southern Mojave Desert.

General Information
Jurisdiction: Joshua Tree National Park
Road status: Roadless; graded access road (2WD)
The climb (southern): 2.3 mi, 940 ft up, 60 ft down one way / easy
The climb (northern): 2.5 mi, 900 ft up, 20 ft down one way / moderate
Main attractions: Views of Queen Valley's boulder piles, bouldering
USGS 7.5' topo map: Malapai Hill
Maps: pp. 469*, 397

Location and Access
Lela Peak is the highest summit in the western Hexie Mountains, overlooking both Queen Valley and Pleasant Valley. The starting point for this climb is the same as for Malapai Hill. Lela Peak is about 2 air miles due east, hidden by the false summit capped with dark rocks at the east end of the pronounced cove in the mountain.

Route Description
The only difficulty in this climb—difficulty being a big word—is circumventing the false summit (~4,525 ft) to get to its east side. This can be done either on its south side or on its north side. Both routes share a common start, across the open cove east of the road. Aim west-southwest, towards the green valley on the false summit's south side. About a mile deep by a mile wide, the cove is a scenic bajada enclosed to the south by a rising ridge of pale granitic lumps, and to the north by a crest of pointed inselbergs. The vegetation is typical Joshua Tree fare, a green garden of creosote, manzanita, and desert almond spiked with silver and diamond chollas, Mojave yucca, and small Joshua trees. From late February to May the hard-packed gravel is bedecked with a congregation of wildflowers covering the alphabet, from aster to desert gold poppies, globemallow, nama, and wooly daisies.

467

After 0.9 mile you will cross a wash coming down from the north-east. This is where the two routes diverge. For the easier route, continue in the same direction (west-southwest), past a thin obelisk—the only shade since the road—up the boulder-strewn wash that scoots around the southern flank of the false summit. The wash soon splits. Take the left fork, a stony drainage on the cusp between a large ravine and a small canyon. Its wash, cluttered with rocks, can be bypassed close by on the tilted north side, where a use trail is starting to emerge. This area is striking when the cacti are blooming, especially the calico cactus and their fluorescent purplish-magenta flowers. At its upper end the canyon opens out to a small playa in full view of Lela Peak. The area up ahead is a billowing plateau, sparsely vegetated, with ground as smooth as sifted gravel. The rest is straightforward, first across the plateau to the foot of the peak, then up to the saddle southwest of it, and finally northeast along the open ridge to the summit.

Thanks to its central position and relatively high elevation, Lela Peak commands fine views of the park in every direction. The unusual viewing angles mystify the landscape and obscure familiar features, but all of the local mountains are showcased, in a complex kaleidoscope of colors and shapes. The most striking element in this vast panorama is the many pyramids of boulders that dot Queen Valley to the west, as mysterious as a township of ancient Maya temples.

For the second route, at the wash 0.9 mile from the start angle left (northeast) along its open strip of sand. Over the next 0.4 mile the

	Dist.(mi)	Elev.(ft)
Lela Peak		
Southern route		
Geology Tour Road	0.0	3,840
Wash crossing	0.9	3,835
Flat at head of south-side cyn	1.5	4,340
Saddle	1.9	~4,580
Lela Peak	2.3	4,723
Northern route		
Geology Tour Road	0.0	3,840
Wash crossing	0.9	3,835
Start of boulder jam bypass	1.45	3,955
Top of boulder jam	1.65	~4,200
Leave wash (NW shoulder)	2.15	~4,430
Lela Peak	2.5	4,723

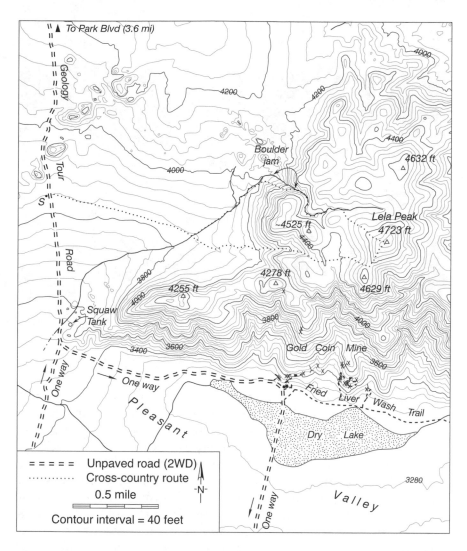

To Park Blvd (3.6 mi)

Geology

Tour

S

Road

One way

Squaw
Tank

Boulder
jam

4632 ft

Lela Peak
4723 ft

4525 ft

4278 ft

4255 ft

4629 ft

Gold Coin Mine

One way

Pleasant

Fried Liver Wash Trail

Dry Lake

Valley

4000
4200
4400
4000
4600
3800
4000
3400
3600
3800
4000
3690
3280

===== Unpaved road (2WD)
············ Cross-country route
0.5 mile
-N-
Contour interval = 40 feet

wash forks twice; take the right fork each time. Near the mountain,
shallow banks rise steeply on both sides. The wash then makes a sharp
90° right bend around a huge boulder, and soon after disappears into a
steep ravine choked under a monumental jumble of giant boulders.
Slithering, crawling, and clawing up this column of smooth rounded
rocks is the most fun on this climb, even though every boulder seems
to have a wish to fall. One of them did, near the top of the jam, a bolt
of granite that came to rest to fashion a delicate window. If this looks
too daunting, leave the wash at the bottom, 50 yards before the sharp
right bend (see map), when you are abreast with a tall conical boulder

Queen Valley's boulder pyramids from boulder jam on north route to Lela Peak

smeared with a patch of chalk on the west bench. Exit the wash and climb the steep, relatively open slope east-southeast, aiming for the canyon at the top of the boulder jam, where it gives way to darker rocks above. There are several ways to enter the canyon in this vicinity.

From there on up the canyon is less steep and still has boulders for about 250 yards, but they are angular, easier to negotiate (Class 2 at most), and they progressively thin down. This canyon is greener than the rest of the mountain, its boulders capturing moisture that attracts catclaw, ephedra, wishbone bush, and manzanita the size of small trees. At the fork, keep left. About half a mile past the boulder jam, leave the wash on the right, and follow Lela Peak's northwestern shoulder up to the summit.

Returning down the jam's pillowy boulders is Lela Peak's greatest offering. The views over Queen Valley's pyramids are even more spectacular than from the summit. In the golden hours of evening, every boulder is sharply highlighted against its own shadow. Down in the cove, the backlit cholla glow in golden fluorescent light. In April, when the paperbag bush are blooming, their countless translucent pods capture the setting sun's rays and light up like Christmas bulbs.

■

MONUMENT MOUNTAIN

Located at the edge of the Sonoran Desert, this remote summit commands far-reaching views into two different deserts, long empty bajadas on one side, and saw-toothed mountains on the other. The incline is modest, up a long series of steps capped with boulders and low outcrops. The area is replete with igneous and metamorphic rocks of all kinds, and host to an interesting combination of plants brought together by the convergence of two worlds.

General Information
Jurisdiction: Joshua Tree National Park
Road status: Roadless; primitive access road (HC)
The climb: 2.9 mi, 1,720 ft up, 130 ft down one way / moderate
Main attractions: Isolated summit overlooking two deserts
USGS 7.5' topo map: Washington Wash
Maps: pp. 473*, 397

Location and Access
The highest point in the Hexie Mountains, Monument Mountain dominates the southeastern tip of the range, its distant pointed summit girdled by a broad shield of sinuous ridges. If it weren't for the primitive road in Smoke Tree Wash, the wide east-west drainage south of the summit that divides the Hexie Mountains from the Cottonwood Mountains, it would be a long hike to it. To get to this road, take Interstate 10 to the Cottonwood Spring Road Exit. This is prime undeveloped country, some 22 miles east of the last busy exit back in Indio, and further still from the next busy exit in Blythe, near the Arizona border. Follow the Cottonwood Spring Road north, up through Cottonwood Canyon along the boundary between the Cottonwood Mountains to the west and the Eagle Mountains to the east. In early spring the lower desert is brilliant with palo verde and ocotillos in bloom. After 6.8 miles you will reach the Cottonwood Visitor Center—the last chance to fill up on water. Just before it, a good graded road on the left side heads north. Follow it 1 mile to a locked gate. The dirt road on the left at the gate is the Pinkham Canyon Road. It curls slowly west by northwest around the Cottonwood Mountains, then skims the edge of Smoke Tree Wash. It is a slow road, hemmed in by healthy creosote, slashed by countless erosion channels that turn the ride into a choppy flight. Even with high clearance it is hard not to scratch bottom

at the deepest trenches. Park after 4.2 miles at a two-car turnout on the left, across from metal stakes lining the road. Monument Mountain is a little west of north, hidden by its own massive foothills.

Route Description

At the road you are in the Sonoran Desert. Monument Mountain, less than 3 air miles away, is in the Mojave Desert. As you cross Smoke Tree Wash north from the road toward the mountain you slip from one desert into the other. This stretch of Smoke Tree Wash has no smoke tree, a denizen of the Sonoran Desert, although there are plenty a few miles downhill. It supports instead a scatter of bright-green desert willow that subsist on the moisture buried beneath its sand. On the north side of the wash, where the plain swells into foothills, you are standing at the edge of the Sonoran Desert. As in celebration of this invisible division, one ultimate grove of ocotillo graces the hillside, their long skinny arms tipped with bright vermillion flames in the spring.

Plated with large rocks, dark and bulky, Monument Mountain looks a little tough from a distance. The ascent follows the ridge that climbs behind the ocotillo grove, which is the mountain's south shoulder. It is a long series of steps capped with rocky outcrops. Somehow there is always a convenient way around the obstacles. The first section is the steepest. It crosses the first two local summits, best bypassed on the west side along sloped causeways of monzonite. These paler exposures are generally relatively clear of large rocks and easier to navigate than the darker outcrops. Above the second summit the main ridge is gained across more open ground. It offers the first views into the desolate northeastern section of the park. The next false summit is very rocky and rougher, but there are a few good routes to circumvent it on the east side. The rest is generally easier, over broader and gentler ridges that offer plenty of options to avoid the hard-rock caps.

This mountain is not spectacular in the classical sense. It is dry, hot, and remote. At midday in the summer the only solid shade is the spiky shadows of Mojave yucca. Shrubs grow a respectable distance from each other. Even in the spring there is no tufts of grass, only diminutive specimens of annuals that bloom for a few weeks and die. We still climb it to satisfy our hunger for unexpected discoveries, because it is wild, secret, and immersed in a hundred square miles of no man's land. There is indeed plenty to enjoy on this unrevered mountain. The igneous rocks are beautiful. Their composition changes from one extreme to the next in just a few steps. There are twisted gneiss, sparkling schists, bright monzonite, and diorite as dark as coal. The flower show is minimalist but delightfully eclectic. At different

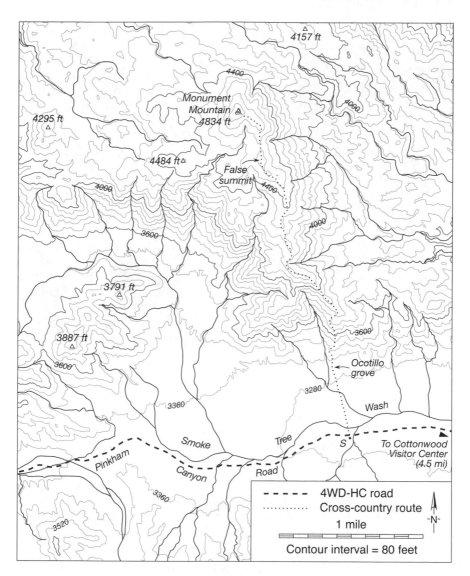

Monument Mountain

	Dist.(mi)	Elev.(ft)
Smoke Tree Wash Road	0.0	3,250
Foot of mountain	0.5	3,320
Main ridge	1.0	3,930
False summit	2.6	~4,600
Monument Mountain	2.9	4,834

Looking up Monument Mountain from the lower reaches of its south shoulder

times chia, lupine, and phacelia cover the purple spectrum; evening primrose, brittlebush, and desert gold poppies supply the complementary yellows; beavertail and calico cactus dazzle with shocking reds; windmills, wishbone bush, and cushion foxtail cactus fill the gap with cotton-candy pinks.

The views are good from the moment you step on the mountain. The ridge provides fine vistas of the Eagle and Cottonwood mountains at first, then of the Hexie Mountains in one direction and the mysterious Coxcomb Mountains in the other. The summit illustrates the sharp contrast between the two provinces it straddles. From the west clockwise to the northeast the Mojave Desert is rippling with rugged crests, from the imposing alignment of the Little San Bernardino Mountains to the Providence Mountains. From the east to the south the Sonoran Desert is far more open, a land of lower mountains, immense bajadas, and shimmering seas of dark-green creosote. On a clear winter day, it may let you peer clear across to the Algodones Dunes, past the dark hump of the Chocolate Mountains. You might even catch a glimpse of Mexico. One desert tells a story of thrusting, upheaval, and creation; the other epitomizes the ravages of endless erosion.

■

PINTO MOUNTAINS

Bookended by the Wonderland of Rocks to the west and the Coxcomb Mountains to the east, the Pinto Mountains are the antithesis of the desert range. They are not a single massif but an agglomerate of multiple loosely connected groups of hills strewn over 800 square miles. Uplifted along the Blue Cut Fault along their southern boundary, they tend to drop more abruptly into Pinto Basin to the south, and more gently into Dale Lake's shallow basin to the north. This fragmentation is mirrored in a surfeit of named summits—fourteen all told—with modest elevations ranging from 2,898 feet to 4,613 feet, although some peaks rise from fairly low valleys and have a good prominence.

The Pinto Mountains are a collage of colorful Mesozoic igneous rocks and Proterozoic metamorphic rocks. Medium-gray biotite quartz monzonite dominates in the north central and eastern range. The western quarter is a mosaic of granite, diorite, gneiss, and more quartz monzonite. Pinto Mountain, the hills directly northwest of it, and the hills east of Ivanhoe Peak, contain a colorful, locally famous formation formerly known as Pinto Gneiss. Widespread in the Transverse Ranges, it is the remnant of a county-size metamorphic complex between 1.65 and 1.70 billion years old shattered by tectonic movements in the Mesozoic. Several sub-units crop out in this range, including the Joshua Tree augen gneiss and suites of quartzite, schist, and granofels. Joshua Tree augen gneiss is one of the region's most attractive rocks, often covered with fine wavy or swirled striations, black and either white, pink, or bluish. Ironically, it is the colorfulness of this then-unnamed gneiss that inspired the name of these mountains long ago, and the name of the mountains that later inspired the name Pinto Gneiss. The only sizable exposure of volcanic rocks is Ivanhoe Peak—it is made of the fine-grained felsite that held most of the Pinto Mountains' gold.

The Pinto Mountains had two mining districts. The Gold Park District, around Music Valley south of Twentynine Palms Mountain, had mostly humbugs, as the name of a nearby mountain suggests. But in the Dale District east of it, several operations brought in decent to exceptional returns. The main properties were the Supply, Nightingale, O.K., Gold Crown, Brooklyn, Virginia Dale, and Carlyle mines. They all worked inclined shafts with a web of drifts, raises, and winzes, and they all had at least one mill. They pulled out mostly free gold, but also silver, lead, iron, copper, and manganese. Although no mine operated continuously, between the late 1880s and 1942 the district was hardly ever idle, and it harvested a fortune—at least 2.1 million dollars. Over time it had three small towns, all named Dale. In the mid-1880s Dale was located at a well on the edge of Dale Lake, at the north end of today's Gold Crown Road off Highway 62. It had a pump house and water tank, cabins and tents, a burro-powered arrastre, and a sizable population working gold placers. Around 1896, when lode mining picked up at the Virginia Dale Mine, the population center moved 4.5 miles to a new location below the mine. A few years later, it moved 3 more miles to near the rich Supply Mine. New Dale boasted several buildings, a post office, a restaurant, and a saloon that served as a hotel. A 100-ton mill and a cyaniding plant were added in the 1910s when the mine was most productive. The district underwent a revival during the Great Depression, then faded during the second world war.

Most of these mines were located in "the bite," the rectangular section in the northern Pinto Mountains that was excluded from the national monument when it was created in 1936. This area is under BLM jurisdiction. The rest of the range—about a third—is in Joshua Tree National Park. The southern part of the bite, contiguous to the park, is preserved in the 24,348-acre Pinto Mountains Wilderness.

This dichotomy rooted in mining and preservation history has created an oddly two-faced range. The north side is lacerated by miles of old mining roads, and illegal bypasses, shortcuts, and extensions are added every year. The south side abounds in the opposite direction: all roads were closed decades ago. Each side attracts a different subspecies of *homo sapiens*. The bite is popular with weekend warriors dressed in camouflage mail-ordered from on-line army-surplus stores, ATV riders hiding behind Darth Vader dust masks, and caravans of four-wheelers hell-bent on finding one more secret mining camp. On the south side you are likely to run into no one at all, or perhaps a lone athletic übermensch powering through his lifelong quest for the little-known, wielding GPS and trekking poles, fueled by a diet of electrolyte water and organic sugar-free granola bars. The Pinto Mountains give us a chance to try both of these immiscible worlds.

■

TWENTYNINE PALMS MOUNTAIN

The second highest summit in the Pinto Mountains, Twentynine Palms Mountain is a prominent thumb-shaped sub-range that overlooks Morongo Basin to the north. This climb is mostly along a road that switchbacks up the mountain's abrupt base, followed by an easy cross-country stretch. Twentynine Palms Mountain stands out for its interesting plant ecology, uncommon ancient schists, ferocious wind, and expansive views of the southern Mojave Desert.

General Information
Jurisdiction: Public lands (BLM)
Road status: Climbing on road and cross-country; 4WD-HC access road
The climb: 2.4 mi, 1,560 ft up, 180 ft down one way/moderate
Main attractions: View of Pinto Mountains and southern Mojave Desert
USGS 7.5' topo maps: Queen Mountain, Twentynine Palms Mountain*
Maps: pp. 479*, 397

Location and Access
On Highway 62 in Twentynine Palms, about a mile east of the town center, turn south on Utah Trail, signed as the north entrance to Joshua Tree National Park. Follow it 1.6 miles to Morning Drive, on the left. Coming from the park, this street corner is 2.5 miles south of the north entrance station. Turn east on Morning Drive and go 0.7 mile to the corner of Bedouin Avenue. Twentynine Palms Mountain is the long ridge rising to the southeast.

At this corner, take the primitive road on the right (south-south-east), which is the Gold Park Road (periodically signed JT 1901). After 1.8 miles, ignoring several side roads used by the locals to reach shooting ranges, JT 1901B splits off on the right. Keep left on JT 1901. After 2 miles the road enters a shallow canyon. At mile 3.0 there is a bedrock exposure that takes practice and high clearance to drive over. At mile 3.6 the road forks. Take the left fork, which climbs a little, then splits after 200 feet. This junction is easy to miss. Take the rockier road that climbs on the left (signed JT 1906). Follow it east across a low broad saddle 1.3 miles to Dog Wash. Turn right up the wash on JT 1909, paralleling Twentynine Palms Mountain to the east. After 1.25 miles (6.25 miles from pavement) an unsigned fork on the left climbs to a radio installation on the mountain's crest about 1.5 miles north of the summit. Drive it 0.45 mile up to the first switchback and park (there is nowhere to park without blocking access between here and a locked gate 0.1 mile further). The Gold Park Road is sandy, and the cutoff to Dog Wash (JT 1906) is rocky and has a few steep grades. It would be heroic to make it without high clearance and four-wheel drive.

Route Description

At 4,562 feet, Twentynine Palms Mountain is not a giant by desert-climbing standards, but most of the climb is along a rough road that makes up for it a little. To negotiate the steep, fault-bound lower flank of the mountain, sharp switchbacks were cut into it, abrupt and rocky enough to defeat a Hummer. After a 0.7-mile ascent the switchbacks end on a ridge that parallels the main crest. Twentynine Palms Mountain becomes visible to the east around this point, the highest of a string of broad open hills sprinkled with low boulders. The summit is separated from the ridge by two steep-walled canyons, making a direct east route difficult. The road offers much easier access, as it climbs north-northeast along the relatively moderate ridge another mile to a pass, circumventing the canyons in the process.

The rest of the route is cross country. The crest can be gained by heading due east from the pass, then followed to the top. A quicker and easier alternative is to stay below the false summits on their west flanks, aiming generally southeast and climbing just enough to skirt below their rockier crowns. On the south side of the 4,442-foot summit Twentynine Palms Mountain comes into view again. It is then a short descent to the shallow wash at the northern foot of Twentynine Palms Mountain, and from there a short 200-foot climb to the summit.

Twentynine Palms Mountain has classic desert geography, in subtle ways different from most. It is part of the region's Precambrian igneous and metamorphic complex, mostly granites but also uncommon schists, their cleaved planes sparkling with gold, silver, or charcoal crystals. In all directions the hills are bare, much more rocks than plants, horizontal outcrops defined by ancient metamorphism poking through them like ribs. The plant diversity does not increase with elevation as it usually does at these mid-elevations, but *decreases*. The washes and lower slopes are covered with yucca, silver and diamond cholla, creosote, saltbush, Mormon tea, wishbone bush, and many other plants. Higher up the selection shrinks to a skeletal creosote-burrobush community peppered with rogue cactus—calico, beavertail, and pincushion. The final slope is mostly a monoculture of dwarf blackbrush growing on scratchy lawns of dry bunch grass, the vermillion heads of scattered barrel cactus the only bright notes. The wind is partly responsible for this inverted botany. When I was there it was

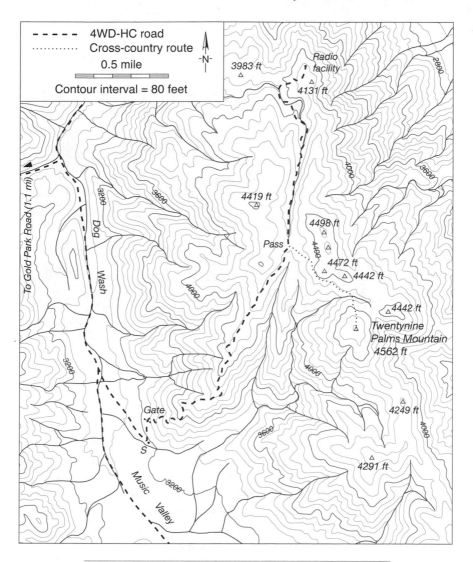

Twentynine Palms Mountain

	Dist.(mi)	Elev.(ft)
Telecom road (1st switchback)	0.0	3,180
Main ridge	0.7	3,840
Pass	1.7	4,250
Bypass false summit	~2.0	~4,380
Wash crossing	2.2	4,280
Twentynine Palms Mountain	2.4	4,562

Pinto Mountains from the summit of Twentynine Palms Mountain

howling up from Music Valley, triggering melodic resonances that justified its name. It was strong enough to challenge my balance and redirect my steps. During most of the day for seven months a year, only a few road cuts and low outcrops in the hills offer slivers of shade. You wished the mountain was a little true to its name and held—forget the other 28—at least one cool shady palm as a relief from the inferno.

The summit is a nice symmetric dome that rolls off in all cardinal directions to aprons of low angular boulders and sweeping views of the southern Mojave Desert. In the early morning the centerpiece is the long chain of the Little San Bernardino and Eagle mountains wrapping around nearly half of the horizon. In the late afternoon the show is stolen by the Pinto Mountains stretching out many miles eastward. There is perhaps no better place to appreciate the extent and sere beauty of this fragmented range. Its northern shores spill out in long parallel ridges into Morongo Basin and the sand-encrusted sink of Dale Lake, brilliant against the Sheep Hole Mountains. The access road, the radio antenna, and all but a wedge of Twentynine Palms are hidden by the mountain, so that in spite of its proximity to civilization this mountaintop gives a gratifying sense of remoteness.

■

PINTO MOUNTAIN

Though not the highest named peak in this range, Pinto Mountain is impressive for its sheer mass and prominence. Its longer approach and a couple of Class-2 scrambles make it also one of the most difficult of the popular climbs in Joshua Tree National Park. The summit provides sweeping views from half a mile up of the corrugated southern fringe of the range, of vast Pinto Basin, and of the entire eastern portion of the park.

General Information
Jurisdiction: Joshua Tree National Park
Road status: Roadless; paved access road
The climb: 4.5 mi, 2,430 ft up, 240 ft down one way / difficult
Main attractions: Dunes, hard scrambles, views of eastern Joshua Tree
USGS 7.5' topo map: Pinto Mountain
Maps: pp. 483*, 397

Location and Access
East from the approximate center of the park, the Hexie and Pinto mountains part and give way to Pinto Basin, a vast valley that occupies a good portion of the park's eastern section. The basin was eroded out of fractured rock along the Blue Cut Fault, the east-west fault line that slices across much of the region. Pinto Mountain is near the south end of the central Pinto Mountains, overlooking Pinto Basin. Coming from the north in the park, work your way on Park Boulevard to the signed Pinto Wye junction. Turn south on the Pinto Basin Road and follow it down through Wilson Canyon 16.1 miles to the parking at the Turkey Flat backcountry board, near Pinto Basin's west end. Coming from the Cottonwood Visitor Center near the south end of the park, this is 13.7 miles, northeast then northwest. All these roads are paved.

Route Description
From Turkey Flat a conical peak rises 4 air miles to the northeast, looming over Pinto Basin's luminous emptiness. This is not Pinto Mountain but its eastern satellite; the true summit is just left of it, hidden by its own mass. A popular route to it is up the eastern ridge of the obvious canyon directly below the eastern satellite. From Turkey Flat it is an easy 2.5-mile walk across Pinto Basin to the mouth of the canyon. The ground is mostly hard-packed, level, silty sand. In the

481

1920s a misguided farmer attempted raising turkey in this overheated and shadeless wilderness. The turkeys were likely dead well before Thanksgiving, but the name stuck. Better equipped animals find Turkey Flat perfectly fine, thank you. We saw lizards, hawks, vultures, and sidewinder tracks. Kangaroo rats are so numerous that we had to constantly circle around their burrows to avoid sinking into them.

One mile in, the route intersects the Pinto Basin Dunes, a singular plural limited to a single, mile-long whaleback dune. It exists thanks to the dark hill just east of it, a piece of bedrock pushed up along the Blue Cut Fault. Only 100 feet high, the hill disturbs the wind just enough to force it to dump its load of sand. The dune is well vegetated with creosote, burrobush, and bunch grass. Following a wet winter it is inundated with wildflowers, many seemingly too extravagant for the frugal desert—the delicate desert lily, attractive birdcage evening primrose, and profuse pink spreads of sand verbena. The wide-open drainage of Pinto Wash just north of the dune is a fierce wind tunnel. When in action it blots out the scenery behind a shroud of high-velocity particles, and every shrub shakes erratically, as if it were possessed.

Pinto Mountain is girdled with high buttressed escarpments that lift straight up from the basin, as if to guard the mountain against the savage winds. The least painful way up is the canyon's east ridge. It starts with a bang, ascending 940 feet over 0.8 mile. Its narrow spine is crowded with darkly varnished daggers of Mesozoic granitic rocks and large colonies of reddish barrel cactus. Small broken rocks litter the slopes. They rest just below the angle of repose and slip underfoot at the slightest provocation. Parts of this ascent border on Class 2—hands help at places, and trekking poles on the way down.

At its summit this first ridge merges with a broader ridge that comes in from the southeast and soon angles north. Along the next half a mile it crosses more gentle, closely spaced low hills. A potpourri of metamorphic rocks from the Mesoproterozoic—hornfels, marble,

Pinto Mountain		
	Dist.(mi)	Elev.(ft)
Pinto Basin Road	0.0	1,790
Top of Pinto Basin Dunes	1.0	1,780
Base of Pinto Mountain	2.5	1,800
Main ridge	3.3	~2,740
Start of steepest section	3.9	~2,960
Pinto Mountain	4.5	3,983

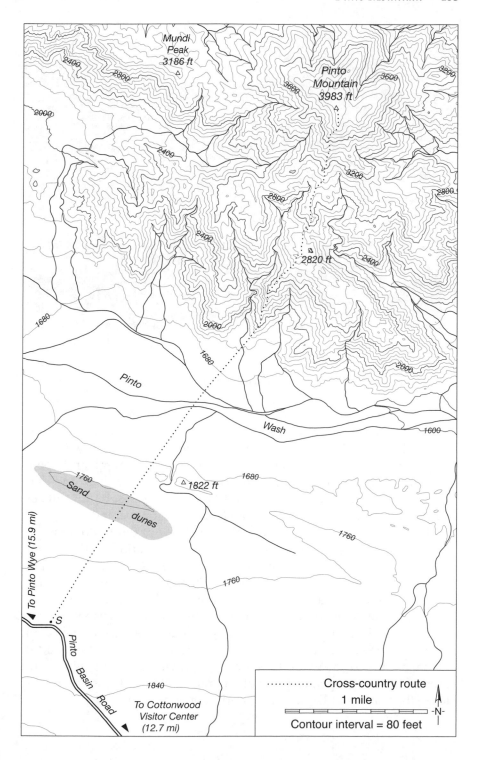

Pinto Mountain in a spring storm, from the middle of Turkey Flat

schists, and quartzite—this uncommonly variegated area may well have inspired Pinto Mountain's name. You meander from hill to hollow across narrow tracts of land delineated by sharp boundaries, a random patchwork of rust, green, blue-gray, and pure white. A primitive trail wiggles up through this contrasted landscape toward the steep hump of Pinto Mountain. The terrain is easier, smooth and open, sparsely covered with creosote and brittlebush, barrel cactus, and diamond cholla. You have just crossed into the Mojave Desert, but tufts of ocotillos linger, tokens of the Sonoran Desert you left behind.

The final pitch, up the south-southwest brow of Pinto Mountain to the summit plateau, is the most arduous. The elevation gain is about the same as the lower pitch, but in less than half the distance. Much of it is a battlefield of small boulders, and the cluster of angular crags about half way up is a good Class-2 scramble. The trail pushes on up through this area, but here too there is nothing solid underfoot. This is an aerial climb, with Pinto Basin filling 180 degrees of the viewshed 2,000 feet below. This last stretch and the broad summit just beyond it encompass the park's wildest geomorphic province, a striking juxtaposition of this wide-open creosote plain and the stolid ranges that encircle it—the Coxcomb, Eagle, Hexie, and Pinto mountains.

■

SHEEP HOLE MOUNTAINS

The Sheep Hole Mountains are a relatively small but very rugged range located just north of the eastern section of Joshua Tree National Park. Northwest-trending like the majority of desert ranges, they are only about 16 air miles long by a little over 3 miles at their widest, yet their prominence exceeds 2,200 feet. When you are in Twentynine Palms just north of the park and look east, you will see them rising like a massive dorsal 20 miles away across the wide-open floor of Morongo Basin. On their far side is remote Cadiz Valley. In spite of their modest size, together with the Wonderland of Rocks in the park they are the southern Mojave Desert's most extraordinary range. The main, northern reach is a gigantic swell of almost nothing but bare granitic rocks carved and polished into spectacular labyrinths of boulder piles and sculpted bedrock. From there southeastward, much of the slender crest is a steep-sided spine crowded with jagged crags and peaks that rise abruptly from sandy bajadas. The combination of steepness and rocky terrain has earned the Sheep Hole Mountains a solid stature in the peak-climbing community. You come here for the pleasure of fighting gravity on hard, convoluted surfaces that demand more stamina, tenacity, strength, and route-finding skills than most desert ranges.

The Sheep Hole Mountains were uplifted as a result of activity in Quaternary time along the Sheep Hole Fault, which follows the western base of the range, and possibly also along the Dry Lakes Fault, along its southeastern base. The mountains' western flank is almost all Jurassic in age, a combination of quartz monzonite, granite, and gneiss. The northern area and the eastern flank are mostly Late Cretaceous granodiorite and granite. The 70-million-year-old pale-gray granodiorite that make up the beautifully jumbled northern head of the range is known as the Sheep Hole Mountains pluton. The finely layered rocks south of the highest summit are Metasedimentary Gneiss of Sheep Hole Mountains, the metamorphosed sedimentary beds that once covered this area extensively. Many rock units are porphyritic:

they are stuffed with large crystals of quartz and feldspar, in certain areas up to four inches long, and occasionally banded with silvery waves of muscovite. The long plutonic ranges that frame Morongo Basin have been a source of considerable volumes of sand that have accumulated over some 20 square miles of valley floor along the Sheep Hole Mountains' southwestern base. There is not enough relief for major dunes to form. But there is enough of it to bury the mountains' foothills under graceful swales of sand.

The Sheep Hole Mountains belong to a small minority of ranges that are largely deprived of valuable metals and minerals, and were practically never mined. Not a single road ever crossed them. The entire range is now protected within the Sheephole Valley Wilderness, itself part of Mojave Trails National Monument. At 188,169 acres, it is the third largest designated wilderness in the California desert. When climbing in this range, you will not be rubbing shoulders with anyone else.

The Sheep Hole Mountains are remarkably barren. They have no springs, scant vegetation, no conifers, not even a Joshua tree. Even in this parched and denuded landscape, many denizens emblematic of the Mojave Desert find ways to subsist—hare, desert tortoise, coyote, a healthy lot of rodents, and lizards and snakes to keep them in check. A small band of bighorn sheep is also perfectly at home on these rough wrinkles of land. The sheep wear the colors of the Mesozoic stones, fawn and pale gray. They blend in so well that you are more likely to hear a clatter of hooves than see them.

The north and south ends of the range are easily accessible from paved roads (Amboy Road and Highway 62). The central area is more difficult to reach, being generally 2 to 4 miles from a road (the Ironage Road along the east side of Dale Lake). The carved crest offers a plethora of peaks to climb. Only two have been officially named, the high point Sheep Hole Mountain (4,613') and Sheep Peak (3,876'), both in the northern half. An inspired climber once traversed the entire crest and unofficially named several prominent summits. In keeping with the range's name, except for North Sheep Peak he used the body parts of a sheep—Loin, Hoof, Pastern, Dock, Cannon, Fetlock, Eye, Stifle, and Toe. From the range's northern tip down 70% of its length, the ridges and slopes are blanketed with hard lumps of jointed blocks. Almost anywhere in this area, you have to fight to move. Only near the southern tip of the mountains, where they have buried themselves up to their shoulders in indolent sand, will you find some reprieve from the endless barrage of standing rocks.

■

SHEEP HOLE MOUNTAIN

This is one of the two or three most strenuous scrambles suggested in this book. From the foot of the mountain the route crosses almost entirely bare granite, first up a sheer ravine clogged with humvee-size boulders, then on a crest overrun by massive outcrops. This is a rare opportunity to indulge in bouldering not just for the fun of it, but also as a means of getting through some of the most awe-inspiring galleries of sculpted stone in the Mojave Desert.

General Information
Jurisdiction: Mojave Trails National Monument (BLM)
Road status: Climbing on old road and cross country; 2WD access road
The climb: 2.2 mi, 2,300 ft up, 120 ft down one way / strenuous
Main attractions: Class-2 and -3 climb on a steep bare-granite mountain
USGS 7.5' topo map: Dale Lake
Maps: pp. 489*, 397

Location and Access
Sheep Hole Mountain is near the northwestern end of the range. Being located near a paved road at the edge of the wilderness, the trailhead is easily accessible. Coming from Twentynine Palms, at the intersection of Highway 62 and Utah Trail (the park's north entrance), drive north on Utah Trail 2 miles to the signed Amboy Road. Turn right on Amboy Road and go 22.3 miles, east then north through Wonder Valley, to Sheep Hole Pass, marked by two radio towers. At the pass, turn right on a good dirt road and go 0.15 mile to the towers. The gas-pipeline road that runs north-south just before the towers marks the approximate western boundary of the Sheephole Valley Wilderness and a private property. Park near the towers and walk from there.

To reach this spot from the north, take Interstate 40 to Ludlow. From the south side of the freeway, drive Route 66 east 28.3 miles to the signed Amboy Road, which is 0.3 mile west of the railroad crossing on the west end of the small community of Amboy. Drive the Amboy Road south 23.5 miles to the side road to the radio towers on the left.

Route Description
From the radio towers, walk the road that heads east across a bajada toward the Sheep Hole Mountains. After 0.2 mile it merges with a road coming in from the right, at the edge of a wide sandy canyon

sunk 50 feet below the bajada. This area gives a good perspective, in both senses of the term, of what is coming up. Half a mile up ahead, the canyon turns into a tight ravine that shoots straight up the mountain to a stately portal of twin peaks—as dubious as it may seem, this precipitous, boulder-choked erosional trench is one of the least difficult routes to Sheep Hole Mountain. The road ends in 0.35 mile at the foot of a low rocky hill. Cross it over the 30-foot saddle in the middle of it, or walk back 250 feet to a fainter road on the right (north) and follow this road as it circles clockwise around the hill. On the far side of the hill, continue up along the canyon's edge 0.3 mile until the rim peters out, then descend over a few boulders into the ravine.

The next part of the climb is punishing. From this point of entry to its upper end near the crest, the ravine is a tidal wave of boulders 1,310 feet high and only 0.6 horizontal mile long. There is very little in the way of a smooth wash, just a sublime chaos of boulders and steep bedrock. Unlike in most bouldery canyons, the average boulder size is enormous—many exceed 10 feet across. You often have to use all limbs for balance on tall boulders, traction on inclined slabs, stemming between vertical surfaces, or mantling over high shelves. When arms get too short, you leap. When there is no way over a boulder, you try under. The saving grace is that the rock is all highly cohesive granodiorite of the Sheep Hole Mountains pluton. It is commonly packed with quartz and feldspar crystals as large as silver dollars, which helps friction. Near its upper end, the ravine squeezes through glistening walls of this pretty stone. Plants are also thankfully scarce. Other than an occasional catclaw, the larger species are mostly harmless creosote, desert lavender, and nolina higher up.

At the top of the ravine, you emerge into another world. The terrain opens up, the slope eases up, and the relentless litany of boulders mercifully eases up. The topography guides you naturally up along a sandy terrace that heads southeast, parallel to and roughly 100 feet below the crest. The terrace climbs across two low ridges and down into the shallow heads of two drainages. After a third of a mile it reaches a saddle on the crest offering the first peek into Cadiz Valley.

From that point forward, the boulders return with a vengeance. The crest area is pure Sheep Hole Mountains fare, acres upon acres of slanting blocks and rock piles too tightly packed to walk. The next rise can be climbed either on its spine or circumvented along the rising base of tall cliffs on the east flank (the route shown on the map). Both approaches end at a pass in full view of the summit a quarter of a mile away. The next tenth of a mile is easy again, down a sandy corridor to the foot of the summit block. The final stretch is the toughest (Class 3),

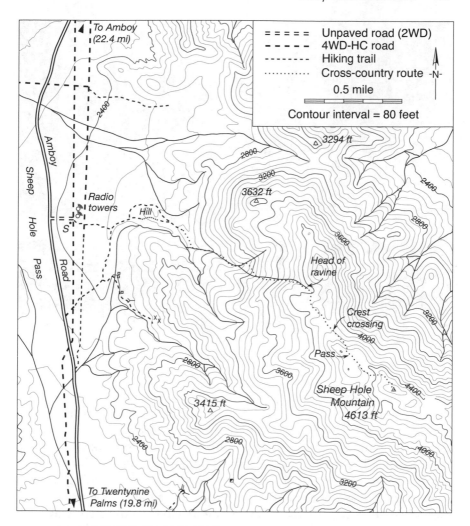

= = = = =	Unpaved road (2WD)
- - - - -	4WD-HC road
---------	Hiking trail
....	Cross-country route

0.5 mile

Contour interval = 80 feet

-N-

Sheep Hole Mountain

	Dist.(mi)	Elev.(ft)
Radio towers	0.0	2,430
End of road at low hill	0.35	2,540
Ravine's wash	0.75	2,675
Leave main wash southeast	~1.05	~3,060
Top of ravine	1.4	3,985
Cross crest to east side	1.75	4,160
Pass at end of east crossing	1.85	4,345
Sheep Hole Mountain	2.2	4,613

Mid-section of the boulder-choked ravine leading up to the crest

up the slight depression in the peak's southwest flank to the crest, then southwest near the crest to the top. Both of these major hurdles epitomize the well-deserved reputation of this range for giant rocks and frequent route finding. Many routes are possible, all too complex to put into words. The crest is locally crowded with colossal blocks that require Class-5 moves. Just a few tens of feet below, climbing usually gets easier (Class 2 and 3). You have to expect small defeats, and occasionally give up hard-earned elevation gains to try a different way.

This climb is exhilarating—heart and lungs pumping hard, the feel of smooth stone, the challenge of navigation, the intimate contact with a spectacular topography, and the satisfaction of finding a passage through this maze of vertical stone. Well before the summit the views are superb. Way down below, jagged ribs of mountains rise from bone-dry aprons of broken stone, sand, and alkali—the Bullion and Pinto mountains on one side, the Calumet and Old Woman mountains on the other. Everywhere, the eroded granites compose a tantalizing landscape, random yet instilled with startling symmetry, whimsical yet formidable. On this mountain replete with first-class scenery, you may find that reaching the summit is secondary to enjoying the ride.

∎

STIFLE PEAK

This enjoyable short traverse explores three adjacent low summits in the scenic southern Sheep Hole Mountains. The terrain is a scaled-down version of the much more rugged northern range, with smaller boulders and easier grades; it gives the opportunity to discover the exceptional topography of this range at the price of a lesser effort. The climb starts and ends in sensual drifts of sand, and the slopes are mantled with extensive displays of granite sculptures. The summits command dramatic views of sand-encrusted Morongo Basin, the Pinto Mountains, and the Sheep Hole Mountains.

General Information

Jurisdiction: Mojave Trails National Monument (BLM)
Road status: Roadless; paved access road
The climb (Toe Peak): 2.0 mi, 920 ft up, 60 ft down one way / easy
The climb (Stifle Pk): 2.9 mi, 1,270 ft up, 440 ft down one way / moderate
Main attractions: Dunes, boulders, views of Sheep Hole & Pinto Mtns
USGS 7.5' topo map: Clarks Pass
Maps: pp. 493*, 397

Location and Access

Toe, Stifle, and Eye peaks are near the south tail of the Sheep Hole Mountains, where Highway 62 curves around the range. Each one can be climbed individually by starting from an optimum point along the highway or the wilderness trail on the range's east side. The route suggested here ascends Stifle Peak via Toe Peak, then goes on to Eye Peak. It is a bit longer, but it spends more time on the panoramic crest.

From its intersection with Utah Trail in Twentynine Palms, drive Highway 62 east 27.8 miles toward the Sheep Hole Mountains, past Dale Lake, to a short, parallel spur up on the right. This is 1 mile before the road makes a 90° left bend around the mountains at Clarks Pass. Between about 4 and 2 miles before the spur, the roughly equidistant summits are easy to identify up ahead. Toe Peak is the southernmost and highest point, Stifle Peak is the next one north, and Eye Peak is the first one north of the deep gap north of Stifle Peak. Park at the spur.

Route Description

From the spur, the easiest route to Toe Peak is up Little Dune Canyon; its mouth is the shallow cleavage in the apron of sand at the

Sheep Hole Mountains looking north from near Toe Peak

base of the Sheep Hole Mountains to the northeast. It is a third of a mile to it, across the broad, braided dry wash between the road and the mountains. In the canyon, you amble up a serpentine corridor confined between steep banks of finely layered sand. It is a pleasant introduction to this range, a bright slice of desert thinly vegetated with creosote, burrobush, and tufts of grass. After 0.6 mile, the sandscape ends suddenly at the mountains' rocky core, and the canyon forks. Take the left fork, which soon angles a sharp right and climbs straight toward the crest. The country rock, a pale-pink granite, has eroded into a deluge of small boulders in the wash, and scenic displays of close-packed knobs up on the slopes. After 0.3 mile, the wash splays out into a steep amphitheater. Aim north to the shallow saddle on the canyon rim, up a 35% slope with scattered boulders. Once on the rim, Toe Peak is 0.4 mile away and less than 250 feet higher, north then northwest up and down the crooked, rocky crest.

From Toe Peak, Stifle Peak is the next hill visible just under a mile to the north-northwest. The gash that splits the two peaks is Big Dune Canyon, the next drainage north (the lone dune resting on its south flank is also visible from Toe Peak). It is a fun traverse to Stifle Peak along the capricious crest. The descent is gentle at first, across nearly

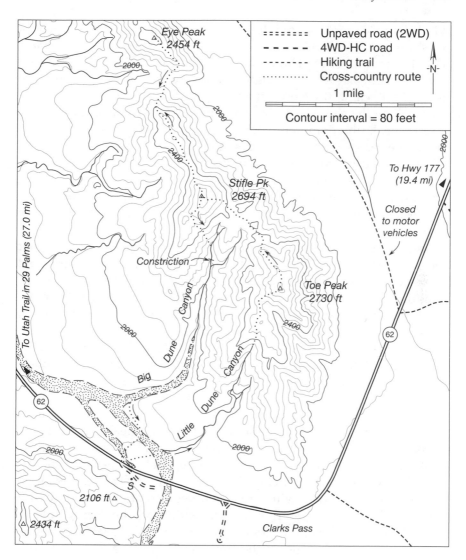

Stifle Peak

	Dist.(mi)	Elev.(ft)
Dirt spur off Highway 62	0.0	1,870
Little Dune Canyon (mouth)	0.3	1,865
Toe Peak	1.95	2,730
Stifle Peak	2.85	2,694
Eye Peak	(1.3)	2,454
Back via Big Dune Canyon	5.0	1,870

black Jurassic diorite worn into crops of crumbling boulders. Then the crest drops 120 feet in 100 yards on a Class-2 incline of mid-size boulders to the head of Big Dune Canyon. This area has two low hills; the first one is bypassed on the right, the second on the left. Just past the second hill, climb the slope straight up to Stifle Peak's east shoulder, then follow the shoulder to the summit. On this whole climb, and up to Eye Peak, the dominant rock is Clarks Pass Granodiorite, a porphyry peppered with black flecks of hornblende and biotite. Erosion has fashioned it into heaps of rounded, patinated boulders of all sizes exposed all over. The pleasure of this traverse lies in moving among these striking sculptures exhibited prominently on the hilly crest.

From the rim of Little Dune Canyon to Stifle Peak and beyond, the crest commands superb views. At first the highlight is the bitterly seared Pinto Mountains to the southwest, their batteries of wrinkled ridges jutting out into Morongo Basin, burnt stone against fiery sand. To the east, Sheephole Valley unfurls past a tiny dry lake to the jagged, bouldery escarpments of the Calumet Mountains. North from Toe Peak, it is the Sheep Hole Mountains that draw the most attention. You gaze 10 miles down the length of an intensely furrowed range bounding in individual headlands, each one studded with sharp summits, the furthest hazy blue with distance. On its west side, the mountains sprout long stringers that peter out in the valley's sands, a pattern echoed in the vast Bullion Mountains on the horizon beyond.

This climb can be extended to include Eye Peak, the lower summit visible beyond and slightly to the right of the twin peaks north of Stifle Peak (1.3 miles and 1,360 feet each way). You will have to go over the twin peaks and descend into a deep saddle barely higher than the surrounding valleys, before finally climbing Eye Peak. The crest is locally steep, narrow, and tiled with larger boulders, and hiking is more difficult. It is then faster to return west then south from the deep saddle.

To return from Stifle Peak, loop back down the peak's southwest shoulder. After 250 yards, at the first small saddle, angle left (southeast) down a sheer ravine. In 0.2 mile it dives down 420 feet over stacked boulders to Big Dune Canyon—a healthy Class 2. Then follow the canyon downhill 1.4 miles to its mouth. It is filled with boulders at first, with occasional brush. You will pass by the upper dune, drop down an easy 6-foot fall at the top of a short constriction (back in pink granite), then skirt wind-rippled sand dunes, before the boulders fully disappear. The lower canyon is a wide river of sand running between islands of desert lavender and smoke trees. From the canyon mouth it is a short walk south back to the spur along the highway.

■

8

WESTERN MOJAVE DESERT

The region. The western quadrant of the Mojave Desert is the area contained between the Sierra Nevada and the Tehachapi Mountains to the west, Panamint Valley and Barstow to the east, Owens Lake to the north, and the San Gabriel Mountains to the south. On the northwest side, the Coso Range and the El Paso Mountains overlook pastoral Owens Valley and the Sierra Nevada's luminous massif. The next range east is the Argus Range, a 50-mile-long barrier that presides one and a half miles above bone-dry Panamint Valley. South of it rises the crescent-shaped Slate Range, huddled around Searles Valley, and southwest from it the smaller Lava and Rand mountains. East from there, along the region's extreme eastern edge, the symmetry breaks down into a random patchwork of isolated mountains with names that bear the temperament of the desert—Robbers Mountain, Black Hills, Pilot Knob, and Eagle Crags. The region's southern half is so different you would think you are somewhere else. The landscape is reduced to an immense plain that reaches out 65 miles from Mojave east to Barstow and beyond, and the same distance again south to the San Gabriels. The northern half is a vivid celebration of America's lusty mountainous deserts. The southern half is the expression of the desert's most forlorn topography, land that seems as flat as a Midwest prairie, punctuated by dusty lakebeds and rare bedrock hills.

Geology. The boundary and striking difference between the northern and southern halves of the region are controlled by the Garlock Fault, a major active fault that cuts eastward right across California. From Fremont Valley near its west end, it skirts successively the south sides of the El Paso Mountains, the Slate Range, and the Owlshead Mountains before petering out 160 miles east in southern Death Valley. North of the fault, the region is Basin and Range country similar to Death Valley, parallel north-trending fault-block mountains tilted upward to sky-raking crests. Between the mountains lie deep youthful valleys not yet overwhelmed by alluvia. The main difference with the Death Valley region is the rocks, influenced by the more westerly location. Death Valley's great Paleozoic sedimentary formations progressively disappear westward, replaced by Mesozoic plutons contemporary with the Sierra Nevada, and broad expanses of volcanic rocks spewed out later, in the Miocene.

The vast alluviated plain south of the Garlock Fault is a large tectonic block bounded to the north by this fault and to the south by the San Andreas Fault. Its basement complex is mostly a granitic batholith, probably also an extension of the Sierra Nevada batholith. In Early Cenozoic times the region was likely one large mountain of elevated basement rock. Widespread torrential rains during the Late Miocene caused severe erosion that broke it up into sub-ranges and deep basins, and subsequently filled the basins with up to thousands of feet of alluvia. All that remains today are these shallow basins sprinkled with irregular low hills. Flooded by pluvial lakes in the Pleistocene, the basins left behind the many dry lakes—Rogers Lake, Koehn Lake, El Mirage Lake, and others—that dot this largely featureless plain.

Protection status. At approximately 7,400 square miles, the western Mojave Desert is the second largest of the desert's quadrants, the least protected, and the most developed. It has no national parks, no monuments, and no preserves. About 46% of the northern half is occupied by the China Lake Naval Air Warfare Center. The base annexed most of the tallest mountains: the core of the Coso Range, the Argus Range's highest crest, two thirds of the Slate Range, and half of the smaller mountains scattered south of it. A few towns neighbor the base, Ridgecrest and China Lake, Inyokern, the small ramshackle old mining towns of Randsburg, Johannesburg, and Red Mountain, and the active mining community of Trona. The rest is mostly public lands, of which only 185,000 acres are protected. The northern tip of the Coso Range and the northwestern flank of the Argus Range have wilderness status. The El Paso Mountains are partially preserved in Red Rock Canyon State Park and the El Paso Mountains Wilderness. The Lava Mountains, farther east, were also granted a small wilderness area.

The southern half is even less privileged. About 15% are taken up by Edwards Air Force Base. North of the base there are three protected

Average temperatures (°F) in the western Mojave Desert							
	Olancha (3,650 feet)		Panamint Springs (1,930 feet)		Ridgecrest (2,290 feet)		Barstow (2,200 feet)	
	Low	High	Low	High	Low	High	Low	High
January	28	52	27	55	31	60	35	59
February	32	58	30	60	35	66	39	63
March	36	63	35	66	39	71	43	70
April	41	71	40	74	45	79	49	76
May	48	80	49	84	53	87	56	86
June	56	90	58	94	60	97	64	95
July	62	96	64	100	66	103	70	101
August	60	94	61	97	65	101	69	100
September	54	87	55	90	58	94	62	92
October	44	76	44	78	48	83	52	80
November	33	62	34	64	37	69	42	67
December	28	53	28	55	30	60	34	58

areas—the Desert Tortoise Natural Area, a wilderness in Grass Valley, and one on Black Mountain, covering jointly 76,000 acres. The rest has been shouldering for decades the burden of our needs for space, food, and renewable energy. The region has six of the fifteen largest cities in area in the state. California City, north of the base, is the third largest, a 204-square-mile grid of mostly dirt streets shared by 14,300 souls. Large tracts around Mojave have been planted with wind turbines up to 25 stories tall and solar "farms" as large as small towns. South of the base, in El Mirage Valley and Antelope Valley, we traded fields of wildflowers for a checkerboard of ranches, strip malls, controlled intersections, and walled-in subdivisions. Only a dozen scattered wildlife and botanical sanctuaries were saved—less than 8,000 acres.

Climate. Being closer to the Pacific Ocean and the Sierra Nevada, the western Mojave Desert enjoys a climate that is year round a little cooler than the rest of the Mojave Desert. It is a little more comfortable in summer, though not by much, and a little less in winter. It rains very little, mostly in winter, between 4.7 inches in Ridgecrest and 7.4 inches in Olancha, and a little more in the mountains. The temperature typically varies from just below freezing to a little above 100°F. Snowfalls are minimal but common on the highest crests of the Coso Range and

Argus Range. The El Paso Mountains can also get a dusting of snow. The mountains east of the El Pasos are much drier.

Mining history. In a desert where most mines were utter failures, the western Mojave Desert stands out for having witnessed several highly successful and record-breaking historic and contemporary mining ventures. Between 1875 and the 1970s, the Darwin district, in the northern Argus Range, produced an estimated $29 million in lead, silver, zinc, and copper. Most of it came out of the Darwin Mine. Since 1872, around 100 million tons of evaporites have been extracted from Searles Lake's extensive deposits near Trona; it is one of the longest continuously active mines in California. The Yellow Aster Mine near Randsburg was one of the desert's richest historic gold properties; its total production exceeded $12 million. The Golden Queen Mine on Soledad Mountain south of Mojave almost matched it, with more than $10 million in gold. The borax mine just north of Boron has exploited continuously since the 1920s a huge lacustrine shale deposited in one of the region's Miocene basins. It is today one of the state's richest mines, consistently supplying nearly half of the world's refined borates and bringing in net annual earnings of a few billion dollars.

Climbing and Regulations. For those of us living on the northern California coast, the western Mojave Desert is the closest desert to home. Climbing mountains there instead of in other parts of the Mojave saves a few precious hours of driving. There is, however, often an inverse relationship between ease and payoff. Because it is closest to large cities, the southern third of the western Mojave Desert is the most developed and most visited. It also happens to be the least mountainous. The few summits there can fulfill our need for a workout and fresh air, but they are no longer suited to nourish our souls. Most mountains elsewhere in the Mojave Desert provide greater satisfaction.

That said, the further north you drive the better the isolation and wildness get. In the middle third of the region the population thins down, and the mountains are higher and rougher. This area has several pleasant summits well worth climbing, especially in the El Paso and Lava mountains, and on Black Mountain. The downside is that this general area is crisscrossed with a large number of roads. The locals love to explore them on ATVs and trucks and tear up their own backyard. Opal Mountain and several other areas have been ruined by irresponsible driving. Target shooting is also a favorite pastime; on a typical weekend, it is not uncommon to hear hundreds of reports an hour all day long. Weekdays are typically much quieter.

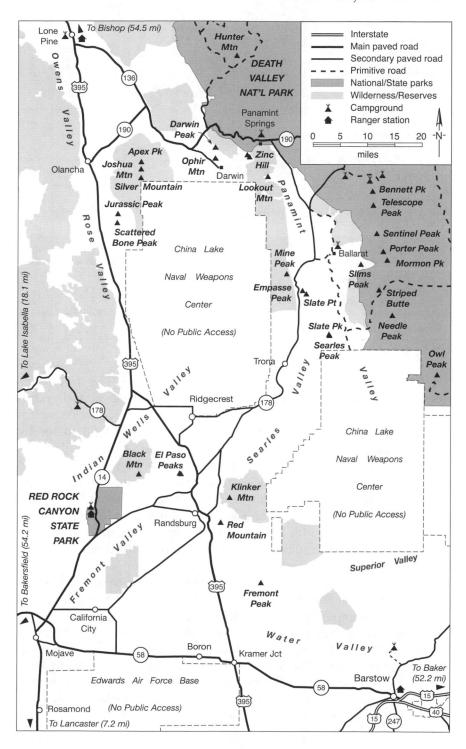

Lone Pine

To Bishop (54.5 mi)

Owens Valley

395

136

190

Darwin Peak

Hunter Mtn

DEATH VALLEY NAT'L PARK

Panamint Springs

190

Olancha

Apex Pk

Joshua Mtn

Silver Mountain

Ophir Mtn

Darwin

Zinc Hill

Lookout Mtn

Bennett Pk

Telescope Peak

Sentinel Peak

Porter Peak

Mormon Pk

Jurassic Peak

Scattered Bone Peak

China   Lake

Naval   Weapons

Center

(No Public Access)

Mine Peak

Empasse Peak

Slate Pt

Slate Pk

Searles Peak

Ballarat

Slims Peak

Striped Butte

Needle Peak

Owl Peak

To Lake Isabella (18.1 mi)

395

Trona

Ridgecrest

178

178

Wells   Valley

Searles   Valley

Panamint

Rose   Valley

Indian

Black Mtn

El Paso Peaks

Klinker Mtn

Red Mountain

China   Lake

Naval   Weapons

Center

(No Public Access)

RED ROCK CANYON STATE PARK

14

Randsburg

Superior   Valley

To Bakersfield (54.2 mi)

Fremont   Valley

395

Fremont Peak

California City

Boron

58

Kramer Jct

Water   Valley

Barstow

To Baker (52.2 mi)

Mojave

58

Edwards   Air   Force   Base

395

15

15

40

247

Rosamond

(No Public Access)

To Lancaster (7.2 mi)

Interstate
Main paved road
Secondary paved road
Primitive road
National/State parks
Wilderness/Reserves
Campground
Ranger station

0   5   10   15   20

miles

-N-

	Restaurant	Groceries	Lodging	Campground	Gas station	Tire repair	Towing	Water
Ballarat				✓				✓
Jawbone Canyon	✓	✓			✓			✓
Boron/Kramer Jct	✓	✓	✓	✓	✓	✓		✓
Lone Pine	✓	✓	✓	✓	✓	✓		✓
Olancha		✓	✓	✓	✓			✓
Panamint Springs	✓	✓	✓	✓	✓			✓
Randsburg/Jo-burg	✓	✓	✓		✓	✓		✓
Red Rock Canyon S. P.				✓				✓
Trona	✓	✓	✓		✓			✓

The very best climbing is in the northern third. The mountains there—the Coso, Argus, and Slate ranges—are the biggest and grandest, stray roads are few, and the wilderness areas provide welcome isolation. This is practically Death Valley country, rugged land shared by very few people. To the west, across Owens Valley, the Sierra Nevada enjoys considerably stronger protection, a seamless quilt of designated wilderness. The Sierra foothills are a spacious transition zone, no longer the Mojave Desert but not quite yet temperate mountain, where coexist bear and cactus, grey pine and Joshua trees, mule deer and creosote bush. Together with Death Valley National Park to the east, they provide a sizable and much needed buffer with civilization.

The undeveloped areas of the western Mojave Desert are almost exclusively the empire of the BLM. Restrictions on camping are few (see *Regulations* in *Part 4*), and there are generally ample opportunities for quiet and remote camps. Each valley has at least one small town or resort offering accommodations and cooked meals for weary hikers—rural Lone Pine in Owens Valley, rustic Panamint Springs in Panamint Valley, funky Trona in Searles Valley, the old-West town of Randsburg on the rim of Fremont Valley, the larger town of Ridgecrest in Indian Wells Valley, and a host of full-service towns in the southern area.

■

COSO RANGE

North from the Navy-base town of Ridgecrest along Highway 395 lies some of the most spectacular scenery in eastern California. As the road traces the western edge of the Mojave Desert, it climbs a long transitional corridor of progressively higher desert valleys—Indian Wells, Rose, then Owens—funneled between the eastern Sierra Nevada's abrupt escarpment to the west and the colorful volcanic dregs of the Coso Range to the east. When you reach the sleepy town of Olancha in Owens Valley 45 minutes later, the Sierras have sprouted dramatic peaks of glistening granite more than 12,000 feet high. The Coso Range has followed suit, on a smaller scale, evolving from low-slung banks of ink-black domed lava and blood-red volcanoes to igneous crags marooned high above shimmering badlands.

Long ago, the China Lake Naval Weapons Center annexed most of the Coso Range and Argus Range complex, like a cookie cutter stamping out a 900-square-mile chunk of dough. Closed for decades to all but relatively limited military uses, this and other reservations now ironically hold some of the best preserved desert tracts in the West. The portion of the Cosos open to the public is the leftover dough outside the cookie cutter—the northwest end of the range—much of it now preserved as the 49,300-acre Coso Range Wilderness. Hiking in this fringe of land bordering military power can be unsettling, in part for fear of accidentally trespassing or witnessing classified maneuvers, and being fittingly deported to Sin City for life. Oddly enough, it is in this wilderness that I encountered my one and only unknown flying object, a gray and white sphere that passed overhead as silently as a paper plane. It was either flying low and slowly, or high and exceedingly fast. As most UFOs, it vanished before I could find my camera. The photograph would have been tabloid-blurry anyway.

The Coso Range substrate is almost all Jurassic and Cretaceous plutonic rocks, likely an outlier of the giant pluton that created the Sierra Nevada directly to the west. About a third of it is overlain by a complex suite of volcanic ruptures—flood-like basaltic lava flows, air-fall pumice, obsidian and perlite domes, cinder cones, ash-flow tuff, lumpy rhyolite and chocolate-brown andesite. They resulted from numerous eruptions spread out between at least 13 million years ago and as recently as 44,000 years ago, possibly much less. Native Americans were no strangers to the Coso Range's continued geothermal activity. The mud pots at Coso Hot Springs, near the center of the range, were sacred to them—*Koso* comes from a Shoshonean word for steam. A few miles west, near Sugarloaf Mountain, lie some of the state's largest aboriginal stone workshops, where they have quarried obsidian since 13,000 years ago and traded it all the way to the coast.

The Coso Range's extraordinary legacy is its strikingly beautiful and prolific rock art—it holds the highest concentration of petroglyphs in the country, numbering well in excess of 35,000. The most extensive sites are inside the naval base. Stretches of canyons have hundreds of figures per mile, bewildering galleries of abstract, zoomorphic, and anthropomorphic drawings incised on patinated basalt walls and boulders, or painted in a palette of black, red, pink, orange, and white. The art is so distinct that it defines its own school—the Coso style. Drawings tend to be more elaborate and use ingenious tricks to render volumes. Large human figures are represented with headdress or ceremonial body paint, and life-size bighorn sheep with characteristic boat-shaped bodies or side-facing horns. Thanks to the secrecy of our weaponry industry, these invaluable sites have been well protected from vandalism. That we may never see them is a small concession to preservation. Escorted tours can be booked at the Maturango Museum in Ridgecrest (patience helps). Many rock-art sites also grace the parts of the range open to the public; the anticipation of a chance encounter with these enigmatic engravings is a highlight of climbing here.

The Coso Range bears many other gems. Its has extensive forests of large Joshua trees, summits with lush toppings of evergreens, small sand dunes, a dozen named peaks, wild extrusive rocks, a colorful serpentine canyon called Vermillion, and grand vistas of Owens Lake and the eastern Sierras. The badlands at the range's northern tip are home to a whole fossilized fauna of mammals that lived here a few millions years ago, when this was a semi-arid grassland interspaced with trees resembling giant sequoias. One of them was *Equus simplicidens*, an equid with a striped skin that might have been the earliest ancestor of the modern horse. The peaceful town of Lone Pine, not too far away, offers the opportunity to enjoy these treasures *and* the luxury of a sit-down meal, and even a bed, at the end of a hard-day's climb.

■

SILVER MOUNTAIN

Silver Mountain might call to mind a sublime spire soaring over a forbidden lost world, perhaps echoing the achingly dramatic American landscapes portrayed by nineteenth-century romantic painters. Far from this idyllic image, Silver Mountain is a squat mesa of dark basalt, dwarfed by the Sierra Nevada rearing up behind it. There is still huge gratification in climbing it. Other than the physical achievement and closeness to nature, the countryside leading up to it is beautiful—first an enchanting canyon, then a serene valley graced by a mature Joshua tree forest, and finally a sensational view of the eastern Sierras.

General Information
Jurisdiction: Coso Range Wilderness (BLM)
Road status: Trail and cross-country climb; dirt access road (HC best)
The climb: 5.8 mi, 2,150 ft up, 240 ft down one way / difficult
Main attractions: Scenic canyon, isolated flat, views of Sierra Nevada
USGS 7.5' topo maps: Centennial Canyon, Upper Centennial Flat
Maps: pp. 505*, 499

Location and Access
Silver Mountain (7,495') is the highest named summit in the section of the Coso Range open to the public. It is located deep in the Coso Range Wilderness, near its southern boundary with the Naval Weapons Center. The easiest access is via the west fork of Centennial Canyon, on the range's north slope. From the junction of Highway 190 and Highway 136, 2 miles south of Lone Pine, drive Highway 190 east 10.0 miles to a primitive road on the right, at a large turnout with a BLM board. From the other direction, this is 2.8 miles west of the signed road to Darwin. This primitive road (SE 75) cuts a straight path south-southwest across Lower Centennial Flat. After 1.5 miles, it splits, just before Gill Corral. Take the right fork, passing to the right of the corral. Stay on SE 75 4.35 miles to the foot of the Coso Range, where a road merges inconspicuously from the right (SE 71) and SE 75 ends. Continue on SE 71, in the same general direction, 0.4 mile to a fork inside Centennial Canyon. Go 0.55 mile on the right fork (signed SE 71) to its end in a wide wash at the wilderness boundary, and park. The road is a washboard down to the corral, then a little rougher to the canyon, with some small rocks but no crown or sand, and it is a little

503

steeper and rockier in the canyon. High-clearance is preferable near the end, but with care a standard-clearance vehicle can make it.

Route Description

The west fork of Centennial Canyon—the wash that climbs west from the end of the road—is a great little corridor that quickly slips into the wilderness and envelops you in familiar surroundings. Its sandy wash wiggles up at a moderate grade between steep hillsides draped in rounded boulders. The rock is a pretty quartz monzonite tinted smoky gray by biotite and hornblende crystals. In the wash, fallen boulders vie for space with a plush spread of shrubs—rabbitbrush and big sagebrush grading into cliffrose, ephedra, and pygmy cedar—and a touch of Joshua trees and pinyon pine. Both plants and boulders are just dense enough to be visually appealing without impeding walking. The wash is interrupted by nearly three dozen piles of boulders and slanted outcrops. Many of them look deceptively hard from a distance, when in fact an easy passage or a quick scramble will often let you through—nature is not usually this cooperative The few occlusions that do require a little climbing are conveniently circumvented by a short trail. Two forks in the canyon call for a decision, 1.85 miles in (the main wash goes left), then 200 feet further (right). A third of a mile further, a beat-up road parallels the wash on the low south bank. In 0.6 mile the road climbs west to the open pass into Joshua Flat, overlooking bouldery hilltops with thick patches of conifers.

Joshua Flat is hardly a flat, more like a billowing valley at the common head of two main drainages that empty into Owens Lake, including striking Vermillion Canyon. It is, however, true to the Joshua part of its name. The valley is carpeted with Joshua trees, many quite old, some over 25 feet tall, with thick apricot bark, deeply notched like on a ponderosa pine. This is a cheerfully green and scenic place, dotted with pine and large cliffrose, filled with a heady sense of remoteness.

Beyond the pass the road cuts northwest into Joshua Flat. Just a quarter of a mile beyond the pass, a burro trail takes off at 11 o'clock. If you miss it, look for a faint side road heading east (right) and walk back 200 feet to the trail. If you still miss it, taking a westerly course across Joshua Flat will do just fine. About half a mile west, on the trail or cross country, Silver Mountain first comes into view—the blackish mesa to the southwest. To the north of it there is first a prone reddish hill, much lower, then Joshua Mountain, then a stand-alone, bell-shaped mountain called Apex Peak. The slightly taller prominence to its right is Bpex Peak; Cpex Peak is hidden behind it. If you have not found the trail, cut a beeline southwest to the saddle between Silver

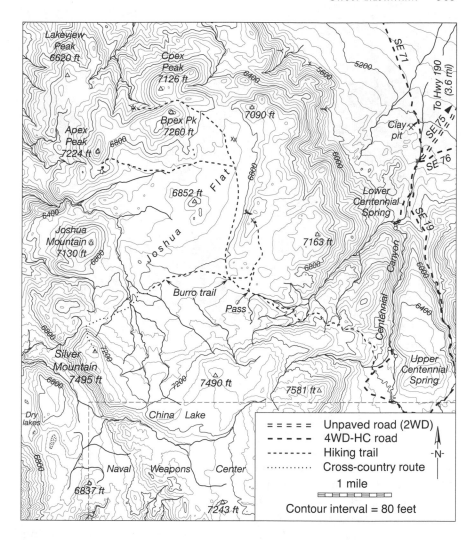

Map labels:
Lakeview Peak 6620 ft
Cpex Peak 7126 ft
SE 71
5200
To Hwy 190 (3.6 mi)
7090 ft
SE 75
Clay pit
Bpex Pk 7260 ft
Apex Peak 7224 ft
6800
6852 ft
Joshua Flat
Lower Centennial Spring
SE 76
SE 19
Joshua Mountain 7130 ft
6800
7163 ft
6400
Burro trail
Pass
Centennial Canyon
6400
Silver Mountain 7495 ft
7200
7490 ft
7581 ft
Upper Centennial Spring
Dry lakes
China Lake
6800
Naval Weapons Center
6837 ft
7243 ft

Legend:
= = = = = Unpaved road (2WD)
- - - - - 4WD-HC road
--------- Hiking trail
.... Cross-country route

-N-

1 mile

Contour interval = 80 feet

Silver Mountain

	Dist.(mi)	Elev.(ft)
Centennial Canyon Rd (end)	0.0	5,580
Old road (right)	2.2	6,700
Pass into Joshua Flat	2.85	~6,940
Burro trail	3.1	6,880
Smaller fork in wash	4.45	6,740
Saddle	5.4	7,014
Silver Mountain	5.8	7,495

Joshua Flat looking northwest at Apex Peak (right) and the Sierra Nevada

Mountain and the reddish hill. Otherwise stay on the trail a total of 1.1 nearly level miles until it fades in a shallow wash. The wash descends 0.25 mile to a smaller fork on the left, next to two low mesas to the west. Walk almost due south up this fork, past the mesas and down into a wash, then west-southwest to the saddle, a distance of 1 mile. The last leg is 0.4 mile south-southeast up the north shoulder of Silver Mountain, at 30% the steepest part of this otherwise fairly easy ascent.

Silver Mountain is a stack of lava flows, each tens of feet thick, that flooded the countryside in broad sheets around 5 million years ago. On the summit plateau the top layer has weathered into a sterile tiling of vesiculated gray basalt. Below it, Joshua Flat's south rim still preserves the smooth surface of a lake of ponded lava. Silver Mountain may not be true to its name, but it packs in stunning views—north to the Inyo Mountains and Owens Lake, east to Joshua Flat and the Argus Range, south to Coso Peak and the off-limits portion of the Coso Range, and west to the Sierra Nevada's monumental crest.

The distance, elevation change, and difficulty to all the other local summits are sensibly the same. A strong hiker can do a loop around Joshua Flat and climb all of them, taking advantage of the old roads, and for a few hours enjoy variations of these sumptuous views.

■

JURASSIC PEAK AND SCATTERED BONE PEAK

> *Jurassic Peak is the high point of a serrated, boulder-capped ridge near the west end of the Coso Range. The boulders make it a fun climb, high along the abrupt western edge of the desert, overlooking the long straight trench of Owens Valley, one of the North America's deepest valleys. Though not very high, the peak and its neighbor Scattered Bone Peak command spectacular views of the eastern Sierra Nevada, covered with snow several months of the year, and of the deep-blue waters of the Haiwee reservoirs.*

General Information
Jurisdiction: Public lands (BLM)
Road status: Climbing on road and cross-country; primitive access road
    (HC/4WD)
The climb: 1.8 mi, 1,050 ft up, 70 ft down one way/moderate
Main attractions: Fun climb on bouldery peak, views of Sierra Nevada
USGS 7.5' topo map: Haiwee Reservoir
Maps: pp. 509*, 499

Location and Access
Jurassic Peak and Scattered Bone Peak are the two named summits on Haiwee Ridge, the north-south sub-range that frames the east side of Owens Valley south of Owens Lake. When driving on Highway 395 a few miles south of Olancha, you will see it rising sharply to the east, a long wall of granitic boulders resting on pale volcanic badlands. The nipple at the ridge's high point is Jurassic Peak. The slightly lower summit less than 2 air miles south of it is Scattered Bone Peak.

Both peaks can be climbed from the saddle between them, which can be reached by road from Little Cactus Flat, a secluded valley on the east side of Haiwee Ridge. To get there, work your way on Highway 395 to the signed Cactus Flat Road, 2.0 miles south of the junction with Highway 190 in Olancha. Drive the Cactus Flat Road east 1.4 miles until the pavement ends, then 0.8 mile to a fork below the North Haiwee Dam. Take the left fork. Proceed 2.15 miles up a hill to a four-way junction at the gated Global Pumice Mine. Continue straight on the main road, signed SE 756, through Little Cactus Flat's scenic Joshua tree woodland. After 5.35 miles, turn right on a smaller road (SE 866, and still Cactus Flat Road). Stay on it 2.45 miles, passing below Jurassic Peak's sheer eastern slope to the right, to a road on the

507

right (SE 766), across from a hill of boulders. This road climbs to the saddle between the two peaks. In dry weather this junction is reachable with a standard-clearance vehicle. Park at the junction.

Route Description

Jurassic Peak. From the junction walk up the windy SE 766 road 0.8 mile to the saddle. It can be driven instead, but you will need more power than most four-wheel-drive SUVs can deliver to negotiate the steep grade just below the saddle. From there the peak is less than a mile up the fairly straight crest to the north. The topography is gentle at first, a low rise of weathered tuffs followed by a gradual descent into a shallow dip. Then the crest steepens markedly toward a false summit, drops into a saddle, and finally shoots up to the true summit. The boulders start part way up the false summit. They are at first interspaced with sandy soil covered with grasses and small cottontop cactus, then locally too densely packed for plants to grow. The general route is obvious, but with so many boulders in the way, the devil is in the details. Finding a route that minimizes the difficulty through this inclined maze of stacked boulders is a good part of the fun, so I will not write too much about it—and hopefully no one will put up cairns and spoil the pleasure. Try the east side of the crest to a little east of the false summit, then west of the crest. It is possible to get there with only one or two short Class-2 moves, including the tilted summit slab, although in general it requires Class-3 moves. The outcrops and boulders are made of a Jurassic-Cretaceous biotite-quartz monzonite that tends to have good grainy surfaces for climbing.

In spite of its modest height, the Haiwee Ridge commands scenic views of the deep-blue Haiwee reservoirs winding across Owens Valley, with Olancha Peak and the long wall of the Range of Light rising more than one and a half vertical miles across the valley. While searching for a route on the west side of the ridge you will be staring tens of miles up and down the Owens Valley corridor, from Little Lake to the south to Owens Lake to the north, slowly turning blue-green

Jurassic Peak and Scattered Bone Peak		
	Dist.(mi)	Elev.(ft)
Road jct in Little Cactus Flat	0.0	4,990
Saddle on Haiwee Ridge	0.8	5,290
Scattered Bone Peak	(0.9)	5,738
Jurassic Peak	1.8	5,952

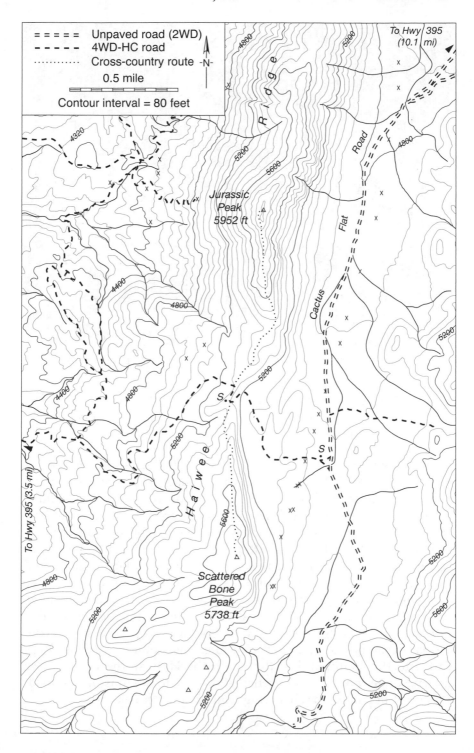

Unpaved road (2WD)
4WD-HC road
Cross-country route -N-
0.5 mile
Contour interval = 80 feet

To Hwy 395
(10.1 mi)

Ridge

Road

Flat

Cactus

Jurassic
Peak
5952 ft

To Hwy 395 (3.5 mi)

Halwee

S

S

Scattered
Bone
Peak
5738 ft

Boulder slopes on the way up to Jurassic Peak (in the middle distance)

after valiant recent efforts to replenish some of its surface water. The summit also has a good view east over little-known Coso Range, held captive by military might.

Scattered Bone Peak. The climb to Jurassic Peak's southern neighbor, Scattered Bone Peak, is similar in distance, vegetation, and vistas, but the terrain is much more subdued. From the road at the saddle, proceed south up the ridge. There is soon an area of granitic boulders, up to a small plug of sedimentary rocks. The rest of the way, the core granite is covered with recent tuff, possibly formed by an avalanche of incandescent ash and gases. It is an even-sloped plateau, peppered with ground-hugging shrubs and occasional beavertail cactus. There *are* scattered bones, left behind by the bighorn sheep who came here, perhaps, for one last grand panorama. The views are indeed excellent, and without the distractions from the boulders they are easier to contemplate than on the Jurassic Peak route. The summit overlooks Rose Valley to the south, and to the north the Haiwee reservoirs' long crooked finger pointing at Owens Valley's pastoral landscape, spreading peacefully under the sheltering wall of the Sierra Nevada.

■

ARGUS RANGE

The Argus Range is one of the longest ranges in California's Mojave Desert. From near the famous Trona Pinnacles in Searles Valley north to just past Panamint Springs in Panamint Valley, it forms the western wall of both valleys for 50 miles. It is an impressive piece of engineering. From Trona north it grows quickly from a hilly ridge to Maturango Peak (8,839'), the apex of a lofty summit block that towers one and a half miles above Panamint Valley, its slopes slashed by deep canyons. Although most of the high country lies inside the China Lake NWC, the range's northern tip and its eastern flanks in Panamint Valley and northern Searles Valley are protected as the 65,726-acre Argus Range Wilderness and offer several named peaks to climb. In historic times, the Argus Range had some of the region's earliest and most lucrative mines. Climbing any of these peaks gives a unique opportunity to explore the many remains of this rich mining past.

The Argus Range is an east-tilted fault block with a complex geological history. In the Paleozoic, as part of the continental margin it was buried under miles of sediments. Deposition stopped in the middle Triassic with the onset of volcanism. Tectonic instabilities started profoundly altering the local terrain in the Permian, and grew stronger through the Triassic into Early Jurassic time. In the Middle Jurassic, as a side effect of the emplacement of the Sierra Nevada batholith, the Hunter Mountain Pluton intruded the region, reaching as far north as the Inyo Mountains. A second one, the Maturango Peak Pluton, squeezed in 22 million years later. These plutons now form the hard crest of the Argus Range. In the latest Jurassic, major structural deformations took place along the northwest-trending Argus Sterling Thrust Fault. Compressional forces shoved the Maturango Peak Pluton eastward over older formations. Mile-size slabs of Paleozoic limestone and Mesozoic volcanic rocks were metamorphosed into marble and mylonite. Volcanism returned in the Late Pliocene and Pleistocene and covered the region with lava and ash. Few ranges offer such a wide spectrum of rocks, conveniently exposed for us when renewed tectonism broke the land into fault blocks a few million years ago.

Being closer to the Pacific Ocean, the Argus Range receives a little more precipitation than many ranges of comparable elevation. Snow blankets its highest summits every winter, and on wet years the snow line reaches below 4,000 feet. Most main canyons have one or more springs with a little permanent surface water. Darwin Canyon, at the north end of the range, is coursed by one of the strongest streams in the region, fed by water collected in a 165-square-mile drainage on the west flank of the range. The Argus Range is home to a small population of bighorn sheep, dangerously outnumbered by the feral burros that drift out of the nearby military base.

The Argus Range's uncontested mining star was Darwin, near the north end of the range. Founded in 1874 following a silver discovery on Ophir Mountain, it quickly became a sizable mining town, with 150 buildings and about 1,000 inhabitants. Organized as the New Coso Mining District, the area had several well-developed mines, including the Defiance, Sterling, Independence, and Lucky Jim. Between 1875 and 1883, the Defiance alone yielded $1,570,000 in silver. Mining slowed down in the 1890s, but it continued for decades, with large bursts around the world wars. By the early 1950s the district's lead-silver-zinc production had topped $29 million, possibly the highest in the California desert. The Lookout Mining district, just east of Darwin, was also rich silver country. The mine that started it was the Modoc, discovered in 1875. Eventually, every major canyon on the east slope had a mine. The heart of the district was the town of Lookout, where two smelters treated the ore from local mines. By 1890 the Modoc had pulled $1.9 million in silver and lead. Its neighbor, the Minnietta Belle Mine, eventually brought in close to $1 million. Like in the New Coso district, many properties became idle in the 1890s, although mining continued until fairly recently. In the 1980s, a gold vein at the Windless Mine was so unbelievably rich that the miners lugged the rocks in backpacks 2 miles down a mule trail to the nearest road!

The last mine to close down was the historic Little Mack, renamed the Golden Eagle, in Thompson Canyon. In the 1990s it was not uncommon to run into its two owners, either hoisting ore out of the tunnel with a winch mounted on their 1940s army truck, or indulging in dinner at Panamint Springs. Listening to them share their invaluable knowledge of the local history was a rare treat. They packed up and left in 1998, but Panamint Springs is still a wonderful place for a tasty dinner after a hard day's climb in the Argus Range.

■

OPHIR MOUNTAIN AND DARWIN PEAK

Famous for their fabulously rich historic silver mines, the Darwin Hills are a free-standing ridge of plump hills whose very names— Ophir Mountain, inspired by the fabled mountain of gold, and Darwin Peak, named after early explorer Darwin French—are an invitation to amble. These two low and easy peaks, less than a mile and 700 feet up each, offer a reflective way to acquaint yourself with the scale, beauty, and history of this little-traveled part of the desert.

General Information
Jurisdiction: Public lands (BLM)
Road status: Climbing on roads and cross-country; 2WD access roads
The climb (Ophir Mountain): 0.9 mi, 510 ft up, 30 ft down one way / easy
The climb (Darwin Peak): 0.8 mi, 620 ft up, 90 ft down one way / easy
Main attractions: Easy climbs, mining history, views of Darwin area
USGS 7.5' topo map: Darwin
Maps: pp. 515*, 499

Location and Access
To reach the Darwin Hills, at the northwest end of the Argus Range, from Olancha in Owens Valley drive Highway 190 east 27.4 miles to the signed turn-off to Darwin (this junction is 17.9 miles west of Panamint Springs). Drive the paved Darwin Road southeast 3.6 miles to a dirt road on the left, at the bottom of a long grade. Ophir Mountain is the high point due east, and Darwin Peak is 2 miles north of it. Follow this signed road (SE 30) 0.6 mile north-northeast to a fork (right), then 0.8 mile, up a gulch that winds east into the Darwin Hills, to a road signed SE 28 on the left. For Ophir Mountain, continue 0.55 mile on SE 30, past a side road on the left, to a rougher road on the right closed to motor vehicles. Park at this junction, or at the crest 0.1 mile further. For Darwin Peak, turn left on SE 28 and go 0.4 mile to the third side road on the right, signed SE 28A. This short side road is quite steep and rough; park at this junction and walk it instead. The other roads are fairly smooth hard-packed dirt free of crown. With a little experience they can be driven with a standard-clearance vehicle.

Route Description
The road on Ophir Mountain climbs gradually across the steep flank of the mountain's northern brow. Here as throughout the Darwin

Hills, the terrain is smooth bulging swells with scant vegetation, mostly low dehydrated shrubs with a serious aversion to chlorophyll. Even cactuses are not fond of the place. The only ornaments are immature Joshua trees, few and far between, only the healthiest granted stubby branches. Wildlife is scarce, although there is little doubt that if you spend a few hours you will come in sight of a burro. The road ends in 0.55 mile at a road cut. A single-track path worn by hooves and very occasional boots picks up at the south end of it. About 0.3 mile long, it heads south, angles right up a low rise, and descends 25 feet to a saddle. It then climbs gently south on the east side of and just below the crest to near the summit, with a short loose slope at the very end.

Ophir Mountain is a fine observatory to take in the size and beauty of four major desert ranges—the Inyo Mountains to the north, the Coso Range to the west, the Argus Range to the east, and behind it, past the pale trench of Panamint Valley, the great Panamint Range itself. Mount Whitney towers to the northwest, its 11,000-foot east face in full view. At the base of Ophir Mountain's furrowed southern slopes lies the half ghost town of Darwin, its cluster of cabins and barracks reduced to toys by distance. One of the smallest towns in the desert, it boasts a population of about 50, not all full-time residents, more mine tailings than trees, and fewer services than on Mars. If you stroll through town, a resident may well materialize out of nowhere to greet you, like children in the Sahara, and lavish you with tall desert tales.

In this dramatic immensity the Darwin Hills seem oddly small and out of place, too far from the closest range. They owe their existence and location, as well as their mineral wealth, to the Coso Range. When the Coso Range batholith boiled up in the Cretaceous, it squeezed a pre-existing stack of Paleozoic strata into an open concave fold known as a syncline. The uplifted west end of the syncline became the Darwin Hills, its east end the northern Argus Range, and its bottom the broad valley drained by Darwin Wash that separates the two—the Darwin Hills are just an extension of the Argus Range. This same batholith also deposited the Darwin Hills' prodigious amounts of silver—8 million ounces—and heavy metals—125,000 tons—exhumed in historic times.

The rocks on Ophir Mountain, Darwin Peak, and most of the Darwin Hills' crest belong to the Keeler Canyon Formation. Deposited in shallow near-shore water in Pennsylvanian and Permian times, it consists mostly of limestone, pebble conglomerate, and calcarenite, a purée of mashed corals and shells. Colorful exposures crop out along the road and crest, auburn or nearly white, often deeply corrugated by the wind, finely striated or imprinted with beautiful eye patterns formed by bluish limestone flowing around oblong tawny inclusions.

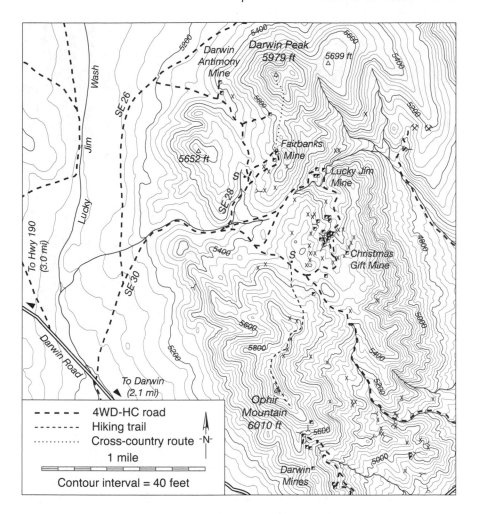

4WD-HC road
Hiking trail
Cross-country route
1 mile
Contour interval = 40 feet

Ophir Mountain and Darwin Peak

	Dist.(mi)	Elev.(ft)
Trailhead on SE 30	0.0	5,525
End of road / start of trail	0.55	5,860
Ophir Mountain	0.9	6,010
Road junction (SE 28-SE 28A)	0.0	5,450
Top of SE 28A road	0.25	5,600
Saddle	0.5	~5,615
Darwin Peak	0.8	5,979

Old cabin at the Christmas Gift Mine; Darwin Peak in background

On the Darwin Peak climb the vegetation, geology, and distance are similar but it is wilder because there is no trail. From the SE 28 road walk up the steep side road (SE 28A) 0.25 mile to its high point, where it curves right just before the Fairbanks Mine. Then head north over a set of low hills, and descend about 60 feet to a saddle. Darwin Peak's southeast shoulder looms up ahead, spiked with sharp outcrops. Aim for the left side of the lowest outcrop, then follow the shoulder to the summit, bypassing the higher outcrops on either side, whichever is less windy that day... Like on Ophir Mountain, the syncline's sheared rim was overturned by the intense pressure from the Coso Range batholith. The outcrops lean to the east, with their top side *older* than their bottom side. The climb is a little steep but easy, over sparse litters of limestone plates and occasional septarian concretions.

The summit of Darwin Peak is a mohawk of overturned blue-gray limestone. The views are much the same as on Ophir Mountain, minus Darwin but with the bonus of a sweeping panorama to the north of the burnt-sienna and blood-red volcanic ledges of Darwin Plateau and the perpendicular gash of Rainbow Canyon. After a winter storm, when a veneer of snow covers the desert summits and the Sierra Nevada are solid white, the spectacle is breathtaking.

■

ZINC HILL

A century ago, when Zinc Hill was one of the state's largest zinc producers, the miners built trails all over the hill's inhospitable slopes to access the high country. The longest of these historic paths is still the best way to reach the mountain's highest summit, across impressively tall volcanic taluses looking out over the high Sierras. Expect a rough access road, surprisingly diverse geology, wild burros, stunning views from the dark summit, and a brisk workout.

General Information
Jurisdiction: Public lands (BLM)
Road status: Climbing on road, trail, and cross-country; access on
      rough primitive road (HC-4WD)
The climb: 2.3 mi, 1,940 ft up, 30 ft down one way/difficult
The loop climb: 5.3 mi, 2,090 ft up loop/difficult
Main attractions: Mining trail, high views of Panamint Valley, mining
USGS 7.5' topo maps: Panamint Springs, Darwin
Maps: pp. 519*, 499

Location and Access
    Zinc Hill is the northernmost main summit in the Argus Range, overlooking northern Panamint Valley. It is accessed from the Darwin Road, once the main thoroughfare connecting Death Valley to the town of Darwin and points west. This road starts on the south side of Highway 190, 1 mile west of Panamint Springs, or 29.7 miles east of Highway 136. Driving it is an adventure in itself. It starts as a broad washboard where even motor homes manage to creep their way to the popular Darwin Falls turnoff. Then it climbs out of Darwin Canyon and turns into a battlefield of rocks. The mountain that soon rises sharply 1,800 feet to the east is Zinc Hill. During the world wars it was extensively exploited for lead, silver, and gold, but its greatest wealth was zinc. The five side roads that branch off along the way lead to these historic mines. The second side road (SE 61), marked by twin ore bins and the stone ruins of a mill and camp, climbs to the Zinc Hill Mine. In the 1910s it was a full-fledged operation serviced by an aerial tramway, an inclined railway, and a mill. The access road is roughest just south of SE 61. Deep holes gape right below jagged bedrock; both high clearance and power are essential. After 5.1 miles the road reaches its high point. Drive 0.2 mile past it, to the right U-shaped curve at

Panamint Lake, Lake Hill, and the Cottonwood Mountains from Zinc Hill

the bottom of the steep grade. The way to Zinc Hill is the rough road that climbs on the left in the curve. Park at this junction.

Route Description

True to miners' general aversion to switchbacks, the old mining road goes straight up a narrow ridge, steep at first, then a gutter of sharp black lava. This area is mostly Pliocene basalt flows; the landscape has the typical looks of volcanic fields—dark, scantily vegetated, more desert-like than most. Absolutely nothing hints that it hides in its folds Darwin Canyon's sheer-walled gorge and luxuriant stream... After 0.75 mile the road crests at a four-way junction. A distinctive pointed hill with horizontal bands of white marble rises a short distance to the east. To its left there is a much taller slope of quartz monzonite outcrops and boulders. This is where the miners found this mountain's riches, at the contact between the marble and this pluton.

Two flat summits separated by a shallow saddle fill the horizon beyond the marble hill. The leftmost summit is Zinc Hill's high point. To get to the miner's trail that climbs almost all the way to it, stay on the main road 150 yards as it drops south to a wash, crosses it, and angles right. The trailhead, marked by a cairn, is 150 yards further again, on the left. If you cannot find it, return to the junction and take

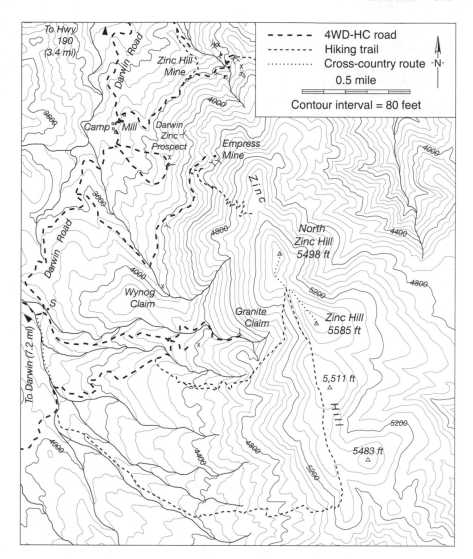

Zinc Hill

	Dist.(mi)	Elev.(ft)
Darwin Canyon Road	0.0	3,675
Jct at top of mining road	0.75	4,235
Mining trail (trailhead)	0.9	4,205
Saddle on crest	2.05	5,340
North Zinc Hill	(0.25)	5,498
Zinc Hill	2.25	5,585

the second road on the right. It winds up into the crooked ravine on the north side of the marble hill. Soon after the road ends below the Granite Prospect (0.5 mile), the wash splits. Scramble up the right fork to the saddle behind the hill, and pick up the trail 40-60 feet above it.

Narrow, rocky, and prone to frequent mood swings, this trail is a treat. It starts as a dim track among squat creosote bush. Rainwater has stripped its thin gravel cover, exposing underlying mosaics of smooth limestone. The trail climbs southeast toward a low rounded ridge, and follows its flank east for a while. Where the slope steepens it switchbacks three times, then angles right toward the peak. Beyond, the terrain is tall, steep, and unstable flows of broken reddish and black basalt, too rough to support anything but scrawny bushes. The trail traverses these giant slides unflinchingly, straight and at a sustained tilt. Below the summit, it readjusts its aim and shoots up to the saddle north of the summit. Since its inception, this trail has been trodden by more burros and coyotes than humans. Without it, the ascent would be unpleasant. With it you get into a rhythm, heart pumping, rocks crunching, steadily riding the avalanche until the ground finally levels off at the saddle on the crest, and Panamint Valley bursts into view.

This is a sight to remember. Far below, the valley floor spreads out for miles, its halo of dunes and long dry lake enclosed by immense alluvial fans. The Cottonwood Mountains loom behind it, their banded walls an open scroll displaying 300 million years of history. From nearly 4,000 feet up, Panamint Springs looks tiny. The two peaks on either side of the saddle, a short cross-country scramble away, offer equally spectacular views. Zinc Hill's highest summit to the south is a crinkled field of basalt, dark and bleak. In the other direction, North Zinc Hill is all granitic, a light-colored hump of rounded boulders artfully displayed on soft sand. It commands even better views of Darwin Plateau to the north, a sprawling aftermath of red volcanics. From anywhere the Sierra Nevada's formidable crest dominates the western horizon, from Olancha Peak to Mount Williamson.

This little trail has more to say. If you stay on it, it will take you on a grand tour of Zinc Hill. From the saddle it wanders south, across volcanic dregs, to a narrow, subdued ridge. Near the south end of the basalt flow the trail veers west and switchbacks down over nicely folded Paleozoic strata. At the foot of the mountain, it follows a straight low ridge for 0.7 mile to finally end, after 3.8 miles, back at the mining road not far below the upper trailhead. To complete the loop, walk the road north 500 feet to where it makes a right hook across a wash. Then hike down the wash 0.4 mile to your starting point.

∎

LOOKOUT MOUNTAIN

Lookout Mountain is the site of the Modoc Mine, one of the richest historic silver mining centers in the region. The short climb to its flat summit on the trail used by miners well over a century ago, past cavernous tunnels, the ruins of the Modoc smelters, and the ghost town of 1880s Lookout, is a rare experience. It gives a glimpse of the life of the men who toiled here to harvest nearly $2,500,000 of silver from the mountain. The view of the Panamint Range is spectacular.

General Information
Jurisdiction: Private claims on BLM land
Road status: Climbing on trails and cross-country; graded access road
The climb: 1.7 mi, 1,350 ft up one way / moderate
Main attractions: Historic silver mine, ghost town, trail climb
USGS 7.5' topo maps: Panamint Springs, Revenue Canyon*
Maps: pp. 523*, 499

Location and Access
Lookout Mountain is a colorful, steep-sided promontory of folded Devonian limestone and dolomite, in the northern Argus Range. With a strong high-clearance four-while-drive vehicle, one can drive a rough stony road right up to its summit, but to climb it on foot all you need is a standard-clearance vehicle. First work your way on Highway 190 to Panamint Springs, 45.2 miles east of Olancha, then to the Panamint Valley Road 2.5 miles east of it. Drive this road 7.4 miles southeast to the signed Minnietta Road on the right. Take this wide graded road 3.6 miles east, over Ash Hill, until it veers north and merges with the Nadeau Trail, signed P 105, coming in from the left. Lookout Mountain rises just to the west. Continue north 0.4 mile to a fork. Angle left on the Nadeau Trail Cutoff, and go 0.35 mile to a junction. The left fork is the way to the summit. It gets rapidly rough, so park at this junction.

Route Description
Lookout Mountain was made famous by a large silver lode discovered near its summit in April 1875. The discovery attracted Senator George Hearst—his son would later build Hearst Castle—who promptly bought into the claims and formed the Modoc Consolidated Mining Company. The area was so rich that after a few veins had been opened, it was incorporated into a new mining district. Inspired by the

open views from the mine, the mountain and the town that grew near the mine were named Lookout. The ore was initially teamed to Panamint City for smelting. In 1876, desert freighter Remi Nadeau delivered to Lookout two 30-ton smelting furnaces. First fired up in October, they produced around 10 tons of silver-lead bullion daily. The charcoal needed to reduce the ore was at first made from pinyon pine logged on this range. By the end of 1876, this scant wood supply was nearly depleted, and Hearst turned to the extensive forest in Wildrose Canyon, across Panamint Valley. Up in the canyon the company erected ten large kilns, which were activated in the spring of 1877. In May, Lookout boasted 30 or 40 houses and stone buildings, three saloons, two general stores, and a bank. Three times a week, a stagecoach connected it to Darwin and Panamint City. By the summer of 1878, the furnaces had churned out over $1,000,000 worth of bullion. For reasons not well understood, the kilns and furnaces were shut down a year later. But there was still plenty of ore, and mining continued. By 1890, the Modoc Mine had produced about $1,900,000, and joined the hall of fame as one of the richest silver mines in the Death Valley region.

In its early history, two shortcuts gave quick access to the mine. The Pack Trail was built for pack animals; the China Wall Trail, much steeper, was for humans. Its namesake is the Chinese employees who built it, and perhaps also its construction: most of it was supported by curvy stone walls, like the Great Wall of China. To get to it from the road junction, hike up the road 0.45 mile to, then in, a steep canyon, to the foot of the tailing and large retaining wall of the Lower Tunnel. Walk up the short tailing to the top of the wall, then go about 25 yards to the left, away from the tunnel. The China Wall Trail starts on the right, just before a cable anchored to the mountain. This narrow foot trail was built to last—and it did. Other than a small landslide and a litter of stones loosened by the local burros, it is essentially intact after 140 years. In 0.4 mile it switchbacks 430 feet up the steep canyon head to a saddle on Lookout Mountain's northeast shoulder, where it joins the Pack Trail. The name Lookout is instantly justified when you reach the saddle and succumb to the first gorgeous view of Panamint Valley.

The trail continues 0.15 mile up the more gentle ridge until it ends at the road at the Modoc Mine. Continue west on the road; be very careful, and avoid walking here at night, as the area has many deep open shafts, including one *right in the middle of the road*. Here as all along the Pack Trail, slag litters the ground. These shiny black pebbles were formed in the smelters when charcoal combined chemically with the silver ore. Four of the Modoc Mine's main tunnels are located along this stretch. Most of the historic production came out of the two

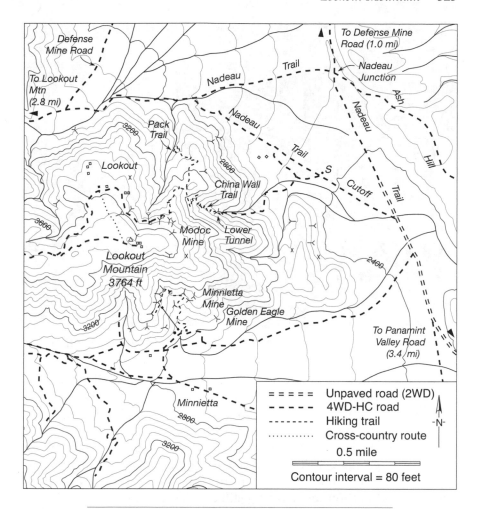

Lookout Mountain

	Dist.(mi)	Elev.(ft)
Nadeau Trail Cutoff	0.0	2,420
Lower end of China Wall Trail	0.5	2,840
Ridge/Jct with Pack Trail	0.9	3,270
Lower end of Pack Trail	(0.35)	~2,980
Nadeau Trail	(0.6)	2,750
Return via Nadeau Tr. Cutoff	(1.3)	2,420
Upper end of Pack Trail/Road	1.05	3,435
Lookout (main building)	1.4	3,580
Lookout Mountain	1.65	3,764

Lookout's main stone building, near the summit of Lookout Mountain

split 500-foot tunnels of Level No. 2, the first adit below the road. The two long, superposed stone platforms on the right side of the road just a little further is the site of the 1876 smelters. Although it is one of the region's oldest ghost towns, Lookout still has five stone buildings and the ruins of at least two dozen more. The largest structure, right by the road past the smelters site, is a prime example of desert mining camp architecture in the 1880s, its two-foot-thick walls of carefully laid angular rocks and portions of its rafters still defying gravity.

From there it is a short walk up the broad ridge (or the road) to the summit. Lookout Mountain was so full of silver that there is a shaft even at its very top, as well as three stone buildings for the miners who liked their room with a view. The barren summit knoll is indeed a spectacular lookout over the 75-mile length of Panamint Valley, from the pale dunes and dry lake in the northern basin to the southern basin's salt pan, all sprawled below the majestic Panamint Range.

To return a different way, hike back to the saddle and go down the Pack Trail. In 0.35 mile it ends at the bottom of a canyon. Continue down waves of white-marble slickrock, then along the canyon's stony wash, to the canyon mouth. The Nadeau Trail Cutoff, which runs just past it, will take you around the tip of the mountain to your vehicle.

■

MINE PEAK

In the middle of the Argus Range stands a little-known summit called Mine Peak, girdled indeed by mines — gold, iron, and pumice — some dating back to the 1870s. It makes for a good little climb into a designated wilderness haunted by wild burros, most of it up a mining road blasted into vivid volcanic rocks. The whole route commands glorious vistas of Panamint Valley and the iconic, nearly two-mile-high western scarp of the Panamint Range.

General Information
Jurisdiction: Argus Range Wilderness (BLM)
Road status: Climbing on trail and cross-country; 2WD dirt access road
The climb: 2.3 mi, 1,790 ft up, 60 ft down one way / moderate
Main attractions: Volcanic geology, views of Panamint Mountains
USGS 7.5' topo maps: Maturango Peak SE, Slate Range Crossing*
Maps: pp. 527*, 499

Location and Access
In its heyday, when the Modoc Mine needed iron-ore flux for its smelters, it turned to a small iron deposit conveniently located just down the road, at the foot of Mine Peak. The property, then known as the Hoot Owl Mine, had a lens of massive hematite and magnetite that met all of its needs. Enough ore was even left behind for another 8,000 tons to be shipped during World War II, then in 1959. Around the 1950s a circuitous road was built to develop a quarry on associated claims. The quarry road, now almost entirely within the Argus Range Wilderness, is the least difficult route to climb Mine Peak.

To reach Panamint Valley from the center of Trona in Searles Valley, drive north on the Wildrose-Trona Road about 14.2 miles to the pass between the two valleys (Slate Range Crossing). Continue down the switchbacks into Panamint Valley 3.1 miles to the primitive Nadeau Trail on the left, which is half a mile before the graded Nadeau Road (paralleled by a small power line). Go 100 yards to a road on the left. Follow it 0.75 mile to the smaller quarry road on the left. Turn left and go 0.2 mile to a small wash crossing, where the quarry road starts climbing steeply into the range. Park here, as the remaining 0.2 mile up this road to the wilderness boundary is very rough. All along these roads Mine Peak is visible to the west, then southwest. There is a washout 0.4 mile from the Nadeau Trail that requires good clearance.

Route Description

From the valley the quarry road climbs along the steep side of a transverse ridge that buttresses the Argus Range. It switchbacks tightly three times, then shoots up a sustained 20% incline. Carved into solid rock with dynamite and steel blades, it is a rough grade trapped between blown-up cliffs on one side and a long drop on the other. When walking on its sharp edge there is an astounding perspective in the vertical depth and breadth of the ridge's precipitous flank. Huge volumes of blasted rocks were unceremoniously shoved over the edge, a manmade landslide of boulders in stasis that spills down to a wash hundreds of feet below. The ridge is all volcanic, a whole suite of andesite ranging from light-gray with inclusions of pale plagioclase, to merlot sprinkled with black biotite crystals. Some road cuts are strikingly bicolored, one half blue-gray, the other a palette of purples laced with white calcite. Erosion and gravity reign supreme over the road. After a heavy downpour, the narrow erosional trench that runs along it channels a stream so energetic that the road's demise seems to be its sole mission in life. In normal weather the foot-deep trench is an awkward yet easier path than the rest of the road, as slippery as marbles.

This is donkey paradise—low human visitation, no NPS forced retirement program, and an asylum protected by military secrecy within trotting distance should things get out of hand. From valley to summit *Equus asinus* droppings are everywhere, in isolated clumps where an animal pooped on the go, in well-fertilized plots at their favorite hangouts. With binoculars you might spot a few of them, motionless mocha specks standing stoically under the sun down below among the valley shrubs. In a face-to-face encounter a shy burro will run away, stop, turn around broadside, and check you out. Accustomed to occasional cars in the valley, on Mine Peak a burro will more likely stare at you with unflinching eyes that dare you to come one step closer.

After a mile the grade reaches its apex 720 feet below Mine Peak. There it angles left, levels off, and moseys on half a mile to a fork at the edge of the quarry. The left fork descends into the quarry, a mess of haulageways bladed into the mountainside. After all the roads and all the damage, unlike the Hoot Owl Mine this area turned out a superb failure—there was nothing up here to harvest. In the middle of this devastation the one structure left is an incongruous wooden outhouse, a farcical memorial to the money that was flushed down the toilet.

The right fork pushes on to a pass just above the quarry, then drops in sheer switchbacks into Water Canyon—a longer but scenic alternative return route. Mine Peak is just up the ridge northwest from the pass, but a spur bristling with vertical outcrops blocks the way. The

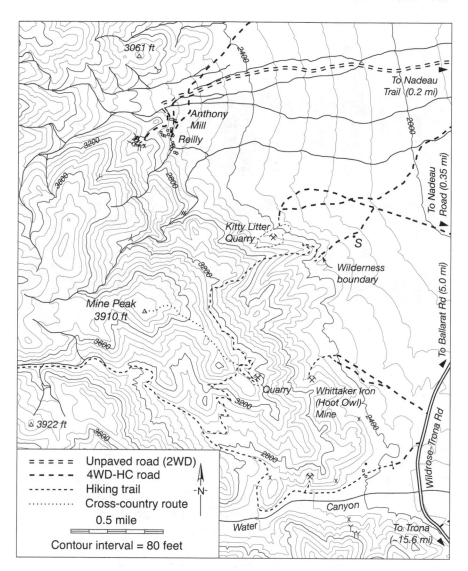

	Dist.(mi)	Elev.(ft)
Mine Peak		
Foot of mountain/grade	0.0	2,180
Top of grade (left bend)	1.05	3,190
Junction at quarry	1.55	3,310
Saddle on crest	1.85	3,500
Mine Peak	2.3	3,910

Manly Peak and South Panamint Playa from Mine Peak

spur can be circumvented by starting 200 yards west of the fork, where three tall mining monuments stand not far above the road. The route is straightforward, northwest past these monuments up across a hillside to the saddle just north of the rocky spur. The slope is mostly dirt with scattered rocks, occasionally steep enough to want to hold onto something. The saddle is an open bridge of land connecting the spur to Mine Peak. The final stretch is up a broad ramp peppered with wind-stunted scrubs, cottontop cactus, and chunks of reddish basalt. When I visited in October the whole mountain had morphed into a sweeping green of new shoots fooled out of dormancy by unexpected rains.

The road, the crest, and eventually the summit deliver increasingly open views of Panamint Valley, its delicate dunes at one end, the ghost of its Ice-Age lake at the other, the skyscraping Panamint Mountains behind it. Someone familiar with this vast range will recognize dozens of places tucked in its giant pleats of stone—peaks named Tuber and Pinto, the wiggly crack of South Park Canyon, the pale fish-shaped imprint of the Hall Canyon Pluton, and the little green spot of Warm Sulphur Springs below Surprise Canyon. This sight is a vivid reminder of what we have been fortunate to visit, and of how much we have yet to discover.

■

SLATE RANGE

North of the town of Mojave there is a lazy byway to Death Valley that unfolds for miles across thinly populated desert. Most of it a two-lane road, it passes through Fremont Valley and the tiny ghost town of Garlock, then wiggles down Poison Canyon, past gray badlands and granite fangs featured in old westerns, into Searles Valley. This is the first of the many long valleys framed by immense mountains that form the mighty Basin and Range. The mountains on Searles Valley's east side are the Slate Range. This is the edge of nowhere: the small community in the valley is Trona, pop. 1,900, the last town for 120 miles.

About 34 miles long, the Slate Range rises to heights of 4,000 feet above Searles Valley's snowy salt flats. Its northern third is made of Paleozoic sedimentary formations partly overlain by Cenozoic basalt. The middle third is almost all granitic rocks, and the southern third a blend of granitic and metamorphic rocks. This mixed geology hosted a surfeit of ores. Precious metals were first identified by brothers Dennis and John Searles during one of the earliest expeditions into the region, in 1861. The following years witnessed a minor rush and the creation of 20-some companies, until the district's mill was burned down by natives in 1866. Between the 1870s and the 1950s, many mines were active, mostly on the west slope. Two of them, the Gold Bottom and Ophir mines, approached the million-dollar mark in lead and silver.

The area's greatest wealth, however, came not from the mountains but from the valley below them. It was John Searles who first recognized the commercial value of the valley's colossal saline deposits, in 1863. Nine years later he started what was probably the state's first borax mine. For 15 years, his outfit scraped raw borax efflorescence off the lake's surface and refined it into borax. Since that era, Searles Lake has been exploited almost continuously, and it has yielded an exceptional suite of minerals. During World War I its potash production went into the manufacture of gunpowder. It also supplies sodium sulfate, phosphoric acid, borax, lithium, bromine, table salt, and the mineral trona after which the town was named. Brine is pumped from deep beds, and its salt content precipitated in solar ponds. Today, Trona is probably the longest active mining town in the California desert. It may well stay alive much longer: its reserves are estimated at $150 billion, more than all the gold recovered in California. The eerie Trona Pinnacles, at the south end of the lake playa, are the spectacular spires of tufa left behind when the lake last dried up.

Since the Slate Range is usually accessed from Searles Valley, a visit here goes hand in hand with a visit to Trona. Molded by its long mining history, Trona is the lone survivor from an extinct era. The alkali lake, on the east side of the one and only artery, is a mine field of injection wells, ditches, ponds, pipelines, rails, dirt roads, mesas of snow-white minerals, and square miles of evaporators. Across the road, the town is a thin spread of modest houses with bare yards enclosed with chain-link fences. A huge processing plant looms over it, a delightfully antiquated multi-story building that spews out white streamers of gas tainted with hydrogen sulfide. At night it is lit up like a spaceship. The town, nicely old-fashioned and eerily empty, has a gas station, a motel, a high school, a general store, a hamburger joint built in half of the town's historic theater, and the ruins of many roadside businesses that died decades ago. Driving through Trona is a liberating trip back in time, a rare treat to a town still free of traffic lights, malls, and glitz.

The southern two thirds of the Slate Range belongs to the China Lake Naval Air Warfare Center, including the two highest named summits, Straw Peak (5,587') and Layton Peak (5,181'). The rest is open to ordinary humans. Although none of it has been protected because of high mineral potential, it has all the natural qualities of a wilderness. The northern tip, overlooking Panamint Valley, is mostly rolling hills and subdued mesas. The granitic areas are characterized by steep upper slopes plated with outcrops and cut by stony canyons. Because all other nearby summits are controlled by the military, this is the only range to view Searles Valley from high up.

Native people have left here an extensive legacy of rock shelters, cairns, quarries, ancient trails, and elaborate flaked stone tools at least 11,000 years old. The most intriguing remains are geoglyphs, giant figures drawn on the ground with boulders. Some geoglyphs are religious symbols rooted in shamanism, others stylized representations of wildlife associated with water. The Slate Range is special in that some of its earthen art was built not on fans but right on the crest. The search for these mysterious figures dedicated to Paleolithic superstitions can add a compelling reason to explore this largely ignored range.

■

SLATE POINT AND EMPASSE PEAK

Strategically located on the Slate Range's northern crest, Empasse Peak and its neighbor Slate Point overlook the beautiful alignment of Panamint Valley and Searles Valley, and the long ranges that frame them. The climbing is just about as easy as it gets, mostly on a good foot trail that samples a variety of interesting geological features, from dry lakes along a small fault to intricate ventifacts.

General Information

Jurisdiction: Public lands (BLM)
Road status: Roadless; access on graded or paved roads
The climb (Slate Point): 1.4 mi, 630 ft up one way / easy
The climb (Empasse Peak): 1.5 mi, 500 ft up, 120 ft down one way / easy
Main attractions: Geology, views of southern Panamint Valley
USGS 7.5' topo map: Slate Range Crossing
Maps: pp. 533*, 499

Location and Access

From near the pass between Searles Valley and Panamint Valley, a narrow gateway known as Slate Range Crossing, a foot trail cuts southeast across the northern Slate Range to end in about 4 miles at a radio tower maintenance road. This trail, which I refer to as Dry Lakes Trail, provides easy access to both Slate Point and Empasse Peak.

To get to the trail's south end, from the center of Trona drive north about 11.3 miles to the signed Quarry Road on the right. Coming from the north, this road is 2.85 miles south of Slate Range Crossing. The Quarry Road splits after 0.4 mile (keep right on BLM road P 4, a good graded road), then again 0.2 mile further (keep right on P 4). Continue east 1.2 miles to the first switchback (a right turn), then south up the switchbacks 1 mile to the first right bend at the crest, where the road veers south. The trailhead is in this bend on the east side. This is a good starting point, especially for novices, the trail being well defined. However, you start from the crest, which has similar views and elevation as the summits, and it dampens the climb's climax. Starting from the first switchback (park on the left side just below the bend), the route described below, is more exciting, and half a mile shorter.

To get to the trail's north end, drive 2.85 miles north of the Quarry Road to Slate Range Crossing, and at the pass turn right onto a primitive road. If your vehicle has standard clearance, park here. Otherwise

Southern Panamint Playa and Panamint Mountains from Slate Point

turn right almost immediately on a rough road with sharp rocks. After 0.2 mile, turn right at a fork. Park at the T junction 120 yards further. The Dry Lakes Trail starts at this junction, heading east-southeast. This is the shortest access to Empasse Peak, visible 1 mile to the southeast.

Route Description

From the first switchback the route is up the narrow ravine that wiggles between the hills to the north. Head down towards it first, and in 100 yards, before getting to its wash, you will run into a foot trail. The trail heads up along the gentle open bench on the east side of the wash, then squeezes between the hills alongside the ravine. In the hills the trail disappears several times, but it does not matter—following the narrow wash is just as easy. A third of a mile into the hills the ravine opens up onto a peculiar valley, straight and narrow, nearly level. The ravine, the valley, and the valley's continuation to the north are all eroded along the weakened plane of a mile-long fault that splits the crest in two. Slate Point first comes into view in this area, a flat ramp of dark basalt rising at the end of the valley. The trail resumes shortly inside the valley. The Dry Lakes Trail comes down from the right and merges with it soon after. If you started at the south end of that trail, this is where you will join in.

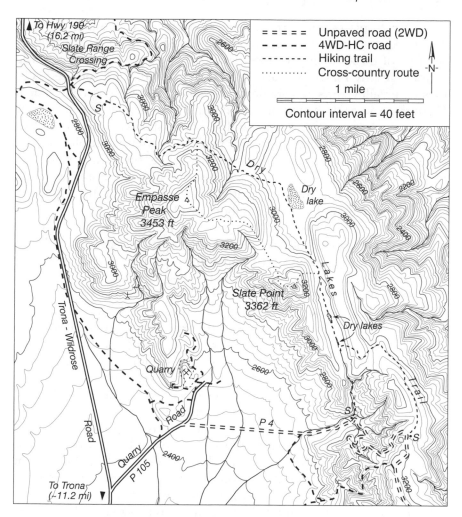

Slate Point and Empasse Peak

	Dist.(mi)	Elev.(ft)
Access road at first switchback	0.0	3,140
Junction with Dry Lakes Trail	0.6	2,770
South trailhead (Quarry Rd)	(1.1)	2,970
Pass (leave trail)	1.1	3,005
Slate Point	(0.3)	3,362
Pass (leave trail)	2.4	3,150
Empasse Peak	(0.5)	3,453
North trailhead (Slate R. Xing)	3.4	3,070

At three places, Quaternary rains flooded the cleft along the fault and filled them with fine sediments. The trail junction is at the tip of the first of these small dry lakes. This one and the second one a little farther are tiny playas of cracked silt littered with dark rounded cobbles. The valley ends at a shallow pass shortly after the second playa. From the pass area, the top of Slate Point is a moderately steep quarter of a mile up its northeastern shoulder, on a stairway of low flattish boulders. Here as along the entire trail, the range is an old field of Cenozoic basalt where only emaciated creosote, burrobush, and saltbush bear the desert's scant green. The restless coalition of heat, wind, rain, quakes, and snow has weathered the lava flow to disjointed pieces, each one sun-baked to a mahogany glaze.

In spite of its modest size, the summit is an outstanding spot. It stands at the apex of Panamint Valley to the north and Searles Valley to the south, arranged head to toe and framed by long ranges in classic Basin and Range geometry. Panamint Valley stands center stage, its long lake of blinding salt showcased against the majestic Panamint Mountains. For their sheer volume alone this is the California desert's greatest range, an immense cordillera that rises nearly two miles above the valley. The only smudge in this grandiose scenery is the infamous Briggs Mine, a gold operation that has been stripping in the middle of the range an area the size of 20 city blocks. Slate Point overlooks a world-class heritage hemorrhaging crushed rocks and cyanide. The Briggs corporate thugs should be let loose in their own excavation, bare feet in their boxer shorts, to see what we have all lost.

The views are similar from Empasse Peak, a broad dome edged with resistant spills of broken basalt. The shortest way from Slate Point is the 1-mile jaunt across the saddle between the summits. One can also return to the trail, and follow it north down into the larger depression that holds the third alluvial lake, colonized by skeletal shrubs. The trail then angles northwest and goes over two low passes. The second pass is on Empasse Peak's northern shoulder, a moderately steep open slope to the summit. This saddle can also be reached by an easy 1-mile walk from the north end of the Dry Lakes Trail. All over this area, the threadbare veneer of stark basalt lets through the mountain's colorful Paleozoic underbelly. It is a remarkably ornate breccia of fawn limestone and dark-gray dolomite cemented with frosty seams of white calcite. Sand-blasted for eons by salt-laden winds blowing from Searles Lake, every surface is textured with rills, crevasses, and prickles, easily drawing blood. Even on the gloomiest wintry day these striking works of art will cheer up a poet's heart.

■

SEARLES PEAK

The highest point in the portion of the Slate Range open to the public, Searles Peak is an action-packed summit to climb. The first segment is an easy amble in a broad and shallow wash, and the second one a hard steep trudge up an awesome little gorge with a lot of character, a delightful unpredictability, and a plethora of minor obstacles. The summit commands a sweeping panorama of Searles Valley, the old mining town of Trona, and the crumpled western front of the Slate Range neatly curled around the valley's dry lake.

General Information
Jurisdiction: Public lands (BLM)
Road status: Roadless; access on primitive HC road
The climb (Searles Peak): 3.3 mi, 2,860 ft up one way / strenuous
The climb (Slate Pk): 4.0 mi, 3,110 ft up, 270 ft down one way / strenuous
Main attractions: Rough canyon route, views of Searles Lake and Trona
USGS 7.5' topo maps: Trona East, Copper Queen Canyon
Maps: pp. 537*, 499

Location and Access
Searles Peak and its neighbor Slate Peak are located at the head of Bundy Canyon, north of Trona in Searles Valley. From the center of town, drive north on the Trona-Wildrose Road about 4.9 miles to the signed Valley Wells Road on the right. When coming from the north, this junction is 9.2 miles south of Slate Range Crossing. Drive the Valley Wells Road east 0.4 mile to a junction near some fenced installations, where the road curves left and straightens out to the northeast as P 39. Stay on it 1.1 miles to a road on the right signed P 33. Follow road P 33 generally east 2.2 miles, to the ruins of the Ophir Mine on the left. Just past it the road angles right and descends 0.25 mile along the foot of the Slate Range to the mouth of Bundy Canyon. There is a track in this canyon but it is illegal; park at the mouth. A standard-clearance vehicle can make it close to the mine; high clearance helps beyond.

Route Description
This is a gratifying climb, almost all of it along Bundy Canyon, a two-faced drainage that starts as a sedate swath and morphs halfway up into a sheer gorge littered with falls and boulders. From the road the wash first winds briefly through a limestone passage. It then cuts a

broad path through the uneventful low foothills of the Slate Range, Searles Peak rearing up ahead in muted browns dotted with silver and charcoal blisters of bare stone. The action starts nearly 2 miles in, where the wash reaches the abrupt face of the mountain. The canyon forks three ways. The short north fork (left) shoots up to a ridge, the middle fork heads east (straight), and the main canyon veers southeast (right). About 0.1 mile before this confluence the wash splits. The left branch leads into the middle fork, the route to the summit.

Trapped in precipitous walls, the middle fork curves through several sharp 90-degree bends, then scores of smaller wiggles as it steepens and narrows to a V-shaped gorge. The entire mountain is plated with outcrops, a symphony of black granite, pale monzonite, and other richly colored subspecies of granitic rocks. The walls are oddly out of kilter, seemingly too slanted to hold themselves together. Literally tons of boulders, recalled by gravity, have crashed down into the wash. At places erosion has not kept up with tectonic uplift, and the canyon floor jumps up 5, 10, or 20 near-vertical feet over resilient ledges. There are about ten falls (Class 2–4), some of them bypassed by a use trail.

It might be easiest to stay in the canyon to its head at the crest, and walk the open crest south to the summit. There is another exit route, however, that cuts down on distance, although it is not terribly easy. About 1.1 miles above the triple fork, where the walls shrink a little, a couple of ill-defined ravines plunge down the very steep south side. Clumps of upright rocks protrude from the slope, white at the bottom, dark grey higher up. Climbing out of the canyon in this vicinity is the shortest route, either up one of the ravines, a ridge between them, or a combination to avoid plants and boulders. This is the most demanding stretch.

After being confined in the canyon, emerging on the bald shoulder overlooking the valley is a liberating experience. From there it is a

Searles Peak		
	Dist.(mi)	Elev.(ft)
Mouth of Bundy Canyon	0.0	2,230
End of narrower passage	0.4	2,400
Triple fork	1.95	~3,100
Leave main wash	~3.05	~4,565
Ridge	3.2	~4,960
Searles Peak	3.3	5,092
Slate Peak	4.0	5,068

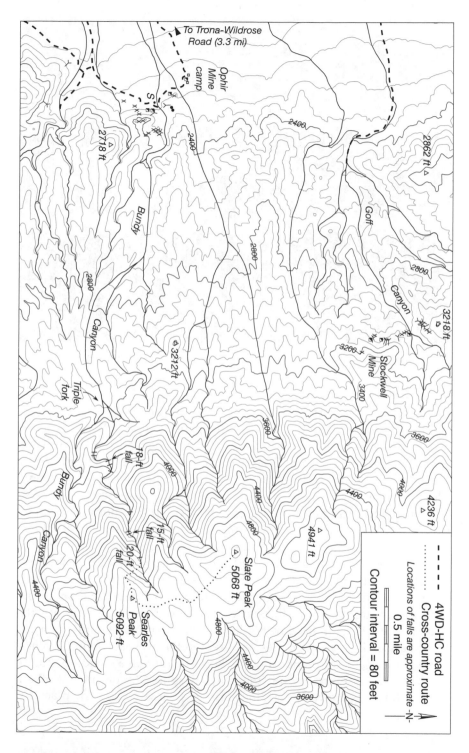

To Trona-Wildrose
Road (3.3 mi)

Ophir
Mine
camp

2862 ft △

2718 ft △

Bundy

Goff

2400

2800

2862 ft △

3218 ft △

Canyon

2800

3212 ft △

Triple
fork

Stockwell
Mine

3200

3400

3600

4000

Bundy

18-ft
fall

15-ft
fall

20-ft
fall

4236 ft △

4000

4400

4000

4400

4941 ft △

Slate Peak
5068 ft △

Searles
Peak
5092 ft △

Canyon

4400

4800

4800

4800

4000

3600

— — —   4WD-HC road
....   Cross-country route
Locations of falls are approximate
0.5 mile
Contour interval = 80 feet
-N-

Sand storm in Searles Valley from the middle fork of Bundy Canyon

short walk to the summit, up a wide, unobstructed ridge. Slate Peak, the next named summit less than a mile to the north-northwest, is reached by an easy stroll up and down a gentle roll of hills.

Had you stood on Searles Peak or Slate Peak during the last Ice Age, when increased rainfall and snow melt from a glaciated Sierra Nevada flooded many desert sinks, you would have been almost completely surrounded by water. At its high stands, Lake Searles was 635 feet deep and extended far enough north to lap the mouth of Bundy Canyon. To the south it formed a single body of water with Lake China and wrapped around the tip of the Slate Range, where it spilled into Panamint Valley and kept it filled with a long lake. The mountains were green with juniper down to the marshlands that flourished along the water's edge. The valleys dried up long ago, but more than a century of mining has brought Searles Valley's Pleistocene lake partly back to life. On a sunny day, the lake's jigsaw of ponds and evaporators sparkles in vibrant shades of blue. On the western shore, Trona's alien plant keeps on plundering the bone-white playa's endless bounty. When the afternoon wind picks up, diaphanous plumes of alkali dust drift across the valley, adding eeriness to an already eerie place.

■

EL PASO MOUNTAINS

Together with the Coso Range, the El Paso Mountains are the Mojave Desert's westernmost sizable range, and the closest to the Sierra Nevada. About 21 miles in length and trending east-northeast, they parallel on their south flank the Garlock Fault, one of California's longest active faults. On this side the mountains' front descends abruptly into Fremont Valley, a closed basin where water drains onto the usually dry playa of Koehn Lake. The north flank is an undulating plateau that slopes more gradually into Indian Wells Valley. Although of modest size and elevation—their high point is an extinct volcano named Black Mountain only 5,412 feet high—the El Paso Mountains stand out for their exceptional diversity. The western tip is known for its superbly colorful badlands and finely fluted cliffs, often featured in western movies. One of the local sedimentary units, the Dove Spring Formation, hosts a sequence of fossils so profuse that it has become a standard reference to date Miocene formations throughout the country. The El Paso Mountains are also home to a few oases, desert tortoise, coyotes, Joshua trees and a few rare plants. It is a haven for raptors, especially red-tailed hawks, Cooper's hawks, and loggerhead shrikes.

Yet what is most special about this range is that it was for centuries an important religious and spiritual center for the Kawaiisu and possibly other desert people. Some 200 cultural sites are scattered on the western flanks of Black Mountain and throughout the range—camp sites, ceremonial centers, toolstone quarries, milling stations, and rock art that date back a hundred centuries. In prehistoric times the heart of the Mountain Kawaiisu's homeland was the Tehachapis and the southern Sierra Nevada. The high mountains offered a greater diversity of game and plants, especially the pinyon-pine nuts central to their diet. The El Paso Mountains were shared by the Mountain Kawaiisu and the Desert Kawaiisu, in particular for hunting and gathering, and for religious ceremonies held on Black Mountain. For at least 700 years, possibly much longer, the Kawaiisu were probably the guardians of this holy range. They lived in small villages, and bivouacked in seasonal camps to hunt, quarry chert, and manufacture stone tools. This ancestral connection permeates the landscape. They left behind a museum of rock art—pictographs, an intaglio, rock alignments, and fine petroglyphs crowded on the desert varnish of multifaceted boulders. The rock art is similar in age to the famous Coso Range petroglyphs, and executed in the same exquisite style, with bighorn sheep portrayed with full, front-facing, bifurcating horns.

About 40% of the El Paso Mountains are protected. The El Paso Mountains Wilderness (23,669 acres) covers the north-central part of the range, while Red Rock Canyon State Park (25,325 acres) straddles the western tip. A large rectangular portion of the central mountains, including almost all of the wilderness and the park's northeast corner, was designated as the Last Chance Archaeological District to recognize the area's exceptional cultural value.

The El Paso Mountains' geology is remarkably diverse. The range is broadly divided into two geographical regions by Last Chance Canyon, the wide drainage that runs along much of its length. North of this canyon, including Black Mountain and extending westward almost to Red Rock Canyon, the terrain is all volcanic, mostly coarse pyroclastics and andesite flows from the Middle Miocene. On the south side of Last Chance Canyon, if you were to hike the crest from end to end, you would come across at least four dozen rock units spanning half a billion years. At the east end you would start with the Late Jurassic Laurel Mountain pluton. You would continue across a miles-long stack of thin metamorphic formations oriented perpendicular to the crest, one at a time through the entire Paleozoic, a potpourri of metamorphosed limestone, chert, argillite, basalt, and conglomerate. You would then cross Permian gneiss on Weiss Mountain and slip into Triassic quartz monzonite and quartz diorite before running into the brilliant sequences of sandstone, arkose, tuff, rhyolite, and basalt that compose Red Rock Canyon's nightmarish landscapes.

Much of this range is unfortunately still open to driving. The proliferation of roads and illegal off-road driving make some areas look as wild as an off-highway-vehicle area, and at times almost as noisy. The proximity to Ridgecrest and other gun-minded towns has also resulted in a significant loss of peacefulness as shooters swarm down to the mountains on evenings and weekends for killing practice. Shell casings discarded by ill-educated hunters and recreational shooters are commonplace. Take a few minutes to clean up after them. It is unlikely that they will change their way.

■

EL PASO PEAKS

> *The El Paso Peaks are a series of small summits on the northeastern crest of the El Paso Mountains, overlooking Indian Wells Valley. The climb is easy, starting from one of the summits and swinging up and down along the crest first on a dirt road, then on a foot trail, with just a couple of short steep grades. Strategically located at the boundary between the desert and the Sierra Nevada, linked to both by strong geological and cultural bonds, this little mountain offers inspirational views of these two ecological extremes.*

General Information
Jurisdiction: Public lands (BLM)
Road status: Hiking from paved road
The climb (highest peak): 0.8 mi, 370 ft up, 170 ft down one way/easy
The climb (4,347-ft peak): 1.25 mi, 410 ft up, 430 ft down one way/easy
Main attractions: A short climb, geology, views of the southern Sierras
USGS 7.5' topo map: El Paso Peaks
Maps: pp. 543*, 499

Location and Access
The El Paso Peaks are located at the northeastern tip of the El Paso Mountains, a few miles south of the town of Ridgecrest. To get there from the north, from the Ridgecrest turn-off on Highway 395 drive 6.8 miles south to a paved road on the right, across from the signed Searles Station Cutoff Road. Coming from the other direction, this junction is 8.0 miles north of the aspiring ghost town of Johannesburg. The paved road services two separate radio facilities. Stay on it 1.5 miles to a fork. The right fork climbs to the first facility, crowned by a white radome on Laurel Mountain. Keep left instead, and go another 1.6 miles, generally west up a curvy grade, to the second facility. This road is accessible to all vehicles, but the asphalt is filled with small sharp rocks and locally potholed, so vehicles with street tires should go slowly. The El Paso Peaks are the low summits about half a mile to the west.

A sign posted at the facility warns that radio-frequency radiation at the site may exceed the safe limit for humans. Since "may exceed" likely means that it does (official safe limits on almost anything toxic to humans tend to be lowered every few years), it is a good idea to park either a little before or past the station to minimize exposure.

Route Description

This is a particularly short climb, less than a mile and all of about 500 feet of elevation change each way. It can be argued that it is not as natural as most, because of the proximity of many dirt roads and the high probability of an encounter with a caravan of heartwarming, gun-toting ATV drivers. Seasoned climbers may even shun this peak. But there is still wildness in it, lots of fresh air, the opportunity for a little physical exercise, and the views are outstanding. Novices may find it empowering, because it is so accessible without being signed.

Directions are simple. From the radio facility the access road continues west as a primitive road, up and down along the crest. After 0.35 mile, where the road veers left and drops down the side of the mountain, the El Paso Peaks Trail picks up ahead, straight up the crest. Butchered by repeated illegal biking, it is a deeply rutted mess. Gravel steals traction on its precipitous incline; zigzagging up the slope next to it makes the ascent safer. At the top the trail levels off, passes by the second highest of the El Paso Peaks (~4,530 ft) on the left, and forks soon after. The left fork ascends a second steep grade, shorter and a little less abrupt. It then circumvents the south side of the highest peak to an overlook on the left, just past the peak's southwestern shoulder. The highest peak is a tenth of a mile cross-country up this shoulder.

This mountain captures the mind not by its grandeur but by its physical and geographic significance. It lies at a continental crossroad, overlooking the world-class glacier-carved Sierra Nevada to the west, sand and creosote desert plains to the north, and processions of imposing desert ranges to the east. The best time to climb this mountain is at the crack of dawn on a cloudless day, when light soaks every peak on the high Sierra's castellated rim before slowly creeping across the valley and touching the desert. The El Paso Peaks were once made of the same miles-thick layers of Paleozoic carbonates as many desert ranges. When the Sierra Nevada pluton was emplaced in the Jurassic, a small satellite pluton intruded land just north of here, and cooked the ancient sedimentary rocks to a whole suite of metamorphic rocks. The ground on the El Paso Peaks ridge is now a smorgasbord of colorful hornfels and pale tactites, a heritage that bridges both provinces. The dichotomy between these two worlds is so intense that it split the Kawaiisu Indians into two cultures, the Mountain Kawaiisu on the Sierra side, and the Desert Kawaiisu on the east side, the El Paso Mountains forming their natural border.

The trail continues past the overlook, snaking lazily along the diminishing spine of the mountain. It passes by one more small peak, then crosses a narrow hogback before reaching the last peak (4,347') in

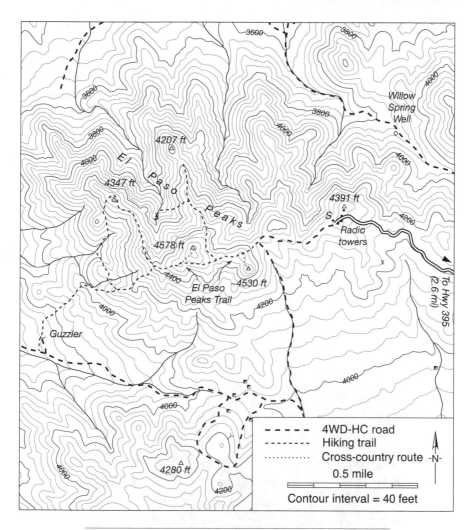

El Paso Peaks

	Dist.(mi)	Elev.(ft)
Radio towers	0.0	4,375
El Paso Peaks Trail	0.35	4,365
Top of steep incline	0.45	4,490
~4,530-ft peak	(0.05)	~4,530
Trail junction	0.55	4,450
Overlook (SW shoulder)	0.7	4,525
El Paso Peak (highest)	(0.1)	4,578
4,347-ft peak	1.25	4,347

this short chain and dropping off the south side to join other local trails.

Even on a small desert mountain, distractions are so plentiful that it is difficult to train our eyes on anything for long. The hills are play-grounds for whiptail lizards and Mojave ground squirrels, under the watchful eyes of ravens and raptors. In May the area is inundated with California buckwheat and the small light-blue daisies of wire lettuce. Each summit offers a slightly different view, north to the towns of Ridgecrest and Inyokern, and a dry lake called China that mere civil-ians hardly every get to see, west of the southern Sierras, or southwest along the fault-bound length of the El Paso Mountains to Koehn Lake, seldom seen from above and striking for its surprisingly large size.

■

Indian Wells Valley and southern Sierra Nevada from El Paso Peak

BLACK MOUNTAIN

The highest summit in the El Paso Mountains, Black Mountain stands at the heart of both the volcanic center that smothered the area under lava in the Miocene, and the holy ground of the Kawaiisu culture that lived here for centuries. The mountain is a tundra of scant grass and shrubs that becomes increasingly invaded by basaltic boulders at higher elevation. The ascent offers a good view of Black Mountain's crater, of the colorful surrounding landscape of rolling hills and abrupt mesas, and of vast Indian Wells Valley.

General Information
Jurisdiction: El Paso Mountains Wilderness (BLM)
Road status: Climbing on trail and cross-country; HC/4WD access
The climb: 2.5 mi, 1,580 ft up, 240 ft down one way/moderate–difficult
Main attractions: An old crater, views of Indian Wells Valley
USGS 7.5' topo map: Garlock
Maps: pp. 547*, 499

Location and Access
Black Mountain is in the central El Paso Mountains, overlooking Indian Wells Valley to the north and west. From the westbound exit on Highway 58 in Mojave, drive Highway 14 north 17.3 miles to the Red Rock Randsburg Road at 1 o'clock. Stay on it 11.1 miles to the Mesquite Canyon Road on the left, at a low swell in the highway. There is a BLM board at the start of the road. Coming from the north, from the Ridgecrest exit on Highway 395 drive 9.9 miles south to the Garlock Road on the right. After 8.3 miles, it merges with the Red Rock Randsburg Road coming in from the left. The Mesquite Canyon Road is 1.1 miles further, on the right. The Mesquite Canyon Road (EP 100) winds up through Mesquite Canyon 3.9 miles to a pass, then goes straight 0.1 mile down to a fork. Turn right on EP 199, go 1.0 mile to the crossing with EP 198, and park. These roads require high clearance, and two outcrops in Mesquite Canyon 1.9–2.0 miles from the highway require four-wheel drive. Black Mountain is the high point on the right side of the broad undulating crest 2 miles to the north-northwest.

Route Description
Black Mountain is an old volcano that was active between about 19 and 15 million years ago, then slipped quietly into extinction. It was

built up by numerous lava flows that spilled all around it and out of the Black Hills just west of it. Referred to as Black Mountain Basalt, this formation is the medium the Kawaiisu Indians favored to create their rich artistic tradition of rock art throughout the central El Paso Mountains. The volcano is geologically old enough that its original slopes are largely obscured by subsequent landslides, now filled with fine erosional material and vegetated, which makes climbing it easier.

A seldom-used road (EP 198) weaves up the first landslide, a broad, mile-long ramp of grass and stones, greened only by occasional creosote and pygmy cedar. Just past the guzzler at the end of the road, a foot trail picks up the short remaining distance to the top of the ramp (4,283'). A sheer escarpment overlooks a sweeping saddle 150 feet below. The trail shoots straight down the scarp's nose, among California buckwheat, indigo bush, and paperbag bush. On the saddle below, it skirts a scenic horseshoe depression lined with puckered badlands, ochre and white, carved in the famous Ricardo Formation that gave us Red Rock Canyon's disturbingly alien formations. An uncommon crop of desert candle grows on the depression's edge, an odd plant resembling a fat white asparagus sprouting tendrils.

The trail ends soon after, on the edge of the ravine that drains south from the crater. This is the one place where a choice is needed—go either across the ravine and up a steep boulder field, or up the equally steep but more open south rim. The two routes converge on the saddle just north of a false summit (4,546'). The rest of the climb is up the steepening eastern edge of the ravine. This is probably where the mountain earned its name, a spread of dark low boulders thickening to a fractured mass of basalt at the crater's rim.

Black Mountain's crater is a disquieting portal into the underground. Its topography still holds memories of the colossal energy that once surged through it. Its suspended basin is imprisoned by congealed lava, boulders on one side, a long disintegrating cliff on the

	Black Mountain	
	Dist.(mi)	Elev.(ft)
Access road	0.0	3,910
End of road at guzzler/trail	0.9	4,230
4283-ft point	1.0	4,283
Ravine crossing/end of trail	1.45	4,320
Crater rim	2.1	5,060
Black Mountain	2.5	5,244

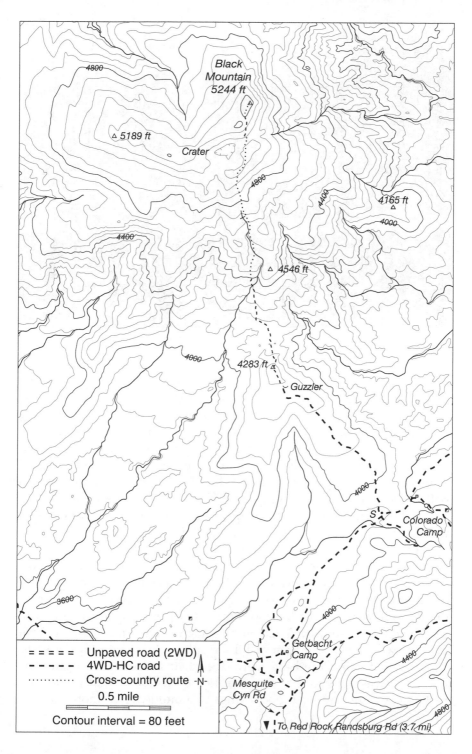

Black
Mountain
5244 ft

△ 5189 ft

Crater

4800

4800

4400

4165 ft
△

4000

4400

△ 4546 ft

4000

4283 ft
△

Guzzler

4000

4000

S

*Colorado
Camp*

3600

4000

*Gerbacht
Camp*

4400

*Mesquite
Cyn Rd*

4800

▼ *To Red Rock Randsburg Rd (3.7 mi)*

===== Unpaved road (2WD)
- - - - - 4WD-HC road
·············· Cross-country route -N-
0.5 mile

Contour interval = 80 feet

Looking northeast across the flank of Black Mountain

other. After 14 million years, erosion has not yet breached it; 100 feet down, it still cups a small playa of ash-colored silt. The summit looms to the north, a sugarloaf of bubble-filled basalt that bulged out during one of its last eruptions. The final ascent is literally breathtaking, up a precipitous, gravelly foot trail that screams up the dome's rocky spine.

Over the course of the day the land becomes filled with anchor points that we carry in our mind. When I was here a brooding storm belted the mountain with gray hail. Then it rained hard, and every wash and ravine was transformed into a gurgling stream of caramel water. An hour later the storm had turned it over to an orchestra of sunlight and playful clouds. The line of pointed hills to the northeast, dripping with red cinder and white siltstone, became a constant pole of attraction. These hills were a harbor for the Kawaiisu, who logged on their abundant boulders an extraordinary lexicon of petroglyphs. On the opposite side of the mountain, sharp mesas sloped down in serried ranks to Red Rock Canyon's magical badlands. The summit itself paraded over an apron of hills rippling down into Indian Wells Valley. By evening the hills were drenched in theatrical light. The mountain was defined that day as much by its shape and plants and rocks as by these sudden mood swings that molded our emotions.

■

LAVA MOUNTAINS AND FREMONT PEAK RANGE

If you drive north on Highway 395 from southern California across the western Mojave Desert's interminable plains, after many flat miles the Fremont Peak Range and Lava Mountains will be first to break the monotony. The Fremont Peak Range is a twisted miniature range capped by a steep stony cone. The Lava Mountains north of it are a particularly colorful coalescence of eroded volcanoes. Although both ranges are littered and lacerated by a senseless network of roads, the central Lava Mountains are preserved as the 36,536-acre Golden Valley Wilderness, with 7,000 additional acres in two proposed extensions. The area is prime habitat for raptors, the Mojave ground squirrel, and a healthy citizenry of desert tortoise. Native Americans visited Golden Valley long ago and left messages on its patinaed basalt, perhaps also attracted by the valley's flamboyant displays of spring wildflowers.

The Lava Mountains were shaped by three major waves of volcanism. Between 11.7 and 10.7 million years ago eruptions from multiple vents gave the area its first coat, mostly dacite and rhyolite tuff. After a hiatus of 400,000 years, a crater nearly 6 miles across opened up in what is now the middle of the range. Off and on over the next 750,000 years it erupted massive andesite and dacite lava flows and domes now known as the Almond Mountain Volcanics. They created the core of the range, including Klinker Mountain, Dome Mountain, and nearby Almond Mountain—the heart of today's Golden Valley Wilderness. Around 6 million years ago, three sets of eruptions smothered the eroding crater under up to 330 feet of viscous lava that rafted 10-foot blocks of andesite. Named Lava Mountains Andesite, this prominent formation caps many of the central summits. When all this began, the Lava Mountains were attached to the El Paso Mountains. Since then, the Lava Mountains and Fremont Peak Range have moved 22 miles east along the Garlock Fault, a major continental fault that slashes 160 miles across eastern California and passes right between the El Paso and Lava mountains. Some lava flows reached the fault and solidified across it. Subsequent lateral motion along the fault cut these straddling flows in two and offset them. The older the flow is, the larger the displacement. These serendipitous markers show that the Garlock Fault has been active for 16.4 million years and clocking on average 14 inches per century—about ten times slower than the San Andreas Fault.

The Fremont Peak Range has a much more complex history involving protracted sedimentation in the Paleozoic, intrusions in the Jurassic-Cretaceous, and extensive erosion until the Eocene. The region was uplifted several times, most recently over the last 5 million years, when its block was slowly tilted to the southwest along a fault at its northeastern base. Only two types of rocks have survived, Mesozoic quartz monzonite and quartz diorite at the northwest and southeast ends of the range, and the Waterman Gneissic Complex in the center. Part of the region's Precambrian basement, this complex was likely formed by crystallization of ancient sedimentary or pyroclastic rocks.

Although the Lava Mountains are deprived of valuable metals, the Fremont Peak Range did have one mine of worth, the Monarch-Rand, at its western base. First developed prior to 1920 and sporadically active until the 1940s, it probably produced a sizable amount of gold. Its history, however, pales compared to the adjacent Rand Mountains, which were among the two or three richest in the California desert. The Rand district boomed three times, for gold in 1895, tungsten in 1904, and silver in 1919. In the late 1890s, the neighboring towns of Randsburg and Johannesburg rivaled for business. Randsburg became one of the greatest boom towns in the West, with several mills, its own railroad, and a population of 3,500 in 1899. The Yellow Aster Mine alone was rich enough to feed a 100-stamp mill. It produced more than $12 million in gold, and the district over $20 million. The tungsten mines generated several million dollars through the 1910s. The richest property, the Papoose Mine, was for a few years the world's largest producer of scheelite (tungsten ore). In 1919, at the start of the silver boom, a third town named Osdick came to life, two miles from Johannesburg. Its star was the California Silver Rand Mine: until it played out in 1929, it put out $13 million. That year, Osdick changed its name to Red Mountain.

Mining was sustained long enough that unlike most, these towns became permanent settlements, still inhabited today and suffused with yesterday's aura. Randsburg stands above the rest, an Old-West town that attracts visitors, with a general store and an ice-cream parlor that have been opened since 1896, an inn and a B&B, antique stores and art galleries fueled by a small artist community, and a lively saloon.

■

KLINKER MOUNTAIN

> *Klinker Mountain is the gutted heart of the crater that laid down the central Lava Mountains in the Miocene. Artfully redesigned since then by nearly 6 million years of erosion, it is now a set of colorful hills and ridges that still traces the symmetry of the former volcano. The climb is convoluted, along a deeply notched skyline liberally littered with boulders and turrets of darkly varnished andesite. The views are gorgeous, encompassing three geomorphic provinces—the Sierra Nevada, the Basin and Range, and the central Mojave Desert—several dry lakes, and the volcano's gaping throat.*

General Information
Jurisdiction: Golden Valley Wilderness (BLM)
Road status: Climbing mostly cross-country; dirt access road (HC)
The climb: 2.5 mi, 1,290 ft up, 120 ft down one way / difficult
Main attractions: Volcanism, erosion, views of Cuddeback Lake
USGS 7.5' topo map: Klinker Mountain
Maps: pp. 553*, 499

Location and Access
Klinker Mountain is approximately in the middle of the Lava Mountains, a few miles northeast of Johannesburg, on Highway 395 about 14 miles south of Ridgecrest. First work your way to the Trona Road, which branches off Highway 395 on the north side 0.9 mile south of Johannesburg, or 0.9 mile north of Red Mountain. Head north on this road 1.3 miles to the unpaved Steam Wells Road (BLM road RM 1444) on the right. This road heads roughly north-northeast down a broad fan. After 0.45 mile it crosses a pipeline road; continue straight. Near the bottom of the road, after 1.75 miles, a road comes in from the left (northwest). The narrower and rougher track on the left very soon after (signed RM 199) is the old aqueduct road coming down from Skillings Well, which supplied water to Randsburg around the 1900s. Follow it 0.6 mile north-northeast up to just below the well's small tailing up ahead. This spur is rocky and requires good clearance. There is a flat area with a small concrete pad to park on the right.

Route Description
From Skillings Well the access road continues up a ravine as a steep, gravelly and rutted track, with barely enough traction for shoes,

let alone for urban vehicles. In 0.2 mile it reaches a low pass on the Lava Mountains' divide and angles 90° left. There are two low pointed hills about 500 yards north, connected by a bridge of level land. Walk the road north about 150 yards, to where it starts descending to the right. Then leave the road and aim for the right side of the land bridge, up a steep slope of volcanic rubble.

This first saddle is a good vantage point to take stock of the lay of the land. You are standing at the southwestern edge of the western Lava Mountains volcano, the crater that spewed out, between 10.5 and 9.4 million years ago, the thick ledges of andesite that form most of the rocks in this part of the range. The hilly ridge climbing to the north was the crater's west rim. It curves around the volcano's old throat to end just past its high point, Dome Mountain (4,974'), the plateau barely visible 3.5 miles to the northeast. Klinker Mountain, its second highest summit (4,562'), is halfway along the rim, hidden from view.

The crater's west rim—the route up Klinker Mountain—has been hit hard by erosion. Since the last eruption 5.8 million years ago, the 350-foot layer of Lava Mountains Andesite that coated it has been all but stripped off. The rim has been dissected into a crown of steep-sided hills standing shoulder to shoulder. Each hilltop sports a crew cut of leftover andesite, hardscrabble outcroppings determined not to accommodate boots. The easiest solution is to bypass each of the next three peaks across their right flanks, circling well below each summit to avoid fallen rocks, and approaching the next saddle from below. The perspective is cunning. As the rim repeatedly throws you off then pulls you back in, in a daisy chain of lopsided arcs, the peaks take turns hiding, never all exposed simultaneously. The volcano reveals itself one piece at a time, in a faultless choreographed tease.

Each hill is higher than the previous one, and each bypass longer. At the end of the third bypass an open hillside of blond grass dips 100 feet to the fourth saddle. On the far side, the ridge shoots straight up to the fourth and last hill (4,512'). Slippery and cluttered with boulders, this is the longest, steepest, and hardest pitch. The easiest way is straight up the middle to the first large pile of boulders, then at 10 o'clock, taking advantage of more open benches to circle widely around the west side of the 4,512-foot peak. Klinker Mountain comes into view only then, a dark mane of angular boulders half a mile away.

After millions of years of nothing but erosion, this land is in its last geological moment. Even so, it holds a strange kind of beauty, every hillside spiked with spires, broken-down chimneys, or glistening blocks of andesite. Way down below, the east rim has been worn into an aggregate of colorful hills that still completes the crater's original

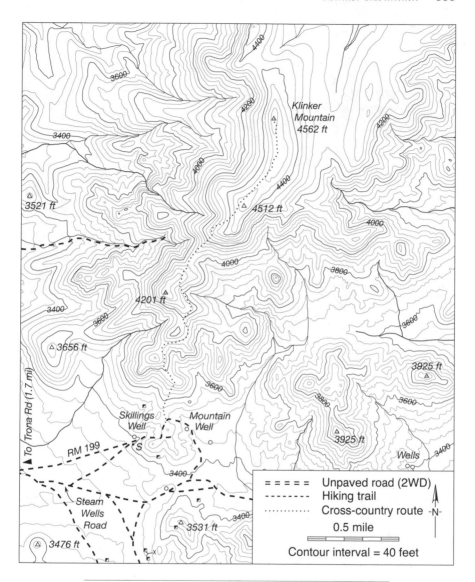

Klinker Mountain

	Dist.(mi)	Elev.(ft)
Skillings Well	0.0	3,390
Leave road, head northwest	0.25	3,530
First saddle	0.5	3,790
Fourth saddle	1.45	4,055
Klinker Mountain	2.5	4,562

Western Lava Mountains crater from Klinker Mountain's summit plateau

circular opening. The wide gap in front of them was ground zero, the two central vents from which the lava welled out of the Earth. The andesite is beautiful, either massive or as breakable as clinker, its fresh cuts gun-metal gray sprinkled with rice-shaped crystals of plagioclase. On the wind-swept ridges, alien symbols run across the face of boulders in perfect symmetry, as if they had been carved by hand.

The summit is a shattered block of Lava Mountains Andesite glazed by eons of sunlight, all angles and points, incapable of hosting even a skinny human butt. We sat as least uncomfortably as we could, a boulder stuck behind each of us. With perseverance came a satisfying sense of completion, giddiness, and sharpened awareness. As we scanned the horizon we shouted out discoveries, competing against a howling wind. To our backs lay the great barrier of the Sierra Nevada. In front of us rose the bluish rampart of the Slate Range and the extraordinary Panamint Range. Off to the southeast, Cuddeback Lake unfolded across the open desert like a wisp of smoke. Beyond it was the pointed hat of Fremont Peak, gateway to the immense plains of the western Mojave Desert. Everywhere we turned that day we saw attractiveness fashioned by the devastating forces of erosion.

■

RED MOUNTAIN

> *The apex of the Lava Mountains, Red Mountain best validates its name when the setting sun torches its lava flanks to a flaming radiance. It is a great little mountain to ascend, partly on roads, the rest cross-country up inclines of basaltic boulders. The summit and its approach overlook one of California's richest historic mining districts and its ghost towns, and the open wedge of jumbled desert mountains between the great Sierras and Death Valley.*

General Information
Jurisdiction: Public lands (BLM)
Road status: Climbing partly on roads; primitive access road (HC)
The climb: 2.1 mi, 1,680 ft up, 210 ft down one way/moderate
Main attractions: Views of western Mojave Desert, history, geology
USGS 7.5' topo map: Red Mountain
Maps: pp. 557*, 499

Location and Access
Rising at the south end of the Lava Mountains and nearly disconnected from the rest of the range, Red Mountain is a stocky prominence just east of the sleepy town by the same name along Highway 395. To get to the starting point, drive Highway 395 to the signed Trona Road, which is 15.7 miles south of the Ridgecrest turn-off and 0.9 mile past Johannesburg, or 0.9 mile north of Red Mountain. Take this road 200 feet to the Red Mountain Road on the right (RM 108). Go east on this primitive road, crossing RM 1555 after 0.6 mile. Very shortly after, there is a split. The Red Mountain Road goes left and gets a little rougher. After 0.5 mile a road joins in from the left (RM 112). It is best to park near this junction. Soon after the road gets very steep, with large holes and rocks and slippery gravel that will stop most drivers.

Route Description
On Red Mountain I ran into a desert tortoise, a venerably old male the size of a serving dish heaped with food. He was lumbering along the road, wobbling with a dinosaur gait, rattlesnake weed smeared on his mouth like green lipstick. He stopped, spotted me, and retracted in his shell as if he were spring-loaded. Fifteen minutes later he emerged ever so slowly, and proceeded to feed on one of my favorite wildflowers. It's hard to get action from a creature that sleeps nine months of

Looking north from the upper section of road on Red Mountain

the year. Other locals—jittery lizards, Mojave ground squirrels, and a baby rattlesnake—made up for it later that day.

The track to Red Mountain's crest, and its more recent extension along the crest, negotiate half the distance and elevation gain to the summit. The weathered roadway, too crude for anything but a dirt bike or an oversized truck, ascends a ridge in three steep waves. It passes beneath a sheer-walled dome of red basalt faced with a checkerboard of rhombohedral cracks. Across from it the slope is an open grove of standing monoliths. Down in the valley the sleepy towns of Red Mountain and Johannesburg, Jo-burg to the locals, are clustered on opposite sides of the Rand Mountains. The abandoned mines that long ago spawned the towns are still prominent, their curved terraces deeply etched into the mountainside. At the crest, the road forks. The road straight ahead ends shortly at a viewpoint, the first of many vistas of the Lava Mountains' pastel palette of red, mocha, and mustard to the northeast. The right fork, signed RM 246 and paralleled briefly by a foot trail, climbs the ridge up to a saddle between twin hills, then descends to a tiny dry lake curiously cupped on a mountain's crest.

The rest of the way is roadless, further motorized incursion thwarted by a 200-foot avalanche of boulders that wraps around the

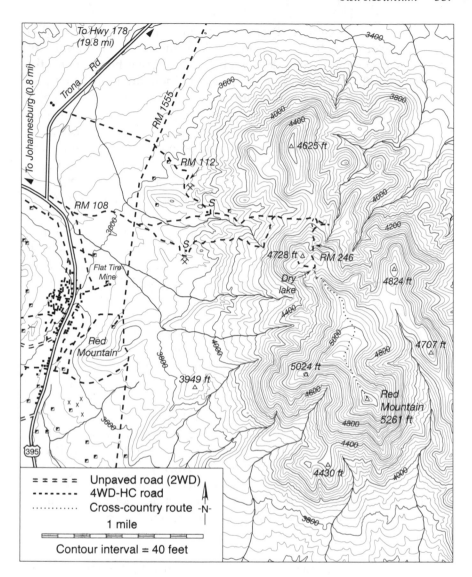

= = = = =   Unpaved road (2WD)
- - - - - - - 4WD-HC road
.... Cross-country route -N-

1 mile

Contour interval = 40 feet

Red Mountain

	Dist.(mi)	Elev.(ft)
Red Mountain Rd at RM 112	0.0	3,790
Crest/road junction	0.7	4,370
Small dry lake/end of road	1.1	4,615
False summit	1.8	~5,185
Red Mountain	2.1	5,261

ridge up ahead. A short trail climbs beyond the lake playa another tenth of a mile to its high point and ends at the base of the boulders. This is the first crux, an aerobic scramble over angular boulders for the most part solidly anchored into the ground. There are plenty of possible routes, most of them Class 1, although a hand occasionally helps.

Above the boulders the ridge morphs abruptly into a broad open plateau that sweeps gently up to a false summit. Up here the mountain has sprouted a motley scratch of fleshy buckwheat, green ephedra and saltbush, and a preponderance of woody plants that want nothing to do with leaves. Boulders take over again at the false summit. On its far side, the rock-cluttered ridge drops into a pronounced saddle. A use trail avoids the difficulty by wiggling between rocks down the dusty slope just east of the ridge line. The second crux, milder than the first, is on the final ascent beyond the saddle—a spine of tall andesite sherds part way up. Some blocks are sharply cleaved, their curved surfaces as smooth as glass, the next thing above them the big Mojave sky. It looks rough from below, but it is not hard to bypass on either side.

Red Mountain holds three odd distinctions. Between 1907 and the mid-1930s, half a dozen USGS geologists climbed here and engraved their names in the summit's low basalt boulders. In spite of all this USGS attention, the USGS benchmark at the summit is virgin—whoever installed it forgot to engrave on it the date and summit's name. The oddest still is the compressed-gas cylinders resting on a concrete pad at the summit, as if a poet had inflated a balloon with helium and vanished into the heavens. On NPS land someone would have held bake sales if that's what it took to remove the junk. On BLM land it may well remain until the Lava Mountains erupt again.

Here on the edge of the desert the seductive symmetry of the Basin and Range breaks down. Red Mountain overlooks not parallel alignments of basins and ranges but a haphazard medley of intertwined mountains and valleys. The south holds an alien view of long and skinny Cuddeback Lake. Behind it rises the pointed profile of the Fremont Peak Range, a cutout layer of a ship riding the emptiness of the western Mojave Desert. On a clear day this normally hazy province opens up to Rogers Lake, where the space shuttle used to land, and the San Gabriel Mountains beyond. To the northeast recede dark layers of ranges, the salt-burnt sinks of Panamint Valley and Death Valley hidden amid their folds. The western horizon is filled by the silvery scarp of the Range of Light. We even steal a glimpse, in the military wilderness to the east, of Pilot Knob's archetypical volcanic mesa and its cohort of craggy hills, last to catch the copper glow of the setting sun.

■

FREMONT PEAK

Climbing Fremont Peak's sharp summit is a short but aerobic affair, first up a beat-up mining road, then along a narrow trail, and finally cross-country up a very steep rock-strewn slope. One of the appeals is the sculpted bluffs of ancient gneiss that form the summit block, which can be climbed on any number of routes, anywhere from an easy walk if you find the right passage to a hard Class-5 climb on vertical faces. The rocky summit is a perfect perch to appreciate the vastness of the western Mojave Desert's central plain.

General Information
Jurisdiction: Public lands (BLM)
Road status: Climbing on road, trail, and cross-country; primitive
    access road (2WD or HC)
The climb: 0.8 mi, 830 ft up one way / moderate
Main attractions: A short, very steep climb to a sculpted summit
USGS 7.5' topo map: Fremont Peak
Maps: pp. 561*, 499

Location and Access
Fremont Peak is the high point of the Fremont Peak Range, about midway between Barstow and Ridgecrest. From Kramer Junction on Highway 58 about 31 miles west of Barstow (or 38 miles east of Highway 14 in Mojave), drive north on Highway 395 13.6 miles to a wide dirt road on the right, with a BLM board a short distance in. This is the Fremont Peak Road. Coming from the north on Highway 395, this junction is 28.7 miles south of the Ridgecrest turn-off, or 13.0 miles south of the Trona Road between Johannesburg and Red Mountain.

The Fremont Peak Road heads roughly northeast, then east, 7.7 miles to the historic Monarch-Rand Mine at the western base of Fremont Peak, clearly visible from the highway. It is first numbered RM 30, then FP 5400. The road that crosses the Fremont Peak Road after 1.2 miles is the old grade of the Randsburg Railway. Between 1898 and 1933 it connected Kramer to Johannesburg to service the rich mines in the Rand Mountains. This intersection was a stop called Fremont. The ruins of its settlement are just south of the intersection.

After 3.8 miles the main road angles left, while the Fremont Peak Road continues straight, and its number changes to FP 5402. The local roads being seriously oversigned, it is hard to get lost if you keep track of these three numbers. After 6.2 miles, turn right where the road splits three ways. The Fremont Peak Road is wide, smooth, hard-packed dirt the whole way, except after heavy rains when short sections turn to muddy ponds. With a standard-clearance vehicle one can easily drive the 7.5 miles up to the FP 5430 crossing, and park at this point. The remaining 0.2 mile to the mine's main shaft is steeper and damaged, and requires high clearance. There is ample space to park by the capped shaft, on the left side of the road. While driving in this area, remember that any road that is *not* signed is closed to motor vehicles.

Route Description
    The huge inclined shaft near the end of the road was the Monarch-Rand Mine's bread and butter. In its heyday it was blasted down to a depth of 100 feet and rich quartz veins were exposed along 225 feet of crosscuts. It produced $600,000 in gold, with a side of silver and copper, a sizable return for the time. In the 1920s, under the new name of Fremont Peak Mine, the shaft was extended 85 feet and half a mile of new crosscuts were sunk, but the production was much more modest. The ore was processed at an on-site mill—the large tank east of the shaft was used for cyaniding—and water was piped in from a well on Cuddeback Lake. All that remains of the mining camp are the imprints of its houses and water tank, everything else having been pumped full of lead—the thousands of spent shells that litter the site may contain more copper than ever came out of the mine.
    Fremont Peak soars just beyond the mine, only half an air mile away but 800 feet higher. Its steep lower slopes are littered with rocks, its upper slopes and crest a pale mass of ancient gneiss sculpted into a profusion of misshapen outcrops. The beauty of climbing here is that it can be done many very different ways, anything from Class-1 hikes to hard scrambles over smaller outcrops and Class-5 climbs up overhanging cliffs. The route described here is the easiest. From the shaft, continue up the road generally west 0.1 mile to a fork. The nearly level

Fremont Peak		
	Dist.(mi)	Elev.(ft)
Monarch-Rand Mine shaft	0.0	~3,755
End of road/trailhead	0.4	~4,060
Leave trail	0.6	~4,225
Break on crest	0.75	~4,520
Fremont Peak	0.8	4,584

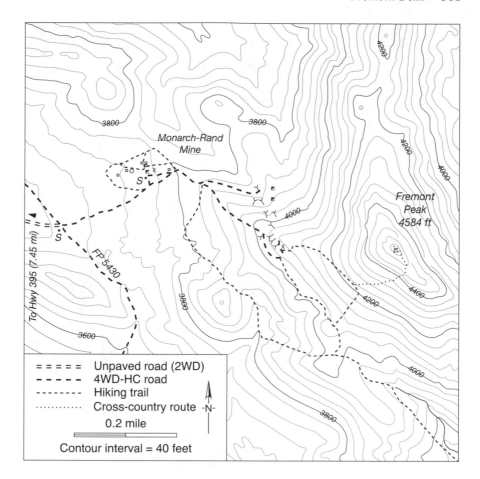

road on the left leads shortly to the mine's western group of workings. The beat-up right fork climbs over bulging eroded bedrock, hooks a left U-turn, then makes a right bend before ending in 0.3 mile. Just before the right bend, take the single-track trail on the right. In 150 feet it splits. Follow the trail on the left (uphill) across the mountain's open southwestern flank 0.2 mile to the trail's high point. The rest of the ascent is cross-country up the 45% slope, east curving to the northeast, over sandy soil and rocks.

At the top the crest is lined with broken bluffs 10 to 25 feet tall (Class 5) separated by boulder-filled couloirs. The only easy way through is to cross over to the far side of the crest at the obvious gap in the bluffs about 150 feet southeast of the summit. The far side has a convenient broad ramp that climbs northwest along the summit block. It passes by a couple of short steep slants (Class 2–3) that can be used

Cuddeback Lake and Lava Mountains from Fremont Peak

to gain the summit, but this is not necessary. If you continue in the same direction past the summit about 100 feet, you will see a shallow trench that gives easy walking access back (southeast) to the summit.

Fremont Peak overlooks the central part of the western Mojave Desert, a stitchery of sprawling basins so vast and shallow that seen from the ground they merge into an endless plain. The closest ranges are the Lava and Rand mountains, more than 10 miles to the northwest. In all other directions the mountains are pushed back tens of miles, reduced to bluish slivers on the horizon. The basins fill the space in between, each one revealed not by topography but by the pale dry lake that occupies its imperceptible depression. A total of eight lakes dot the landscape—the three lakes in Superior Valley, Rogers Lake, Harper Lake, and unnamed others. Cuddeback Lake stretches out to the north, a curvy playa seemingly coming out of the Fremont Peak Range like a genie freed from its lamp. Part of the experience of climbing Fremont Peak is discovering this immense desert deprived of mountains—from the ground while driving to the peak, and from above while on the mountain.

■

BIBLIOGRAPHY

Further Reading

Casebier, D. G. *Mojave Road Guide: An Adventure Through Time*. Essex, Ca.: Tales of the Mojave Road Publishing Company. Tales of the Mojave Road No. 22, 1999.

Chalfant, W. A. *The Story of Inyo*. Stanford, Ca.: Stanford Univ. Press, 1953.

Digonnet, M. *Hiking Western Death Valley National Park*. Palo Alto, Ca.: self-published, 2007.

Digonnet, M. *Hiking the Mojave Desert*. Palo Alto, Ca.: self-published, 2013.

Digonnet, M. *Hiking Death Valley*. 2nd ed. Palo Alto, Ca.: self-published, 2016.

Ferris, R. S. *Death Valley Wildflowers*. Pathfinder Books, 2016.

Greene, S. *Death Valley Book of Knowledge*. New York: iUniverse, Inc., 2009.

Ingram, S. *Cacti, Agaves, and Yuccas of California and Nevada*. Los Olivos, Ca.: Cachuma Press, 2008.

Knute, A. *Plants of the East Mojave: Mojave National Preserve*. Barstow, Ca.: Mojave River Valley Association, 2002.

Lingenfelter, R. E. *Death Valley and the Amargosa: A Land of Illusion*. Berkeley, Ca.: University of California Press, 1986.

MacKay, P. *Mojave Desert Wildflowers*. Guilford, Conn.: The Globe Pequot Press, 2013.

Vredenburgh, L. M., G. L. Shumway, and R. D. Hartill. *Desert Fever*. Canoga Park, Ca.: Living West Press, 1981.

Wiseman, J. *ASA Survival Guide*. 3rd ed. New York, NY: HarpersCollins Publishers, 2014.

Zdon, A. *Desert Summits*. 2nd ed. Bishop, Ca.: Spotted Dog Press, Inc., 2006.

Sources

Armstrong, A. K., *et al.* "Mineral resources of the Nopah Range wilderness study area, Inyo County, California." *USGS Bull.* 1709, 1987.

Aubury, L. E. "The Copper resources of California." *Cal. St. Mining Bureau Bull.* 50 (1908): 19–23, 325–340.

Blank, M. *Overpowered*. New York, NY: Seven Stories Press, 2014.

Calzia, J. P. *Igneous Geology of a Part of the Southeastern Owlshead Mountains, San Bernardino County, California*: Master's thesis, Univ. of Southern California, Los Angeles, Ca., 1974.

Calzia, J. P., *et al.* "Mineral resources of the Kingston Range wilderness study area, San Bernardino County, California." *USGS. Geol. Survey Bull.* 1709 (1987): 1–31.

Campbell, E. A., and B. E. John. "Crustal extension and the peak Colorado River gravity high, southern Sacramento Mountains, California: A preliminary correlation." *Open-File Rept.* 94-236, 1994.

Cardiff, S. W., and J. V. Remsen, Jr. "Breeding avifaunas of the New York Mountains and Kingston Range: Islands of conifers in the Mojave Desert of California." *Western Birds* 12 (1981): 73–86.

Carr, M. D., et al. "Bedrock geologic map of the El Paso Mountains in the Garlock and El Paso Peaks 7-1/2' quadrangles, Kern County, California." *USGS Map* I-2389, 1997.

Cloudman, H. C., et al. "San Bernardino County—Tulare County." *Rept. of the State Mineralogist* 15 (1915–1916): 773–852.

Collier, M. *An Introduction to the Geology of Death Valley.* Death Valley, Ca.: Death Valley Natural History Association, 1990.

Corsetti, F. A., and A. J. Kaufman. "The relationship between the Neoproterozoic Noonday Dolomite and the Ibex Formation: New observations and their bearing on 'Snowball Earth'." *Earth-Science Rev.* 73 (2005): 63-78.

Cowie, S., P. Baird, and A. C. MacWilliams. "Mine documentation in the Standard Mining District, Mojave National Preserve, California." *The Digital Archaeological Record, Publications in Anthropology* 88, 2006.

Crawford, J. J. "Mines and Mining Products of California." *Annual Rept. of the State Mineralogist* 12 (1894): 21-141.

Crawford, J. J. "Mines and Mining Products of California." *Annual Rept. of the State Mineralogist* 13 (1896): 32-185, 230, 319–330, 606–609.

Curry, H. D. "Turtlebacks in the central Black Mountains, Death Valley, California." *Cal. Div. Mines Bull.* 170 (1954): 53-59.

Dibblee, T. W., Jr. "Areal geology of the western Mojave Desert, California." *USGS Prof. Paper* 522, 1967.

Dibblee, T. W., Jr. "Geology of the Fremont Peak and Opal Mountain quadrangles, California." *Cal. Div. of Mines & Geol. Bull.* 188, 1968.

Diggles, M. F., et al. "Mineral resources of the El Paso Mountains wilderness study area, Kern County, California." *U. S. Geol. Survey Bull.* 1708-C, 1985.

Diggles, M. F., et al. "Mineral resources of the Golden Valley wilderness study area, San Bernardino County, California." *USGS Bull.* 1708-D, 1985.

Dohrenwend, J. C., et al. "K-Ar dating of the Cima Volcanic Field, eastern Mojave Desert, California: Late Cenozoic volcanic history and landscape evolution." *Geol.* 12, No. 3 (1984): 163–167.

Dorr, E. P. Sworn affidavit, *Cal. Mining J.* 10, No. 3 (1940): 37.

Evans, J. R., G. C. Taylor, and J. S. Rapp. "Mines and mineral deposits in Death Valley National Monument, California." *Cal. Div. Mines & Geol. Spec. Rept.* 125 (1976): 1-61.

Fiero, B. *Geology of the Great Basin*. Reno, Nev.: Univ. of Nevada Press, 1986.

Fumal, T. E., *et al.* "Timing of large earthquakes since A.D. 800 on the Mission Creek strand of the San Andreas Fault Zone at Thousand Palms Oasis, near Palm Springs, California." *Bull. Seism. Soc. Am.* 92, No. 7 (2002): 2841–2860.

Garfinkel, A. P., and H. Williams, *Handbook of the Kawaiisu. Wa-hi Sina'avi* Publications, 2011.

Greene, L. W., and J. A. Latschar. *Historic Resource Study: A History of Mining in Death Valley National Monument*. Denver, Co.: National Park Service, 1981.

Greene, L. W. *Historic Resource Study: A History of Land Use in Joshua Tree National Monument*. Denver Service Center, 1983.

Hall, W. E. "Geology of the Panamint Butte quadrangle, California." *USGS Bull.* 1299 (1971): 1–67.

Hall, W. E., and E. M. MacKevett, Jr. "Geology and ore deposits of the Darwin quadrangle, Inyo County, California." *USGS Prof. Paper* 368, 1962.

Hall, W. E., and H. G. Stephens. "Economic geology of the Panamint Butte quadrangle and Modoc district, Inyo County, California." *Cal. Div. Mines & Geol. Spec. Rept.* 73 (1963): 1–39.

Hazzard, J. C. "Paleozoic section in the Nopah and Resting Springs Mountains, Inyo County, California." *Cal. J. of Mines and Geol.* 33 (1937): 273-339.

Hensher, A. "The historical mining towns of the eastern Mojave Desert." In *Old Ores: Mining History in the Eastern Mojave Desert*. R. E. Reynolds, Ed., Abstracts from the 2005 Desert Symposium (2005): 28–40.

Hewett, D. F. "Geology and mineral resources of the Ivanpah quadrangle, California and Nevada." *USGS Prof. Paper* 275, 1956.

Holm, D. K., *et al.* "The Death Valley turtlebacks reinterpreted as Miocene-Pliocene folds of a major detachment surface." *J. of Geol.* 102, No. 6 (1994): 718–727.

Horne, S. P., and R. Musser-Lopez. "Rock art portal to passage: An ancient desert footpath near Needles, California." *Pacific Coast Archaeological Soc. Quaterly* 51, No. 1 (2015): 83–95.

Howard, K. A., *et al.* "Mineral resources of the Bristol/Granite Mountains wilderness study area, San Bernardino County, California." *USGS Bull.* 1712-C (1987): 1–18.

Hunt, C. B., and D. R. Mabey. "Stratigraphy and structure, Death Valley, California." *USGS Prof. Paper* 494-A, 1966.

Jaeger, E. C. *Desert Wildlife*. Stanford, Ca.: Stanford Univ. Press, 1950.

John, B. E. "Geologic map of the Chemehuevi Mountains area, San Bernardino County, California and Mohave County, Arizona." *Open-*

File Rept. 87-666, 1987.

Johnson, B. K. "Geology of a part of the Manly Peak quadrangle, southern Panamint Range, California." *Univ. of Cal. Pub. in Geol. Sci.* 30, No. 5 (1957): 353–424.

Killian, H. M. *Geology of the Marble Mountains, San Bernardino County, California*: Master's thesis, Univ. of Southern California, Los Angeles, Ca., 1964.

Knott, J. R., *et al.* "Upper Neogene stratigraphy and tectonics of Death Valley—a review." *Earth-Science Rev.* 73 (2005): 245–270.

Koch, R. D., *et al.* "Mineral resources and resource potential of the Owlshead Mountains wilderness study area, San Bernardino County, California." *USGS Open-File Rept.* 84–755, 1984.

Kroeber, A. L. *Handbook of the Indians of California.* Bureau of American Ethnology Bulletin No. 78. Washington, D.C., 1925.

Lanner, R. M. *Conifers of California.* Los Olivos, Ca.: Cachuma Press, 2008.

Lightfoot, K. G., and O. Parrish. *California Indians and their Environment: An Introduction.* Berkeley, Ca.: Univ. of California Press, 2009.

Lynton, E. D. "Sulphur deposits of Inyo County, California." *Cal. J. Min. of Mines and Geol.* 34 (1938): 563–590.

MacMahon, J. A. *Deserts.* National Audubon Society Nature Guides, New York: Alfred A. Knopf, Inc., 1997.

McAllister, J. F. "Geology of mineral deposits in the Ubehebe Peak quadrangle, Inyo County, California." *Cal. Div. of Mines and Geol. Spec. Rept.* 42 (1955): 1–63.

McAllister, J. F. "Geologic maps and sections of a strip from Pyramid Peak to the southeast end of the Funeral Mountains, Ryan quadrangle, California." In *Guidebook Death Valley Region, Ca. and Nev.* Shoshone, Ca.: Death Valley Pub. Co., 1974: 81-83.

McCurry, M., D. R. Lux, and K. L. Mickus. "Neogene structural evolution of the Woods Mountains volcanic center, East Mojave National Scenic Area." *San Bernardino County Museum* A 42, No. 3 (1995): 75–80.

Miller, D. M., and J. L. Wooden. "Field guide to Proterozoic geology of the New York, Ivanpah, and Providence Mountains, California." *USGS Open-File Rept.* 94–674, 1994.

Miller, J. M. G. "Glacial and syntectonic sedimentation: The Upper Proterozoic Kingston Peak Formation, southern Panamint Range, eastern California." *Geol. Soc. Am. Bull.* 96, No. 12 (1985): 1537–1553.

Munz, P. A. *Introduction to California Desert Wildflowers.* Revised Edition. California Natural History Guides, 2004.

Myrick, D. F. *Railroads of Nevada and Eastern California. Volume II: The Southern Roads.* Reno, Nev.: Univ. of Nevada Press, 1991.

Nadeau, R. *The Silver Seekers.* Santa Barbara, Ca.: Crest Publishers, 1999.

Niemi, N. A. *Extensional Tectonics in the Basin and Range Province and the Geology of the Grapevine Mountains, Death Valley Region, California and*

Nevada. Doctoral thesis, Calif. Inst. of Technology, Pasadena, Ca., 2002.

Noble, L. F. "Structural features of the Virgin Spring area, Death Valley, California." *Geol. Soc. Am. Bull* 52, No. 7 (1941): 941–999.

Norman, L. A., and R. M. Stewart. "Mines and mineral resources of Inyo County, California." *Cal. J. of Mines and Geol.* 47 (1951): 17–223.

Novitsky-Evans, J. M. *Geology of the Cowhole Mountains, Southeastern California*. Doctoral thesis, Rice Univ., Houston, Texas, 1978.

Nyborg, T. G., and V. L. Santucci. "The Death Valley National Park paleontological survey." National Park Service, *Geol. Resources Tech. Rept.*, 1999.

Palmer, A. R., and R. B. Halley. "Physical stratigraphy and trilobite biostratigraphy of the Carrara Formation (Lower and Middle Cambrian) in the southern Great Basin." *USGS Prof. Paper* 1047, 1979.

Palmer, T. S. *Place Names of the Death Valley Region in California and Nevada*. Morongo Valley, Ca.: Sagebrush Press, 1980.

Petterson, R., *et al.* "The Neoproterozoic Noonday Formation, Death Valley region, California." *Geol. Soc. Am. Bull.* 123, No. 7/8 (2011): 1317–1336.

Plotkin, H., *et al.* "The Old Woman, California, IIAB iron meteorite." Meteoritics & Planetary Sci. 47, No. 5 (2012): 929–946.

Powers, A. "Gold or Just a Fever?" *Los Angeles Times*, September 11, 2006.

Reynolds, M. W. "Geology of the Grapevine Mountains, Death Valley, California: A Summary." In *Guidebook: Death Valley Region, California and Nevada*, Shoshone, Ca.: Death Valley Pub. Co., 1974: 91-97.

Rogers, A. K. "Temporal patterns of archaic land use in the El Paso Mountains, Kern County, California." *Proc. of Soc. Cal. Archaeology* 19 (2006): 173-184.

Rothfuss, E. L. "Death Valley Burros." In *Proceedings, Third Death Valley Conference on History & Prehistory*. J. Pisarowicz, ed. Death Valley, Ca.: Death Valley Natural History Association (1992): 182–206.

Smith, E. I., *et al.* "Stratigraphy and geochemistry of volcanic rocks in the Lava Mountains, California: Implications for the Miocene development of the Garlock fault." *Geol. Soc. of Am. Memoir* 195 (2002): 151–160.

Spencer, J. E. *Geology and Geochronology of the Avawatz Mountains, San Bernardino County, California*. Doctoral thesis, Cambridge, Ma.: Mass. Inst. of Technology, 1981.

Stevens, C. H., and P. Stone. "The Pennsylvanian-Early Permian Bird Spring carbonate shelf, southeastern California: Fusulinid biostratigraphy, paleographic evolution, and tectonic implications." *Geol. Soc. Am. Spec. Papers* 429, 2007.

Stewart, K. M. "A brief history of the Chemehuevi Indians." *Kiva* 34, No. 1 (1968): 9–27.

Stock, C. "Mammalian fauna from the Titus Canyon Formation, California." *Carnegie Institute of Washington Pub.* 584 (1949): 229–244.

Taylor, R. J. *Desert Wildflowers of North America.* Missoula, Mt.: Mountain Press Publishing Company, 1998.

Theodore, T. G. "Geology and mineral resources of the East Mojave National Scenic Area, San Bernardino County, California." *USGS Bull.* 2160, 2007.

Thomas, K., T. Keeler-Wolf, J. Franklin, and P. Stine. "Mojave Desert ecosystem program: Central Mojave vegetation database." *USGS Science for a Changing World,* Sacramento, California, 2004.

Trent, D. D., and R. W. Hazlett. *Joshua Tree National Park Geology.* Twentynine Palms, Ca.: Joshua Tree Nat. Park Assoc., 2002.

Tucker, W. B. *Rept. of the State Mineralogist* 17 (1920): 333–374; 18 (1921): 273–305; 20 (1924): 92–95, 196–200; 22 (1926): 453–539; and 26 (1930): 202–325.

Tucker, W. B., and R. J. Sampson. *Rept. of the State Mineralogist* 30 (1934): 324–325; 27 (1931): 262–401; 28 (1932): 329–376; 34 (1938): 368–500; 36 (1940): 22–28, 53–81; 37 (1941): 584–587; and 39 (1943): 66–69, 126–138, 427–549.

Wilshire, H. G., *et al.* "Mineral resources of the Cinder Cones wilderness study area, San Bernardino County, California." *USGS Bull.* 1712-B (1987): 1–13.

Wright, L. A. "Talc deposits of the southern Death Valley-Kingston Range region, California." *Cal. Div. Mines & Geol. Spec. Rept.* 95 (1968):1–79.

Wright, L. A., and B. W. Troxel. "Geology of the northern half of the Confidence Hills 15-minute quadrangle, Death Valley region, eastern California: The area of the Amargosa Chaos." *Cal. Div. Mines & Geol.,* Map Sheet 34 (1984).

Wright, L. A., *et al.* "Mines and mineral deposits of San Bernardino County, California." *Cal. J. Mines and Geol.* 49, Nos. 1 and 2 (1953): 49–257.

Wrucke, C. T., *et al.* "The Butte Valley and Layton Well thrusts of eastern California: Distribution and regional significance." *Tectonics* 14, No. 5 (1995): 1165–1171.

■

SUMMARY TABLE OF CLIMBS

Summit	Elev.	Round-trip distance	Elev. gain	Pages
Alaska Hill	~5,873'	3.0 mi	1,610'	303
Alaska Hill (loop)	~5,873'	4.9 mi	2,060'	303
Apex Peak	7,224'	13.5 mi	2,420'	503
Ashford Peak	3,547'	5.8 mi	2,510'	123
Avawatz Peak	6,154'	14.2 mi	5,580'	73
Barber Peak	5,504'	1.8 mi	950'	277
Bennett Peak	9,980'	3.0 mi	2,050'	179
Bighorn Mountain	5,894'	5.8 mi	1,210'	411
Black Mountain	5,244'	5.0 mi	1,820'	545
Bpex Peak	7,260'	12.2 mi	2,200'	503
Cady Peak	4,627'	6.4 mi	2,010'	385
Castle Peak	3,842'	3.8 mi	1,160'	375
Chaparrosa Peak	5,541'	5.6 mi	1,550'	415
Chemehuevi Peak	3,694'	7.6 mi	2,040'	355
Chloride Cliff (mining tr.)	5,279'	9.2 mi	4,600'	95
Chloride Cliff (road)	5,279'	4.6 mi	1,140'	95
Cima Dome	5,745'	3.6 mi	420'	331
Cima Dome (loop)	5,745'	6.6 mi	770'	331
Clark Mountain	7,930'	3.6 mi	1,970'	307
Coffin Peak	5,490'	2.5 mi	910'	119
Con Peak	2,621'	12.4 mi	2,970'	211
Cowhole Mountain	2,247'	3.8 mi	1,280'	345
Dante Peak	5,704'	0.8 mi	230'	115
Darwin Peak	5,979'	1.6 mi	710'	513
Desert Hound Peak	4,472'	13.8 mi	3,990'	127
Dove Peak	5,829'	5.6 mi	1,240'	253
Eagle Peak	3,308'	3.0 mi	1,660'	351
Eagle Rocks	5,780'	1.8 mi	550'	267
Eagle Rocks (loop)	5,780'	2.1 mi	540'	267
Eastern Butte	2,750'	1.7 mi	670'	89
East Ord Mountain	6,168'	2.8 mi	1,950'	405
East Queen Mountain	5,677'	3.9 mi	1,260'	453
El Paso Peak	4,578'	1.6 mi	540'	541
El Paso Peaks (4,347')	4,347'	2.5 mi	840'	541

Summit	Elev.	Round-trip distance	Elev. gain	Pages
Empasse Peak	3,452'	3.0 mi	620'	531
Eureka Peak (road)	5,518'	0.3 mi	60'	425
Eureka Peak (trail)	5,518'	9.4 mi	1,800'	425
Eye Peak	2,454'	8.3 mi	3,070'	491
Fountain Peak	6,988'	4.8 mi	2,840'	281
Fremont Peak	4,584'	1.6 mi	830'	559
Goat Mountain	5,168'	3.6 mi	1,230'	404
Granite Mountain	6,762'	17.6 mi	4,400'	295
Grapevine Peak	8,738'	6.6 mi	3,060'	80
Guitar Mountain	5,003'	4.0 mi	1,020'	250
Hackberry Mountain	5,390'	2.0 mi	1,030'	245
Hackberry Mtn (loop)	5,390'	3.1 mi	1,160'	245
Hart Peak	5,543'	4.0 mi	1,180'	231
High Table Mtn West End	4,793'	9.0 mi	920'	235
Hunter Mountain	7,455'	2.0 mi	400'	165
Inspiration Peak	5,570'	2.0 mi	830'	435
Joshua Mtn (Coso Range)	7,130'	11.8 mi	2,150'	503
Joshua Mountain (JTNP)	3,682'	2.7 mi	1,190'	457
Jurassic Peak	5,952'	3.6 mi	1,120'	507
Kessler Peak	6,163'	3.8 mi	1,175'	321
Kessler Peak (loop)	6,163'	4.2 mi	1,285'	321
Keys Peak	4,483'	7.2 mi	640'	449
Kingston Peak	7,336'	8.8 mi	3,600'	69
Klinker Mountain	4,562'	5.0 mi	1,410'	551
Kokoweef Peak	6,040'	0.7 mi	500'	313
Kokoweef Peak (loop)	6,040'	2.4 mi	880'	313
Last Chance Mtn (long)	8,456'	6.8 mi	3,630'	135
Last Chance Mtn (short)	8,456'	5.0 mi	3,120'	135
Lead Peak	5,856'	4.0 mi	780'	139
Leaning Rock	7,342'	3.6 mi	1,620'	157
Lela Peak (northern route)	4,723'	2.5 mi	920'	467
Lela Peak (southern route)	4,723'	2.3 mi	1,000'	467
Little Cowhole Mtn (nth)	1,699'	2.2 mi	590'	341
Little Cowhole Mtn (sth)	1,699'	2.5 mi	690'	341
Lookout Mountain	3,764'	3.3 mi	1,350'	521
Lookout Mountain (loop)	3,764'	3.7 mi	1,350'	521
Lost Burro Peak	6,097'	2.6 mi	1,200'	161
Lost Horse Mountain	5,313'	4.4 mi	900'	443
Lost Horse Mtn (loop)	5,313'	6.7 mi	1,200'	443

Summit	Elev.	Round-trip distance	Elev. gain	Pages
Malapai Hill	4,280'	1.6 mi	520'	463
Marble Peak	2,467'	3.0 mi	1,450'	379
Mine Peak	3,910'	4.6 mi	1,850'	525
Monument Mountain	4,834'	5.8 mi	1,850'	471
Mormon Peak	8,270'	2.4 mi	1,250'	197
Mount Hephestus	3,763'	7.2 mi	1,030'	338
Mount Minerva Hoyt	5,405'	8.8 mi	2,050'	429
Mount Palmer	7,958'	11.4 mi	4,620'	79
Mount Perry	5,716'	9.0 mi	2,690'	115
Needle Peak	5,803'	7.6 mi	2,780'	205
Nevares Peak	2,859'	12.2 mi	3,080'	101
New York Peak	7,532'	5.0 mi	2,330'	257
Noon Peak	4,238'	2.8 mi	1,450'	63
North Castle Butte	5,896'	6.2 mi	1,370'	253
North Leaning Rock	~7,250'	4.8 mi	2,050'	157
North New York Peak	7,463'	4.6 mi	2,060'	257
North Zinc Hill	5,498'	4.6 mi	1,880'	517
Old Woman Mountain	5,325'	4.0 mi	2,240'	365
Old Woman Statue	5,105'	7.2 mi	2,700'	369
Ophir Mountain	6,010'	1.8 mi	540'	513
Owl Lake Viewpoint	3,300'	7.1 mi	1,650'	215
Owl Peak	4,666'	3.8 mi	1,270'	219
Pahrump Peak	5,740'	7.8 mi	3,470'	59
Palm Grove Overlook	~890'	4.0 mi	1,010'	111
Pinto Mtn (N. Y. Mtns)	6,142'	4.6 mi	1,170'	261
Pinto Mtn (Pinto Mtns)	3,983'	9.0 mi	2,570'	481
Porter Peak	9,101'	6.8 mi	2,920'	197
Providence Peak	6,612'	4.8 mi	2,810'	285
Pyramid Peak	6,703'	9.8 mi	3,790'	105
Quail Mountain	5,813'	11.4 mi	2,820'	429
Queen Mountain	5,687'	3.9 mi	1,230'	453
Red Cathedral	~980'	2.2 mi	550'	111
Red Mountain	5,261'	4.2 mi	1,890'	555
Red Top Peak	3,017'	3.1 mi	1,470'	89
Ryan Mountain	5,457'	2.8 mi	1,070'	439
Scattered Bone Peak	5,738'	3.4 mi	500'	507
Searles Peak	5,092'	6.6 mi	2,860'	535
Sentinel Peak	9,634'	17.0 mi	7,080'	187
Sheep Hole Mountain	4,613'	4.4 mi	2,420'	487

Summit	Elev.	Round-trip distance	Elev. gain	Pages
Silver Mountain	7,495'	11.6 mi	2,390'	503
Silver Peak	6,368'	11.0 mi	4,050'	291
Slate Peak	5,068'	8.0 mi	3,380'	535
Slate Point	3,362'	2.8 mi	630'	531
Sleeping Beauty	3,979'	5.2 mi	1,690'	389
Slims Peak	7,115'	5.6 mi	2,600'	193
South Teutonia Peak	~5,735'	4.2 mi	940'	327
Spring Peak	3,342'	5.0 mi	1,250'	215
Spring Peak (loop)	3,342'	5.5 mi	1,560'	215
Stepladder Mountain	2,926'	9.6 mi	1,400'	361
Stifle Peak (loop)	2,694'	5.0 mi	1,320'	491
Stifle Peak (via Toe Peak)	2,694'	5.7 mi	1,710'	491
Striped Butte	4,774'	1.2 mi	840'	201
Striped Butte (loop)	4,774'	2.4 mi	930'	201
Striped Mountain	5,958'	2.2 mi	980'	317
Table Mountain	6,178'	2.0 mi	1,050'	271
Table Mountain (loop)	6,178'	5.3 mi	1,300'	271
Telescope Peak (via ridge)	11,049'	29.2 mi	12,320'	182
Telescope Peak (via trail)	11,049'	12.8 mi	3,480'	179
Teutonia Peak	5,755'	3.8 mi	900'	327
Thimble Peak	6,381'	3.6 mi	1,690'	85
Tin Mountain	8,953'	6.6 mi	4,310'	149
Toe Peak	2,730'	3.9 mi	980'	491
Towne Peak	7,287'	6.8 mi	2,860'	169
Twentynine Palms Mtn	4,562'	4.8 mi	1,740'	477
Twin Cone	3,222'	1.3 mi	470'	335
Ubehebe Peak	5,678'	5.2 mi	2,410'	143
Ubeshebe Peak	5,520'	4.4 mi	1,810'	143
Ute Peak (cross-country)	4,908'	2.8 mi	1,240'	235
Ute Peak (trail)	4,908'	14.0 mi	1,810'	235
Wahguyhe Peak	8,228'	3.0 mi	2,000'	80
Warren Peak	5,103'	6.0 mi	1,160'	421
West Ord Mountain	5,525'	3.3 mi	1,580'	401
White Top Mountain	7,607'	2.5 mi	1,050'	153
Wildrose Peak	9,064'	8.4 mi	2,580'	175
Woods Mountain	5,590'	6.0 mi	1,930'	241
Zinc Hill	5,585'	4.6 mi	1,970'	517
Zinc Hill (loop)	5,585'	5.3 mi	2,090'	517

INDEX

573